HISTORICAL DICTIONARIES OF RELIGIONS, PHILOSOPHIES, AND MOVEMENTS
Edited by Jon Woronoff

1. *Buddhism,* by Charles S. Prebish, 1993
2. *Mormonism,* by Davis Bitton, 1994
3. *Ecumenical Christianity,* by Ans Joachim van der Bent, 1994
4. *Terrorism,* by Sean Anderson and Stephen Sloan, 1995
5. *Sikhism,* by W. H. McLeod, 1995
6. *Feminism,* by Janet K. Boles and Diane Long Hoeveler, 1995
7. *Olympic Movement,* by Ian Buchanan and Bill Mallon, 1995
8. *Methodism,* by Charles Yrigoyen Jr. and Susan E. Warrick, 1996
9. *Orthodox Church,* by Michael Prokurat, Alexander Golitzin, and Michael D. Peterson, 1996
10. *Organized Labor,* by James C. Docherty, 1996
11. *Civil Rights Movement,* by Ralph E. Luker, 1997
12. *Catholicism,* by William J. Collinge, 1997
13. *Hinduism,* by Bruce M. Sullivan, 1997
14. *North American Environmentalism,* by Edward R. Wells and Alan M. Schwartz, 1997
15. *Welfare State,* by Bent Greve, 1997
16. *Socialism,* by James C. Docherty, 1997
17. *Bahá'í Faith,* by Hugh C. Adamson and Philip Hainsworth, 1998
18. *Taoism,* by Julian F. Pas in cooperation with Man Kam Leung, 1998

Historical Dictionary of the Bahá'í Faith

Hugh C. Adamson
and
Philip Hainsworth

Historical Dictionaries of Religions, Philosophies, and Movements, No. 17

The Scarecrow Press, Inc.
Lanham, Md., & London
1998

SCARECROW PRESS, INC.

Published in the United States of America
by Scarecrow Press, Inc.
4720 Boston Way
Lanham, Maryland 20706

British Library Cataloguing in Publication Information Available

Library of Congress Cataloging-in-Publication Data

Adamson, Hugh C.
Historical dictionary of the Bahā'ī Faith / Hugh C. Adamson and Philip Hainsworth.
p. cm. — (Historical dictionaries of religions, philosophies, and movements ; no. 17)
Includes bibliographical references.
ISBN 0-8108-3353-0 (alk. paper)
1. Bahai Faith—History—Dictionaries. I. Hainsworth, Philip. II. Title. III. Series.
BP327.A33 1998
297.9'3'03—dc21 97-2610

ISBN 0-8108-3353-0 (cloth : alk. paper)

The paper used in this publication meets the minimum requirements of American National Standard for Information Sciences—Permanence of Paper for Printed Library Materials, ANSI Z39.48–1984.
Manufactured in the United States of America.

Contents

Editor's Foreword

Only about a century-and-a-half old, the Bahá'í Faith is one of the younger religions to be dealt with in this series. Although of recent origin, it has grown most vigorously and already counts 6,000,000 members. Its geographic expansion is even more impressive, with members living in nearly every country and territory in the world. Coming later, the Bahá'ís have not ignored their predecessors and have built on the beliefs of Judaism, Christianity, Islám, Buddhism and other faiths. They also look forward and actively address many present-day issues, such as democracy, racial and sexual equality, economic development, environmental protection, human rights and peace.

Despite this, the Bahá'í Faith is not as well known as it should be. So it is hoped that this historical dictionary will contribute to spreading knowledge of the religion among outsiders while permitting members to deepen their understanding. This book presents the Founders and numerous leaders and pioneers, many of the basic principles and precepts, aspects of organization and administration, and significant events of its history. Several timelines trace the evolution and various appendices provide essential data. Of particular interest is a substantial bibliography.

This volume was written by Hugh Adamson and Philip Hainsworth. Both are Bahá'ís with very considerable experience, not only in the United Kingdom, where they reside, but in other communities as well. Hugh Adamson has long been the Secretary General of the National Spiritual Assembly of the Bahá'ís of the United Kingdom, and Philip Hainsworth has served in various capacities in the National Spiritual Assembly, including Chairman. Equally important, they have written and lectured extensively on the Bahá'í Faith both for members and nonmembers. That has stood them in good stead while producing this informative *Historical Dictionary of the Bahá'í Faith*.

Jon Woronoff
Series Editor

Preface

The Bahá'í Faith came into being in the middle of the 19th century with a well-recorded and voluminously documented history. As such, the authors had great difficulty in choosing what to include and what to exclude. This is an historical dictionary, and history is about people. Obviously, a great many entries (and people who have contributed significantly to the historical development of the Bahá'í Faith) have had to be left out due to the limits of space. As a general rule, we have elected to exclude people who are living, despite their many contributions to the development of the Bahá'í Faith.

Also, in an effort to conserve space, the authors have made no attempt at a comprehensive review of the lives, teachings, family and sufferings of the three Central Figures of the Bahá'í Faith (the Báb, Bahá'u'lláh and 'Abdu'l-Bahá) or Shoghi Effendi (the Guardian of the Bahá'í Faith). We did so on the premise that these details may be easily obtained from the many publications that are readily available (a bibliography of major works dealing with their lives and teachings is appended). An overview of the major historical events relating to Their lives and the evolution of the Bahá'í Faith can, however, be found in the five chronological "Timelines" (the Báb and Bahá'u'lláh, 'Abdu'l-Bahá, Shoghi Effendi, the Chief Stewards the Interregnum and the Universal House of Justice), which precede the main dictionary entries. While not in any way meant to be definitive, these timelines should nonetheless assist researchers and readers alike in identifying major historical events and the source documents relating to them.

If we have minimized textual entries relating to the Central Figures, we have tried on the other hand to give a little more space to the people who followed Them—souls who gave a lifetime of service to the Bahá'í Faith and in so doing significantly influenced the historical development of Bahá'u'lláh's Cause (due to the limits of space and the targeting of a mainly Western audience, a great many of the early Oriental heroes and heroines have been passed over lightly or, sadly, not mentioned at all). Of particular note, however, are the entries about the 50 Hands of the Cause of God and the inclusion of their photographs. Presently there is no other such detailed survey of their lives in any one publication.

We would very much have liked to include a great many more photographs but the limits of space imposed a constraint in this area. We are grateful to the Universal House of Justice, audio visual department for providing of the bulk of the photographs used in the book. With the exception of the three living Hands of the Cause of God who are currently all resident at the Bahá'í World Centre in Haifa, and three ex-members of the Universal House of Justice, space has not allowed us to refer to an extremely large number of individuals who have given outstanding services to the Faith.

The reader will quickly recognize that the body of this work is replete with quotations from Bahá'u'lláh, 'Abdu'l-Bahá and Shoghi Effendi. There are two reasons we have chosen this method of presentation.

First, in His Will and Testament, Bahá'u'lláh appointed His Son 'Abdu'l-Bahá as the sole Interpreter of His Words (a step taken to avoid disunity and schism). 'Abdu'l-Bahá, in turn, in His Will and Testament, appointed His grandson Shoghi Effendi to the position of "Guardian" of the Bahá'í Faith and the sole Interpreter of matters not already pronounced on by Bahá'u'lláh or Himself. This means that "authoritative" statement(s) on the meaning of Bahá'u'lláh's Writings can only be found in the Writings of Bahá'u'lláh, (i.e., His own interpretation of passages of Scripture), or the commentaries of 'Abdu'l-Bahá and/or Shoghi Effendi. As such, interpretation of Bahá'í Writings is forbidden to everyone else. Of course, anyone may hold an opinion(s) as to the meaning of any given passage, but individuals have no right to insist on the correctness of their position. By preferring the words of Bahá'u'lláh, 'Abdu'l-Bahá and/or Shoghi Effendi throughout this dictionary, the authors have then offered the reader access to authoritative meaning, rather than speculative viewpoint.

Second, the use of quotation throughout allows readers immediate access to source materials, thereby allowing them to decide whether they wish to access the originals for further contextual analysis. Considerable care has been taken to cite all quotations and to provide references to sources where further information can be found on a wide range of the issues covered in this work. This should, hopefully, allow researchers to turn quickly to primary and secondary sources with minimal additional research. The source referencing system we have used is a "numbered list style." The system works as follows: [3:4] refers to page 4 of citation number 3 in the citation list at the end of the dictionary.

Considerable effort went into the compilation of a bibliography of historical source materials that we hope will be of value to both researchers and casual browsers alike. In this regard we have included a section on biographies containing much personal historical information that is of enormous help to researchers in understanding the historical development of the Cause (given that this is often the only source of such information).

The most comprehensive source of bibliographical materials is William Collins's major work entitled *Bibliography of English Language Works on the Bábí and Bahá'í Faiths 1844-1985*.[1] Serious researchers will find Collins's painstakingly researched book invaluable to their work. Given the rise in usage of the Internet/World Wide Web we have included a number of the more important WWW site URLs and FTP sites for those wishing to access Bahá'í materials via that media. The Bahá'í World Centre operates an FTP site from which all of the English-language Bahá'í Sacred Writings can be downloaded at no cost. The site also contains a large number of other materials.

Lee Nelson's Windows software entitled *Refer—Multiple Author Refer System: Indexing and Retrieval Software* offers those with computers complete access to English-language Bahá'í Writings in electronically searchable format. Serious researchers will find much of value in Bernal Schooley's *Immerse*. This 32-bit software contains over 200 books and texts from not only Bahá'í sources but also the entirety of the Bible, the Qur'án, The Bhagavad-Gita and the Dhammapada.

We are indebted to the Universal House of Justice for their consent to reproduce the unpublished article entitled "The Epochs of the Formative Age," as well as the definitions of oriental terms found in Bahá'í as published in several issues of *The Bahá'í World*.[11:735ff] The definitions have been inserted directly into the body of the dictionary and are identified by a "📖" mark in the citation reference (i.e., [11:735 📖]).

American spelling has been used throughout the text except where a quotation uses English spelling (in which case the original has been retained). Readers will note that pronouns referring to the Báb, Bahá'u'lláh and 'Abdu'l-Bahá are capitalized throughout in keeping with Bahá'í practice. The system of transliteration used is that specified by Shoghi Effendi for use within the Bahá'í Community by Bahá'ís. [2 :734] The authors are indebted to Dr. Christopher Buck for the provision of a typeface developed by him (New World Transliterator) whereby the transliteration of certain Persian letters (Ḍ, ḍ, Ṭ, ṭ, Ẓ, ẓ, Ḥ, ḥ, Ṣ, ṣ) was made possible within the text.

The pronunciation of Persian words is according to the following schema: [2 :895f]

a	as in account	I	as (e) in best
á	as in arm	í	as (ee) in meet
u	as (o) in short	ú	as (oo) in moon
aw	as in mown	dh	like z
z	like z	ẓ	like z
ḍ	like z	th	like ss
s	like ss	ṣ	like ss
Zh	like s in pleasure	Kh	like ch in loch
gh	as q	H	like h
ḥ	like h	'	means pause
'	means pause		

As its authors we are only too aware of the many shortcomings of this work and, as such, we offer it as a beginning effort rather than a final product.

Introduction

The *Encyclopaedia Britannica, 1995 Book of the Year*, indicates that the Bahá'í Faith has been established in 210 countries, territories and dependencies—with Christianity in 260, Islam in 184 and Judaism in 134. The 1997 geographic distribution of the Bahá'í Faith places it much closer to Christianity insofar as there are Bahá'ís resident in 245 countries, territories and dependencies. In addition, selections of its Scripture are available in more that 820 languages, and its adherents have been enrolled from more than 2,200 different tribes and ethnic groups. That it has such a wide global spread in less than a century and a half not only demonstrates its right to be classed as an independent world religion but also its need to be examined as a unique religious phenomenon.

Its three Central Figures, The Báb, Bahá'u'lláh and 'Abdu'l-Bahá, were born in Persia (modern Írán) in the first half of the 19th century. It bears a relationship to Shí'ah Islám similar to that which Christianity had to Judaism. The combined period of the Writings of the Central Figures span more than 77 years—from 1844 to 1921. Its source Writings are in four languages—ancient classical Persian, modern Persian, classical Arabic and modern Arabic. Together they form "Bahá'í Scripture." Coupled with the Writings of Shoghi Effendi, the Guardian of the Bahá'í Faith, mostly in English but also in Arabic, Persian and French, they provide the authentic text.

Historical Background

Towards the end of the 18th century a learned and saintly Muslim, Shaykh Aḥmad-i-Aḥsá'í, believed that a great world teacher, whose appearance had been prophesied in the scriptures of the world's great religions, would shortly make himself known. He moved from his home town to Karbilá, a holy city in Iráq, and attracted a group of students to his teachings. Shortly before his death in 1826 he appointed his star pupil, Siyyid Káẓim-i-Rashtí, as his successor to continue to instruct his students and prepare them for the coming of the "Promised One" or Qá'im.

Siyyid Káẓim taught his pupils to look for certain signs that would be manifest in this Promised One: He would be of noble lineage—a Siyyid (a descendant of the Prophet Muhammad); He would be young but possessed of innate knowledge; His learning would not be from Shaykh Aḥmad but from God; He would be of medium height, would abstain from smoking and would be of extreme devoutness and piety. He then urged his followers to scatter far and wide to seek for the Promised One who, he told them, was even then alive.

One pure-hearted student, an eager searcher after truth and a brilliant scholar, Mullá Ḥusayn-i-Bushrú'í, was sent by Siyyid Káẓim on a special mission to Írán. By the time Mullá Ḥusayn returned his master had died. On Siyyid Káẓim's instruction his students were preparing to begin their search for the Promised One. Mullá Ḥusayn, with several friends, spent forty days in prayer and fasting, and then he set off with his brother and nephew to begin their search. Mullá Ḥusayn felt drawn toward the beautiful city of Shíráz, famous for its poets, its flower gardens and its nightingales—and it was to that city that he traveled with several other companions. He arrived dusty, hungry and tired at the gates of Shíráz late one afternoon. Sending his companions ahead into the town to look for food and accommodation, Mullá Ḥusayn lingered for a while, and in due course he was approached by a young stranger who welcomed him to the city as though he was a long-lost friend. His demeanor impressed Mullá Ḥusayn most favorably and when the stranger invited him to his house for refreshment, Mullá Ḥusayn explained that his companions were expecting him to join them and that he felt it best not to accept the kind invitation. To this the stranger replied, "Commit them to the care of God. He will surely protect and watch over them." Mullá Ḥusayn went with his new friend, Siyyid 'Alí-Muḥammad, the Báb, to his house in the city.

According to Shoghi Effendi in *God Passes By,* his history of the first Bahá'í century:

> The opening scene of the initial act of this great drama was laid in the upper chamber of the modest residence of the son of a mercer of Shíráz, in an obscure corner of that city. The time was the hour before sunset, on the 22nd day of May, 1844. The participants were the Báb, a twenty-five year old Siyyid, of pure and holy lineage, and the young Mullá Ḥusayn, the first to believe in Him. Their meeting immediately before that interview seemed to be purely fortuitous. The interview itself was protracted till the hour of dawn. The Host remained closeted alone with His guest, nor was the sleeping city remotely aware of the import of the conversation they held with each other. No record has passed to posterity of that unique night save the fragmentary but highly illuminating account that fell from the lips of Mullá Ḥusayn. "I sat spellbound by His utterance, oblivious of time and of those who awaited me," he himself has testified, after describing the nature of the questions he had put to his Host and the conclusive replies he had received from Him, replies which had established beyond the shadow of a doubt the validity of His claim to be the promised Qá'im. "Suddenly the call of the

Mu'adhdhin, summoning the faithful to their morning prayer, awakened me from the state of ecstasy into which I seemed to have fallen. All the delights, all the ineffable glories, which the Almighty has recounted in His Book as the priceless possessions of the people of Paradise—these I seemed to be experiencing that night.... Sleep had departed from me that night. I was enthralled by the music of that voice which rose and fell as He chanted; now swelling forth as He revealed verses of the Qayyúmu'l-Asmá', again acquiring ethereal, subtle harmonies as He uttered the prayers He was revealing. At the end of each invocation, He would repeat this verse: "Far from the glory of thy Lord, the All-Glorious, be that which His creatures affirm of Him! And peace be upon His Messengers! And praise be to God, the Lord of all beings!"

"This Revelation," Mullá Ḥusayn has further testified, "so suddenly and impetuously thrust upon me, came as a thunderbolt which, for a time, seemed to have benumbed my faculties. I was blinded by its dazzling splendor and overwhelmed by its crushing force. Excitement, joy, awe, and wonder stirred the depths of my soul. Predominant among these emotions was a sense of gladness and strength which seemed to have transfigured me. How feeble and impotent, how dejected and timid, I had felt previously! Then I could neither write nor walk, so tremulous were my hands and feet. Now, however, the knowledge of His Revelation had galvanized my being. I felt possessed of such courage and power that were the world, all its peoples and its potentates, to rise against me, I would, alone and undaunted, withstand their onslaught. The universe seemed but a handful of dust in my grasp. I seemed to be the voice of Gabriel personified, calling unto all mankind: "Awake, for, lo! the morning Light has broken. Arise, for His Cause is made manifest. The portal of His grace is open wide; enter therein, O peoples of the world! For He Who is your promised One is come!" [5:5]

The Dispensation of the Báb (1844—1863)

The religion thus inaugurated by the Báb was known as the Bábí Faith and had a fourfold objective—to fulfill the promises of Islám, bring a new spirit amongst the people, annul the laws of the Qur'án and prepare the world for the coming of the Promised One of all religions—"Him Whom God shall make Manifest." During the following 40 days, 16 more students of Siyyid Káẓim independently reached the city and recognized the Báb. The 18th disciple was Ṭáhirih, a well-known poetess who recognized Him in a dream and wrote to Him declaring her allegiance. Collectively these souls were designated the Letters of the Living. The Báb called upon them to scatter throughout the country and spread His Teachings and thereby prepare the people for the coming of that Promised One. He told them that they would face extreme opposition, torture and even death as a reward for their efforts—and this they did, with reports of as many as 20,000 meeting their death in the following years.

The Báb Himself faced immediate opposition, but somewhat surprisingly He retained relative freedom to teach His Faith—which spread with such tremendous rapidity that both the religious authorities and the representatives of government rose up against Him and the Bábís. Following his arrest he was imprisoned for three years (in Chihríq and Máh-Kú) leading eventually to his execution at noon on 9 July 1850 before a multitude in the northern town of Tabríz.

His actual martyrdom was accompanied by several significant events. In the moments leading up to His execution He was in His prison cell giving some final instructions to one of His amanuensis. At the hour appointed by His executioners it was commanded by Sám Khán, the Christian Colonel in charge of the regiment of 750 soldiers that He must come immediately to the square in order that the sentence might be carried out. The Báb advised him that He had not finished his instructions and that until He had no force on earth could remove Him. Sám Khán expressed his personal reservations about the rôle that had been thrust on him. He said that were the Báb to be Who He claimed to be He would surely have it within His power to prevent His execution. By way of response the Báb assured him that he should carry out his orders and, if his intention was sincere, the Almighty was surely able to relieve him from his perplexity. The Báb was then taken to the place of execution, the regiment lined up in three rows and the command to fire given. When the smoke from the rifle muzzles cleared it was found that the shots had merely severed the ropes, and the Báb had disappeared. After great confusion He was eventually found back in His original cell engaged in conversation with His amanuensis. When the authorities came into the cell He informed them that He had now completed his task and that they were free to carry on with their task. Sám Khán refused to take any further part in the execution, resigned his position and marched his men away. Another regiment was found and this time carried out the task without further difficulty. The bodies of the Báb and His companion were riddled with bullets though their faces were little marred. The corpses were thrown in the moat of the city, and it was stated by the authorities that dogs had devoured the bodies. The precious Remains were in fact recovered by His followers and remained hidden in various places for more than half a century until, on 'Abdu'l-Bahá's instruction, they were delivered to the Holy Land for proper interment.

The Dispensation of Bahá'u'lláh (1863—1892)

Among the high-ranking Bábís was a nobleman of Ṭihrán—Mírzá Ḥusayn 'Alí. He took a leading part in organizing a gathering (Conference) of Bábís in an area known as Badasht in 1849. The Conference was initially called to plan for the release of the Báb, but this did not prove possible. However, it was during this gathering that the new religion severed irrevocably its ties with Shí'ih Islám. This happened when Ṭáhirih, in a symbolic gesture, appeared before the assembled participants unveiled. During the Conference Mírzá Ḥusayn 'Alí gave the participants a new name, Himself assuming the title of Bahá'u'lláh.

The execution of the Báb did little to stem the opposition to the Bábís, and their persecution continued unabated, with many being killed for their adherence to His Cause. Two years after His death two of His followers, blaming the Sháh for the unceasing persecutions, made a futile and ill-conceived attempt on his life. The outcome was predictable, and a renewed outbreak of persecution immediately took root. In order to stem the loss of life Bahá'u'lláh immediately offered Himself as a ransom. He was arrested and cast into the Síyáh-Chál (Black Pit) prison in Ṭihrán. It was in this foul prison that He received the first intimation of His Divine Station and Mission (described in some detail in the Dictionary entry under His Name.) Though no evidence could be found against Him, Bahá'u'lláh was stripped of His possessions and given one month to remove Himself and His family from the country. Although offered asylum in Russia, He accepted banishment to Baghdád and arrived there after a most difficult journey in April 1853.

In the ten years following His arrival in Baghdád, the leaderless and divided Bábí community was changed through His influence into a dynamic united group. Indeed, it attracted the favorable attention of the local populace and its many officials, so much so that the Persian government persuaded the Turkish authorities to exile Bahá'u'lláh once again, this time to Constantinople and to Edirne (Adrianople.)

Immediately before His departure, Bahá'u'lláh, His family and close companions spent 12 days in what became known as the Riḍván Garden on the banks of the River Tigris. During this time He announced publicly that He was the long-awaited "Promised One." The arrival of Bahá'u'lláh in the Riḍván Garden began what has come to be recognized as the holiest and most significant of all Bahá'í festivals, the Riḍván Festival, commemorating the Declaration of His Mission to His companions. This public announcement may be regarded as the prelude to His later proclamation of that same Mission to the world and its rulers from Adrianople. The departure of Bahá'u'lláh from the Garden, at noon, on the 3rd of May, 1863, witnessed scenes of tumultuous enthusiasm no less spectacular and even more touching than those that greeted Him when leaving His house in Baghdád. Believers and unbelievers alike sobbed and lamented. The chiefs and notables who had congregated were struck with wonder. Mounted on a red roan stallion of the finest breed and leaving behind Him a bowing multitude of admirers, He rode forth on the first stage of a journey that was to carry Him to the city of Constantinople. After a brief stay in Constantinople, Bahá'u'lláh and His family were moved on to Adrianople. His presence in that town attracted many to His Cause, and it was there that the followers began to be known as Bahá'ís rather than Bábís. While in Adrianople Bahá'u'lláh began to write what was to become a series of letters to the rulers and kings of the earth.

It was also in Adrianople that the long-standing opposition of his half-brother Azal (Mírzá Yaḥyá) came to a head. When the government banished Him still further from Persia, this time to the prison city of 'Akká, Palestine, they decided to split the group of exiles. Azal and some of his followers, as well as a few faithful Bahá'ís, were sent to Cyprus while Bahá'u'lláh and the main group were sent to 'Akká, Palestine. Bahá'u'lláh left for Palestine by ship and reached 'Akká on the 31st of August,1868. On arrival in that prison city His party met with a great hostility from the local inhabitants—who had been advised that a group of vile and despicable criminals was about to arrive. Indeed, on arrival, an edict imposing perpetual banishment was read aloud from the steps of the mosque as a warning to the populace that they should have nothing to do with the prisoners.

Bahá'u'lláh was first placed in the Citadel (a prison within the prison) in a small cell completely open to the elements. It was in this prison, which he designated "The Most Great Prison," that His youngest son, Mírzá Mihdí, accidentally fell through a skylight to his death. Notwithstanding this tragedy, and under appalling circumstances, He continued to write letters to the kings and leaders of the world, calling on them to accept His Station and Teachings. Two years later He was removed to a series of houses in the city where He was kept under close arrest. Throughout this entire period He continued to reveal messages of guidance, including the *Kitáb-i-Aqdas* (Book of Law.)

Gradually, His eldest son, 'Abdu'l-Bahá, became the one on whom the responsibility fell for the general affairs of the exiles, for negotiations with officials, for continually seeking to improve the conditions under which the exiles lived and for attending to the needs of the growing number of pilgrims who began to arrive in the city hoping to catching a glimpse of their Beloved.

Eventually the positive changes that had taken place among the people and officials in Baghdád, Constantinople and Adrianople began to be seen in 'Akká, and when, after nine years, 'Abdu'l-Bahá rented a property outside the city and (with great difficulty) persuaded His father to move to it, no voice was raised in opposition, and He left the city for Mazra'ih. Two years later 'Abdu'l-Bahá secured a more spacious dwelling, the Mansion of Bahjí, for Bahá'u'lláh and his family. 'Abdu'l-Bahá remained in 'Akká to attend to the many details of the day-to-day administration of His Father's Faith.

Two years before He passed away, Bahá'u'lláh allowed a visiting Cambridge Orientalist, Edward Granville Browne, to stay with Him at Bahjí as His guest. The visit, lasting five days (15-20 April 1890) has provided the only known Western pen-portrait of Bahá'u'lláh:

> "The face of Him on Whom I gazed," is the interviewer's memorable testimony for posterity, "I can never forget, though I cannot describe it. Those piercing eyes seemed to read one's very soul; power and authority sat on that ample brow.... No need to ask in whose presence I stood, as I bowed myself before one who is the object of a devotion and love which kings might envy and emperors sigh for in vain." "Here," the visitor himself has testified, "did I spend five most memorable days, during which I enjoyed unparalleled and unhoped-for opportunities of holding intercourse with those who are the fountain-heads of that mighty and wondrous spirit, which works with invisible but ever-increasing force for the transformation and quickening of a people who slumber in a sleep like unto death. It was, in truth, a strange and moving experience, but one whereof I despair of conveying any save the feeblest impression." [5:194]

Browne also recorded the following written report of the Words spoken by Bahá'u'lláh:

> Praise be to God that thou hast attained!... Thou hast come to see a prisoner and an exile.... We desire but the good of the world and happiness of the nations; yet they deem us a stirrer up of strife and sedition worthy of bondage and banishment.... That all nations should become one in faith and all men as brothers; that the bonds of affection and unity between the sons of men should be strengthened; that diversity of religion should cease, and differences of race be annulled—what harm is there in this?... Yet so it shall be; these fruitless strifes, these ruinous wars shall pass away, and the 'Most Great Peace' shall come.... Do not you in Europe need this also? Is not

> this that which Christ foretold?... Yet do we see your kings and rulers lavishing their treasures more freely on means for the destruction of the human race than on that which would conduce to the happiness of mankind.... These strifes and this bloodshed and discord must cease, and all men be as one kindred and one family.... Let not a man glory in this, that he loves his country; let him rather glory in this, that he loves his kind....[98:157]

In the last years of His life Bahá'u'lláh made four visits to Haifa, during which time He instructed 'Abdu'l-Bahá concerning the exact Spot where He should build the Shrine to receive the remains of the Báb. Bahá'u'lláh passed away on 29th May 1892 and was buried in a room in the vicinity of the Mansion at Bahjí. This is now the Qiblih of the Bahá'í world to which the believers turn daily while saying their obligatory prayers.

'Abdu'l-Bahá—Center of the Covenant (1892—1921)

The Will and Testament of Bahá'u'lláh designated His eldest Son, 'Abdu'l-Bahá as His successor and the sole Interpreter of His Writings.

He was very well known and highly respected in 'Akká and Haifa, but the attacks on His good name by His enemies and by disaffected members of His own family resulted in periods of great personal restriction. Indeed, the situation was so difficult that it was not until 1898 that the first band of Western pilgrims were able to visit Him in 'Akká. It was these pilgrims who spread the news to Europe and America that the Promised One had come.

Notwithstanding the restrictions imposed on Him as a prisoner, the construction of the Báb's Sepulcher, whose foundation stone had been laid by Him on the site blessed and selected by Bahá'u'lláh, went on without interruption. Neither did 'Abdu'l-Bahá allow obstacles, no matter how formidable they appeared, to interfere with the daily flow of Tablets (letters) that poured forth from His pen. He wrote and dictated answers to a vast number of letters, reports, inquiries, prayers and confessions of faith received from countless followers and admirers in both the East and the West. Eyewitnesses have testified that, during that period of His life, they had known Him to write, with His own Hand, no fewer than 90 Tablets in a single day and to pass many a night, from dusk to dawn, alone in His bed-chamber engaged in a correspondence that the pressure of His manifold responsibilities had prevented Him from attending to in the daytime.

During these years, in the heyday of His life and in the full tide of His power, He, with inexhaustible energy, marvelous serenity and unshakable confidence, initiated and prosecuted the varied enterprises associated with His ministry. In these years He conceived the plan for and implemented the construction of the first Bahá'í House of Worship in 'Ishqábád in Turkistán. Moreover, despite the disturbances that agitated His native country, He issued instructions for the restoration of the holy and historic House of the Báb in Shíráz. Also, chiefly through His constant encouragement, the initial measures were taken for the purchase of land for the construction of the Mother Temple of the West at Wilmette on the shore of Lake Michigan.

He was freed in 1908 and during the next five years devoted His last energies to traveling in Egypt, France, the British Isles, the United States, Canada, Germany and Hungary in order to share the Message of His Father. His epic journeys in these lands are recorded in some detail in the timelines that form part of this dictionary.

Immediately following WW I 'Abdu'l-Bahá sent a series of Tablets to the American Bahá'ís calling on them to undertake the spiritual conquest of the planet. These Tablets became known as the *Tablets of the Divine Plan* and listed the countries in the world to which He called the believers to settle and carry the Message of Bahá'u'lláh. Although a few souls immediately responded and blazed the way for the thousands who eventually followed, it was Shoghi Effendi who initiated the process in a systematic manner.

'Abdu'l-Bahá passed away on the 28th of November 1921 in Haifa, Palestine and was buried in the Shrine of the Báb in an adjacent vault to the east of the building.

Shoghi Effendi—Guardian of the Bahá'í Faith (1921—1957)

The Will and Testament of 'Abdu'l-Bahá appointed Shoghi Effendi, His eldest grandson and the great grandson of Bahá'u'lláh, as Guardian of the Bahá'í Faith. In that same Document He designated the Guardian the infallible interpreter of the Bahá'í Writings and specified his duties of the Guardian and relationship to the Universal House of Justice (on which Body he was to serve as Chairman.) He also enunciated the operating structure of the Bahá'í Administrative Order specified in the Writings of Bahá'u'lláh.

The world order designated in the Writings of Bahá'u'lláh, expanded and clarified in the Will and Testament of 'Abdu'l-Bahá and elaborated on by Shoghi Effendi, is unique. Leadership rests in elected bodies and not in the hands of any individual—there is no priesthood. As such, it is necessary to attempt briefly to explain the character and functions of the twin pillars that support this administrative structure—the institutions of the Guardianship and of the Universal House of Justice. Shoghi Effendi described them as follows:

> It should be stated, at the very outset, in clear and unambiguous language, that these twin institutions of the Administrative Order of Bahá'í should be regarded as divine

> in origin, essential in their functions and complementary in their aim and purpose. Their common, their fundamental object is to insure the continuity of that divinely-appointed authority which flows from the Source of our Faith, to safeguard the unity of its followers and to maintain the integrity and flexibility of its teachings. Acting in conjunction with each other these two inseparable institutions administer its affairs, coordinate its activities, promote its interests, execute its laws and defend its subsidiary institutions. Severally, each operates within a clearly defined sphere of jurisdiction; each is equipped with its own attendant institutions—instruments designed for the effective discharge of its particular responsibilities and duties. Each exercises, within the limitations imposed upon it, its powers, its authority, its rights and prerogatives. These are neither contradictory, nor detract in the slightest degree from the position which each of these institutions occupies. Far from being incompatible or mutually destructive, they supplement each other's authority and functions, and are permanently and fundamentally united in their aims.[126:148]

In 1937, in line with the guidance set out in the *Tablets of the Divine Plan*, Shoghi Effendi called upon the National Spiritual Assembly of United States and Canada to launch a systematic plan to achieve certain specified objectives throughout the American continent. This call saw the adoption by that community of the first Seven Year Plan. This was followed by similar plans in India and Burma, the British Isles, Egypt and Sudan, Germany and Austria, Persia and Iráq. In 1951 the British Bahá'ís were called upon to initiate the first international campaign of teaching in Africa. This culminated in 1953 with the launch of the Ten Year Global Campaign (or Crusade.) The object of this world-wide campaign was to take the Faith to every country mentioned by 'Abdu'l-Bahá in His Divine Plan. Also, it was designed to raise the number of National Spiritual Assemblies to the level necessary for the election of the Universal House of Justice.

Shoghi Effendi passed away in London on the 4th of November 1957 and was buried in the New Southgate Cemetery, Barnet. His passing came slightly before the mid-point of the Global Crusade. This left the embryonic Bahá'í Community without a leader, and had it not been for the heroic efforts and sterling leadership of the Hands of the Cause of God, the new-born Faith may well have degenerated into numberless sects. Fortuitously, Shoghi Effendi in a letter dated only a few weeks before his passing (2 October 1957) wherein he appoint the 3rd (and final) contingent of Hands, he referred to them as

"...the Chief Stewards of Bahá'u'lláh's embryonic World Commonwealth, who have been invested by the unerring Pen of the Center of His Covenant with the dual function of guarding over the security, and of insuring the propagation, of His Father's Faith." [6:127] Under the unerring guidance and leadership of the Hands, the Bahá'í Community remained united and accomplished every one of the goals assigned by the Plan. Indeed, the Crusade was an overwhelming success, and the only parts of the world not opened to the Faith were those where antipathetic governments would not allow Bahá'ís to enter to teach.

Universal House of Justice (1963—)

The essential conditions for the election of the Universal House of Justice having been reached by 1963, the Hands of the Cause of God called for its election; they disqualified themselves from membership lest they be seen to be seeking personal self advancement. The elections took place in Haifa in April 1963. Almost immediately, the House of Justice launched its first Global Plan, which maintained the momentum of teaching, "pioneering" and consolidation along the paths outlined by Shoghi Effendi. This pattern has continued with the issuance of a series of plans by the Universal House of Justice. The Universal House of Justice is the Supreme Head of the Bahá'í Faith and the Institution under which all other Bahá'í Institutions fall. It adopted a Constitution 26 November 1972 and now governs its affairs according to that document. [142]

Bahá'í Institutions

Writing about the administrative structure in a statement to the United Nations in 1947, Shoghi Effendi described it as follows:

> The Faith which this order serves, safeguards and promotes is...essentially supernatural, supranational, entirely non-political, non-partisan, and diametrically opposed to any policy or school of thought that seeks to exalt any particular race, class or nation. It is free from any form of ecclesiasticism, has neither priesthood nor rituals and is supported exclusively by its avowed adherents. Though loyal to their respective governments, though imbued with the love of their own country, and anxious to promote at all times its best interests, the followers of the Bahá'í Faith nevertheless, viewing mankind as one entity, and profoundly attached to its vital interests, will not hesitate to subordinate every particular interest, be it personal, regional or national to the over-riding interests of the generality of mankind, knowing full well that in a world of interdependent peoples and nations the advan-

tage of the part is best to be reached by the advantage of the whole, and that no lasting results can be achieved by any of the component parts if the general interests of the entity itself are neglected." [44:6]

Bahá'í Institutions are composed of two main types: those that are elected (the Rulers) and those that are appointed (the Learned.)

The Elected Arm (Rulers)

All adult believers (21 years and older) participate in the election processes.

Local administrative bodies, presently known as local Spiritual Assemblies, are elected every year on the 21st of April in all local districts that have nine or more adult believers. Elections are by secret ballot and without nomination or electioneering.

The process of electing the national body takes a different form. Delegates are elected from adult Bahá'ís on a proportional representation basis to attend an annual convention later in the Riḍván period (21 April to 2 May) to elect the nine members of the national body, the National Spiritual Assembly.

International elections for the Universal House of Justice take place in the Holy Land every five years. The delegates' body is composed of the members of the National Spiritual Assemblies elected in the previous year.

The Appointed Arm (Learned)

The "appointed" arm allows an element of continuity that is subject to but not a part of the elected arm. During His lifetime, Bahá'u'lláh appointed a few believers distinguished for their outstanding services to the Faith as "Hands of the Cause of God." 'Abdu'l-Bahá, although possessing the authority to appoint Hands, did not do so. In His Will, 'Abdu'l-Bahá stipulated that the Guardian had the authority to appoint Hands of the Cause. Shoghi Effendi's first appointments were by way of posthumous announcement. It was not until December 1951 that he appointed the first contingent of living Hands of the Cause. By the time of his death the total number of Hands came to 50 and the authority to appoint more died with him.

In order to preserve the functions of an appointed arm, the Universal House of Justice, through legislation, created Continental Boards of Counsellors. Counsellors have the delegated power to appoint assistants known as Auxiliary Board members (a body first created by Shoghi Effendi to assist the Hands of the Cause of God.) The work of the Continental Boards of Counsellors is directed by the International Teaching Centre—a body that reports directly to the Universal House of Justice. For the most part Auxiliary Board members have a geographical area of responsibility and can, in turn, appoint assistants.

A New World Order*

There are no clergy in the Bahá'í Faith; its growth and development rests with its institutions as supported by the individual Bahá'í. To teach the Faith (share the Message) is an obligation placed upon every Bahá'í, each according to his/her capacity and opportunity. Their aim is to establish the new world order enunciated in the Teachings of Bahá'u'lláh:

> The world's equilibrium hath been upset through the vibrating influence of this most great, this new World Order. Mankind's ordered life hath been revolutionized through the agency of this unique, this wondrous System—the like of which mortal eyes have never witnessed.... Immerse yourselves in the ocean of My words, that ye may unravel its secrets, and discover all the pearls of wisdom that lie hid in its depths. Take heed that ye do not vacillate in your determination to embrace the truth of this Cause—a Cause through which the potentialities of the might of God have been revealed, and His sovereignty established. With faces beaming with joy, hasten ye unto Him. This is the changeless Faith of God, eternal in the past, eternal in the future. Let him that seeketh, attain it; and as to him that hath refused to seek it—verily, God is Self-Sufficient, above any need of His creatures.[78:118f]

The fact that within a century and a half of its birth the Bahá'í Faith has been established in nearly every country, territory and dependency in the world, without benefit of paid missionaries or clergy, is indeed a testimony to the enthusiasm and dedication of those who have embraced it. Their history and beliefs are set out in more detail in the pages that follow.

The Epochs of the Formative Age[1]

Introduction

In disclosing the panoramic vision of the unfoldment of the Dispensation of Bahá'u'lláh, Shoghi Effendi refers to three major evolutionary stages through which the Faith must pass—the Apostolic or Heroic Age (1844-1921) associated with the Central Figures of the Faith; [3:4] the Formative or Transitional Age (1921-onward), [4:156] the "hall-mark" [4:98] of which is the rise and establishment of the Administrative Order, based on the execution of the provisions of 'Abdu'l-Bahá's Will and Testament; [3:5] and the Golden Age which will represent the "consummation of this glorious Dispensation." [4:156] Close examination of the details of Bahá'í history reveals that the individual Ages are comprised of a number of periods—inseparable parts of one integrated whole. [5:xv]

In relation to the Heroic Age of our Faith, the Guardian, in a letter dated 5 June 1947 to the American Bahá'ís, specified that this Age consisted of three epochs and described the distinguishing features of each: "...the Apostolic and Heroic Age of our Faith fell into three distinct epochs, of nine, of thirty-nine and of twenty-nine years' duration, associated respectively with the Bábí Dispensation and the ministries of Bahá'u'lláh and 'Abdu'l-Bahá. This Primitive Age of the Bahá'í Era, unapproached in spiritual fecundity by any period associated with the mission of the Founder of any previous Dispensation, was impregnated, from its inception to its termination, with the creative energies generated through the advent of two independent Manifestations and the establishment of a Covenant unique in the spiritual annals of mankind." [3:4]

The Formative Age, in which we now live and serve, [4:98] was ushered in with the passing of 'Abdu'l-Bahá. [5:xiv] Its major thrust is the shaping, development and consolidation of the local, national and international institutions of the Faith. [5:324] It is clear from the enumeration of the tasks associated with the Formative Age that their achievement will require increasingly mature levels of functioning of the Bahá'í community: "During this Formative Age of the Faith, and in the course of present and succeeding epochs, the last and crowning stage in the erection of the framework of the Administrative Order of the Faith of Bahá'u'lláh—the election of the Universal House of Justice—will have been completed, the Kitáb-i-Aqdas, the Mother-Book of His Revelation, will have been codified and its laws promulgated, the Lesser Peace will have been established, the unity of mankind will have been achieved and its maturity attained, the Plan

[1] Prepared by the Research Department of the Universal House of Justice—January 1986 (Reprinted with the kind permission of the Universal House of Justice).

conceived by 'Abdu'l-Bahá will have been executed, the emancipation of the Faith from the fetters of religious orthodoxy will have been effected, and its independent, religious status will have been universally recognized,..."[3:6]

The epochs of the Formative Age mark progressive stages in the evolution of the organic Bahá'í community and signal the maturation of its Institutions, thus enabling the Faith to operate at new levels and to initiate new functions. The timing of each epoch is designated by the Head of the Faith, and given the organic nature of evolutionary development, the transition from one epoch to another may not be abrupt, but may well occur over a period of time. This is the case, for example, in relation to both the inception of the Formative Age and the end of its first epoch. In relation to the former, the passing of 'Abdu'l-Bahá is the transitional event most often identified with the close of the Heroic Age and the beginning of the Formative Age. [5:xiv] However, the Guardian also asserts that the Apostolic Age of the Faith concluded "more particularly with the passing (in 1932) of His well-beloved and illustrious sister the Most Exalted Leaf—the last survivor of a glorious and heroic age." [4:98] With regard to the termination of the first epoch of the Formative Age, Shoghi Effendi has placed this between the years, 1944 [3:5] and 1946. [6:89]

Before describing the individual epochs of the Formative Age, it is important to comment on the use of the term "epoch" in the writings of the Guardian. In a letter dated 18 January 1953, written on his behalf to a National Spiritual Assembly, it is explained that the term is used to apply both to the stages in the Formative Age of the Faith, and to the phases in the unfoldment of 'Abdu'l-Bahá's Divine Plan. We are currently in the fourth epoch of the Formative Age[2] and the second epoch of 'Abdu'l-Bahá's Divine Plan. [8:25] (The first epoch of the Divine Plan began in 1937 with the inception of the First Seven Year Plan of the North American Bahá'í community, and concluded with the successful completion of the Ten Year Crusade in 1963. The second epoch of 'Abdu'l-Bahá's Divine Plan commenced in 1964 with the inauguration of the Nine Year Plan of the Universal House of Justice.)

The primary focus of this statement is on the epochs of the Formative Age of the Dispensation of Bahá'u'lláh.

The First Epoch of the Formative Age: 1921—1944/46

The first epoch of this Age witnessed the "birth and the primary stages in the erection of the framework of the Administrative Order of the Faith." [3:5] The epoch was characterized by concentration on the formation of local and national institutions in all five conti-

---

[2] Unpublished letter dated 2 January 1986 written by the Universal House of Justice to the Bahá'ís of the World.

nents, [6:19] thereby initiating the erection of the machinery necessary for future systematic teaching activities. This epoch was further marked by the launching, at the instigation of the Guardian, of the First Seven Year Plan (1937-1944) by the American Bahá'í community. This Plan, drawing its inspiration from the *Tablets of the Divine Plan*, represented the first systematic teaching campaign of the Bahá'í community and inaugurated the initial stage of the execution of 'Abdu'l-Bahá's Divine Plan in the Western Hemisphere. [3:5]

The Second Epoch of the Formative Age: 1946—1963

This epoch extended the developments of the first epoch by calling for the "consummation of a laboriously constructed Administrative Order," [3:6] and was to witness the formulation of a succession of teaching plans designed to facilitate the development of the Faith beyond the confines of the Western Hemisphere and the continent of Europe. [3:6] This epoch was distinguished, in the first instance, by the simultaneous and often spontaneous prosecution of Bahá'í national plans in both the East and the West. [6:13] For example, in a letter written at Naw-Rúz 105 B.E. to the Bahá'ís in the East, the beloved Guardian listed the specific plans undertaken by the United States, British, Indian, Persian, Australian and New Zealand, and Iráqí National Spiritual Assemblies, and indicated that this concerted action signalized the transition into the second epoch of the Formative Age.[3] The internal consolidation and the administrative experience gained by the National Assemblies was utilized and mobilized by the Guardian with the launching of the Ten Year World Crusade[3:140]—a crusade involving the simultaneous prosecution of 12 national plans. The plans derived their direction from 'Abdu'l-Bahá's Divine Plan, and the goals were assigned by Shoghi Effendi from the World Center of the Faith. [6:151ff] A second distinguishing feature of this epoch was the "rise" [6:13] and "steady consolidation" [6:13] of the World Center of the Faith.

The second epoch thus clearly demonstrated the further maturation of the institutions of the Administrative Order. It witnessed the appointment of the Hands of the Cause, [6:18ff] the introduction of Auxiliary Boards, [6:44] and the establishment of the International Bahá'í Council. [6:7f] The culminating event of the epoch was the election of the Universal House of Justice in 1963. It further demonstrated the more effective and co-ordinated use of the administrative machinery to prosecute the goals of the first global spiritual crusade, and the emergence in ever sharper relief of the World Center of the Faith.

---

[3] Unpublished: Tawqí'át-I-Mubárakih, 102-109 B.E. (Ṭihrán: Bahá'í Publishing Trust, 125 B.E.) pp.99-188. Letter dated Naw-Rúz 105 B.E. to the Bahá'ís of the East.

The Third Epoch of the Formative Age: 1963-1986

In addressing the British National Spiritual Assembly in 1951, the Guardian foreshadowed "world-wide enterprises destined to be embarked upon, in future epochs of that same (Formative) Age, by the Universal House of Justice." [9:261] In announcing the Nine Year Plan, "the second of those world-encircling enterprises destined in the course of time to carry the Word of God to every human soul," [8:14] the Universal House of Justice embarked upon the process anticipated by the Guardian and proclaimed the commencement of the third epoch of the Formative Age, an epoch which called the Bahá'ís to a yet more mature level of administrative functioning, consistent with the expected vast increase in the size and diversity of the community, its emergence as a model to mankind, and the extension of the influence of the Faith in the world at large. The House of Justice, in a letter dated October 1963, stated: "Beloved friends, the Cause of God, guarded and nurtured since its inception by God's Messengers, by the Center of His Covenant, and by His Sign on earth, now enters a new epoch, the third of the Formative Age. It must now grow rapidly in size, increase its spiritual cohesion and executive ability, develop its institutions, and extend its influence into all strata of society. We, its members, must, by constant study of the life-giving Word, and by dedicated service, deepen in spiritual understanding and show to the world a mature, responsible, fundamentally assured, and happy way of life, far removed from the passions, prejudices, and distractions of present-day society." [8:17f]

The period of the third epoch encompassed three world plans, involving all National Spiritual Assemblies, under the direction of the Universal House of Justice, namely, the Nine Year Plan (1964-1973), the Five Year Plan (1974-1979), and the Seven Year Plan (1979-1986.) This third epoch witnessed the emergence of the Faith from obscurity[4] and the initiation of activities designed to foster the social and economic development of communities.[5] The institution of the Continental Boards of Counsellors was brought into existence [8:139] leading to the establishment of the International Teaching Center.[6] Assistants to the Auxiliary Boards were also introduced.[7] At the World Center of the Faith, the historic construction and occupation of the Seat of the Universal House of Justice was a crowning event.[8]

---

4 Unpublished letter dated 19 May 1983 written by the Universal House of Justice to the Bahá'ís of the World.

5 Unpublished letter dated 20 October 1983 written by the Universal House of Justice to the Bahá'ís of the World.

6 Unpublished letter dated 8 June 1973 written by the Universal House of Justice to the Bahá'ís of the World.

7 Unpublished letter dated 8 June 1973 written by the Universal House of Justice to the Continental Board of Counsellors, and 7 October 1973 to the Bahá'ís of the World.

8 Unpublished telex dated 1 February 1983 written by the Universal House of Justice to the

The Fourth Epoch of the Formative Age: 1986—

In a letter dated 2 January 1986 written by the Universal House of Justice to the Bahá'ís of the World, the Supreme Body announced the inception of the fourth epoch of the Formative Age. It highlighted the significant developments that had taken place in the "organic growth of the Cause of God"[9] during the course of the recently completed third epoch, by assessing the readiness of the Bahá'í community to begin to address the objectives of the new Six Year Plan scheduled to begin on 21 April 1986, and outlined the general aims and characteristics of this new Plan. Whereas national plans had previously derived largely from the World Center, in this new epoch the specific goals for each national community will be formulated, within the framework of the overall objectives of the Plan, by means of consultation between the particular National Spiritual Assembly and the Continental Board of Counsellors. As the Universal House of Justice states: "This new process... signalizes the inauguration of a new stage in the unfoldment of the Administrative Order. Our beloved Guardian anticipated a succession of epochs during the Formative Age of the Faith; we have no hesitation in recognizing that this new development in the maturation of Bahá'í institutions marks the inception of the fourth epoch of that Age." [10]

Future Epochs

The tasks that remain to be accomplished during the course of the Formative Age are many and challenging. Additional epochs can be anticipated, each marking significant stages in the evolution of the Administrative order and culminating in the Golden Age of the Faith.[3:6] The Golden Age, itself, will involve "successive epochs" [6:155] leading ultimately to the establishment of the Most Great Peace, to the World Bahá'í Commonwealth and to the "birth and efflorescence of a world civilization." [3:6]

Bahá'ís of the World.

[9] Unpublished letter dated 2 January 1986 written by the Universal House of Justice to the Bahá'ís of the World.

[10] Unpublished letter dated 2 January 1986 written by the Universal House of Justice to the Bahá'ís of the World.

Timeline[1]—The Báb and Bahá'u'lláh

1817-11-12	Birth of Bahá'u'lláh, the hour of dawn, Ṭihrán, Írán. [10:12]
1819-10-20	Birth of the Báb (Siyyid 'Alí-Muḥammad) in Shíráz, Írán. [10:14,72]
1842	Marriage of the Báb to Khadíjih-Bagum. [10:76]
1844-05-23	Declaration of the Báb to Mullá Ḥusayn-i-Bushrú'í (the Bábu'l-Báb (gate of the Gate)) two hours and 11 minutes after sunset. The Báb was aged 25 years, four months and four days old. [10:57ff]
1844-05-23	Birth of 'Abdu'l-Bahá. [11:586]
1844-08	Mullá Ḥusayn (through Mullá Muḥammad) delivers a scroll from the Báb to Bahá'u'lláh in Ṭihrán. [10:104]
1844-10	The Báb receives Mullá Ḥusayn's first letter from Mashad conveying Bahá'u'lláh's response to His Divine Message. [10:107]
1844-10/ 1845-03	The Báb undertakes a pilgrimage to Mecca in the company of Quddús, arriving nine days later. [10:129]
1844-12-20	The Báb, taking hold of the ring on the door of the Kabah, proclaims three times the words: "I am that Qá'im whose advent you have been awaiting." [12:71]
1845-01-10	The Báb arrives in Medina. [10:140]
1845-09-23	The Báb is placed under arrest at the home of His uncle Ḥájí Mírzá Siyyid 'Alí in Shíráz. [10:151]
1846	Bahíyyih Khánum (daughter of Bahá'u'lláh; full sister of 'Abdu'l-Bahá) is born in Ṭihrán, Írán.
1846-09	The Báb proceeds from Shíráz to Iṣfáhán. [10:159]
1847-03-29	The Báb is imprisoned for 20 days in Kulayn after being summoned by Muḥammad Sháh to Ṭihrán. [10:226]
1847-04-01	Bahá'u'lláh sends a letter and gifts to the Báb in Kulayn. [10:227]
1847-07	The Báb is imprisoned in the fortress of Máh-Kú, Ádhirbáyján for nine months. [10:230, 243]
1847-11/12	Bahá'u'lláh is imprisoned for a few days after He was seen helping the Bábís of Qazvín. [10:299]
1848-03-20	Mullá Ḥusayn arrives at Máh-Kú on foot from Mashad to visit the Báb. [10:256]

1 Dates are listed by year followed (where known) by month and day; periods of a month or more are separated by a "/".

1848-04-10	The Báb is transferred to the fortress of Chihríq, Ádhirbáyján. [10:301]
1848-06/07	Conference of Badasht (22 days).[10:288]
1848-07	The Báb is summoned to Tabríz, Ádhirbáyján, for interrogation and subsequent incarceration. [10:315]
1848-07-21	On the instructions of the Báb, Mullá Ḥusayn hoists the Black Standard and with 202 followers leaves Mashad for Shaykh Ṭabarsí. [10:324]
1848-10/1849-05	The Mázindarán upheaval occurs at Shaykh Ṭabarsí near Bárfurúsh and in the forest of Mázindarán; Mullá Ḥusayn, Quddús and some one half of the Letters of the Living lose their lives. [10:324ff]
1848-10-10	Mullá Ḥusayn arrives at Bárfurúsh. [10:329]
1848-10-12	Mullá Ḥusayn arrives at Shaykh Ṭabarsí. [10:343]
1848-10	Bahá'u'lláh visits and inspects Shaykh Ṭabarsí and instructs Mullá Ḥusayn to send Mullá Mihdíy-i-Khu'í with six companions to Sárí to demand the release of Quddús. [10:349]
1848-11	Quddús arrives at Fort Ṭabarsí after Mullá Ḥusayn secures his release from Sárí. [10:354]
1848-12	Bahá'u'lláh is again imprisoned, this time in Ámul, preventing Him from joining the Báb's followers in Shaykh Ṭabarsí. He suffers the bastinado on behalf of His companions (who were spared through His actions). [10:369]
1849-02-02	Mullá Ḥusayn is killed at Fort Ṭabarsí. [10:380]
1849-05-16	Quddús is killed in Bárfurúsh. [10:410]
1850	Seven Martyrs of Ṭihrán are executed. [10:446]
1850-06-29	Execution of Vaḥid takes place in Nayríz. [10:494]
1850-07-09	The Báb is executed in the Barrack Square, Tabríz at noon. His mangled remains are exposed on the edge of the moat outside the city. [10:510ff]
1850-07-11	The remains of the Báb are removed and taken by Ḥájí Sulaymán Khán to a silk factory owned by one of the Bábí's in Mílán. [10:517ff]
1850-07-12	Remains of the Báb are placed in a wooden coffin and taken to "a place of safety." Subsequently, on Bahá'u'lláh's instructions, they are moved to Ṭihrán and placed in the shrine of the Imám-Zadíh Ḥasan. They are later removed to the home of Ḥáji Sulaymán

Khán in the Sar-Chashmih quarter of Ṭihrán and from there to the shrine of the Imám-Zadíh Ma'ṣúm. [10:519ff]

1851-01-08	Ḥujjat, The Proof, (Mullá Muḥammad-'Alí of Zanján) is killed in Zanján. [10:573]
1851-08-30	Bahá'u'lláh visits the holy city of Karbilá, 'Iráq. [10:582ff]
1852-08	Ṭáhirih is killed in Ṭihrán. [13:95ff]
1852-08-15	Two Bábí's (Ṣádiq-i-Tabrízí and Fatḥu'lláh-i-Qumí) attempt to assassinate Náṣiri'd-Dín Sháh outside his imperial court at Níyávarán. [10:599]
1852-08-16	Bahá'u'lláh is arrested Níyávarán, taken to Ṭihrán and imprisoned in the Siyáh-Chál (Black Pit.) He is 36 years old. This imprisonment lasts four months. It is during this time that the "Maid of Heaven" came to Bahá'u'lláh to invest Him with His Mission as the Manifestation of God for this Age. [10:607,631], [5:101]
1853-01-12	Bahá'u'lláh's exiles begin with His banishment to Baghdád. He is accompanied by members of His family, the more important of whom are: His wife Navváb, His nine-year-old son, 'Abdu'l-Bahá, His seven-year-old daughter Bahíyyih Khánum, as well as two of His brothers, Mírzá Músá (called Áqáy-i-Kalím) and Mírzá Muḥammad-Qudí. [5:104,108ff]
1853-04-08	Bahá'u'lláh arrives in Baghdád. At first He resides in Káẓimayn, three miles north of the city. Soon He moves to rented accommodations in the house of Ḥájí 'Alí-Madad. Works (revealed during this period include): Qullu'ṭ-Ṭa'ám. [5:109]
1854-04-10	Bahá'u'lláh departs for Sulaymánníyyih, Kurdistán. Before reaching Sulaymánníyyih, Bahá'u'lláh lives for a period on the Sar-Galú mountain. His family moves to the house of Sulaymán-i-Ghannám to await His return. Works: Prayers; Qaṣidiy-i-Varqa'íyyih; Sáqí-Az-Ghayb-i-Baqá. [14:115]
1856-03-19	Bahá'u'lláh returns to Baghdád from His two-year retreat to Sulaymánníyyih. And resides in the house of Sulaymán-i-Ghannám. Works (1856-1862): Tafsír-i-Hurúfát-i-Muqaṭṭah'ih; Ṣaḥífy-i-Shaṭṭiyyih; Haft-Vádí (Seven Valleys); Tafsír-i-Hú; Lawḥ-i-Javáhiru'l-Asrár, Lawḥ-i-Ḥúríyyih; Kitáb-i-Íqán (Book of Certitude); Kalimát-i-Maknúnih (Hidden Words.)[14:122]
1862	Bahá'u'lláh transfers His residence to the house of Riḍá Big for about one year. Works: Lawḥ-i-Sayyáḥ. [11:582]

1863-03-26	Bahá'u'lláh departs from Mazra'iy-i-Vash-shásh. Works: Subḥána-Rabbíya'l-A'lá; Shikkar-i-Shikan-Shavand; Húr-i-'Ujáb; Halih-Halih-Yá Bishárat, Ghulámu'l-Khuld; Az-Bágh-i-Iláhí; Báz-Áv-u-Bidih-Jámí; Malláḥu'l-Quds (Holy Mariner); Súriy-i-Ṣabr.[11:582]
1863-04-21	Declaration of Bahá'u'lláh (in Baghdád) is made to a few followers as the "One proclaimed and promised by the Báb."
1863-04-22	Public declaration of Bahá'u'lláh takes place in the Garden of Riḍván (Najíbíyyih) on the shores of the River Tigris.[11:583]
1863-04-22	Commencement of Bahá'u'lláh's exile from Baghdád for Constantinople. He arrives in the Garden of Riḍván (Najíbíyyih) where He spends 12 days.[11:583]
1863-04-30	Bahá'u'lláh's family joins Him in the Garden of Riḍván.
1863-05-03	Bahá'u'lláh leaves the Riḍván Garden at noon to begin the next phase of His exile. Works: Lawḥ-i-Hawdaj (while approaching Sámsún on the last day of overland travel).[11:583]
1863-05-09	Bahá'u'lláh departs for Constantinople.[11:583]
1863-06	Bahá'u'lláh moves to the house of Kháníy-i-Amru'lláh near Sulṭán-Salím Mosque. Works: Alvaḥ-i-Laylatu'l-Quds, Munájatháy-i-Ṣíyám (Prayers for fasting).
1863-08-13	Bahá'u'lláh leaves Sámsún by steamer for Constantinople.[5:157]
1863-08-14	The steamer carrying Bahá'u'lláh calls at Sinope.[5:157]
1863-08-15	The steamer carrying Bahá'u'lláh calls at Anyábulí.[5:157]
1863-08-16	Bahá'u'lláh arrives in Constantinople about noon. Residences include: Constantinople, house of Shamsí Big (near Khirgih Sharíf Mosque) for one month; house of Vísí Páshá (near Sulṭán Muḥammad Mosque) for three months. Works: Subḥánika-Yá-Hú, Lawḥ-i-'Abdu'l-Azíz Va-Vukalá.[5:157],[11:583f]
1863-12-01	Bahá'u'lláh departs for Adrianople.[11:584]
1863-12-12	Bahá'u'lláh arrives in Adrianople. He stays three nights at the Khán-i-'Aráb, a two-storey caravanserai, near the house of 'Izzat-Áqá. Works: Súriy-I-Aṣḥab; Lawḥ-i-Ḥajj I; Lawḥ-i-Ḥajj II.[11:584]
1863-12-15	Bahá'u'lláh moves to a house in the Murádíyyih quarter near Takyiy-i-Mawlaví for one week. Works: Kitáb-i-Badí,' Súriy-i-Mulúk (Tablet of the Kings.)[11:584]

1863-12-23	Bahá'u'lláh moves again to another house in Murádíyyih where He stays for about six months. Works: Lawḥ-i-Ru'ya, Súriy-i-Amr, Súriy-i-Damm. [11:584]
1864	Bahá'u'lláh moves to the house of Amru'lláh (north of Sulṭán-Salím Mosque), for about three months. Works: Lawḥ-i-Nápulyún I (1st Tablet to Napoleon III.)[11:584]
1865	Bahá'u'lláh moves to the house of 'Izzat-Áqá for 11 months. Works: Lawḥ-i-Sulṭán (Tablet to the Sháh of Persia), Lawḥ-i-Nuqṭih. [11:584]
1867-68	Remains of the Báb are removed from the shrine of the Imám-Zadíh Ma'ṣúm by Mullá 'Alí Akbar-i-Shahmírzádi and Jamál-i-Burújirdí, on the instructions of Bahá'u'lláh, to "another spot," the walls of a dilapidated building, Masjid-i-Mashá'u'lláh, on the road to Chashmih-'Alí. The next day, hearing that they had been discovered, the remains are moved to the house of Mírzá Ḥasan-i-Vazír (son-in-law of Ḥájí Mírzá Siyyid 'Alíy-i-Tafríshí) where they stay for 14 months. [15:21]
1868-07-26	Sulṭán 'Abdu'l-'Azíz issues a public farmán that condemns Bahá'u'lláh (and members of His family) to perpetual banishment, strict incarceration and forbids them from meeting among themselves and/or with local inhabitants. [5:179], [14:284]
1868-08-12	Bahá'u'lláh departs on the final stage of His exile to 'Akká, Palestine.[11:584]
1868-08-30	Bahá'u'lláh arrives in Port Said in the morning and leaves the same day for Jaffa, Haifa where He stays for a few hours before leaving by sail boat for 'Akká. [11:585]
1868-08-31	Bahá'u'lláh arrives in 'Akká. During His time in 'Akká He stays in the following houses: Barracks (two years, two months five days) House of Malik and House of Rabí'ih (three months), House of Manṣúr (two or three months), House of 'Abbúd (Kitáb-i-Aqdas revealed), Mazra'ih, Qaṣr (Mansion of Bahjí.) Works: Kitáb-i-Aqdas, Lawḥ-i-Nápulyún II (2nd Tablet to Napoleon III), Lawḥ-i-Malikih (Tablet to Queen Victoria), Lawḥ-i-Malik-i-Rús (Tablet to the Czar), Súriy-i-Haykal, Lawḥ-i-Burhán, Lawḥ-i-Ibn-i-Dhi'b (Epistle to the Son of the Wolf), Lawḥ-i-Páp (Pope).[11:585]
1868-1870	Custody of the remains of Báb is given to Ḥájí Sháh Muḥammad-i-Manshádí, surnamed Amínu'l-Bayán,

	and they are hidden beneath the floor of the inner sanctuary of the shrine of the Imám Zádih Zayd where they lie until Bahá'u'lláh instructs Mírzá Asadu'lláh-i-Iṣfáhání to move them to other locations in Ṭihrán. [15:21]
1870-06-23	Bahá'u'lláh's son, Mírzá Mihdí, dies as a result of a fall through a skylight on the roof of the Barracks, 'Akká. [11:585]
1877-06	Bahá'u'lláh leaves 'Akká and moves to Mazra'ih. [11:585]
1879-09	Bahá'u'lláh leaves Mazra'ih and moves to Bahjí. [11:585]
1890	Bahá'u'lláh's tent is raised on Mount Carmel. Bahá'u'lláh visits Mount Carmel four times, the longest visit lasting three months. [5:194]
1890-04-15/20	Prof. E. G. Browne of Cambridge is granted four interviews with Bahá'u'lláh at Bahjí over five days. [5:194]
1892-05-29	Ascension of Bahá'u'lláh, aged, 74 occurs eight hours after sunset (03:00 A.M.) in the Mansion of Bahjí. [5:221-233]

Timeline—'Abdu'l-Bahá

1844-05-23	Birth of 'Abdu'l-Bahá takes place in Ṭihrán.[16:9]
1883-12-10	Possibly the first mention is made of Bahá'í Faith in the United States in a newspaper—*The Sun*, published in New York City, under a column heading of *The Babs and Their Prophet*.[17:227]
1893-09-23	First major public mention is made of the Bahá'í Faith in America—a paper written by Rev. Henry Jessup, DD, director of Presbyterian Missionary Operations in North Syria and read by Rev. George A. Ford of Syria at the World Parliament of Religions in Chicago.[11:586]
1894	Mr. Thornton Chase—first American believer—is enrolled (as designated by 'Abdu'l-Bahá). 'Abdu'l-Bahá surnames him 'Thábit—the Steadfast.[18:36]
1894-02	First Bahá'í Center is established in the West (Chicago).[19:179]
1894-07-04	Green Acre opens, culminating in the raising of a flag of World Peace by Miss Sarah Farmer.[20:151]
1898	'Abdu'l-Bahá gives instructions to Mírzá Asad-u'lláh regarding the transportation of the remains of the Báb to Palestine.[15:21]
1898-03-31	Fifty lunar years after His execution in Tabríz, the remains of the Báb arrive in the Holy Land (via Iṣfáhán, Kirmánsháh, Baghdád and Damascus).[15:21]
1898-11	'Abdu'l-Bahá ends the period of mourning for Bahá'u'lláh by opening His Tomb to pilgrims.[5:275]
1898-12-10	First Western pilgrims (the Getsingers) visit 'Abdu'l-Bahá.[16:67]
1898-12-20	Second Western pilgrim group arrives in 'Akká (among whom were Phoebe Hearst, Mrs. Thornburgh, Mrs. May Bolles (Maxwell) and (possibly) Robert Turner).[16:68]
1899-01	Purchase is made of the land designated by Bahá'u'lláh as the Resting Place of the Báb, and the construction is started of a marble sarcophagus by the Burmese believers in accordance with 'Abdu'l-Bahá's suggestion. 'Abdu'l-Bahá lays the Cornerstone of the Shrine.[15:21]
1901-08-20	Following a long period of relative freedom, 'Abdu'l-Bahá is reimprisoned in 'Akká.[11:586][16:94]

1902	First Bahá'í Publishing Society is formed in Chicago; *Bahá'í News* is inaugurated developing later into *Star of the West* magazine.[5:261]
1902-11-28	Construction begins on the first Bahá'í House of Worship in "Ishqábád, Russia.[11:586][16:108]
1903-06-07	'Abdu'l-Bahá writes to the House of Spirituality of Chicago advising them to begin construction of the first Mashriqu'l-Adhkár in the West.[22:64]
1907-11-26	First (North American) Mashriqu'l-Adhkár Convention meeting is held in Chicago. A Temple Committee of nine members is appointed to locate a suitable site.[19:179]
1908-03-22	Second (North American) Mashriqu'l-Adhkár Convention meeting (22/23) takes place, resulting in the formation of the "Bahá'í Temple Unity." The convention adopts a constitution and elects an executive board charged with the purchase of land and the erection of the temple.[22:67]
1908-04-09	Two plots of land are purchased at a cost of $2,000 (with an option to purchase another 12) for the North American Mashriqu'l-Adhkár by the House of Spirituality of Chicago (the lots are subsequently transferred to the Bahá'í Temple Unity).[22:67]
1908-09	'Abdu'l-Bahá is released from His incarceration by the "Young Turks".[11:586]
1909-03	Bahá'í Temple Unity is formed as an "incorporated religious corporation" in the state of Illinois. An Executive Board is elected by representatives from 36 U.S. cities to hold properties and full legal authority to proceed with the construction of the Mashriqu'l-Adhkár.[17:137]
1909-03-21	'Abdu'l-Bahá places remains of the Báb in His final resting place on Mount Carmel, Israel.[15:21] The first Convention of the Bahá'ís of the United States and Canada is held.[23:137]
1910-03-21	The Bahá'í magazine—*Bahá'í News* is founded by Alfred Windust and Gertrude Buikema in Chicago and renamed *Star of the West* in 1911.[20:190]
1910	'Abdu'l-Bahá visits Egypt.[16:131]
1910-09	——leaves Egypt for Palestine.[11:586]
1911-08-11	——boards the S. S. *Corsica* for Marseilles thereby beginning the first of two epic journeys to the West.[16:139]

1911-09-04	——arrives in London (following a few days rest at Thonon-les-Bains).[16:140] Except for a few days in Bristol, He resides in the home of Lady Blomfield, 97 Cadogan Gardens, London, where He receives many guests and visitors.[24:33] He visits the Lord Mayor of London (on the invitation of the mayor) in the Mansion House.[24:109]
1911-09-08	——meets with "friends" during a Unity Meeting in the home of Miss Ethel Rosenberg.[24:44]
1911-09-09	——visits Vanners, Byfleet.[24:85]
1911-09-10	——gives a public address in the City Temple, Holborn, London.[24:19] This is the first time He has spoken to a public audience.[16]
1911-09-13	——gives a short discourse in the home of Mrs. Thornburgh-Cropper.[24:46]
1911-09-17	——addresses the congregation of St. John the Divine Church, Westminster.[24:19,21]
1911-09-23	—— gives a short discourse in the home of Mrs. Thornburgh-Cropper.[24:48]
1911-09-23/25	——visits Bristol where He stays in the Clifton Guest House, Clifton.[24:81]
1911-09-28/29	——second visit to Vanners, Byfleet.[24:86] On this occasion He visits the Brooklands aviation grounds.[24:99]
1911-09-30	——gives a discourse in the Theosophical Headquarters at the request of their president, Mrs. A. Besant.[24:19,27]
1911-09-29	Some 460 people gather in the Passmore Edwards' Settlement, Tavistock Place, London at the invitation of Mrs. Thornburgh-Cropper to bid farewell to 'Abdu'l-Bahá on the eve of His departure for Paris.[24:33]
1911-10-01	'Abdu'l-Bahá unites Regina Núr Maḥal Khánum and Mírzá Yuhanna Dáwud in marriage. He says to them: "Never have I united anyone in marriage before, except My own daughters."[24:77]
1911-10-03	——arrives in Paris and remains for approximately nine weeks. He resides at 4 Avenue de Camoën in the area of Quai de Passy, Paris, where He speaks daily to a gathering of interested people in His salon. His morning addresses are recorded in the book *Paris Talks*.[25]

1911-11	——addresses the Theosophical Society and elaborates 11 central principles of Bahá'í Teachings.[25:127] These are restated in a variety of ways during subsequent morning meetings.[25:135ff]
1911-11-09	——speaks at L'Alliance Spiritualiste, Salle de l'Athénée, St. Germain, Paris.[25:83]
1911-11-10	—— speaks at 15 Rue Greuze, Paris.[25:88]
1911-11-26	——speaks at Church of Pastor Wagner, Foyer de l'Âme, Paris.[25:119]
1911-12-01	——speaks at 15 Rue Greuze, Paris, His last meeting in Paris.[25:168]
1911-12-02	——departs for Egypt.[16:167]
1911-12	——returns to Egypt where He takes up residence in Ramlih. He winters in Egypt before leaving for America in March of the next year.[16:171]
1912	Green Acre Fellowship is given control of the Green Acre Properties in Eliot, Maine.[22:89]
1912	Lake shore tract of 293 feet frontage is contracted at $17,000 (Wilmette).[22:68]
1912-03-25	'Abdu'l-Bahá sails on the steamship S. S. *Cedric* from Alexandria for New York (via Naples).[16:171]
1912-03-26	Shoghi Effendi, eldest grandson of 'Abdu'l-Bahá and later the Guardian of the Bahá'í Faith, is required to leave the ship (due to a diagnosed eye infection).[16:171]
1912-04-11	'Abdu'l-Bahá arrives in New York where He takes up residence in the Hotel Ansonia.[16:172] Later in the day He visits the home of Mr. and Mrs. Edward B. Kinney, 780 West End Ave., N.Y.[26:1]
1912-04-12	——visits the home of Mr. and Mrs. Howard MacNutt, 935 Eastern Parkway, Brooklyn, N.Y.[26:2] Later that day He visits the studio of Miss Phillips, 39 West 67th St., N.Y.[26:5]
1912-04-13	——visits the home of home of Mr. and Mrs. Alexander Morten, 141 East 101st St., N.Y.[26:7]
1912-04-14	——gives His first public address in America in the Church of the Ascension, Fifth Ave., and 10th St., N.Y.[26:9] Later that day He addresses the Union Meeting of Advanced Thought in the Carnegie Lyceum, West 57th St., N.Y.[26:11]
1912-04-15	——visits the home of Mr. Montford Mills, 327 West End Ave., N.Y.[26:14]
1912-04-16	——addresses the Bahá'í friends of New Jersey in the Hotel Ansonia, Broadway and 73rd St., N.Y.[26:16]

1912-04-17 ——speaks in the Hotel Ansonia, Broadway and 73rd St., N.Y.[26:18] Later that day He visits the home of Mr. and Mrs. Kinney.[26:20]

1912-04-18 ——visits the home of Mr. and Mrs. Marshall L. Emery, 273 West 90th St., N.Y.[26:20] He attends a play, *The Terrible Meek* about the crucifixion of Christ, in the Little Theater, 44th St., N.Y.

1912-04-19 ——speaks in Earl Hall, Columbia University.[26:26] Later that day He addresses the residents of the Bowery Mission, 227 Bowery, N.Y.[26:30] At the end of this meeting 'Abdu'l-Bahá stands at the Bowery entrance to Mission Hall shaking hands with each one of the 400—500 men attending and placing a piece of silver in each hand.[16:177]

1912-04-20 —travels to Washington, D.C., where He and an interpreter are guests in the home of Mr. and Mrs. Arthur J. Parsons, 1700 18th Street Northwest.[16:179] That evening He addresses a meeting of the Orient-Occident-Unity Conference in the public library.[26:32]

1912-04-21 ——speaks in Studio Hall, 1219 Connecticut Ave.[26:34] Later that day He speaks in the Universalist Church, 13th and L Streets.[26:36]

1912-04-22 ——visits the home of Mr. and Mrs. Parsons.[26:40]

1912-04-23 ——speaks at Howard University.[26:41]

1912-04-23 ——visits the home of Mr. and Mrs. Parsons.[26:44] Later that day He speaks in the Metropolitan African Methodist Episcopal Church, M St.[26:46]

1912-04-24 ——addresses a Children's Reception in Studio Hall;[26:49] Later that day He visits the home of Mr. and Mrs. Parsons followed by a visit to the home of Mrs. Andrew Dyer, 1937 13th St., NW.[26:51]

1912-04-24 ——at Mr. Bell's invitation visits Alexander Graham Bell in his home and stays overnight.[16:183]

1912-04-25 ——receives former U.S. President Theodore Roosevelt;[16:184] speaks to the Theosophical Society in the home of Mr. and Mrs. Parsons as well as receiving other visitors.[26:55] Later that evening He attends a dinner hosted in His honor by the Turkish Ambassador, Yúsuf Ḍíyá Pá<u>sh</u>á.[16:183]

1912-04-27 Lee McClung, treasurer of the United States, has lunch with 'Abdu'l-Bahá; later that day He attends a farewell dinner hosted by Mrs. Parsons; among the guests are Admiral Peary of North Pole fame, eminent judges, members of Congress and representatives of foreign governments.[16:184]

1912-04-28 'Abdu'l-Bahá receives a number of important ambassadorial and ministerial callers (including the British Ambassador, James Bryce, later Viscount Bryce). He leaves by train for Chicago in the late afternoon.[16:184]

1912-04-29 ——arrives in Chicago and takes up residence in the Plaza Hotel.[16:185]

1912-04-30 Fifth (North American) Mashriqu'l-Adhkár Convention (29 April-1 May), Chicago; 'Abdu'l-Bahá is present.[22:68]

1912-04-30 'Abdu'l-Bahá addresses a number of different meetings, including: the Bahá'í Convention, Drill Hall, Masonic Temple, Chicago; a Public Meeting concluding Convention of Bahá'í Unity Temple;[26:62] a gathering in Hull House, Chicago;[26:64] and, the Fourth Annual Conference of the National Association for the Advancement of Colored People, Handel Hall, Chicago.[26:66]

1912-05-01 ——gives an Address at the Dedication of the Mashriqu'l-Adhkár grounds.[26:67] Dedication of (North American) Mashriqu'l-Adhkár ground is by 'Abdu'l-Bahá and the laying of the cornerstone by Him.[16:186]

1912-05-02 ——Hotel Plaza, Chicago, gives two discourses;[26:68,75] Hotel LaSalle, Chicago, Federation of Women's Clubs;[26:70] Hotel LaSalle, Chicago, Bahá'í Women's Reception.[26:74]

1912-05-03 ——Hotel Plaza, Chicago, gives two discourses;[26:80, 81] the Association of East Indians makes a presentation to 'Abdu'l-Bahá expressing their gratitude at His visit to North America.[16:188]

1912-05-04 ——speaks at Northwestern University Hall, Chicago, Theosophical Society.[26:83]

1912-05-05 ——speaks at Hotel Plaza, Chicago, children's meeting;[26:88] Plymouth Congregational Church, 935 East 50th St., Chicago;[26:90] All-Souls Church, Lincoln Center, Chicago.[26:93]

1912-05-06 ——leaves Chicago for Cleveland; gives an address at Euclid Hall, stays in the Euclid Hotel.[26:97] Later that day He visits the Sanitarium of Dr. C. Swingle.[26:100]

1912-05-07 ——leaves for Pittsburgh; on arrival at the Hotel Schenley He gives a public address.[26:101]

1912-05-08 ——returns to Washington, D.C., where He stays in rented accommodation at 14 Harvard Street.[16:189]

1912-05-11 ——leaves by train for New York where He takes up residence in an apartment in the Hudson Apartment House, 227 Riverside Drive, N.Y.;[16:190] later that day He gives an address.[26:107]

1912-05-12 ——speaks at Unity Church, Montclair, N.J.;[26:109] He then addresses a meeting of International Peace Forum in Grace Methodist Episcopal Church, West 104th St., N.Y.[26:112]

1912-05-13 ——attends a reception by New York Peace Society in the Hotel Astor.[26:118]

1912-05-14 ——goes to the Conference on Peace and Arbitration, Lake Mohonk, and stays for three days.[16:193]

1912-05-19 ——speaks in the Church of the Divine Paternity, Central Park West, N.Y.;[26:122] speaks in the Brotherhood Church, Bergen and Fairview Aves., Jersey City, N.J.[26:125]

1912-05-20 ——addresses the Woman's Suffrage meeting in the Metropolitan Temple, 7th Ave., and 14th St., N.Y.[26:128]

1912-05-22 ——travels to Boston and remains there until the 26th. In addition to His public addresses He also visits the al-Ḥalqadath-Dhahabíyyah (The Golden Circle) the largest association of Syrians in the U.S. at that time. Later that day He visits Worchester by car.[16:198]

1912-05-23 ——speaks in the home of Mr. and Mrs. Francis W. Breed, 367 Harvard St., Cambridge, Mass.[16:199][26:133]

1912-05-24 ——addresses the Free Religious Association at the Unitarian Conference, Ford Hall, Boston.[16:199][26:138]

1912-05-25 ——makes a farewell address at Huntington Chambers, Boston.[26:134]

1912-05-26 ——leaves Boston at noon, by train, arriving in New York at 6 P.M. He goes straight to the home of Mr. and Mrs. Kinney and from there to address the congregation of Mount Morris Baptist Church, 5th Ave., and 126th St. He is very tired and has to lean on a pillar when He rises to speak.[16:201]

1912-05-28 ——attends a reception in the Metropolitan Temple.[26:145]

1912-05-29 ——speaks in the home of Mr. and Mrs. Kinney.[26:148]

1912-05-30 ——speaks in the Theosophical Lodge, N.Y.[26:151]

1912-05-31 ——speaks in the Town Hall, Fanwood, N.J.[26:155]

1912-06-01 ——has first sitting for the portrait painted by Miss Juliet Thompson in her studio in New York.[27:299]

1912-06-02 ——speaks at Church of the Ascension, N.Y.[26:157]

1912-06-03 ——visits Milford, Penn. and stays overnight.[16:208]

1912-06-04 ——returns to New York and takes up residence for the duration of His stay in the home of Mr. and Mrs. Champney, 309 West 79th Street, N.Y.[16:208]

1912-06-08 ——speaks in the home of Mr. and Mrs. Champney,[26:166] and then leaves for Philadelphia. On arrival He is so tired that He has to cancel some of His engagements.[16:209]

1912-06-09 ——speaks in the Unitarian Church, 15th St., and Girard Ave., Philadelphia;[26:167] and then in the Baptist Temple, Broad and Berks Streets.[26:171]

1912-06-10 ——returns to New York.[16:212]

1912-06-11 ——speaks to the Open Committee meeting in the home of Mr. and Mrs. Kinney;[26:178] later that day He gives two discourses.[26:178,181]

1912-06-12 ——speaks in the home of Mr. and Mrs. Kinney.[26:182]

1912-06-15 ——speaks in the home of Mr. and Mrs. Kinney.[26:184]

1912-06-16 ——speaks in the Fourth Unitarian Church, Beverly Road, Flatbush, Brooklyn;[26:185] speaks in the home of Mr. and Mrs. Howard MacNutt, 935 Eastern Parkway, Brooklyn. He has lunch with Mr. and Mrs. MacNutt;[26:189] later that day He speaks in the Central Congregational Church, Hancock St., Brooklyn.[26:192]

1912-06-17 ——speaks in the home of Mr. and Mrs. Kinney.[26:199]

1912-06-18 A motion picture is made of 'Abdu'l-Bahá in the home of Mr. and Mrs. Howard MacNutt;[16:220] 'Abdu'l-Bahá speaks in the home of Mr. and Mrs. Kinney.[26:200]

1912-06-19 'Abdu'l-Bahá names New York City the "City of the Covenant." On the same day He designates Mrs. Lua Getsinger a "Herald of the Covenant."[16:220]

1912-06-20 ——speaks in the home of Mr. and Mrs. Kinney.[26:201]

1912-06-23 ——visits Montclair, N.J. He stays for a week; with one overnight visit to Newark.[16:221][26:205]

1912-06-29 ——visits West Englewood, N.J. He attends a "Unity Feast" held outdoors, on properties owned by the Wilhelms, during which many unique photographs are taken. He stays overnight.[16:223, 225][26:208]

1912-06-30	——motors to Morristown, N.J., lunching in the home of Mr. Topakiyan, the consul-general for Persia. He returns to New York later that evening.[16:226]
1912-07-01	——gives two discourses in the home of Mr. and Mrs. Kinney.[26:211,213]
1912-07-05	——gives two discourses in the home of Mr. and Mrs. Kinney.[26:213,215]
1912-07-06	——speaks in the home of Mr. and Mrs. Kinney.[26:220]
1912-07-14	——speaks in the All Souls Unitarian Church, 4th Ave., and 20th St., N.Y.[26:224]
1912-07-15	——speaks in the home of Mrs. Florian Krug, 830 Park Ave., N.Y.[26:230]
1912-07-17	——presides over the marriage of Grace Robarts and Harlan Ober.[16:230]
1912-07-22	——is received by Prince Muḥammad-'Alí Pás͟há, brother of the Khedive of Egypt.[16:230]
1912-07-23	——travels to Boston;[16:232] gives a talk in the Hotel Victoria.[26:233]
1912-07-24	——pays a second visit to the al-Ḥalqadat͟h-D͟hahabíyyah;[16:232] addresses the Theosophical Society in The Kensington, Exeter and Boylston Streets.[26:234]
1912-07-25	——speaks in the Hotel Victoria.[26:239]
1912-07-26	——travels to Dublin, N.H. where He resides at an estate owned by Mr. and Mrs. Parsons.[16:234]
1912-08-05	——speaks at the Dublin Inn, Dublin.[26:240]
1912-08-06	——speaks in home of Mr. and Mrs. Parsons.[26:242]
1912-08-14	——speaks in home of Mr. and Mrs. Parsons.[16:239]
1912-08-15	Mrs. Parsons hosts a farewell meeting with musical recitation.[16:239]
1912-08-16	'Abdu'l-Bahá travels by car to Green Acre, Eliot, Maine, and within minutes of arrival gives a discourse to a large group of people. He then visits Sarah Farmer in a sanitarium in Portsmouth. On His return to Green Acre He gives one of the longest talks of His entire tour.[16:240f][26:247]
1912-08-17	——gives four discourses at Green Acre.[26:255ff]
1912-08-20	Fred Mortensen arrives at Green Acre.[16:247]
1912-08-23	'Abdu'l-Bahá leaves for Malden where He stayed in the home of Miss Wilson. Enroute He called again at the Portsmouth sanitarium to visit Miss Farmer.[16:251f]
1912-08-25	——addresses the New Thought Forum, in the Metaphysical Club, Boston.[26:270]

1912-08-26	——speaks at Franklin Square House, Boston.[26:274]
1912-08-27	——addresses the Metaphysical Club.[26:278]
1912-08-29	——speaks in the home of Madame Morey, 34 Hillside Ave., Malden, Mass.[26:283]
1912-08-30	——arrives in Montréal, Canada and stays the night in the home of Mr. and Mrs. William Sutherland Maxwell, 716 Pine Avenue West. He then moves to the Windsor Hotel.[28][16:256] On arrival He goes for a drive and on noticing the Roman Catholic Church of Notre Dame He goes in.[16:260]
1912-09-01	——at the request of Mr. And Mrs. Birk, neighbors of the Maxwells, He visits their nine-year-old daughter who was an invalid, and holds her in His arms; she later recovered;[16:261] speaks at the Church of the Messiah;[26:291] gives two discourses in the home of Mr. and Mrs. Maxwell.[26:296]
1912-09-02	——speaks in the in the home of Mr. and Mrs. Maxwell.[26:296,300]
1912-09-03	——gives and address in Coronation Hall.[16:264]
1912-09-05	—— gives and address in St. James Methodist Church.[16:264]
1912-09-09	——leaves Montréal for Buffalo, N.Y. several days behind schedule because of ill health; He changes trains in Toronto and gets out and walks for a few moments on the station platform.[16:265]
1912-09-11	——speaks in the Church of the Messiah, North and Mariner Streets, Buffalo.[16:266]
1912-09-11	——visits Niagara Falls.[16:266]
1912-09-12	——departs for Chicago by train[16:266] where He is greeted by a large throng of people, then He is driven to the home of Mrs. Corinne True, 5358 Kenmore Avenue.[16:297]
1912-09-14	——speaks at the Theosophical Society, Chicago.[16:297]
1912-09-15	——travels by train to Kenosha, Wisconsin. On arrival He addresses the Bahá'í friends and then gives a public presentation in the evening in the Congregational Church.[16:267]
1912-09-16	——speaks in home of Mr. and Mrs. Corinne True;[26:314] following which He leaves for Minneapolis, Minnesota, where He stays in Suite 603 of the Plaza Hotel.[16:273]

1912-09-19 ——addresses the Commercial Club, Minneapolis; speaks in the Jewish Reform Temple, 10th Street and 5th Avenue South.[16:274]

1912-09-20 ——speaks in home of Mr. Albert L. Hall, 2030 Queen Ave., South, Minneapolis;[26:319] speaks in the home of Dr. and Mrs. Clement Woolson, 870 Laurel Ave., St. Paul, Minnesota.[26:323]

1912-09-21 ——leaves Minneapolis and stays overnight in Omaha, Nebraska.[16:279]

1912-09-22 ——visits the home of William Jennings Bryan (the future secretary of state in the Wilson administration) in Lincoln, Nebraska. Mr. Bryan was not home (he was campaigning on Woodrow Wilson's behalf); however, 'Abdu'l-Bahá meets with his wife and daughter.[16:279]

1912-09-23 ——arrives in Denver, Colorado and stays in the Shirley Hotel.[16:280]

1912-09-24 ——speaks in the home of Mrs. Sidney Roberts, Sherman St., Denver.[26:328]

1912-09-25 ——speaks in the Second Divine Science Church, 3229 West 38th Ave., Denver.[26:331]

1912-09-27 ——leaves Denver for California.[16:283]

1912-09-28 ——stays overnight in Glenwood Springs where He goes to the mineral baths and has lunch on the lawn of the Colorado Hotel; He leaves by train at midnight.[16:283]

1912-09-29 ——decides to visit Salt Lake City, Utah; where He stays in the Kenyon Hotel.[16:284]

1912-09-30 ——visits the Agricultural Conference and Exhibition, which is in progress and orders flower seeds for the gardens around the Bahá'í Shrines in the Holy Land.[16:284]

1912-10-01 ——reaches in San Francisco around midnight and stays in a house at 1815 California Street.[16:286]

1912-10-01 Final payment 12 land lots for (North American) Mashriqu'l-Adhkár.[22:72]

1912-10-06 ——speaks in a Unitarian Church in San Francisco.[16:286]

1912-10-07 ——addresses the Japanese Young Men's Christian Association in the Japanese Independent Church, Oakland.[26:337]

1912-10-08 ——speaks in the Palo Alto Unitarian Church, Stanford University, Palo Alto.[16:295]

1912-10-10 ——addresses the Open Forum in San Francisco.[26:349]

1912-10-12	——speaks in Temple Emmanu-El, 450 Sutter St., San Francisco.[26:355]
1912-10-12	——speaks in the home of Mrs. Goodall.[16:307]
1912-10-13	——for three days the guest of Mrs. Phoebe Hearst, who had led the first party of American pilgrims to visit Him in 'Akká.[16:307]
1912-10-16	——attends a 19-Day Feast in the home of Mrs. Goodall and Mrs. Cooper in Oakland.[16:309]
1912-10-17	——discovers His signet ring is missing and for the rest of His sojourn signs (instead of sealing) every Tablet He writes or dictates.[16:309]
1912-10-18	——travels to Los Angeles to visit the grave of Thornton Chase. Traveling to the cemetery by tram car, He visits the grave on 19 October.[16:309]
1912-10-21	——returns to San Francisco.[16:310]
1912-10-23	——visits Oakland for the last time.[16:311]
1912-10-24	——leaves San Francisco for Sacramento.[16:311]
1912-10-25	——speaks in the Assembly Hall, Hotel Sacramento, Sacramento.[26:365]
1912-10-26	——speaks in the Assembly Hall, Hotel Sacramento;[26:371] He then departs California by train for Chicago.[16:316]
1912-10-28	——stays overnight in Denver where He speaks in the home of Mrs. Roberts and also the Church of the Messiah.[16:316]
1912-10-31	——arrives in Chicago;[16:317] speaks in the Hotel Plaza.[26:375]
1912-11-01	——speaks in the home of Mr. and Mrs. Corinne True.[26:371]
1912-11-03	——speaks in the Hotel Plaza; gives an address in the Englewood Church and then another in the Congregational Church; attends a 19-Day Feast in the home of Mrs. Davis.[16:318]
1912-11-05	——speaks in the Grand Hotel, Cincinnati, Ohio. A banquet is prepared in His honor.[26:382]
1912-11-06	——speaks in the Grand Hotel, Cincinnati, Ohio; He leaves for Washington D.C. on the noon train. On arrival He takes up residence in the home of Mr. and Mrs. Parsons;[16:318] in the afternoon He speaks in the Universalist Church, 13th and L Streets.[26:384]
1912-11-07	——gives two discourses in the home of Mr. and Mrs. Parsons.[26:391,394]

1912-11-08 ——gives an address in the Eighth Street Temple, Jewish Synagogue, Washington, D.C.[26:397]

1912-11-09 ————gives two discourses in the home of Mr. and Mrs. Parsons;[26:405,410] attends a Bahá'í Banquet in His honor in Rauscher's Hall. 'Abdu'l-Bahá presents everyone present with flowers and sweets. This is the first Bahá'í interracial banquet.[26:413]

1912-11-10 ——speaks in the home of Mr. and Mrs. Parsons;[26:416] speaks in the home of Mr. and Mrs. Joseph H. Hannen, 1252 8th St., NW, Washington D.C.;[26:420] speaks at 1901 18th St. and NW, Washington D.C.[26:423]

1912-11-11 ——leaves for Baltimore by train; on arrival He addresses a number of people in a hotel; He then addresses the congregation of a Unitarian Church followed by lunch in the home of Mr. and Mrs. Struven; in the afternoon He departs for Philadelphia where He meets and talks with Bahá'ís in the station before boarding a third train for New York City, (which reaches its destination at 01:00 hours the next morning).[16:328]

1912-11-12 ——receives guests in His residence (the home of Mr. and Mrs. Champney, 309 West 78th Street is placed at His disposal); regular meetings are also held in the home of Mrs. Krug, during the day and the home of Mr. and Mrs. Kinney, in the evenings.[16:329]

1912-11-15 ——speaks in the home of Miss Juliet Thompson, 48 West 10th St., N.Y.[26:426]

1912-11-16 ——gives an address in the home of Mr. and Mrs. Champney.[26:432]

1912-11-17 —— gives an address in the Genealogical Hall, 252 West 58th St., N.Y.[26:433]

1912-11-18 ——speaks in the home of Mr. and Mrs. Frank K. Moxey, 575 Riverside Drive, N.Y.; visits J. Pierpont Morgan's library and inscribes a blessing to him for his philanthropy.[26:437]

1912-11-23 ——attends a banquet in His honor in the Great Northern Hotel, 118 West 57th St., N.Y.;[26:442] speaks in the home of Mr. and Mrs. Champney.[16:331]

1912-11-29 ——speaks in the home of Mr. and Mrs. Kinney.[26:444]

1912-12-02 ——gives two discourses in the home of Mr. and Mrs. Kinney.[26:448,449]

1912-12-03 ——speaks in the home of Mrs. Florian Krug;[26:453] He addresses Mr. Edward J. Kinney's Bible class in the Kinney home and gives a general discourse to those gathered.[26:454,456]

1912-12-04 ——addresses the Theosophical Society, 2228 Broadway, N.Y.[26:458]

1912-12-05 ——gives a discourse on board the S. S. *Celtic*, N.Y. to those who have come to bid Him farewell on the day of departure for Europe;[26:464] sails for England.[16:337]

1912-12-13 ——arrives in Liverpool, England and stays in the Adelphi Hotel.[16:343]

1912-12-14 ——speaks at Theosophical Society, Liverpool.[16:343]

1912-12-15 ——speaks in Pembroke Chapel, Liverpool.[16:343]

1912-12-16 ——leaves Liverpool by train for London where He stays at 97 Cadogan Gardens, London (the apartment home of Lady Blomfield). He receives an almost constant stream of visitors (amongst whom was Mrs. Emily Pankhurst.)[16:343f]

1912-12-17 ——addresses a reception held in His honor by Miriam Thornburgh-Cropper.[16:344]

1912-12-18 ——receives Professor Edward Granville Browne, the noted Cambridge Orientalist, the only Westerner to have been received by Bahá'u'lláh.[16:346]

1912-12-20 ——Mushíru'l-Mulk, the Persian Minister in London calls on 'Abdu'l-Bahá during the course of the afternoon; 'Abdu'l-Bahá speaks in the Westminster Hotel, London. (Sir Thomas Barclay in the Chair.)[16:347]

1912-12-22 ——attends a performance of Alice Buckton's mystery play, *Eager Heart*, at Church House, Westminster.[16:348]

1912-12-24 ——gives a series of long interviews to a number of newspaper reporters.[16:348]

1912-12-25 ——visits Lord Lamington in the afternoon; that evening visits a Salvation Army hostel where He donates 20 guineas to the hostel for an extra evening meal. He inspects the sleeping accommodation of the hostel and visits a children's home.[16:351]

1912-12-26 ——speaks on the subjects of prayer, evil and the progress of the soul at 97 Cadogan Gardens.[25:177]

1912-12-27 ——goes for a walk in Hyde Park and Kensington Gardens followed by a reception arranged by Lady Blomfield.[16:352]

1912-12-29 The Maharajah of Jalawar visits 'Abdu'l-Bahá; in the afternoon 'Abdu'l-Bahá speaks in the home of Miss Annie Gamble; later that evening He speaks from a Methodist pulpit at Kingsway House.[16:352]

1912-12-30 ——attends a Nineteen-Day Feast in the home of Mrs. Robinson.[16:352]

1912-12-31 ——arrives at Manchester College, Oxford University, Oxford for meetings arranged on the initiative of Dr. T. K. Cheyne; 'Abdu'l-Bahá meets separately with Dr. Cheyne and also has lunch with him and his wife; the meeting is presided over by the Principal of the College, Dr. E. Estlin Carpenter.[16:352ff]

1913-01-02 'Abdu'l-Bahá addresses a meeting arranged by Mrs. Despard for a number of her colleagues in the Suffragette Movement.[16:354]

1913-01-04 ——speaks on the "Four Kinds of Love" at 97 Cadogan Gardens.[25:179]

1913-01-06 ——travels to Edinburgh on the invitation of Dr. and Mrs. Alexander Whyte. He arrives at Edinburgh Waverley Station at 5:00 P.M. He stays in the Whyte home, West Register House, 7 Charlotte Square. 'Abdu'l-Bahá receives a continual stream of visitors.[29:65ff]

1913-01-07 ——visits Castle Hill and the Outlook Tower museum where He is received by Professor Sir Patrick Geddes, the founder and president of the Outlook Tower Society. Later that day He drives down the Royal Mile and past Holyrood Palace; that evening He addresses the Esperanto Society in the Freemasons' Hall, 96 George Street, Edinburgh.[29:73ff]

1913-01-08 ——under the auspices of the Outlook Tower Society, 'Abdu'l-Bahá gives an address in Rainy Hall, New College (Divinity Faculty). That evening He attends a recital of Handel's *Messiah* in St. Giles Cathedral.[29:85ff]

1913-01-09 ——addresses a gathering of suffragettes and a number of prominent men opposed to them (7 Charlotte Square); that evening he is the dinner guest of the Theosophical Society, 28 Great King Street; after dinner He addresses the society.[29:101ff]

1913-01-10 ——returns to London.[29:109ff]

1913-01-11 ——speaks at Caxton Hall, Westminster.[16:368]

1913-01-12	——speaks in the Friends' Meetinghouse, St. Martin's Lane;[25:173] attends a dinner in His honor in the home of Sir Richard and Lady Stapley.[16:369]
1913-01-14	——speaks in a Congregational Church in the East End of London; attends a dinner in His honor hosted by the Persian Minister (Mus͟híru'l-Mulk) at the Legation in London.[16:368]
1913-01-15	——travels to Bristol where He stays in the Clifton Guest House (which belonged to Mr. and Mrs. Tudor-Pole). He addresses a gathering in the Guest House that evening.[16:369]
1913-01-16	——returns to London.[16:370]
1913-01-17	——tells Mrs. Gabrielle Enthoven that He would give her a play, *Drama of the Kingdom*. Mrs. Enthoven allows Mary Basil Hall (Lady Blomfield's daughter) to write it (it was published in London in 1933).[16:388,497ff]
1913-01-18	——visits the Mosque in Woking, Surrey, England. Before speaking in the court outside the mosque (which was too small to hold the assembled participants, He lunches with a number of Muslim and Christian notables). Ameer 'Alí Syed (then a member of the Judicial Committee of the Privy Council; as well as the author of *The Spirit of Islám*) also addresses the gathering.[16:370]
1913-01-19	'Abdu'l-Bahá is the luncheon guest of Rev. Dr. R. J. Campbell.[16:371]
1913-01-20	——attends an afternoon reception in His honor in the home of Dr. Felix Moscheles; is the dinner guest of a Rajput Prince; speaks in the Higher Thought Center—His last engagement in London.[16:371]
1913-01-21	——leaves London for Paris where He stays in a house rented for Him by M. Hippolyte Dreyfus-Barney at 30 Rue St. Didier. A constant stream of visitors visit with Him in the drawing-room.[16:373]
1913-01-27	The Persian Minister in Paris, the Mumtázu's-Salṭnih, 'Abduṣ-Ṣamad K͟hán calls on 'Abdu'l-Bahá; as a matter of courtesy and in conformity with custom, 'Abdu'l-Bahá returns his call that same day.[16:374]
1913-01-28	Aḥmad Pás͟há and Munír Pás͟há, prominent Ottomans; the latter of which was Sulṭán 'Abdu'l-Hamíd's ambassador in Paris, call on 'Abdu'l-Bahá.[16:374]

1913-01-29 Rashíd Páshá, an ex-válí of Beirut and a fierce persecutor of 'Abdu'l-Bahá under the old regime, calls on Him and shows great reverence and contrition; 'Abdu'l-Bahá returns his call that same day.[16:375]

1913-01-31 Íránian students call on 'Abdu'l-Bahá; He speaks in the home of M. Mme. Dreyfus-Barney; this is part of a series of weekly meetings that take place in other homes as well, notably M. et Mme. Scott's and Miss Edith Sanderson's.[16:377]

1913-02-06 ——visits Versailles. That evening He is entertained by the music, song and art of Professor 'Ináyatu'lláh Khán.[16:376]

1913-02-12 ——the guest of the Esperantists at a banquet in His honor in the Hôtel Moderne; He delivers an address.[16:377]

1913-02-13 ——addresses the Theosophists.[16:377]

1913-02-17 ——speaks separately in the homes of three Bahá'ís; that evening He visits Pasteur Monnier's Theological Seminary and answers his questions.[16:377]

1913-02-21 ——speaks in the Salle de Troyes to the L'Alliance Spiritualiste.[16:378]

1913-03-09 Professor and Mrs. E.G. Browne visit Him.[16:379]

1913-03-19 'Abdu'l-Bahá moves from the Dreyfus-Barney home to a hotel in Rue Lauriston, near the Place de l'Étoile.[16:379]

1913-03-21 ——celebrates Naw-Rúz and entertains guests at lunch (many of them Eastern notables). Later that day, accompanied by M. Hippolyte Dreyfus-Barney, He calls on the Íránian Legation; He closes the day by giving a discourse in the home of M. Mme. Dreyfus-Barney.[16:379]

1913-03-30 ——leaves Paris and travels to Stuttgart; He arrives on 1 April and stays in the Hotel Marquardt.[16:379]

1913-04-03 ——speaks in the upper hall of the City (Burger) Museum, Stuttgart.[16:380]

1913-04-04 ——visits a children's meeting in Esslingen.[16:382]

1913-04-05 ——addresses a number of meetings and in the evening speaks to the Esperanto Society; He ends the day by having dinner in the home of Herr Eckstein.[16:383]

1913-04-06	——gives an address in the Hotel Marquardt. He is driven to the Black Forest and meets with Bahá'ís in Wangenburg where photographs are taken. He gives a discourse in the Obere Museum. He dines that evening in the home of Miss F. Knobloch and Fräulein Döring.[16:383]
1913-04-07	——visits Bad Mergentheim at the request of Consul Schwarz who owns the hotel and mineral bath.[16:383]
1913-04-08	——returns to Stuttgart and lunches in the home of Consul and Frau Schwarz.[16:384]
1913-04-09	——leaves Stuttgart by train for Budapest (changing trains in Vienna). He stays in the Hotel Ritz.[16:384]
1913-04-10	Well-known academics call upon 'Abdu'l-Bahá. Among them are: Dr. Agnas Goosen, Rector of the University, Professor Julius Germanus and Dr. Alexander Giesswein, M.P. Sirdar Omrah Singh also calls and expresses the regrets of Professor Arminius Vambéry who is too ill to leave his house. That evening 'Abdu'l-Bahá addresses the Theosophical Society.[16:385]
1913-04-11	'Abdu'l-Bahá receives a delegation from the Turkish Association. That afternoon He returns the call of Professor Ignaz Goldziher and others. Later He delivers a discourse in the Old Building of Parliament (at that time a museum).[16:386]
1913-04-12	The President of the Túránian Society calls on 'Abdu'l-Bahá. That afternoon 'Abdu'l-Bahá visits Professor Vambéry.[16:386]
1913-04-13	Despite failing health, Professor Vambéry tries to visit 'Abdu'l-Bahá but finds Him absent visiting Professor Robert A. Nadler, and later in the day Sirdar Omrah Singh. Later that evening, despite a blizzard, 'Abdu'l-Bahá delivers a discourse in His hotel.[16:387]
1913-04-14	'Abdu'l-Bahá delays His departure at the request of the president of the Túránian Society to address a meeting organized by him in the hall of the Old Parliament Building. The delay allows Him to return Professor Vambéry's visit (much to the professor's delight). 'Abdu'l-Bahá attends a dinner party in the home of 'Alí 'Abbás Áqá where guests include the Ottoman Consul-General.[16:387]
1913-04-15	——is prevented from traveling to Vienna by a severe cold.[16:387]
1913-04-19	——leaves Budapest and travels to Vienna where He stays in the Grand Hotel.[16:388]

1913-04-19 ——calls upon the Turkish Ambassador who insists He stay for lunch. Following lunch He returns to His Hotel where He is greeted by Frau Tyler and Herr Kreuz who request Him to give a discourse. He consents and that evening speaks in the Theosophical Hall. In the afternoon He goes for a walk and gives money to a charity collector as well as to some children playing in the park.[16:388]

1913-04-20 ——is the guest of the Persian Minister and the Turkish Ambassador, respectively.[16:388]

1913-04-21 The Persian Minister calls on 'Abdu'l-Bahá in the morning. Later that day He goes for a drive and in the evening addresses the Theosophical Society.[16:388]

1913-04-23 Íránian residents call on 'Abdu'l-Bahá. That evening He addresses the Theosophists for the third time.[16:388]

1913-04-24 'Abdu'l-Bahá returns to Stuttgart from Vienna. He arrives in the early hours of the next day and stays in the Hotel Marquardt. He is unwell for most of this second week in Stuttgart.[16:389]

1913-04-25 ——speaks in the Burger Museum (despite extremely poor health).[16:389]

1913-04-27 A number of children are brought to visit 'Abdu'l-Bahá at His Hotel.[16:390]

1913-05-01 After addressing the Bahá'ís in three groups, 'Abdu'l-Bahá returns to Paris where He stays in the Hôtel California, Rue Colbert, near the Bibliothèque Nationale. As usual, He receives a large number of visitors on a daily basis.[16:391]

1913-05-18 'Abdu'l-Bahá is taken to the famous racecourse at Longchamps where He walks with Dr. Muḥammad Khán (one of the Íránian Bahá'ís then resident in Paris). That evening He dines with M. Mme. Richard until midnight.[16:393]

1913-05-22 ——visits an eminent member of the Persian aristocracy. Later that day He visits Mme. Jackson and receives Albert Dawson, editor of the *Christian Commonwealth*.[16:394]

1913-05-23 Bahá'ís visit 'Abdu'l-Bahá offering flowers in celebration of His birthday but He tells them that the day must be considered only the anniversary of the Declaration of the Báb—an event He celebrates that night in the home of M. Mme. Dreyfus-Barney.[16:394]

1913-05-27 ——returns to the hotel in Rue Lauriston.[16:394]

1913-05-30 ——speaks in the home of M. Mme. Dreyfus-Barney.[16:395]

1913-06-01 Mírzá 'Alí-Akbar-i-Nakhjavání arrives from the Holy Land and informs 'Abdu'l-Bahá that a large number of pilgrims there await His return.[16:395]

1913-06-06 Ahmad 'Izzat Páshá, a member of Sultán 'Abdu'l-Hamíd's inner circle calls on 'Abdu'l-Bahá.[16:395]

1913-06-12 'Abdu'l-Bahá leaves His hotel at 8:00 A.M. for the train station where He addresses Bahá'ís before taking the noon train for Marseilles. The train reaches Marseilles at midnight and 'Abdu'l-Bahá stays overnight in a hotel next to the station.[16:395]

1913-06-13 ——sails aboard the P&O steamer S. S. *Himalaya* from Marseilles for Port Said, Egypt at 9:00 A M.[16:395]

1913-06-27 Mírzá Ja'far-i-Rahmáníy-i-Shírází invites the Bahá'ís in Port Said to dinner; they eat under a canvas tent, and 'Abdu'l-Bahá serves the food.[16:399]

1913-07-17 'Abdu'l-Bahá moves to Alexandria where He stays for two weeks in the Hotel Victoria in Ramlih before moving into rented accommodation in the proximity of the Mazlúm Páshá Station.[16:400]

1913-08-01 Bahíyyih Khánum and Shoghi Effendi (the sister and grandson of 'Abdu'l-Bahá) arrive in Ramlih from Haifa.[16:401]

1913-08-17 'Abbás Hilmí Páshá ('Abbás II), the Khedive of Egypt, calls on 'Abdu'l-Bahá for the third time, followed a month later by his brother, Prince Muhammad-'Alí.[16:401]

1913-12-02 'Abdu'l-Bahá boards a Lloyd Triestino boat and sets sail for Haifa (stopping enroute in Port Said and Jaffa.)[16:402]

1913-12-05 ——His early afternoon arrival in Haifa concludes His epic travels in Europe and North America.[16:402]

1913-12-06 ——visits the Shrine of the Báb, a large group of pilgrims is present; 'Abdu'l-Bahá directs them to the eastern foreroom of the Shrine while He enters the western foreroom alone).[16:403]

1914-02-02 Final payment made on the Wilmette lakeshore tract.[22:72]

1915 Eighth (North America) Mashriqu'l-Adhkár Convention meeting and First Bahá'í Congress in San Francisco, Calif.[22:69]

1916-03-26 'Abdu'l-Bahá reveals the first of the *Tablets of the Divine Plan* (Alváḥ-i-Tablíghí-i-Ámríká), in the house at Bahjí. This first Tablet is addressed to the Bahá'ís of nine northeastern states: Maine, New Hampshire, Rhode Island, Connecticut, Vermont, Pennsylvania, Massachusetts, New Jersey and New York.[16:420]

1916-03-27 ——reveals the second of the *Tablets of the Divine Plan*, in the garden adjacent to the Shrine of Bahá'u'lláh at Bahjí. It is addressed to the Bahá'ís of 16 southern states: Delaware, Maryland, Virginia, West Virginia, North Carolina, South Carolina, Georgia, Florida, Alabama, Mississippi, Tennessee, Kentucky, Louisiana, Arkansas, Oklahoma and Texas.[16:421]

1916-03-29 ——reveals the third of the *Tablets of the Divine Plan*, outside the house in Bahjí. It is addressed to the Bahá'ís of 12 central states: Michigan, Wisconsin, Ill., Ohio, Minnesota, Iowa, Missouri, North Dakota, South Dakota, Nebraska and Kansas.[16:421]

1916-04-01 ——reveals the fourth of the *Tablets of the Divine Plan*, in His room in the house in Bahjí. This fourth Tablet is addressed to the Bahá'ís of 11 western states: New Mexico, Colorado, Arizona, Nevada, Utah, California, Wyoming, Montana, Idaho, Oregon and Washington.[16:421]

1916-04-05 ——reveals the fifth of the *Tablets of the Divine Plan*, in the garden adjacent to the Shrine of Bahá'u'lláh at Bahjí. It is addressed to the Bahá'ís of Canada, Newfoundland, Prince Edward Island, Nova Scotia, New Brunswick, Quebec, Manitoba, Alberta, Ontario, Saskatchewan, British Columbia, Yukon, Mackenzie, Ungava, Keewatin, Franklin Islands and Greenland.[16:421]

1916-04-08 ——reveals the sixth of the *Tablets of the Divine Plan*, in the garden outside the Shrine of Bahá'u'lláh at Bahjí. It is addressed to the Bahá'ís of the United States and Canada.[16:421]

1916-04-11 ——reveals the seventh of the *Tablets of the Divine Plan*, in His room in the house in Bahjí. It is addressed to the Bahá'ís of the United States and Canada.[16:421]

1917-02-02 ——reveals the eighth of the *Tablets of the Divine Plan*, in His room in the house in Bahjí. It is addressed to the Bahá'ís of the United States and Canada.[16:421]

1917-02-02 ——reveals the ninth of the *Tablets of the Divine Plan*, in Ismá'íl Áqá's room in the house of 'Abdu'l-Bahá in Haifa. It is addressed to the Bahá'ís of the nine northeastern states.[16:422]

1917-02-03 ——reveals the tenth of the *Tablets of the Divine Plan*, in the Ismá'íl Áqá's room in the house of 'Abdu'l-Bahá in Haifa. It is addressed to the Bahá'ís of the 16 southern states.[16:422]

1917-02-08 ——reveals the eleventh of the *Tablets of the Divine Plan*, in the room of Bahá'u'lláh in the house of 'Abbúd in 'Akká. It is addressed to the Bahá'ís of the 12 central states.[16:422]

1917-02-15 ——reveals the twelfth of the *Tablets of the Divine Plan*, in the room of Bahá'u'lláh in the house of 'Abbúd in 'Akká. It is addressed to the Bahá'ís of the 11 western states.[16:422]

1917-02-21 ——reveals the thirteenth of the *Tablets of the Divine Plan*, in the room of Bahá'u'lláh in the house of 'Abbúd in 'Akká. It is addressed to the Bahá'ís of Canada.[16:422]

1917-03-08 ——reveals the fourteenth (and final) of the *Tablets of the Divine Plan*, in the summer-house (Ismá'íl Áqá's room in the house of 'Abdu'l-Bahá in Haifa.) It is addressed to the Bahá'ís of the United States and Canada.[16:422]

1918-09-23 General Allenby's (British) forces take Haifa and Allenby cables London that 'Abdu'l-Bahá is safe.[16:425]

1918-12-23 Aḥmad Sohráb (one of 'Abdu'l-Bahá's secretaries) is sent to the United States to deliver the *Tablets of the Divine Plan*.[16:433]

1919-02 Passing of Hand of the Cause of God Ḥájí Mirzá Muḥammad Taqiy-i-Abhari.

1919-04-26/30 Bahá'í Temple Unity Annual Meeting (Convention) during which the *Tablets of the Divine Plan* are released to the Bahá'í community.

1919-10-04 On the invitation of Major Williamson, the acting Military Governor of Haifa, 'Abdu'l-Bahá goes aboard the warship H.M.S. *Marlborough*.[16:440]

1919-12-17 'Abdu'l-Bahá reveals a Tablet to the Central Organization For A Durable Peace at the Hague.[16:438]

1920-04-27 Louis Bourgeois's design of the North American Mas͟hriqu'l-Ad͟hkár is selected during National Convention.[22:72]

1920-09-24	Work begins on the site of the Mashriqu'l-Adhkár.
1920-09-27	'Abdu'l-Bahá is invested with the insignia of a Knight Commander, Order of the British Empire, for His humanitarian work in relieving distress and famine during WW I. The investiture is in the garden of the Military Governor of Haifa.[16:443]
1921-01-05	(North American) Mashriqu'l-Adhkár structural engineer and superintendent of construction appointed.[22:73]
1921-03-19	——the building permit is granted by Village of Wilmette.[22:74]
1921-05-19	As instructed by 'Abdu'l-Bahá, first Convention(s) are held for Amity Between the Colored and White Races (19-21 May) in Washington D.C. Similar conventions are held in Philadelphia, Dayton, Green Acre, Brooklyn, Boston, Chicago, Montréal, New York, Seattle and Portland.) Race Amity Conventions.[20:22, 200ff]
1921-11-28	Passing of 'Abdu'l-Bahá at 1 A.M.

Timeline—Shoghi Effendi

1897-03-01	Birth of Shoghi Effendi in the house of 'Abdu'lláh Pá<u>sh</u>á, 'Akká. [30:2]
1920-04	Shoghi Effendi leaves Haifa to study at Balliol College, Oxford. On the instruction of 'Abdu'l-Bahá he spends time in a sanitarium in Neuilly before proceeding to England in the month of July. [16:433]
1920-10-11	——attends the first lecture of *Logic* course (given by Mr. Ross, M.A.). [31:36]
1920-10-12	—— attends the first lecture of the *Political Economy* course (given by Sir T. H. Penson, M.A.);——attends the first lecture of the *Eastern Question* course (given by F. F. Urquhart, M.A.). [31:36]
1920-10-13	——attends the first lecture of the *Social and Industrial Questions* course (given by the Rev. Carlyle). [31:36]
1920-10-14	——attends the first lecture of the *Political Science* course (given by the Rev. Carlyle). [31:36]
1920-10-15	——attends the first lecture of the *Social and Political Problems* course (given by Mr. Smith). [31:36]
1920-10-16	——attends the first lecture of the *English Economic History since 1688* course (given by Sir T. H. Penson, M.A.). [31:36]
1920-10-19	——attends the first lecture of the *Relations of Capital and Labor* course (given by Mr. Clay, New College). [31:36]
1921-11-28	Bahíyyih <u>Kh</u>ánum cables the office of Major Tudor-Pole, 61 St. James's Street London, saying: "His Holiness 'Abdu'l-Bahá ascended to the Kingdom of Abhá. Please inform friends." The cable arrives at 09:30 A.M. 29 November. Shoghi Effendi arrives around noon that day and while waiting for Tudor-Pole to arrive in his office he reads the cable which was lying open on the desk. He collapses and is taken to the home of Miss Grand and put to bed for a few days. A similar cable is dispatched to the North American Bahá'í community through Mr. Roy Wilhelm in New York. Messages of condolence flood in from around the world (from, among others, Winston Churchill, then secretary of state for the colonies).[31:39]
1921-12-16	Shoghi Effendi sails for Haifa with Lady Blomfield and his sister Rouhangeze. [31:42]

1921-12-29 ——arrives in Haifa by train from Egypt (where his boat had docked at 5:20 P.M. [31:42]

1922-01-03 The Will and Testament of 'Abdu'l-Bahá designates Shoghi Effendi as the successor to 'Abdu'l-Bahá and the Head of the worldwide Bahá'í community: "The Guardian of the Faith...," "the expounder of the words of God...," "the Sign of God on earth..." among other titles. Shoghi Effendi instructs that the Will and Testament be read aloud later that same day (but not in his presence) to nine men, mostly members of his family, and the seals, signature and writing shown to them (by way of proof that the Will was genuine). He gives instructions that a true copy should be made by one of those present. [31:43ff, 46]

1922-01-07 On Shoghi Effendi's instruction, but without his presence, 'Abdu'l-Bahá's Will and Testament is read to a gathering of Bahá'ís from Persia, India, Egypt, England, Italy, Germany, America and Japan. [31:46]

1922-01-07 Bahíyyih Khánum cables the Persian Bahá'í community, announcing Shoghi Effendi as the successor to 'Abdu'l-Bahá. [31:47]

1922-01-16 Bahíyyih Khánum cables the most important content of 'Abdu'l-Bahá's Will and Testament to the Bahá'í world (via the United States): "In Will Shoghi Effendi appointed Guardian of Cause and Head of House of Justice." [31:48] Shoghi Effendi immediately begins the duties of his new rôle and writes his first letters as Guardian (separate communications to the Persian, American and Japanese Bahá'ís). [31:52]

1922-01-30 Covenant Breakers (Badí'u'lláh and others) seize the keys of the Shrine of Bahá'u'lláh from the Bahá'í caretaker, thereby asserting Muḥammad 'Alí's (half-brother of 'Abdu'l-Bahá) right as lawful custodian. The governor of 'Akká demands that the keys be turned over to him and refuses to return the keys to either party. [31:53]

1922-03-05 Shoghi Effendi sends his first letter to the Bahá'ís of the world referring to the mission of the Cause and to the formation of local and national Spiritual Assemblies. [9:3ff]

1922-04-05 Shoghi Effendi leaves Haifa for the Bernese Oberland with his eldest cousin. In the words of Bahíyyih Khánum, Shoghi Effendi had left "in order to rest and recuperate, and then return to the Holy Land to render his services and discharge his responsibilities." The *Star of the West* subsequently carried a facsimile of a letter written by Shoghi Effendi communicating his decision to place Bahíyyih Khánum at the Head of the Cause in his absence. [31:57]

1922-04-08 Bahíyyih Khánum writes a letter to Bahá'ís explaining the current situation with respect the Guardian. [31:57]

1922-12-15 Shoghi Effendi returns to the Holy Land to resume his duties as Guardian. [31:63]

1922-12-16 ——writes to America, "Prolonged though this period has been, yet I have strongly felt ever since this New Day has dawned upon me that such a needed retirement, despite the temporary dislocations it might entail, would far outweigh in its results any immediate service I could have humbly tendered at the Threshold of Bahá'u'lláh"; [31:63] he also writes to the Bahá'ís of Great Britain care of the members of the Spiritual Council conveying the same sentiments. [9:9]

1922-12-23 ——first letter to the newly elected National Spiritual Assembly of the United States and Canada (which replaced the Bahá'í Temple Unity); [31:64] also writes his first letter to the Bahá'ís of Great Britain care of the Bahá'í Council in reply to the first letter he receives from the West after his return. [9:11]

1923-03-12 ——calls for the establishment of national and local Bahá'í Funds. [31:330]

1923-06 For health reasons, Shoghi Effendi again leaves Haifa for a prolonged stay in Switzerland. [31:72]

1923-11 ——returns to Haifa. [31:73]

1925-02 Shoghi Effendi conceives, in discussion with Mrs. Stannard, of the International Bahá'í Bureau (to be sited in Geneva, Switzerland).[31:249]

1925-05-10 Divisional session of the religious court of Beba, decides cases No. 913, 814 (1923) and 915 (1924); Bahá'í religion is a religion independent of Islám, Kowno, Saayedeh (District of Soweif), Egypt. [5:365]

1925-11-22 Passing of Dr. John E. Esslemont in Haifa, Israel. [32:xxii]

1925-11-30 Shoghi Effendi appoints Dr. Esslemont to the rank of a Hand of the Cause of God. [32:xxii]

1926-01-30 Miss Martha Root secures the first of eight audiences (covering the period January 1926 to February 1936) with Her Royal Highness Queen Marie of Rumania in Controceni Palace, Bucharest. Queen Marie becomes

	the first monarch to accept the Faith of Bahá'u'lláh. [5:387, 33-35]
1926-04-29	National Spiritual Assembly of United States and Canada approves incorporation as a "Voluntary Trust" with a "Declaration of Trust" and attendant "By-Laws." Adopted during San Francisco Annual Convention (29 April to 2 May 1926).[20:89]
1926-07-16	The National Spiritual Assembly of the United States writes to the Shah of Persia pleading for justice on behalf of the persecuted Bahá'í community there. [20:37,287]
1926-08-27	Queen Marie of Rumania writes for the first time to Shoghi Effendi (in response to a letter from him).[20:173]
1927-04-04	Incorporation of the National Spiritual Assembly of the Bahá'ís of United States and Canada.[20:89ff]
1928-05-27	Passing of Hand of the Cause of God Ḥájí Abu'l-Ḥasan. [32:xxii]
1928-06	Russian law expropriating religious edifices is applied to the Mashriqu'l-Adkár of 'Ishqábád, Turkistán. The use of the building as a house of worship is continued on a five-year lease. [36:34ff]
1928-09-11	National Spiritual Assembly Bahá'ís of 'Iraq submits a petition to the Permanent Commission of the League of Nations for protection and aid in the return of the House occupied by Bahá'u'lláh during His sojourn in Baghdad. [36:50ff]
1929-03-04	Council of the League of Nations, Geneva, Switzerland, adopts a resolution directing the Mandatory Power (Great Britain) "to make representations to the government of 'Iráq" to return Houses occupied by Bahá'u'lláh to the National Spiritual Assembly of 'Iráq. [36:50ff]
1929-05-04	Bahá'í Community of Haifa petitions Palestinian authorities for official recognition as a community with full powers to administer its own affairs in the same way as other religious communities. The petition is granted. [5:355]
1929-11-27	Muḥammad-'Alí and family leave the Mansion of Bahjí and restoration work begins. [5:356]
1930-04-08	Registration in Haifa, Palestine of the National Spiritual Assembly of the Bahá'ís of the United States and Canada as a recognized Religious Society in Palestine, under the name the National Spiritual Assembly of the Bahá'ís of the United States and Canada—Palestine Branch. The Association comprises Shoghi Effendi

	Rabbání and Ruhí Afnán. [17:165ff]
1930-07-04	Shoghi Effendi completes his translation of the Kitáb-i-Íqán (The Book of Certitude); this is the first of the Works that he translates. [31:214]
1931-04	Completion of the main superstructure of the (North American) Mashriqu'l-Adkár. [17:188ff]
1931-05-01	Dedication of the first Bahá'í House of Worship in the Western World (the Mother Temple) and the first devotional service in the new structure on the 19th anniversary of the dedication of the grounds by 'Abdu'l-Bahá. [17:188ff]
1931-12-14	National Spiritual Assembly United States and Canada writes to the Prime Minister of Egypt, drawing his attention to the persecution of the Egyptian Bahá'í community and asking the adoption of a decree recognizing the Egyptian Bahá'í community as a religion in its own right. [17:166ff]
1932-03-31	New York Spiritual Assembly incorporated using Constitution and By-laws to be used as a model by other Assemblies throughout the world. [17:158ff]
1932-07-15	Passing of the Greatest Holy Leaf, Bahíyyih Khánum. [5:108, 37:169]
1933-10-23	Passing of Keith Ransom-Kehler in Iṣfáhán, Persia; Shoghi Effendi appoints her a Hand of the Cause of God. [32:xxii]
1936-03-11	Shoghi Effendi writes the letter subsequently published as *The Unfoldment of World Civilization* to the "beloved of God and the handmaids of the Merciful throughout the West." [31:213]
1937-03-25	Marriage of Shoghi Effendi to Mary Maxwell in the room of Bahíyyih Khánum in the house of 'Abdu'l-Bahá. His mother cables America and Persia, "Announce Assemblies celebration marriage beloved Guardian Inestimable honor conferred upon handmaid of Bahá'u'lláh Rúḥíyyih Khánum Miss Mary Maxwell. Union of East and West proclaimed by Bahá'í Faith cemented. Ziaiyyih mother of the Guardian." [31:151]
1937-04	The first Seven Year Plan (1937—1944) is launched in the United States.[38:7, 9, 39, 40:385ff, 41:25]
1938-04-28	Shoghi Effendi cables Bahá'í Conventions regarding the passing of Munírih Khánum, wife of 'Abdu'l-Bahá. [9:118, 42:259ff]
1938-07-04	——cables National Spiritual Assembly of India,

Pákistán and Burma approving their decision to launch their first Six Year Plan (1938—1944.) [40:403, 43:70ff]

1938-12-25 ——writes the letter subsequently published as "The Advent of Divine Justice" to the "beloved of the Lord and the handmaids of the Merciful throughout the United States and Canada." [39]

1939-03-11 Grand Muftí of Egypt (the highest exponent of Islámic Law in Egypt) issues a fatvá (judgment) stating clearly that the Bahá'í religion is quite separate and independent of Islám (i.e., a religion in its own right).[5:366ff]

1939-09-28 Passing of Martha Root in Honolulu. [32:xxii, 42:643]

1939-10-03 Shoghi Effendi appoints Martha Root (posthumously) to the rank of a Hand of the Cause of God. [32:xxii]

1939-11-24 Following Shoghi Effendi's guidance, the first Bahá'í in the British Isles to appeal for noncombatant service after the outbreak of WW II, Philip Hainsworth, appears before a court in Leeds, England and has his appeal granted, thereby establishing a precedent that was accepted for other Bahá'ís in the British Isles and in other countries when called into the armed forces. This is the first time an individual Bahá'í has the Bahá'í Faith recognized as the legal basis for a court appeal. It is also the first time an army has to issue a name tag (dog tag) with "Bahá'í" on it. [42:84]

1939-12-05 The remains of Bahá'u'lláh's wife, Navváb, the Most Exalted Leaf, and His son, Mírzá Mihdí, the Purest Branch, are transferred to the precincts of the Shrine of the Báb. [5:188, 42:245ff]

1939-12-24 The remains of Navváb and Mírzá Mihdí are laid in state in the Shrine of the Báb. [5:188, 42:245ff]

1939-12-25 The remains of Navváb and Mírzá Mihdí are reinterred together in the Bahá'í Monument Gardens on Mount Carmel. [5:188, 42:245ff]

1940-03-01 Passing of May Bolles Maxwell in Buenos Aires.

1940-06-02 Shoghi Effendi, Rúḥíyyih Kh̲ánum and Mr. Maxwell leave St. Malo for Southampton, England. [31:178]

1940-07-28 ——departs from England for Cape Town, South Africa, on board the S. S. *Cape Town Castle* with 'Rúḥíyyih Kh̲ánum and her father. Shoghi Effendi and Rúḥíyyih Kh̲ánum proceed overland to Khartoum where they are rejoined by Mr. Maxwell.[31:179f]

1940-10 ——arrives back in Haifa. [31:181]

1941-02-17	Passing of Hand of the Cause of God John Henry Hyde-Dunn in Sydney, Australia. [32:xxii]
1941-03-28	Shoghi Effendi writes the letter subsequently published as *The Promised Day is Come* to "Friends and fellow-heirs of the Kingdom of Bahá'u'lláh." [44]
1942-03-13	Passing of Hand of the Cause of God Siyyid Muṣṭafá Rúmí. [32:xxii]
1942-06-25	Shoghi Effendi appoints 'Abdu'l-Jalíl Bey Sa'ad to the rank of a Hand of the Cause of God. (d. Egypt, 25 June 1942).[32:xxii]
1942-08-14	U.S. quartermaster general approves the use of the Greatest Name on stones marking the graves of Bahá'ís killed in WW II and who are buried in military or private cemeteries. [45:475]
1944-01-22	Shoghi Effendi finishes *God Passes By* (originally titled *Prospect and Retrospect*).
1944-05-23	Celebrations of the Centenary of the Declaration of the Báb.
1944-05-25	Shoghi Effendi cables his approval of the British National Spiritual Assembly's adoption their first Six Year Plan (1944-1950) as follows: "Welcome spontaneous decision advise formation nineteen Spiritual Assemblies spread over England Wales Scotland Northern Ireland and Eire praying signal victory." [9:169, 40:393]
1945-05	National Spiritual Assembly of Germany and Austria adopt a Five Year Plan (1948—1953).[40:412]
1945-07-14	Shoghi Effendi appoints Siyyid Muṣṭafá Rúmi to the rank of a Hand of the Cause of God. [32:xxii]
1946-01-09	National Spiritual Assembly of India, Pákistán and Burma adopt a Four Year Plan (1946—1950).[40:403]
1946-04	Second American Seven Year Plan (1946—1953) (launched following a two year respite). [38:87ff, 40:395, 41:33]
1946-10-11	National Spiritual Assembly of Írán adopts a Four Year Plan (1946—1950).[40:405]
1946-11-22	Shoghi Effendi advises Amelia Collins by cable that she is a Hand of the Cause of God and that she is the first to be told during her lifetime. He advises that the announcement is to be held pending his discretion (which was 24 December 1951).[31:258]
1946-12-13	——appoints Muḥammad Taqíy-i-Isfáhání to the rank of a Hand of the Cause of God. (d. Egypt, 13 December 1946).[32:xxii]
1947-03-14	——writes to the National Spiritual Assembly of Aus-

tralia and New Zealand encouraging them to adopt a Plan (Six Year Plan (1947—1953)). [9:69f, 40:407]

1947-04c National Spiritual Assembly of the United States and Canada is accredited as an NGO (Nongovernmental Organization) with the United Nations. [11:378ff]

1947-04c The National Spiritual Assembly of Iráq adopts a Three Year Plan (1947—1950).[40:407]

1948-04-14 Shoghi Effendi writes to the first National Spiritual Assembly of Canada (about to be formed during Convention later that month) congratulating them and urging them to adopt a Five Year Plan. [40:409, 46:7]

1948-05 The National Spiritual Assembly of Egypt adopts a Five Year Plan (1948—1953).[40:411]

1949-01-21 Shoghi Effendi meets with Prime Minister Ben Gurion of Israel. [31:174, 289]

1949-03-07 ——announces that work would begin on the Shrine of the Báb on the Spot chosen by Bahá'u'lláh.[31:174, 289] A superstructure, comprising a colonnade and arcade, an octagon above, a drum with 18 windows and a golden dome and lantern, is to be built on the existing building.

1950-04 ——announces to the National Spiritual Assembly of the Bahá'ís of the British Isles the launch of the *Africa Plan* (1951—1953). [9:245, 40:413]

1950-12-16 Mazra'ih is leased from the Israeli authorities; Shoghi Effendi announces to the Bahá'í world that the keys to Mazra'ih have been delivered to him. [31:290] This he says, anticipated the "opening door to pilgrimage." [6:7]

1951-01-09 Shoghi Effendi announces the appointment of the 1st International Bahá'í Council (forerunner of the Universal House of Justice): 'Amatu'l-Bahá Rúḥíyyih Khánum (liaison between Shoghi Effendi as Guardian of the Bahá'í Faith and the Council), Amelia Collins (Vice-President), Ugo Giachery, Member at Large, Luftu'lláh Ḥakim (Eastern Assistant Secretary), Leroy Ioas, Secretary General, Mason Remey (President), Ethel Revell (Western Assistant Secretary), Jessie Revell (Treasurer), Ben Weedon, and Gladys Weedon. [6:7, 47:395]

1951-04 Shoghi Effendi writes the National Spiritual Assembly of India, Pákistán and Burma approving the launch of their Nineteen-Month Plan (1951-1953.) [40:403, 43:149]

1951-04-03 Passing of Hand of the Cause of God Corrine True in

	Chicago. [32:xxiii]
1951-07-30	Passing of Hand of the Cause of God Louis Gregory in Eliot Maine. [32:xxii]
1951-08-05	Shoghi Effendi appoints Louis Gregory to the rank of a Hand of the Cause of God. [32:xxii]
1951-12-20	Passing of Hand of the Cause of God Roy C. Wilhelm in North Lovell, Maine. [32:xxii]
1951-12-23	Shoghi Effendi appoints Roy C. Wilhelm to the rank of a Hand of the Cause of God. [32:xxii]
1951-12-24	——appoints first contingent of (12) Hands of the Cause of God (previous appointments having been posthumous): Dorothy B. Baker, Amelia E. Collins, ‘Alí-Akbar Furútan, Ugo Giachery, Hermann Grossman, Horace Holley, Leroy C. Ioas, William Sutherland Maxwell, Ṭarázu’lláh Samandarí, George Townshend, Valíyu’lláh Varqá. Cables of appointment were sent the previous day. [32:xxiii]
1952-02-29	——appoints second contingent of (six) Hands of the Cause of God: Clara Dunn, Adelbert Mühlschlegel, Shu’u’lláh ‘Alá’í, Dhikru’lláh Khádem, Corrine True and Siegfried Schopflocher. Cables of appointment were sent the previous day. [32:xxiii]
1952-03-08	——announces the members of and enlargement of the International Bahá’í Council: ‘Amatu’l-Bahá Rúḥíyyih Khánum, Mason Remey, Amelia Collins, Ugo Giachery, Leroy Ioas, Jessie and Ethel Revell and Lufṭu‘lláh Ḥakim. [47:395]
1952-03-25	Passing of Hand of the Cause of God William Sutherland Maxwell in Montréal. [32:xxiii]
1952-03-26	Shoghi Effendi appoints ‘Amatu’l-Bahá Rúḥíyyih Khánum as a Hand of the Cause of God (replacing her illustrious father). [32:xxiv]
1952-04	One Year Plan Central America. (1952—1953) [40:414]
1952-04-26	——appoints John Henry Dunn to the rank of a Hand of the Cause of God. (b. 5 March 1855, d. 17 February 1941.) [32:xxii]
1952-10	Centenary Celebrations birth of Bahá’u’lláh’s Mission in the Síyáh-Chál. [6:34]
1952-10-08	Shoghi Effendi announces the Ten Year Crusade (1953—1963) to be conducted by 12 National Spiritual Assemblies. [3, 40:417ff, 47]
1953-02-12/18	First International Teaching Conference, Kampala, Uganda, Africa. Hand of the Cause of God Leroy Ioas

	represents Shoghi Effendi. [6:26]
1953-03	Knights of Bahá'u'lláh: Soheil, Mehdi and Ursula Samandarí, arrive in Italian Somaliland. [47:449ff]
1953-04-21	Ten Year Crusade (1953—1963) (International Bahá'í Teaching and Consolidation Plan) launched. Nine National Spiritual Assemblies exist at that time. [6:40, 41:45, 48:253ff]
1953-05	Knight of Bahá'u'lláh: Robert Powers Jr., arrive in the Mariana Islands. [47:449ff]
1953-05-01	Bahá'í dedication of North American Mashriqu'l-Adkár. [48:515ff]
1953-05-02	Public dedication of North American Mashriqu'l-Adkár. [48:515ff]
1953-05-03/06	All American Bahá'í (Second) Intercontinental Teaching Conference, Chicago. The Guardian is represented by Hand of the Cause of God 'Amatu'l-Bahá Rúḥíyyih Khánum. [6:33]
1953-06	Knights of Bahá'u'lláh: Ghulam Ali Kurlawala, Daman; Jack Huffman, Kodiak Island; Dunduzu Chisiza, Ruanda-Urundi; Mary and Rex Collison, Ruanda-Urundi; 'Izzatu'lláh Zahrá'í, Southern Rhodesia. [47:449ff]
1953-07	Knights of Bahá'u'lláh: Roshan Aftabi, Goa; Feroza Yaganegi, Goa; Arthur and Ethel Crane, Key West; Rose Perkal, Kodiak Island; Saeed Nahvi, Pondicherry; Eyneddin and Tahereh 'Alá'í, Southern Rhodesia. [47:449ff]
1953-07-21/26	Third Bahá'í Intercontinental Teaching Conference, Stockholm, Sweden. Hand of the Cause of God Ugo Giachery represents Shoghi Effendi. [6:33]
1953-07-27	Passing of Hand of the Cause of God Siegfried Schopflocher in Montréal (b. 1877, Switzerland.)[32:xxiii]
1953-08	Knights of Bahá'u'lláh: Elaine and Jenabe Caldwell, the Aleutian Islands; Virginia Orbison, the Balearic Islands; Abbas Vakil, Cyprus; Eskil Ljungberg, the Faroe Islands; Fred Schechter, French Somaliland; Amin and Sheila Banání, Greece; Salisa Kennani, Karikal; Shirin Noorani, Karikal; Amir Huschmand Manutscherhri, Liechtenstein; Mildred Clark, the Lofoten Islands; Loyce Lawrence, the Lofoten Islands; Shyam Behari Lai, Pondicherry; Edythe MacArthur, the Queen Charlotte Islands; Udai Narain Singh, Sikkim. [47:449ff]
1953-09	Knights of Bahá'u'lláh: Grace Bahovec, Baranof Island;

Helen Robinson, Baranof Island; Cora Oliver, British Honduras; Ziaoullah Asgarzadeh, the Channel Islands; Hugh and Violet McKinley, Cyprus; K. Gale and J. Jameson Bond, Franklin; Max Kanyerezi, French Equatorial Africa; Elsa Grossmann, Frisian Islands; Doris Richardson, Grand Manan Island; Carole and Dwight Allen, Greece; Dick Stanton, Keewatin; Howard J. Snider, Key West; Ella Duffield, Madeira; Elizabeth Hopper, Madeira; Sara Kenny, Madeira; Adah Schott, Madeira; Kathleen Weston, the Magdalen Islands; Nellie French, Monaco; Manoutchehr Hezari, Morocco (International Zone); Hormoz Zendeh, Morocco (International Zone); Julius Edwards, Northern Territories Protectorate; Hilda and Jose Xavier Rodriques, Portuguese Guinea; Tabandeh Payman, San Marino; Brigitte Hasselblatt, the Shetland Islands; Joan and R. Ted Anderson, the Yukon. [47:449ff]

1953-10 Completion of the construction of the Shrine of the Báb. [48:235]

1953-10 Knights of Bahá'u'lláh: William Danjon, Andorra; Lois and Richard Nolen, the Azores; V. Gail and Gerald Curwin, the Bahama Islands; Ethel Holmes, the Bahama Islands; Elizabeth and Frederick Laws, Basutoland; Enoch Olinga, British Cameroons; Malcolm King, British Guiana; Shirley Wade, British Honduras; Gertrude Eisenberg, the Canary Islands; George and Marguerite True, the Canary Islands; Frederick and Jean Allen, Cape Breton Island; Grace and Irving Geary, Cape Breton Island; Zunilda de Palacios, Chiloé Island; Edith Danielson, the Cook Islands; Rolf Haug, Crete; Elinor and Robert Wolf, Dutch Guiana; Elly Becking, Dutch New Guinea; Eberhard Friedland, French Guiana; Geertrui Ankersmit, the Frisian Islands; Ursula von Braun, the Frisian Islands; Geraldine Craney, the Hebrides; Adela I. de Torma and Salvador Torma, Juan Fernandez Island; Earle Render, the Leeward Islands; Ben and Gladys Weedon, the Leeward Islands; Frances Heller, Macao; Lionel Peraji, Mahé; Una Townshend, Malta; R. Katherine Meyer, the Margarita Islands; Elsie Austin, Morocco (International Zone); Hossein and Nosrat Rowhani Ardekani, Morocco (International Zone); Bertha Dobbins, the New Hebrides; Charles Dunning, the Orkney Islands; Opal Jensen, Reunion; Amín Baṭṭah, Rio de Oro; Ola Pawlowska, St. Pierre & Miquelon; Carol, Florence,

	Gerrold, Stanley and Susan Bagley, Sicily; Emma Rice, Sicily; Gretta Lamprill, the Society Islands; Gladys Parke, the Society Islands; Ted Cardell, South West Africa; Claire Gung, Southern Rhodesia; Earleta and John Fleming, Spanish Morocco; Alyce Janssen, Spanish Morocco; Luella McKay, Spanish Morocco; Bahia and Fawzi Zeinol-Abedin, Spanish Morocco; Muḥammad Musṭṭafá, Spanish Sahara; Esther Evans, the Windward Islands; Lillian Middlemast, the Windward Islands. [47:449ff]
1953-10-07/15	Fourth Bahá'í Intercontinental Teaching Conference, New Delhi, India. Hand of the Cause of God Mason Remey represents Shoghi Effendi. [6:33]
1953-11	Knights of Bahá'u'lláh: Khodadad M. Fozdar, the Andaman Islands; Virginia Breaks, the Caroline Islands; Evelyn Baxter, the Channel Islands; Samira Vakil, Cyprus; Matthew Bullock, the Dutch West Indies; Labíb and Habíb Iṣfahání, French West Africa; Olga Mills, Malta; Ottilie Rhein, Mauritius; Ali Akbar Hassanzadeh, Shayesteh and Abbas Rafii-Rafsandjani, Morocco (International Zone); Shokat Nahvi, Pondicherry; Marie Ciocca, Sardinia; Kamil 'Abbás, the Seychelles; Jean and Tove Deleuran, the Balearic Islands; Gulnar Aftabi, Diu; Kaykhusraw Dehmobedi, Diu; Bahiya Rowhani, Diu; Adib and Wahida Baghdadi, Hadhramaut; Carl and Loretta Scherer, Macao. [47:449ff]
1953-12-06	Shoghi Effendi appoints Hand of the Cause of God Jalál Kházeh. [32:xxiv]
1953-12-13	The State of Israel establishes a separate Department for the Bahá'í Faith within the Ministry of Religious Affairs. [49:64]
1954-01	Knights of Bahá'u'lláh: Andrew and Nina Matthisen, the Bahama Islands; Charles Ioas, the Balearic Islands; Howard and Joanne Menking, the Cape Verde Islands; Dulcie Dive, the Cook Islands; Munir Vakil, the Kuria-Muria Islands; Elizabeth Bevan, Rhodes; Lilian Wyss, the Samoa Islands; Adul Rahman Zarqani, the Seychelles; Kenneth and Roberta Christian, Southern Rhodesia; Stanley Bolton Jr., the Tonga Islands; Jean Sevin, the Tuamotu Archipelago. [47:449ff]
1954-01-10	Passing of Hand of the Cause of God Dorothy Baker in a plane crash into the Mediterranean Sea (b. Newark, 21 December, 1898). [32:xxiii]
1954-02	Knights of Bahá'u'lláh: Gail Avery, Baranof Island;

Audrey, John and Patrick Robarts, Bechuanaland; Harry Clark, Brunei; Charles Duncan, Brunei; John Leonard, the Falkland Islands; Feriborze Roozbehyan, Gambia; Ḥusayn Ḥalabí, Hadhramaut; Bernard Guhrke, Kodiak Island; Charles and Mary Dayton, the Leeward Islands; David Schreiber, the Leeward Islands; Raḥmatu'lláh and Írán Muhájir, the Mentawai Islands; Azizullah and Shamsi Navidi, Monaco; Elise Schreiber, St. Thomas Island; Elena and Roy Fernie, the Gilbert and Ellice Islands; Khodarahm Mojgani, Mahé; Qudratollah Rowhani, Mahé; Gretta Jankko, the Marquesas Islands; Olivia Kelsey, Monaco; Florence Ullrich, Monaco; Leland Jensen, Reunion; Alvin and Gertrude Blum, the Solomon Islands. [47:449ff]

1954-03-19 Shoghi Effendi appoints Paul E. Haney as a Hand of the Cause of God. [32:xxiv]

1954-04 ——appoints the first Auxiliary Board members to act as deputies to the Hand of the Cause of God. Africa: John Allen, Elsie Austin, Muḥammad Musṭaphá Soleiman, 'Alí Nakhjavání, Jalál Nakhjavání, John Robarts, William Sears, Valeria Wilson, 'Azíz Yazdí; America:—Esteban Canales, Rowland Estall, William de Forge, Florence Mayberry, Margery McCormick, Katherine McLaughlin, Sarah Pereira, Gayle Woolson, Margot Worley; Asia: Agnes Alexander, 'Abbás 'Alí Butt, Abu'l-Qásim Faizí, Elena Marsella (Fernie), Kazim Kazimzadeh, Carl Scherer, Daod Toeg; Europe: Tove Deleuran, Dorothy Ferraby, Angeline Giachery, Anna Grossmann, Louis Hénezet, Marion Hofman, Eugen Schmidt, Elsa Steinmetz, Joel Marangella; Australasia: H. Collis Featherstone, Thelma Perks. [6:59, 48:40f]

1954-04 Knights of Bahá'u'lláh: Elinore Putney, the Aleutian Islands; Benedict Eballa, Ashanti Protectorate; Albert Buapiah, British Togoland; Edward Tabe, British Togoland; John Fozdar, Brunei; Lex Meerburg, Dutch New Guinea; John and Marjorie Kellberg, the Dutch West Indies; Meherangiz Munsiff, the French Cameroons; Samuel Njiki, the French Cameroons; David Tanyi, French Togoland; Gayle Woolson, the Galapagos Islands; Howard Gilliland, Labrador; Bruce Matthews, Labrador; Kay Zinky, the Magdalen Islands; Mary L. and Richard Suhm, Morocco (International Zone); Evelyn and Richard Walters, Morocco (International Zone); Martin Manga, Northern Territories Protectorate; Sohrab Payman, San Marino; John and Valera Allen, Swaziland; Bula Mott Stewart, Swaziland. [47:449ff]

1954-04-25 Shoghi Effendi receives the first official visit of the Israeli President and Mrs. Ben Zvi in the home of 'Abdu'l-Bahá. [31:293]

1954-05 Knights of Bahá'u'lláh: Fahimah and Sabri Elias, French Somaliland; Mavis Nymon, French Togoland; Vivian Wesson, French Togoland; Haik Kevorkian, the Galapagos Islands; Cynthia Olson, the Mariana Islands; Elizabeth Stamp, St. Helena; Elise Schreiber, Spanish Guinea; Ardishir Faroodi, Bhutan; Shapoor Rowhani, Bhutan; Louise Groger, Chiloé Island; Florence and Harold Fitzner, Portuguese Timor; Violet Hoehnke, the Admiralty Islands; Shoghi Riaz Ruhany, the Canary Islands; John Mitchell, Malta; Jose Marques, Portuguese Timor; Dudley and Elsa Blakely, the Tonga Islands; Mehraban Sohaili, the Comoro Islands; Marcia Atwater, the Marshall Islands; Mírzá Áqá Khán Kamálí-Saristání, Socotra Island. [47:449ff]

1955-05-04 Shoghi Effendi announces appointment of Sylvia Ioas to the International Bahá'í Council, thereby raising its number to nine. [47: p.395]

1955-05-26 ——accompanied by 'Amatu'l-Bahá Rúḥíyyih Khánum, pays a return visit to the president of Israel in Jerusalem. [31:293]

1955-06 Knights of Bahá'u'lláh: Frank Wyss, the Cocos Islands; Udai Narain Singh, Tibet; Daniel Haumont, the Loyalty Islands. [47:449ff]

1955-11-12 Passing of Hand of the Cause of God Valíyu'lláh Varqá (b. 1884.)[32:xxiii]

1955-11-15 Shoghi Effendi appoints 'Alí-Muḥammad Varqá as a Hand of the Cause of God. [32:xxiv]

1956-04 Knight of Bahá'u'lláh: Mary Zabolotny, Anticosti Island. [47:449ff]

1956-05-20 Passing of Louisa Matthew Gregory, wife of Hand of the Cause of God Louis Gregory. The couple were married at the suggestion of 'Abdu'l-Bahá during His visit to the U.S. They were the first inter-racial Bahá'í marriage in the West. [47:876]

1957-03-25 Passing of Hand of the Cause of God George Townshend in Dublin, Ireland (b. 14 June 1876, Dublin.)[32:xxiii]

1957-03-27 Shoghi Effendi appoints Agnes Alexander as a Hand of the Cause of God. [32:xxiv]

1957-05 Knight of Bahá'u'lláh: Puva Murday, the Chagos Archipelago. [47:449ff]

1957-07 Knights of Bahá'u'lláh: Margaret Bates, the Nicobar Islands; Jeanne Frankel, the Nicobar Islands. [47:449ff]

1957-10-02 Shoghi Effendi cables appointment third (and last contingent) of (eight) Hands of the Cause of God; Abu'd-Qásim Faizí, John Robarts, William Sears, Enoch Olinga, John Ferraby, Ruḥmatu'lláh Muhajír, Collis Featherstone and Ḥasan Bályúzí. [32:xxiii]

1957-11-04 Passing of Shoghi Effendi, Guardian of the Bahá'í Faith, in London. 'Amatu'l-Bahá Rúḥíyyih Khánum telephones Hands of the Cause of God Ḥasan Balyúzí (who in turn phones John Ferraby) and Ugo Giachery advising them of the passing of Shoghi Effendi. Later that afternoon a call is placed to Leroy Ioas in Haifa. [32:25] Mr. Ioas seals and secures the Guardian's apartment and office (as well as the Shrines of the Báb, Bahá'u'lláh and the Mansion at Bahjí) until such time as an official search could be made for Shoghi Effendi's Will and Testament. 'Amatu'l-Bahá Rúḥíyyih Khánum cables the tragic news to the Bahá'í World. [31:446f, 47:207]

1957-11-05 'Amatu'l-Bahá Rúḥíyyih Khánum cables all National Spiritual Assemblies advising that the funeral of Shoghi Effendi will take place on Saturday 9 November in London. [47:216]

1957-11-09 The funeral of Shoghi Effendi in the Great Northern London Cemetery takes place at 2:00 P.M. [47:207ff]

Timeline—Chief Stewards—Interregnum

1957-11-10	'Amatu'l-Bahá Rúḥíyyih Khánum cables Bahá'í World asking for Memorial Meetings to be held on 18 November in memory of Shoghi Effendi.[31:447]
1957-11-12	——The Chief Stewards (Hands of the Cause of God) cables National Spiritual Assemblies calling on them to remain united within the framework of the Cause.[31:450]
1957-11-18	Memorial ceremony held for Shoghi Effendi in the Shrine of Bahá'u'lláh at 2:00 P.M.[32:27]
1957-11-18/25	The first Conclave of the Hands of the Cause of God held at the Mansion of Bahjí, 'Akká.[32:27]
1957-11-19	Nine Hands of the Cause of God (the five who sealed his safe and desk plus Horace Holley, Músá Banání, Ḥasan Bályúzí and 'Alí-Muḥammad Varqá) enter the office of Shoghi Effendi at 9:00 A.M. and search his safe and desk for a Will and Testament. An Official Statement, signed by them, is issued stating that no Will and Testament had been found and, therefore, no heir could be designated.[32:27]
1957-11-25	Unanimous Proclamation (signed by 26 of the Hands, the 27th member Corinne True being absent due to ill health) is issued to the Bahá'í World by all 27 Hands stating that no Will and Testament had been found and, as the Chief Stewards of the Faith and in accordance with the provisions of 'Abdu'l-Bahá's Will and Testament, that they had appointed nine from among their number to act on their behalf as Custodians of the Bahá'í World Faith (with full powers and authority to act on behalf of the Faith) until such time as the Universal House of Justice could be elected in conformity with the Bahá'í Writings.[32:28]
1957-11-25	Hands issue a Unanimous Certification naming the body of nine Custodian Hands: 'Amatu'l-Bahá Rúḥíyyih Khánum, Mason Remey, Amelia Collins, Leroy Ioas, Ḥasan Bályúzí, 'Alí-Akbar Furútan, Jalál Kházeh, Paul Haney and Adelbert Mühlschlegel. Ugo Giachery is appointed as an alternate member to fill any temporary vacancy that occurred.[32:31]
1957-11-25	Hands issue a Resolution setting out the principles applying to the relations between the Hands and the nine Custodians as well as to their activities. A second

resolution was issued setting forth the relationship of the Hands with the other Institutions of the Bahá'í Faith.[32:32]

1957-11-25 Hands issue a Proclamation to the Bahá'ís of the East and West advising that no Will and Testament has been found and therefore no heir appointed. The Proclamation also advises the Bahá'í World of the steps taken by the Hands to preserve and protect the unity of the Cause until the Universal House of Justice can be elected, as well as to ensure that the work initiated by Shoghi Effendi in the Ten Year Crusade is actively and faithfully pursued.[32:35]

1957-11-30 Affidavit issued by Hand of the Cause of God Corinne True declaring her to be in full agreement with the Unanimous Proclamation issued by the other Hands on 25 November 1957.[32:30]

1957-12-02 The Hands ask National Spiritual Assemblies to undertake steps to secure the legal recognition of the Hands of the Cause in the Holy Land (Custodians) under the name of "The Custodians of the Bahá'í World Faith" and asking for National Spiritual Assemblies to pledge allegiance to the body of the Custodians.[32:40]

1957-12-05 Hands cable Bahá'í World announcing transfer of all remaining properties in the vicinity of the Shrine of Bahá'u'lláh to the Israel Branch of the United States National Assembly.[32:50]

1957-12-25 Hands cable Bahá'í World advising demolition of the house adjacent and to the Mansion of Bahjí (which had been occupied by Covenant Breakers).[32:51]

1958-01-01 Hands cable Bahá'í World calling for the entire Community to refrain from religious festivity for a period of nine months from the day of Shoghi Effendi's death.[32:55]

1958-01-23 Intercontinental Conference, Kampala, Uganda.[32:56]

1958-03-12 Intercontinental Conference, Sydney, Australia.[32:72]

1958-04-21 Under supervision of the Hands the National Spiritual Assembly of France elected.[32:86]

1958-05-02 Intercontinental Conference, Chicago.[32:90]

1958-06-12 The Hands in the Holy Land issue a "Statement regarding the Guardianship."[32:100]

1958-07 Knight of Bahá'u'lláh: Paul Adams, Spitsbergen.[47:449ff]

1958-07-25 Intercontinental Conference, Frankfurt, Germany.[32:102]

1958-08-24 Hands cable Bahá'í World that pilgrimages to the Holy Land would again be permitted.[32:110]

1958-09-21 Intercontinental Conference, Djakarta, Singapore.[32:111]

1958-11-01 Hands announce completion of the monument on Shoghi Effendi's grave.[32:116]

1958-11-21 Second Conclave of the Hands of the Cause, Bahjí.[32:108]

1958-11-30 Hands issue a Conclave Message (through National Spiritual Assemblies) to the Bahá'í Community.[32]

1959-04-21 Under supervision of the Hands the new National Spiritual Assemblies of Turkey, Burma, Austria and the South Pacific Regional National Spiritual Assembly are elected.[32:148ff]

1959-08 Knight of Bahá'u'lláh: John Z. T. Chang, Hainan.[47:449ff]

1959-09 Knights of Bahá'u'lláh: Catherine Heward Huxtable and Clifford Huxtable, the Gulf Islands.[47:449ff]

1959-11-07 Message is issued to the Bahá'ís of the East and the West (via National Spiritual Assemblies) by the Hands from their third Conclave. This message announces the plans and procedure for the election of the Universal House of Justice on 21 April 1963 in Holy Land. The message also provides for the election of an International Bahá'í Council at Riḍván 1961.[32:166]

1960-04-28 Hands cable National Spiritual Assemblies advising that Mason Remey issued a statement claiming that he was the second Guardian and calling upon believers everywhere to repudiate this "misguided action." Only the National Spiritual Assembly of France voted to accept Remey's claim (eight members were in favor; four subsequently repented and cabled the Hands for forgiveness). Some 15 individual believers decided to follow Remey (10 in France and five in the United States).[32:196]

1960-04-29 The United States National Convention sends a cable to the Hands pledging the loyalty of the body of the believers and completely rejecting Remey's claims. Over the next 22 days all other National and Regional Spiritual Assemblies or National Conventions pledge their complete loyalty (with the exception of France): 29 April, Austria, Benelux, Scandinavia and Finland; 30 April, Alaska, Argentina Bolivia Chile Paraguay and Uruguay, Australia, Burma, India, and South Pacific Islands, as well as the Australian National Convention; 1 May, Brazil, Peru, Colombia, Ecuador and Venezuela, and the United States, as well as Alaskan and Greater Antilles National Conventions; 2 May, Central America, Mexico and Panama, North East Asia, South East Asia; 3 May, Canada and Pakistan, as well as the Canadian and South Pacific Islands National Conventions; 4 May, Arabian Peninsula; 5 May, Central and East Africa, Írán and Italo-Swiss; 8 May, the British Isles; 9 May, North East Africa; 10 May, Germany; 12 May, South and West Africa; 13 May Turkey; 14 May New Zealand; 16 May, the Iberian Peninsula; 17 May, North West Africa; 21 May, 'Iráq. [32:199ff]

1960-04-30 Hands write to Mason Remey conveying the text of their cable to the Bahá'í World thereby rejecting his claim.[32:197]

1960-05-05 Hands write to the National Spiritual Assembly of France advising that they are sending Hand of the Cause of God Abu'l Qásim Faizí to meet with them to take whatever steps are felt by him to be necessary to protect the Faith in France. The Assembly is subsequently dissolved and the five members who accepted Remey's claim declared ineligible for re-election. In the interim, the local Spiritual Assembly of Paris, which remained loyal, takes over as the Central Assembly for France.[32:197]

1960-05-10 The Hands write to National and Regional Spiritual Assemblies throughout the world advising them that Remey's claim to be the second Guardian strips him of his rank as a Hand. The letter calls upon the Bahá'ís everywhere to have no association with Remey.[32:198]

1960-05-13 International Bahá'í Council cables its loyalty and complete rejection of Remey's claims per resolution made at its 27 April 1960 meeting.[32:207]

1960-07-12 Passing of Hand of the Cause of God Horace Holley in Haifa (b. Torrington, Conn. 7 April 1887).[32:xxiii]

1960-07-26 In a letter to all National Spiritual Assemblies, the Hands expell Mason Remey from the Cause and declare him a Covenant Breaker.

1960-10-15 The Hands write to all National Spiritual Assemblies in detail setting out a systematic refutation of Remey's claim.[32:231]

1960-10-18 Fourth Conclave of the Hands of the Cause of God, Bahjí.[32:229]

1960-11-18	Passing of Hand of the Cause of God Clara Dunn in Sydney, Australia.[32:245]
1960-11-20	The cornerstone of the Mother Temple of Europe (Langenhain, near Frankfurt, Germany), is laid during a ceremony attended by nearly 1,000 Bahá'ís and guests.[32:241]
1961-01-14	Dedication of the Mother Temple of Africa, Kampala, Uganda.[32:249f]
1961-04-01	Passing of Hand of the Cause of God Amelia Collins, Haifa (b. Pittsburgh 1 November 1861.)[32:xxiii]
1961-04-21	The Hands call for the election 21 Latin American National Spiritual Assemblies: Argentina, Bolivia, Brazil, Chile, Colombia, Costa Rica, Cuba, Dominican Republic, Ecuador, El Salvador, Guatemala, Haiti, Honduras, Jamaica, Mexico, Nicaragua, Panama, Paraguay, Peru, Uruguay and Venezuela.[32:255, 274]
1961-04-21	Election by the members of pre-Riḍván National and Regional Spiritual Assemblies of International Bahá'í Council ('Ali Nakhjavání, President, Charles Wolcott, Secretary General, Sylvia Ioas, Vice-President, Ian Semple, Assistant Secretary, Borrah Kavelin, Member-at-large, Lotfu'llah Ḥakim, Ethel Revell, Jessie Revell, Treasurer, Mildred Mottahedeh).[32:285ff][47:397]
1961-06-25	First full meeting of the International Bahá'í Council in Haifa.[32:285ff]
1961-06-25	The Hands convene a joint meeting with the newly elected International Bahá'í Council and give to them their operating mandate.[32:285ff]
1961-09-14	Dedication of the Mother Temple of the Antipodes, Sydney, Australia.[32:309]
1961-10-15/11-02	Fourth Conclave Meeting of the Hands of the Cause of God in Bahjí.[32:313]
1962-01-01	Passing of the Hand of the Cause of God Amelia Collins, in Haifa, Israel.[32:xxiii, 333]
1962-04-21	Eleven new independent European National Spiritual Assemblies elected: Belgium, Denmark, Finland, Holland, Italy, Luxembourg, Norway, Portugal, Spain, Sweden and Switzerland (these are in addition to the National Spiritual Assemblies of the British Isles, France, Germany and Austria).[32:352]
1963-04	Completion of the Ten Year Crusade.[32:340ff]
1963-04-09	The Hands cable all National Spiritual Assemblies calling on them to ask the Bahá'í community, either

individually or in groups, to unite in prayers beginning sundown on 21 April to beseech God to inspire and guide the delegates in their votes for the Universal House of Justice.[32:420]

1963-04-09 Sixth Conclave of the Hands of the Cause of God.[32:403]

1963-04-12 Hands write the International Bahá'í Council expressing deep gratitude and appreciation for the services rendered by its members (that institution being rendered superfluous by the upcoming election of the Universal House of Justice.) They also set out in detail the program for the World Congress to be held immediately following the election. The letter also gave guidance with respect to the position agreed by the Hands of the Cause of God regarding their eligibility for service as members of the Universal House of Justice.[32:421]

1963-04-21 Election of the Universal House of Justice.[32:424]

1963-05-09 Hands draw up principles governing the relationship of the five in the Holy Land to the full body.[32:426]

1963-05-19 Hands cable all National Conventions expressing loving appreciation for the dedication that resulted in the triumphant conclusion of the Ten Year Crusade and setting out their new operating format.[32:427]

1963-06-07 The Hands of the Cause of God submit their official report on the proceeding of the First International Convention to the Universal House of Justice.[32:429]

1963-06-07 The Universal House of Justice legally terminated the legal entity known as "The Custodians of the Bahá'í World Faith."[32:433]

Timeline—Universal House of Justice

1963-04-21/23	Election of the Universal House of Justice—First International Convention—representatives of 56 National and Regional Assemblies gather for the election in the House of 'Abdu'l-Bahá, 7 Haparsim Street, Haifa. Casting of ballots begins at 9:30 A.M., on Sunday 21 April. The members of the first Universal House of Justice are (in order of the number of votes received): Charles Wolcott, 'Alí Nakhjavání, H. Borrah Kavelin, Ian Semple, Luftfu'lláh Ḥakim, David Hofman, Hugh Chance, Amoz Gibson, Ḥushmand Fathe-Azam. Convention sessions on 22-23 April take place in the Beit Harofe Auditorium, 2 Wingate Avenue, Haifa.[32:424]
1963-04-28/05-02	First Bahá'í World Congress—Celebration of the Most Great Jubilee in London (Royal Albert Hall).[50:57]
1963-04-30	Presentation of the first Universal House of Justice and the reading of its first message to the Bahá'ís of the World in the Royal Albert Hall, London.[8:1]
1963-06-07	The Universal House of Justice legally terminates the legal entity known as "The Custodians of the Bahá'í World Faith."
1963-10	——announces Nine Year Plan (1963—1972).[8:14] The Third Epoch of the Formative Age is announced.[8:17]
1963-10-06	——issue statement *"no way to appoint or legislate to make it possible to appoint a second Guardian to succeed Shoghi Effendi."*[8:11]
1964-04-21	Nine Year Plan launched.[8:12, 22][50:101]
1964-07-04	Dedication of the Mother Temple of Europe, Langenhain, Germany.[8:28]
1965-04-21	Announcement is made about holding six intercontinental conferences in October 1965; also calling of oceanic conferences.[8:65][50:221]
1965-07-22	Passing of Hand of the Cause of God Leroy C. Ioas, Haifa.[32:xxiii]
1967-09/10	Celebration of the Centenary of the Revelation of the Súriy-i-Mulúk.
1967-10	Luftfu'lláh Ḥakim resigns as a member of the Universal House of Justice due to health problems. Because new elections are to be held in six months a by-election is not called.
1967-10	Inauguration of major proclamation campaign by the

presentation of a special edition of "The Proclamation of Bahá'u'lláh" to 140 leads of state by the Universal House of Justice.[8:116][50:195ff]

1967-10-05/10 Intercontinental Conference, Chicago. Hand of the Cause of God Ṭarázu'lláh Samandarí represents the Universal House of Justice.[50:229]

1967-10-06/09 Intercontinental Conference, Sydney, Australia. Hand of the Cause of God Ugo Giachery represented the Universal House of Justice.[50:239] Intercontinental Conference, Kampala, Uganda. Hand of the Cause of God 'Alí Akbar Furútan represents the Universal House of Justice.[50:243] Intercontinental Conference, Frankfurt, Germany. Hand of the Cause of God Paul Haney represents the Universal House of Justice.[50:249]

1967-10-07/09 Intercontinental Conference, New Delhi, India. Hand of the Cause of God Abu'l Qásim Faizí represents the Universal House of Justice.[50:253] Intercontinental Conference, Panama City, Panama. Hand of the Cause of God 'Amatu'l-Bahá Rúḥíyyih Khánum represents the Universal House of Justice.[50:223]

1968 Following earthquake damage, the Mashriqu'l-Adhkár of 'Ishqábád is demolished on order of the Soviet authorities.[50:479]

1968-02-19 His Highness Malietoa Tanumafili II, head of state of Western Samoa embraces the Faith of Bahá'u'lláh. He was the first ruling monarch to do so.[51:180]

1968-04-22 Second International Convention—representatives of 81 National and Regional Assemblies gather for the election of the Universal House of Justice in the Beit Harofe, Haifa. The members of the second Universal House of Justice were (in order of the number of votes they received): Amoz Gibson, 'Alí Nakhjavání, Ḥushmand Fathe-Azam, Ian Semple, Charles Wolcott, David Hofman, H. Borrah Kavelin, Hugh Chance and David Ruhe.[51:565]

1968-06-21 Establishment of the Continental Boards of Counsellors by the Universal House of Justice. The members (36) of the first Boards: Northwestern Africa (3):—Ḥusayn Ardikání, Muḥammad Kebdani, William Maxwell; Central and East Africa (5):—Oloro Epyeru, Kolonario Oule, Isobel Sabri, Mihdí Samandarí, 'Azíz Yazdí; Southern Africa (3):—Seewoosumbur-Jeehoba Appa, Shídán Fatḥ-I-'Aẓam, Bahíyyih Ford; North America (3):—Lloyd Gardner, Florence Mayberry, Edna True; Central America (3):—Carmen de Burafato,

Central America (3):—Carmen de Burafato, Artemus Lamb, Alfred Osborne; South America (3):—Athos Costas, Hooper Dunbar, Donald Witzel; Western Asia (5):—Masíḥ Farhangí, Mas'úd Khamsí, Hádí Raḥmání, Manúchihr Salmánpúr, Sankaran-Nair Vasudevan; Southeast Asia (3):—Yan Lee Leong, Khudárahm Paymán, Chellie Sundram; Northeast Asia (2):—Rúḥu'lláh Mumtází, Vicente Samaniego; Australasia (3):—Suhayl 'Alá'í, Howard Harwood, Thelma Perks; Europe (3):—Erik Blumenthal, Dorothy Ferraby, Louis Hénuzet.[49:4][51:611]

1968-07-07 Passing of Hand of the Cause of God Hermann Grossman in Germany.[51:416]

1968-08-10 Passing of Luftu'lláh Ḥakim, member of the Universal House of Justice, in Haifa.[51:430]

1968-09-02 Passing of Hand of the Cause of God Ṭarázu'lláh Samandarí, in Haifa.[51:410]

1968-08-23/25 First Oceanic Conference, Palermo, Sicily in commemoration of the 100th anniversary of Bahá'u'lláh's journey on the Mediterranean Sea (from Galipoli to 'Akká).[49:10] [51:73]

1968-08-31 Commemoration of 100th anniversary of the arrival of Bahá'u'lláh in the Holy Land.

1968-11 Knight of Bahá'u'lláh: Fereidun Khazrai, Romania.

1969-07-10 The number of Continental Board of Counsellors on the Northwest Asia and South America Boards is increased by one member each, bringing the total number of Counsellors to 38.[49:28]

1970-05-27 Bahá'í International Community accorded category II consultative status with the United Nations Economic and Social Council (ECOSOC).[11:587][49:50][51:358]

1970-04-21 Number of Continental Board of Counsellors on Western Asia Board is raised by one and in Europe by two; bringing the total number of Counsellors to 41.[49:52]

1970-06-23 Commemoration of the 100th anniversary of the death of Mírzá Mihdí, "The Purest Branch."[11:587][51:159ff]

1970-08-14/15 Oceanic and Continental Conference La Paz, Bolivia. Hand of the Cause of God 'Amatu'l-Bahá Rúḥíyyih Khánum represents the Universal House of Justice.[51:317] Oceanic and Continental Conference Rose Hall, Mauritius. Hand of the Cause of God William Sears represents the Universal House of Justice.[51:317]

1971-01-01 Passing of Hand of the Cause of God Agnes B. Alexan-

1971-01-01	Passing of Hand of the Cause of God Agnes B. Alexander, Honolulu, Hawaii.[51:423]
1971-01-01/03	Oceanic and Continental Conference Monrovia, Liberia. Hand of the Cause of God 'Amatu'l-Bahá Rúḥíyyih Khánum represents the Universal House of Justice.[51:318] Oceanic and Continental Conference Singapore. Hand of the Cause of God Enoch Olinga represents the Universal House of Justice.[51:319]
1971-05-21/23	Oceanic and Continental Conference Kingston, Jamaica. Hand of the Cause of God Dhikru'lláh Khádem represents the Universal House of Justice.[51:320] Oceanic and Continental Conference Suva, Fiji Islands. Hand of the Cause of God Ruḥmatu'lláh Muhajír represents the Universal House of Justice.[51:320]
1971-09-03/05	Oceanic and Continental Conference Sapporo, Japan. Hand of the Cause of God 'Alí Akbar Furútan represents the Universal House of Justice.[51:321] Oceanic and Continental Conference Reykjavik, Iceland. Hand of the Cause of God William Sears represents the Universal House of Justice.[51:322]
1971-09-04	Passing of Hand of the Cause of God Músá Banání in Kampala, Uganda.[51:421]
1971-11-26/28	Commemoration of the 50th anniversary of the passing of 'Abdu'l-Bahá.[51:107ff]
1971-12-17	Completion of Obelisk, Mt. Carmel, marking site of a future Mashriqu'l-Adkár.[11:587]
1972-04-29/30	Dedication of the Mother Temple of Latin America, Panama.[51:633]
1972-11-26	Adoption of a Constitution by the Universal House of Justice.[11:587][51:555f]
1973-03-15	The house at Mazra'ih (the Farm) is purchased. Bahá'u'lláh lived in this house for two years from June 1877 before moving to the Mansion at Bahjí.[49:112]
1973-04-21	Third International Convention—representatives of 113 National and Regional Assemblies gather for the election of the Universal House of Justice in the Beit Harofe, Haifa. The members of the third Universal House of Justice were (in order of the number of votes received): 'Alí Nakhjavání, Ḥushmand Fathe-Azam, Amoz Gibson, Ian Semple, David Hofman, Charles Wolcott, H. Borrah Kavelin, David Ruhe and Hugh Chance.[52:392]

1973-04-21	Publication of "A Synopsis and Codification of the Laws and Ordinances of the Kitáb-i-Aqdas."[51:87ff]
1973-06-05	International Teaching Center is established by the Universal House of Justice. Its membership includes all the Hands of the Cause of God and three Counsellors (Hooper Dunbar, Florence Mayberry and 'Azíz Yazdí.)[52:413]
1973-09-05	Passing of Hand of the Cause of God John Ferraby in Cambridge, England.[52:511]
1974-01-14	Universal House of Justice announces the purchase of the house of Abdu'lláh Pásha, the home of 'Abdu'l-Bahá in 'Akká and the birthplace of Shoghi Effendi.
1974-02-04	Passing of Mason Remey (Covenant Breaker).
1974-02-07	Announcement by the Universal House of Justice of the selection of the design for its Permanent Seat.[52:397ff]
1974-04-21	Five Year Plan launched.[52:107ff][53:71ff]
1976-03-08	Bahá'í International Community granted consultative status with United Nations Children's Fund (UNICEF).[52:337]
1976-07-05/08	International Teaching Conference Helsinki, Finland. Hand of the Cause of God Ugo Giachery represents the Universal House of Justice.[53:129]
1976-07-23/25	International Teaching Conference Anchorage, Alaska. Hand of the Cause of God Collis Featherstone represents the Universal House of Justice.[53:130]
1976-08-03/06	International Teaching Conference Paris, France. Hand of the Cause of God 'Amatu'l-Bahá Rúḥíyyih Khánum represents the Universal House of Justice.[53:131]
1976-10-15/17	International Teaching Conference Nairobi, Kenya. Hand of the Cause of God William Sears represents the Universal House of Justice.[53:133]
1976-11-27/30	International Teaching Conference Hong Kong. Hand of the Cause of God 'Alí Akbar Furútan represents the Universal House of Justice.[53:135]
1977-01-19/22	International Teaching Conference Auckland, New Zealand. Hand of the Cause of God Abu'l Qásim Faizí represents the Universal House of Justice.[53:136]
1977-01-27/30	International Teaching Conference Bahia, Brazil. Hand of the Cause of God Enoch Olinga represents the Universal House of Justice.[53:137]
1977-02-	International Teaching Conference Merida, Mexico.

04-06	Hand of the Cause of God Paul Haney represents the Universal House of Justice.[53:139]
1977-06	Commemoration of the Centenary of the termination of Bahá'u'lláh's Confinement in the prison-city of 'Akká.[53:51ff]
1977-10-17	Foundation stone laid in New Delhi for the Mother Temple of the Indian subcontinent.[53:368]
1978-04-29	Fourth International Bahá'í Convention—representatives of 123 National and Regional Assemblies gather for the election of the Universal House of Justice in the Haifa Auditorium. The members of the Universal House of Justice were (in order of the number of votes received): 'Alí Nakhjavání, Ḥushmand Fathe-Azam, Amoz Gibson, Ian Semple, David Ruhe, David Hofman, Charles Wolcott, Hugh Chance and H. Borrah Kavelin.[53:293]
1978-07	Knight of Bahá'u'lláh: Helmut Winkelbach, White Russia.
1979-01-27	Foundation stone laid in Samoa for the first Mashriqu'l-Adhkár of the Pacific Islands by His Highness Malietoa Tanumafili II.[53:371ff]
1979-04-21	Seven Year Global Crusade Plan launched.[2:81ff]
1979-07-04	The Universal House of Justice announces the appointment of Anneliese Bopp to the International Teaching Center.
1979-09-16	Passing of Hand of the Cause of God Enoch Olinga, sadly murdered with four members of his family in Uganda.[2:618]
1979-12-29	Passing of Hand of the Cause of God Ruḥmatu'lláh Muhajír in Ecuador.[2:651]
1980-02-12	Passing of Hand of the Cause of God Ḥasan M. Bályúzí in London.[2:635]
1980-07-29	Passing of Hand of the Cause of God Adelbert Mühlschlegel in Athens, Greece.[2:611]
1980-11-04	The Universal House of Justice announces the melding of the 12 Continental Boards of Counsellors into five Zones (63 Counsellors) in effect from 26 November 1980 (Zone 1, Africa, 15 Counsellors; Zone 2, the Americas, 16 Counsellors; Zone 3, Asia, 16 Counsellors; Zone 4, Australasia, including the Hawaiian Islands and Micronesia, seven Counsellors; Zone 5, Europe, nine Counsellors).[2:475ff]

1980-11-19	Passing of Hand of the Cause of God Abu'l-Qásim Faizí.[2:659]
1982-05-14	Passing of Amoz Gibson, member of 1st Universal House of Justice, in Haifa, Israel.[2:665]
1982-06-27/29	International Conference in Dublin Ireland. Hand of the Cause of God Collis Featherstone represents the Universal House of Justice.[2:41ff]
1982-07-15	Universal House of Justice announces election of Mr. Glenford Mitchell to their Membership.
1982-08-06/08	International Conference in Quito, Ecuador. Hand of the Cause of God Paul Haney represents the Universal House of Justice.[2:157]
1982-08-19/22	International Conference in Lagos, Nigeria. Hand of the Cause of God John Robarts represents the Universal House of Justice.[2:158]
1982-09-02	International Conference in Canberra, Australia. Hand of the Cause of God Ugo Giachery represents the Universal House of Justice.[2:159]
1982-09-02/05	International Conference in Montréal, Canada. Hand of the Cause of God 'Amatu'l-Bahá Rúḥíyyih Khánum represents the Universal House of Justice.[2:161]
1982-12-03	Passing of Hand of the Cause of God Paul Haney in a car accident in Haifa.[2:613]
1983-01-31	The Universal House of Justice officially occupies its Permanent Seat on the slopes of Mount Carmel.[11:588]
1983-04	House of 'Abdu'lláh Páshá opened to pilgrims for the first time since the time of 'Abdu'l-Bahá.[11:588]
1983-04-29	Fifth International Convention—representatives of 133 National and Regional Assemblies gather for the election of the Universal House of Justice. The election took place in the Concourse of the Seat while the consultative sessions were held in the Haifa Auditorium. The members of the Universal House of Justice were (in order of the number of votes received): 'Alí Nakhjavání, Ḥushmand Fathe-Azam, Ian Semple, David Ruhe, Glenford Mitchell, David Hofman, H. Borrah Kavelin, Charles Wolcott and Hugh Chance.[2:461]
1983-05-19	The Universal House of Justice raises the number of resident members of the International Teaching Center to nine: Hands of the Cause of God 'Amatu'l-Bahá Rúḥíyyih Khánum and 'Alí Akbar Furútan and Counsellors Anneliese Bopp, Magdalene Carney, Hooper

Dunbar, Mas'úd Khamsí, Peter Khan, Isobel Sabrí and 'Azíz Yazdí. The term of office for Counsellor members of the International Teaching Center was set at five years with effect from 23 May immediately following the International Bahá'í Convention.[2:477]

1983-08-29 The Government of Írán announce the banning of the Bahá'í Administration in Írán; the Bahá'ís are left free to practice their beliefs provided they do not teach their faith to others, form local Spiritual Assemblies or take part in administrative activities.[2:249ff][11:177ff]

1984-09-01 Dedication of the Mashriqu'l-Adhkár of the Pacific Islands in Apia, Western Samoa.[11:548]

1984-11-16 Passing of Hand of the Cause of God Shu'u'lláh 'Alá'í.[11:593]

1985-10-24 Universal House of Justice releases statement entitled the "Promise of World Peace" to the peoples of the world.[11:324]

1986-01-02 Universal House of Justice announces the opening phase of the Fourth Epoch of the Formative Age of the Faith.[54:39]

1986-04-21 Six Year Plan launched.[11:23ff]

1986-11-13 Passing of Hand of the Cause of God Dhikru'lláh Khádem.

1986-12-24 Dedication of the Mother Temple of the Indian subcontinent, New Delhi, India.

1987-01-26 Passing of Charles Wolcott in Haifa, member of the Universal House of Justice.

1987-03-21 Universal House of Justice announces election of Peter Khan to their Membership.

1988-04-21 Sixth International Convention—representatives of 132 National and Regional Assemblies gather for the election of the Universal House of Justice in the Haifa Auditorium. The members of the Universal House of Justice were (in order of the number of votes received): 'Alí Nakhjavání, Glenford Mitchell, Ḥushmand Fathe-Azam, Ian Semple, Peter Khan, David Ruhe, Hugh Chance, Hooper Dunbar, and Adíb Taherzadeh. David Hofman and Borrah Kavelin announced their retirement prior to the election.

1988-05-23 The Universal House of Justice announces the appointment of a nine-resident Counsellor membership International Teaching Center.

1988-12	Knight of Bahá'u'lláh: Mr. Sean Hinton arrives in Mongolia.
1988-12-18	Passing of H. Borrah Kavelin, member of the Universal House of Justice, in Albuquerque, N.M.
1989-07-05	Passing of Hand of the Cause of God Ugo Giachery in Western Samoa.
1990-02-20	Passing of Hand of the Cause of God Jalál Kházeh.
1990-03	Abbas and Rezvanieh Katirai (Knights of Bahá'u'lláh) arrive on Sakhalin—thereby completing the goals of the Ten Year Crusade.
1990-03-29	Bahá'í International Chinese Symposium held in San Francisco.
1990-06-14	Bahá'í International Chinese Symposium, Kingston, Jamaica.
1990-06-27	First Sino-American Conference on Women's Issues, Beijing.
1990-09-29	Passing of Hand of the Cause of God H. Collis Featherstone in Kathmandu, Nepal.
1991-06-18	Passing of Hand of the Cause of God John Robarts.
1992-03-25	Passing of Hand of the Cause of God William Sears.
1992-04-21	Bahá'í Holy Year commenced.
1992-04-21	Universal House of Justice announces worldwide application of the Law of Ḥuqúqu'lláh.
1992-05-28/29	Centenary Commemoration of the Ascension of Bahá'u'lláh in Haifa and Bahjí. Laying of the Scroll of Honor recording the names of the Knights of Bahá'u'lláh into the threshold of His Shrine.
1992-11-22	Second Bahá'í World Congress, City of the Covenant, New York City.
1993-04-21	The Three Year Plan is launched (1993-1996).
1993-04-29	Seventh International Convention—representatives of 132 National and Regional Assemblies gathered for the election of the Universal House of Justice in the Haifa Auditorium. The members of the Universal House of Justice were (in order of the number of votes received): 'Alí Nakhjavání, Ian Semple, Adíb Taherzadeh, Hooper Dunbar, Ḥushmand Fathe-Azam, Glenford Mitchell, Peter Khan, Farzám Arbáb and Douglas Martin. Hugh Chance and David Ruhe announced their retirement prior to the election.
1996-04-21	The Four Year Plan is launched (1996-2000).

List of Acronyms

BIC	Bahá'í International Community
CBC	Continental Board of Counsellors
HCG	Hands of the Cause of God
LSA	Local Spiritual Assembly
NSA	National Spiritual Assembly
ECOSOC	Economic & Social Council (United Nations.)
UN	United Nations
UNICEF	United Nations International Children's Emergency Fund
U.K.	United Kingdom
U.S.	United States (of America)
WW I	World War One
WW II	World War Two

THE DICTIONARY

A

AB Father. [11:735]

ABÁ See **ABÚ**. [11:735]

'ABÁ A loose, sleeveless cloak or mantle, open in the front. [11:735]

'ABBÁS EFFENDI The name often given to 'Abdu'l-Bahá (q.v.) by non-Bahá'ís.

'ABBAS-RIḌA, KÁMIL (1911-1980) (Knight of Bahá'u'lláh) An Iráqi believer who served on the local Spiritual Assembly of Baghdád and then the National Spiritual Assembly of Iráq. In 1953 he pioneered (see **PIONEER**) to the Seychelles Islands for which service he was designated a Knight of Bahá'u'lláh (q.v.). In 1957 he was appointed an Auxiliary Board member. In 1966 he assisted his father (Muḥammad Ḥusayn Rawḥání) in the transference of the remains of the father of Bahá'u'lláh, Mírzá Buzurg, to a Bahá'í cemetery. He served for nearly 20 years as Secretary of the National Spiritual Assembly of Iráq. He was arrested in Baghdád in 1973 and sentenced to life imprisonment for his belief in Bahá'u'lláh (q.v.). He passed away a few months after his release in 1980. [2:722]

'ABD Servant, bondsman, worshipper (of God). [11:735]

'ABDU'L-BAHÁ (The Center of the Covenant; The Master) Bahá'u'lláh's eldest surviving son and His appointed Successor. Known to the outside community as 'Abbás Effendi and knighted in 1920 as Sir 'Abdu'l-Bahá 'Abbás. He was born in Ṭihrán, Írán, on 23 May 1844, the same day that the Báb made His Declaration in Shíráz. He accompanied Bahá'u'lláh throughout His exile and increasingly took on much responsibility for the family and for the Bahá'ís, acting as Bahá'u'lláh's deputy when dealing with the public and officials.

He received several titles from Bahá'u'lláh—"The Most Great Branch;" "The Mystery of God;" "The Master." After the passing of Bahá'u'lláh, He adopted for Himself the name 'Abdu'l-Bahá (Servant of Bahá). Shoghi Effendi wrote of His unique characteristics as follows:

> He it was Whose tender soul had been seared with the ineffaceable vision of a Father, haggard, disheveled, freighted with chains, on the occasion of a visit, as a boy

of nine, to the Siyáh-Chál of ^ihrán. Against Him, in His early childhood, whilst His Father lay a prisoner in that dungeon, had been directed the malice of a mob of street urchins who pelted Him with stones, vilified Him and overwhelmed Him with ridicule.... He it was Who, in His inconsolable grief at His separation from an adored Father, had confided to Nabíl, as attested by him in his narrative, that He felt Himself to have grown old though still but a child of tender years. His had been the unique distinction of recognizing, while still in His childhood, the full glory of His Father's as yet unrevealed station, a recognition which had impelled Him to throw Himself at His feet and to spontaneously implore the privilege of laying down His life for His sake....

On Him Bahá'u'lláh, as the scope and influence of His Mission extended, had been led to place an ever greater degree of reliance, by appointing Him, on numerous occasions, as His deputy, by enabling Him to plead His Cause before the public, by assigning Him the task of transcribing His Tablets, by allowing Him to assume the responsibility of shielding Him from His enemies, and by investing Him with the function of watching over and promoting the interests of His fellow-exiles and companions....

He it was Who had been chiefly instrumental in providing the necessary means for Bahá'u'lláh's release from His nine-year confinement within the city walls of 'Akká, and in enabling Him to enjoy, in the evening of His life, a measure of that peace and security from which He had so long been debarred....

He alone had been accorded the privilege of being called "the Master," an honor from which His Father had strictly excluded all His other sons. Upon Him that loving and unerring Father had chosen to confer the unique title of "Sirru'lláh" (the Mystery of God), a designation so appropriate to One Who, though essentially human and holding a station radically and fundamentally different from that occupied by Bahá'u'lláh and His Forerunner, could still claim to be the perfect Exemplar of His Faith, to be endowed with super-human knowledge, and to be regarded as the stainless mirror reflecting His light.... On Him, at a later period, the Author of the Kitáb-i-Aqdas, in a celebrated passage, subsequently elucidated in the "Book of

> My Covenant," had bestowed the function of interpreting His Holy Writ, proclaiming Him, at the same time, to be the One "Whom God hath purposed, Who hath branched from this Ancient Root."
>
> And now to crown the inestimable honors, privileges and benefits showered upon Him, in ever increasing abundance, throughout the forty years of His Father's ministry in Baghdád, in Adrianople and in 'Akká, He had been elevated to the high office of Center of Bahá'u'lláh's Covenant, and been made the successor of the Manifestation of God Himself—a position that was to empower Him to impart an extraordinary impetus to the international expansion of His Father's Faith, to amplify its doctrine, to beat down every barrier that would obstruct its march, and to call into being, and delineate the features of, its Administrative Order, the Child of the Covenant, and the Harbinger of that World Order whose establishment must needs signalize the advent of the Golden Age of the Bahá'í Dispensation.[5:240ff]

The arrival of 15 visitors from America to 'Abdu'l-Bahá in the last days of 1898 dramatically changed the development of the Bahá'í Faith when they returned to the West. Shoghi Effendi described this journey as follows:

> The return of these God-intoxicated pilgrims,... was the signal for an outburst of systematic and sustained activity, which, as it gathered momentum, and spread its ramifications over Western Europe and the states and provinces of the North American continent, grew to so great a scale that 'Abdu'l-Bahá Himself resolved that, as soon as He should be released from His prolonged confinement in 'Akká, He would undertake a personal mission to the West.[5:259]

The opportunity came in 1910 when He left for Egypt but was unable to carry on His journey to London until 1911, where He arrived on 4 September. Describing this journey, Shoghi Effendi wrote:

> 'Abdu'l-Bahá was at this time broken in health. He suffered from several maladies brought on by the strains and stresses of a tragic life spent almost wholly in exile and imprisonment. He was on the threshold of three-score years and ten. Yet as soon as He was released from His forty-year long captivity, as soon as He had laid the Báb's body in a safe and permanent resting-place, and His mind

> was free of grievous anxieties connected with the execution of that priceless Trust, He arose with sublime courage, confidence and resolution to consecrate what little strength remained to Him, in the evening of His life, to a service of such heroic proportions that no parallel to it is to be found in the annals of the first Bahá'í century.[5:279]

After about a month in England, nine weeks in Paris and three months back in Egypt, He sails to New York, arriving there on 11 April 1912. Following a prolonged tour of eight months He returns to England, then again to Paris and, after brief visits to Germany, Hungary, Austria, Paris and Egypt, returned to Haifa on 5 December 1913. See **TIMELINE—'ABDU'L-BAHÁ**.

During WW I 'Abdu'l-Bahá was again subjected to oppressive and humiliating restrictions by the Turkish authorities. They even threatened to crucify Him and raze the Tomb of Bahá'u'lláh to the ground. During this time He was able to help feed large numbers of the Palestinian population (a course of action that resulted in His receiving a knighthood from the British Government). Also during this time he wrote and dispatched the *Tablets of the Divine Plan* (q.v.) to the Bahá'ís of North America.

In the spring of 1918 Lady Blomfield (London, England) received a deeply disturbing telephone message "'Abdu'l-Bahá in serious danger. Take immediate action." She went at once to Lord Lamington, who put the matter into the hands of the Right Honourable Arthur Balfour, secretary of state for foreign affairs, and a cable was immediately sent to General Allenby, "Extend every protection and consideration to 'Abdu'l-Bahá, His family and His friends, when British march on Haifa." When Allenby took Haifa, several days before it was believed possible for him to do so, he cabled London, "Have today taken Palestine. Notify the world that 'Abdu'l-Bahá is safe." This remarkable episode is reported in Lady Blomfield's book, *The Chosen Highway.* [55]

'Abdu'l-Bahá passed away in Haifa in the early hours of 28 November 1921. To the very end He carried on His normal activities, receiving, on the afternoon before He died, the Muftí of Haifa, the mayor and head of the police and inquiring, before He retired at night, after the health of every member of His household, of the pilgrims and of the friends in Haifa. 'Abdu'l-Bahá's contributions to His Father's Faith were summarized by Shoghi Effendi:

> 'Abdu'l-Bahá, ... had erected the standard of His Father's Faith in the North American continent, and established an impregnable basis for its institutions in Western Europe, in the Far East and in Australia. He had, in His works, Tablets and addresses, elucidated its principles,

interpreted its laws, amplified its doctrines, and erected the rudimentary institutions of its future Administrative Order. In Russia He had raised its first House of Worship, whilst on the slopes of Mt. Carmel He had reared a befitting mausoleum for its Herald, and deposited His remains therein with His Own hands. Through His visits to several cities in Europe and the North American continent He had broadcast Bahá'u'lláh's Message to the peoples of the West, and heightened the prestige of the Cause of God to a degree it had never previously experienced. And lastly, in the evening of His life, He had through the revelation of the *Tablets of the Divine Plan* issued His mandate to the community which He Himself had raised up, trained and nurtured, a Plan that must in the years to come enable its members to diffuse the light, and erect the administrative fabric, of the Faith throughout the five continents of the globe.[5:323f]

'ABDU'L-BAHÁ, ASCENSION OF A Bahá'í Holy Day commemorating the time of His passing (1 A.M. 28 November 1921). It is one of the two Holy Days on which work is not suspended.

'ABDU'L-BAHÁ, SHRINE OF When 'Abdu'l-Bahá built the square fortresslike building to house the Remains of the Báb on the site on Mount Carmel pointed out to Him by Bahá'u'lláh, He made it with six rooms (see below). When He passed away His remains were entombed in the center room of the three northern ones—on the side nearest to 'Akká. The other two are places for the private prayer and meditation of the pilgrims and visitors. The Shrine of 'Abdu'l-Bahá is frequently open to the public, but guides ensure that the silence and dignity of this Holy Place is maintained.

'ABDU'L-BAHÁ, WILL AND TESTAMENT OF The Will and Testament of 'Abdu'l-Bahá is a central document in the creation of the Administrative Order (q.v.). Shoghi Effendi details its importance as follows:

> The triple impulse generated through the revelation of the Tablet of Carmel by Bahá'u'lláh and the Will and Testament as well as the *Tablets of the Divine Plan* bequeathed by the Center of His Covenant—the three Charters which have set in motion three distinct processes, the first operating in the Holy Land for the development of the institutions of the Faith at its World Center and the other two, throughout the rest of the Bahá'í world, for its propagation and the establishment of its Administrative Order" [6:84]

The Charter which called into being, outlined the features and set in motion the processes of, this Administrative Order is none other than the Will and Testament of 'Abdu'l-Bahá, His greatest legacy to posterity, the brightest emanation of His mind and the mightiest instrument forged to insure the continuity of the three ages which constitute the component parts of His Father's Dispensation. The Covenant of Bahá'u'lláh had been instituted solely through the direct operation of His Will and purpose. The Will and Testament of 'Abdu'l-Bahá, on the other hand, may be regarded as the offspring resulting from that mystic intercourse between Him Who had generated the forces of a God-given Faith and the One Who had been made its sole Interpreter and was recognized as its perfect Exemplar. The creative energies unleashed by the Originator of the Law of God in this age gave birth, through their impact upon the mind of Him Who had been chosen as its unerring Expounder, to that Instrument, the vast implications of which the present generation ... is still incapable of fully apprehending. This Instrument can, if we would correctly appraise it, no more be divorced from the One Who provided the motivating impulse for its creation than from Him Who directly conceived it.... The Administrative Order which this historic Document has established, it should be noted, is, by virtue of its origin and character, unique in the annals of the world's religious systems. No Prophet before Bahá'u'lláh... has established, authoritatively and in writing, anything comparable to the Administrative Order which the authorized Interpreter of Bahá'u'lláh's teachings has instituted, an Order which, by virtue of the administrative principles which its Author has formulated, the institutions He has established, and the right of interpretation with which He has invested its Guardian, must and will, in a manner unparalleled in any previous religion, safeguard from schism the Faith from which it has sprung. Nor is the principle governing its operation similar to that which underlies any system, whether theocratic or otherwise, which the minds of men have devised for the government of human institutions. Neither in theory nor in practice can the Administrative Order of the Faith of Bahá'u'lláh be said to conform to any type of democratic government, to any system of autocracy, to any purely aristocratic order, or to any of the various theocracies... which mankind has witnessed in the past. It incorporates within its structure certain elements which are to be found in each of the three recognized forms of secular government, is devoid of the defects which each of them inherently possesses, and blends the salutary truths which each undoubtedly contains without vitiating in any way the integrity of the Divine verities on which it is essentially founded...these are among the features which combine to set apart the Order identified with the Revelation of Bahá'u'lláh from any of the existing systems of human government.[5:325ff]

'Abdu'l-Bahá, Who incarnates an institution for which we can find no parallel whatsoever in any of the world's recognized religious systems, may be said to have closed the Age to which He Himself belonged and opened the one in which we are now laboring. His Will and Testament should thus be regarded as the perpetual, the indissoluble link which the mind of Him Who is the Mystery of God has conceived in order to insure the continuity of the three ages that constitute the component parts of the Bahá'í Dispensation.[4:143f] See **THREE CHARTERS**.

ABHÁ The superlative of "Bahá" (Glory) and means "Most Glorious." See **ALLÁH'U'ABHÁ; BAHÁ'U'L-ABHÁ.** [11:735📖]

ABHÁ BEAUTY Bahá'u'lláh.

ABHÁ KINGDOM The spiritual world into which the soul passes after death.

ABÍ See **ABÚ**. [11:735📖]

ABJAD NOTATION system whereby each letter of the Arabic alphabet is assigned a specific numerical value. [11:735📖]

ABLUTIONS The washing of the hands and face required before the reciting of the obligatory prayers.

ABÚ Father of. [11:735📖]

A<u>DH</u>ÁN Muslim call to prayer. [11:735📖]

Á<u>DH</u>IRBÁYJÁN Northwestern province of Írán, where the Báb was imprisoned. The provincial capital is Tabríz.

ADÍB Refined, cultured, learned; writer, scholar, man of letters. [11:735📖]

'ADL Justice. See **BAYTU'L-'ADL-I-A'ẒAM.** [11:735📖]

ADMINISTRATION The name by which Bahá'ís refer to the administrative and organizational operating structure of the Bahá'í Faith.

ADMINISTRATIVE ORDER, BAHÁ'Í The name given to the institutions that form the operating structure of the Bahá'í Faith. The Administrative Order was designated by Bahá'u'lláh, elaborated and established in the "Will and Testament" of 'Abdu'l-Bahá, developed by Shoghi Effendi during his lifetime as Guardian and now being followed and further developed by the Universal House of Justice. The "twin pillars" of the Administrative Order are the Guardianship and the Universal House of Justice. It includes the local and national Spiritual Assemblies (in the future to be designated 'Houses of Justice'), the Universal House of Justice, the Guardianship, the Institutions of the Hands of the Cause, the International Teaching Center, the Continental Board of Counsellors, the Auxiliary Boards and their Assistants.

Shoghi Effendi wrote of the Administrative Order:

> This new-born Administrative Order incorporates within its structure certain elements which are to be found in each of the three recognized forms of secular government, without being in any sense a mere replica of any one of them, and without introducing within its machinery any of the objectionable features which they inherently possess. It blends and harmonizes... the salutary truths which each of these systems undoubtedly contains.... The Administrative Order of the Faith of Bahá'u'lláh must in no wise be regarded as purely democratic in character inasmuch as the basic assumption which requires all democracies to depend fundamentally upon getting their mandate from the people is altogether lacking in this Dispensation. In the conduct of the administrative affairs of the Faith, in the enactment of the legislation necessary to supplement the laws of the Kitáb-i-Aqdas, the members of the Universal House of Justice, it should be borne in mind, are not... responsible to those whom they represent, nor are they allowed to be governed by the feelings, the general opinion, and even the convictions of the mass of the faithful, or of those who directly elect them. They are to follow, in a prayerful attitude, the dictates and promptings of their conscience. They may, indeed they must, acquaint themselves with the conditions prevailing among the community, must weigh dispassionately in their minds the merits of any case presented for their consideration, but must reserve for themselves the right of an unfettered decision.[4:152f]

ADMINISTRATIVE RIGHTS All registered Bahá'ís possess certain community rights such as: the right for adult (aged 21 and over) Bahá'ís to vote in Bahá'í elections; to serve on Bahá'í administrative bodies; to attend Nineteen Day Feasts (q.v.); to have a Bahá'í marriage ceremony; to contribute to the Bahá'í Funds. Where an individual breaches Bahá'í law in a flagrant manner, his/her "rights" may be wholly or partially withdrawn as a sanction; restoration depends on the person correcting his/her behavior.

ADRIANOPLE (Edirne) A city in European Turkey, almost on the border with Greece, to which Bahá'u'lláh was exiled in 1863. It was while He was in Adrianople that He began writing to the kings and rulers of the day advising them of His advent. See **TABLETS TO THE KINGS**.

AFNÁN (Twigs) The name given to the descendants of the two brothers of the Báb's wife, as well as the Báb's maternal uncles.

AFRUKHTIH, YOUNESS (-1948) An early Persian believer. He served 'Abdu'l-Bahá as Secretary and translator in 'Akká for a period of nine years (1900-1909.) He is perhaps best known for his translation of the responses given by 'Abdu'l-Bahá to questions posed by Laura Clifford Dreyfus-Barney (q.v.) in 'Akká. She subsequently published the material under the title *Some Answered Questions*. [56] He traveled extensively throughout America and Europe as a teacher of the Cause. [48:679]

ÁGHÁ Originally lord, nobleman; officer, commander; placed after a woman's name Ágh́á is a courtesy title comparable with Áqá (q.v.). It may also form a part of a compound proper name. [11:735📖]

AGHṢÁN (Branches) The family and descendants of Bahá'u'lláh. 'Abdu'l-Bahá was named "The Most Great Branch" and took precedence over Mírzá Muḥammad-'Alí, "The Greater Branch." See appended **GENEALOGIES**.

A.H. Anno Hegirae (in the year of the Emigration): denotes the Muslim Era, reckoned from the year of Muḥammad's flight from Mecca to Medina in A.D. 622. See **HIJRAT**. [11:735📖]

'AHD Covenant, bond, treaty; The Covenant (of God). [11:735📖]

AKBAR Greater, greatest. See **ALLÁH-U-AKBAR; KABÍR**. [11:735📖]

'AKKÁ A city on the coast of Israel to which Bahá'u'lláh was exiled from Edirne in 1868. At that time it was a penal colony serving the Turkish Empire. On arrival, Bahá'u'lláh and His family were imprisoned in the barracks for two years, two months, and five days. During this period His younger son, Mírzá Mihdí (q.v.), fell through a skylight to his death while rapt in prayers. Bahá'u'lláh continued to write letters to the rulers, including His letter to Queen Victoria (1870), and many other 'Tablets. In this city 'Abdu'l-Bahá was married and received His first Western pilgrims (1898-99) and where Shoghi Effendi was born in 1897. Bahá'u'lláh passed the last years of His life in Bahjí (several miles outside the city). It was here that He passed away (1892) and is buried. 'Abdu'l-Bahá remained in 'Akká until 1910 when He moved to Haifa following His release. Bahá'u'lláh was released from the prison but continued to live in the city. See **BAHÁ'U'LLÁH**.

A'LÁ Most Exalted. See **ḤAḌRAT-I-'LÁ; QALAM -I-'LÁ.** [11:735]

AL-ABHÁ The Most Glorious. See **BAHÁ'U'L-ABHÁ.** [11:735]

'ALÁ'Í, GENERAL SHU'Á'U'LLÁH (1889-1984) (Hand of the Cause of God) He was born in Ṭihrán, Írán on 16 November 1889 into a theological environment. His father held several theological degrees and was expected to become a divine in accordance with family tradition, but when his close friend became a Bahá'í he attempted to bring him back into the Muslim faith. In trying to do so he himself became convinced of the truth of the Bahá'í religion. Proclaiming it with fervor, he was in his native village condemned to death as a heretic and fled to Ṭihrán where he eventually became a physician in the court of the Sháh. When 'Alá'í was seven years old his father received a letter from 'Abdu'l-Bahá, who passed it to his son to commit to memory; its contents became the blue-print for his life. The letter contained such sentences as: "O flame of the love of God... beseech thou the Lord to enable thee to give illumination and enlightenment, to brighten the horizons and to consume the world with the fire of the love of God. I hope that thou mayest attain such a station, nay surpass it." [57:593] 'Alá'í studied first at home, then attended the newly opened Bahá'í school in Ṭihrán. He then went to medical college but eventually left to study accountancy. At the age of 19 he was appointed financial officer of the police department and later, during WW I, he served as the treasurer of the Ministry of Justice. For 25 years he was comptroller and chief financial officer to the army, rising to the rank of general. During this time he carried out many important official assignments, as his trustworthiness and integrity were proverbial. He was elected to the local Spiritual Assembly of Ṭihrán in 1913 and served on that body for the next 30 years. When the National Spiritual Assembly of the Bahá'ís of Írán came into being in 1934, he was elected to that body and served on it until he was appointed a Hand of the Cause in the 2nd contingent in February 1952. He attended the first four Intercontinental Conferences of 1953 and visited centers in the United States, Germany, Italy, Switzerland, Holland, India, Pakistan, North Africa and the Middle East. In 1956 he toured centers in India, Ceylon, Indonesia and Malaya and participated in the first Southeast Asia Teaching Conference in August of that year. Within Írán he managed the extensive properties in that land and carried out important negotiations with the Government. He also represented the Guardian and later the World Center at the inaugural Conventions of Pakistan (1957); Columbia and Jamaica (1961) and Ceylon (1962.) In 1959-60 he visited centers in India, Pakistan, Hong Kong, Macau, Japan, Vietnam and Malaya. In 1961 he traveled to centers in the United States, France, Belgium, Holland, Germany,

Italy, Switzerland and Turkey. The 1970s saw very turbulent times in Írán in which he was intimately involved, but his international travels continued, with visits to the United Kingdom and Europe. In Germany he presented Bahá'í literature to many distinguished orientalists for their state and university libraries. He was able to visit the Holy Land for important consultations, attended the International Convention of 1978 and settled in France later that year. He attended the National Convention of Austria in 1979 and moved on to Scottsdale, Arizona in January 1981. There, on the 96th anniversary of his birth, he passed away surrounded by his family and friends. The Universal House of Justice cabled:

> Grieved announce passing Hand Cause Shu'á'u'lláh 'Alá'í 16 November thus ending more than seventy years uninterrupted dedicated services Threshold Bahá'u'lláh. He was tower strength Cradle Faith where he served eminently, devotedly in its emerging administrative institutions since their inception. His membership many decades National Assembly frequently as Chairman bears witness trust Bahá'ís Írán placed his noble person. His exemplary courage representing interests Faith high places, his integrity performing official duties enhanced prestige beloved Faith he so diligently sincerely championed entire life. His manifold achievements crowned honor appointment Hand Cause 29 February 1952. This enabled him extend services Faith international arena. Supplicating Sacred Threshold progress radiant soul Abhá Kingdom. Advise hold memorial gatherings Bahá'í world including all Mashriqu'l-Adhkárs.[57:594]

ALCOHOL Forbidden except for medical use. See **DRUGS**.

ALEXANDER, AGNES BALDWIN (1875-1971) (Hand of the Cause of God) Born in Honolulu, Hawaii of Christian missionary heritage on 21 July 1875. In 1900 she traveled to Rome where she encountered the Bahá'í Faith. While in Rome she was attracted to a lady and her two daughters because of their "radiant happiness" and though they did not mention the full nature of their faith to her, after three days she spontaneously announced to the lady, Mrs. Charlotte Dixon, "Christ is on this earth!" To which Mrs. Dixon replied "Yes, I can see by your face that you know it." [51:424] She wrote of her instinctive declaration of faith to 'Abdu'l-Bahá on 26 November 1900. Later she made contact with some Bahá'ís in Paris and while living in Milan received a loving letter from May Bolles. She then moved to Paris and after some time decided to take her newfound faith to her homeland (Hawaii.) On the morning before leaving she received a letter from 'Abdu'l-Bahá in which He admonished her to be like a divine bird, return to Hawaii, spread the wings of sanctity over the island, warble melodies in praise of God's cause, seeking souls to be attracted as moths to a lighted lamp, and be the means of making Hawaii illumined by the Light of God. [58:10] She arrived, to "open" the islands to the Faith, on 26 December 1901. She remained in Hawaii for 12 years, and in her published *Memoirs* tells stories of the early believers. They included the second Bahá'í from the Island—Clarence Hobron Smith (also from a missionary background); Dr. George Augur (one of 'Abdu'l-Bahá's 19 Disciples); and Kanichi Yamamoto—the first Japanese to accept the Faith. With the same intuitive knowledge that led her to accept the Faith without direct awareness of it, she began to study of Japan and its culture. In early 1913 her parents passed away, her sister left the island and she went to Canada to spend a month with the Maxwells before going to New York. During this time she received a letter from 'Abdu'l-Bahá written just as she was leaving Hawaii in which He encouraged her to take the Faith to Japan. Although the hazards of wartime travel necessitating changes in her plans, she arrived in Japan in 1914 and made it her base for the next 23 years. In 1921 she spent a month in Korea where she introduced the Faith to many waiting souls. Although she traveled widely, she was never able to reach the Holy Land in time to meet 'Abdu'l-Bahá. In 1924 she accompanied Martha Root to China where they spoke of the Faith to Sun Yatsen. She also traveled, proclaiming the Faith, to Taiwan, Hong Kong, the Philippines, the United States, Canada and Europe. Much of her teaching was in Esperanto. In 1937 she visited the Holy Land, where Shoghi Effendi lavished her with praise and appreciation for her outstanding teaching and pioneering services. Not until 1950 was she able to return to Japan. By this time she had served the Faith for 50 years, but she was as enthusiastic as ever. At 54 years of age she had climbed Mount Fuji with a band of Buddhist pilgrims; at 85 she had accompanied a Bahá'í to the mountains of Luzon in the Philippines, riding for hours in a jeep. On several occasions she went from cell to cell in the national prison of Manila, teaching and giving solace to prisoners, "because Bahá'u'lláh had been a prisoner." On 27 March 1957 she was appointed a Hand of the Cause.

Over the years she received approximately 100 letters from Shoghi Effendi, and she was able successively to serve 'Abdu'l-Bahá, the Guardian and the Universal House of Justice. Although free from personal financial worries, she lived very frugally, expending little on herself and always giving to the Faith and to others in need. Wherever she traveled, however, she always regarded Hawaii as her home. When the islands were able to elect their first National Spiritual Assembly, just over 62 years after she had first taken the Faith there, she attended as the representative of the Universal House of Justice. In 1957 she witnessed the formation of the Regional National Spiritual Assembly of the Bahá'ís of Northeast Asia with its seat in Tokyo and was a member of that body until 1963. During those years she visited the Holy Land to attend the meetings of the Hands of the Cause. In 1963 she attended the World Congress in London immediately after the election of the Universal House of Justice. In 1965, about to attend the World Congress of Esperantists, she fell and broke her hip—sadly, she was never again able to walk alone. With no word of complaint she stated positively that God had a purpose in confining her to a Tokyo hospital for two years. However, unable to walk and write, she felt 'Abdu'l-Bahá now wished her to return to Hawaii. Because she was 92 years old, very frail, with failing memory, her friends were concerned about her ability to undertake such a long journey. She was adamant, however, and disposed of her trunks full of books, writings and relics and returned to a place prepared for her almost opposite her childhood home in Honolulu, where she passed away quietly on 1 January 1971. She was buried only a few miles from the other distinguished Hand, Martha Root. The Universal House of Justice cabled:

> Profoundly grieved passing illumined soul Hand Cause Agnes Alexander long-standing pillar Cause Far East, first bring Faith Hawaiian Islands. Her long dedicated exemplary life service devotion Cause God anticipated by Center Covenant selecting her share May Maxwell imperishable honor mention Tablets Divine Plan. Her unrestrained unceasing pursuit teaching obedience command Bahá'u'lláh, exhortations Master, guidance beloved Guardian shining example all followers Faith. Her passing severs one more link Heroic Age. Assure family friends ardent prayers holiest Shrine progress radiant soul. Request all National Spiritual Assemblies hold memorial meetings...[51:430] [59:158ff] [60:1]

'ALÍ The first Imám and rightful successor of Muḥammad; also the fourth Caliph according to the Sunnah. [11:735🕮]

ALLÁH God. [11:735🕮]

ALLÁH-U-ABHÁ "God is Most Glorious, God is All-Glorious." Used as a greeting among Bahá'ís.

ALLAH'U'AKBAR God is Most Great: Muslim salutation and opening words of the call to prayer, superseded by **ALLÁH-U-ABHÁ** as a greeting among the Bahá'ís during the Adrianople period. [11:735🕮]

ALLEN, JEANNE GWENDOLIN (1911-1969) (Knight of Bahá'u'lláh) An early (1940) Canadian believer who in 1963 pioneered with her husband (Fredrick Allen) to Cape Breton Island for which they were designated Knights of Bahá'u'lláh. [51:458]

ALLEN, JOHN WILLIAM (1907-1980) (Knight of Bahá'u'lláh) An American believer who in 1954 pioneered with his wife (Valera) to Swaziland for which they were designated Knights of Bahá'u'lláh. He served as a member of the Regional National Spiritual Assembly of Southern Africa; later he served as a member of the National Spiritual Assembly of Swaziland. While visiting Haifa he assisted Ugo Giachery in driving the stakes and stretching the strings to lay out the location of the International Archives Building on Mount Carmel (the first building to form part of the Arc (q.v.). In 1954 he was appointed an Auxiliary Board member (q.v.) for Northern and Southern Rhodesia, Nyasaland and Mozambique. [2:725]

AL-MADÍNAH Literally The City (of the Prophet). See **MECCA.** [11:735📖]

ALMOND, MAYSIE [47:936] (-1960) **ALMOND, PERCY MEADE** [51:489] (1890-1970) The Almonds were the first two believers in South Australia (1923). Maysie served as a member of the first local Spiritual Assembly of Adelaide; Percy served on the first National Spiritual Assembly of Australia and New Zealand (1934).

ALTASS, FLORENCE ELIZABETH (1884-1982) An early British believer who met the Faith in her early teens. Following "nursing care" training she found herself working in the Austrian Imperial Court of the House of Habsburg to nurse a lady-in-waiting. As time passed she became well liked by the Archduke Franz-Ferdinand and the Archduchess and was able to share with them many "Bahá'í ideas." In 1913 while on a visit to Edinburgh she attended a Bahá'í meeting in the home of Dr. and Mrs. Alexander Whyte where she met 'Abdu'l-Bahá (who was a guest in the Whyte's home). Her one meeting with 'Abdu'l-Bahá formed the theme of many poems she wrote during her life. She served in later life as a member of the local Spiritual Assemblies of Horsham and Hastings. She was active in the promotion of the Cause throughout her long life. [2:788]

AMANUENSIS (secretary) A person who wrote down or copied the words revealed by the Báb, Bahá'u'lláh and 'Abdu'l-Bahá.

'AMATU'L-BAHÁ Maidservant of Bahá. [11:735📖]

'AMATU'L-BAHÁ RÚḤÍYYIH KH̲ÁNUM, MADAME MARY RABBÁNÍ. (1910-) (Widow of Shoghi Effendi; Hand of the Cause of God) Born in Canada in 1910 to William Sutherland Maxwell and May Ellis Bolles Maxwell, she had the most illustrious of Bahá'í parents. From her earliest childhood Mary was active in teaching the Faith. At the age of nine she formally presented the "first" and "second" Tablets to Canada of the *Tablets of the Divine Plan* to the 1919 Annual Convention in New York.[51:461]

During a pilgrimage in 1937 Shoghi Effendi (q.v.) asked Mrs. Maxwell for her daughter's hand in marriage. From the beginning of her marriage until the passing of Shoghi Effendi in 1957 she served as his secretary.

On 9 January 1951 the International Bahá'í Council (q.v.) was appointed by Shoghi Effendi with 'Amatu'l-Bahá Rúḥíyyih Khánum as liaison member between Shoghi Effendi and the Council. On the passing of May in 1940, Mr. Maxwell was invited to live in Haifa, on his passing She was appointed a Hand of the Cause on 26 March, 1952.

She attended the Intercontinental Conference, Chicago-Wilmette, Ill., April-May 1953 as representative of the Guardian; and, after his passing, fulfilled his wish that she should be his representative at the second Intercontinental Conference in Kampala, Uganda, January 1958.

From his passing in 1957 until the election of the Universal House of Justice in April 1963 she was a member of the Nine Hands of the Cause in the Holy Land and has continued to live in the House in Haifa, which was the home of 'Abdu'l-Bahá and in which she lived all her married life. A year after Shoghi Effendi's passing she supervised the construction of the monument at his grave in London and began to attend a series of meetings as representative of the World Center of the Faith—1959 Conference of European Hands of the Cause, Copenhagen; 1960 Conventions of United States and Canada; 1961 Dedication of Bahá'í Houses of Worship, Kampala in January and of Sydney, Australia in September; toured centers in Uganda, Kenya and Tanganyika January—February 1961, and centers in Australia, Malaya, Indonesia, Vietnam, Cambodia, Thailand and Burma September-October 1961; European Hands of the Cause, Conference, Luxembourg, December. 1962. After the passing of Shoghi Effendi, the main purpose of her life was to travel and carry the message of Bahá'u'lláh and the love of Shoghi Effendi to as many peoples of the world as possible—from the highest in every land to the most primitive of villagers in the remotest of areas. Notable among these travels were trips to India, Southeast Asia, the Indian Ocean, Africa, Europe and Central and South America, visiting places where neither Bahá'í teachers nor Hands of the Cause had been. Commencing in February 1964 she traveled almost 55,000 miles in nine months in India. This took her to all but three states and included visiting some remote and almost extinct tribes, she was received by the president, the prime minister and many notables, distinguished officials and leaders of thought. She also attended several conventions and broke off to attend the dedication of the Mother Temple of Europe in Frankfurt, Germany in July. In 1967 she visited Sikkim, India, and the Indian Ocean islands of Reunion, Madagascar and Mauritius and in 1972 she visited the Seychelles. During this period she also visited the Intercontinental Conference in Panama, 1967 after which she spent seven months visiting the tribal areas of Panama, Bolivia, Peru, Ecuador, Chile, Argentina, Paraguay, Venezuela, Colombia and Brazil. These trips often took place under the most arduous conditions, including transport by truck, jeep, on foot or horseback, along tortuous mountain trails at high altitudes, sometimes in rain and mud, often sleeping in the most primitive houses in hammocks or on the floor. In 1968 she visited Surinam and Guyana. From 1970-1973 she made four journeys throughout Africa, which became known as "The Great Safari." Interrupted only by visits to other parts of the world to attend functions of historic importance to the Bahá'í world, she visited most parts of East, West, South and Central Africa. She was by then in her mid-sixties and drove her Land Rover for well over half of the 36,000 miles of her journeys.

Between 1973 and 1976, she visited India, Bangladesh, Burma, Hong Kong, the United States and Canada. In 1975, by which time she had already visited 109 countries, she took a team of filmmakers to visit the indigenous tribes of the Amazon Basin and produced a two-hour documentary film, *The Green Light Expedition*, with English, Spanish and Persian commentaries. In August 1976 she attended the largest International Conference to date when over 6,000 Bahá'ís met in Paris. After this she spent some time in Bermuda and in 1977 returned to India, followed by visits to Australia and an eight month round-the-world trip, followed by a nine-week tour of Australasia, when she represented the Universal House of Justice at the laying of the foundation stone of the Bahá'í House of Worship in Samoa. Her travels continued, and in 1980 she visited Europe and Canada where she directed, edited and narrated the two-hour documentary film she had written, *The Pilgrimage*. January 1981 found her attending a conference for Counsellors in Panama followed by a tour of Central America and the Caribbean, where she was received by many dignitaries and a host of tribal villagers. She completed an almost one-year tour with a visit to Canada. Commencing 11 August 1982 she went on a tour of Canada, Greenland and Iceland where she again was well received by many dignitaries and senior officials and met with many hundreds of North American Indians and Eskimos. After visiting conferences and centers in Europe in mid-1983, she set out on an extensive tour of Asia and Australasia in April 1984 which included the dedication of the Samoan Temple. In January 1985, after more visits to South America and Panama she was in New York by 22 November to present the *Promise of World Peace* to the Secretary-General of the United Nations. In 1988, at the age of 78, she undertook a grand tour of China and Mongolia, and in 1992 she visited the Soviet republics.

Throughout her travels, in her lectures and using her personal funds she has actively campaigned for the protection of the environment. She has been associated with the top officials of the World Wide Fund for Nature and at St. James's Palace, London on 28 July 1994 shared the platform with HRH The Duke of Edinburgh at a World Forestry Charter gathering.

Her books include the weighty study of her husband's life and mission, The Priceless Pearl [31] and its sister volume, The Guardian of the Bahá'í Faith; [30] Prescription for Living; Twenty-five Years of Guardianship; [61] and The Ministry of the Custodians. 1957-1963. [156]

As the First Lady of the Bahá'í Faith, she continues, now past her mid-eighties, to leave the Holy Land to attend special historic gatherings and to teach and proclaim the Faith of Bahá'u'lláh.

AMIH Maid (servant), handmaid(en). [11:735]

AMÍN Faithful, trustworthy, honest; Trustee. [11:735]

AMÍR Prince, ruler; commander, governor. [11:735]

ANCIENT BEAUTY A title of Bahá'u'lláh.

ANCIENT OF DAYS God.

ANÍS Literally companion, friend, associate; appellation given by the Báb to Mírzá Muḥammad-'Alíy-i-Zunúzí, the youthful disciple who shared His martyrdom. [11:735]

APOSTLES OF BAHÁ'U'LLÁH (Pillars of the Faith) While in His *Tablets of the Divine Plan* (q.v.), 'Abdu'l-Bahá addressed the Bahá'ís of North America and referred to them as "Apostles of Bahá'u'lláh," Shoghi Effendi listed 19 distinguished early Íránian Bahá'ís as "Pillars of the Faith" or "Apostles of Bahá'u'lláh," and it is to these the title is normally applied. See appended list of **APOSTLES**.

APPA, SEEWOOSUMBUR JEEHOBA (1912-1981) A Mauritian believer (1956) who served on the first local Spiritual Assembly of Vacoas and in 1964 was elected to the first National Spiritual Assembly of the Indian Ocean. That same year he was appointed an Auxiliary Board member for the Indian Ocean region, and in 1968 he was made a member of the Continental Board of Counsellors for the South African Zone. [2:754]

ÁQÁ Master; The Master; title given by Bahá'u'lláh to 'Abdu'l-Bahá. Also used preceding a name in an honorific sense: Mister, Sir. [11:735]

AQDAS Most holy. See **KITÁB-I-AQDAS**. [11:735]

ARC A section of Mount Carmel, Haifa, Israel, on which the world center of the Bahá'í Faith has been developed. The Shrine of the Báb (and of 'Abdu'l-Bahá); the Monuments of the Greatest Holy Leaf, her Mother and her younger Brother; the International Archives and the Seat of the Universal House of Justice have been established for many years, the Seat being the last to be built. In 1989 architectural plans were adopted for further development and beautification of the mountain. This included the construction of additional administrative buildings and gardens: the Seat of the International Teaching Center, the Center for the Study of the Sacred Texts, the International Library, an extension to the International Archives and 19 terraced gardens. The major portion of the work was completed in 1997. All buildings employ the most advanced technology for differing heating and cooling requirements, with special air treatment to filter polluted gases and particulates, especially for the Archives. This provides complete sterile conditions for the preservation of the Holy Writings. Underground parking and communication facilities are incorporated. Nine terraces and fountains will make a ceremonial approach to the Shrine of the Báb from the foot of Mount Carmel; with underground reservoirs and irrigation systems will be installed. The existing main road that runs up Mount Carmel (Hatzionut Avenue) passes through the site, and detailed arrangements had to be made with the many departments of the municipality of Haifa to permit the road to be lowered and a bridge constructed to allow the unbroken development of the Terraces. Access from the avenue enables the public to enter a landscaped courtyard from which they can enter a Public Information Center with a164-seat auditorium and reception area. All this and an office of security is being built under Terrace 11. It is of tremendous significance to the Bahá'ís that this work, which is the source of astonishment and admiration to the people of Israel and thousands of visitors, is entirely funded by the Bahá'ís themselves. It is the sacrificial participation of the worldwide Bahá'í community that is enabling this colossal enterprise to forge ahead on God's Holy Mountain.

ARCHIVES, BAHÁ'Í INTERNATIONAL Situated on the Arc, this building houses the personal relics of Bahá'u'lláh, the Báb and 'Abdu'l-Bahá, including Their portraits and Their original manuscripts. Bahá'í pilgrims (q.v.) are allowed to view these relics and archives.

ARḌ Earth, land, territory.

ARMSTRONG, LEONORA STIRLING (Holsapple) (1895-1980) An early American believer who, following the death of her mother in 1890, was raised by her grandmother, who taught her the Faith.

Following the unveiling of the *Tablets of the Divine Plan* [62] to the 1919 Bahá'í Convention in New York, she wrote to 'Abdu'l-Bahá offering her services in the pioneering field. She shared the Tablet she received by way of reply from 'Abdu'l-Bahá with Miss Martha Root (q.v.) who promptly urged her to go to Brazil (where Miss Root had been the first Bahá'í visitor in 1919.) Miss Armstrong arrived in Rio de Janeiro in February 1921 and immediately moved to Santos, just south of Rio. Three months after her arrival in Santos she received a second Tablet from 'Abdu'l-Bahá (written just before His passing) in which He referred to her as a "Herald of the Kingdom." It was addressed with nothing more than "Brazil. To the Maidservant of God, Leonora Stirling Holsapple"— somehow it was delivered to her! For the next six decades she traveled extensively throughout Brazil. She established the Faith in Rio de Janeiro and São Paulo. In 1927 she became the first Bahá'í to visit and proclaim the Cause in Colombia, Venezuela, Curaçao, Trinidad, Barbados, Haiti and British Guiana. She translated a large volume of Bahá'í literature and Writings into Portuguese and later into Spanish. In 1941 she married an Englishman, Harold Armstrong, who joined her in her efforts to promote the Cause. In 1973 she was appointed a member of the Continental Board of Counsellors in South America. According to 'Amatu'l-Bahá Rúḥíyyih Khánum, Shoghi Effendi considered Leonora "as one of the Faith's most outstanding and most distinguished believers in the West." [2:733]

ARNADÓTTIR, HÓLMFRÍDUR (1873-1955) The first (1924) and, during her lifetime, the only Bahá'í in Iceland. She translated *Bahá'u'lláh and the New Era* into Icelandic. [47:942]

ARPUSHANA, FRANCISCO PIMIENTA (-1966) (First Guajiro Martyr) An Indian of the Guajira area of Colombia, he was the chief of the Arpushana clan and embraced the Cause in 1964. Sadly, he was murdered in 1966 for his efforts to bring peace and harmony to the clans in the area. [50:319]

'ASGHARZÁDIH, ḌIÁ'U'LLÁH (1880-1956) (Knight of Bahá'u'lláh) An early Persian believer who made his first pilgrimage to the Holy Land in 1903. At that time he brought with him a silk carpet that 'Abdu'l-Bahá laid in the Inner Shrine of Bahá'u'lláh. During the time of Shoghi Effendi, with Ḍiá'u'lláh's approval, the carpet was presented to the Wilmette Temple, where it now hangs in Foundation Hall. Following his second pilgrimage, Ḍiá'u'lláh pioneered to Great Britain from 1925 to 1940; for 14 years he served there on the National Spiritual Assembly. He again pioneered during the Ten Year Crusade to Jersey (for which service he received the title Knight of Bahá'u'lláh.) [47:881]

'ASHÚRÁ Tenth day of the month of Muharram, anniversary of the martyrdom of the Imám Husayn. [11:735]

ÁSÍYIH KHÁNUM See **NAVVÁB.**

ASSEMBLY An essential institution of the Administrative Order composed of nine adult Bahá'ís elected annually by secret ballot from among the body of adult believers. Assemblies function at both local (local Spiritual Assembly) and national (National Spiritual Assembly) levels.

ASSISTANTS TO THE AUXILIARY BOARDS MEMBERS As their title indicates they assist Auxiliary Board Members (q.v.). Unlike other appointed "Board" members (Counsellors and Auxiliary Board Members) assistants may serve also on the elected bodies. See **AUXILIARY BOARD MEMBERS; CONTINENTAL BOARDS OF COUNSELLORS.**

AUGUR, DR. GEORGE JACOB (1853-1936) (Disciple of 'Abdu'l-Bahá) He was born in 1853, became a homeopathic physician and lived with his wife Ruth in Oakland, California before moving to Honolulu. Ruth's sister, Mrs. Otis, heard of the Faith from Elizabeth Muther in 1904 and then spent some time with Helen Goodall while in Oakland, embraced the Cause on her return to Honolulu and began to hold regular meetings at her home. Soon afterwards he and Ruth became Bahá'ís. When Mrs. Otis left Hawaii early in 1907 they started to hold the meetings in their home. He began a correspondence with 'Abdu'l-Bahá in early 1909, and during the following years he was encouraged to make a second visit to Japan, this time to try to establish the Faith in that land. Several Bahá'ís had been to Japan, but when he went there in May 1914 and stayed for 10 months he became the first resident Bahá'í. On 6 November 1914 Agnes Alexander joined him, and a week later they held the first Bahá'í meeting in Japan, which three other people attended. He returned to Ruth in Honolulu in April 1915, stayed there for six months and then they returned together on 12 October 1915. After visiting Honolulu and returning, they finally resettled back in Honolulu and were there when "Father and Mother" Dunn spent some time in the area when on their way to "open" Australia to the Faith in January 1920. The Augurs received several letters from 'Abdu'l-Bahá that paid wonderful tribute to their services in Hawaii and Japan as well as their dedicated efforts to hold regular meetings in their home until 1927 when he retired due to ill health. He passed away after a stroke at the age of 73 on 14 September 1927. Ruth remained constant in her service to the Faith until her death in Oakland, California on 21 April 1936.

AUXILIARY BOARD An Institution of the appointed arm of the Bahá'í Administrative Order initiated by the Guardian in 1954 to assist the Hands of the Cause. In 1968 the Universal House of Justice appointed Continental Boards of Counsellors and placed the Auxiliary Boards under their direct jurisdiction. The Counsellors were also authorized to appoint Auxiliary Board members on a geographical basis. In 1973 the Universal House of Justice extended further authority allowing Auxiliary Board members to appoint Assistants. Each geographical area normally has two Boards, one for "Propagation" and one for "Protection." The main responsibility of the propagation Board members is to encourage individual Bahá'ís, local Spiritual Assemblies and Groups in their teaching work, in the achievement of the goals of their plans and in their contributions to Bahá'í funds. Protection Board members are mainly concerned with the protection of the Faith from attack by those who are not Bahá'ís and/or by Covenant Breakers. They are also responsible for assisting believers to deepen in their Bahá'í knowledge and loyalty to the Covenant and to promote the unity of the Bahá'í communities. They do not become involved in the administrative decision-making, or pass judgements, though they may give advice and mature counsel. In exceptional instances only are they permitted to be members of local or national spiritual assemblies; if elected they must make a choice between being an Assembly or a Board member. If elected to the Universal House of Justice they cease to be Members of the Board.

AUXILIARY LANGUAGE See **UNIVERSAL AUXILIARY LANGUAGE.**

AYÁDÍ Literally hands; Hand(s) of the Cause. [11:735]

AYYÁM Days.. [11:736]

AYYÁM-I-HÁ The name given to the four Intercalary Days, (five in a Leap Year) which fall just before the last month in the year in the Bahá'í Calendar. The four or five days are devoted to spiritual preparation for the Fast, for extending hospitality, feasting, charitable works and gift giving.

AZAL, MÍRZÁ YAḤYÁ half-brother of Bahá'u'lláh, known also as **SUBḤ-I-AZAL.** He broke away from Bahá'u'lláh, caused Him untold sufferings, including trying to take His life by poison, and made claims to be the true Manifestation of God. He and a few of his followers, known as Azalís, were exiled to Cyprus when Bahá'u'lláh was sent to 'Akká. He died in Cyprus in 1912.

A'ẒAM Greatest. See **BAYTU'L-'ADL-I-A'ẒAM**; **ISM-I-A'ẒAM**; **ṢADR-A'ẒAM.** [11:736]

'AẒÍM Literally mighty, great, glorious. [11:736]

B

BÁB (The Primal Point) (The Qá'im) (The Gate) Born in S̲h̲íráz, Írán on 20 October 1819 as Siyyid 'Alí- Muḥammad, He was raised by His maternal uncle as 'Abdu'l-Bahá explained:

> the Báb was a young merchant of the Pure Lineage.... and when after a few years His father Siyyid Muḥammad-Riḍa died, He was brought up in S̲h̲íráz in the arms of His maternal uncle Mírzá Siyyid 'Alí. On attaining maturity He engaged in trade in Bús̲h̲ihr, first in partnership with His maternal uncle and afterwards independently. On account of what was observed in Him He was noted for godliness, devoutness, virtue, and piety, and was regarded in the sight of men as so characterized.[63:4]

He married K̲h̲adíjih-Bagum (q.v.) in 1842, and they had one son who died in infancy. He announced that He was the Báb (The Gate) to Mullá Ḥusayn (q.v.) during the night of 22-23 May 1844. See **SÚRIH OF JOSEPH**.

The inception of the Bábí and the Bahá'í Faiths and the beginning of the Bahá'í Era is described in the following passage:

> The opening scene of the initial act of this great drama was laid in the upper chamber of the modest residence of the son of a mercer of S̲h̲íráz, in an obscure corner of that city. The time was the hour before sunset, on the 22nd day of May, 1844. The participants were the Báb, a twenty-five year old Siyyid, of pure and holy lineage, and the young Mullá Ḥusayn, the first to believe in Him. Their meeting immediately before that interview seemed to be purely fortuitous. The interview itself was protracted till the hour of dawn. The Host remained closeted alone with His guest, nor was the sleeping city remotely aware of the import of the conversation they held with each other. No record has passed to posterity of that unique night save the fragmentary but highly illuminating account that fell from the lips of Mullá Ḥusayn. "I sat spellbound by His utterance, oblivious of time and of those who awaited me," he himself has testified, after describing the nature of the questions he had put to his Host and the conclusive replies he had received from Him, replies which had established beyond the shadow of a doubt the validity of His claim to be the promised Qá'im....

> Sleep had departed from me that night. I was enthralled by the music of that voice which rose and fell as He chanted; now swelling forth as He revealed verses of the Qayyúmu'l-Asmá, again acquiring ethereal, subtle harmonies as He uttered the prayers He was revealing....
>
> "This Revelation," Mullá Ḥusayn has further testified, "so suddenly and impetuously thrust upon me, came as a thunderbolt which, for a time, seemed to have benumbed my faculties. I was blinded by its dazzling splendor and overwhelmed by its crushing force. Excitement, joy, awe, and wonder stirred the depths of my soul. Predominant among these emotions was a sense of gladness and strength which seemed to have transfigured me...."
>
> A more significant light, however, is shed on this episode, marking the Declaration of the Mission of the Báb, by the perusal of that "first, greatest and mightiest" of all books in the Bábí Dispensation, the celebrated commentary on the Súrih of Joseph, the first chapter of which, we are assured, proceeded, in its entirety, in the course of that night of nights from the pen of its divine Revealer. The description of this episode by Mullá Ḥusayn, as well as the opening pages of that Book attest the magnitude and force of that weighty Declaration. A claim to be no less than the mouthpiece of God Himself, promised by the Prophets of bygone ages; the assertion that He was, at the same time, the Herald of One immeasurably greater than Himself.[5:5f]

Sixteen searchers, all male, followed Mullá Ḥusayn, and with the poetess Ṭáhirih (q.v.), who recognized the Báb in a dream, became known as the "Letters of the Living." Shoghi Effendi described the Báb's relationship to them in these words:

> He enjoined them to observe the utmost caution and moderation in their behavior, unveiled the loftiness of their rank, and stressed the magnitude of their responsibilities. He recalled the words addressed by Jesus to His disciples, and emphasized the superlative greatness of the New Day. He warned them lest by turning back they forfeit the Kingdom of God, and assured them that if they did God's bidding, God would make them His heirs and spiritual leaders among men. He hinted at the secret, and announced the approach, of a still mightier Day, and bade them prepare themselves for its advent. He called to remembrance the triumph of Abraham over Nimrod, of

> Moses over Pharaoh, of Jesus over the Jewish people, and of Muhammad over the tribes of Arabia, and asserted the inevitability and ultimate ascendancy of His own Revelation.[5:8]

The Teachings of this new Revelation inflamed the clergy, and the whole country of Írán was in turmoil. State officials and the religious leaders combined in their attempts to exterminate this new faith that was sweeping the country, and the persecutions that had become intensified almost immediately. The Báb Himself made a pilgrimage to Mecca where in December 1844 He publicly proclaimed His Mission. After His return to Shíráz He was arrested, His books and documents confiscated and He was released on condition He leave the city. For a time, until He was sent to the prison of Máh-Kú (q.v.)—some three years—He was relatively free to teach His Faith but the remaining three years of His life He spent in captivity. He was in Ma-Ku for nine months then transferred to the fortress of Chihríq (q.v.). See **BADASHT.** It was from Chihríq that He was taken to Tabríz for execution. Summarizing this period Shoghi Effendi wrote:

> The period of the Báb's banishment to the mountains of Ádhirbáyján, lasting no less than three years, constitutes the saddest, the most dramatic, and in a sense the most pregnant phase of His six year ministry. It comprises His nine months' unbroken confinement in the fortress of Máh-Kú, and His subsequent incarceration in the fortress of Chihríq, which was interrupted only by a brief yet memorable visit to Tabríz.... It corresponds to the most critical stage of the mission of Bahá'u'lláh, during His exile to Adrianople... and is paralleled by the darkest days of 'Abdu'l-Bahá's ministry in the Holy Land... Shíráz had been the memorable scene of the Báb's historic Declaration; Iṣfáhán had provided Him, however briefly, with a haven of relative peace and security; whilst Ádhirbáyján was destined to become the theater of His agony and martyrdom. These concluding years of His earthly life will go down in history as the time when the new Dispensation attained its full stature, when the claim of its Founder was fully and publicly asserted, when its laws were formulated, when the Covenant of its Author was firmly established, when its independence was proclaimed, and when the heroism of its champions blazed forth in immortal glory. For it was during these intensely dramatic, fate-laden years that the full implications of the station of the Báb were disclosed to His disciples, and formally announced by Him in the capital of Ádhirbáyján, in the

presence of the Heir to the Throne; that the Persian Bayán, the repository of the laws ordained by the Báb, was revealed; that the time and character of the Dispensation of "the One Whom God will make manifest" were unmistakably determined; that the Conference of Badasht proclaimed the annulment of the old order; and that the great conflagrations of Mázindarán, of Nayríz and of Zanján were kindled.[5:17]

BÁB, DECLARATION OF Commemorated as one of the nine Holy days when work is suspended, it took place when Siyyid 'Alí Muḥammad, the Báb, at two hours and 11 minutes after sunset on the evening of 22 May 1844 announced to His visitor, Mullá Ḥusayn-i-Bárfurúshi (q.v.) that He was the Promised One awaited by Islám. This date marks the beginning of the Bábí religion, the opening of the Bahá'í Dispensation and of the Bahá'í Era.

BÁB, MARTYRDOM OF The execution of the Báb took place at noon on 9 July 1850 in the barrack square of Tabríz, Northern Írán. It is commemorated as one of the Nine Holy Days in the Bahá'í Calendar.

Summarizing the scene just prior to His execution, Shoghi Effendi wrote:

> The waves of dire tribulation that violently battered at the Faith, and eventually engulfed, in rapid succession, the ablest, the dearest and most trusted disciples of the Báb, plunged Him... into unutterable sorrow. For no less than six months the Prisoner of Chihríq, His chronicler has recorded, was unable to either write or dictate. Crushed with grief by the evil tidings that came so fast upon Him, of the endless trials that beset His ablest lieutenants, by the agonies suffered by the besieged and the shameless betrayal of the survivors, by the woeful afflictions endured by the captives and the abominable butchery of men, women and children, as well as the foul indignities heaped on their corpses, He, for nine days, His amanuensis has affirmed, refused to meet any of His friends, and was reluctant to touch the meat and drink that was offered Him. Tears rained continually from His eyes, and profuse expressions of anguish poured forth from His wounded heart, as He languished, for no less than five months, solitary and disconsolate, in His prison.
>
> The pillars of His infant Faith had, for the most part, been hurled down at the first onset of the hurricane that had been loosed upon it. Quddús, immortalized by Him as

Ismu'lláhi'l-Ákhir (the Last Name of God) ... such a man had, in the full bloom of his youth, suffered, in...Bárfurúsh, a death which even Jesus Christ, as attested by Bahá'u'lláh, had not faced in the hour of His greatest agony. Mullá Ḥusayn, the first Letter of the Living, surnamed the Bábu'l-Báb (the Gate of the Gate); designated as the "Primal Mirror;" on whom eulogies, prayers and visiting Tablets of a number equivalent to thrice the volume of the Qur'án had been lavished by the pen of the Báb...

Such a one had likewise, in the prime of his manhood, died a martyr's death at Ṭabarsí. Vaḥíd, pronounced in the Kitáb-i-Íqán to be the "unique and peerless figure of his age," a man of immense erudition and the most preeminent figure to enlist under the banner of the new Faith, to whose "talents and saintliness," to whose "high attainments in the realm of science and philosophy" the Báb had testified ... had already, under similar circumstances, been swept into the maelstrom of another upheaval, and was soon to quaff in his turn the cup drained by the heroic martyrs of Mázindarán. Hujjat, another champion of conspicuous audacity, of unsubduable will, of remarkable originality and vehement zeal, was being, swiftly and inevitably, drawn into the fiery furnace whose flames had already enveloped Zanján and its environs. The Báb's maternal uncle, the only father He had known since His childhood, His shield and support and the trusted guardian of both His mother and His wife, had, moreover, been sundered from Him by the ax of the executioner in Ṭihrán. No less than half of His chosen disciples, the Letters of the Living, had already preceded Him in the field of martyrdom. Ṭáhirih, though still alive, was courageously pursuing a course that was to lead her inevitably to her doom.... A fast ebbing life, so crowded with the accumulated anxieties, disappointments, treacheries and sorrows of a tragic ministry, now moved swiftly towards its climax. The most turbulent period of the Heroic Age of the new Dispensation was rapidly attaining its culmination. The cup of bitter woes which the Herald of that Dispensation had tasted was now full to overflowing. Indeed, He Himself had already foreshadowed His own approaching death. In ... one of His last works, He had alluded to the fact that the sixth Naw-Rúz after the declaration of His mission would be the last He was destined to celebrate on earth.... Forty days before His final depar-

> ture from Chihríq He had even collected all the documents in His possession, and placed them, together with His pen-case, His seals and His rings, in the hands of Mullá Báqir ... to deliver them to Bahá'u'lláh in Ṭihrán. [5:49ff]

The miracle that occurred at this time is attested by many independent witnesses and is described in some detail by Shoghi Effendi:

> An official ... had abruptly interrupted the last conversation which the Báb was confidentially having in one of the rooms of the barracks with His amanuensis Siyyid Ḥusayn, and was drawing the latter aside, and severely rebuking him, when he was thus addressed by his Prisoner: "Not until I have said to him all those things that I wish to say can any earthly power silence Me. Though all the world be armed against Me, yet shall it be powerless to deter Me from fulfilling, to the last word, My intention." To the Christian Sám Khán—the colonel of the Armenian regiment ordered to carry out the execution—who, seized with fear lest his act should provoke the wrath of God, had begged to be released from the duty imposed upon him, the Báb gave the following assurance: "Follow your instructions, and if your intention be sincere, the Almighty is surely able to relieve you of your perplexity."...Sám Khán accordingly set out to discharge his duty. A spike was driven into a pillar which separated two rooms of the barracks facing the square. Two ropes were fastened to it from which the Báb and one of his disciples ... were separately suspended. The firing squad ranged itself in three files, each of two hundred and fifty men. Each file in turn opened fire until the whole detachment had discharged its bullets. So dense was the smoke from the seven hundred and fifty rifles that the sky was darkened. As soon as the smoke had cleared away the astounded multitude of about ten thousand souls, who had crowded onto the roof of the barracks, as well as the tops of the adjoining houses, beheld a scene which their eyes could scarcely believe. The Báb had vanished from their sight! Only his companion remained, alive and unscathed, standing beside the wall on which they had been suspended. The ropes by which they had been hung alone were severed. "The Siyyid-i-Báb has gone from our sight!" cried out the bewildered spectators. A frenzied search immediately ensued. He was found, unhurt and unruffled,

> in the very room He had occupied the night before, engaged in completing His interrupted conversation with His amanuensis. "I have finished My conversation with Siyyid Ḥusayn" were the words with which the Prisoner, so providentially preserved, greeted the appearance of the farrá<u>sh</u>-ba<u>sh</u>í, "Now you may proceed to fulfill your intention." Recalling the bold assertion his Prisoner had previously made, and shaken by so stunning a revelation, the farrá<u>sh</u>-ba<u>sh</u>í quitted instantly the scene, and resigned his post. Sám <u>Kh</u>án, likewise, remembering, with feelings of awe and wonder, the reassuring words addressed to him by the Báb, ordered his men to leave the barracks immediately, and swore, as he left the courtyard, never again, even at the cost of his life, to repeat that act.[5:52]

Another regiment was called in and the execution carried out. Shoghi Effendi wrote of the closing of the Báb's Ministry:

> Thus ended a life which posterity will recognize as standing at the confluence of two universal prophetic cycles, the Adamic Cycle stretching back as far as the first dawnings of the world's recorded religious history and the Bahá'í Cycle destined to propel itself across the unborn reaches of time for a period of no less than five thousand centuries. The apotheosis in which such a life attained its consummation marks, as already observed, the culmination of the most heroic phase of the Heroic Age of the Bahá'í Dispensation. It can, moreover, be regarded in no other light except as the most dramatic, the most tragic event transpiring within the entire range of the first Bahá'í century. Indeed it can be rightly acclaimed as unparalleled in the annals of the lives of all the Founders of the world's existing religious systems. [5:54f]

BÁB, SHRINE OF It was in 1891 when Bahá'u'lláh made one of His few visits to Haifa that He pointed out to 'Abdu'l-Bahá the actual spot where the Remains of the Báb should be placed. In 1898 'Abdu'l-Bahá gave instructions for the casket that contained the remains of the Báb and His disciple (who was shot with Him) to be brought to 'Akká where it was concealed under the bed of the Greatest Holy Leaf in the House of 'Abdu'lláh Páshá. It arrived in January 1899, and later that year 'Abdu'l-Bahá laid the foundation stone for the Shrine. In the meantime the Bahá'ís of Rangoon, Burma, had begun to prepare a marble sarcophagus, and this was then shipped to Haifa. After a great many difficulties, the building was completed in 1909 and on Naw-Rúz the remains were entombed with deep emotion by 'Abdu'l-Bahá. Years later the

Guardian had three additional rooms added that were used to house some archives. Sutherland Maxwell (q.v.) was asked to design a superstructure for the original square building. The design was developed under the guidance of Shoghi Effendi, a model was completed and displayed in May 1944, contracts were placed in Italy for granite columns in 1948, the foundations were completed and work began in 1949 and the work was completed by October 1953. The new work was built around the original Shrine and comprised a colonnade and arcade, an octagon above, a drum of the dome with 18 lancet windows, one for each of the Letters of the Living and crowned with a dome and lantern clothed in golden tiles. Describing this the Guardian wrote:

> For, just as in the realm of the spirit, the reality of the Báb has been hailed by the Author of the Bahá'í Revelation as "The Point round Whom the realities of the Prophets and Messengers revolve," so, on this visible plane, His sacred remains constitute the heart and center of what may be regarded as nine concentric circles ... The outermost circle in this vast system ... is none other than the entire planet. Within the heart of this planet lies the "Most Holy Land," acclaimed by 'Abdu'l-Bahá as "the Nest of the Prophets" and which must be regarded as the center of the world.... Within this Most Holy Land rises the Mountain of God of immemorial sanctity ... Reposing on the breast of this holy mountain are the extensive properties permanently dedicated to, and constituting the sacred precincts of, the Báb's holy Sepulcher. In the midst of these properties, recognized as the international endowments of the Faith, is situated the most holy court, an enclosure comprising gardens and terraces which at once embellish, and lend a peculiar charm to, these sacred precincts. Embosomed in these lovely and verdant surroundings stands in all its exquisite beauty the mausoleum of the Báb, the shell designed to preserve and adorn the original structure raised by 'Abdu'l-Bahá as the tomb of the Martyr-Herald of our Faith. Within this shell is enshrined that Pearl of Great Price, the holy of Holies, those chambers which constitute the tomb itself, and which were constructed by 'Abdu'l-Bahá. Within the heart of this holy of Holies is the tabernacle, the vault wherein reposes the most holy casket. Within this vault rests the alabaster sarcophagus in which is deposited that inestimable jewel, the Báb's holy dust. So precious is this dust that the very earth surrounding the edifice enshrining this dust has been extolled by the Center of Bahá'u'lláh's Covenant, in

> one of His Tablets in which He named the five doors belonging to the six chambers which He originally erected after five of the believers associated with the construction of the Shrine, as being endowed with such potency as to have inspired Him in bestowing these names, whilst the tomb itself housing this dust He acclaimed as the spot round which the Concourse on high circle in adoration. [3:95f]

BÁB, STATION Of the station occupied by the Báb and the significance of His appearance, Shoghi Effendi wrote:

> The Báb, acclaimed by Bahá'u'lláh as the "Essence of Essences," the "Sea of Seas," the "Point round Whom the realities of the Prophets and Messengers revolve," "from Whom God hath caused to proceed the knowledge of all that was and shall be," Whose "rank excelleth that of all the Prophets," and Whose "Revelation transcendeth the comprehension and understanding of all their chosen ones," had delivered His Message and discharged His mission. He Who was, in the words of 'Abdu'l-Bahá, the "Morn of Truth" and "Harbinger of the Most Great Light," Whose advent at once signalized the termination of the "Prophetic Cycle" and the inception of the "Cycle of Fulfillment," had simultaneously through His Revelation banished the shades of night that had descended upon His country, and proclaimed the impending rise of that Incomparable Orb Whose radiance was to envelop the whole of mankind. He, as affirmed by Himself, "the Primal Point from which have been generated all created things," "one of the sustaining pillars of the Primal Word of God," the "Mystic Fane," the "Great Announcement," the "Flame of that supernal Light that glowed upon Sinai," the "Remembrance of God" concerning Whom "a separate Covenant hath been established with each and every Prophet" had, through His advent, at once fulfilled the promise of all ages and ushered in the consummation of all Revelations. He the "Qá'im" (He Who ariseth) promised to the Shí'ahs, the "Mihdí" (One Who is guided) awaited by the Sunnís, the "Return of John the Baptist" expected by the Christians, the "Ushídar-Máh" referred to in the Zoroastrian scriptures, the "Return of Elijah" anticipated by the Jews, Whose Revelation was to show forth "the signs and tokens of all the Prophets", Who was to "manifest the perfection of Moses, the radiance of Jesus and the patience of Job" had appeared, proclaimed His Cause, been mercilessly persecuted and died gloriously.

The 'Second Woe," spoken of in the Apocalypse of St. John the Divine, had, at long last, appeared, and the first of the two "Messengers," Whose appearance had been prophesied in the Qur'án, had been sent down. The first "Trumpet-Blast", destined to smite the earth with extermination, announced in the latter Book, had finally been sounded. "The Inevitable," "The Catastrophe," "The Resurrection," "The Earthquake of the Last Hour," foretold by that same Book, had all come to pass. The "clear tokens" had been "sent down," and the "Spirit" had "breathed," and the "souls" had "waked up," and the "heaven" had been "cleft," and the "angels" had "ranged in order," and the "stars" had been "blotted out," and the "earth" had "cast forth her burden," and "Paradise" had been "brought near," and "hell" had been "made to blaze," and the "Book" had been "set," and the "Bridge" had been "laid out," and the "Balance" had been "set up," and the "mountains scattered in dust." The "cleansing of the Sanctuary," prophesied by Daniel and confirmed by Jesus Christ in His reference to "the abomination of desolation," had been accomplished. The "day whose length shall be a thousand years," foretold by the Apostle of God in His Book, had terminated. The "forty and two months," during which the "Holy City," as predicted by St. John the Divine, would be trodden under foot, had elapsed. The "time of the end" had been ushered in, and the first of the "two Witnesses" into Whom, "after three days and a half the Spirit of Life from God" would enter, had arisen and had "ascended up to heaven in a cloud." The "remaining twenty and five letters to be made manifest," according to Islámic tradition, out of the "twenty and seven letters" of which Knowledge has been declared to consist, had been revealed. [5:57f]

BÁBÍ A follower of the Báb; of or pertaining to the Revelation of the Báb. It was during the latter part of Bahá'u'lláh's stay in Adrianople that His followers became known as Bahá'ís rather than Bábís. Some believe that over 20,000 Bábís have been martyred for their faith—often after torture at the hands of the Muslim clergy and the Íránian government whose only object was to make them recant.

BÁBÍ DISPENSATION A period covering the time from the Declaration of the Báb in May 1844 until the Declaration of Bahá'u'lláh, during Riḍván, 1863.

BÁBU'L-BÁB The Gate of the Gate: title of Mullá Ḥusayn. [11:736🕮]

BACKBITING Along with calumny, backbiting is forbidden by Bahá'u'lláh. Described by Him as "grievous error ... inasmuch as backbiting quencheth the light of the heart, and extinguisheth the life of the soul." [64:193] 'Abdu'l-Bahá said, "If any soul speak ill of an absent one, the only result..." will be that "... he will dampen the zeal of the friends and tend to make them indifferent. For backbiting is divisive." [65:230]

BACKWELL, RICHARD (1914-1972) An early (1944) British believer. During the period 1946 to 1950 he pioneered successively to Nottingham, Newcastle, Glasgow and Edinburgh. He served as a member of the National Spiritual Assembly of the British Isles from 1947 to 1955. He served for a number of years as part-time manager of the Bahá'í Publishing Trust, during which time he compiled *Principles of Bahá'í Administration,* [66] *The Covenant of Bahá'u'lláh,* [67] and *Pattern of Bahá'í life* [68] (his last book, *The Christianity of Jesus,* was published posthumously in 1972. [69]) He also served as editor of the *British Bahá'í Journal* on two separate occasions. In 1951 he (and his wife Vida Johnson) pioneered to British Guiana (now Guyana) where he was a member of the first Spiritual Assembly of Georgetown, paving the way for the formation of the National Spiritual Assembly of Guyana, Surinam and French Guiana. In 1961 he returned with his wife to England and in 1963 pioneered to Northern Ireland where he served on the first Spiritual Assembly of Larne Rural District. In 1963 he was again elected to the British National Spiritual Assembly and served on it until his appointment as an Auxiliary Board member in 1968. [51:525][60:270]

BADA<u>SH</u>T, CONFERENCE OF A gathering convened by the Báb for some 81 of His followers in mid-1848. It lasted for 22 days, during which several significant events took place. In the absence of the Báb, Who was imprisoned in the fortress of <u>Ch</u>ihríq, the organization and leading rôle fell to Mírzá Ḥusayn 'Alí. The first event can be seen to be one of the objectives of the Conference—"...to make a sudden, a complete and dramatic break with the past, with its order, its ecclesiasticism, its traditions and ceremonials," [5:31] each participant was given a new name by Mírzá Ḥusayn 'Alí. The last Letter of the Living (q.v.) became known as "Quddús" and Qurratu'l-'Ayn as "Ṭáhirih," while Mírzá Ḥusayn 'Alí was henceforth entitled "Bahá'u'lláh." After much discussion with many differing opinions, the climax of the conference came when Ṭáhirih, to demonstrate her rejection of the old laws and customs, appeared before the assembled believers unveiled—her face uncovered for all to see. This caused great upset among those present and some fled in dismay, one tried to cut his throat and some faint-hearted ones fell away entirely from their belief in the Báb's

Cause. According to one historian, "when those who had remained steadfast left the hamlet it was to go out into a world (which), for them, was greatly changed.... They were determined to assert their freedom from the fetters of the past." [12:169]

BADÍ CALENDAR The calendar originated by the Báb on which the Bahá'í calendar is based.

BADÍ' (Martyr) (Apostle of Bahá'u'lláh) (Wonderful) Born Áqá Buzurg-i-Níshápúrí, he was later given the title, Badí' (unique, wonderful). Reputed to be a wild, unruly, youth and son of a devoted Bábí, he had no interest in his father's affairs until, during the visit to his home of a traveling teacher, Mullá Muḥammad-i-Zarandí (Nabíl), he listened to some verses from a long poem by Bahá'u'lláh and was so entranced that he devoted the balance of his life to serving Him. Eventually reaching Bahá'u'lláh, having gone on foot from Mosul to 'Akká, he was entrusted with the delivery of a letter (Tablet) from Bahá'u'lláh to Náṣiri'd-Dín Sháh. Badí,' full of joy, laughter, gratitude and forbearance, walked from Haifa where he had received the Tablet, almost alone, as instructed by Bahá'u'lláh, for four months until he reached Ṭihrán where he was able to deliver the message to the Sháh at one of his summer camps. He was tortured to reveal the names of other Bábís and then put to death while he laughed with joy at the efforts of his torturers. Steadfast to the end, he achieved the crown of martyrdom while still only 17 years of age. Bahá'u'lláh added to his name another title, Fakhru'sh-Shuhadá—The Pride of Martyrs; he was also designated an Apostle of Bahá'u'lláh.

BAGDÁDÍ, ZIA (-1937) Named Zia at birth by Bahá'u'lláh (in later life called "Mabsoot" (the happy one) by Bahá'u'lláh). Following his arrival in America in 1909 (as a medical student; graduating in 1911). He became associate editor of the *Star of the West* magazine in 1911; later he prepared the Persian pages section of the magazine. He remained in America until his death in 1937. [37:535]

BAGHDÁD The city in Iráq to which Bahá'u'lláh was exiled from Írán in 1853 and where He lived until His further exile to Turkey in 1863.

BAGLEY, STANLEY T. (1912-1993) (Knight of Bahá'u'lláh) An American believer who pioneered to Sicily, for which he was designated a Knight of Bahá'u'lláh. He also lived or taught in Belgium, France, Guadeloupe and Martinique. [11:319]

BAGUM Lady (of rank), dame, Begum; placed after a woman's given name, Bagum is a courtesy title comparable with (see) **BIG.** [11:736]

BAHÁ (Glory) The Greatest Name. A title by which Bahá'u'lláh is known.

BAHÁ'Í A follower of Bahá'u'lláh. Of, or pertaining to, the Revelation of Bahá'u'lláh. It was first used while Bahá'u'lláh was in exile in Adrianople.

BAHÁ'Í CENTER See **ḤAẒÍRATU'L-QUDS**.

BAHÁ'Í CYCLE See **CYCLE**.

BAHÁ'Í ERA The period of the Bahá'í Dispensation that began with the Declaration of the Báb and will end with the appearance of the next Manifestation of God. Bahá'u'lláh promises that this next appearance will not happen for at least 1,000 years. (See the section entitled "The Epochs Of The Formative Age" immediately before the Dictionary for a detailed analysis of **EPOCHS**.)

BAHÁ'Í FAITH The independent world religion founded by Bahá'u'lláh.

BAHÁ'Í INTERNATIONAL COMMUNITY Two years after its inauguration, the United Nations formally recognized the Bahá'í International Community in three significant ways. First, the United Nations Commission on Palestine requested from Shoghi Effendi a statement on the relationship between the Bahá'í Faith and the Holy Land. Second, the National Spiritual Assembly of the Bahá'ís of the United States and Canada set up a United Nations Committee and became affiliated with the UN Office of Public Information as a national Non Governmental Organization. Third, the National Spiritual Assembly submitted two statements to the Economic and Social Council (ECOSOC)—one to the Human Rights Commission and the other to the Commission on the Status of Women (1947).

The following year the United States National Spiritual Assembly registered the Bahá'í International Community on behalf of the eight National Spiritual Assemblies then in existence as an international NGO. The entity known as the Bahá'í International Community was enlarged each year as new National Spiritual Assemblies came into being. In 1949 the Bahá'í International Community was asked to submit proposals for the UN Prayer Building and in 1954 submitted proposals for revisions to the UN Charter.

In 1967 the responsibility for the Bahá'í International Community was taken over by the Universal House of Justice, by which time there were some 56 National Spiritual Assemblies, (with 113 by 1973; 149 in 1987 and 174 in 1996.)

The close relationships between the Bahá'í International Community and the UN developed rapidly, and significant events took place almost yearly from 1970, when the Bahá'í International Community was granted consultative status with Economic and Social Council. From that time it presented papers and statements to almost every international and regional conference. During the years that followed the total number of presentations on a wide variety of subjects became most impressive, over 200 during the 1980s alone. From a total of about 26 areas of interest we find some on Disarmament; Human Rights; Racial Discrimination; Social Development; Status of Women; Youth; Children; World Food; Population; Law of the Sea; Nuclear Energy; Outer Space; Narcotic Drugs and Crime Prevention.

In 1973 the Bahá'í International Community became affiliated to the UN Environmental Program with an office in Nairobi; in 1976 it obtained consultative status with UNICEF; in 1980 it opened an office in the International Center in Vienna and a major suboffice in Geneva. In 1987 the Bahá'í International Community became the sixth major religion to join the World Wide Fund for Nature in its campaigns for the conservation of nature and the environment.

The Bahá'í International Community was called upon to play a very considerable rôle in all the preparations for the series of summits that began with the one on the child, New York (1990); the Earth Summit, Rio (1992); Population, Cairo (1994); Social Development, Copenhagen (1995) Women, Beijing (1995); and Habitat II, the city summit in Istanbul, June 1996. It also produced statements for the World Conference on Education for All (1990); the drafting of the Universal Code of Environmental Conduct (1990); International Legislation for Environment and Development (1991); The Earth Charter (1991); World Citizenship (1992); A Global Strategy and Action-Plan for Social Development (1994). These were followed in 1995 by three major works, *The Prosperity of Humankind* (22 January 1995); an 87-page book for use in Beijing, *The Greatness Which Might Be Theirs*; and a statement for the 50th Anniversary celebrations in New York—"Turning Point for All Nations" (October 1995). Under the direction of the Universal House of Justice it continues to keep the global Bahá'í community well informed about the Faith's involvement with the work of the United Nations, producing guidance notes and presenting appropriate statements for international and regional conferences, which then become available for use at national and local levels.

BAHÁ'Í TEMPLE UNITY The first national Bahá'í institution in the embryonic Bahá'í Administration. Formed in Chicago in March 1909 at a convention of 39 delegates representing 36 cities in accordance with guidance given by 'Abdu'l-Bahá. It was legally incorporated as a religious body in Illinois and had full authority to hold the title of the Bahá'í Temple property and carry out its construction and raise the necessary funds. The Bahá'í Temple Unity was taken over by the National Spiritual Assembly of the Bahá'ís of the United States and Canada when it was formed in 1925.

BAHÁ'U'L-ABHÁ The Glory of the Most Glorious. [11:736]

BAHÁ'U'LLÁH (The Glory of God) The Prophet-Founder of the Bahá'í Faith. Born 12 November 1817 in Núr, Mázindarán, Írán to Mírzá Buzurg-i-Vazír (q.v.) and Khadíjih Khánum (q.v.). His family name was Mírzá Ḥusayn-'Alí. Shoghi Effendi wrote about His ancestry:

> He derived His descent, on the one hand, from Abraham (the Father of the Faithful) through his wife Katurah, and on the other from Zoroaster, as well as from Yazdigird, the last king of the Sásáníyan dynasty. He was moreover a descendant of Jesse, and belonged, through His father, Mírzá 'Abbás, better known as Mírzá Buzurg—a nobleman closely associated with the ministerial circles of the Court of Fatḥ-'Alí Sháh—to one of the most ancient and renowned families of Mázindarán. [5:94]

He was living in Ṭihrán in 1844, and when He received a message sent to Him by the Báb through Mullá Ḥusayn He immediately accepted the claim of the Báb. Although He and the Báb never met, They corresponded and, as Mírzá Ḥusayn-'Alí, He became known as a leader of the Bábís. It was during the Conference of Badasht that He became known as Bahá'u'lláh. After an abortive attempt on the life of the Sháh by two misguided Bábís in 1853, Bahá'u'lláh was imprisoned for four months in the Siyáh-Chál, and it was there that He received the first experience of His call to proclaim a new revelation. A passage in His own words throws some light on His experience:

> During the days I lay in the prison of Ṭihrán, though the galling weight of the chains and the stench-filled air allowed Me but little sleep, still in those infrequent moments of slumber I felt as if something flowed from the crown of My head over My breast, even as a mighty torrent that precipitateth itself upon the earth from the summit of a lofty mountain. Every limb of My body would, as a result, be set afire. At such moments My tongue recited what no man could bear to hear.[70:22]

Shoghi Effendi elaborate on Bahá'u'lláh's first experience of Revelation in *God Passes By*:

> He thus describes those breathless moments when the Maiden, symbolizing the "Most Great Spirit" proclaimed His mission to the entire creation: "While engulfed in tribulations I heard a most wondrous, a most sweet voice, calling above My head. Turning My face, I beheld a Maiden—the embodiment of the remembrance of the

> name of My Lord—suspended in the air before Me. So rejoiced was she in her very soul that her countenance shone with the ornament of the good-pleasure of God, and her cheeks glowed with the brightness of the All-Merciful Pointing with her finger unto My head, she addressed all who are in heaven and all who are on earth, saying: 'By God! This is the Best-Beloved of the worlds, and yet ye comprehend not. This is the Beauty of God amongst you, and the power of His sovereignty within you, could ye but understand. This is the Mystery of God and His Treasure, the Cause of God and His glory unto all who are in the kingdoms of Revelation and of creation, if ye be of them that perceive.' ... This thing is not from Me, but from One Who is Almighty and All-Knowing. And He bade Me lift up My voice between earth and heaven, and for this there befell Me what hath caused the tears of every man of understanding to flow.... This is but a leaf which the winds of the will of Thy Lord, the Almighty, the All-Praised, have stirred.... His all-compelling summons hath reached Me, and caused Me to speak His praise amidst all people. I was indeed as one dead when His behest was uttered. The hand of the will of Thy Lord, the Compassionate, the Merciful, transformed Me." "By My Life!" He asserts in another Tablet, "Not of Mine own volition have I revealed Myself, but God, of His own choosing, hath manifested Me." And again: "Whenever I chose to hold My peace and be still, lo, the Voice of the Holy Spirit, standing on My right hand, aroused Me, and the Most Great Spirit appeared before My face, and Gabriel overshadowed Me, and the Spirit of Glory stirred within My bosom, bidding Me arise and break My silence." [5: 101f]

Through the persistent and decisive intervention of the Russian minister, Prince Dolgorouki, the testimony established by competent tribunals as to Bahá'u'lláh's noncomplicity in the attack on the S͟háh and the efforts of His family and friends, He was released from prison but soon afterwards was sentenced to exile leaving to Him the right to choose His destination. Shoghi Effendi continues the story:

> The S͟háh's edict, equivalent to an order for the immediate expulsion of Bahá'u'lláh from Persian territory, opens a new and glorious chapter in the history of the first Bahá'í century. Viewed in its proper perspective it will be even recognized to have ushered in one of the most eventful and momentous epochs in the world's religious history.

> It coincides with the inauguration of a ministry extending over a period of almost forty years—a ministry which, by virtue of its creative power, its cleansing force, its healing influences, and the irresistible operation of the world-directing, world-shaping forces it released, stands unparalleled in the religious annals of the entire human race. It marks the opening phase in a series of banishments, ranging over a period of four decades, and terminating only with the death of Him Who was the Object of that cruel edict. The process which it set in motion, gradually progressing and unfolding... finally carried Him as far as the shores of the Holy Land, thereby fulfilling the prophecies recorded in both the Old and the New Testaments, redeeming the pledge enshrined in various traditions attributed to the Apostle of God and the Imáms who succeeded Him, and ushering in the long-awaited restoration of Israel to the ancient cradle of its Faith.... This enforced and hurried departure of Bahá'u'lláh from His native land, accompanied by some of His relatives, recalls in some of its aspects, the precipitate flight of the Holy Family into Egypt; the sudden migration of Muḥammad, soon after His assumption of the prophetic office, from Mecca to Medina;... and above all the banishment of Abraham from Ur of the Chaldees to the Promised Land—a banishment which, in the multitudinous benefits it conferred upon so many divers peoples, faiths and nations, constitutes the nearest historical approach to the incalculable blessings destined to be vouchsafed, in this day, and in future ages, to the whole human race, in direct consequence of the exile suffered by Him Whose Cause is the flower and fruit of all previous Revelations. [5:106f]

During the years 1854-1856, He left for an unknown destination and actually went secretly into the mountains of Sulaymáníyyih where He lived as a dervish until 'Abdu'l-Bahá traced Him and persuaded Him to return. After His return, the Bábí Faith, under Bahá'u'lláh's leadership, began to attract the attention of a large number of people, including scholars, renowned clerics and government officials, all enamored by the person of Bahá'u'lláh and His uplifting teachings and explanations of the new religion. Then suddenly, in April 1863, He was told He must renew His exile and leave for Constantinople in Turkey. On the eve of His further exile to Constantinople He moved into a garden alongside the river Tigris and it was here, from 21 April until 2 May that He proclaimed His Mission to be the One not only promised by the Báb but by all the other world religions. Thus was actually born the Bahá'í Faith This period has since been commemorated annually as the Festival of Riḍván with the First, Ninth and 12th Days being three of the nine Bahá'í Holy Days during which all work is suspended. (See **RIḌVÁN**) Shoghi Effendi wrote that "of the exact circumstances attending this Declaration we, alas, are but scantily informed."

> As to the significance of that Declaration let Bahá'u'lláh Himself reveal to us its import. Acclaiming that historic occasion as the "Most Great Festival," the "King of Festivals," the "Festival of God," He has, in His Kitáb-i-Aqdas, characterized it as the Day whereon "all created things were immersed in the sea of purification," whilst in one of His specific Tablets, He has referred to it as the Day whereon "the breezes of forgiveness were wafted over the entire creation." "Rejoice, with exceeding gladness, O people of Bahá! ... as ye call to remembrance the Day of supreme felicity." Such is the inebriating effect of the words of God upon the Revealer of His undoubted proofs that His pen can move no longer.
>
> And again:
>
> The Divine Springtime is come, O Most Exalted Pen, for the Festival of the All-Merciful is fast approaching.... Take heed lest anything deter Thee from extolling the greatness of this Day.... This is the Day whereon the unseen world crieth out: "Great is thy blessedness, O earth, for thou hast been made the footstool of thy God, and been chosen as the seat of His mighty throne" ... "Arise, and proclaim unto the entire creation the tidings that He who is the All-Merciful hath directed His steps towards the Riḍván and entered it.... This is the Day whereon He Who is the Desire of all nations hath shed upon the kingdoms of the unseen and of the seen the splendors of the light of His most excellent names, and enveloped them with the radiance of the luminaries of His most gracious favors, favors which none can reckon except Him Who is the Omnipotent Protector of the entire creation." [5:153ff]

Bahá'u'lláh's time in Turkey, first in Constantinople and then in Adrianople (Edirne) witnessed some of the most heart-breaking events of His life, with the rebellion of His half-brother, Mírzá Yaḥyá, who not only corrupted the text of the Writings of the Báb and conspired to take over the leadership of the Bábís, but even administered poison to Bahá'u'lláh, the effects of which lasted until the end of His life. It still proved to be a period of tremendous significance. Shoghi Effendi writes of it:

> Though He Himself was bent with sorrow, and still suffered from the effects of the attempt on His life, and though He was well aware a further banishment was probably impending, yet, undaunted by the blow which His Cause had sustained, and the perils with which it was encompassed, Bahá'u'lláh arose with matchless power, even before the ordeal was overpast, to proclaim the Mission with which He had been entrusted to those who, in East and West, had the reins of supreme temporal authority in their grasp. The day-star of His Revelation was, through this very Proclamation, destined to shine in its meridian glory, and His Faith manifest the plenitude of its divine power.... A period of prodigious activity ensued which, in its repercussions, outshone the vernal years of Bahá'u'lláh's ministry. "Day and night," an eyewitness has written, "the Divine verses were raining down in such number that it was impossible to record them. Mírzá Áqá Jan wrote them as they were dictated, while the Most Great Branch was continually occupied in transcribing them. There was not a moment to spare." "A number of secretaries," Nabíl has testified, "were busy day and night and yet they were unable to cope with the task."[5:170f] (See **TABLETS TO THE KINGS**.)

On 12 August 1868 Bahá'u'lláh with His family and other exiles were sent to Gallipoli and from there to 'Akká via Alexandria, Port Said, Jaffa and Haifa, arriving at the Prison City on 31 August. Mírzá Yaḥyá and his supporters—"Azalís", were sent to Cyprus with four of Bahá'u'lláh's followers while several Azalís accompanied Bahá'u'lláh. It was in Adrianople that the followers of Bahá'u'lláh began to be known as "Bahá'ís."

The prison in which the exiles were incarcerated was the old Citadel of 'Akká, adjacent to the sea and surrounded by a moat. Shoghi Effendi described the general situation:

> 'Akká, the ancient Ptolemais, the St. Jean d'Acre of the Crusaders, that had successfully defied the siege of Napoleon, had sunk, under the Turks, to the level of a penal colony to which murderers, highway robbers and political agitators were consigned from all parts of the Turkish empire. It was girt about by a double system of ramparts; was inhabited by a people whom Bahá'u'lláh stigmatized as "the generation of vipers;" was devoid of any source of water within its gates; was flea-infested, damp and

honey-combed with gloomy, filthy and tortuous lanes. "According to what they say," the Supreme Pen has recorded in the Lawh-i-Sulṭán, "it is the most desolate of the cities of the world, the most unsightly of them in appearance, the most detestable in climate, and the foulest in water. It is as though it were the metropolis of the owl." So putrid was its air that, according to a proverb, a bird when flying over it would drop dead. Explicit orders had been issued by the Sultan and his ministers to subject the exiles, who were accused of having grievously erred and led others far astray, to the strictest confinement. Hopes were confidently expressed that the sentence of life-long imprisonment pronounced against them would lead to their eventual extermination.[5:185f] (See **'AKKÁ**).

On the 23 June 1870 Bahá'u'lláh's youngest son, Mírzá Mihdí (q.v.), the Purest Branch, fell through a skylight and suffered injuries that proved fatal. Shoghi Effendi recalls the event and its significance:

> His dying supplication to a grieving Father was that his life might be accepted as a ransom for those who were prevented from attaining the presence of their Beloved. In a highly significant prayer, revealed by Bahá'u'lláh in memory of His son—a prayer that exalts his death to the rank of those great acts of atonement associated with Abraham's intended sacrifice of His son, with the crucifixion of Jesus Christ and the martyrdom of the Imám Ḥusayn—we read the following: "I have, O my Lord, offered up that which Thou hast given Me, that Thy servants may be quickened, and all that dwell on earth be united." And, likewise, these prophetic words, addressed to His martyred son: "Thou art the Trust of God and His Treasure in this Land. Erelong will God reveal through thee that which He hath desired."[5:188]

While He was in the House of 'Údí Khammár, which was adjacent to, and later became a part of, the House of 'Abbúd, Bahá'u'lláh revealed the Kitáb-i-Aqdas. Shoghi Effendi wrote of this as:

> What may well rank as the most signal act of His ministry—the promulgation of the Kitáb-i-Aqdas. Alluded to in the Kitáb-i-Íqán; the principal repository of that Law which the Prophet Isaiah had anticipated, and which the writer of the Apocalypse had described as the "new heaven" and the "new earth," as "the Tabernacle of God,"

> as the "Holy City," as the "Bride," the "New Jerusalem coming down from God," this "Most Holy Book," whose provisions must remain inviolate for no less than a thousand years, and whose system will embrace the entire planet, may well be regarded as the brightest emanation of the mind of Bahá'u'lláh, as the Mother Book of His Dispensation, and the Charter of His New World Order. [5:213]

He passed away in the Mansion of Bahjí at three hours after midnight on 29 May 1892. His Will and Testament was read in the presence of witnesses nine days later. See **BAHÁ'U'LLÁH, WILL AND TESTAMENT OF**.

In his survey of the first Bahá'í century, Shoghi Effendi writes of the

> dynamic process, divinely propelled, possessed of undreamt-of potentialities, world-embracing in scope, world-transforming in its ultimate consequences, which had been set in motion by the Báb and which "acquired a tremendous momentum with the first intimations of Bahá'u'lláh's dawning Revelation amidst the darkness of the Siyáh-Chál of Ṭihrán. It was further accelerated by the Declaration of His mission on the eve of His banishment from Baghdád. It moved to a climax with the proclamation of that same mission during the tempestuous years of His exile in Adrianople. Its full significance was disclosed when the Author of that Mission issued His historic summonses, appeals and warnings to the kings of the earth and the world's ecclesiastical leaders. It was finally consummated by the laws and ordinances which He formulated, by the principles which He enunciated and by the institutions which He ordained during the concluding years of His ministry in the prison-city of 'Akká."[5:237]

Many works covering the life and writings of Bahá'u'lláh have been published in English but the following should, in particular, be referenced: *God Passes By* [5]; *Bahá'u'lláh—The King of Glory* [14]; *The Revelation of Bahá'u'lláh;* [71][72][73] *Bahá'u'lláh—The Prince of Peace;* [75] and *Robe of Light: The Persian Years of the Supreme Prophet Bahá'u'lláh* [76] See **ADRIANOPLE; 'AKKÁ; BADASHT; BAGHDÁD; BAHJÍ; SIYÁH-CHÁL.**

BAHÁ'U'LLÁH, ASCENSION OF Commemorating the anniversary of the passing of Bahá'u'lláh that took place at three hours after midnight on the 29 of May 1892. It is one of the nine Holy Days on which work is suspended.

BAHÁ'U'LLÁH, COVENANT OF The purpose of the Covenant made by Bahá'u'lláh is to protect the Faith from disunity. 'Abdu'l-Bahá was clearly appointed as the Successor of Bahá'u'lláh, the sole Interpreter of His Writings and the "Center of His Covenant" in the *Kitáb-i-'Ahdí.* [77] See **BAHÁ'U'LLÁH, WILL & TESTAMENT; COVENANT BREAKERS; COVENANT, GREATER AND LESSER.**

BAHÁ'U'LLÁH, DECLARATION OF The period of 12 days in the Garden of Riḍván, Baghdád, April 21 to May 2 1863 during which Bahá'u'lláh made the claim that He was the Promised One of all religions and thereby bringing into being what is now known as the Bahá'í Faith. The first, ninth and 12th days of this period are three of the nine Holy Days on which work is suspended.

BAHÁ'U'LLÁH, SHRINE OF For the last 13 years of His life, Bahá'u'lláh lived in the Mansion of Bahjí, a few miles to the north of 'Akká off the Beirut road (see **BAHJÍ; PILGRIM**), and when He passed away on 29 May 1892, He was buried beneath the floor of a room in a house adjacent to the Mansion. This is, for the Bahá'ís, the Qiblih, the Holiest Spot on Earth, the only one of the three Holy Places for pilgrimage presently available and described by 'Abdu'l-Bahá as the Most Holy Shrine.

BAHÁ'U'LLÁH, WILL & TESTAMENT OF (*Kitáb-i-'Ahd*) Shoghi Effendi refers to this "unique and epoch-making document" in which Bahá'u'lláh clearly reaffirms 'Abdu'l-Bahá as His Successor in the following words:

> To direct and canalize these forces let loose by this Heaven-sent process, and to insure their harmonious and continuous operation after His ascension, an instrument divinely ordained, invested with indisputable authority, organically linked with the Author of the Revelation Himself, was clearly indispensable. That instrument Bahá'u'lláh had expressly provided through the institution of the Covenant, an institution which He had firmly established prior to His ascension. This same Covenant He had anticipated in His Kitáb-i-Aqdas, had alluded to it as He bade His last farewell to the members of His family, who had been summoned to His bed-side, in the days immediately preceding His ascension, and had incorporated it in a special document which He designated as "the Book of My Covenant," and which He entrusted, during His last illness, to His eldest son 'Abdu'l-Bahá. Written entirely in His own hand... this unique and epoch-making Document, designated by Bahá'u'lláh as His "Most Great Tablet," and alluded to by Him as the "Crimson Book" in His "Epistle to the Son of the Wolf," can find

no parallel in the Scriptures of any previous Dispensation... For nowhere in the books pertaining to any of the world's religious systems... had any single document establishing a Covenant endowed with an authority comparable to the Covenant which Bahá'u'lláh had Himself instituted.[5:237f] See **COVENANT** and **COVENANT OF BAHÁ'U'LLÁH**.

BAHÁ'U'LLÁH, WORLD ORDER OF A central element of Bahá'í teachings is its reference to a new World Order—the basis for which is established in the Writings of Bahá'u'lláh and 'Abdu'l-Bahá and described in some detail by Shoghi Effendi. The words of Bahá'u'lláh set the pattern: "The world's equilibrium hath been upset through the vibrating influence of this most great, this new World Order. Mankind's ordered life hath been revolutionized through the agency of this unique, this wondrous System—the like of which mortal eyes have never witnessed." [78:118]

Summarizing its evolution, Shoghi Effendi wrote: "The first epoch witnessed the birth and the primary stages in the erection of the framework of the Administrative Order of the Faith—the nucleus and pattern of its World Order according to the precepts laid down in 'Abdu'l-Bahá's Will and Testament, as well as the launching of the initial phase of the world-encompassing Plan bequeathed by Him to the American Bahá'í Community.... It witnessed on the one hand, the emergence and the laying of the groundwork of that embryonic World Order whose advent was announced by the Báb in the Bayán, whose laws were revealed by Bahá'u'lláh in the Kitáb-i-Aqdas, and whose features were delineated by 'Abdu'l-Bahá in His Will and Testament. It was marked ... by the launching, in the Western Hemisphere, of the first stage of a Plan whose original impulse was communicated by the Herald of our Faith in His Qayyúmu'l-Asmá to whose implications the Author of the Bahá'í Revelation alluded in His Tablets, and whose Charter was revealed by the Center of His Covenant in the evening of His life." [3:5]

In his summary of the state of the Faith on the Passing of Bahá'u'lláh, Shoghi Effendi wrote:

> God's new-born Faith, the cynosure of all past Dispensations, had been fully and unreservedly proclaimed. The prophecies announcing its advent had been remarkably fulfilled. Its fundamental laws and cardinal principles, the warp and woof of the fabric of its future World Order, had been clearly enunciated. Its organic relation to, and its attitude towards, the religious systems which preceded it had been unmistakably defined. The primary institutions, within which an embryonic World Order was

destined to mature, had been unassailably established. The Covenant designed to safeguard the unity and integrity of its world-embracing system had been irrevocably bequeathed to posterity. The promise of the unification of the whole human race, of the inauguration of the Most Great Peace, of the unfoldment of a world civilization, had been incontestably given.[5:223]

Describing some of its features Shoghi Effendi wrote:

I feel it, however, incumbent upon me by virtue of the responsibility attached to the Guardianship of the Faith, to dwell more fully upon the essential character and the distinguishing features of that world order as conceived and proclaimed by Bahá'u'lláh.... I consider it my duty to warn every beginner in the Faith that the promised glories of the Sovereignty which the Bahá'í teachings foreshadow, can be revealed only in the fullness of time, that the implications of the Aqdas and the Will of 'Abdu'l-Bahá, as the twin repositories of the constituent elements of that Sovereignty, are too far-reaching for this generation to grasp and fully appreciate. I cannot refrain from appealing to them who stand identified with the Faith to disregard the prevailing notions and the fleeting fashions of the day, and to realize as never before that the exploded theories and the tottering institutions of present-day civilization must needs appear in sharp contrast with those God-given institutions which are destined to arise upon their ruin.... It is towards this goal—the goal of a new World Order, Divine in origin, all-embracing in scope, equitable in principle, challenging in its features—that a harassed humanity must strive.... To claim to have grasped all the implications of Bahá'u'lláh's prodigious scheme for world-wide human solidarity, or to have fathomed its import, would be presumptuous on the part of even the declared supporters of His Faith. To attempt to visualize it in all its possibilities, to estimate its future benefits, to picture its glory, would be premature at even so advanced a stage in the evolution of mankind. All we can reasonably venture to attempt is to strive to obtain a glimpse of the first streaks of the promised Dawn that must, in the fullness of time, chase away the gloom that has encircled humanity. All we can do is to point out, in their broadest outlines, what appear to us to be the guiding principles underlying the World Order of Bahá'u'lláh, as amplified and enunciated by 'Abdu'l-Bahá, the Center of His Covenant with all mankind and the appointed Interpreter and Expounder of His Word.... The central, the underlying aim which animates it is the establishment of the New World Order as adumbrated by Bahá'u'lláh. The methods it employs, the standard it inculcates, incline it to neither East nor West, neither Jew nor Gentile, neither rich nor poor, neither white nor colored. Its watchword is the unification of the human race; its standard the "Most Great Peace"; its consummation the advent of that golden millennium—the Day when the kingdoms of this world shall have become the Kingdom of God Himself, the Kingdom of Bahá'u'lláh.[4:16,34f,157]

BAHÍYYIH KHÁNUM (the Greatest Holy Leaf) (1846-1932) Distinguished not only in her own right as the only daughter of Bahá'u'lláh and for the purity of her life, a generosity, a love, at once disinterested and undiscriminating and a forgiving nature, but also as the only woman ever to be Head of a world religion (which she was called upon to assume when, soon after the passing of 'Abdu'l-Bahá, in the earliest days of the Guardianship, Shoghi Effendi was obliged for a short while to leave the Holy Land). Described by him as having "a saintly life which history will acknowledge as having been endowed with a celestial potency that few of the heroes of the past possessed ... and as an object worthy of the admiration of all mankind." He paid further testimony in remarkably poetic terms, "In the innermost recesses of our hearts, we have reared for thee a shining mansion that the hand of time can never undermine, a shrine which shall frame eternally the matchless beauty of thy countenance, an altar whereon the fire of thy consuming love shall burn for ever." [2:45] She was born in Ṭihrán, 1846 and died July 1932. She is buried in the Bahá'í Gardens on Mount Carmel, Haifa, Israel. [79] See **VARAQIY-I-'ULYÁ**.

BAHJÍ The "Place of Delight" is situated on the plain of 'Akká and gave its name to the Mansion that was the final residence of Bahá'u'lláh (from 1879 to 1892). It was while living here that He revealed many of His outstanding works, described by Shoghi Effendi as "among the choicest fruits which His mind has yielded and which mark the consummation of His forty-year-long ministry." Here in 1890 He received E. G. Browne, the Cambridge orientalist, some sentences from whose description of that meeting, were quoted at the 1893 Conference of Religions in Chicago. When Bahá'u'lláh passed away 29 May 1892 He was interred in a small house in the precincts of the Mansion and that became the Qiblih of the Bahá'í Faith, its holiest spot on earth and the major focus for the Bahá'í pilgrims who visit the Holy Land every year. The beautification of the large area of land purchased around the Shrine has continued in the pattern that Shoghi Effendi began during his lifetime. See **PILGRIMAGE**.

BAILEY, ELLA (1864-1953) (Martyr) An early American believer. She met 'Abdu'l-Bahá during His visit to America and was much loved by Him and, later, by Shoghi Effendi. She traveled widely as a teacher of the Cause and was elevated by Shoghi Effendi to the rank of "Martyr" following her death. [43:224][48:685]

BAKER, DOROTHY BEECHER (1898-1954) (Hand of the Cause of God) Born in Newark, New Jersey, 21 December 1898. She was the granddaughter of "Mother Beecher," a Bahá'í at the turn of the century who took her to see 'Abdu'l-Bahá in New York in 1912. Dorothy was too shy to speak during that meeting although she wrote afterwards to Him stating that she wished to serve the Cause. 'Abdu'l-Bahá responded that He would pray that God would grant her desire. She developed into a most eloquent, persuasive and convincing teacher for small groups or large audiences, and in addition to an inimitable charm she had a sincerity that was with her always—she was an ardent Bahá'í first, last and at all time.

As a public speaker she was much in demand, traveled throughout the United Sates and Canada and became well known for her interracial concerns—during one year alone she lectured in 90 colleges throughout the South proclaiming fearlessly the principle of the oneness of mankind. She was called upon by the Guardian to travel in Central and South America, which she toured on several occasions, as well as visiting Europe. She was also a most competent administrator and served as a member of the United States National Spiritual Assembly for 16 years (Chairman for four of them). After being appointed a Hand of the Cause her service intensified, and she was present with other Hands at the series of four International Teaching Conferences called for 1953, the first one in Kampala, Uganda, which she attended immediately following her long-awaited pilgrimage to the Holy Land. At this Conference that some of the Hands met each other for the first time.

In that same year she was again elected to the National Spiritual Assembly of the United States, and such was the spirit of the times that five of the nine members resigned to go pioneering. Throughout the whole of her married life her husband, Frank (q.v.), whom she married in 1921, was her mainstay and supporter. A friend once wrote about Frank, "I don't believe the extent to which he sacrificed to make it possible for Dorothy to do all the things she did is generally realized. He loved her very much, and he loved being with her ... I've always felt that in many ways he was an unsung hero of the Faith." Frank himself is on record of having confided to another Hand, "First of all, she's not just my wife. She's my queen. I would never consider her my equal. As far as her services go, my main recollections are of packing and unpacking. I send her off on a teaching trip and when she returns I help her unpack. Those moments when we're home together are the sweetest moments of my life." [80:273-4]

During September 1953 she attended the last of the Intercontinental Conferences in New Delhi, India. While she was there Frank was continuing with their plans to move and settle in Grenada, Windward Isles. Following the very successful Conference, Dorothy and some other Hands were asked by the Guardian to stay over for some time to travel teach in various locations throughout India. At that time the Bakers had homes in the United States and in Lima, Peru. To relocate to Grenada they were in the process of selling both houses. During that period Frank wrote to a friend: "...Dorothy will be home about December 14th....This will probably be our last long separation—hope so at any rate as I miss her more than on any of her other trips..." Due to a very intensive teaching and lecture tour throughout India and a final day of meetings in Karachi, Pákistán on 9 January 1954 Dorothy was not able to keep to that timetable. On the 10th she flew to Beirut and then in Rome where she posted her final reports to Shoghi Effendi and left at 9.31AM. The plane exploded south of Elba, killing all on board. The Guardian cabled:

> Hearts grieved lamentable untimely passing Dorothy Baker, distinguished Hand Cause, eloquent exponent its teachings, indefatigable supporter its institutions, valiant defender its precepts. Long record outstanding service enriched annals concluding years heroic opening epoch Formative Age Bahá'í dispensation. Fervently praying progress soul Abhá Kingdom. Assure relatives profound loving sympathy. Noble spirit reaping bountiful reward. Advise hold memorial gathering Temple befitting her rank imperishable services. [40:653-7][48:670]

BAKER, EFFIE (1880-1968) The first Australian believer (1922), she embraced the Cause through the efforts of Father and Mother Dunn. She served Shoghi Effendi for a period of 11 years in Haifa, where she took a great many photographs. About 1930 at the request of Shoghi Effendi she visited and photographed historical places in Persia, Syria and 'Iráq (many of which were included by Shoghi Effendi in the first edition of the *Dawn-Breakers*.) [10] In 1937 she returned permanently to Australia. [50:320]

BAKER, FRANK ALBERT (1889-1963) An early American believer of German family origin, he was the husband and staunch sup porter of Hand of the Cause of God Dorothy Beecher Baker. He pioneered to Grenada in the West Indies. [50:321][60:271] See **BAKER, DOROTHY BEECHER.**

BAKER, RICHARD ST. BARBE (1889-1982) Widely known as "the Man of the Trees," he achieved wide international recognition and an award of Office, Order of the British Empire, for his forestry and environmental work. In 1922, while living in Kenya, he created the embryonic organization that was to become "The Men of the Trees"; in 1979 His Royal Highness the Prince of Wales became patron of the organization (now known as International Tree Foundation). Shoghi Effendi was the first person to become a life member of the organization. Through his inspiring environmental work St. Barbe (as he was mainly known) was a powerful advocate of the Cause. [2:802][60:166]

BALYÚZÍ, ḤASAN MUVAQQAR (1908-1980) (Hand of the Cause of God) He was born on 7 September 1908 in Shíráz, Írán into a very distinguished Bábí/Bahá'í family. He was related to the Guardian through a common great-grandfather, Ḥájí Mírzá Abu'l-Qásim and was therefore a member of the Afnán family. His superb mastery of the English language is perhaps due to the fact that he was brought up from the age of four in a "diplomatic" environment—his father being at one time the governor of the Gulf Ports and Islands. Two scholarly friends of his father tutored him in Persian, Arabic and history. When his father was exiled to India during WW I he learned Urdu and pursued his studies of English in Bishop's College, Poona. After returning to Írán, where his father died in 1921, he was sent, at the age of 17, to the Preparatory School of the American University of Beirut where he met Shoghi Effendi, who confirmed him in the Bahá'í Faith. Having taken a Bachelor's degree in chemistry and a Master's degree in diplomatic history, he left Beirut to take his M.S. (Economics) at the London School of Economics. He achieved this in 1935, but the outbreak of WW II cut short his studies for a doctorate. In 1932, before leaving the Near East, he went on pilgrimage to Haifa (the last time he met Shoghi Effendi). In April 1933, within a few months of his arrival in London, he was elected to the British National Spiritual Assembly, where he served until February 1960. While still in Beirut he had been a leading light in the activities of the various university societies, including the Bahá'í Society and continued after he left to encourage the other students by, in the words of one, "his beautiful letters." Himself encouraged by the Guardian to remain similarly active in the Bahá'í administrative, teaching and consolidating work in the British Isles, he rapidly established his reputation as a brilliant speaker; a loving, wise and humorous counselor; a powerful writer and an indefatigable administrator. Working for the Persian Section of the BBC he wrote many special features, such as talks on current affairs, English writers and history, translating English poetry and short stories and assisting in productions of Shakespeare and a series on English by radio. He produced more than 1,000 radio programs on Írán, its history and literature and some of his translations of English literature became part of modern Persian literature and coined many words now currently in use; "He made new and different uses of old words to convey new meanings." [2:640]

In 1941 he married Mary (Molly) Brown and with the birth of their first son, Molly had to abandon a promising career in ballet. They had five sons, and her devotion to the family and support of Ḥasan throughout their nearly 40 years of marriage enabled him to continue his outstanding services in so many fields. His dedication to the Guardian is summed up in two brief instances. Once, when asked how he could do so much and carry out so many engagements, he nodded to his chair and desk in his room and said, "Many nights I sit there all night and do not go to bed," and when asked how he could subject himself to such continuous hardship, he replied, "Whenever I think of what our beloved Guardian is doing for us I am ashamed of how little we are doing in response and sleep escapes my eyes." [2:642] The second was when his mother died in Írán, and he inherited substantial wealth and properties there, which meant he could live in comfort and ease if he went to live back at home. However, he explained to a friend, "I am only interested in serving the Cause wherever the beloved Guardian wants me to serve, and I am not a bit interested in all that belongs to me in Írán." [2]

In 1953 he convened and attended at the Guardian's insistence the First Intercontinental Conference in Kampala, Uganda. Also, as Chairman of the British National Spiritual Assembly, he attended the Stockholm Conference later that year. His next trip overseas was to preside at the opening of the 1956 Convention in Kampala, when the Regional National Spiritual Assembly of the Bahá'ís of Central and East Africa was elected. He was appointed a Hand of the Cause of God in the last contingent in October 1957. The first responsibility he had to assume after his appointment was to work with his fellow Hands John Ferraby and Ugo Giachery in giving assistance to Shoghi Effendi's wife ('Amatu'l-Bahá Rúḥíyyih Khánum) in arranging the funeral following his unexpected demise in London on 4 November 1957.

During the first Conclave of the Hands of the Cause in the Holy Land, Ḥasan was one of the nine chosen by 'Amatu'l-Bahá Rúḥíyyih Khánum to unseal the Guardian's apartment and after a thorough search reported to the others that, "no Will or Testament of any nature whatsoever executed by Shoghi Effendi had been found."

During all the long, emotional and grief-stricken consultations when every word spoken had to be translated into English and Persian, the burden of translation fell to Ḥasan and Abu'l-Qásim Faiẓí. Although appointed with Faiẓi to be one of the Nine to reside in the Holy Land, he was unable to settle his personal affairs to make this possible. He would from time to time spend weeks, sometimes months, in Haifa. One of his outstanding contributions at that time was in preparing of the World Center Archives for their housing in the special building designed for them on Mount Carmel, particularly in the identification of the original Bahá'í Writings and other sacred materials. As a fellow Hand, himself a Persian scholar stated, "I have met many Bahá'í scholars in Írán but he was to me one of the outstanding figures ... I have never found in my life such a modest and humble man as Balyúzí ... I loved him dearly." Another Hand wrote after working closely with him in Haifa, "His life of service and spiritual obedience and sacrifices remain an effulgent example to emulate." [2:645]

Throughout his life he would cheer anyone in his company with his unique sense of humor, equally seen in his English stories and jokes and in his stories of Persia. In the months following the passing of the Guardian he was a tower of strength, visiting communities and conferences in the British Isles to help the friends to overcome the shock of his death and to keep them on the right pathway to carry out the plans he had given to them.

During the period of 1958 to June 1964 he attended some 10 conferences of European Hands of the Cause and their Auxiliary Board Members and met often with National Spiritual Assembly members, contributing wise and practical advice. To these European travels should be added his visits in April 1961 to Ecuador and Peru for their first annual Conventions, which were followed by a crossing of Canada, when he met with many Indian tribes. His time at home was characterized by his numerous visits to teaching conferences and summer schools and Bahá'í communities throughout the British Isles where he never failed to inspire the friends and deepen their knowledge of the Faith and leave them strengthened to serve with renewed vigor. By 1960, however, his health was causing increasing concern, and he had to contend repeatedly with various kinds of illnesses and injury. His researches and writing continued, and the real extent of his scholarship was revealed in his many publications.

Outstanding among these were: Bahá'u'lláh; Edward Granville Browne and the Bahá'í Faith; [155] 'Abdu'l-Bahá, The Center of the Covenant of Bahá'u'lláh; [16] The Báb, the Herald of the Day of Days; [12] Muhammad and the Course of Islám; [156] and Bahá'u'lláh—The King of Glory. [14] It was his custom to work on two or three books at the same time so that he was relieved of concentrating on a single manuscript. He would write far into the night and turn to reading for background or to research as a break from writing. He would submit all his books to the publisher in his own handwriting, even the quotations, to ensure that his choice of deletions would be observed. References from other scholars are numerous to his encyclopedic mind and his knowledge of the Faith, of Persian history, literature and culture, of 19th and 20th century Írán and its leading figures, and of current developments in the world—political, artistic or literary. Typical are: "His fluency in Persian, English, Arabic, French as well as familiarity with some other language had made him ... unique among orientalists"; "...he produced a monumental work on Islam which will eclipse most of the books on this subject"; "his gem-like books will remain among the most outstanding writings to enlighten the paths of seekers for centuries to come." [2:650] Even while writing his works in English he had three books in Persian published in Írán, and his copious notes enabled some of his works to be published posthumously. His large collection of books donated for scholarly research now form the basis for the Afnán Trust Library (currently held in storage at the Bahá'í Publishing Trust, Ketton, England, until a permanent site can be found). They are a testimony to the depth of his own studies as well as his burning desire to give all in the service of the Faith, which occupied so many of his waking hours right up to his death. It had been his intention to personally take a leather-bound copy of his last book to place it on the Threshold of the Shrine of Bahá'u'lláh at Bahjí. When the first copy reached England early in February 1980 he had it sent unseen for binding. However, he never saw it, as he had a stroke and passed away on 12 February; he was buried in a special plot near to the grave of his beloved Guardian on 15 February and his son, Robert, carried the book to Israel in the following month to carry out his father's wishes. The Universal House of Justice released the following message: "With broken hearts announce passing dearly loved Hand Cause Ḥasan Balyúzí. Entire Bahá'í world robbed one of its most powerful defenders, most resourceful historians. His illustrious lineage, his devoted labors Divine Vineyard, his outstanding literary works combine in immortalizing his honored name in annals beloved Faith. Call on friends everywhere hold memorial gatherings. Praying Shrines his exemplary achievements, his steadfastness patience humility, his outstanding scholarly pursuits will inspire many devoted workers among rising generations follow his glorious footsteps." [2:650]

BANÁNÍ, MÚSÁ (1886-1971) (Hand of the Cause of God) He was born into a Jewish family in Baghdád in 1886. His father died when he was four, and he migrated to Persia when only 12. The grim struggle for existence left him no opportunity for schooling and to the end of his life could only read and write in Arabic and Persian, written in the Hebrew script he had learned as a very small child.

In Persia his elder brother accepted the Faith but it was of no interest to him until in 1911, while resident in Kirmánsháh, some distinguished Bahá'ís were visiting the area and were photographed with local Bahá'ís, including his brother. The visitors were arrested and maltreated and the photograph used to round up the local Bahá'ís pictured to force them to recant their Faith. During this process Músá was mistakenly arrested because he resembled to his brother. By convincing the authorities that he was not in fact a Bahá'í he was able to obtain his release but he had been deeply moved by the refusal to recant, in spite of cruel torture, of his cell-mate—a frail old man. He subsequently reproached himself for denouncing a Faith about which he knew nothing, and as a result of his efforts to learn more he became a Bahá'í. His conversion amazed his associates, particularly his decision to marry only a Bahá'í so that his children might have a firm Bahá'í upbringing. Several years later when he married, it became known that his wife's father was one of those Bahá'í teachers who visited Kirmánsháh and were instrumental in his interest in the Faith.

In 1934 he made his first pilgrimage to the Holy Land, which created an intense flame of love and loyalty to Shoghi Effendi. This remained the hallmark of his character until the end of his life. The Guardian, recognizing the simplicity, directness, unbounded energy and spiritual potential of Músá Banání, surprised one group of pilgrims, who could not understand why he should speak glowingly of an unlettered man, stated that he "is one equal to a thousand." His particular qualities were recognized in Persia when he was on the committee for identifying and acquiring historic sites associated with the Cause and particularly with the purchase and restoration of the house of Bahá'u'lláh in Ṭihrán.

Although his business enterprise and activity had made him a man of considerable means, when the Guardian called in 1950 for pioneers for Africa, Músá abruptly ended all his business concerns and with the full approval of the Guardian left Persia for London to prepare for pioneering to East Africa. Accompanied by his wife, Samihih; his daughter, Violette; his son-in-law, 'Alí Nakhjavání; his grand-daughter, Bahíyyih and an English Bahá'í, Philip Hainsworth, he left London for Dar-es-Salaam where the party received their final destination instructions. They arrived in their pioneer post of Kampala, Uganda on 2 August 1951.

When the Guardian announced the reopening of pilgrimages, Músá and Samihih were encouraged by the other pioneers to go on an early pilgrimage, for by this time the teaching work was beginning to bear fruit. Towards the end of his pilgrimage, the Guardian advised Músá that he had announced to the Bahá'í world his appointment as a Hand of the Cause. This was in the second contingent, 29 February 1952. The remainder of his life was dedicated to carrying out the detailed wishes of the Guardian in the expansion of the Faith throughout the whole African Continent. He did this with his customary zeal and sense of urgency despite some severely disabling illnesses. Serious eye surgery with the eventual loss of sight in one eye; paralysis of one side of his body, and amputation of one leg hindered his energetic service, but the radiant quality of his faith overwhelmed and conquered all. He participated in the Intercontinental Conferences in Kampala; Wilmette; Stockholm and New Delhi in 1953; and in Kampala and Frankfurt in 1958. He represented the Guardian at the Conventions in Africa for the elections of the Regional National Spiritual Assemblies of Central and East Africa; South and West Africa; Northwest Africa and Northeast Africa in April-May 1956, respectively in Kampala, Johannesburg, Tunis and Cairo.

Músá Banání was directly involved in the purchase of the Ḥaẓíratu'l-Quds in Kampala and the African Temple site in Kampala. Through his encouragement and his direction of the work of his Auxiliary Board Members, the Bahá'í enrollments throughout Africa during the 1950s exceeded those in any other part of the world; the Guardian called him "The Father of Africa" and "The Lion of Africa." Towards the end of his life while he lay paralyzed and bedridden, his prayers, like a great beating heart, supported and sustained the teaching work, and he passed away in Kampala on 2 September 1971 and was buried in his favorite spot in the vicinity of the Kampala House of Worship. The Universal House of Justice cabled:

> Profoundly mourn passing dearly loved Hand Cause Músá Banání. Recall with deep affection his selfless unassuming prolonged services Cradle Faith, his exemplary pioneering Uganda culminating his appointment as Hand Cause Africa and praise beloved Guardian as spiritual conqueror that continent. Interment his remains African soil under shadow Mother Temple enhances spiritual lustre that blessed spot. Fervently praying Shrines progress his noble soul. May Africa now robbed staunch venerable promoter defender Faith follow his example cheer his

heart Abhá Kingdom. Convey family most tender sympathies advise hold memorial meetings all communities Bahá'í world befitting gatherings Mother Temples. [51:421]

BANÍ-HÁSHIM Literally Sons of Háshim (great-grandfather of Muḥammad), clan of Quraysh from which Muḥammad was descended.

BATTRICK, JEANNETTE HILDA (1922-1978) A British believer (c.1951) who along with her husband (Owen) pioneered extensively in the promotion of the Cause. In 1957 she and her family moved to Edinburgh for six months to reestablish the local Spiritual Assembly. In 1960 she pioneered for 10 months to Luxembourg before returning to teach in Edinburgh, Cardiff, Belfast, Dublin, London and the North Sea islands of Shetland and Orkney. In 1967 the family decided to pioneer to the South Pacific and set out for that region via New Zealand. While her husband went on to the Solomon Islands to assist in building that community (with the eventual aim of gaining a foothold in New Caledonia), Jeannette remained in New Zealand where she was elected to the National Spiritual Assembly in April 1968. She was reelected the following year but left to settle with her husband in New Caledonia. From 1971 to 1975 she served on the National Spiritual Assembly of the Southwest Pacific. In 1975 the family moved back to Auckland after an 18-month pioneering stay in Ouvea, Loyalty Islands. In 1976 her husband was appointed a member of the Continental Board of Counsellors, and Jeannette served as his secretary until her death in 1978. [53:471][60:274]

BAQÍYYATU'LLÁH Remnant of God: traditional appellation of the Qá'im, derived from the Qur'án; designation of the Báb as the Promised One of Islám and applied by Him to Bahá'u'lláh.

BAXTER, EVELYN (1883?-1969) (Knight of Bahá'u'lláh) An early (1923) British believer who embraced the Cause through the reading of Bahá'í books alone (i.e., she had not met a Bahá'í to discuss matters). She served on a the local Spiritual Assembly of London and then the National Spiritual Assembly of the British Isles before pioneering during the Six Year Plan (first to Birmingham and then to Nottingham, Hove, Oxford and Cardiff.) Her final pioneer move took her in 1953 to the Channel Islands (Jersey) for which she was designated a Knight of Bahá'u'lláh. [51:456]

BAYÁN Literally exposition, explanation, lucidity, eloquence, utterance: title given by the Báb to His Revelation and two of His Writings, one in Persian, the other in Arabic. [11:736📖]

BAYT House. [11:736📖]

BAYTU'L-'ADL-I-A'ẒAM The Supreme House of Justice: a title of the Universal House of Justice. [11:736📖]

B.E. Bahá'í Era: denotes the Badí' calendar, reckoned from the year of the Báb's declaration of His Mission in 1844. [11:736]

BECKER, MATILDA (Betty) (1887-1974) An early (1933) American believer, she helped form the first local Spiritual Assembly in Kansas City (1935). In 1939 she pioneered to Alaska where she settled in Anchorage in March 1941 (following unsuccessful efforts to establish herself in Juneau and Sitka). She was elected in 1943 to the first local Spiritual Assembly of Anchorage, which was also the first in Alaska. In 1959, at the age of 72, she again pioneered, this time to Valdivia, Chile. In 1960 she moved to Punta Arenas, Chile—the southernmost outpost of the Faith. In 1945 she served on the first local Spiritual Assembly of Punta Arenas (one of the first in South America).[52:538][60:275]

BEDIKIAN, VICTORIA (1879-1955) An early American believer. She met 'Abdu'l-Bahá during His visit to America and in 1927 spent three months as the guest of Shoghi Effendi in Haifa. She traveled widely throughout the United States following the death of her husband in 1945 and in later years entered into an extensive international correspondence with Bahá'ís in India, Pákistán, Burma, Ceylon, Southeast Asia, Indonesia and the Islands of the Indian Ocean. [47:884]

BEETON, JAMES HENRY ISAAC (1907-1975) The first (1971) Cape Barren Islander to embrace the Cause, he helped form the first local Spiritual Assembly of the Bahá'ís of Glenorchy, Tasmania, Australia. [52:551]

BEGGING and giving to beggars is forbidden in Bahá'u'lláh's book of laws, the *Kitáb-i-Aqdas.* He has made useful work obligatory, and it ranks as worship. He wrote, "Waste not your time in idleness and sloth. ... Occupy yourselves with that which profiteth yourselves and others ... The most despised of men in the sight of God are those who sit idly and beg." [81:30] In that same Book, Bahá'u'lláh also states that if a person is not able to work to earn a living, the House of Justice and the wealthy must make the necessary provision. The rich are exhorted to engage in charity to the needy. [81] See **SERVICE.**

BELCHER, EDWARD (1900-1985) An American believer (1931) who embraced the faith after a dream in which 'Abdu'l-Bahá came to him. In 1938 he pioneered from his home in Binghamton, New York, to Syracuse, New York to assist in the formation of the first (1939) local Spiritual Assembly of that town. In 1943 he pioneered to Sioux Falls, South Dakota and later moved on to Los Angeles. In 1955 he pioneered to Uruguay where he was the first Bahá'í to settle in Salto. In 1958 he pioneered to Minas and lived there until the formation of the first (1966) local Spiritual Assembly in Minas (the second local Spiritual Assembly to form in Uruguay). In 1966 he moved on to Pando to assist in the formation of a local Spiritual Assembly in that town. He remained in Pando until his death in 1985. [11:657]

BENKE, GEORGE ADAM (-1932) (Martyr) A pioneer from Germany to Sofia, Bulgaria, he was designated by Shoghi Effendi as "the first European martyr for the Faith." [82:263]

BIG Literally lord, prince, governor, bey: placed after the given name, Big was used as a courtesy title for middle-ranking officials. See KHÁN. [11:736]

BISHÁRÁT Glad Tidings.

BISMILLÁHI'R-RAḤMÁNI'R-RAḤIM In the name of God, the Compassionate, the Merciful: an invocation that is prefixed to all but the ninth Súrih (chapter) of the Qur'án and composed (in Arabic) of 19 letters. [11:736]

BLACKWELL, ELLSWORTH (1902-1978) An American believer (1934) who served for a time on the National Spiritual Assembly of the United States and whose pioneer activities spanned nearly 25 years from 1940 until his death. In 1940 he, along with his wife (Ruth Browne) pioneered to Haiti on three separate occasions. In 1940 they went for a period of three years, returning in 1950 and again in 1960 (remaining until 1975.) He was a member of the first (1942) local Spiritual Assembly of Port-au-Prince and in 1961 served on the first National Spiritual Assembly of Haiti. He was later appointed the first Auxiliary Board member in Haiti. In 1975 he and his wife again pioneered, this time to Malagasy Republic on the island of Madagascar where he was elected to the National Spiritual Assembly in 1976-1977. In 1977 he and his wife pioneered to the Republic of Zaire. [53:452][60:279]

BLAKE, CECILIA KING (1911-1980) A Panamanian believer who embraced the Cause in 1957 and immediately pioneered to the Chitré Zone. On several occasions she served as a member of the National Spiritual Assembly of Panama. She traveled widely throughout Central America pioneering at the end of the Ten Year Crusade (1961) to Nicaragua, where she helped form the first (1961) local Spiritual Assembly of Bluefields. In the 1970s she resettled in Costa Rica. [2:723]

BLAKELY, DUDLEY MOORE (1902-1982) (Knight of Bahá'u'lláh) An early (1920) American believer who traveled widely throughout Latin America in the promotion of the Cause. In 1954 he and his wife (Elsa) pioneered to Tonga for which they were designated Knights of Bahá'u'lláh. [2:810]

BLESSED BEAUTY, THE (Bahá'u'lláh) A title used by the Bahá'ís.

BLOMFIELD, LADY SARA LOUISA (Sitarih Khánum) (1859-1939) Lady Blomfield was an eminent British Bahá'í. She was born in Ireland and married a distinguished architect some 30 years her senior, Sir Arthur William Blomfield. They had two daughters, Mary Esther and Rose Ellinor Cecilia. When Sir Arthur died in 1899, Lady Blomfield with her two daughters moved from their London house. Later she began to develop a deep respect for the Christianity as taught by Basil Wilberforce, then the Archdeacon of Westminster, and she would take her daughters every Sunday to St. John's, Westminster to hear him preach. Some eight years after the death of Sir Arthur, Lady Blomfield and her daughter Mary were in Paris where they attended a reception at the home of Madam Lucien Monod. It was here that she met Miss Bertha Herbert, who introduced her to the Bahá'í Message, saying "If I look happy it is because I am happy. I have found the desire of my heart." Asked to say more, Miss Herbert said, "It is true! True! We have been taught to believe that a great Messenger would again be sent to the world. He would set forth to gather together all the peoples of good will in every race, nation, and religion on the earth. Now is the appointed time! He has come! He has come!" Miss Herbert explained that there was a woman in Paris who had recently visited 'Abdu'l-Bahá and said that a meeting could be arranged for her to hear more. The woman was Miss Ethel Jenner Rosenberg (q.v.) who had, in the summer of 1899, become the second Bahá'í to enroll in the British Isles. The Blomfields met with Miss Rosenberg and the first French Bahá'í, the scholar, Hippolyte Dreyfus. During this meeting Lady Blomfield embraced the Bahá'í Message. On returning to London the Blomfields contacted Ethel Rosenberg and Mrs. Thornburgh-Cropper (q.v.) and dedicated themselves to spreading the Faith in England. They were then living at 97 Cadogan Gardens, London, and in early August 1911 when 'Abdu'l-Bahá visited Great Britain she invited Him to stay at her house. 'Abdu'l-Bahá left London for Paris on 3 October 1911, and Lady Blomfield, her daughters and a friend, Miss Beatrice Marion Platt, followed Him, took notes of His talks and published them under the title, *Paris Talks.* [25] She subsequently wrote *The Chosen Highway*, telling how she first heard of the Faith and of her meetings with 'Abdu'l-Bahá. [55]

When WW I began the Blomfields were living in Geneva and moved to Paris to work for the French Red Cross. In the spring of 1918 she received a telephone message that disturbed her greatly: "'Abdu'l-Bahá in serious danger. Take immediate action." She went at once to Lord Lamington, who put the matter into the hands of the Right Honorable Arthur Balfour, secretary of state for foreign affairs, and a cable was immediately sent to General Allenby, "Extend every protection and consideration to 'Abdu'l-Bahá, His family and His friends, when British march on Haifa." [5:306] The Turks had threatened to crucify 'Abdu'l-Bahá but when Allenby took Haifa, several days before it was believed possible for him to do so, he cabled London, "Have today taken Palestine. Notify the world that 'Abdu'l-Bahá is safe." [5:306] Around 1920 Lady Blomfield decided to spend part of each year in Geneva, and it was there that she befriended Eglantyne Jebb, founder of the "Save the Children Fund," and set up an assisting group, the "Blomfield Fund" under the sponsorship of Lord Weardale in London. During this time that she used her considerable influence to get the five-point text, drawn up by the "Save the Children Fund International," of the "Geneva Declaration" accepted by the League in 1924 and that eventually became expanded into the Declaration of the Rights of the Child by the United Nations General Assembly in 1959.

When Shoghi Effendi came to England to perfect his studies of English at Balliol College, Oxford, he became very close to Lady Blomfield. She accompanied Shoghi Effendi to Haifa in December 1921, following the news of the passing of 'Abdu'l-Bahá. For several months she remained in the Holy Land assisting Shoghi Effendi in his new and heavy rôle as Guardian of the Bahá'í Faith. To the very end of her life she remained dedicated to the service of her beloved Faith. In addition to her teaching she served for eight of the first 11 years on the National Spiritual Assembly of the British Isles. She died on 31 December 1939. Shoghi Effendi immediately sent the following cable: "Profoundly grieve passing dearly beloved outstanding coworker Sitárih Khánum. Memory her glorious services imperishable. Advise English community hold befitting memorial gatherings. Assure relatives my heartfelt sympathy loving fervent prayers." [42:651][83:101][60:29]

BLUM, ALVIN J. (1912-1968) (Knight of Bahá'u'lláh) An early (1937) American believer, he pioneered within America during the first Seven Year Plan and later (after several visits) he moved with his family to New Zealand. In 1954 he pioneered to the Solomon Islands for which service he was designated a Knight of Bahá'u'lláh. [51:439]

BLUM, GERTRUDE (1909-1993) (Knight of Bahá'u'lláh) An early (1927) American believer and her husband (Alvin) who were designated Knights of Bahá'u'lláh for their pioneer move to the Solomon Islands in 1954. She served on the National Spiritual Assembly of Australia and New Zealand as well as the first Regional Spiritual Assembly of the South Pacific Ocean. In 1989 she was made a Member of the British Empire (MBE) for her services to the community and to the Bahá'í Faith. [11:319]

BLUNDELL, HUGH K. (1884-1976) An early New Zealand believer of British birth. His parents came into the Cause through the efforts of Father and Mother Dunn, who were invited to hold meetings in the Blundell home during their first (1923) visit to that country. In 1925 Hugh, although not yet a declared Bahá'í (he became a Bahá'í the following year), was among the first party of Australasian pilgrims to visit the Holy Land. He served on the local Spiritual Assembly of Auckland from 1927 onwards and was a member of the National Spiritual Assembly of Australia and New Zealand for some time. In 1957 he was appointed as the first Auxiliary Board member in New Zealand, an appointment he held for 11 years, traveling extensively in the promotion of the Cause throughout New Zealand and the Pacific Islands. [53:422]

BLUNDELL, SARAH (1850-1934) An early English believer who moved with her family to New Zealand. She became a Bahá'í in 1922 shortly after a visit by the Dunns. In 1925 she was one of the first party of Australasian pilgrims to visit the Holy Land. [23:496][60:283]

BODE, EDWARD L. (1906-1976) An American believer who pioneered (1946) with his wife (Mary) to Rio de Janeiro during the first Seven Year Plan, where they helped form the first local Spiritual Assembly. They also assisted in the formation of the Bahá'í Publishing Trust for the Portuguese language. During the period 1949-50 they traveled extensively in Holland and Portugal. From 1954 to 1956 they pioneered to Mexico, followed by a brief stay in the Canal Zone, Panama and then returned to the United States. In 1959 they moved to Holland again and stayed for a period of nine years, for five of which Edward served as a member of the National Spiritual Assembly. In 1969 they took up a pioneer post in Funchal, Madeira. [52:566]

BODE, MARY HOTCHKISS (1896-1969) An early American believer who met 'Abdu'l-Bahá when still a child during His visit to America. He named her "Ruqíyyih" ("lofty" or "exalted") and revealed several Tablets in her name. In 1919, together with her sister Helen Hotchkiss Lielnors (named "Laṭífih" ("pure" or "radiant") by 'Abdu'l-Bahá) she formally presented the first and second sections of the *Tablets of the Divine Plan* to the southern states. In 1946 she and her husband (Edward Bode) pioneered to Brazil and assisted in the formation of the first local Spiritual Assembly in that country. In 1948 they moved to Chile and then Panama, Mexico, Portugal and Holland. In 1969 they moved to Funchal in the Madeira Islands. [51:460]

BOLTON, MARIETTE GERMAINE (Roy) (1900-1968) An early (c.1924) Australian believer of French Canadian birth. She helped establish many local Spiritual Assemblies and was Secretary of the Spiritual Assembly of Australia and New Zealand from 1948 to 1951. In 1952 she and her husband donated their home in Yerrinbool to the National Spiritual Assembly, a donation which saw the creation of the first official cultural center Bahá'í Summer and Winter School. [51:435]

BOLTON, STANLEY WILLIAM (1892-1966) (Knight of Bahá'u'lláh) An early Canadian believer who in 1924 moved to Australia (as a representative of the Fuller Brush Company) became a Bahá'í shortly after his arrival. In the early 1930s, due to the Depression, he was forced to return to the U.S. where he and his wife qualified as chiropractors and returned to Australia. In 1953 he and his wife were given the privilege of representing Australia and New Zealand at the dedication of the Wilmette Temple. On their return they visited Haifa as pilgrims and brought back from that visit gifts from Shoghi Effendi for the Community: among which was a cream fez worn by 'Abdu'l-Bahá. He served on the National Spiritual Assembly of Australia for 17 years, frequently as Chairman. [50:323]

BOON, CHOO YEOK (1945-1976) The first (early 1960s) Sino-Thai of Malaysia to embrace the Cause. He was a member of the National Spiritual Assembly of Malaysia at the time of his premature death. [53:405]

BOSCH, JOHN DAVID (1855-1946) An early American believer of Swiss birth. He met 'Abdu'l-Bahá on several occasions. He deeded his property in Geyserville, California to the National Spiritual Assembly of the Bahá'ís of the United States, and this became the first Bahá'í School in the west. [84:488][60:285]

BOSCH, LOUISE (1870-1952) An early American believer of Swiss birth, she was the wife of John David Bosch. She was among the pilgrim group of 1909 which met 'Abdu'l-Bahá in 'Akká. [48:705]

BOWMAN, AMELIA (1897-1976) An American believer (1933) who pioneered (1947) to Europe during the second Seven Year Plan. In 1947 she moved to Sweden where she helped form the first (1948) local Spiritual Assembly of Stockholm. In 1949 she pioneered to Norway and settled in Oslo. In 1952 she transferred to Bergen where she helped form the first (1955) local Spiritual Assembly of that city. In 1957 she relocated to France for two years where she served s a member of the National Teaching Committee. She returned to Norway in 1959 and assisted in the formation of the first (1962) local Spiritual Assembly of Stavanger. In 1962 she was elected a member of the first National Spiritual Assembly of Norway and served until 1967. [53:409]

BRANCHES See A<u>GH</u>ṢÁN.

BRAUNS-FOREL, MARTA (1888-1948) The daughter of Dr. Auguste Forel and an early European believer. [84:481]

BRAY, JOSEPH GRANDIN (1887-1939) A early American believer. [42:672]

BREAKS, VIRGINIA (1906-1993) (Knight of Bahá'u'lláh) An American believer (1947) who in 1953 pioneered to Chuuk, Eastern Caroline Islands for which service she was designated a Knight of Bahá'u'lláh. She remained on the island until 1987, serving for some time as an Auxiliary Board member. [11:320]

BREAKWELL, THOMAS (1872-1902) The first English Bahá'í. Born in Woking, Surrey, 31 May 1872, Thomas was the youngest of five children and was educated in the ordinary state school in Woking before he moved with the family to the United States. He found a well-paid and responsible post in a southern cotton mill that was run on child labor. Due to his high salary, he was able to spend long summer vacations in Europe. In the summer of 1901, on a steamship crossing to France he made friends with a Mrs. Milner, who noted his interest in Theosophy and felt moved to invite him to go with her to meet a special friend in Paris. This special friend was May Ellis Bolles (q.v.)—one of the first pilgrims from the West to visit 'Abdu'l-Bahá in 'Akká. Thomas and Mrs. Milner returned to their respective homes in Europe and the United States on fire with the desire to spread their newly found Faith but May Bolles had been asked by 'Abdu'l-Bahá to stay in Paris for the time being. Her mother disapproved of May's wholehearted dedication to her new religion and wished in the summer of 1901 to take her to Brittany. She had written to 'Abdu'l-Bahá on May's refusal to leave Paris, but He still did not wish her to leave. It was at this juncture that Mrs. Milner arrived with Thomas Breakwell. May described her first sight of him, "It was like looking at a veiled light. I saw at once his pure heart, his thirsty soul, and over all was cast the veil which is over every soul until it is rent asunder by the power of God in this day," and in another report, he was "of medium height, slender, erect, and graceful with intense eyes and an indescribable charm.... I discerned a very rare person of high standing and culture, simple, natural, intensely real in his attitude toward life and his fellowmen... he asked to see me the following day." [83:66] When Breakwell returned, he showed remarkable insight into the Faith, accepting its teachings and absorbing its history. She told him of her visit to 'Abdu'l-Bahá and as she later wrote, "his heart was filled with such longing that all his former life was swept away, he gave up his journey, canceled his plans and had but one hope in life, to be permitted to go himself and behold the face of 'Abdu'l-Bahá.... He wrote the following supplication, "My Lord, I believe, forgive me, Thy servant Thomas Breakwell." [83:67]

Breakwell and a friend set off for Egypt in anticipation of acceptance as May had sent his petition with her eager support and request for the answer to be sent to Port Said. That very evening when May went to collect her mail she found a cablegram from 'Abdu'l-Bahá, "You may leave Paris at any time!" The visit with 'Abdu'l-Bahá—the first visit of an English pilgrim—set Breakwell on fire, and he rapidly freed himself from all his earthly possessions. When he told 'Abdu'l-Bahá of the child labor in his factory, the Master had said, "Cable your resignation," [83:68] which he did with joy in his heart. On his return to Paris he threw himself into the teaching work with all his energy and enthusiasm, and such was his overflowing love and depth of understanding that many enrolled. His parents, having moved back to England, came over to Paris with the intention of persuading him to return to London with them. He told his father that he could not leave, as 'Abdu'l-Bahá had asked him to stay in Paris, and such was his loving treatment of his father that he too wrote a letter of supplication to 'Abdu'l-Bahá. Breakwell's health was rapidly declining, and he was found to have advanced consumption. He wrote, "Suffering is a heady wine; I am prepared to receive that bounty which is the greatest of all; torments of the flesh have enabled me to draw much nearer to my Lord..." [83:70] This was in a letter to 'Abdu'l-Bahá's Secretary, Dr. Yúnis Khán, and a few days after the letter was received, Breakwell died, on 13 June 1902—'Abdu'l-Bahá appeared to know long before the official news reached Him. Deeply grieved, 'Abdu'l-Bahá revealed a prayer of visitation for Breakwell [83:71-72] and gave it to two translators to put into English with the instruction to translate it well so that whoever read it would weep. Its words are heartbreaking yet joyful in the assurances they contain of the exalted spiritual station that Breakwell had attained.

About a year after his passing, 'Abdu'l-Bahá received an envelope that contained a letter and a violet attached to a postcard. On the card, written in gold ink was written, "He is not dead. He lives on in the Kingdom of God" and at the bottom of the card, "This flower was picked from Breakwell's grave." In the enclosed letter it said, "Praise be to the Lord that my son left this world for the next with the recognition and love of 'Abdu'l-Bahá." [83:71-72]

BRITTINGHAM, ISABELLA (1852-1924) (Disciple of 'Abdu'l-Bahá) She was born on 21 February 1852, the daughter of an Episcopal clergyman. She married James D. Brittingham in 1886 and attended her first Bahá'í study class in 1898. Almost immediately on accepting the Faith she began to travel to teach it. In September 1901 she visited 'Abdu'l-Bahá in 'Akká. After her visit she wrote a scholarly instructive essay, *The Revelation of Bahá'u'lláh* that was published in 1902 by the Bahá'í Publishing Society. Whenever she witnessed a new declaration of faith she would, week after week, send off their letters to 'Abdu'l-Bahá, Who on one occasion said laughingly, "Mrs. Brittingham was our Bahá'í-maker." One such distinguished person who studied the Faith with her was Dr. Susan Moody (q.v.) who later rendered heroic services to the Faith as a doctor, educator and Bahá'í teacher in Ṭihrán, Írán. Mrs. Brittingham received the full support of her husband, James, who was not able to accompany her on her teaching trips. She made her second pilgrimage to the Holy Land in October 1909. She continued her traveling for the Faith to the end of her life and, in the home of the Revell sisters in Philadelphia, she dictated 11 letters to Jessie Revell (q.v.) on the evening of 28 January 1924 and then passed away later that same evening.

BROWN, RUTH RANDALL (1887-1969) An early (1912) American believer, she met 'Abdu'l-Bahá while lying on a sick bed with what was considered an incurable illness. On meeting her 'Abdu'l-Bahá said to her three times, "You are not sick, you are the healthiest person here." From that point the healing began, and she became an ardent believer. She and her husband (Harry Randall) contributed the funds (1922) for the construction of the Pilgrim House built opposite the House of 'Abdu'l-Bahá in Haifa. In 1953 she pioneered with her second husband (Mr. Bishop Brown) to Durban, South Africa. [51:463][60:299]

BROWNE, EDWARD GRANVILLE (1862-1926) The Cambridge scholar who studied and wrote about the Bábí and Bahá'í Faiths and who had been granted an interview with Bahá'u'lláh. He wrote

> The face on whom I gazed I can never forget, though I cannot describe it. Those piercing eyes seemed to read one's very soul; power and authority sat on that ample brow; while the deep lines on the forehead and face implied an age which the jet-black hair and beard flowing down in indistinguishable luxuriance almost to the waist seemed to belie. No need to ask in whose presence I stood, as I bowed myself before one who is the object of a devotion and love which kings might envy and emperors sigh for in vain.[5:194]

When the Bahá'ís refused to become involved in Íránian politics, Browne transferred his interest to the Azalís, though his translation of *A Traveller's Narrative* [62] and the report of his interview with Bahá'u'lláh have earned him a place in Bahá'í history.

BULLOCK, MATTHEW W. (1891-1972) (Knight of Bahá'u'lláh) An American believer (1940) who was elected to the National Spiritual Assembly of the United States in 1952. He traveled extensively at his own expense promoting the Faith. In 1955 he pio neered to Curaçao, Dutch West Indies and in so doing helped form the first Spiritual Assembly there. He was designated a Knight of Bahá'u'lláh for his pioneer move. [51:535][60:301]

BURIAL, BAHÁ'Í According to Bahá'í law the body, having been the temple of the spirit, must be respected, treated with honor and buried, not cremated. The body must be buried within an hour's journey from the place of death; it is wrapped in a shroud of silk or cotton and on a finger is placed a ring carrying a special inscription. The coffin should be of crystal, stone or hard fine wood and a specific Prayer for the Dead is said or chanted before interment. This formal prayer and the ring are obligatory for only those Bahá'ís who have attained the age of maturity (15 years). The coffin is placed in the ground so that the face of the body looks towards the Qiblih (Bahjí). The recitation of the special prayer is the only obligatory part of the funeral service, and the family may have additional readings, music, speeches if they wish.

BUSEY, GARRETA HELEN (1893-1976) An American believer (1934) who traveled extensively in North America and Europe in the promotion of the Cause. Her main contribution to the Cause was through her work in the field of Bahá'í publications: she served on the editorial staffs of *World Order* magazine, *Bahá'í News* and the *Bahá'í World*. [53:423]

BUTT, ABBASALLY (1894-1959) An early Indian believer who was called to the Holy Land by 'Abdu'l-Bahá to assist in the translation of His tablets to the Western believers and their letters to Him. The beginning of WW I forced his return to India, where he was for many years the Chairman of the National Spiritual Assembly of India, Pákistán and Burma. He was the first member of the Asian Auxiliary Board appointed in India. [47:885][60:304]

BUZURG-I-VAZÍR, MÍRZÁ; Mírzá 'Abbás of Núr (-1839) The father of Bahá'u'lláh. He was well known for his charm, character and the beauty of his calligraphy.

C

CABEZAS, EMMA (1895-1992) An early (1947) Chilean Bahá'í, she served as a member of the first (1961) National Spiritual Assembly of Chile. [57:274]

CALAMITIES AND CRISES In the latter part of the 19th century Bahá'u'lláh warned about the problems facing humankind. He wrote, in part:

> The world is in travail and its agitation waxeth day by day. Its face is turned toward waywardness and unbelief.

Such shall be its plight that to disclose it now would not be meet and seemly. Its perversity will long continue. And when the appointed hour is come, there shall suddenly appear that which shall cause the limbs of mankind to quake. Then, and only then, will the Divine Standard be unfurled, and the Nightingale of Paradise warble its melody. [85:118]

In 1983 the Universal House of Justice wrote:

Both within and without the Cause of God, powerful forces are operating to bring to a climax the twin tendencies of this portentous century. Among the many evidences which reveal this process may be cited ... the continual increase of lawlessness, terrorism, economic confusion, immorality and the growing danger from the proliferation of weapons of destruction, and on the other, the world-wide, divinely propelled expansion, consolidation and rapid emergence into the limelight of world affairs of the Cause itself, a process crowned by the wonderful efflorescence of Mount Carmel, the mountain of God, whose Divine springtime is now so magnificently burgeoning.[86:126]

In 1949 Shoghi Effendi wrote through his secretary:

No doubt to the degree we Bahá'ís the world over ... strive to spread the Cause and live up to its teachings, there will be some mitigation to the suffering of the peoples of the world. But it seems apparent that the great failure to respond to Bahá'u'lláh's instructions, appeals and warnings issued in the 19th Century, has now sent the world along a path, and released forces, which must culminate in a still more violent upheaval and agony. The thing is out of hand, so to speak, and it is too late to avert catastrophic trials. [86:129]

Earlier, in 1933, he wrote to an individual believer describing the forces of darkness that beset the society of that day: Whatever our shortcoming may be, and however formidable the forces of darkness which besiege us today, the unification of mankind as outlined and insured by the World Order of Bahá'u'lláh will in the fullness of time be firmly and permanently established. This is Bahá'u'lláh's promise, and no power on earth can in the long run present or even retard its adequate realization. The friends should, therefore, not lose hope, but fully conscious of their power and their role they should persevere in their

> mighty efforts for the extension and the consolidation of Bahá'u'lláh's universal Dominion on earth. [86:330]

In 1969 the Universal House of Justice wrote to the Bahá'ís of the world:

> In the worsening world situation, fraught with pain of war, violence and the sudden uprooting of long-established institutions, can be seen the fulfillment of the prophecies of Bahá'u'lláh and the often repeated warnings of the Master and the beloved Guardian about the inevitable fate of a lamentably defective social system, an unenlightened leadership and a rebellious and unbelieving humanity. Governments and peoples of both the developed and developing nations, and other human institutions, secular and religious, finding themselves helpless to reverse the trend of the catastrophic events of the day, stand bewildered and overpowered by the magnitude and complexity of the problems facing them. At this fateful hour in human history many, unfortunately, seem content to stand aside and ring their hands in despair or else join in the Babel of shouting and protestation which loudly objects, but offers no solution to the woes and afflictions plaguing our age. Nevertheless a greater and greater number of thoughtful and fair-minded men and women are recognizing in the clamor of contention, grief and destruction, now reaching such horrendous proportions, the evidences of Divine chastisement, and turning their faces towards God are becoming increasingly receptive to His Word. Doubtless the present circumstances, though tragic and awful in their immediate consequences, are serving to sharpen the focus on the indispensability of the teachings of Bahá'u'lláh to the needs of the present age, and will provide many opportunities to reach countless waiting souls, hungry and thirsty for Divine guidance.[86:132f]

CALENDAR, BAHÁ'Í Also known as the **BADÍ CALENDAR**. It was instituted by the Báb and approved by Bahá'u'lláh, Who stated that it should commence with the New Year's day of the year of the Báb's Declaration (21 March 1844.) It is based on the solar year of 365 days, five hours and 50 minutes with Naw-Rúz (New Year) beginning on the spring equinox (usually 21 March but if it takes place after sunset on the 21st, then Naw-Rúz is celebrated on the 22nd. The Calendar consists of 19 months of 19 days each. The 19th month is one of fasting and is preceded by the four Intercalary Days (five in a leap year) known as Ayyám-i-Há. The Bahá'í day begins and ends at sunset. The names of the months are taken from the names of God invoked in a prayer said during the month of fasting in Shí'ih Islám. See appended Badí' Calendar for a listing of the Bahá'í calendar events.

CALIPH Vicar, deputy: successor of the Prophet Muḥammad, supreme civil and spiritual head of the Islámic world, a title claimed by successive dynasties. [11:736]

CALUMNY Ranks in the Bahá'í Faith along with backbiting (q.v.). It is the act of speaking maliciously, making false charges to damage another person's reputation.

CARAVANSERAI (-SERA, -SARY) See **KHÁN**. [11:736]

CENTRAL FIGURES the Báb, Bahá'u'lláh and 'Abdu'l-Bahá are referred to by Shoghi Effendi as the three Central Figures of the Bahá'í Faith.

CENTRE OF THE COVENANT A title given to 'Abdu'l-Bahá. See **CITY OF THE COVENANT; BAHÁ'U'LLÁH, COVENANT OF.**

CHASE, THORNTON (1847-1912) (Disciple of 'Abdu'l-Bahá; surnamed Thábit [Steadfast]) He was born in Springfield, Massachusetts, 22 February 1847. In June 1894 when a traveling insurance salesman in Chicago, he met an oriental gentleman who introduced him to the Bahá'í Faith. Later that same year, along with four others, he embraced the Cause and began actively to teach. He thus became not only the first American to become a Bahá'í but the first enrolled believer in the Western world. He visited 'Abdu'l-Bahá in 'Akká in 1907, and shortly after his return he was transferred to California where his teaching of the Bahá'í Faith intensified. He published several books, letters and poems before his death on 30 September 1912, in Los Angeles. When 'Abdu'l-Bahá was in America that year and learned of his passing He made a special journey to Inglewood Cemetery, and after some words of prayer said, "This is a personage who will not be forgotten. For the present his worth is not known, but in the future it will be inestimably dear. His sun will be ever shining, his star will ever bestow the light." [83:11]

CHASTITY The highest standard of behavior is expected of a Bahá'í. The writings of Shoghi Effendi are most explicit on this theme:

> A chaste and holy life must be made the controlling principle in the behavior and conduct of all Bahá'ís, both in their social relations with the members of their own community, and in their contact with the world at large. It must adorn and reinforce the ceaseless labors and meritorious exertions of those whose enviable position is to propagate the Message, and to administer the affairs, of the Faith of Bahá'u'lláh. It must be upheld, in all its integrity and implications, in every phase of the life of those

who fill the ranks of that Faith, whether in their homes, their travels, their clubs, their societies, their entertainments, their schools, and their universities. It must be accorded special consideration in the conduct of the social activities of every Bahá'í summer school and any other occasions on which Bahá'í community life is organized and fostered. It must be closely and continually identified with the mission of the Bahá'í youth, both as an element in the life of the Bahá'í community, and as a factor in the future progress and orientation of the youth of their own country. Such a chaste and holy life, with its implications of modesty, purity, temperance, decency, and clean-mindedness, involves no less than the exercise of moderation in all that pertains to dress, language, amusements, and all artistic and literary avocations. It demands daily vigilance in the control of one's carnal desires and corrupt inclinations. It calls for the abandonment of a frivolous conduct, with its excessive attachment to trivial and often misdirected pleasures. It requires total abstinence from all alcoholic drinks, from opium, and from similar habit-forming drugs. It condemns the prostitution of art and of literature, the practices of nudism and of companionate marriage, infidelity in marital relationships, and all manner of promiscuity, of easy familiarity, and of sexual vices. It can tolerate no compromise with the theories, the standards, the habits, and the excesses of a decadent age. Nay rather it seeks to demonstrate, through the dynamic force of its example, the pernicious character of such theories, the falsity of such standards, the hollowness of such claims, the perversity of such habits, and the sacrilegious character of such excesses. [39:29f]

In another passage he wrote:

It must be remembered, however, that the maintenance of such a high standard of moral conduct is not to be associated or confused with any form of asceticism, or of excessive and bigoted puritanism. The standard inculcated by Bahá'u'lláh, seeks, under no circumstances, to deny anyone the legitimate right and privilege to derive the fullest advantage and benefit from the manifold joys, beauties, and pleasures with which the world has been so plentifully enriched by an All-Loving Creator. [39:33]

CHEE, LEONG TAT (1910-1972) A Malaysian believer who served on the first Spiritual Assembly of Malacca. He served as treasurer of the Regional Spiritual Assembly of South East

Asia from 1957 until 1964. He had the privilege of being the only Malaysian believer to participate in the election of the first Universal House of Justice in 1963. In 1964 he was elected to the first National Spiritual Assembly of Malaysia, and later that same year he was appointed as an Auxiliary Board member—the first Malaysian to serve in that capacity. In 1969, despite failing health, he and his wife pioneered to Singapore in an effort to raise up a National Spiritual Assembly in that country (a goal that was realized in 1972).[51:527][60:416]

CHIHRÍQ The fortress in northeastern Írán where the Báb had been imprisoned for most of the last two years of His life and from which He wrote many of His important works. One of the main objectives of the Conference of Badasht (q.v.) was to find a way to free the Báb from this prison.

CHIPOSI, LEONARD (1928-1993) One of the earliest (1956) indigenous believers in Zimbabwe he served as a member of two National Spiritual Assemblies: South Central Africa (1964-1970) followed by Zimbabwe (1970-1973.) [11:320]

CHOSEN BRANCH 'Abdu'l-Bahá.

CHRISTIAN, ROBERTA KALEY (1913-1971) (Knight of Bahá'u'lláh) An early (1936) American believer. She and her husband, William Kenneth Christian (q.v.), were designated Knights of Bahá'u'lláh for their pioneer move to Southern Rhodesia. Following the death of her husband in 1959 she pioneered to Alaska to complete a goal of the Nine Year Plan. [51:497]

CHRISTIAN, WILLIAM KENNETH (1913-1959) (Knight of Bahá'u'lláh) An early American believer and member of the National Spiritual Assembly of the United States for several years. In 1953 he and his family pioneered first to Southern Rhodesia (for which service he and his wife, Roberta Kaley Christian (q.v.), were designated Knights of Bahá'u'lláh,) then to Athens, Greece, and finally to Indonesia (where he was the first Bahá'í to be buried in the Bahá'í burial ground in Djakarta). [47:906]

CIVILIZATION, DIVINE The civilization that, according to Bahá'í writings, will result from the establishment of the World Order of Bahá'u'lláh:

> The Revelation of Bahá'u'lláh, whose supreme mission is none other but the achievement of this organic and spiritual unity of the whole body of nations, should, if we be faithful to its implications, be regarded as signalizing through its advent the coming of age of the entire human race. It should be viewed not merely as yet another spiritual revival in the ever-changing fortunes of mankind, not only as a further stage in a chain of progressive Revelations, nor even as the culmination of one of a series of re

current prophetic cycles, but rather as marking the last and highest stage in the stupendous evolution of man's collective life on this planet. The emergence of a world community, the consciousness of world citizenship, the founding of a world civilization and culture ... should, by their very nature, be regarded, as far as this planetary life is concerned, as the furthermost limits in the organization of human society, though man, as an individual, will, nay must indeed as a result of such a consummation, continue indefinitely to progress and develop. [4:163]

CLARK, MILDRED EILEEN (1892-1967) (Knight of Bahá'u'lláh) An American believer who pioneered to many locations: in 1946 she pioneered to Norway where in 1948 she served on the first local Spiritual Assembly of Oslo; in 1950 she pioneered to the Netherlands; in 1952 to Luxembourg; in 1953 she moved to Svolvaer, Lofoten Islands—for which she was designated a Knight of Bahá'u'lláh. [50:303]

CLERGY There is no clergy in the Bahá'í Faith nor leadership by individuals. The administration of the Bahá'í community rests in elected bodies. Bahá'u'lláh forbids monasticism and living in seclusion, commands priests to marry and prohibits the confession of sins. See **ADMINISTRATION**.

COBB, STANWOOD (1881-1982) An early (1906) [87:Vol.15,No.1] American believer who met 'Abdu'l-Bahá in Haifa in 1908 and again in 1910 when he was a guest in His home on the first visit and in the pilgrim house on the second. He met the Master again in both France and the United States. During his life he published some 20 books on religion, philosophy and education, as well as several books of verse. In 1924 he was appointed editor of *Star of the West* and its successor *World Order* until 1939. He continued to lecture on Bahá'í subjects well into his 100th year. [2:815][60:317]

COLLINS, AMELIA ENGELDER (Milly) (1873-1962) (Hand of the Cause of God; the only Hand who was informed of her rank before it was bestowed: she was advised of her rank by Shoghi Effendi in 1947 but not publicly appointed until 24 December 1951 (in the first contingent appointees).) She was born in Pittsburgh, Pennsylvania on 7 June 1873 of a German Lutheran clergyman. She was the seventh of a family of 14 children. She became a Bahá'í towards the end of the life of 'Abdu'l-Bahá, and she received a letter from Him dated 6 December 1919 that set the pattern of her life. When 'Abdu'l-Bahá passed away and His Will appointing Shoghi Effendi was read she turned to him and was known to say, "How I prayed that God would help me to make him happy," [47:834] and often said, "To see the Guardian smile just once was worth a lifetime of suffering." [47:834] Shoghi Effendi himself in numerous letters and messages referred to her "indomitable spirit of faith and love," her "single-minded and wholehearted devotion" and her "self-sacrificing efforts" examples that "will live and influence many a soul." [47:835]

In 1923 she made her first pilgrimage to the Holy Land. Shortly after her husband died in 1937, she made her second pilgrimage.

Milly was elected to the National Spiritual Assembly of the United States and Canada in 1924 and served on it for many years. She was also most active in travel teaching and visiting most centers in the States and Canada as well as those in South and Central America. By living simply, allowing herself no luxuries, she was an outstanding benefactress, but rarely spoke of the generous contributions she made. She was frequently the first to respond to a call from the Guardian, and most contributions were known only to God, to the Guardian and to Milly herself. There were even many she herself could not remember. However many were of such significance that the Guardian publicly acknowledged them, particularly properties on Mount Carmel; the American Temple and its dependencies; temple sites in Latin America, Europe and Asia; the developments around the Bahá'í Holy Places in Israel and the purchase of national Bahá'í headquarters and endowments in five continents. In his last message to the Bahá'í world the Guardian referred to Milly's "munificent donation" [6:112] towards the building of Houses of Worship in Europe, Africa and Australia.

The traveling she did on behalf of the National Spiritual Assembly and for the Guardian himself was frequently mentioned in letters to her by the Guardian, and one such reads, "The Bahá'ís, East and West, North and South, admire and are thankful for such signal services... Be happy, and persevere in your exemplary and historic services." [47:838]

In January 1947 Milly received a letter from Shoghi Effendi, the contents of which she had to keep locked in her heart for almost five years. He not only appointed her as a Hand of the Cause but as one of the Nine Hands who, according to the terms of the Will of 'Abdu'l-Bahá, were to serve the Guardian in a very special capacity. In the words of his secretary, the Guardian is quoted as saying "So you see you are not only worthy to be a Hand of the Cause, but have rendered a service which ordinarily would be performed by this select body of nine. You must realize that by his conferring this rank upon you is not as an inducement to you to perform future tasks, but as a well-deserved recognition of those already performed..." [47:839] His own postscript to the letter con tains the following excerpts: "The high rank you now occupy and which no Bahá'í has ever held in his own lifetime has been conferred solely in recognition of the manifold services you have already rendered.... Indeed the character of this latest and highly significant service you have rendered places you in the category of the Chosen Nine who, unlike the other Hands of the Cause, are to be associated directly and intimately with the cares and responsibilities of the Guardian of the Faith." [47:839]

In January 1951 the International Bahá'í Council (q.v.) was appointed by Shoghi Effendi with Milly as vice-president. This appointment required her to live in Haifa though she had to return to the United States for some time for treatment for arthritis. In December of that year she carried out some special assignments for the Guardian in Turkey and Cairo, which she executed though ill and in constant pain through her increasingly crippling arthritis. Shoghi Effendi made public the news of her appointment as a Hand with the announcement of the first contingent later that month. She was appointed to accompany 'Amatu'l-Bahá Rúḥíyyih Khánum to the 1953 All-America Conference in Chicago and as his representative to the European Intercontinental Conference in Frankfurt, Germany, in July 1958. By that time Shoghi Effendi had passed away, and her tribute to him at the close of that Conference gave a unique insight into his life and work. It was subsequently published for the benefit of future generations and concluded with a most moving appeal, "Let us not fail him, for he never failed us. Let us never forget him, for he never forgot us."

On 20 November 1960 she returned to Germany to complete the trust given to her by Shoghi Effendi—to lay the cornerstone of the European Bahá'í House of Worship. She returned to Haifa after an overseas visit in October 1961 to attend the annual meeting of the Hands of the Cause where, in spite of an arm broken in a fall that required hospitalization and severe illness, she was able to go to all but one of the sessions.

On 1 January 1962 she passed away in the arms of 'Amatu'l-Bahá Rúḥíyyih Khánum and was buried in the Bahá'í Cemetery at the foot of Mount Carmel. To the U.S. National Spiritual Assembly the Hands of the Cause cabled:

> With deepest regret share news Bahá'í World passing dearly loved Hand Cause outstanding benefactress Faith Amelia Collins. Unfailing support love devotion beloved Guardian darkest period his life brought her unique bounty his deep affection esteem confidence and honor direct association work world Center. Signal services every field Bahá'í activity unforgettable. Purchase site future Mashriqu'l-Adhkár Mount Carmel, generous gifts has-

tening construction Mother Temples four continents, acquisition national Ḥaẓíratu'l-Quds, endowments, constant support home-fronts, world-wide teaching enterprises, among her munificent donations. Urge national assemblies hold memorial gatherings particularly Temples, commemorate her shining example ceaseless services maintained until last breath.[47:835]

COLLISON, MARY GALE (1892-1970) (Knight of Bahá'u'lláh) An early (1923) American believer of Canadian birth. She and her husband made a 17,000-mile teaching trip by automobile across the United States in 1928, visiting a large number of Bahá'í communities enroute. In 1952 she and her husband pioneered to Uganda. In 1953 they were the first American believers to arise in response to the Ten Year Crusade call for pioneers and moved to Ruanda-Urundi, for which service they were each designated a Knight of Bahá'u'lláh. In 1955 they returned to Uganda where they served as Custodians (until 1966) of the Mother Temple of Africa (Mas͟hriqu'l-Ad͟hkár) after its dedication in 1961. [51:486]

COLLISON, REGINALD (Rex) (1884-1983) (Knight of Bahá'u'lláh) Rex was born in central Ohio in 1884 and married Mary Gale in 1920. They accepted the Bahá'í Faith together in 1923. He retired in 1945 as Chief of Research and Professor Emeritus at Cornell University after 33 years in plant research and associated studies. He then moved with his wife to a house they owned in Geyserville and in 1952 pioneered to Uganda, where for about a year they were caretakers of the Ḥaẓíratu'l-Quds in Kampala. Leaving to pioneer with a student friend, Duduzu Chisiza, they settled in Ruanda-Urundi, where their names were in the first list of Knights of Bahá'u'lláh announced by Shoghi Effendi. When they returned to Kampala, Rex was walking across the newly bulldozed piece of land where the Bahá'í Temple was to be erected and picked up a piece of stone which he said was an stone-age hand ax. This was sent for identification and carbon-dating to Nairobi and confirmed as being a 20,000 year old artifact. In 1966 they returned home to Geyserville where Rex continued to serve, give lectures and hold firesides. Although Mary died in 1970 Rex carried on actively until he was almost 100 years old. He had a radiant nature and like one of the pieces of his hobby, he was "a gemstone finely cut and supremely polished." See **COLLISON, MARY GALE.** [11:595]

COMMUNITY, BAHÁ'Í Used in three ways—to refer to those Bahá'ís who live in a local or national Bahá'í administrative unit or to the Bahá'ís worldwide.

CONCLAVE OF THE HANDS OF THE CAUSE When Shoghi Effendi passed away in November 1957 the Hands of the Cause (q.v.) held a meeting in the Holy Land to determine the future of the

Cause. These meetings were continued annually until the election of the Universal House of Justice.

CONCOURSE ON HIGH The name found in Bahá'í Writings for the Prophets and holy souls in the spiritual world. The "Supreme Concourse" and the "Celestial Concourse" are also used in this context. For example, 'Abdu'l-Bahá wrote in one of His Prayers: "...These souls are Thy heavenly army. Assist them and, with the cohorts of the Supreme Concourse, make them victorious, so that each one of them may become like unto a regiment and conquer these countries through the love of God and the illumination of divine teachings." [62:34]

CONSOLIDATION A term used by Bahá'ís to describe the process whereby they deepen in their Faith, follow more closely its precepts and assume their teaching and administrative responsibilities. See **DEEPENING.**

CONSTANTINOPLE (Istanbul) The city in Turkey to which Bahá'u'lláh was exiled from Bag͟hdád in 1863. He remained there for four months and was then sent to Adrianople (q.v..)

CONSULTATION The technique of discussion used throughout Bahá'í administration. Bahá'u'lláh wrote: "The heaven of divine wisdom is illumined with the two luminaries of consultation and compassion. Take ye counsel together in all matters, inasmuch as consultation is the lamp of guidance which leadeth the way, and is the bestower of understanding."[77:168] In the "Notes" section of the first English language version of the Kitáb-i-Aqdas, the Universal House of Justice have indicated that "Bahá'u'lláh has established consultation as one of the fundamental principles of His Faith and has exhorted the believers to 'take counsel together in all matters'. Shoghi Effendi states that the 'principle of consultation ... constitutes one of the basic laws' of the Bahá'í Administrative Order." [81:Notes, 190]

It is also encouraged for all decision-making, even in business and within the family. It involves the sharing of ideas in a spirit of love and harmony while encouraging full and frank discussion with a healthy clash of opinions but without the clash of personalities. 'Abdu'l-Bahá said that

> consultation must have for its object the investigation of truth. He who expresses an opinion should not voice it as correct and right but set it forth as a contribution to the consensus of opinion, for the light of reality becomes apparent when two opinions coincide. A spark is produced when flint and steel come together. Man should weigh his opinions with the utmost serenity, calmness and composure. Before expressing his own views he should carefully consider the views already advanced by others. If he finds

> that a previously expressed opinion is more true and worthy, he should accept it immediately and not willfully hold to an opinion of his own. By this excellent method he endeavors to arrive at unity and truth. Opposition and division are deplorable. It is better then to have the opinion of a wise, sagacious man; otherwise, contradiction and altercation, in which varied and divergent views are presented, will make it necessary for a judicial body to render decision upon the question. Even a majority opinion or consensus may be incorrect. A thousand people may hold to one view and be mistaken, whereas one sagacious person may be right. Therefore, true consultation is spiritual conference in the attitude and atmosphere of love. Members must love each other in the spirit of fellowship in order that good results may be forthcoming. Love and fellowship are the foundation. [26:72f]

When a decision is reached, either in unanimity or by majority vote, it becomes the decision of the collective body and, as such, is obeyed by that body, thereby maintaining complete unity. Parties to the decision are called upon to give their unqualified active support, thus ensuring that where an incorrect decision has been taken and implemented it will quickly become apparent and reopened without losing the essential unity of the body.

CONTINENTAL BOARDS OF COUNSELLORS An institution created by the Universal House of Justice in 1968 to extend into the future the functions of the Hands of the Cause as they had decided that it could see "no way in which additional Hands of the Cause could be appointed."[49:6] The members are presently appointed every five years and are not eligible for election to any Bahá'í administrative body except the Universal House of Justice. If so elected, a Counsellor ceases to be a member of the Board. They direct the Auxiliary Board members of their respective continents, consult with and collaborate with National Spiritual Assemblies, and keep the Universal House of Justice and Hands of the Cause fully informed of the state of the Faith in their areas. They may be appointed by the Universal House of Justice to the International Teaching Center, and they then must relinquish their membership of their Continental Board. See **AUXILIARY BOARDS.**

CONVENTION, NATIONAL The annual gathering of delegates in every national Bahá'í community at which the National Spiritual Assembly is elected. In the larger national Bahá'í communities there are preliminary unit, area, district, state or other conventions that elect the delegates for the national convention. The number of delegates for each national community is established by the Universal House of Justice, and the responsible National Spiritual Assembly determines the size of these subnational conventions so that, on a proportional representation basis of adult Bahá'ís, each such subconvention has one delegate. Normally the annual convention is held during the Riḍván Festival (21 April-2 May) and the delegates consult on the affairs of the national community and midway in the proceedings, elect the National Spiritual Assembly. With regard to the proceedings themselves, Shoghi Effendi indicated "the necessity of adopting the essential method of a full, frank and unhampered consultation between the National Assembly and the assembled delegates." He went on to stress that

> It is the vital duty of the delegates to unburden their hearts, state their grievances, disclose their views, and explain their motives. It is the vital duty of the national Assembly to give earnest, prompt and prayerful consideration to the views of the delegates, weigh carefully their arguments and ponder their considered judgements, before they resort to voting and undertake to arrive at a decision according to the dictates of their conscience. They should explain their motives and not dictate: seek information and invite discussion. [86:18]

> How great the privilege, how delicate the task of the assembled delegates whose function it is to elect such national representatives as would by their record of service ennoble and enrich the annals of the Cause! If we but turn our gaze to the high qualifications of the members of Bahá'í Assemblies, as enumerated in 'Abdu'l-Bahá's Tablets, we are filled with feelings of unworthiness and dismay, and would feel truly disheartened but for the comforting thought that if we rise to play nobly your part every deficiency in our lives will be more than compensated by the all-conquering spirit of His grace and power. Hence it is incumbent upon the chosen delegates to consider without the least trace of passion and prejudice, and irrespective of any material consideration, the names of only those who can best combine the necessary qualities of unquestioned loyalty, of selfless devotion, of a well-trained mind, of recognized ability and mature experience. [88:87f]

CONVENTION, INTERNATIONAL The Constitution of the Universal House of Justice provides for the election of that Body every five years. These conventions have been held in Haifa since April

1963. The delegates to the convention are the members of the National Spiritual Assemblies then serving; they consult on many topics of vital importance to the Faith worldwide and elect the members for the Universal House of Justice from among all the adult male Bahá'ís in the world.

COOKSON, ALEXE (1918-1980) A believer who was born in the Outer Hebrides island of Harris, Scotland and embraced the Cause in 1964 in Wanganui, New Zealand. She was a member of the National Spiritual Assembly of New Zealand for 10 years (1958-1968), during eight of which she served as Secretary. She was appointed an Auxiliary Board member in 1968. [2:730][60:322]

COOPER, ELLA GOODALL (1870-1951) (Disciple of 'Abdu'l-Bahá) An early American believer. She met 'Abdu'l-Bahá on several occasions, including during a pilgrimage to 'Akká in 1908. Following this she copublished (with her mother, who was on pilgrimage with her) an account of their experiences entitled *Daily Lessons Received at Acca—January, 1908.* [89] Shoghi Effendi wrote on her passing, "Deeply grieved at sudden passing of herald of the Covenant, Ella Cooper, dearly loved handmaid of 'Abdu'l-Bahá, greatly trusted by Him. Her devoted services during concluding years of Heroic Age and also Formative Age of Faith unforgettable. Assure relatives, friends, deepest sympathy for loss. Praying for progress of her soul in Abhá Kingdom." [48:681][83:21][59:9ff]

COVENANT BREAKERS A person who accepts the Bahá'í Faith believes in Bahá'u'lláh as its Founder and in the line of succession through 'Abdu'l-Bahá, as the designated Center of His Covenant (1892-1921); Shoghi Effendi as His appointed successor, (Guardian of the Bahá'í Faith, 1921-1957); and the Universal House of Justice, (since its election in 1963). One who accepts and then publicly denies this succession, rebels against the Head of the Faith or Center of the Covenant or works to undermine the Covenant may be declared a "Covenant Breaker" and expelled from the Community. This is a very rare occurrence and is only taken after a great deal of tolerance has been shown, loving care expended to help the believer to realize the wrong that is being done, the danger of this rebellion to that believer's immortal soul and the serious consequences that will ensue if he or she persists in the actions deemed to be against the Cause. Expulsion of a believer from the Faith can only be exercised by the Hands of the Cause with the approval of the Universal House of Justice. Bahá'ís are forbidden to associate with Covenant Breakers, for as 'Abdu'l-Bahá explained that just as certain physical diseases are contagious, "likewise spiritual diseases are also infectious. If a consumptive should associate with a thousand safe and healthy persons, the safety and health of these thousand persons would not affect the consumptive and would not cure him. ... but when this consumptive associates with those thousand souls, in a short time the disease of consumption will infect a number of those healthy persons." While they must shun the Covenant Breakers completely, they are to pray for them, as "these souls are not lost forever." [86:183] It would appear, then, that the main cause of this spiritual disease is related to the ego of the individual; the desire for leadership, for authority that gradually dominates the person. There have been several in the times of Bahá'u'lláh, of 'Abdu'l-Bahá and of Shoghi Effendi.

One of the most powerful of those who, on the passing of Bahá'u'lláh, opposed 'Abdu'l-Bahá was His own brother, Mírzá Muḥammad 'Alí; later referred to as the Arch-Breaker of Bahá'u'lláh's Covenant. Mírzá Muḥammad 'Alí had been designated by Bahá'u'lláh to be next in line in succession to 'Abdu'l-Bahá, and he would, had he remained firm in the Covenant, been Head of the Faith for many years after the passing of 'Abdu'l-Bahá, instead of living and dying in ignominy. (For a detailed discussion of the activities associated with Muḥammad 'Alí see *The Covenant of Bahá'u'lláh.*) [90]

The first Bahá'í teacher to settle in America was a Syrian doctor, Ibráhím George Khayru'lláh, who in February 1894 began conducting classes in Chicago with considerable success. Early in 1898 he was invited to move to New York City, where he brought into the Faith a large number of highly intelligent, cultured, respected believers, most of whom remained faithful when he turned against 'Abdu'l-Bahá and openly sought leadership for himself. (The activities of Ibráhím Khayru'lláh are detailed comprehensively in Robert Stockman's excellent history of the early American Bahá'í community: *The Bahá'í Faith in America—Origins 1892-1900.*) [18]

During Shoghi Effendi's ministry, the main Covenant Breaker was Aḥmad Sohrab, a one-time secretary of 'Abdu'l-Bahá who was originally sent to the States as a cook for a well-known Bahá'í teacher. He settled there and became an outstanding and charismatic speaker. Sohrab could not accept the appointment of Shoghi Effendi as Guardian of the Faith and began systematically and strenuously to undermine the growing administrative structure of the Faith as developed by Shoghi Effendi. Sohrab was eventually expelled from the Faith and continued to oppose the Cause for many years until he died in April 1958 with every hope frustrated, every plan extinguished and every ambition thwarted. (For summary details of Sohrab's activities see Adib Taherzadeh: *The Covenant of Bahá'u'lláh.*) [90]

In more recent times, 1960, a most distinguished Hand of the Cause, Charles Mason Remey (q.v.) laid claim to be the second

Guardian. This preposterous claim, so clearly contrary to all the Sacred Texts, was made almost 30 months after he was one of the nine Hands chosen to reside in the Holy Land after the passing of Shoghi Effendi, and one of the 27 living Hands of the Cause to sign the proclamation that the Guardian had not left a will and not appointed a successor, nor could he have done as there was no one able to qualify for consideration according to the Will and Testament of 'Abdu'l-Bahá. Remey thereby relinquished his right to be regarded as a Hand of the Cause, and his claim was not only repudiated by every one of his fellow Hands but by all the National Spiritual Assemblies of the world. He was declared a Covenant Breaker on 26 July 1960. What made this case so incomprehensible and painful to those who knew and respected him was his history of long service to the Faith. (For a discussion of the activities associated with Remey see the letters of the Hands of the Cause of God in *The Ministry of the Custodians, 1957-1963;* [156] Adib Taherzadeh: *The Covenant of Bahá'u'lláh.*) [90]

COVENANT, CITY OF THE When on 19 June 1912 'Abdu'l-Bahá spoke in New York of Bahá'u'lláh's *Tablet of the Branch*, He declared that His own station was that of the "Center of the Covenant" and that that city, New York, was the "City of the Covenant." See **'ABDU'L-BAHÁ; COVENANT**.

COVENANT, DAY OF THE (26 November) One of the two Bahá'í Holy Days on which work is not suspended. It commemorates the appointment of 'Abdu'l-Bahá as the Center of the Covenant. It was so designated by 'Abdu'l-Bahá, Who said that this day should be used instead of a celebration of His birthday—which falls on the same day as the Declaration of the Báb.

COVENANT, GREATER AND LESSER In the Bahá'í Writings it is stated that there are two forms of Covenant:

> First is the covenant that every Prophet makes with humanity or, more definitely, with His people that they will accept and follow the coming Manifestation Who will be the reappearance of His reality. The second form of covenant is such as the one Bahá'u'lláh made with His people that they should accept the Master. This is merely to establish and strengthen the succession of the series of Lights that appear after every Manifestation. Under the same category falls the covenant the Master made with the Bahá'ís that they should accept His administration after Him.[86:181]

See **BAHÁ'U'LLÁH, COVENANT OF; COVENANT BREAKERS.**

COY, GENEVIEVE LENORE (1886-1963) An early American believer who visited 'Abdu'l-Bahá in 'Akká in 1920. In 1922, with the approval of 'Abdu'l-Bahá, she moved to Ṭihrán, Írán as director of the Tarbíyat School for girls. On her return to the United States she served for many years on the Spiritual Assembly of New York City. During those years she also served as a senior administrator and chairman of the Program Committee of Green Acre Bahá'í School. In 1958 she pioneered to Salisbury, Rhodesia (now Harare, Zimbabwe). [50:326][91:199][60:325]

CRADLE OF THE ADMINISTRATION—America Shoghi Effendi wrote: "Indeed so preponderating has been the influence of its members in both the initiation and the consolidation of Bahá'í administrative institutions that their country may well deserve to be recognized as the cradle of the Administrative Order which Bahá'u'lláh Himself had envisaged and which the Will of the Center of His Covenant had called into being." [5:329]

CRADLE OF THE FAITH—Írán (Persia) Birthplace of the Bahá'í Revelation.

CUELLAR, YVONNE LIEGEOIS (1896-1983) The first (1940) Bolivian believer of French birth. She served with her husband (Col. Arturo Cuellar Echazu, who in 1946 became a Bahá'í through her efforts) on the first local Spiritual Assembly of La Paz (also the first in Bolivia). She proclaimed the Faith widely by way of radio programs on Radio Illimani and Radio Bolivar of La Paz. In 1947 she arranged for an audience (and presentation of a Bahá'í book) to the Bolivian President, Enrique Hertzog, which in turn led to the official recognition of the Cause by the Bolivian Government later in 1947. She and her husband made substantial contributions towards the translation of Bahá'í literature into the Spanish language. In 1953 she moved to the United States but returned to Bolivia in 1956 at the request of the National Spiritual Assembly of that country. In 1958 she traveled to France to help with the formation of the National Spiritual Assembly there. In 1969 she returned to the United States but continued to visit Bolivia and other countries. [11:619]

CULVER, JULIA (1861-1950) An early American believer who traveled throughout Europe with Miss Martha Root. On settling in Geneva she took on responsibility for the financial upkeep of the "Bahá'í International Bureau" in Geneva (with the assistance of a donation of £6.00 per month from Shoghi Effendi). [84:507]

CYCLE (Era, Ages, Epochs) The Bahá'í Cycle, as designated by Bahá'u'lláh, is a period lasting at least 5,000 centuries. [5:55] The Bahá'í Era comprises the Dispensations of the Báb and Bahá'u'lláh. The Dispensation of Bahá'u'lláh will last at least 1,000 years. [81:32]

> The first seventy-seven years of the preceding century, constituting the Apostolic and Heroic Age of our Faith,

> fell into three distinct epochs, of nine, of thirty-nine and of twenty-nine years' duration, associated respectively with the Bábí Dispensation and the ministries of Bahá'u'lláh and of 'Abdu'l-Bahá.... The last twenty-three years of that same century coincided with the first epoch of the second, the Iron and Formative, Age of the Dispensation of Bahá'u'lláh—the first of a series of epochs which must precede the inception of the last and Golden Age of that Dispensation—a Dispensation which, as the Author of the Faith has Himself categorically asserted, must extend over a period of no less than one thousand years, and which will constitute the first stage in a series of Dispensations, to be established by future Manifestations, all deriving their inspiration from the Author of the Bahá'í Revelation, and destined to last, in their aggregate, no less than five thousand centuries.[3:31-34]

See the section entitled *The Epochs Of The Formative Age* immediately before the Dictionary for a detailed analysis of **EPOCHS**.

CYCLE, PROPHETIC The period of time that began with Adam during which a great number of Manifestations of God appeared Who prophesied the coming of Bahá'u'lláh. This Cycle has been succeeded by the Era of Fulfillment (The Bahá'í Era).

D

DALVÁND, SHÁHÍN (Shírín) (1956-1983) (Martyr) A young Bahá'í who was executed along with other coreligionists in Shíráz, Írán, by the government in June 1983, for refusing to recant her belief in Bahá'u'lláh. [11:600]

DANIELSEN, EDITH MAY MILLER (1909-1984) (Knight of Bahá'u'lláh) An American believer who embraced the Cause in 1949 (to be followed in 1951 by her husband, Theodore.) In 1953 she pioneered under the Ten Year Crusade to the Cook Islands for which service she was designated a Knight of Bahá'u'lláh. She left the Cook Islands half way through the Ten Year Crusade returning first to the United States and then moving on to New Zealand—where she was elected to the first (1968) National Spiritual Assembly of New Zealand. She subsequently returned to the United States for a final time, passing away there in Kirkland, Washington on 29 January 1984. [11:625]

DÁRÚGHIH High Constable. [11:736]

DARVÍSH (Religious) mendicant, dervish, Muslim mystic. See **SÚFÍ**. [11:736]

DAUGHERTY, ORPHA MAUD (1912-1985) An American believer who embraced the Cause in 1944 while living in Hawaii. In 1945 she returned to Seattle, Washington from where she traveled widely throughout the United States in the promotion of the Cause. In 1960 she settled in the Philippines on the island of Cebu, where she found employment as a radio announcer. She was elected to the first National Spiritual Assembly of the Philippines in 1964. In 1965 she was appointed an Auxiliary Board member for Eastern Asia, moved to Thailand and traveled widely throughout Laos visiting hill tribes and by canoe on rivers in Sarawak and Brunei. She lived for a while in Ceylon and visited Vietnam and Cambodia. In 1967 she pioneered to Taiwan where she remained until 1969 when she was requested to move to Macau. In 1970 she returned to the Philippines and in 1974 to Hiroshima, Japan. In 1982 she moved to Korea where in October 1984 she "...climbed a mountain to bring the message of Bahá'u'lláh to Chong Hak Dong—the People of the Pure White Crane—a community of people who, about half a century ago, isolated themselves on a Korean mountaintop to await word of a great prophet." Many of these people embraced the Cause. [11:666]

DAWE, ETHEL (1902-1954) An early Australian believer who came to the Faith through her cousin Maysie Almond. In 1937 she was appointed temporary collaborator for Australia to the League of Nations and visited Geneva in that capacity. She met Shoghi Effendi in 1938, who entrusted her to carry a lock of Bahá'u'lláh's hair as a gift to the Australian believers. [47:940]

DAWLIH State, government. [11:736📖]

DAWN-BREAKERS The martyrs and heroes of the early days of the Faith—followers of the Báb, so named because of their association with the beginnings of the new age. Shoghi Effendi wrote of them as follows:

> We behold, as we survey the episodes of this first act of a sublime drama, the figure of its Master Hero, the Báb, arise meteor-like above the horizon of Shíráz, traverse the somber sky of Persia from south to north, decline with tragic swiftness, and perish in a blaze of glory. We see His satellites, a galaxy of God-intoxicated heroes, mount above that same horizon, irradiate that same incandescent light, burn themselves out with that self-same swiftness, and impart in their turn an added impetus to the steadily gathering momentum of God's nascent Faith.[5:3]

Their inspiring story is told in the book, *The Dawn-Breakers* [10] by Nabíl-i-'Aẓam (translated from Persian into English by Shoghi Effendi). This book also describes the rôle of Bahá'u'lláh as a Bábí up to His banishment to Baghdád.

DAYYÁN Literally conqueror, ruler; Judge (an epithet of the Godhead). [11:736]

de FORGE, WILLIAM (1899-1963) An American believer who traveled widely as a teacher of the Faith. In 1954 he was among the first contingent of Auxiliary Board members appointed by the Hands of the Cause of God. This appointment led him to travel throughout the United States, Canada, Alaska and most of the Latin American republics. He also traveled widely through Europe, where he died in 1963. [50:330]

de MATAMOROS, MARCIA STEWARD (1904-1966) (Knight of Bahá'u'lláh) An American believer who embraced the Faith in 1938, she pioneered to Santiago, Chile during the first Seven Year Plan. She later moved to Honduras where she entered into correspondence over a number of years with Shoghi Effendi. In 1954 she pioneered to the Marshall Islands—for which service she was designated a Knight of Bahá'u'lláh. Her final pioneer move was to San Salvador, El Salvador. [50:304]

DEAN, SIDNEY I. (1920-1971) An American believer who pioneered to Hong Kong, India (where he was principal of the New Era Bahá'í School in Panchgani), Taiwan, Hawaii, Kenya and Zambia. [51:508]

DEATH, LIFE AFTER According to Bahá'í Writings this earthly life is the second stage of the development of the human soul—the first being from conception to birth. It is during this experience of the soul in the material body that it develops through the exercise of its free will, those spiritual qualities that will equip it for its "real" life in the world of the spirit to which it evolves after physical death. Whereas the physical body decomposes, the soul has eternal life and in the world of the spirit continues to develop in its journey towards God. The true nature of this afterlife cannot be fully understood but glimpses of what this may be like are given by Bahá'u'lláh and 'Abdu'l-Bahá. For example, Bahá'u'lláh in the Hidden Words writes: "I have made death a messenger of joy to thee. Wherefore dost thou grieve? I made the light to shed on thee its splendor. Why dost thou veil thyself therefrom?" [92:32] Again, in another place, He writes: "The world beyond is as different from this world as this world is different from that of the child while still in the womb of its mother. When the soul attaineth the Presence of God, it will assume the form that best befitteth its immortality and is worthy of its celestial habitation." [93:157]

DECLARATION A statement of belief, made verbally or in writing or by signature on a suitably worded card or other document in which the new declarant accepts the Stations of the Báb,

Bahá'u'lláh and 'Abdu'l-Bahá and all that They have revealed. The Universal House of Justice explained: "The declarants need not know all the proofs, history, laws and principles of the Faith, but in the process of declaring themselves they must in addition to catching the spark of faith, become basically informed about the Central Figures of the Faith, as well as the existence of laws they must follow and an administration they must obey." [86:73]

DEEDS, ACTIONS Bahá'u'lláh stated: "The triumph of this Cause hath depended, and will continue to depend, upon the appearance of holy souls, upon the showing forth of goodly deeds, and the revelation of words of consummate wisdom." [39:83] And again, "Verily I say unto thee: Of all men the most negligent is he that disputeth idly and seeketh to advance himself over his brother. Say, O brethren! Let deeds, not words, be your adorning." [92:5]

DEEPENING Shoghi Effendi wrote through his secretary: "To deepen in the Cause means to read the writings of Bahá'u'lláh and the Master so thoroughly as to be able to give it to others in its pure form." [8:88-9] And, "In their efforts to achieve this purpose they must study for themselves, conscientiously and painstakingly, the literature of their Faith, delve into its teachings, assimilate its laws and principles, ponder its admonitions, tenets and purposes, commit to memory certain of its exhortations and prayers, master the essentials of its administration, and keep abreast of its current affairs and latest developments." [39:41]

DEPUTIZATION "Center your energies" are Bahá'u'lláh's words, "in the propagation of the Faith of God. Whoso is worthy of so high a calling, let him arise and promote it. Whoso is unable, it is his duty to appoint him who will, in his stead, proclaim this Revelation." [39:66f] These words led to the establishment of the principle of deputatization that is the provision of financial support for a pioneer or teacher by another person.

DETACHMENT Submission to the will of God, seeking His good pleasure, ridding oneself of pride in one's knowledge, position, accomplishments all combine in the achievement of true detachment: "Should a man," Bahá'u'lláh Himself reassures us,

> wish to adorn himself with the ornaments of the earth, to wear its apparels, or partake of the benefits it can bestow, no harm can befall him, if he alloweth nothing whatever to intervene between him and God, for God hath ordained every good thing, whether created in the heavens or in the earth, for such of His servants as truly believe in Him. Eat ye, O people, of the good things which God hath allowed you, and deprive not yourselves from His wondrous bounties. Render thanks and praise unto Him, and be of them that are truly thankful." [93:276]

And, in another place, "The essence of detachment is for man to turn his face towards the courts of the Lord, to enter His Presence, behold His Countenance, and stand as witness before Him." [77:155]

DEVELOPMENT, SOCIAL AND ECONOMIC Many of the teachings of the Bahá'í Faith are of immediate importance to development issues, but these demand that spiritual development should go hand-in-hand with material development. Of particular significance are the social teachings relating to universal education, the equality of men and women, the requirement for all government officials to observe a rectitude of conduct, the use of techniques of consultation (q.v.) in the solution of problems and in making decisions, the establishment of economic justice, the abolition of the extremes of poverty and wealth, the need for unity and the recognition of the oneness of mankind. The development of the Bahá'í Administrative Order throughout the globe provides a network of local and national Bahá'í administrative bodies that reached every country of the world by the 1990s and enables them to propagate these principles on a global scale.

In 1983 the Universal House of Justice addressed the "Bahá'ís of the World" stating that: "the process of this development should be incorporated into its regular pursuits." In this same letter the establishment of an Office of Social and Economic Development was announced to "assist [it] to promote and coordinate the activities of the friends throughout the world in this new field." Development projects specifically initiated by the Bahá'ís were encouraged to start at the grass-roots level and were to receive their driving force from those sources rather than from top-imposed programs and plans. Since that time the number of projects has blossomed into thousands; specifically in the fields of education, agriculture, forestry, medical care and the stimulation of the arts, crafts, traditional music and dancing of indigenous peoples. Particularly impressive have been the contributions throughout the world in pursuing the objectives of "Agenda 21" of the Earth Summit 1992, those of the Copenhagen Summit on Social Development and the Global Platform for Action of the Fourth International Conference on Women, Beijing, 1995.

A publication by the Bahá'í International Community, *The Prosperity of Humankind* [94] was prepared in time for use at the 1995 Summit in Copenhagen on Social Development. Some 250 Bahá'ís from over 40 countries took part in the activities associated with the Copenhagen Summit. Four thousand copies of this publication (in English, Danish, French and Spanish) were distributed, and along with 15,000 copies of a companion statement, *World Citizenship* [95] in nine languages were among some 37,000 copies or more of Bahá'í materials. Bahá'ís have been very active in all the preparatory committees of all the United Nations World Summit meetings, particularly with those that involved development in its many aspects.

DHABÍḤ Literally slain, sacrificed, offered up. [11:736]

DHIKR Mention, remembering; remembrance of God; praise and thanksgiving; recital of the names of God, religious exercise or ceremony; The Qur'án. The Word of God. Plural: Adhkár; see **MASHRIQU'L-ADHKÁR.** [11:736]

DISCIPLES OF 'ABDU'L-BAHÁ Nineteen outstanding Bahá'ís from the West given this title by the Guardian. They were also known by him as "Heralds of the Covenant." See appended list of the **DISCIPLES.**

DISPENSATION Frequently used in Bahá'í writings in relation to the period of time during which the laws and teachings of a Manifestation of God endure. For example, the Dispensation of the Báb began with His Declaration on 23 May 1844 and ended with the Declaration of Bahá'u'lláh at Riḍván 1863. According to Bahá'u'lláh His Dispensation will last at least 1,000 years.

DIVE, DULCIE BURNS (-1962) (Knight of Bahá'u'lláh) An early New Zealand believer who pioneered to the Cook Islands, for which she was designated a Knight of Bahá'u'lláh. She was a member for some years of the National Spiritual Assembly of Australia and New Zealand and then the regional Spiritual Assembly of the South Pacific. [47:925]

DIVORCE Is strongly condemned in Bahá'í writings but is allowed in cases of extreme antipathy and aversion on the part of either spouse following a year of waiting (or "year of patience") during which time every effort should be made by the couple (with spiritual and professional counseling) to effect a reconciliation.

DODGE, ARTHUR PILLSBURY (1849-1915) (Disciple of 'Abdu'l-Bahá) Of English ancestry (1629) Arthur numbered Major Richard Dodge of Bunker Hill fame and General Grenville M. Dodge of the Union Pacific Railroad among his forbears. During the American Civil War he served as a drummer boy under his father, Colonel Simon Dodge. Born on 28 May 1849 he often heard his parents and grandparents speak about the Millennium, and he himself became a passionate searcher after truth. After working as a journalist he studied law and gained admission to the bars of New Hampshire and Massachusetts. With a friend he founded three illustrated magazines and had plans for a fourth "to educate the public unawares." This required capital, which he did not possess, so he made contact with George M. Pullman, the inventor and manufacturer of Pullman Palace Cars. While not providing him with the capital necessary, Pullman did show him an abandoned invention of a steam-driven motor car and suggested that Arthur tried to develop it. Having had no engineering experience but being possessed of an inquiring mind, he re-engineered the car in ways that made it commercially viable. Early in 1896, despite a cash offer of some ten million dollars for a controlling interest in his Kinetic Power Company, he refused and tried to set up his business in Boston. This failed, and he returned to Chicago where almost immediately he came in touch the Bahá'í teacher, Dr. Ibráhím Khayru'lláh. In early 1898 he moved to New York and invited Khayru'lláh to join him. In the company of such celebrated future believers as the Brittinghams, the MacNutts, Lillian Kappes and Hooper Harris, many meetings were held in the Dodges' home. The Dodges went to the Holy Land in August 1900 and called in London on the way home, where Arthur gave the Bahá'í Message to Canon Wilberforce of Westminster Abbey (who was later to arrange for 'Abdu'l-Bahá to speak in London in St. John's Smith Square). He also had talks with Professor E. Dennison Ross and Professor E. G. Browne (q.v.) who had met Bahá'u'lláh in 1890. Browne translated some precious letters that he (Arthur) had received from 'Abdu'l-Bahá. On returning to New York the Dodges once again threw themselves into teaching the Bahá'í Faith and organized many very large public meetings.

In 1901 he wrote a short book on the "cause and purpose of our being on earth"—*The Truth of It.* He continued to develop his motor car and eventually bought a factory and a small farm on the Delaware River. This farm became the Dodges' summer home, but in 1907, the electrification of street and elevated railroads, combined with the Wall Street panic, resulted in the loss of his large fortune. Since he had become so absorbed in spreading the Faith this no longer meant much to him. On the 14 March 1915, 14 believers signed a declaration constituting themselves the founder members of the first Bahá'í Assembly of Hempstead, Nassau, State of New York, and nine of the signatories had the last name of Dodge. Arthur received his last letter from the Holy Land dated 12 August 1915; and he read it out with difficulty (as he had a tube in his throat) to a meeting in his home on 10 October, typed out a notice of a meeting that he hoped to hold on the following Sunday afternoon. Soon after 7 A.M. on the next morning, he passed away. After his death Shoghi Effendi referred to him as one of "that immortal galaxy now gathered in the glory of Bahá'u'lláh" who "will for ever remain associated with the rise and establishment of His Faith in the American continent, and will continue to shed on its annals a lustre that time can never dim."[4:81]

DOKTOROGLU, SAMI (1901-1979) An early (c.1925) Turkish believer. He was a member of the first (1952) local Spiritual Assembly of Istanbul; he served also as an Auxiliary Board member and was the trustee of the Ḥuqúqu'lláh in Turkey. In Turkish history books he is noted as the founder of travel agencies in Turkey. [2:684]

DOWRY The payment of a dowry by the groom to the bride is stipulated by Bahá'u'lláh in His Book of Laws (the Kitáb-i-Aqdas) [81] as a requirement for Bahá'í marriage. At the time of writing, this law has not yet been put into general effect.

DREAMS While the majority of dreams are of no significance, Bahá'u'lláh did address the phenomena. He wrote that "it is the most mysterious of the signs of God amongst men." [77:187-8] Shoghi Effendi elaborated as follows:

> That truth is often imported through dreams no one who is familiar with history, especially religious history, can doubt. At the same time dreams and visions are always colored and influenced more or less by the mind of the dreamer and we must beware of attaching too much importance to them. The purer and more free from prejudice and desire our hearts and minds become, the more likely is it that our dreams will convey reliable truth, but if we have strong prejudices, personal likings and aversions, bad feelings or evil motives, these will warp and distort any inspirational impression that comes to us.... In many cases dreams have been the means of bringing people to the truth or of confirming them in the Faith. We must strive to become pure in heart and "free from all save God." Then our dreams as well as our waking thoughts will become pure and true. We should test impressions we get through dreams, visions or inspirations, by comparing them with the revealed Word and seeing whether they are in full harmony therewith.[86:513-14]

DREYFUS-BARNEY, HIPPOLYTE (-1928) (Disciple of 'Abdu'l-Bahá) He was introduced to the Bahá'í Faith by May Ellis Bolles, later May Maxwell (q.v.) in 1901 and thereby became the first French Bahá'í. He married another Bahá'í introduced to the Faith by May—an American living in Paris, Laura Clifford Barney (q.v.) and adopted the surname "Dreyfus-Barney." He was a scholar of some note and learned Persian and Arabic to enable him to translate the Writings of Bahá'u'lláh and 'Abdu'l-Bahá. He visited the Holy Land on several occasions and kept closely in touch with 'Abdu'l-Bahá as well as being in attendance during His visits to Europe. He was the first European Bahá'í to visit Írán and undertook extensive journeys for the Faith in Canada, the United States and North Africa and as far east as India, Burma, Indo-China and Japan. In his field of scholarship he made several significant contributions to Bahá'í literature and translated much of the Bahá'í Writings into French. He gave valuable assistance to Shoghi Effendi in the efforts to obtain justice for the Bahá'ís in Iráq and Egypt in the early years of the Guardianship. When he passed away after a slow and painful illness in December 1928, Shoghi Effendi wrote a lengthy "Appreciation" which included "...His gifts of unfailing sympathy and penetrating insight, his wide knowledge and mature experience, all of which he utilized for the glory and propagation of the Message of Bahá'u'lláh, will be gratefully remembered by future generations who, as the days go by, will better estimate the abiding value of the responsibilities he shouldered for the introduction and consolidation of the Bahá'í Faith in the Western world.... To me ... he was a sustaining and comforting companion, a most valued counsellor, an intimate and trusted friend." [Bahá'í Year Book, 1930 #275:210][59:155ff]

DREYFUS-BARNEY, LAURA CLIFFORD (1879-1974) Born in 1879 into a family of artists and scholars, daughter of Alice Barney, gifted poetess, painter, dramatist, musician, architect and craftswoman whose paintings are to be found in most of the important museums of the United States and who gave to the city of Washington, the "Neighborhood-House." Laura was living in Paris when she became acquainted with May Ellis Bolles (see **MAXWELL, MAY**). Around 1900 she embraced the Cause and subsequently visited 'Abdu'l-Bahá on many occasions. It was soon after this that she introduced her mother to the Faith, who then joined her on a pilgrimage to the Holy Land in 1905. She had a keen intelligence, logical mind and investigating nature and devoted her whole life from her adolescence to improving human relations, bringing together peoples of different races, classes and nations. She was a brilliant speaker and made several trips around the world lecturing on the necessity of a united world. Those who knew her over a period of many decades testified that her undaunted zeal for the objective of the brotherhood of man remained alive and glowing to the very last day of her life on earth.

As one of the early pilgrims from the West who visited 'Abdu'l-Bahá, she was privileged to spend long periods of time with Him and His immediate family. It was during the years 1904-1906 that she was permitted to put certain questions to 'Abdu'l-Bahá. On one occasion He said to her, "I have given you my tired moments." Shoghi Effendi referred to this monumental work on many occasions, such as when mentioning Laura Barney, "whose imperishable service was to collect and transmit to posterity in the form of a book, *Some Answered Questions*, 'Abdu'l-Bahá's priceless explanations, covering a wide variety of subjects, given to her in the course of an extended pilgrimage to the Holy Land..." [5:260] and, "It was at this juncture that that celebrated compilation of His table talks, published under the title *Some Answered Questions*, was made, talks given during the brief time He was able to spare, in the course of which certain fundamental aspects of His Father's Faith were elucidated, traditional and rational proofs of its validity adduced, and a great variety of subjects regarding the Christian Dispensation, the Prophets of God, Biblical prophecies, the origin and condition of man and other kindred themes authoritatively explained..." [5:260,268] This work was first published in London in 1908. It was such an important book that the distinguished French scholar, the first French Bahá'í, Hippolyte Dreyfus, offered to translate it into French. It was during their collaboration on this translation that they decided to marry (1911) and adopted the name "Dreyfus-Barney." They undertook many other joint activities in the service of the Faith, which included visits to the prison fortress of Máh-Kú and other parts of Persia, 'Ishqábád, Russian Turkistán, Indo-China and other parts of Eastern Asia.

'Abdu'l-Bahá referred to her on numerous occasions, and she received many presents from the ladies of the household in the Holy Land, which were eventually entrusted to Ugo Giachery to deliver to the Universal House of Justice. Another outstanding service she rendered was the purchasing of the land and the construction of a suitable home for 'Abdu'l-Bahá and His family (No. 7 Haparsim Street, Haifa; subsequently the home of Shoghi Effendi.)

It is not possible in a work of this nature to list all Laura's services in America, Europe and other parts of the world. During WW I she served in Paris in the American Ambulance Corps and after the War gave her full support to the League of Nations, representing in that body the International Council of Women. She was the only woman named by the League Council to sit on the sub-committee of experts on education—a post she held for many years. On 23 July 1925 she was appointed *Chevalier de la Légion d'Honneur* and subsequently served on many international committees. In the 1930s she served on numerous international bodies particularly those connected with education and educational cinematography. Under the auspices of the International Institute of Educational Cinematography of the League of Nations she convened the first congress for women, held in Rome in 1934, specializing in the dissemination of educational material for peace by means of motion pictures. At this Congress she was elected one of the six vice-presidents and in 1937 was elected President of the Peace and Arbitration Commission of the International Council of

Women. After the death of her husband in December 1928, her efforts for the Faith actually intensified. In 1941 she was a member of the American delegation to the Conference on Cultural Cooperation, Havana, Cuba. During WW II she was delegate of the French National Committee of Women to the Commission on Racial Affairs and on the formation of the United Nations she became an officer of the Commission of the Council of Women for the Control and Reduction of Armaments, located in Geneva. In the years that followed she was very active in the United Nations Economic and Social Council in Geneva. Towards the end of her life she lived in Paris; she suffered much from rheumatism, but her mind was as alert as ever.

She died on 18 August 1974 within five years of the centenary of her birth. She is buried in the Passy Cemetery of Paris. The Universal House of Justice cabled this tribute: "Ascension distinguished maidservant Laura Dreyfus-Barney further depletes small band promoters Faith Heroic Age. Member first historic group Paris taught by May Maxwell she achieved immortal fame through compilation *Some Answered Questions* unique entire field religious history. Offering ardent prayers Sacred Threshold progress her soul Abhá Kingdom. Urge all communities France hold memorial gatherings gratitude outstanding achievement." [52:535][59:80ff]

DRUGS Alcohol, habit-forming drugs and all intoxicants are forbidden in the Bahá'í Faith except where prescribed for medical treatment by a competent physician. 'Abdu'l-Bahá wrote particularly strongly against alcohol, hashish and opium. [65:149]

DUFFIELD, ELLA WARDEN (1873-1962) (Knight of Bahá'u'lláh) An American believer who pioneered to Madeira in 1953 (for which she was designated a Knight of Bahá'u'lláh) and then at the request of the European Teaching Committee of the United States she moved to France. [47:922]

DUNNING, CHARLES WILLIAM (1885-1967) (Knight of Bahá'u'lláh) An English (Yorkshire) Bahá'í who embraced the Faith at the age of 63, he pioneered first to Belfast (1948), then to Sheffield and finally to the Orkney Islands (1953) for which latter service he was designated a Knight of Bahá'u'lláh. Ill health eventually forced him to move to Cardiff. He met Shoghi Effendi in Haifa in January 1957. [50:305][60:333]

E

EBO, ANTÓNIO FRANCISCO (-1977) The first (1956) Angolan believer of the KiMbundu tribe, he served as a member of the first (1956) local Spiritual Assembly of Luanda and in 1957 as a member of the first local Spiritual Assembly of Malange. In the 1940-1950s he was well known for his radio programs on the Bahá'í Faith, which were broadcast in Esperanto. [53:432]

ECHTNER, VUK (1905-1994) Born in Southern Bohemia, he was one of the first (c.1944) believers in Czechoslovakia. During the late 1950s he was incarcerated for two years for his beliefs. [11:320]

ECONOMIC PROBLEMS, SPIRITUAL SOLUTION TO One of the social teachings of the Bahá'í Faith is the abolition of the extremes of poverty and of wealth, and this will be achieved by both taxation and by voluntary giving (which in turn depends upon the spiritual transformation of the people). Both are found in the Bahá'í community. No funds for Bahá'í purposes are accepted from non-Bahá'ís but all contributions to the Bahá'í funds (q.v.) are voluntary and are left to the conscience of the believer. Even the Bahá'í tax of Ḥuqúqu'lláh is only paid after the believer has individually assessed his/her standard of living so here also the principle of sacrifice is given expression. Shoghi Effendi wrote:

> There are practically no technical teachings on economics in the Cause, such as banking, the price system, and others. The Cause is not an economic system, nor can its Founders be considered as having been technical economists. The contribution of the Faith to this subject is essentially indirect, as it consists in the application of spiritual principles to our present-day economic system. Bahá'u'lláh has given us a few basic principles which should guide future Bahá'í economists in establishing such institutions which will adjust the economic relationships of the world. [86:550]

EDUCATION, NATURE OF Bahá'u'lláh taught that each individual soul is absolutely unique and is endowed with capacities and talents not possessed by others. The purpose of education is to discover and develop these individual gifts so that each person may achieve fulfillment by doing those things for which he/she was created. The position of the teacher and educator therefore ranks very highly in Bahá'í understanding. Bahá'u'lláh wrote: "Regard man as a mine rich in gems of inestimable value. Education can, alone, cause it to reveal its treasures, and enable mankind to benefit therefrom." [93:260] And, "The learned of the day must direct the people to acquire those branches of knowledge which are of use, that both the learned themselves and the generality of mankind may derive benefits therefrom. Such academic pursuits as begin and end in words alone have never been and will never be of any worth." [77:169]

EDUCATION, UNIVERSAL As ignorance and lack of education erect barriers among the human race, education should be universal. Every father has the obligation to have his children educated; if he is unable to do this the representatives of the people (government; spiritual assemblies) should provide for this vital need of every child. Males and females should follow a like curriculum and have the same opportunities. Should resources be limited, girls should be given priority as the education of women, as the first trainers of the next generation, is more important than that of men. Not only should all children have the opportunity for education but the basis of the teaching should be that mankind is one, and all are citizens of one world.

EDWARDS, HERMIONE VERA KEENS-DOUGLAS (1908-1981) A Grenadian who embraced the Cause in 1958 in Monrovia, she served on the first local Spiritual Assembly of Monrovia. In 1964 she was appointed an Auxiliary Board member. Between 1964 and 1979 she wrote monthly letters to the believers in Gambia, Senegal, Sierra Leon, Liberia, Ivory Coast, Upper Volta, Ghana, Nigeria and Mali. [2:778]

EGGLESTON, HELEN LATIMER (Whitney) (1892-1979) An early (1909) American believer who along with her husband (Lou) started the Louhelen Bahá'í School. In 1948 they deeded the nine-acre property and buildings to the National Spiritual Assembly. Both Helen and Lou were tireless administrators of the school from its inception; during the years of their service many thousands of people passed through it, and all were made to feel special by the Egglestons. [2:675]

EGGLESTONE, LOU W. (1872-1953) An early (1930) American believer who along with his wife (Helen) in 1931 started the Louhelen Bahá'í School near Davison, Michigan.[48:712][60:335]

EGO Through his secretary Shoghi Effendi wrote:

> Self has really two meanings, or is used in two senses, in the Bahá'í writings; one is self, the identity of the individual created by God. This is the self mentioned in such passages as "he hath known God who hath known himself" etc. The other self is the ego, the dark, animalistic heritage each one of us has, the lower nature that can develop into a monster of selfishness, brutality, lust and so on. It is this self we must struggle against, or this side of our natures, in order to strengthen and free the spirit within us and help it to attain perfection. Self-sacrifice

means to subordinate this lower nature and its desires to the more Godly and noble side of ourselves. Ultimately, in its highest sense, self-sacrifice means to give our will and your all to God to do with as He pleases. Then He purifies and glorifies our true self until it becomes a shining and wonderful reality.... The ego is the animal in us, the heritage of the flesh which is full of selfish desires. By obeying the laws of God, seeking to live the life laid down in our teachings, and prayer and struggle, we can subdue our egos. We call people "Saints" who have achieved the highest degree of mastery over their ego.... Life is a constant struggle, not only against forces around us, but above all against our own "ego." We can never afford to rest on our oars, for if we do, we soon see ourselves carried down stream again.... Sometimes ... people fail because of a test they just do not meet, and often our severest tests come from each other. Certainly the believers should try to avert such things, and if they happen, remedy them through love.... The only people who are truly free of the "dross of self" are the Prophets, for to be free of one's ego is a hallmark of perfection. We humans are never going to become perfect, for perfection belongs to a realm we are not destined to enter. However, we must constantly mount higher, seek to be more perfect. [86:113f]

ELECTIONS Leadership in the Bahá'í community lies in the spiritual assemblies (local and national) and the Universal House of Justice. All elections are carried out by secret ballot without nominations, canvassing or electioneering and in an atmosphere of prayer. Electors are urged to keep before them the guidance given by Shoghi Effendi: "Hence it is incumbent upon the chosen delegates to consider without the least trace of passion and prejudice, and irrespective of any material consideration, the names of only those who can best combine the necessary qualities of unquestioned loyalty, of selfless devotion, of a well-trained mind, of recognized ability and mature experience." [96:88] And, "I do not feel it to be in keeping with the spirit of the Cause to impose any limitations upon the freedom of the believers to choose those of any race, nationality or temperament, who best combine the essential qualifications for membership of administrative institutions. They should disregard personalities and concentrate their attention on the qualities and requirements of office, without prejudice, passion or partially. The Assembly should be representative of the choicest and most varied and capable elements in every Bahá'í community." [86:9-10]

The results of Bahá'í elections are based on a plurality vote, which is that the nine members with the highest number of votes constitute the elected body. Tied votes are decided between those who have tied by further secret balloting. Elections for officers of the elected bodies are by a majority vote of the elected or appointed members.

ELSTON, MARY ASHLEY (1898-1974) An (c.1950) American believer pioneered to East Africa in 1952. Throughout her time there she lived in Uganda and Tanzania, helping to form local Spiritual Assemblies in each country. She was elected to the first National Spiritual Assembly of Tanzania and served for a number of years as its Secretary. [52:530]

ENROLLMENT Each National Spiritual Assembly determines the methods to be used in the area of its jurisdiction for the registering of its declared believers. See **DECLARATION**.

EPISTLE A letter but often used in Bahá'í writings for specific letters from Bahá'u'lláh to particular individuals. For example, *Epistle to the Son of the Wolf,* [70] the last large volume revealed by Bahá'u'lláh in Bahjí in 1891; it contains many quotations from His previous Writings and was translated into English by Shoghi Effendi. For a detailed discussion of the epistolary style of writing see Ann Boyles's essay *The Epistolary Style of Shoghi Effendi.* [97:9]

EQUALITY OF MEN AND WOMEN Bahá'u'lláh wrote: "the Pen of the Most High hath lifted distinctions from between His servants and handmaidens, and, through His consummate favors and all-encompassing mercy, hath conferred upon all a station and rank of the same plane." [98:357]

'Abdu'l-Bahá stated: "There is no doubt that when women obtain equality of rights, war will entirely cease among mankind." [26:175] and

> In reality, God has created all mankind, and in the estimation of God there is no distinction as to male and female. The one whose heart is pure is acceptable in His sight, be that one man or woman.... Furthermore, the education of woman is more necessary and important than that of man, for woman is the trainer of the child from its infancy. If she be defective and imperfect herself, the child will necessarily be deficient; therefore, imperfection of woman implies a condition of imperfection in all mankind, for it is the mother who rears, nurtures and guides the growth of the child.... Again, it is well established in history that where woman has not participated in human affairs the outcomes have never attained a state of completion and perfection. On the other hand, every influential undertaking of the human world

wherein woman has been a participant has attained importance.... The world of humanity consists of two parts: male and female. Each is the complement of the other. Therefore, if one is defective, the other will necessarily be incomplete, and perfection cannot be attained. There is a right hand and a left hand in the human body, functionally equal in service and administration. If either proves defective, the defect will naturally extend to the other by involving the completeness of the whole; for accomplishment is not normal unless both are perfect. If we say one hand is deficient, we prove the inability and incapacity of the other; for single-handed there is no full accomplishment. Just as physical accomplishment is complete with two hands, so man and woman, the two parts of the social body, must be perfect. It is not natural that either should remain undeveloped; and until both are perfected, the happiness of the human world will not be realized. [26:133-34]

ERICKSON, LOUISE M. (-1960) An early Swedish believer who learned of the Faith while in the United States (where she met 'Abdu'l-Bahá in 1912 in New York). On her return to Sweden she arranged (in cooperation with Mrs. Rudd-Palmgren) for the translation into Swedish of *Bahá'u'lláh and the New Era.* She also "gave the Message" to the Swedish Head of State, Carl Lindhagen. On hearing what she had to say he said, "Louise, the Crown Prince must know about this." He promptly telephoned the Royal Palace and arranged an interview, which lasted two hours with the Crown Prince. [47:913]

ESSLEMONT, JOHN EBENEZER (1874-1925) (Hand of the Cause of God, Disciple of 'Abdu'l-Bahá) The first Western Bahá'í to be appointed a Hand of the Cause of God. He was a medical practitioner from Scotland who ran a clinic in Bournemouth, England. He was introduced to the Bahá'í Faith in 1914. By that time he was well recognized in the medical field and had practiced in Australia and South Africa. As a student he had contracted tuberculosis, and he devoted his time to applying new techniques to its treatment and eventually developed a scheme for its total eradication. One of his principal concerns was the need for a state medical service, and with a number of his associates he set up the State Medical Service Association in 1912, which produced the Dawson Report, which in turn became the foundation of the British National Health Service.

Esslemont was a proficient linguist, fluent in French, Spanish and German, a keen advocate of Esperanto and, after accepting the Bahá'í Faith, a student of Arabic and Persian. His name is known world-wide through his seminal work, *Bahá'u'lláh and the*

New Era, [99] the first nine chapters of which were written during WW I and submitted to 'Abdu'l-Bahá for His comments. 'Abdu'l-Bahá encouraged him to complete the book and bring it to Him in the Holy Land. He first met 'Abdu'l-Bahá on 6 November 1919 but due to a serious deterioration in his health was unable to attend many of 'Abdu'l-Bahá's talks. He returned to England at end of January 1920 and by August had completed his book. It was first published by George Allen and Unwin in September 1923 and has since become a basic textbook on the Faith and has been printed in many languages. By that time Esslemont had returned to Aberdeen and then again to Bournemouth as his health was again deteriorating.

In 1924 he was invited by Shoghi Effendi to visit Haifa again and he arrived there in November and became fully involved in assisting the Guardian in his work in translating the Writings of Bahá'u'lláh. He also served as his English-language secretary.

On the 22 November 1925, he passed away in Haifa at the early age of 51. Shoghi Effendi cabled the British National Spiritual Assembly: "Beloved Esslemont passed away. Communicate friends and family distressing news. Urge believers dedicate special day for universal prayer and remembrance." [9:40]

On 30 November 1925 Shoghi Effendi wrote a glowing tribute to the Bahá'í world, which included the following passages:

> His close association with my work in Haifa, in which I had placed the fondest hopes, was suddenly cut short. His book, however—an abiding monument to his pure intention—will, alone, inspire generations yet unborn to tread the path of truth and service as steadfastly and as unostentatiously as was trodden by its beloved author. The Cause he loved so well, he served even unto his last day with exemplary faith and unstinted devotion. His tenacity of faith, his high integrity, his self-effacement, his industry and painstaking labors were traits of a character the noble qualities of which will live, and live forever after him. To me personally he was the warmest of friends, a trusted counsellor, an indefatigable collaborator, a lovable companion ... by the beauty of his character, by his knowledge of the Cause, by the conspicuous achievements of his book he has immortalized his name, and by sheer merit deserved to rank as one of the Hands of the Cause of God."[96:97][40:459][83:171][60:337]

ESTRADA, SALOMÓN PACORA ("Blue Mountain") (1889-1969) One of the first (1938) of Inca descent to embrace the Cause, he played an important rôle in spreading the teachings throughout Mexico and South America. [52:568][51:466]

ESTY, FRANCES (1878-1963) An early American believer who in 1930 arranged for the painting of a portrait of 'Abdu'l-Bahá by the Polish-American artist, Sigismond Ivanowski. [37:76][50:333]

EVIL is not seen in Bahá'í teachings as a positive force in its own right but, rather, as the absence of good (in the same way that darkness is the absence of light). 'Abdu'l-Bahá said:

> In creation there is no evil; all is good. Certain qualities and natures innate in some men and apparently blameworthy are not so in reality. For example, from the beginning of his life you can see in a nursing child the signs of greed, of anger and of temper. Then, it may be said, good and evil are innate in the reality of man, and this is contrary to the pure goodness of nature and creation. The answer to this is that greed, which is to ask for something more, is a praiseworthy quality provided that it is used suitably. So if a man is greedy to acquire science and knowledge, or to become compassionate, generous and just, it is most praiseworthy. If he exercises his anger and wrath against the bloodthirsty tyrants who are like ferocious beasts, it is very praiseworthy; but if he does not use these qualities in a right way, they are blameworthy.... Then it is evident that in creation and nature evil does not exist at all; but when the natural qualities of man are used in an unlawful way, they are blameworthy.[56:215]

And

> the intellectual realities, such as all the qualities and admirable perfections of man, are purely good, and exist. Evil is simply their non-existence. So ignorance is the want of knowledge; error is the want of guidance; forgetfulness is the want of memory; stupidity is the want of good sense. All these things have no real existence. [56:263]

Shoghi Effendi had this to say on the subject:

> We know absence of light is darkness, but no one would assert darkness was not a fact. It exists even though it is only the absence of something else. So evil exists too, and we cannot close our eyes to it, even though it is a negative existence. We must seek to supplant it by good, and if we see an evil person is not influenceable by us, then we should shun his company for it is unhealthy. [86:403]

EVOLUTION 'Abdu'l-Bahá explained that change is a basic law of the universe:

> Know that nothing which exists remains in a state of repose—that is to say, all things are in motion. Everything is either growing or declining; all things are either coming from non-existence into being, or going from existence into non-existence. So this flower, this hyacinth, during a certain period of time was coming from the world of non-existence into being, and now it is going from being into non-existence. This state of motion is said to be essential—that is, natural; it cannot be separated from beings because it is their essential requirement, as it is the essential requirement of fire to burn.... Thus it is established that this movement is necessary to existence, which is either growing or declining. Now, as the spirit continues to exist after death, it necessarily progresses or declines; and in the other world to cease to progress the same as to decline; but it never leaves its own condition, in which it continues to develop. [56:233]

'Abdu'l-Bahá also said that man, whatever his shape or form, has always been a distinct species:

> as man in the womb of the mother passes from form to form, from shape to shape, changes and develops, and is still the human species from the beginning of the embryonic period—in the same way man, from the beginning of his existence in the matrix of the world, is also a distinct species—that is, man—and has gradually evolved from one form to another. Therefore, this change of appearance, this evolution of members, this development and growth, even though we admit the reality of growth and progress, does not prevent the species from being original. Man from the beginning was in this perfect form and composition, and possessed capacity and aptitude for acquiring material and spiritual perfections, and was the manifestation of these words, "We will make man in Our image and likeness." [56:193f]

EXEMPLAR, PERFECT See **'ABDU'L-BAHÁ.**

EZIUKWU, ISAAC (1934-1973) Born in Nigeria, he was one of the first people (1956) to embrace the Cause in Bangui, Central African Republic. In 1962 he was a member of the first local Spiritual Assembly of Bangui. He pioneered to Gabon at the beginning (1964) of the Nine Year Plan and in 1961 served on the first local Spiritual Assembly of Libreville. [52:522][60:343]

F

FACEY, JAMES VASSAL (1896-1975) He was among the first five people to embrace the Cause in Panama (1945) and helped form the first local Spiritual Assembly of Colón, Panama. He was elected a member of the first Regional Spiritual Assembly of Central America and the Antilles in 1951; in 1961 he was elected to the first National Spiritual Assembly of Panama and served as its Treasurer until his retirement in 1968. [52:556]

FAIẒÍ, ABUL-QÁSIM (1906-1980) (Hand of the Cause of God) He was probably born in 1906 (he himself did not know the date). He preferred to be known simply as "Faiẓí" and did not like birthdays other than those of the Manifestations of God to be celebrated. His early years were spent in the fundamentalist Moslem environment of Qum, Írán. He moved later with his parents to Ṭihrán. Though not a Bahá'í, his father allowed Faiẓí to go to a Bahá'í School where he excelled in studies and in sports. His fellow students, many of whom became life-long friends, loved and respected him. Through his association with Bahá'í students and the example shown by his dedicated teachers. He became a Bahá'í, a commitment that gained the approval of his mother though herself a devout Muslim. She subsequently learned that her other child, Faiẓí's elder brother, had become a Bahá'í in another part of Persia and many years later she too became a firm believer. In 1927 he went to the American University, Beirut, Lebanon and shortly after arriving went on pilgrimage to Haifa where he met Shoghi Effendi, to whom he instantly, completely and forever surrendered his heart. From that moment to the end of his life, he had but one desire, to serve the Guardian, becoming selfless in this servitude. The great love he cherished for the Guardian was the source of his own inspiration and flowed out from him to countless of other souls. With a kindred soul, Ḥasan Balyúzí (see **BALYÚZÍ, ḤASAN MUVAQQAR**) they organized a multitude of activities in Beirut, and when they visited Haifa together the Guardian would encourage them in every way. Intending to return to Írán after his studies to work in the Bahá'í school where he had accepted the Faith, his plans were shattered as he had first to do two years compulsory military service. Three weeks before that was completed, all the Bahá'í schools were closed down by the government as the National Spiritual Assembly had decided not to open them on Bahá'í Holy Days. He reluctantly accepted a post with the Anglo-Íránian Oil Company, with a good salary and every prospect for advancement. This did not appeal to him as he wanted to give all his life in service to the Faith. When the Bahá'ís in a remote village, Najafábád, needed a volunteer teacher, he gave up his job to go there. When reading of this in a report from the National Spiritual Assembly, the Guardian wrote, "This spontaneous decision will attract divine confirmation and is a clear proof of the high endeavor, the pure motive, and the self-sacrifice of that favored servant of the divine Threshold. I am extremely pleased and grateful to him and I pray from the depths of my heart for the success of that active, radiant youth." [2:661]

In the five years he remained in Najafábád he went from house to house teaching the children of all ages, training teachers to carry on after he left, transcribing Bahá'í writings in a beautiful calligraphy, listening to the older Bahá'ís tell of the early struggles for their Faith. He also helped set up a library, encouraged the Bahá'ís to build a public bath, as there were no private baths and the Bahá'ís were forbidden entry to the one owned by Muslims, traveling to teach in nearby towns and translated for visitors from other countries when they came to the nearby larger towns. He was asked by the National Spiritual Assembly to move to Qasvín, where he stayed for a year and then, responding to a call to pioneer outside of Persia, moved with his wife to Baghdád in the winter of 1941 to try to obtain a visa for one of the countries of the Arabian Peninsula. During the year they had to wait, living in very straitened circumstance due to wartime conditions, he threw himself into teaching and continued to collect stories of the early days of the Faith from the time of Bahá'u'lláh's exile in that city; under these dire conditions he was a ray of joy with his ever ready humor, his patience and absolute dedication. After exhausting his meager savings he was offered a job in Bahrain, but this was withdrawn after his arrival when it was learned that he was a Bahá'í. The family had two children and had to meet test after test, yet the terrible heat, lack of water, proper food and every means of comfort, as well as the hostility of the fanatical populace, could not shake his determination to stay. Gradually his sincere love for his fellows won the hearts of many, and large numbers became his friends. He received many young visiting Bahá'ís who were to pioneer in other lands and his correspondence with them and with their parents developed. This was extended to pioneers in other parts of the world. He would share with them news of the teaching work, quotations from the Writings, anecdotes to make them laugh, and, in addition, wrote many articles and literary works for publication. The Guardian wrote of him: "The unceasing meritorious services of that radiant youth in these past years illumine the Cause of God and set an example for all to follow..." and referred to him as the "Spiritual Conqueror of Arabia." [2:664]

Before he left in 1957 there was a National Spiritual Assembly in Arabia, and he lived to see five others established in the area. In 1953 he attended the Intercontinental Conference in New Delhi and then accompanied a Hand of the Cause as a translator on a visit to Australasia. He was in Europe when, in the last contingent, he was appointed a Hand in October 1957. A few weeks later he was completely shattered by the news of the passing of Shoghi Effendi. After attending the funeral he lost all desire to live but kept going to complete the tasks that the Guardian had given to him and threw himself into the service of the Hands of the Cause in the Holy Land where he was chosen to be one of the nine resident there. His health suffered, and although in and out of the hospital he continued to be a liaison between those Hands who did not understand English and their Persian colleagues. He corresponded widely in Persian and English and was proficient in Arabic and French. The burden of his writing was very heavy. He was also very much in demand in the Holy Land, meeting with the pilgrims and taking them to the Bahá'í Holy Places. In addition to this he traveled throughout the world, representing the Universal House of Justice at numerous conferences and conventions; he defended the Faith against the attacks of the Covenant Breakers; he visited National Spiritual Assemblies to counsel them; he met with heads of state and world leaders, addressed many public meetings, conducted study classes and above all, encouraged the youth with his inspirational stories and published works. He never ceased his writing of letters even when he was too ill to receive visitors. Even among his last papers were a few gifts—quotations from the Writings in his own calligraphy with a note, "For the dear pilgrims."

Among his best-known works are: Payám-i-Dúst va Bahár-i-Ṣad-u-Bíst; Dástán-i-Dústán; The Priceless Pearl (translated into Persian); Three Meditations on the Eve of November the 4th; Explanation of the Greatest Name; Our Precious Trusts; The Wonder Lamp; and Stories from the Delight of Hearts (translation).[2:665]

On 20 November 1980 the Universal House of Justice cabled:

> Hearts filled with sorrow passing indefatigable self-sacrificing dearly loved Hand Cause God Abu'l-Qásim Faiẓí. Entire Bahá'í world mourns his loss. His early outstanding achievements in Cradle Faith through education children youth stimulation friends promotion teaching work prompted beloved Guardian describe him as luminous distinguished active youth. His subsequent pioneering work in lands bordering Íran won him appellation spiritual conqueror those lands. Following his appointment Hand Cause he played invaluable part work Hands Holy Land. Traveled widely penned his literary works continued his extensive inspiring correspondence with

high and low, young and old, until after long illness his soul was released and winged its flight Abhá Kingdom. Call on friends everywhere hold befitting memorial gatherings his honor, including special commemorative meetings his name Houses of Worship all continents. May his shining example consecration continue inspire his admirers every land. Praying Holy Shrines his noble radiant soul may be immersed in ocean Divine mercy continue its uninterrupted progress in infinite worlds beyond.[2:659]

FAITH The following excerpts from Bahá'í Scripture throw light on the Bahá'í approach to this far-reaching subject. Basically, faith requires not only belief but also action: "The essence of faith is the abundance of deeds; he whose words exceed his deeds, know verily his death is better than his life."[77:156] "True belief in God and recognition of Him cannot be complete save by acceptance of that which He hath revealed and by observance of whatsoever hath been decreed by Him and set down in the Book by the Pen of Glory."[77:50] "For the faith of no man can be conditioned by any one except himself."[93:143] "If religion and faith are the causes of enmity and sedition, it is far better to be nonreligious, and the absence of religion would be preferable; for We desire religion to be the cause of amity and fellowship."[26:232] "By faith is meant, first, conscious knowledge, and second, the practice of good deeds."[100:550] "If religion is opposed to reason and science, faith is impossible; and when faith and confidence in the divine religion are not manifest in the heart, there can be no spiritual attainment."[26:299] "...the love that flows from man to God. This is faith, attraction to the Divine, enkindlement, progress, entrance into the Kingdom of God, receiving the Bounties of God, illumination with the lights of the Kingdom, This love is the origin of all philanthropy; this love causes the hearts of men to reflect the rays of the Sun of Reality."[25:180] "The first sign of faith is love. The message of the holy, divine Manifestations is love; the phenomena of creation are based upon love; the radiance of the world is due to love; the well-being and happiness of the world depend upon it, Therefore, I admonish you that you must strive throughout the human world to diffuse the light of love." [26:337] "For faith, which is life eternal, is the sign of bounty, and not the result of justice, The flame of the fire of love, in this world of earth and water, comes through the power of attraction and not by effort and striving. Nevertheless, by effort and perseverance, knowledge, science and other perfections can be acquired; but only the light of the Divine Beauty can transport and move the spirits through the force of attraction." [56:130]

FANTOM, MARY TILTON (1879-1972) The first Hawaiian to embrace the Cause. She served on the first local Spiritual Assembly of Maui (1928).[51:529]

FARMÁN Order, command, edict, royal decree. [11:737]

FARMER, SARAH J. (1847-1916) (Disciple of 'Abdu'l-Bahá) She will be known to posterity not only as a Disciple of 'Abdu'l-Bahá but as the originator of the concept of the establishment of the first universal platform in America. This, which, during its first 33 years, developed into the Green Acre school and conference center, comprising some 200 acres along the banks of the Piscataqua River in Eliot, Maine, four miles up from the sea and opposite the city of Portsmouth, New Hampshire. One writer said of her in 1928, "she stands as the actual fulfiller of Emerson in terms of applied influence" and "The roll of speakers who have taken part in the Green Acre Conferences represent well-nigh the flower of modern liberal thought." It was typical of her vision that when opening the Center on 4 July 1894 she raised, at the end of the ceremony, a flag of World Peace. Two years after the opening, she found and embraced the Faith. She went immediately to see 'Abdu'l-Bahá in 'Akká to offer her services to Him. The letters He addressed to her during subsequent years continued to guide her in her work. When He came to America in 1912 He spent a week in August at Green Acre (although Sarah herself was by this time confined to a sanitarium in Portsmouth, which she left for a few hours to welcome Him). Green Acre continues to flourish and develop as a Bahá'í school thereby fulfilling the vision of this remarkable woman and in accordance with the guidance given by 'Abdu'l-Bahá in its earliest days.

FARRÁSH Footman, lictor, attendant. [11:737]

FARRÁSH BÁSHÍ The head farrásh. [11:737]

FARAKH A unit of measurement, approximately 3-4 miles or nearly 5½ kilometers. [11:737]

FASTING The 19th month of the Bahá'í Calendar—'Alá' (2-20 March) is the Bahá'í month of Fasting. No food or drink is taken between sunrise and sunset on each of the 19 days. Those exempted are those below the "age of maturity" (15); those who are weak from illness or age (70 is the age stated); travelers; women who are pregnant, nursing or menstruating; and those engaged in heavy labor. Shoghi Effendi wrote through his secretary: "It essentially is a period of meditation and prayer, of spiritual recuperation, during which the believer must strive to make the necessary readjustments in his inner life, and to refresh and reinvigorate the spiritual forces latent in his soul. Its significance and purpose are fundamentally spiritual in character. Fasting is symbolic, and a reminder of abstinence from selfish and carnal desires." [86:233]

FÁṬIMIH Daughter of the Prophet Muḥammad, wife of the Imám 'Alí and mother of the Imám Ḥusayn. [11:737]

FÁṬIMIH KHÁNUM (Mahd-i-'Ulyá) (1828-1904) A cousin of Bahá'u'lláh who became His second wife in Ṭihrán in 1849. She had six children of whom four survived, and all traveled with Bahá'u'lláh in all His exiles. This wife, her daughter and three sons all violated the Covenant of Bahá'u'lláh, rejected 'Abdu'l-Bahá and caused untold sufferings to Him and to all the faithful followers. She survived Bahá'u'lláh by 12 years. See **GENEALOGIES**.

FÁṬIMIH UMM-SALAMIH See **ṬÁHIRIH**.

FATVÁ A legal pronouncement or decree by a Muslim Muftí. [11:737]

FEAST, NINETEEN DAY An institution inaugurated by Bahá'u'lláh in the Kitáb-i-Aqdas: "Verily, it is enjoined upon you to offer a feast, once in every month, though only water be served; for God hath purposed to bind hearts together, albeit through both earthly and heavenly means."[81:40]

This injunction has become the basis for the holding of monthly Bahá'í festivities and as such constitutes the ordination of the Nineteen Day Feast. In the Arabic Bayán the Báb called upon His followers to gather together once every nineteen days to show hospitality and fellowship. Bahá'u'lláh here confirms this and notes the unifying rôle of such occasions. 'Abdu'l-Bahá and Shoghi Effendi after Him have gradually unfolded the institutional significance of this injunction. 'Abdu'l-Bahá emphasized the importance of the spiritual and devotional character of these gatherings. Shoghi Effendi, besides further elaborating the devotional and social aspects of the Feast, has developed the administrative element of such gatherings and, in systematically instituting the Feast, has provided for a period of consultation on the affairs of the Bahá'í community, including the sharing of news and messages. In answer to a question as to whether this injunction is obligatory, Bahá'u'lláh stated it was not (Q & A number 48.) Shoghi Effendi in a letter written on his behalf further comments: "Attendance at Nineteen Day Feasts is not obligatory but very important, and every believer should consider it a duty and privilege to be present on such occasions."[81:202]

Ideally, these are to be held on the first day of each Bahá'í month. All members of the community meet together with any visiting Bahá'ís and consult during part of the Feast. The first part is of a devotional nature mainly with readings and prayers from the Writings of Bahá'u'lláh, the Báb and 'Abdu'l-Bahá. The second part is the consultative section during which correspondence and/or messages are studied, the local Spiritual Assembly presents its report and consultation follows on the affairs of the community. The Treasurer reports on the state of the local fund. All believers have the opportunity to participate in the consultation, and recommendations may be made to the local Spiritual Assembly or through them to the National Spiritual Assembly. Only Bahá'ís are permitted to attend the Feast. Believers are urged to consider it most important to attend though attendance is not obligatory. The third part of the Feast is social, when refreshments are served. 'Abdu'l-Bahá wrote: "As to the Nineteen Day Feast, it rejoiceth mind and heart. If this Feast be held in the proper fashion, the friends will, once in nineteen days, find themselves spiritually restored, and endued with a power that is not of this world."[101:8] See **UNITY FEAST**.

FEATHERSTONE, H. COLLIS (1913-1990) (Hand of the Cause of God) Born in Quorn, S. Australia on 5 May 1913. He was educated in Adelaide where he founded a precision engineering business that he owned for over 35 years. During this time he became widely recognized in the industry for his excellent workmanship and business integrity. He married Madge Green in 1938, and they had five children. The Featherstones learned of the Faith together from Bertha Dobbins and accepted it in December 1944.

In 1945, Collis wrote the first of many letters to the Guardian, and his zeal and enthusiasm for teaching developed to the extent that he began to travel long distances to attend meetings. He and Madge were on the first local Spiritual Assembly of their district of Woodville in 1948, which was only the sixth Assembly in Australia and New Zealand. The following year he went to the Annual Convention and was elected to the National Spiritual Assembly, on which he served until 1962.

In 1953 the Featherstones were able to attend the New Delhi Intercontinental Conference and then go on pilgrimage. When Hand of the Cause Mother Dunn appointed her first two Auxiliary Board Members, Collis was one of these souls. He was elevated to rank of Hand of the Cause in the last contingent in October 1957 and participated in the Intercontinental Conference, Sydney, in March 1958. He represented the World Center at the inaugural convention of the South Pacific Islands in April 1958 and during the next three years visited centers in Ceylon, Malaya, Indonesia, Thailand, Burma, Pakistan, Írán, Italy, Germany, France, England, the United States, Hawaii, Honduras, Nicaragua, Guatemala, San Salvador, Mexico, India, Arabian Peninsula and Iráq and thereafter bore the burden of responsibility for the whole of the vast area of Australia, New Zealand, Papua New Guinea and the islands of the South Pacific. He visited remote outposts, attended conferences, conventions and summer schools and often represented first the Hands of the Cause of God and later the

Universal House of Justice. In the ensuing years he continued with visits to Europe, Canada, the United States, Alaska, Eastern Asia, and the Western Pacific. In 1976 he started off on a round-the-world trip from a conference in Anchorage, Alaska to East and Southern Africa and Bahá'í communities in the Indian Ocean and methodically visited numerous other countries. In 1977 he and Madge moved from Adelaide to Rockhampton, Central Queensland and during the last 14 years of his life he made a total of 243 visits to 95 countries on all continents. Throughout all these years of traveling he had many radio interviews and met with many dignitaries and highly placed officials to share with them the Bahá'í teachings. In 1979 he made his third African journey. On all these worldwide tours he was accompanied by his wife. In 1983 they had a particularly successful tour of the Philippines, Japan, Korea, Taiwan, Hong Kong, Macau, Thailand, Malaysia, Singapore and several cities in Australia. This was the pattern of their lives and continued right up to the end of his life.

In September 1990, he and Madge planned to visit Pakistan, Thailand, Burma, Nepal, India, Bangladesh, Malaysia and then go back to Sydney. Travel difficulties and visa problems allowed for only the visits to Thailand and Nepal. Immediately prior to leaving Australia, he was telephoned with a request to attend a special activity in Fiji. He responded immediately in his usual way and leaving himself four days to leave their home in Rockhampton, Australia, fly to Suva, Fiji, attend various functions and get back, giving themselves only another four days to prepare for the long Asian journey. He was very tired and developed a cough on the return flight that persisted throughout his Thailand visit. His brief but busy tour of Nepal was to be followed by a flight to New Delhi at 7 A.M. on 26 September, but he developed chest pains during the night of the 25th and was taken to the hospital early that morning. Collis seemed to be much improved and on the 28th was discussing plans to attend a Youth Conference in Lahore, Pakistan, but he passed away mid-morning of Saturday, 29 September. He was buried in an underground vault in the foothills of the Himalayas in the Bahá'í Cemetery "on the top of the world." The Universal House of Justice cabled on 1 October 1990:

> Deeply grieved announce passing valiant Hand Cause God Collis Featherstone while visiting Kathmandu, Nepal course extensive journey Asia. His notable accomplishments as staunch, fearless defender Covenant, his unceasing commitment propagation Cause all parts world, especially Pacific Region, his unremitting perseverance fostering establishment local, national institutions Administrative Order., his exemplary devotion to Writings

Faith, his outstanding personal qualities unswerving loyalty, enthusiasm, zeal and dedication, distinguish his manifold services throughout many decades. Offering prayers Holy Shrines bountiful reward his radiant soul Abhá Kingdom. Advise Friends everywhere hold befitting memorial gatherings, particularly in Mashriqu'l-Adhkár, recognition his magnificent achievements.

FERNIE, ROY (1922-1964) (Knight of Bahá'u'lláh) An American believer born in the Panama Canal Zone (son of the owner of the C. Fernie Steamship Company) who became a Bahá'í in 1953 (for which his father disinherited him). He pioneered to the Gilbert and Ellice Islands in 1953 and was thus designated a Knight of Bahá'u'lláh. [50:308][60:345]

FERRABY, DOROTHY (1904-1994) An early (c.1934) British believer, she served for many years as a member of the National Spiritual Assembly of the British Isles and was a member of the first Auxiliary Board in Europe. During the period 1957-1963 she served at the World Center. (She was the wife of Hand of the Cause of God John Ferraby who was during that time a "Hand resident in the Holy Land.") In 1968 she was appointed a member of the Continental Board of Counsellors in Europe and served for 17 years in that capacity. [11:320]

FERRABY, JOHN (1914-1973) (Hand of the Cause of God) Born in Southsea, England on 9 January 1914 of Jewish background. He had a classical education—King's College, Cambridge and heard of the Faith from a friend when living in London. He found a book in the local library and finally located the Bahá'ís who, because of the intense bombing raids on London, were only able to visit the Bahá'í Center for called meetings. After a couple of meetings he accepted the Faith and immediately became very active; in less than one year he was a member of the London local Spiritual Assembly and the National Spiritual Assembly of the British Isles.

In 1943 he married a fellow member of the National Spiritual Assembly and in 1946 was elected its Secretary. In 1950 he became its first full-time Secretary and the first resident secretary of the National Ḥaẓíratu'l-Quds when it was purchased in the fall of 1954. For many years he was also manager of the British Bahá'í Publishing Trust and was most active in the teaching field and on several national committees.

From 1951 to 1956 he was very involved in the work of the Africa campaign, which included much contact with government bodies. He wrote one of the two booklets that were to become the basic literature for translation into more than 100 African languages.

He attended the Intercontinental Conference in Frankfurt, Germany, 1958, the Convention that elected the National Spiritual Assembly of Austria, 1959, and the election of the National Spiritual Assembly of Norway, 1962. He was on pilgrimage in the Holy Land in January 1955, which inspired him on his return to write his major work *All Things Made New.*

He was appointed a Hand in the last contingent, October 1957 and as such was very heavily involved in the arrangements associated with the funeral of Shoghi Effendi. Attending the first gathering of the Hands of the Cause in the Holy Land following the funeral he remained there for over three months. In December 1959 he went to reside in Haifa, where he remained until the election of the Universal House of Justice in April 1963. He then returned to England and resided in Cambridge, where for a few years he worked as a Hand dealing with secretarial matters and traveling a great deal. For the remainder of his life, his health prevented his active service but right up to his death in September 1973, the Bahá'í Faith was his first concern, as it had been throughout all of his 42 years as a Bahá'í. The Universal House of Justice cabled: "Regret sudden passing Hand Cause John Ferraby. Recall long services Faith British Isles crowned elevation rank Hand Cause valuable contribution Bahá'í literature through his book "All Things Made New." Requesting befitting gatherings Mashriqu'l-Adhkárs memorial meetings all communities Bahá'í world." [102]

FIORENTINI, PROFESSOR. MARIO (1887-1967) An Italian believer who was introduced to the Faith during a visit to Haifa in the early 1940s. He embraced the Cause in 1948 in Rome and became a member of the first Spiritual Assembly of that city. In 1953 he was elected to the Italo-Swiss National Spiritual Assembly. In 1964 he was appointed an Auxiliary Board member. [50:336][60:349]

FIRDAWS Garden, Paradise. [11:737📖]

FIRESIDE A meeting, usually held in a home, for the study and teaching of the Bahá'í Faith. Shoghi Effendi encouraged the Bahá'ís personally to host one of these meetings as frequently as possible. He wrote, through his secretary to an individual believer: "The principle of the fireside meeting, which was established in order to permit and encourage the individual to teach in his own home, has been proven the most effective instrument for spreading the Faith" [104:30] and "the most effective method of teaching is the Fireside group, where new people can be shown Bahá'í hospitality, and ask all questions which bother them. They can feel there the true Bahá'í spirit—and it is the spirit that quickeneth." [104:33]

FIRMÁN See **FARMÁN**. [11:737📖]

FITZNER, HAROLD THOMAS (1893-1969) (Knight of Bahá'u'lláh) An early (1927) Australian believer, he was for sometime chairman of the National Spiritual Assembly of Australia and New Zealand. In 1954 he pioneered to Dili, Portuguese Timor for which service he was designated a Knight of Bahá'u'lláh. [51:449]

FITZNER, SARAH FLORENCE (1906-1980) (Knight of Bahá'u'lláh) An early (1927) Australian believer of Welsh birth. In 1931 she married Harold Fitzner in one of the first Bahá'í marriages in Australia. In 1954 she pioneered to Dili, Portuguese Timor for which service she was designated a Knight of Bahá'u'lláh. [2:727]

FOZDAR, KHODADAD M. (1898-1958) (Knight of Bahá'u'lláh) The first Indian Parsi to become a believer c.1925. He pioneered to Singapore in 1935 where he later started a free school teaching underprivileged women to read and write. In 1953 he pioneered to the Andaman Islands and received the title Knight of Bahá'u'lláh. [47:892]

FREE WILL 'Abdu'l-Bahá made it clear that this refers to the freedom given by God to man to choose whether or not to recognize Him and to obey His commands. He said:

> Some things are subject to the free will of man, such as justice, equity, tyranny and injustice, in other words, good and evil actions; it is evident and clear that these actions are, for the most part, left to the will of man. But there are certain things to which man is forced and compelled, such as sleep, death, sickness, decline of power, injuries and misfortunes; these are not subject to the will of man, and he is not responsible for them, for he is compelled to endure them, But in the choice of good and bad actions he is free, and he commits them according to his own will. For example, if he wishes, he can pass his time in praising God, or he can be occupied with other thoughts. He can be an enkindled light through the fire of the love of God, and a philanthropist loving the world, or he can be a hater of mankind, and engrossed with material things. He can be just or cruel. These actions and these deeds are subject to the control of the will of man himself; consequently, he is responsible for them. [56:248]

FUJITA, SAICHIRO (1886-1976) The second (1905) Japanese Bahá'í to embrace the Cause in Oakland, California. He met 'Abdu'l-Bahá in Chicago (where he was invited by the Master to join Him for dinner) in Kenosha. 'Abdu'l-Bahá invited him to accompany Him to California—a request he acceded to without hesitation. It was during 'Abdu'l-Bahá's visit that Fujita (as he was known to everyone) expressed the desire to return with 'Abdu'l-Bahá to the Holy Land and to serve Him. 'Abdu'l-Bahá accepted the offer and said he would send for him when circumstances permitted. For the next seven years Fujita lived with the True family, during which time he received many Tablets from 'Abdu'l-Bahá. Finally, in 1919, he received the long-awaited invitation to go to Haifa where, with the exception of a three-month visit to his family in Japan, he remained continuously until 1938 serving first 'Abdu'l-Bahá and then Shoghi Effendi. In 1938, just prior to the outbreak of WW II, Shoghi Effendi sent him to Japan where he remained for the next 17 years—returning to Haifa in 1955 and remaining there until his death in 1976. [53:407]

FUNDS (of the Faith) Contributions to the various funds of the Bahá'í Faith are accepted only from registered believers. There are funds for the conduct of local, national, regional and international purposes, and there are those for special projects such as the building of a Bahá'í House of Worship, the Bahá'í World Center on Mount Carmel, for the deputatization of pioneers and travel teachers. All the responses to the appeals and statements of needs are left entirely to the individual believer who makes his/her donation in confidence to the appropriate authority. No pressure is placed on any believer, and what is given is a measure of that person's wish to sacrifice for the good of the Faith. Shoghi Effendi wrote through his secretary: "We must be like the fountain or spring that is continually emptying itself of all that it has and is continually being refilled from an invisible source. To be continually giving out for the good of our fellows undeterred by the fear of poverty and reliant on the unfailing bounty of the Source of all wealth and all good—this is the secret of right living." [104:32]

FURÚTAN, 'ALÍ AKBAR (1905-) (Hand of the Cause of God) Born in 1905, in Sabrizva, Khurusan, Persia where his father was the first Bahá'í in the family. His mother and grandmother became Bahá'ís later. In 1914 he moved with his family to 'Ishqábád, Russia and attended the elementary Bahá'í boys' school where, on his graduation at age 14, he was asked to teach the children of the first grade. He did this until 1922 when he began his secondary education. This was completed in 1925 and he went to work as Principal of the Bahá'í Schools for a year prior to going on to the University of Moscow (where he graduated in psychology and education). Returning to Írán in 1930 he married Ata'íyyih Azíz-Khurasání and had two daughters (Parvine and Írán).

Always active in the Faith, he traveled widely throughout the Caucasus region even while young and taught also in Leningrad and other Russian cities. In Írán he and his wife settled in Susan, where they established a Bahá'í school for girls and another for boys, which eventually had an attendance of about 700 students.

In 1933 he was appointed Principal of the Tarbíyat School for boys in Ṭihrán. In 1934 Rezá Sháh Pahlavi issued an order to close all the Bahá'í Schools in Írán. That same year saw the election of the first National Spiritual Assembly of the Bahá'ís of Írán. He was elected a member and served for a great many years on that Assembly as well as the local Spiritual Assembly of Ṭihrán—often as Secretary of both bodies.

In 1941 he, his wife, mother and daughter went on his first pilgrimage to the Holy Land. In 1946 the Íránian Radio and Broadcasting Service invited him to give a series of lectures on children's education, the text of which was published as *Essays on Education* which subsequently was published in English as *Mothers, Fathers and Children.*

He was elevated to Hand of the Cause in the first contingent, 24 December 1951 and is therefore, at the time of writing, the longest-serving surviving Hand.

He participated in all four of the first Intercontinental Conferences, held in 1953—Kampala February; Chicago, April-May; Stockholm, July; and New Delhi, October. During 1953-54 he visited centers in the United States, Canada, France, Spain and Portugal and more than 40 centers in Australasia. He represented Shoghi Effendi at the convention of Southeast Asia in April 1957 and was one of the Nine Hands of the Cause resident in the Holy Land, 1957-1963. He visited centers in Persia and Turkey from November 1959 to April 1960 and represented the World Center at the conventions of Brazil and Uruguay in April 1961. Following this he visited centers in Argentina, British Isles and Cyprus. Although his many duties in the Holy Land included assisting with the pilgrimage program, during 1963-1968 he undertook teaching trips in Turkey, Írán, East Africa and Ethiopia and wrote a pamphlet answering the attacks made on the Bahá'ís in his native Írán. Again in 1973 and 1975 he toured Western Europe and was for five months in Írán in 1974. In 1976 his travels took him to the United States and Canada, India and Hong Kong. In 1977 he visited England, the United States, Canada, Alaska, Japan and Írán and went on to Western Europe in 1978. His travels continued throughout the 1980s mostly in Europe but it was not until 1990 that he was able to fulfill his long-held wish to return to Russia where he visited 'Ishqábád, Dushanbe, Samarkand, Mary, Tashkent, Leningrad and Murmansk and witnessed the re-formation, after a lapse of more than 60 years, of the first local Spiritual Assembly of Moscow. A year later he represented the Universal House of Justice at the election of the first Spiritual Assembly of the Soviet Union and the following year, the Regional Assembly of the Baltic States and the National Spiritual Assembly of the Bahá'ís of Hungary. During that Holy Year, 1992, he attended the Second Bahá'í World Congress in New York City. He presently resides in Haifa where he is a member of the International Teaching Center and assists with the pilgrims' program.

G

GAIL, MARZIEH (-1993) The daughter of the first Bahá'í marriage between a Persian father ('Alí-Kuli Khán [q.v.]) and an American mother (Florence Breed Khán [q.v.]). She was renowned for her literary skills and wrote and translated many works. During a 10 year stay in Europe she served on the National Spiritual Assembly of Austria and also helped to form several local Spiritual Assemblies. [11:320]

GAMBLING is forbidden in the Bahá'í Faith.

GARDEN OF RIḌVÁN See **BAHÁ'U'LLÁH, DECLARATION.**

GARDNER, LLOYD G. (1915-1985) An early Canadian believer who embraced the Cause in 1938 in Toronto. In 1948 he was elected to the first National Spiritual Assembly of Canada on which he served for some 20 years. In 1968 he was appointed to the newly formed Continental Board of Counsellors in North America and served from 1980 onwards as Trustee of the Continental Fund for the Americas. [11:663]

GEARY, MABEL GRACE [50:310] (1888-1965) (Knight of Bahá'u'lláh); **GEARY, IRVING** [11:652] (1887-1984) (Knight of Bahá'u'lláh) In 1937 the Gearys agreed to allow a visiting Bahá'í (Mabel Ives) to hold meetings in their home in Moncton, New Brunswick, Canada. During the course of these meetings they embraced the Cause and in 1938 formed the first local Spiritual Assembly of Moncton (which was also the first in the Atlantic Provinces of Canada). They later pioneered to Prince Edward Island where they served as members of the first (1944) Spiritual Assembly of Charlottetown. In 1953 they pioneered to Cape Breton Island for which they were designated Knights of Bahá'u'lláh.

GETSINGER, EDWARD CHRISTOPHER (1866-1935) One of the earliest American believers. He and his wife came into the Faith through Ibráhím Khayru'lláh (q.v.). Dr. Getsinger was one of the State of Michigan's official delegates to the World Congress of Scientists, Chicago's World Fair in 1893 (at which the Bahá'í Faith was mentioned for the first time in public in the States). He and his wife, Lua, were among the first western pilgrims to visit 'Abdu'l-Bahá (10 December 1898). It was following the continual solicitation of Dr. Getsinger that 'Abdu'l-Bahá consented to a recording of His voice on a phonograph record (subsequently brought to America by Dr. Getsinger).[23:493][59:9ff][60:362]

GETSINGER, LOUISA AURORA MOORE (Lua) (1871-1916) (Disciple of 'Abdu'l-Bahá) One of the earliest Bahá'ís in the United States. Along with her husband, Edward, she heard about the Cause in 1896 and embraced it in 1897. In that same year she and her husband were invited to visit Mrs. Phoebe Hearst at her hacienda (see **TURNER, ROBERT**). Mrs. Hearst, the wealthy widow of Senator George Hearst, was introduced to the Faith by Lua and began to make plans to go to the Holy Land. Prior to all this, Lua had introduced the Faith to May Ellis Bolles, who became the first believer in France and later in Canada, and earned the name "Livá" (Banner) [5:257] from 'Abdu'l-Bahá. She was later designated "The mother teacher of the West," and "Herald of the dawn of the Day of the Covenant" by Shoghi Effendi.[5:257] She shone among those early American Bahá'ís. During her life of service she was on occasion a special emissary for 'Abdu'l-Bahá; she went on pilgrimage again in 1902 and stayed for more than a year to teach English in the household of the Master, she traveled to teach the Faith in India and in Egypt and died there in 1916, where she is buried in Cairo in the next grave to Apostle of Bahá'u'lláh, Mírzá Abu'l-Faḍl.

GIACHERY, ANGELINE (-1980) Born in Sweden, she embraced the Cause in early 1920s while visiting friends in Boston. She married Ugo Giachery (q.v.) in 1926 in New York City. In 1948 she served on the first local Spiritual Assembly of Rome. In 1954 she was appointed an Auxiliary Board member and served in that capacity until 1964. During that time she traveled widely throughout not only Italy but also Corsica, Malta, Rhodes, Greece, Monaco and Switzerland. In 1964 she returned to the United States and traveled extensively in the promotion of the Cause. She passed away in 1980. [2:717]

GIACHERY, UGO R. (-1995) (Hand of the Cause of God) He was born in Palermo, Sicily. He was educated there and received a Doctorate in Chemistry. He served with distinction in WW I and lived for many years in the United States where he accepted the Bahá'í Faith.

He and his wife pioneered to Rome in 1947. In 1948 he was appointed by Shoghi Effendi as his personal representative for all the work in Italy associated with the construction of the superstructure of the Shrine of the Báb on Mount Carmel, Haifa. He was in the first contingent of the Hands of the Cause, appointed in December 1951, and in 1952 Shoghi Effendi appointed him as "Member at Large" of the International Bahá'í Council. In 1953 he became Chairman of the first National Spiritual Assembly of the Bahá'ís of Italy and Switzerland. He was the Guardian's representative at the Intercontinental Conferences of Stockholm in 1953 and Chicago in 1958. For a number of years he was the Bahá'í Observer to the United Nations Economic and Social Council in Geneva. Throughout his life he also worked translating Bahá'í literature into Italian.

When the building of the International Archives on Mount Carmel began in 1954, he was once again appointed the Guardian's personal representative in Italy. For his distinguished and dedicated services to the Faith in the Holy Land, the Guardian honored him by naming the southwestern door of the original Shrine the "Báb-i-Giachery."

After the passing of Shoghi Effendi, his travels for the Faith intensified, and he began to visit the Far East, Australia and the Pacific Islands as well as Europe and the Americas. He returned to live in the United States in 1964 and played a prominent rôle in an international proclamation campaign in 1968 (when he presented a special volume of the Writings of Bahá'u'lláh to the Vatican via Cardinal Paolo Morella on 9 April).

Prior to this he had visited the Intercontinental Conference in Sydney in October 1967 and was in Samoa when, on the 27th he was able to present a copy of the same volume of Bahá'u'lláh's Writings to His Highness Malietoa Tanumafili II of Western Samoa. The book was so warmly received by the monarch that by early December Dr. Giachery had received letters stating that His Highness wished to become a Bahá'í. The Universal House of Justice asked Ugo to revisit Samoa and discuss this historic decision with the Malietoa. During that visit the Malietoa confirmed his belief and in so doing became the first reigning monarch to embrace the Faith. The very close relationship that developed between the Hand and the Malietoa was unique. On one occasion, when His Highness was visiting London, Dr. Giachery accompanied Him, along with members of the United Kingdom National Spiritual Assembly, on the first visit by a monarch to the Grave of Shoghi Effendi. In April 1989 Dr. Giachery arrived in Samoa for a prolonged visit and was met as he stepped off the plane by the Malietoa. He lived in Samoa for three months, but his health suffered and he was often in great pain; during this time, the Malietoa visited him frequently as well as receiving him officially at His Residence.

Dr. Giachery made plans to return to his home in Monaco but on 5 July his condition seriously deteriorated, and he was admitted to the hospital where he passed away the same evening. He was buried in a beautiful spot overlooking the House of Worship at

Tiapapata, Apia, Western Samoa where, on 12 July 1989 a very moving ceremony was attended by the Malietoa, the Prime Minister and four members of Cabinet, many local dignitaries and over 200 Bahá'ís from the Pacific communities. The Universal House of Justice cabled on 27 September 1989:

> Deeply grieved loss valiant, indefatigable, dearly-loved, distinguished Hand Cause Dr. Ugo Giachery. His passing in course historic visit Samoa adds fresh laurels to crown already won during ministry beloved Guardian, and reinforces spiritual distinction vast Pacific region, already blessed by interment four other Hands. His magnificent accomplishments as Member at Large of International Bahá'í Council in connection raising superstructure Shrine of the Báb, which prompted Guardian to name one of the doors of that noble edifice after him, his painstaking efforts in promoting on the local, national and international levels, paramount interests of the Faith, his notable achievement in establishment Italo-Swiss National Spiritual Assembly on eve of launching Ten Year Crusade, his outstanding qualities of zeal, fidelity, determination and perseverance, which characterized imperishable record his arduous labors—all combine to richly adorn annals Faith over period his superb, assiduous exertions, and undoubtedly assure him bountiful reward in Kingdom on High. Advise all National Spiritual Assemblies hold befitting memorial gatherings his name, particularly in Mashriqu'l-Adhkár in recognition his unique position, splendid services. [105]

GIBSON, AMOZ EVERETT (1918-1982) (Member first Universal House of Justice) A tireless American believer who before (and even after) his election to the first Universal House of Justice in 1963 traveled widely throughout North America, Persia, Europe and Mexico in the promotion of the Cause. Although born into a Bahá'í family (his parents accepted the Cause in 1912), he did not himself register as a Bahá'í until 1944. Born to a mother whose grandfather was a full-blooded Creek Indian and a Scots-Irish father whose mother was a mulatto slave, Amoz spend many years living and working among the North American Indian peoples. In 1959 he was appointed an Auxiliary Board member for the western United States and traveled widely in that region as well as to Jamaica and Haiti. In 1960 he was elected to the National Spiritual Assembly of the United States and in 1961 represented them at the dedication of the Mother temple of Africa in Kampala, Uganda. In 1963 he was elected to the first Universal House of

Justice. He served as a member of that Body for 13 years until his "in office" death in 1982. [2:666]

GILLEN, CHARLOTTE THOMAS ZUTAVERN (1869-1962) An early (1901) American believer, she met 'Abdu'l-Bahá in Chicago in 1912. She turned a shovelful of earth in the name of Alaska during the laying of the foundation stone of the Wilmette Temple. She later received two Tablets from 'Abdu'l-Bahá. In 1959, at the age of 90, she pioneered to Alaska where she lived for a year. [50:341][60:369]

GILLESPIE, JOHN BIRKS ("Dizzy") (1917-1993) This renowned jazz trumpeter embraced the Cause in 1968 and spoke widely of it during his many public performances. [57:274]

GOALS In the mid 1930s Shoghi Effendi called on the National Spiritual Assembly of the United States and Canada to carry out a campaign with specific objectives or goals. From this initiative the first Seven Year Plan was launched at Riḍván 1937. All goals were achieved by Riḍván 1944. Following this example, other National Spiritual Assemblies were given or adopted teaching plans with goals assigned to them by Shoghi Effendi. The last was his Ten Year Plan or Global Crusade, launched at Riḍván 1953 and completed, under the direction of the Hands of the Cause, after his passing, at Riḍván, 1963. Since that time the Universal House of Justice has continued the practice of launching global plans, each with specific goals of expansion and consolidation, such as Nine, Five, and Seven Year Plans. All these were based upon, or were supplementary to, the goals listed by 'Abdu'l-Bahá in His *Tablets of the Divine Plan* (q.v.) revealed by Him during WW I and given to the Bahá'ís of North America in 1919. See **PLANS; SHOGHI EFFENDI; TIMELINE—UNIVERSAL HOUSE OF JUSTICE**.

GOD The creation can reflect one or more attributes of the Creator; the human race, uniquely, has the capacity to reflect all the attributes of God. The purpose of religion is to reveal those attributes, just as the purpose of education is to help mankind to develop these in each human being. The purpose of life on this earth is to struggle to achieve those latent perfections through service to one's fellow man and the recognition of, and obedience to, the Manifestation of God for His day and age. Bahá'u'lláh wrote:

> To every discerning and illuminated heart it is evident that God, the unknowable Essence, the Divine Being, is immensely exalted beyond every human attribute, such as corporeal existence, ascent and descent, egress and regress. Far be it from His glory that human tongue should adequately recount His praise, or that human heart comprehend His fathomless mystery. He is, and hath ever been, veiled in the ancient eternity of His Essence, and

will remain in His Reality everlastingly hidden from the sight of men.... The door of the knowledge of the Ancient of Days being thus closed in the face of all beings, the Source of infinite grace ... hath caused those luminous Gems of Holiness to appear out of the realm of the spirit, in the noble form of the human temple, and be made manifest unto all men, that they may impart unto the world the mysteries of the unchangeable Being, and tell of the subtleties of His imperishable Essence.[93:47]

GOD, ATTRIBUTES OF According to both the Báb and Bahá'u'lláh human beings cannot comprehend the nature of God the Creator. God may only be known through His attributes such as love, mercy, justice, trustworthiness, wisdom, etc. The transcendence of God is captured in these passages from the Báb:

> Immeasurably exalted art Thou, O my God, above the endeavours of all beings and created things to praise Thee and recognize Thee. No creature can ever comprehend Thee as beseemeth the reality of Thy holy Being and no servant can ever worship Thee as is worthy of Thine unknowable Essence. Praise be unto Thee; too high is Thine exalted Self for any allusions proceeding from Thy creatures ever to gain access unto Thy presence.
>
> Whenever, O my God, I soared into Thy holy atmosphere and attained the inmost spirit of prayerfulness unto Thee, I was led to recognize that Thou art inaccessible and that no mention of Thee can ever reach Thy transcendent court. Therefore I turn towards Thy Loved Ones—They upon Whom Thou hast graciously conferred Thine Own station that They might manifest Thy love and Thy true knowledge. Bless Them then, O my God, with every distinction and goodly gift which Thy knowledge may reckon within the domain of Thy power.
>
> O my God, my Lord and my Master! I swear by Thy might and glory that Thou alone and no one else besides Thee art the ultimate Desire of all men, and that Thou alone and none other save Thee art the Object of adoration. O my God! The paths of Thine inaccessible glory have prompted me to voice these words and the ways of Thine unattainable heights have guided me to make these allusions. Exalted art Thou, O my God! The evidences of Thy revelation are too manifest for me to need to refer to aught else save Thyself, and the love I cherish for Thee is far sweeter to my taste than the knowledge of all things

and freeth me from the need to seek anyone's knowledge other than Thine....

All majesty and glory, O my God, and all dominion and light and grandeur and splendour be unto Thee. Thou bestowest sovereignty on whom Thou willest and dost withhold it from whom Thou desirest. No God is there but Thee, the All-Possessing, the Most Exalted. Thou art He Who createth from naught the universe and all that dwell therein. There is nothing worthy of Thee except Thyself, while all else but Thee are as outcasts in Thy holy presence and are as nothing when compared to the glory of Thine Own Being.

Far be it from me to extol Thy virtues save by what Thou hast extolled Thyself in Thy weighty Book where Thou sayest, "No vision taketh in Him but He taketh in all vision. He is the Subtile, the All-Perceiving." Glory be unto Thee, O my God, indeed no mind or vision, however keen or discriminating, can ever grasp the nature of the most insignificant of Thy signs. Verily Thou art God, no God is there besides Thee. I bear witness that Thou Thyself alone art the sole expression of Thine attributes, that the praise of no one besides Thee can ever attain to Thy holy court nor can Thine attributes ever be fathomed by anyone other than Thyself.

Glory be unto Thee, Thou art exalted above the description of anyone save Thyself, since it is beyond human conception to befittingly magnify Thy virtues or to comprehend the inmost reality of Thine Essence. Far be it from Thy glory that Thy creatures should describe Thee or that any one besides Thyself should ever know Thee. I have known Thee, O my God, by reason of Thy making Thyself known unto me, for hadst Thou not revealed Thyself unto me, I would not have known Thee. I worship Thee by virtue of Thy summoning me unto Thee, for had it not been for Thy summons I would not have worshipped Thee. Lauded art Thou, O my God, my trespasses have waxed mighty and my sins have assumed grievous proportions. How disgraceful my plight will prove to be in Thy holy presence. I have failed to know Thee to the extent Thou didst reveal Thyself unto me; I have failed to worship Thee with a devotion worthy of Thy summons; I have failed to obey Thee through not treading the path of Thy love in the manner Thou didst inspire me. Thy might

> beareth me witness, O my God, what befitteth Thee is far greater and more exalted than any being could attempt to accomplish. Indeed nothing can ever comprehend Thee as is worthy of Thee nor can any servile creature worship Thee as beseemeth Thine adoration. So perfect and comprehensive is Thy proof, O my God, that its inner essence transcendeth the description of any soul and so abundant are the outpourings of Thy gifts that no faculty can appraise their infinite range. [145:200ff]

Every created thing has been made the recipient of at least one of these signs or attributes of God, but each human being, uniquely in creation, has been endowed with the capacity to reflect all these attributes and may therefore be said to be made in the "image" of God. This capacity may only be developed through the influence of those Whom God has created to reveal these attribute in their fullest form—the Manifestations of God, the Founders of the world's revealed religions. See **GOD, MANIFESTATION OF.**

GOD, KINGDOMS OF A description used in Bahá'í Writings for the different levels in creation, such as the mineral, the vegetable, the animal and the human kingdoms. From Bahá'í Scripture we find:

> If we look with a perceiving eye upon the world of creation, we find that all existing things may be classified as follows: First—Mineral—that is to say matter or substance appearing in various forms of composition. Second—Vegetable—possessing the virtues of the mineral plus the power of augmentation or growth, indicating a degree higher and more specialized than the mineral. Third—Animal—possessing the attributes of the mineral and vegetable plus the power of sense perception. Fourth—Human—the highest specialized organism of visible creation, embodying the qualities of the mineral, vegetable and animal plus an ideal endowment absolutely minus and absent in the lower kingdoms—the power of intellectual investigation into the mysteries of outer phenomena. The outcome of this intellectual endowment is science, which is especially characteristic of man. This scientific power investigates and apprehends created objects and the laws surrounding them. It is the discoverer of the hidden and mysterious secrets of the material universe and is peculiar to man alone. The most noble and praiseworthy accomplishment of man therefore is scientific knowledge and attainment. [106:242]
>
> In the world of existence man has traversed successive degrees until he has attained the human kingdom. In

each degree of his progression he has developed capacity for advancement to the next station and condition. While in the kingdom of the mineral he was attaining the capacity for promotion into the degree of the vegetable. In the kingdom of the vegetable he underwent preparation for the world of the animal and from thence he has come onward to the human degree or kingdom. Throughout this journey of progression he has ever and always been potentially man. [107:63]

As existence can never become non-existence, there is no death for man; nay, rather, man is everlasting and ever-living. The rational proof of this is that the atoms of the material elements are transferable from one form of existence to another, from one degree and kingdom to another, lower or higher. For example, an atom of the soil or dust of earth may traverse the kingdoms from mineral to man by successive incorporations into the bodies of the organisms of those kingdoms. At one time it enters into the formation of the mineral or rock; it is then absorbed by the vegetable kingdom and becomes a constituent of the body and fiber of a tree; again it is appropriated by the animal, and at a still later period is found in the body of man. Throughout these degrees of its traversing the kingdoms from one form of phenomenal being to another, it retains its atomic existence and is never annihilated nor relegated to non-existence. Non-existence therefore is an expression applied to change of form, but this transformation can never be rightly considered annihilation, for the elements of composition are ever present and existent as we have seen in the journey of the atom through successive kingdoms, unimpaired; hence there is no death; life is everlasting. So to speak, when the atom entered into the composition of the tree, it died to the mineral kingdom, and when consumed by the animal, it died to the vegetable kingdom, and so on until its transference or transmutation into the kingdom of man; but throughout its traversing it was subject to transformation and not annihilation. [106:263-264]

When we were in the mineral kingdom, although endowed with certain gifts and powers, they were not to be compared with the blessings of the human kingdom. In the matrix of the mother we were the recipients of endowments and blessings of God, yet these were as nothing compared to the powers and graces bestowed upon us after birth into this human world. Likewise if we are born from the matrix of this physical and phenomenal environment into the freedom and loftiness of the life and vision spiritual, we shall consider this mortal existence and its blessings as worthless by comparison. [106:266f]

Just as the vegetable kingdom is unaware of the world of man, so we, too, know not of the Great Life hereafter that followeth the life of man here below. Our non-comprehension of that life, however, is no proof of its non-existence. The mineral world, for instance, is utterly unaware of the world of man and cannot comprehend it, but the ignorance of a thing is no proof of its non-existence. [106:341]

GOD, MANIFESTATION OF The title given in Bahá'í Writings to the Founders of the world's revealed religions; mentioned particularly are Abraham; Buddha; Zoroaster; Moses; Christ; Muhammad; the Báb and Bahá'u'lláh. Noah, Húd and Sálih are also mentioned. Bahá'u'lláh stated that another Divine Manifestation would not appear for at least 1,000 years. As mankind, the creation, will never be able fully to comprehend the nature of its Creator, God's purpose becomes known through a knowledge of His Manifestation. This Manifestation of God in a perfect human frame is described by Bahá'u'lláh:

These Tabernacles of Holiness, these Primal Mirrors which reflect the light of unfading glory, are but expressions of Him Who is the Invisible of the Invisibles. By the revelation of these Gems of Divine virtue all the names and attributes of God, such as knowledge and power, sovereignty and dominion, mercy and wisdom, glory, bounty, and grace, are made manifest. These attributes of God are not, and have never been, vouchsafed specially unto certain Prophets, and withheld from others. Nay, all the Prophets of God, His well-favored, His holy and chosen Messengers are, without exception, the bearers of His names, and the embodiments of His attributes. They only differ in the intensity of their revelation, and the comparative potency of their light. Even as He hath revealed: "Some of the Apostles We have caused to excel the others." It hath, therefore, become manifest and evident that within the tabernacles of these Prophets and chosen Ones of God the light of His infinite names and exalted attributes hath been reflected, even though the light of some of these attributes may or may not be outwardly revealed from these luminous Temples to the eyes of men. That a certain attribute of God hath not been outwardly manifested by these Essences of Detachment doth in no wise imply that they who are the Day Springs of God's attributes and the Treasuries of His holy names did not actually possess it. Therefore, these illuminated Souls, these beauteous Countenances have, each and every one of them, been endowed with all the attributes of God, such as sovereignty, dominion, and the like, even though to outward seeming they be shorn of all earthly majesty.

These sanctified Mirrors, these Day Springs of ancient glory, are, one and all, the Exponents on earth of Him Who is the central Orb of the universe, its Essence and ultimate Purpose. From Him proceed their knowledge and power; from Him is derived their sovereignty. The beauty of their countenance is but a reflection of His image, and their revelation a sign of His deathless glory. They are the Treasuries of Divine knowledge, and the Repositories of celestial wisdom. Through them is transmitted a grace that is infinite, and by them is revealed the Light that can never fade. [85:46ff]

See **REVELATION; PROGRESSIVE REVELATION.**

GOD, UNITY OF The significance given to this theme is emphasized by the fact that 'Abdu'l-Bahá made it the main subject in His first public address given in the City Temple, London, England. Of this occasion Shoghi Effendi wrote:

'Abdu'l-Bahá's first public appearance before a western audience significantly enough took place in a Christian house of worship, when, on September 10, 1911, He addressed an overflowing congregation from the pulpit of the City Temple. Introduced by the Pastor, the Reverend R. J. Campbell, He, in simple and moving language, and with vibrant voice, proclaimed the unity of God, affirmed the fundamental oneness of religion, and announced that the hour of the unity of the sons of men, of all races, religions and classes had struck. [5:283]

In Bahá'u'lláh's own words:

Know thou assuredly that the essence of all the Prophets of God is one and the same. Their unity is absolute. God, the Creator, saith: There is no distinction whatsoever among the Bearers of My Message. They all have but one purpose; their secret is the same secret. To prefer one in honor to another, to exalt certain ones above the rest, is in

> no wise to be permitted. Every true Prophet hath regarded His Message as fundamentally the same as the Revelation of every other Prophet gone before Him.[85:78]

Shoghi Effendi again refers at length to this unity in his letter of 21 March 1932 addressed to the Bahá'ís of the United States and Canada:

> Let no one, however, mistake my purpose. The Revelation, of which Bahá'u'lláh is the source and center, abrogates none of the religions that have preceded it, nor does it attempt, in the slightest degree, to distort their features or to belittle their value. It disclaims any intention of dwarfing any of the Prophets of the past, or of whittling down the eternal verity of their teachings. It can, in no wise, conflict with the spirit that animates their claims, nor does it seek to undermine the basis of any man's allegiance to their cause. Its declared, its primary purpose is to enable every adherent of these Faiths to obtain a fuller understanding of the religion with which he stands identified, and to acquire a clearer apprehension of its purpose. It is neither eclectic in the presentation of its truths, nor arrogant in the affirmation of its claims. Its teachings revolve around the fundamental principle that religious truth is not absolute but relative, that Divine Revelation is progressive, not final. Unequivocally and without the least reservation it proclaims all established religions to be divine in origin, identical in their aims, complementary in their functions, continuous in their purpose, indispensable in their value to mankind. "All the Prophets of God," asserts Bahá'u'lláh in the *Kitáb-i-Íqan*, "abide in the same tabernacle, soar in the same heaven, are seated upon the same throne, utter the same speech, and proclaim the same Faith." From the "beginning that hath no beginning," these Exponents of the Unity of God and Channels of His incessant utterance have shed the light of the invisible Beauty upon mankind, and will continue, to the "end that hath no end," to vouchsafe fresh revelations of His might and additional experiences of His inconceivable glory. To contend that any particular religion is final, that "all Revelation is ended, that the portals of Divine mercy are closed, that from the daysprings of eternal holiness no sun shall rise again, that the ocean of everlasting bounty is forever stilled, and that out of the Tabernacle of ancient glory the Messengers of God have

ceased to be made manifest" would indeed be nothing less than sheer blasphemy. [4:57]

While in Paris, 'Abdu'l-Bahá said:

All religious laws conform to reason, and are suited to the people for whom they are framed, and for the age in which they are to be obeyed.... Religion has two main parts: (1) The Spiritual. (2) The Practical. The spiritual part never changes. All the Manifestations of God and His Prophets have taught the same truths and given the same spiritual law. They all teach the one code of morality. There is no division in the truth. The Sun has sent forth many rays to illumine human intelligence, the light is always the same. The practical part of religion deals with exterior forms and ceremonies, and with modes of punishment for certain offenses. This is the material side of the law, and guides the customs and manners of the people. [25:141]

See **UNITY; ONENESS OF MANKIND; PROGRESSIVE REVELATION.**

GOLFER, PAUL (1886-1961) An early German believer. He met 'Abdu'l-Bahá in Stuttgart in 1913 and later received a Tablet from Him. He visited Shoghi Effendi in 1936. He was for many years a member of the National Spiritual Assembly of Germany and Austria. He was a moving force following WW II in securing recognition of the Bahá'í Faith in Germany. [47:933]

GOMEZ, LUISA MAPA (1892-1977) Born into a prominent family in Talisay, Negros Occidental, Philippines, Luisa embraced the Cause in 1953. In 1964 she was elected to the first National Spiritual Assembly of the Philippines and served until 1975 (often as treasurer).[53:442]

GOODALL, HELEN MIRRELL (1864-1922) (Disciple of 'Abdu'l-Bahá) She was born in Maine and moved to San Francisco in 1864 where in 1868 she married Edwin Goodall. They had one daughter, Ella. In 1898 she learned of the Faith but before she could investigate fully, the teacher with whom she was to study, Lua Getsinger, had gone with Mrs. Hearst and others on pilgrimage to the Holy Land. Not willing to wait for their return, Helen and Ella went by train in September 1898 to New York to study with another Bahá'í teacher. Sadly, however, Helen became ill and could not leave her room. When she recovered sufficiently to return to California, Ella responded to a call from Mrs. Hearst to join the pilgrims in Cairo, and she and a friend left in February 1899. On arrival she spent most of March in 'Akká. On her return she found that her mother had already attracted a small group to the Faith

In Oakland, and over the years their house became a center for visiting speakers.

In 1904 Ella married Dr. Charles Miner Cooper and in late 1907 mother and daughter received permission to visit 'Abdu'l-Bahá. They reached 'Akká on 4 January 1908. They continued jointly to serve the Faith. In 1909 when Edwin died Helen and her son Arthur moved to the same house as Ella and her husband. When 'Abdu'l-Bahá came to America the ladies accompanied Him to many places, and He once remarked about Helen, "God has certain treasures hidden in the world which He reveals when the time comes. She is like one of those treasures." [91:27] When in San Francisco 'Abdu'l-Bahá asked Helen to visit Him every morning and remain all day if possible. 'Abdu'l-Bahá, in 1920 gave permission for Helen and Ella to visit Haifa again, and although Helen was very frail they reached there on 21 October. When 'Abdu'l-Bahá passed away on 21 November 1921, it was remembered that Helen had often been heard to say to her friends and family that as soon as the Master had left this world she hoped to do the same, and she passed away on 19 February 1922. The Guardian in *God Passes By* [5:257] and in *America and the Most Great Peace* [4:81] has referred to the consecrated, imperishable services of Helen S. Goodall.

GOSSIP See **BACKBITING.**

GOVERNMENT, OBEDIENCE TO Bahá'ís are forbidden to participate in any subversive activity, and it is one of the laws of the Faith that they must be obedient to the laws of the government of the country in which they live. 'Abdu'l-Bahá: "Let them obey the government and not meddle in political affairs, but devote themselves to the betterment of character and behavior, and fix their gaze upon the Light of the world." [65:319]

Shoghi Effendi wrote on the same subject: "Absolute impartiality in the matter of political parties should be shown by words and by deeds, and the love of the whole humanity, whether a Government, or a nation, which is the basic teaching of Bahá'u'lláh, should also be shown by words and by deeds." [104:56-57]

> For whereas the friends should obey the government under which they live, even at the risk of sacrificing all their administrative affairs and interests, they should under no circumstances suffer their inner religious beliefs and convictions to be violated and transgressed by any authority whatever. A distinction of a fundamental importance must, therefore, be made between spiritual and administrative matters. Whereas the former are sacred and inviolable and hence cannot be subject to compromise, the latter are secondary and can consequently be given up

> and even sacrificed for the sake of obedience to the laws and regulations of the government. Obedience to the state is so vital a principal of the Cause that should the authorities in ... decide to-day to prevent Bahá'ís from holding any meeting or publishing any literature they should obey.... But, as already pointed out, such an allegiance is confined merely to administrative matters which if checked can only retard the progress of the Faith for some time. In matters of belief, however, no compromise whatever should be allowed, even though the outcome of it be death or expulsion. [86:446]

> [N]o loyal believer should under any circumstances commit himself in any way to a political program or policy formulated and upheld by a political party for affiliation with such a party necessarily entails repudiation of some principles and teachings of the Cause, or partial recognition of some of its fundamental verities. The friends should, therefore, keep aloof from party politics. What they should mainly keep away from under all circumstances and in all its forms is partisanship. [86:443]

GRAEFFE, ETTY (1897-1969) An early Belgian believer who became a Bahá'í in America during the 1940s. She was one of the first contingent of American pioneers to set out for Europe during the first Seven Year Plan. She moved to Switzerland and following the direction of Shoghi Effendi set up an office under the adjunct of the International Bahá'í Bureau. Throughout her Bahá'í life she traveled and pioneered extensively within Europe. [51:453]

GREATEST HOLY LEAF see **BAHÍYYIH <u>KH</u>ÁNUM.**

GREATEST NAME Of the names or attributes of God there is said to be one which is "hidden" and the Bahá'ís believe that it is revealed in the name, "Bahá," which means splendor, light or glory. Derivatives of this such as "Alláh'u'Abhá" is used as a greeting between Bahá'ís and is repeated 95 times once per day. A calligraphical form designed by Mishkín-Qalam is used as a revered wall-hanging in many Bahá'í homes. Another form is used on the Bahá'í ring-stone.

GREEN ACRE BAHÁ'Í SCHOOL On a property in Eliot, Maine, donated to the Bahá'í Faith by Sarah Farmer (q.v.). It opened as a Bahá'í Summer School in 1929.

GREENLEAF, CHARLES (1856-1920) (Disciple of 'Abdu'l-Bahá) He heard of the Faith from Thornton Chase and with his wife, Elizabeth who were in turn students of Dr. Ibráhím <u>Kh</u>ayru'lláh. After some time their teacher made a suggestion to his class that they send a petition to 'Abdu'l-Bahá asking Him to confer infalli bility on Khayru'lláh for the West. Elizabeth refused to sign this letter, and later, when Khayru'lláh left the Faith, they realized the wrongness of his suggestion. Those who signed the letter drifted away, and those who remained firm in their Faith became the founders of the American Bahá'í community. Charles and his wife were indefatigable in their services to the Faith. Rosemary and Emeric Sala wrote an essay about this dedicated couple, *The Greenleafs: An Eternal Union*, and in 1921 another writer wrote of Charles, "He was a giant in mind and body, and a guide to great numbers of souls in their search for the Truth. He was one of the three recognized pillars of strength of the Cause in the early days—being closely associated with Thornton Chase and Arthur S. Agnew." [91:102-3] In 1907 Charles received a most powerful and confirmatory letter from 'Abdu'l-Bahá that contained the sentence, "Thy services and those of thy revered wife are acceptable in the Kingdom of Abhá, for ye have made your home a nest for the birds of God, and have engaged in teaching the Cause of God." Charles passed away on the 24 May 1920. [87:Vol ii, No. 19, p.321-2]

GREEVEN, INEZ MARSHALL COOK (1889-1983) A direct descendant of John Marshall, one of the signatories to the Declaration of Independence, she embraced the Cause in 1919. She traveled twice to visit 'Abdu'l-Bahá in Haifa. In 1926 she married Max Greeven, who embraced the Faith the next year. She moved with her husband to Europe in 1930 and returned to the United States when Holland was invaded in 1940. [11:608]

GREEVEN, MAX (1869-1951) An early American believer. It was through his efforts (acting on the request of the Spiritual Assembly of New York) that a specially bound set of Bahá'í Writings was presented to the Emperor of Japan (c.1928). In 1930 he moved to Bremen, Germany, where he was responsible for publishing a number of Bahá'í titles in Dutch. In the years following the Nazi ascent to power he was in the forefront of the work with the Ministry of Church Affairs in an effort (albeit unsuccessful) to have them rescind the edict curtailing Bahá'í activities. In 1937 he was forced to move to Holland, and Shoghi Effendi advised that all further appeal efforts should be foregone lest they have the effect of displeasing still further the Nazi authorities. [46:909]

GREGORY, ERNEST (1899-1978) A British believer (1951), he was the third local resident of Sheffield to embrace the Cause. He served as a member of the National Spiritual Assembly of the British Isles from 1954 to 1963. In 1963 he accepted an appointment as an Auxiliary Board member and served in that capacity until 1974. During that time he traveled widely throughout the British Isles, Iceland and the Faroes in the promotion of the

Cause. From 1974 until his death in 1978 he and his wife served at the Bahá'í World Center in Haifa. [53:455]

GREGORY, LOUIS G. (1874-1951) (Hand of the Cause of God) Born in Charleston, South Carolina, 6 June 1874, he was the son of a freed slave who passed away when he was five years old. His mother later remarried and his stepfather apprenticed him to a tailor and later helped him to attend Fisk University, where he obtained scholarships and worked cleaning, pressing, tailoring and as a waiter during the vacations. He went on to study law at Howard University, then he practiced with James A. Cobb, who later became a judge of the district court with Louis moving into the United States Treasury Department. Judge Cobb later wrote of Louis, "I knew him as a student, teacher, practicing lawyer, lecturer and friend, and in each capacity he was strong and understanding. In other words he was a fine student, a lovely character and a person with a great mind which he devoted to the betterment of mankind.... In fact, he was one of those who enriched the life of America." [40:650]

He learned of the Bahá'í Faith in 1908 while employed with the government. He later visited 'Abdu'l-Bahá in Egypt and again in Haifa and 'Akká. The inspiration of the first message Louis received from 'Abdu'l-Bahá set the course of his life for the next 43 years: "...I hope that thou mayest become the Herald of the Kingdom, become the means whereby the white and colored peoples shall close their eyes to racial differences and behold the reality of humanity, and that is the universal unity which is the oneness of the kingdom of the human race, the basic harmony of the world and the appearance of the Bounty of the Almighty." [40:650f]

According to one writer, "It is probable that no individual teacher in the Faith traveled more extensively throughout the United States than Mr. Gregory. Living in the utmost simplicity, sacrificing at every turn, he spoke in schools, colleges, churches, forums, conferences, and with individuals throughout the land. With a marvelous blending of humility and courage, of tenderness and adamantine firmness and steadfastness, he met high and low, rich and poor, educated and ignorant ... he spoke in Protestant, Catholic, and Jewish schools and before nondenominational groups, and everywhere he was accepted..." [40:652] For more than 35 years he was the mainspring behind the work for Race Amity; he was for many years a member of the National Spiritual Assembly of the Bahá'ís of the United States; he shone not only as a speaker and a writer but also as an administrator.

When he passed away on 30 July 1951 Shoghi Effendi cabled: "Profoundly deplore grievous loss dearly beloved, noble-minded, golden-hearted Louis Gregory, pride example Negro adherents

Faith, keenly feel loss one so loved, admired and trusted by 'Abdu'l-Bahá. Deserves rank first Hand of the Cause of his race. Rising generation African continent will glory in his memory and emulate his example." [3:163][48:666][59:156f][60:371]

GREGORY, LOUISA MATHEW (1866-1956) Born in England she moved to America in 1912. She met 'Abdu'l-Bahá in Egypt, Paris and America. At His suggestion she married Louis Gregory (q.v.) in New York in 1912. 'Abdu'l-Bahá officiated at their wedding. In 1927 she traveled extensively in Europe (while her husband devoted himself to similar extensive travel in America.) She faced a great deal of bigotry and prejudice during her marriage to Louis, which she faced bravely and with dignity. [47:876]

GROSSMAN, ELSA MARIA (1896-1977) (Knight of Bahá'u'lláh) Born in Argentina of German parentage, she returned to Germany with her family 1909 where, in 1919 or 1920, she embraced the Cause. She was imprisoned briefly for her faith during WW II. In 1953 she pioneered to Westerland, Frisian Islands for which service she was designated a Knight of Bahá'u'lláh. During her years on these islands she translated the following materials into German: *Gleanings from the Writings of Bahá'u'lláh* and (in collaboration with her brother, Hand of the Cause of God Hermann Grossmann [q.v.]) *The Proclamation of Bahá'u'lláh* and *Paris Talks*. [53:440]

GROSSMANN, ANNA (1905-1984) An early (1921) German believer, she married her childhood sweetheart Hermann Grossmann (later a Hand of the Cause of God) in 1924. She and her husband lived in Germany throughout the war years. After the war she was elected to the National Spiritual Assembly of Germany and Austria and served as its Secretary. In 1954 she was appointed an Auxiliary Board member. She accompanied her husband on several of his teaching trips and generally supported him throughout the entire period he functioned as a Hand of the Cause of God. Following his death she joined her son as a pioneer in Finland. After serving for several years on the easternmost local Spiritual Assembly (Savonlinna) in Europe she died on 12 June 1984. [11:639]

GROSSMANN, HERMANN (1899-1968) (Hand of the Cause of God) Born of German parents in Rosario, Argentine on 16 February 1899 his environment was one of love and tolerance. The family returned to Germany when Hermann was 10 years old. Towards the end of WW I he served in the German army. In 1924 he studied political science and the arts and obtained a doctorate in political science in Hamburg. In the summer of 1920 he heard of the Faith from Grace and Harlan Ober (q.v.). He and Lina and George Adam Benke almost immediately accepted the truth of this new message, and they rapidly became devotees. In his enthusiasm Hermann wrote to 'Abdu'l-Bahá and received back from Him a most significant letter dated 9 December 1920.

After continuing his studies of the Faith in Leipzig he returned to Hamburg where he witnessed the acceptance of the Faith by his mother and sister. He married another Bahá'í, Anna, and settled in Neckargemünd where he built the house that was to become the focal point for Bahá'í activities and lived there with his parents, his sister, wife and children.

During the remainder of his life he translated many of the Bahá'í Writings from English into German, published several major writings on the Faith in German and for some years published a monthly magazine in Esperanto.

In 1937 Hermann, his wife and sister, went on pilgrimage to the Holy Land. During WW II he, along with his fellow Bahá'ís suffered much persecution, most of the early Bahá'í compilations were seized and destroyed by the Gestapo, and he and his sister suffered imprisonment. Their home, however, escaped destruction and from the small amount of material on the Faith he had been able to preserve, he was able to prepare new compilations that served the new German Bahá'í community that emerged after the war.

In December 1951 he was in the first contingent of Hands of the Cause to be appointed by Shoghi Effendi and in spring 1957 he and Anna went on their second pilgrimage.

The most important works that came from his pen were: The Dawn of a New Age; A Change-over to Unity; What is the Bahá'í Religion? and God's Covenant in Revealed Religions.

After the passing of Shoghi Effendi in November 1957 he made a noticeable contribution to the consultations that followed when the Hands met in the Holy Land. One Hand wrote that Herman's breadth of vision and capacity to find a judicious balance were a valued factor. In 1959 the Hands asked him to return to South America to help the two Regional National Spiritual Assemblies there, as each had the enormous responsibility of guiding five countries. He suffered ill-health, but after traveling around the continent and to some of the countries in the interior he was able to report that ten new National Spiritual Assemblies could be formed in 1961.

In January 1960 he visited the continent again, this time with Anna, spending more that seven months there and yet again, during the Bahá'í election time in 1961. Finally in 1962, "distinct signs of exhaustion had begun to show," and "Once more it was his galvanizing enthusiasm and iron will that took him from place to place to bring to a good end one of his most difficult tasks." [51:420]

In spite of his weakened health he was able to witness the election of the Universal House of Justice in April 1963 and to participate in the World Congress in the Albert Hall, London, which immediately followed, but his travels became shorter and less frequent and he passed away on 7 July 1968. The Universal House of Justice cabled:

> Deeply regret announce passing Hand Cause Hermann Grossmann greatly admired beloved Guardian. His grievous loss deprives company Hands Cause outstanding collaborator and world community staunch defender promoter Faith. His courageous loyalty during challenging years tests persecutions Germany, outstanding services South America immortalized annals Faith. Invite all National Spiritual Assemblies hold memorial gatherings befitting his exalted rank exemplary services.[51:416][60:377]

GROUPS, BAHÁ'Í Communities with fewer than nine adult Bahá'ís normally constitute a "Bahá'í Group." They have no administrative status although they are encouraged to hold "feasts" and have a fund and teaching plans in preparation for the time when numbers permit them to assume Assembly status.

GUARDIAN, THE See **SHOGHI EFFENDI**.

GUNG, CLAIRE (Kleine) (1904-1985) (Knight of Bahá'u'lláh) An early (1939) British believer of German birth, she pioneered nine times over 39 years (five times in Great Britain and four times in Africa). In 1946 she pioneered to Northampton and became a member of the first local Spiritual Assembly formed during the British Six Year Plan (1944-1950). Subsequently she pioneered to Cardiff where she was again a member of the first local Spiritual Assembly of the city; she then moved on to Brighton, followed by Belfast. In 1950 she was the first British believer actually to leave in response to Shoghi Effendi's call for pioneers to go to Africa as part of the Two Year Plan (1951-1953), an action that won for her the accolade "Mother of Africa." She settled first in Lushoto, Tanganyika (now Tanzania), where she established the first multiracial kindergarten known as "Auntie Claire." After two years she moved to Nairobi, Kenya, where she served on the first local Spiritual Assembly of that country. Two years later she again moved, this time to Salisbury, Southern Rhodesia (now Harare, Zimbabwe), for which she was designated a Knight of Bahá'u'lláh. Approximately 18 months later she moved to Limbe, Nyasaland (now Malawi), and finally in 1957, for a period of 28 years, to Kampala, Uganda. At her passing in 1985 the Universal House of Justice cabled:

Deeply grieved news passing devoted maidservant God, Knight of Bahá'u'lláh, Claire Gung. Her distinguished record services Holy Cause as first pioneer leave her home community signalising inauguration African Campaign in response to beloved Guardian's call won her accolade "Mother of Africa." Her notable achievements in pioneer fields in United Kingdom, Tanzania, Kenya, Zimbabwe, Malawi and Uganda deserve high praise particularly her contributions to education children spiritual heart Africa. Praying Holy Shrines progress her noble soul Abhá Kingdom. May valiant souls arise from Africa' s fertile soil follow in her footsteps. [11:653]

GHUṢN Literally Branch: son or male descendant of Bahá'u'lláh. (Plural **AGHṢÁN**). [11:737]

GHUṢN-I-AṬHAR The Purest Branch: title conferred by Bahá'u'lláh on Mírzá Mihdí, brother of 'Abdu'l-Bahá, who died in the Most Great Prison 'Akká. [11:737]

GHUṢN-I-A'ẒAM The Most Great Branch: title conferred by Bahá'u'lláh on 'Abdu'l-Bahá. [11:737]

H

ḤADÍTH Literally report, account; Prophetic Tradition. The whole body of the sacred tradition of the Muslims.

ḤAḌRAT Literally presence. Placed before a name, in the form of Ḥaḍrat-i-—, the word is a courtesy signifying "His Majesty," "His Holiness." [11:737]

ḤAḌRAT-I-'ALÁ His Holiness, The Most Exalted One; a title of Bahá'u'lláh. [11:737]

HÄFNER, OTTO (1908-1978) An early European believer who met 'Abdu'l-Bahá on two separate occasions: the first time when he was three in Paris, and the second when he was five in Esslingen. Photographs of the period show 'Abdu'l-Bahá embracing him. Otto went on in later life to serve the Cause with loyalty and devotion. He was a member of the National Spiritual Assembly of Germany for some 20 years (serving throughout as Treasurer) and a member of the local Spiritual Assembly of Esslingen until the end of his life. [53:473]

HAIFA A major city and port in northern Israel. It was visited four times by Bahá'u'lláh, and was the city that for many years was the home of 'Abdu'l-Bahá and Shoghi Effendi and that today is the administrative world center of the Bahá'í Faith. See **ARC; MOUNT CARMEL.**

ḤÁJÍ, ḤÁJJ A Muslim who has performed a pilgrimage to Mecca. [11:737]

ḤÁJÍ ABU'L-ḤASAN (Ḥájí Amín) Appointed posthumously by Shoghi Effendi to the rank of a Hand of the Cause of God. He was also an Apostle of Bahá'u'lláh and Trustee of the Ḥuqúqu'lláh.

ḤÁJÍ ÁKHÚND (1842-1910) (Hand of the Cause of God) The son of a Mullá he was born about 1842 and became a Bábí when he was in his late teens. He readily accepted Bahá'u'lláh, suffered imprisonment and torture and was called upon by Bahá'u'lláh to travel in Persia deepening the believers in their Faith. He was the recipient of many letters from Bahá'u'lláh and eventually referred to as a Hand. He passed away in Ṭihrán in 1910.

ḤÁJÍ MÍRZÁ ḤASAN-I-ADÍB (1839-1919) (a Hand of the Cause of God and an Apostle of Bahá'u'lláh) Before accepting the Faith in his early forties in 1889, he was distinguished in the learned circles surrounding the Persian royal family, and in recognition of his outstanding accomplishments in the field of literature was given the title "Adíbu'l-'Ulamá" (The Literary man of the Muslim Divines). Such were the qualities of his scholarship that on accepting the Faith, his literary output reached new heights of sublimity and he gave the rest of his life in service to the Faith until he passed away in Ṭihrán in 1919. Although he never met with Bahá'u'lláh, He designated him a Hand of the Cause after a very short time as a Bahá'í, and under the guidance of 'Abdu'l-Bahá he continued to teach and write inspiring poetry, proofs of the truth of the Faith and historical works. He played an important rôle in the formation of the first Spiritual Assembly of the Bahá'ís of Ṭihrán and served for some time as its Chairman. He was also designated an Apostle of Bahá'u'lláh.

ḤÁJÍ MÍRZÁ MUḤAMMAD-TAQÍ-I-AFNÁN (—) (an Apostle of Bahá'u'lláh) A cousin of the Báb and son of Ḥájí Mírzá Siyyid Muḥammad to whom Bahá'u'lláh revealed the *Kitáb-i-Íqan*. He was one of the eminent members of the Afnán family and had the title Vakílu'd-Dawlih. He became a highly respected merchant in the city of Yazd, and not long before the passing of Bahá'u'lláh he purchased some properties in 'Ishqábád, Turkistán (where a nucleus of Persian Bahá'í families was developing into a strong Bahá'í community.) Bahá'u'lláh wished that one of these properties be used as the site for a Bahá'í House of Worship and, after His death (1892) Muḥammad-Taqí moved to 'Ishqábád and was responsible for the erection of the first Bahá'í House of Worship (Mashriqu'l-Adhkár.) He left that city in 1907 when the building was completed and went to serve 'Abdu'l-Bahá in the Holy Land where he passed away and was buried on the slopes of Mount

Carmel. He was of such a joyous and delightful personality that from the time of his stay in Baghdád he was known as "Kabír-i-Afnán."

ḤÁJÍ MÍRZÁ MUḤAMMAD-TAQIY-I-AHBARÍ (known as Ibn-i-Abhár) (-1917) (Hand of the Cause of God) While living in Qazvín, his father and family, already Bábís, became Bahá'ís about the time Bahá'u'lláh was beginning His Proclamation to the Kings in Adrianople (1868.) He traveled extensively throughout Persia, Caucasia, Turkmenistan and India and suffered imprisonment for his Faith. At the time of the passing of Bahá'u'lláh he was in prison in Ṭihrán and, for a time, wore the same heavy and notorious chains that had been placed on Bahá'u'lláh some 40 years previously. The first Central Spiritual Assembly was formed in Ṭihrán in 1897 in the presence of the other Hands. He finally settled there, and his wife—the daughter of Ḥájí Akhúnd (q.v.) helped found the first Girls' School. In 1907 he traveled to India in the company of two of the early American Bahá'ís. He passed away in Ṭihrán in 1917.

ḤÁJÍ MUḤAMMAD-'ALÍY-BÁRFURÚSHÍ See **QUDDÚS.**

ḤÁJÍ MULLÁ 'ALÍ-AKBAR-I-SHAHMIRZÁDÍ See **ḤÁJÍ ÁKHÚND.**

ḤAKÍM, DR. ARASTÚ KHÁN (1877-1934) The first Bahá'í from a Jewish background. He learned of the Faith from Ṭáhirih. [37:414]

ḤAKÍM, LUṬFU'LLÁH (1888-1968) (Member Universal House of Justice) He met 'Abdu'l-Bahá in 1911 while in London studying physiotherapy and became a friend of Dr. Esslemont (q.v.) (who was at that time studying the Faith). He received many Tablets from 'Abdu'l-Bahá and was eventually summoned by Him to serve in Haifa. In 1920 'Abdu'l-Bahá entrusted His grandson, Shoghi Effendi, to Luṭfu'lláh's safe-keeping when he was sent to England to study. Luṭfu'lláh was in Haifa when 'Abdu'l-Bahá passed away in 1921 and was one of those to greet Shoghi Effendi on his return to that city. In 1924 he returned to Persia where he worked for a time as an assistant in the clinic of Dr. Susan I. Moody (q.v.). In 1950, with Shoghi Effendi's approval, he returned to England. In 1951 he was summoned by Shoghi Effendi to Haifa and in 1952 was appointed by him to the first International Bahá'í Council. In 1963 he was elected a member of the first Universal House of Justice. In October 1967 he asked to be released from service due to ill health, but as it was only six months from the second International Convention, no by-election was held. He died in August 1968 and the Universal House of Justice cabled on 12 August 1968:

> Following cable sent National Spiritual Assembly Persia "Grieve announce passing Luṭfu'lláh Ḥakím dedicated servant Cause God. Special missions entrusted him full

confidence reposed in him by Master and Guardian his close association with early distinguished believers East West including his collaboration Esslemont his services Persia British Isles Holy Land his membership appointed and elected International Bahá'í Council his election Universal House of Justice will always be remembered immortal annals faith Bahá'u'lláh. Inform believers hold befitting memorial meetings all centres. Convey all members his family expressions loving sympathy assurance prayers progress his radiant soul Abhá Kingdom." Request hold memorial gathering Mother Temple West. [51:430]

ḤALABÍ, ḤUSAYN (1921-1979) (Knight of Bahá'u'lláh) An Íránian believer who in 1954 pioneered to Hadhramaut for which service he was designated a Knight of Bahá'u'lláh. [2:707]

HANDS OF THE CAUSE OF GOD The Bahá'í Faith has eliminated the internal conflicts which throughout past ages have characterized religious communities in the arena of those who are recognized for their learning and wisdom and those who are given the authority to govern, which were often reflected in hostility between church and state, priests and kings, intellectuals and the establishment. The overconcentration of power seen when priests or doctors of religious law have both powers of interpretation and of legislative and governing authority has no place in Bahá'í administration.

The Bahá'í community has no clergy, and all leadership and administrative powers are vested in elected bodies functioning at local, national and international levels. (See **UNIVERSAL HOUSE OF JUSTICE; ASSEMBLY.**) To provide a long-term overview of Bahá'í affairs, to maintain the continuity of guidance, to be uninvolved in periodic elections, to be regarded as the "learned" as different from the "rulers," Bahá'u'lláh established a unique institution, the "Hands of the Cause of God." Some He appointed in His own lifetime, others were appointed posthumously, while the sole authority to appoint living "Hands" was given by 'Abdu'l-Bahá to Shoghi Effendi, the Guardian of the Faith. After the passing of Shoghi Effendi no Hands could be appointed, and the Universal House of Justice created a new institution, the "Continental Board of Counsellors" (q.v.) to continue the principle of specially appointed individuals. These two "arms" of the Bahá'í Administration (q.v.) may therefore be regarded as the "elected" and the "appointed." Bahá'u'lláh wrote, "Blessed are the rulers and learned in Bahá'u'lláh." [77:221]

Shoghi Effendi wrote, "the 'learned' are, on the one hand, the Hands of the Cause of God and, on the other, the teachers and diffusers of His teachings who do not rank as Hands, but who have attained an eminent position in the teaching work. As to the 'rulers' they refer to the members of the local, national and international Houses of Justice." [81:245]

The Universal House of Justice wrote in 1972, "The existence of institutions of such exalted rank, comprising individuals who play such a vital rôle, who yet have no legislative, administrative or judicial authority, and are entirely devoid of priestly functions or the right to make authoritative interpretations, is a feature of Bahá'í administration unparalleled in the religions of the past." [2:473]

Bahá'u'lláh appointed four Hands to serve Him in His own lifetime, but 'Abdu'l-Bahá, while describing their station and functions, did not Himself appoint any additional Hands. He did, however, refer to four outstanding teachers of the Faith as Hands after their passing. In His Will and Testament, 'Abdu'l-Bahá wrote,

> The Hands of the Cause of God must be nominated and appointed by the guardian of the Cause of God. All must be under his shadow and obey his command ... The obligations of the Hands of the Cause are to diffuse the Divine Fragrances, to edify the souls of men, to promote learning, to improve the character of all men and to be, at all times and under all conditions, sanctified and detached from earthly things. They must manifest the fear of God by their conduct, their deeds and their words.[2:474]

From the time of 'Abdu'l-Bahá's passing in 1921 and taking up his appointment as Guardian, Shoghi Effendi over 30 years appointed 10 Hands posthumously and then, in December 1951 appointed a contingent of 12 living Hands. This was followed by the appointment of a further 12 and a final group of eight in October, 1957 barely a month before he passed away unexpectedly. In his letter of this final contingent he described them as the "Chief Stewards of Bahá'u'lláh's embryonic World Commonwealth." [6:127] See **APPENDIX—APPOINTMENT OF THE HANDS OF THE CAUSE OF GOD (BY CONTINGENT).**

HANEY, MARY IDA (Pankhurst) "Mariam" (1872-1965) An early (1900) American believer, she met 'Abdu'l-Bahá in 'Akká in 1909. He subsequently named her "Mariam" by which she was then known. He also blessed her unborn son, Paul, who was later to become a Hand of the Cause of God. She also met 'Abdu'l-Bahá during His visit to America in 1912. In later years she was associate editor of the Bahá'í magazine *Star of the West*; she later served on the editorial board that produced the first two volumes of the *Bahá'í World* yearbook. [50:343][83:139][59:189ff][60:384]

HANEY, PAUL EDMUND (1909-1982) (Hand of the Cause of God) Paul has the distinction of having been "on pilgrimage" before he was born in August 1909—his parents, married in 1893, had become Bahá'ís in 1900 and were among the first believers in America to visit 'Abdu'l-Bahá in 'Akká at a time when Paul's mother was carrying him in her womb. His parents came from God-fearing religious stock of the Methodist tradition, and once they accepted the Bahá'í Faith their commitment to 'Abdu'l-Bahá was total. Paul, their only child, was brought up with his whole being dedicated to the Covenant established with 'Abdu'l-Bahá. It was 'Abdu'l-Bahá who had given his mother the name "Mariam," which she always used, and it was 'Abdu'l-Bahá who gave His own name, "'Abdu'l-Bahá" to the child as his "real" name but he used "Paul" for the outside world. In a letter to Mariam, we find these phrases: "The new-born babe is blessed, and acceptable in the Divine Kingdom ... I ask God that my namesake, may grow and develop day by day and that his radiant face, may be illumined with the light of the greatest bestowal." [2:614]

As he went through school, his mother's loving education and the bestowal of 'Abdu'l-Bahá caused him to flourish spiritually, and there was a pure-heartedness about him which seemed an essential, unforced part of his nature. It was natural that he should grow up in Bahá'í service, following the example of his mother (his father died when Paul was barely 12 years old). At 22 he was appointed to the National Teaching Committee of the National Spiritual Assembly of the Bahá'ís of the United States and Canada. By 1934 he had studied at night school and then at Northwestern University and become a professional economist, publishing his first article, *The Economic Organization of Society in the New World Order.*

He became a member of the first National Youth Committee of the United States and was elected to the National Spiritual Assembly of the United States and Canada in 1946, remaining on it when Canada elected its own National Spiritual Assembly in 1948, and served as its Chairman from 1950 to 1957. During these years Paul represented the National Spiritual Assembly at the formation of several goal National Spiritual Assemblies—Canada (1948); the Regional National Spiritual Assembly of the Bahá'ís of South America (1951); and the Regional National Spiritual Assembly of the Bahá'ís of Italy and Switzerland (1953).

His stature in the Bahá'í world was such that it came as little surprise when on 19 March 1954 Shoghi Effendi announced his elevation to rank of Hand of the Cause, which was in a special announcement and not as part of a large contingent. He continued his international services to the Faith, representing the National Spiritual Assembly of the United States at the Convention in South and West Africa (1956) and representing the Guardian at the first Alaskan Convention in Anchorage (1957.)

Paul married Helen Margery Wheeler in July 1942 and the couple went to live in Washington not far from Mariam. They remained there until they moved to Haifa in 1958 when Paul was called upon to be one of the Nine Hands residing in the Holy Land. This required the utmost dedication from Paul; not only was he to be far away from his beloved mother, but in his professional life, he was within sight of appointment to a very high and well-paid position. His mother is on record as having written to a close friend, "The beloved Paul is so pure-hearted, so conscientious, so noble a soul that when this great blessing and honor came to him ... he said he could not live with himself had he not accepted this tremendous spiritual bounty ... naturally I miss Paul—the pure-hearted—but I believe I am with him daily in his service. Distance is no real separation when there is understanding and love." [2:617] Mariam passed away on 1 September 1965.

From the time Paul moved to Haifa until the end of his life, his total energies were concentrated on service to the Cause. He prepared a definitive statement on the Hands of the Cause and their activities up to the election of the Universal House of Justice; played an important part in the drafting of the messages of explanation and encouragement that flowed from the Hands of the Cause in Haifa; he traveled the world as their representative; he attended conventions of old-established national and newly inaugurated national Spiritual Assemblies; he presented a significant paper on the importance of the World Center of the Bahá'í Faith to the 1963 Jubilee Conference in the Albert Hall and was one of the five Hands of the Cause invited by the Universal House of Justice to remain in the Holy Land to carry out special duties and act as advisors to them. One such position was appointment to the editorial committee that was responsible for the gathering of information from the entire Bahá'í world and rewriting and editing it for distribution to all the National Spiritual Assemblies. He represented the Universal House of Justice in visiting communities throughout the world. In the words of one writer: "Paul Haney, distinguished, incorruptible, adamantine in his defense of the Covenant, sound in his judgment and greatly loved by Bahá'ís everywhere ... he attended diplomatic and governmental functions in Jerusalem as representative of the Bahá'í World Center." [2:617]

He played a great part in the development of the Continental Boards of Counsellors and the International Teaching Center and participated in all four of the International Conventions that took place during his lifetime. In August 1982 he represented the Universal House of Justice at a Continental Conference in Quito, Ecuador and on his return, delighted all the Bahá'ís at the World Center with his characteristically jovial, spiritually uplifting and informative account of his visit. Within three months all were shocked and grief-stricken when he was killed in a car accident in Haifa. The Universal House of Justice cabled the Bahá'í world:

> With stricken hearts announce sudden irreparable loss through automobile accident 3 December highly distinguished greatly prized Hand Cause God staunch defender Covenant Paul Haney. This distinguished servant Bahá'u'lláh was blessed childhood through attainment presence 'Abdu'l-Bahá. His natural gentleness, genuine humility, unaffected unbounded love, his uprightness, integrity, his single-minded devotion Cause since youthful years, his unfailing reliability meticulous attention detail characterized his historical services both national and international levels. Spanning more than half century his tireless labors included long-time membership American National Assembly. Since 1954 he consecrated his energies as member unique company Chief Stewards Faith and later as member body Hands Cause residing Holy Land at one of most crucial periods Bahá'í history. Last decade his earthly life was fully dedicated development newly formed International Teaching Center. Generations yet unborn will glory in his imperishable achievements and be inspired by his unique fortitude. Ardently supplicating Holy Threshold progress his noble soul Abhá Kingdom. Advise hold throughout Bahá'í world including all Mas͟hriqu'l-Ad͟hkárs memorial gatherings befitting his high rank and his meritorious services. [2:617]

HANNEN, JOSEPH H. (-1919) (Disciple of 'Abdu'l-Bahá) He was introduced to the Bahá'í Faith at the turn of the century by his wife, Pauline Knobloch Hannen, who had herself just become a Bahá'í within three days of hearing of it and who witnessed a similar acceptance by her mother and her two sisters, Fannie and Alma. Joseph and Pauline were two rare souls, teaching at every level of society and to people from every background. They healed the sick, consoled the distressed, visited prisoners in jail and taught children and the aged. Wherever they went were a healing and harmonizing influence. They made their pilgrimage to the Holy Land in 1909 and later published the story of the inspiration they received there in a pamphlet, *'Akká Lights.* When 'Abdu'l-Bahá was in America, He graced their home in Washington and received a host of visitors on 12 November 1912 less than a month before He left America. "Brother Joseph" died suddenly in 1919, leaving his widow to carry on their outstanding record of service.

HANNEN, PAULINE KNOBLOCH (-1939) An early (1903) American believer (the daughter of Amalie Knobloch) she met 'Abdu'l-Bahá during a visit to Haifa in 1909 and again during His visit to America in 1912. A published account of her 1909 visit was printed in leaflet form (*'Akká Lights*). She received several Tablets from 'Abdu'l-Bahá. [108][42:660][59:137ff]

ḤARAM Sanctuary, sacred precinct or court. See **ḤILL.** [11:737🕮]

ḤARAM-I-AQDAS The Most Holy Court; a description given by Shoghi Effendi to the northwestern quadrant of the garden surrounding the Shrine of Bahá'u'lláh. [11:737🕮]

HARRIS, HOOPER (1866-1934) An early American believer who traveled to India to share the Message. Shoghi Effendi wrote on his passing: "His passing in these early days of the formative period of our faith is, indeed, a severe loss not only to his friends and relatives but also mainly to the American followers of the movement who had found in his person not only a real and sincere fellow-believer but also an active and capable exponent of the teachings and principles of the Cause." [23:486][59:36ff]

ḤAWDAJ Howdah: a litter carried by a camel, mule, horse or elephant for traveling. [11:737🕮]

HAYDEN, ROBERT EARL (1913-1980) He was born Asa Bundy Sheffey; following the separation and divorce of his parents, while still an infant, he was renamed by his foster parents, William and Sue Ellen Hayden. It was not until he was 40 years old that he discovered that it was not his legal name; he made it legal in 1978. He embraced the Faith in 1943 and during his Bahá'í life served as a member of the local Spiritual Assemblies of Nashville, Tennessee and Falls Church, Virginia. He was a gifted, internationally recognized poet and in 1980 was invited to the White House to read his poetry to President and Mrs. Carter. He traveled widely giving readings of his poetry. From 1968 until his death he was an associate editor of *World Order* Bahá'í magazine. [2:716]

ḤAẒÍRATU'L-QUDS (The Sacred Fold) The name by which local and national Bahá'í centers are known. The national Ḥaẓíratu'l-Quds is the seat of the National Spiritual Assembly and the pivot of all national Bahá'í administrative activity. Ideally, as the Bahá'í Faith develops, it will, in addition to the Ma<u>sh</u>riqu'l-A<u>dh</u>kár (q.v.) provide the seat for the secretariat, the treasury, the archives, the library, the publishing office, a council chamber, an assembly hall, and accommodation for visitors.

HEALING Bahá'u'lláh commands His followers when ill to consult competent physicians. In Bahá'í understanding healing is possible by several means—physical medicine; psychological treatment; prayer; and through spiritual healing. In a table discussion early in the 1900s 'Abdu'l-Bahá said,

> Now let us speak of material healing. The science of medicine is still in a condition of infancy; it has not reached maturity. But when it has reached this point, cures will be performed by things which are not repulsive to the smell and taste of man—that is to say, by aliments, fruits and vegetables which are agreeable to the taste and have an agreeable smell. For the provoking cause of disease—that is to say, the cause of the entrance of disease into the human body—is either a physical one or is the effect of excitement of the nerves.... But the principal causes of disease are physical, for the human body is composed of numerous elements, but in the measure of an especial equilibrium.... As long as this equilibrium is maintained, man is preserved from disease; but if this essential balance, which is the pivot of the constitution, is disturbed, the constitution is disordered, and disease will supervene.... For instance, there is a decrease in one of the constituent ingredients of the body of man, and in another there is an increase; so the proportion of the equilibrium is disturbed, and disease occurs.... When by remedies and treatments the equilibrium is re-established, the disease is banished.... All the elements that are combined in man exist also in vegetables; therefore, if one of the constituents which compose the body of man diminishes, and he partakes of foods in which there is much of that diminished constituent, then the equilibrium will be established, and a cure will be obtained. So long as the aim is the readjustment of the constituents of the body, it can be effected either by medicine or by food. ... It is, therefore, evident that it is possible to cure by foods, aliments and fruits; but as today the science of medicine is imperfect, this fact is not yet fully grasped. When the science of medicine reaches perfection, treatment will be given by foods, aliments, fragrant fruits and vegetables, and by various waters, hot and cold in temperature.[56:257ff]

HEART Frequently used in Bahá'í Writings as a symbol of the spiritual center of an individual. Bahá'u'lláh wrote: "My first counsel is this: Possess a pure, kindly and radiant heart, that thine may be a sovereignty ancient, imperishable and everlasting." [92:A1] "Thy heart is My home; sanctify it for My descent." [92:A57] "In the garden of thy heart plant naught but the rose of love, and from the nightingale of affection and desire loosen not thy hold." [92:2]

'Abdu'l-Bahá wrote: "In this day, to thank God for His bounties consisteth in possessing a radiant heart, and a soul open to the promptings of the spirit. This is the essence of thanksgiving." [65:179]

HEAVEN AND HELL In the Bahá'í Faith these terms do not refer to material places but are conditions of a soul, which may experience them in this world or in the next. "Heaven" is taken as being in a condition of nearness to God after striving to acquire virtues while still on this earth and in exercise of its free will. "Hell" is the awareness of one's deprivation of these virtues and being remote from God. Shoghi Effendi wrote through his Secretary to a believer in 1947: "Heaven and hell are conditions within our own beings." [109:48]

HERALD, THE The Báb.

HIDDEN WORDS OF BAHÁ'U'LLÁH, THE This work was revealed in Arabic and Persian by Bahá'u'lláh in Baghdád in 1858. They were described by Shoghi Effendi as:

> a marvelous collection of gem-like utterances, the "Hidden Words" with which Bahá'u'lláh was inspired, as He paced, wrapped in His meditations, the banks of the Tigris. "The significance of this dynamic spiritual leaven cast into the life of the world for the reorientation of the minds of men, the edification of their souls and the rectification of their conduct can best be judged by the description of its character given in the opening passage by its Author: 'This is that which hath descended from the Realm of Glory, uttered by the tongue of power and might, and revealed unto the Prophets of old. We have taken the inner essence thereof and clothed it in the garment of brevity, as a token of grace unto the righteous, that they may stand faithful unto the Covenant of God, may fulfill in their lives His trust, and in the realm of spirit obtain the gem of Divine virtue.'"[5:140]

HIJRAT, HIJRA(H) Literally Emigration; Hegira: the date of Muḥammad's flight from Mecca to Medina in A. D. 622: the basis of the Islámic chronology. [11:737📖]

ḤILL Nonsacred ground, an antonym of Ḥaram (q.v.). [11:737📖]

HIM WHOM GOD SHALL MAKE MANIFEST References made by the Báb to "Him Whom God will make manifest"; in short, the One Who would appear in the future and for Whom He was pre paring the way. Understood by the Bahá'ís to refer to Bahá'u'lláh. See **PROMISED ONE OF ALL AGES.**

HIPP, SUZETTE (1901-1984) Through the efforts of Honor Kempton she became the first (1947) believer to embrace the Cause in Luxembourg. She served as a member of the first (1949) local Spiritual Assembly of Luxembourg-Ville (also the first in Luxembourg). She also served on the first (1962) National Spiritual Assembly of Luxembourg. Throughout her life she pioneered within Luxembourg to assist with the formation of local Spiritual Assemblies: Ettlebruck, Kopstal-Bridel, Walferdange. [11:641]

HOAR, WILLIAM H. (—) (Disciple of 'Abdu'l-Bahá) A prominent Bahá'í teacher whose home in Fanwood, New Jersey was visited by 'Abdu'l-Bahá on 31 May 1912.

HOFMAN, MARION HOLLEY She was born in California on 17 May 1910. She and her mother heard of the Faith from May Maxwell (q.v.) in 1917. Although brought up as a Bahá'í, while at university she lost her belief in God until her faith was regained after studying with Keith Ransome-Kehler in 1932. She became very active in teaching, writing and administration and served on the United States National Teaching Committee throughout the first Seven Year Plan in 1937. With an already distinguished record of service she went to England in 1945 to marry David Hofman (later a member of the Universal House of Justice) whom she had met many years previously while he was in the United States. Together they pioneered to Northampton, Birmingham, Oxford, Cardiff and Watford. During this time they both served on the National Spiritual Assembly and the National Teaching Committee. Also during this time she continued her travel and teaching (and was known to be a brilliant speaker); raised two children and took on a large amount of the editorial and business arrangements of her husband's publishing firm (George Ronald).

In 1954 she was appointed as one of the first two Auxiliary Board members for the Hand of the Cause George Townshend. This extended her travels to many of the developing Bahá'í communities in Europe. On the election of her husband to the Universal House of Justice in 1963 she was obliged to completely take over the running of the publishing business and, eventually, to relinquish her membership of the National Spiritual Assembly and the Auxiliary Board to join him in Haifa. On arrival, on the request of the Universal House of Justice, she used her deep knowledge of the Faith and capacities for meticulous research on their behalf.

When her husband retired from service at the Bahá'í World Centre, they resettled in Oxford, where she again became involved in teaching, giving study classes in Norway, Sweden, Holland,

Czechoslovakia and Ireland right into her 80s. In a tribute by the National Spiritual Assembly of the Bahá'ís of the United Kingdom on her passing in December 1995 they wrote:

> Her understanding of the World Order of Bahá'u'lláh was unique and greatly enhanced by the answers to her questions given at the dinner table by Shoghi Effendi when on pilgrimage. When she returned to England from Haifa she continued to endear herself to all with whom she came into contact and her service to the Faith only lessened as her health deteriorated. Only future historians will be able to do justice to her unforgettable contributions to the progress of the Faith made during more than sixty years of her life. (*Bahá'í Journal* United Kingdom January 1996)

> The Universal House of Justice cabled:

> Profoundly lament loss dearly loved, highly admired, stalwart handmaiden Bahá'u'lláh Marion Hofman now gathered glory Abhá Kingdom. Community Most Great Name robbed of one of its tireless promoters whose accomplishments were praised beloved Guardian. Her service National Teaching Committee United States during first Seven Year Plan, National Spiritual Assembly British Isles, First Auxiliary Board Europe, and at World Centre Faith lovingly remembered. Her promotion teaching, pioneering plans throughout British Community, her notable contribution enrichment Bahá'í literature, her indomitable faith, unswerving devotion Covenant coupled with her loving nature, unflagging zeal and radiant spirit, greatly aided advancement Cause God. Confident her distinguished labours extending over period six decades British Isles, United States will inspire present future generation Bahá'í 'emulate shining example her life. Assure fervent prayers Holy Shrines progress her noble soul. Convey our loving sympathy members her family. Advise hold befitting memorial meetings her honour throughout British Isles.

HOKAFONU, MOSESE (1927-1979) A Tongan (Tongatapu Island) believer who donated the land for the national Ḥaẓíratu'l-Quds. In 1968 he was appointed an Auxiliary Board member and traveled extensively in the islands of the South Pacific in the promotion of the Cause. [2:686]

HOLLEY, DORIS (Pascal) (1894-1983) An early (1913) American believer of Irish birth she married Horace Holley (q.v.). Following the death of her husband in 1960 she moved in 1961 to Neuchâtel,

Switzerland, where she remained as a pioneer for seven years before moving to Lausanne. In 1971 she moved to Limerick, Ireland, and then to Dun Laoghaire in 1976 to save the local Spiritual Assembly. In 1980 she moved to Greystones for the purpose of forming the local Spiritual Assembly of County Wicklow. [2:822]

HOLLEY, HORACE HOTCHKISS (1887-1960) (Hand of the Cause of God) Born in Torrington, Connecticut, 7 April 1887; majored in literature at Williams College, Williamstown, Massachusetts in 1909. He traveled, studied and worked in Europe until the war broke out in 1914. On the voyage to Europe he met a young artist whom he married in Paris and from whom he heard of the Bahá'í Faith. While living in Italy in 1911 they learned of the visit of 'Abdu'l-Bahá to Thonon-les-Bains, France and were able to meet Him there and subsequently in Paris. It was in Paris that his first two books of poems were published, and it was there that he founded and became director of the Ashur Gallery of Modern Art. Back in the United States, Horace's first book on the Bahá'í Faith, *Bahá'ísm—The Modern Social Religion*, was published in 1913, and he moved to New York with his family in 1914. For the next 46 years his hand was never idle—poetry, books, articles, advertising material, editorials, lectures, compilations of Bahá'í scripture and a vast correspondence carried out for the American National Spiritual Assembly of which he was the Secretary for 34 of the 36 years he was a member.

The administration of the Bahá'í Faith was for the most part developed by Shoghi Effendi writing to the American Bahá'ís through Horace. It was Horace, who, on receipt of a letter from the Guardian, would study it, give it a title and divide it into chapters with subtitles and produce it for the Bahá'í world. The close collaboration between Horace and the Guardian is reflected in one of the many personal letters Shoghi Effendi wrote to him:

> My dearest co-worker: I have lately followed your activities and efforts, as reflected in the minutes of the meetings you sent me, with true satisfaction and pleasure ... Your personal contribution to so many aspects and phases of the Movement, performed so diligently, so effectively and so thoroughly are truly a source of joy and inspiration to me. How much I feel the need of a similar worker by my side in Haifa, as competent, as thorough, as methodical as alert as yourself. You cannot and should not leave your post for the present. Haifa will have to take care of itself for some time.[47:853]

It was never to be, however, and in 1925 Horace gave up earning his living in various companies to devote his entire life to Bahá'í service. The partnership that developed between Horace and the Guardian of the Bahá'í Faith was dealt with in depth by the writer of his "In Memoriam" in *Bahá'í World*: "That it worked so well, bore such fruit and survived the acid test of time, is a great compliment to the two people involved. For Shoghi Effendi was not dealing with a sycophant but a man of strong personality, views and capacity, and Horace was not dealing with a mere leader but a divinely inspired, infallibly guided spiritual ruler" [47:854]

Although constantly overworked, writing, editing, lecturing, participating in symposia and being the pivot around which all the administrative work of the U.S. National Spiritual Assembly revolved, he kept up his close correspondence with the Guardian who, in turn poured out his encouragement and appreciation. "Your ready pen, your brilliant mind, your marvelous vigor and organizing ability, above all your unwavering loyalty are assets that I greatly value and for which I am deeply grateful."(1931.) [47:854ff] "Assure you my ever deepening admiration your unrivaled services..."(1933) [47:854ff]

A heart attack in 1944 left him with weakening health, but he attended the first Canadian National Convention in 1948 and the Convention in 1951 in Panama City when the first Central American National Spiritual Assembly was elected. He was in the first contingent of live Hands of the Cause and was able to attend the Intercontinental Conferences in 1953; in Kampala; Stockholm; Chicago and New Delhi. It was in December of that year that for the first time Horace went on pilgrimage and met the Guardian. When the Guardian passed away Horace was in hospital and unable to attend the funeral in London. Virtually an invalid, he attended the first and most vital meeting of the Hands of the Cause in the Holy Land in December 1957 after the passing of the Guardian and was largely responsible for the Proclamation that came to the Bahá'í world after that meeting. The decision was taken at that time that Horace should resign from the U.S. National Spiritual Assembly and go to reside in the Holy Land. He and his wife arrived in Israel on 31 December 1959, and he passed away after a brief six months on 12 July 1960. The Hands of the Cause, in their capacity as Custodians of the Bahá'í Faith, sent the following message to the Bahá'í world, "Grieved announce passing Haifa much loved distinguished Hand Cause Horace Holley outstanding champion Faith since days Master, praised by beloved Guardian for unique contribution development Administrative Order. His indefatigable services protection teaching administrative fields culminating service Holy Land inspiring example present future generations Bahá'ís."[47:849ff][91:214][60:388]

HOLMES, ETHEL MAY BOWMAN (1904-1972) (Knight of Bahá'u'lláh) An American believer who pioneered with her husband to the outer islands of the Bahamas in 1953 (for which service they were designated Knights of Bahá'u'lláh).[51:523]

HOLMLUND, MARIE CIOCCA (1929-1968) (Knight of Bahá'u'lláh) An American believer (1949) of Italian parentage. In 1953 she pioneered to Cagliari, Sardinia for which service she was designated a Knight of Bahá'u'lláh. [51:437]

HOLY DAYS, BAHÁ'Í Eleven special days in the year that commemorate significant events and on nine of which work is suspended. See **BAHÁ'Í CALENDAR**.

HOLY PLACES The Bahá'ís regard the Houses of the three Central Figures of the Faith and their Shrines as being of special significance—the most sacred spot on earth being the Shrine of Bahá'u'lláh, Bahjí, Israel. This and the houses of the Báb in Shíráz, Írán and that of Bahá'u'lláh in Baghdád, Iráq are places for pilgrimage. Other places regarded as holy include the Shrine of the Báb and the Shrine of 'Abdu'l-Bahá in Haifa, Israel, and the Shrines of the other revered members of Bahá'u'lláh's Family on Mount Carmel, the Mansion at Bahjí and the Grave of Shoghi Effendi, London. On the general theme of Holy Places, 'Abdu'l-Bahá wrote: "Holy places are undoubtedly centers of the outpouring of Divine grace, because on entering the illumined sites associated with martyrs and holy souls, and by observing reverence, both physical and spiritual, one's heart is moved with great tenderness." [86:539]

HOLY SPIRIT Used in Bahá'í Writings to indicate the outpouring from God to His Manifestations. Just as the nature of God is unknowable, so also is the nature of the Holy Spirit and so is frequently referred to in all dispensations in some symbolic form, such as the dove that "descended" upon Jesus; the Angel Gabriel who appeared to Muḥammad; the voice of God that "spoke" with Moses through the burning bush. Bahá'u'lláh refers to the "Maid of Heaven" when writing of His call to arise to proclaim His Mission. It is through the power of the Holy Spirit that God's Manifestations infuse all mankind with the capacity to evolve spiritually and carry out His purpose.

HOPPER, ELIZABETH G. (1883-1967) (Knight of Bahá'u'lláh) An American believer who pioneered in 1953 to Funchal, Madeira Islands for which service she was designated a Knight of Bahá'u'lláh. She remained at her post, despite great hardship and suffering, until her death in 1967. [50:311]

HORNELL, KATHLEEN (Lady Hornell) (1890-1977) An early (1923) British believer, she served as a member of the British National Spiritual Assembly from 1936 until 1945. She also served as a member of the local Spiritual Assembly of London from 1932 until 1945 except for one year during WW II when she lived in Torquay (and even then she served on that local Spiritual Assembly). She traveled extensively throughout the country promoting the Cause and pioneered to such places as Nottingham, Belfast and then Bangor, Northern Ireland, where she served on the first (1959) local Spiritual Assembly. In 1960 she pioneered to Venice and remained there until 1965 when she pioneered on to Cagliari, Sardinia. Towards the end of her life she returned to England to live with her son-in-law, Hand of the Cause of God, Ḥasan Balyúzí and her daughter, Molly Balyúzí. She died in London in September 1977 and was buried in the vicinity of the grave of Shoghi Effendi. The Universal House of Justice cabled

> Passing Lady Hornell robs British Community one of few remaining links early days Faith. Her unwavering faith constant dedicated services pioneer teaching administration fields over so many years assure her high station annals Cause provide shining example present future generations. Advise hold befitting memorial meeting. Assure ardent prayers Sacred Threshold progress her loving soul Abhá Kingdom. [53:443]

HOUSES OF JUSTICE The Universal House of Justice was ordained by Bahá'u'lláh Who described its functions; these were further explained by 'Abdu'l-Bahá and by Shoghi Effendi (see **GUARDIAN, THE**). The local and national Spiritual Assemblies will in future be designated "Houses of Justice." Shoghi Effendi wrote:

> The importance, nay the absolute necessity of these local Assemblies is manifest when we realize that in the days to come they will evolve into the local Houses of Justice.... The matter of Teaching, its direction, its ways and means, its extension, its consolidation, essential as they are to the interests of the Cause, constitute by no means the only issue which should receive the full attention of these Assemblies ... other duties, no less vital to the interests of the Cause, devolve upon the elected representatives of the friends in every locality.... They must endeavor to promote amity and concord amongst the friends, efface every lingering trace of distrust, coolness and estrangement from every heart, and secure in its stead an active and whole-hearted co-operation for the service of the Cause. They must do their utmost to extend at all times the helping hand to the poor, the sick, the disabled, the orphan, the widow, irrespective of color, caste and creed.... They must promote by every means in their power the

> material as well as the spiritual enlightenment of youth, the means for the education of children, institute, whenever possible, Bahá'í educational institutions, organize and supervise their work and provide the best means for their progress and development. They must undertake the arrangement of the regular meetings of the friends, the feasts and the anniversaries, as well as the special gatherings designed to serve and promote the social, intellectual and spiritual interests of their fellow-men.... They must supervise in these days when the Cause is still in its infancy all Bahá'í publications and translations, and provide in general for a dignified and accurate presentation of all Bahá'í literature and its distribution to the general public. [96:37ff] See **ADMINISTRATION ORDER, BAHÁ'Í.**

HUFFMAN, EVELYN (1911-1978) She and her husband (Vern, 1906-1978) were among the early (1945) believers in Alaska. A year or so after becoming Bahá'ís they moved from Anchorage (which was the only Bahá'í community in Alaska at that time) to a property about 10 miles from the town and in so doing formed the nucleus of what was to be the second local Spiritual Assembly in Alaska. In 1957 Evelyn was elected to the first National Spiritual Assembly of Alaska and served as its Secretary for seven of her 10 years on that body. The land on which the Alaskan National Ḥaẓíratu'l-Quds is build was donated by the Huffmans. In 1965 they pioneered to Prince of Wales Island. Following the death of her husband (1974) Evelyn served for one year at the Bahá'í World Center (1976-1977). She returned to Alaska, and despite her deteriorating health, she continued her teaching activities among the Indian and Eskimo peoples. [53:467]

ḤUJJAT Literally proof, argument, reason. [11:737📖]

HUMAN RIGHTS 'Abdu'l-Bahá said:

> Bahá'u'lláh teaches that an equal standard of human rights must be recognized and adopted. In the estimation of God all men are equal; there is no distinction or preferment for any soul in the dominion of His justice and equity."[106: 240f]

> And again,

> The Bahá'í Cause covers all economic and social questions under the heading and ruling of its laws. The essence of the Bahá'í spirit is that, in order to establish a better social order and economic condition, there must be allegiance to the laws and principles of government.... The

governments will enact these laws, establishing just legislation and economics in order that all humanity may enjoy a full measure of welfare and privilege; but this will always be according to legal protection and procedure. Without legislative administration, rights and demands fail, and the welfare of the commonwealth cannot be realized. [26:238]

In February 1947 the National Spiritual Assembly of the Bahá'ís of the United States and Canada presented to the Human Rights Commission a Statement on behalf of the eight National Spiritual Assemblies then in existence, entitled *A Bahá'í Declaration of Human Obligations and Rights* [110] that set out in four chapters the Bahá'í position on this subject. After the Universal Declaration of Human Rights, great emphasis for the following 50 years was placed on "rights" rather than upon "obligations." It was only in the lead-up to the 50th anniversary of the United Nations that attention began to be drawn to the obligations and responsibilities of the individual. The 1947 Bahá'í document was far too advanced in concept to be adopted in full as the following extract indicates:

> World order has become legally possible, socially imperative, and divinely ordained. The principle of federation has already united previously independent communities diverse in race, language, religion and size of population. The nations can find just expression for their legitimate rights and needs through proportionate representation in a supranational body. Until world citizenship is guaranteed as a social status, the human rights and privileges developed in the past are undermined by the disruption of modern society.[110:11]

Further developing this theme, the Bahá'í International Community, as an outcome of the Earth Summit, June 1992, presented a statement to the first session of the Commission on Sustainable Development, June 1993, entitled *World Citizenship—A Global Ethic for Sustainable Development.* Referring to the educational programs called for in Agenda 21, this document states,

> Based on the principle of the oneness of the human race, they should cultivate tolerance and brotherhood, nurturing an appreciation for the richness and importance of the world's diverse cultural, religious and social systems and strengthening those traditions that contribute to a sustainable, world civilization. They should teach the principle of "unity in diversity" as the key to strength and wealth both for the nations and for the world community.

> They should foster an ethic of service to the common good and convey an understanding of both the rights and the responsibilities of world citizenship.

In a statement issued in time for wide use at the Social Development Summit, Copenhagen, 1995, the Bahá'í International Community wrote:

> At the heart of the discussion of a strategy of social and economic development, therefore lies the issue of human rights. The shaping of such a strategy calls for the promotion of human rights to be freed from the grip of the false dichotomies that have for so long held it hostage. Concern that each human being should enjoy the freedom of thought and action conducive to his or her personal growth does not justify devotion to the cult of individualism that so deeply corrupts many areas of contemporary life.[94:10f]

ḤUQÚQU'LLÁH—THE RIGHT OF GOD Ḥuqúqu'lláh is ordained by Bahá'u'lláh both as a spiritual obligation and a bounty. Clear guidelines are given by Him in His Book of Law (Kitáb-i-Aqdas) and amplified by 'Abdu'l-Bahá, Shoghi Effendi and by the Universal House of Justice. The payment of Ḥuqúqu'lláh is based on the gold standard. The amount due is 19 percent of income after living expenses. Each believer, individually must decide on what "standard of living" is to be observed before the required 19 percent is paid. This therefore combines the freedom of the individual with the compulsory payment and allows for the full expression of each Bahá'í to determine how much of an element of sacrifice is involved. The Bahá'í Writings make it clear that no one should ever feel forced to pay, nor may a Bahá'í be solicited for payment. The use of the funds raised by this payment is for the promotion of the Faith and for charitable purposes. There is a difference made between the normal contributions to the Bahá'í Fund (q.v.) and Ḥuqúqu'lláh, as the latter is seen, as the name implies, to be "the right of God," while ordinary donations are entirely in the province of the believer to determine when, how much and to which Fund, contributions are made. Bahá'ís believe that the payment of Ḥuqúqu'lláh actually purifies the possessions of those who pay it. Bahá'u'lláh wrote:

> It is clear and evident that the payment of the Right of God is conducive to prosperity, to blessing, and to honor and Divine protection. Well is it with them that comprehend and recognize this truth and woe betide them that believe not. And this is on condition that the individual should observe the injunctions prescribed in the Book with the utmost radiance, gladness and willing acquies-

cence. It behoveth you to counsel the friends to do that which is right and praiseworthy. Whoso hearkeneth to this call, it is to his own behoof, and whoso faileth bringeth loss upon himself. Verily our Lord of Mercy is the All-Sufficing, the All-praised.[86:340]

Bahá'u'lláh Himself answered a question concerning the precedence of Ḥuqúqu'lláh as a payment:

Thou hast asked which is to take precedence: the Ḥuqúqu'lláh, the debts of the deceased, or the cost of burial. It is God's command that the cost of burial take precedence, then payment of debts, then the Right of God. Verily He is the One Who will pay due recompense, the All-Rewarding, the All-Generous. If the property is not equal to the debts, the estate must be distributed in direct proportion to each debt. The settlement of debts is a most important command set forth in the Book. Well is it with him who ascendeth unto God, without any obligations to Ḥuqúqu'lláh and to His servants. It is evident that the Ḥuqúqu'lláh hath priority over all other liabilities. [86:306]

'Abdu'l-Bahá wrote:

The Lord, as a sign of His infinite bounties, hath graciously favored His servants by providing for a fixed money offering ('Ḥuquq), to be dutifully presented unto Him, though He, the True One and His servants have been at all times independent of all created things, and God verily is the All-Possessing, exalted above the need of any gift from His creatures. This fixed money offering, however, causeth the people to become firm and steadfast and draweth Divine increase upon them. It is to be offered through the Guardian of the Cause of God, that it may be expended for the diffusion of the Fragrances of God and the exaltation of His Word, for benevolent pursuits and for the common weal. [111:15]

ḤUSAYN The third Imám, second son of 'Alí and Fáṭimih, martyred on the plains of Karbilá in A.D. 680. [11:737📖]

ḤUSAYNÍYYIH A place where the martyrdom of the Imám Ḥusayn is mourned or where Muslim passion-plays may be presented. The term is the designation that was given to Bahá'u'lláh's Most Great House in Baghdád after its forcible occupation by the Shí'ah community. [11:737📖]

HUTCHINSON-SMITH, JEAN (1886-1979) An early (1941) Australian believer who traveled widely in the United Kingdom and

Europe. She was the first (1959) Australian believer to visit the Japanese Bahá'í community. [2:681]

HUXTABLE, CATHERINE HEWARD (1932-1967) (Knight of Bahá'u'lláh) Born in England, she moved with her family to Canada in 1939. Although confined to a wheelchair, she pioneered with her husband several times: first to Regina, Saskatchewan (1957), then to the Gulf Islands (1959), for which service she was designated a Knight of Bahá'u'lláh. In 1965 she and her husband pioneered to St. Helena. [50:313]

HYDE-DUNN, CLARA ("Mother Dunn") (1869-1960) (Hand of the Cause of God) Born in London, England on 12 May 1869 the sixth child of a London policeman, Thomas Holder, and an Irish mother, she settled in the United States and met John Henry Hyde-Dunn (q.v.) when she was in her late thirties

In 1932, after over a decade of dedicated travel teaching with her husband throughout Australia, she went alone on pilgrimage to the Holy Land. Together, they subsequently witnessed in 1934 the formation of the first National Spiritual Assembly of the Bahá'ís of Australia and New Zealand.

With the passing of Hyde in 1941 she continued her teaching with unabated vigor. As the last remaining link in Australia with 'Abdu'l-Bahá she had a particularly important rôle to play. This became apparent when, in the second contingent to be appointed as Hands of the Cause and aged 84, she assumed her increased responsibilities with enthusiasm.

Frail in body but with a remarkable memory and a vibrant personality, she attended the Intercontinental Conference in New Delhi in October 1953 and a summer school in New Zealand in 1954 and later in that year, every state in Australia. In 1957, as representative of the Guardian, she attended the convention when the first National Spiritual Assembly of the Bahá'ís of New Zealand was elected. On the passing of the Guardian she attended the first Conclave of the Hands of the Cause in Bahjí, Israel, and was able, as appointed by the Guardian before he died, to participate in the Australian Intercontinental Conference when the foundations of the House of Worship were dedicated. Her scintillating wit inherited from her Irish mother remained fresh until her passing in November 1960 in Sydney, where she was laid to rest beside her husband—unique in Bahá'í history—two Hands of the Cause, man and wife, pioneers and the openers of a Continent, together in one grave.

On 21 November the Hands of the Cause sent the following cable to the U.S. National Spiritual Assembly: "Grieve announce passing Hand Cause Clara Dunn distinguished member American Bahá'í Community who with Hyde-Dunn spiritual conqueror Australia, responded Master's appeal Divine Plan arose carried Faith Antipodes, rendered unique unforgettable pioneer service over forty year period. Advise hold memorial gathering Temple." [32:245][47:859][91:153][60:331]

HYDE-DUNN, JOHN HENRY (1855-1941) (Hand of the Cause of God) Born in London, 5 March 1855, the son of a pharmacist (interestingly, he had childhood contact with Charles Dickens). In early adult life he engaged in business in Great Britain and Europe and emigrated to the United States. On arrival in America he came in contact with the Bahá'í Faith and immediately accepted it. He maintained close contact with such outstanding Bahá'í teachers as Lua Getsinger, Thornton Chase and Helen S. Goodall. As a traveling salesman he moved around the country teaching the Faith, but his real confirmation came with his meeting with 'Abdu'l-Bahá in San Francisco in the autumn of 1912.

Fanny, his first wife, had become a Bahá'í but died in 1911 before the visit of 'Abdu'l-Bahá. Some time after Hyde's meeting with the Master he married Clara, a Bahá'í who had settled in San Francisco where their "open house" became a center of Bahá'í teaching and hospitality. The couple were reading one of 'Abdu'l-Bahá's messages to America in 1918 (*Tablets of the Divine Plan*) when, as Hyde later wrote, "His appeal was so penetrating and thrilling it pierced our hearts....Mother [Clara] looked up and said, 'Shall we go Father? [Hyde] 'Yes' was my reply, and no further discussion took place." [40:553]

They decided to "open" Australia; stopped on their way there for two months in Honolulu and landed in Sydney 18 April 1919. Hyde was not in very good health, and Clara was the first one to obtain employment but after five months Hyde applied for and was given employment that took him all over Australia and to New Zealand to enable him to carry the Bahá'í message and with sufficient income for Clara to leave her job and travel with him. They lived for various periods in New South Wales; Victoria; Western Australia; and Queensland. They were responsible for the foundation of several local Spiritual Assemblies and witnessed the formation of a National Spiritual Assembly in 1934. When he died in Sydney on 17 February 1941 the National Spiritual Assembly's obituary contained many tributes to "Father" Dunn which included. "It was not alone the great message of which he was the bearer that arrested attention but in addition, the unearthly light that suffused his whole personality when giving the message, endowing him with a quality which set him on a spiritual plane to which others were blindly groping, a height reached only through the surrender of personal will and ambition..." [40:555]

In his cable to America, Shoghi Effendi wrote: "I share your sorrow in the loss and participate in your rejoicings for the triumph of beloved Father Dunn. The magnificent career of this veteran warrior of the Faith of Bahá'u'lláh reflects the purest lustre of the world historic mission conferred upon American community by 'Abdu'l-Bahá ... Advise hold national memorial gathering ... befitting the rank of Australia's spiritual conqueror." [112:45]

To the Australian National Spiritual Assembly Shoghi Effendi wrote on 19 April 1941 that the community had "lost a great leader...The influence he has exercised will however continue to live, and the example he has set will inspire the rising generation to perform deeds as great and brilliant as those which will ever remain associated with his name. Our dear friend, Mr. Hyde-Dunn, will, from his exalted station intercede on your behalf, and you should, on your part strive to emulate one whom Bahá'í historians will recognize and acclaim as Australia's spiritual conqueror." [113:39]

When, in February 1952, Clara Dunn was appointed a Hand of the Cause of God, the Guardian, in response to an inquiry from Australia, cabled, "Hyde-Dunn regarded as Hand." [45:593][91:153]

I

-I- (-i-) Sound inserted in pronunciation (though not represented in Persian script) at the end of a word to indicate that the following word stands in a possessive or adjectival relation to it. [11:737📖]

IBN Son. [11:737📖]

ÍL Clan, tribe. [11:737📖]

IMÁM Head, chief, leader. (1) Muslim cleric who leads the congregation in prayer. (2) Title applied by the Shí'ahs to each of the 12 successors of Muḥammad in the line of 'Alí. [11:737📖]

IMÁM-JUM'IH Muslim clergyman who performs the Friday prayers, the chief Imám in a town or city; chief of the mullás, who recites the Friday prayers for the sovereign. [11:737📖]

IMÁM-ZÁDIH Descendant of an Imám or his shrine. [11:737📖]

INDEPENDENT SEARCH AFTER TRUTH Shoghi Effendi wrote that the independent search after truth needs to be "unfettered by superstition or tradition" [5:281] and that it is one of the cardinal social principles of the Bahá'í Faith. 'Abdu'l-Bahá explained that this was one of the first principles of Bahá'u'lláh and said: "Among these teachings is the independent investigation of reality, so that the world of humanity might be saved from the darkness of imitation and attain to the truth." [107:28f] And again,

> Among these teachings was the independent investigation of reality so that the world of humanity may be saved from the darkness of imitation and attain to the truth; may tear off and cast away this ragged and outgrown garment.... and may put on the robe woven in the utmost purity and holiness in the loom of reality. As reality is one and cannot admit of multiplicity, therefore different opinions must ultimately become fused into one. [65:298]

> Man must cut himself free from all prejudice and from the result of his own imagination, so that he may be able to search for truth unhindered. Truth is one in all religions, and by means of it the unity of the world can be realized. All the peoples have a fundamental belief in common. Being one, truth cannot be divided, and the differences that appear to exist among the nations only result from their attachment to prejudice. If only men would search out truth, they would find themselves united. [25:129]

INFALLIBILITY Bahá'ís understand there to be two kinds of infallibility (freedom from error): that which is "conferred" and that which is "inherent." Inherent infallibility rests only with the Manifestation of God that Bahá'u'lláh describes in the *Kitáb-i-Aqdas* as "He doeth whatsoever He Willeth." [81: 36]

'Abdu'l-Bahá explains this:

> Infallibility is of two kinds: essential infallibility and acquired infallibility. In like manner there is essential knowledge and acquired knowledge; and so it is with other names and attributes. Essential infallibility is peculiar to the supreme Manifestation, for it is His essential requirement, and an essential requirement cannot be separated from the thing itself. The rays are the essential necessity of the sun and are inseparable from it. Knowledge is an essential necessity of God and is inseparable from Him. Power is an essential necessity of God and is inseparable from Him. If it could be separated from Him, He would not be God. If the rays could be separated from the sun, it would not be the sun. Therefore, if one imagines separation of the Most Great Infallibility from the supreme Manifestation, He would not be the supreme Manifestation, and He would lack the essential perfections. But acquired infallibility is not a natural necessity; on the contrary, it is a ray of the bounty of infallibility which shines from the Sun of Reality upon hearts, and grants a share and portion of itself to souls. ... To epito

> mize: essential infallibility belongs especially to the supreme Manifestations, and acquired infallibility is granted to every holy soul. For instance, the Universal House of Justice ... will be under the protection and the unerring guidance of God. If that House of Justice shall decide unanimously, or by a majority, upon any question not mentioned in the Book, that decision and command will be guarded from mistake. Now the members of the House of Justice have not, individually, essential infallibility; but the body of the House of Justice is under the protection and unerring guidance of God: this is called conferred infallibility. [56:171ff]

While Bahá'u'lláh therefore had the "Most Great Infallibility," infallibility was conferred by Him on 'Abdu'l-Bahá and the Universal House of Justice, and by 'Abdu'l-Bahá on Shoghi Effendi acting as Guardian. In this respect, however, Shoghi Effendi wrote: "The infallibility of the Guardian is confined to matters which are related strictly to the Cause and interpretation of the teachings; he is not an infallible authority on other subjects, such as economics, science, etc." [104:34f]

IN-SHÁ'A'LLÁH If God wills. [11:737📖]

INSTITUTIONS Several types of institutions exist within the Bahá'í community: Spiritual Assemblies, the Nineteen-Day Feast, Continental Boards of Counsellors, Auxiliary Boards, Mashriqu'l-Adhkár, the International Teaching Center, various "Funds," Ḥuqúqu'lláh, summer schools and such bodies that draw their authority (existence) directly from Bahá'í Writings or from decisions of the Universal House of Justice. They are usually referred to as "Institutions of the Faith" as they possess a substantial measure of permanence. As the World Order of Bahá'u'lláh unfolds, more of these are established and become an integral part of Bahá'í understanding, but they must all have this same authoritative origin.

INTELLECT Much is written in Bahá'í Writings about the capacity for rational thought. Some of the writings of 'Abdu'l-Bahá are particularly descriptive:

> All the powers and attributes of man are human and hereditary in origin, outcomes of nature's processes, except the intellect, which is supernatural. Through intellectual and intelligent inquiry science is the discoverer of all things. It unites present and past, reveals the history of bygone nations and events, and confers upon man today the essence of all human knowledge and attainment throughout the ages. By intellectual processes and logical

> deductions of reason, this super-power in man can penetrate the mysteries of the future and anticipate its happenings. [26:49]

> Science is the first emanation from God toward man. All created beings embody the potentiality of material perfection, but the power of intellectual investigation and scientific acquisition is a higher virtue specialized to man alone. [107:60]

> [W]e find in him (humankind) justice, sincerity, faithfulness, knowledge, wisdom, illumination, mercy and pity coupled with intellect, comprehension, the power to grasp the realities of things and the ability to penetrate the truths of existence. [107:110]

> God's greatest gift to man is that of intellect, or understanding.... The understanding is the power by which man acquires his knowledge of the several kingdoms of creation, and of various stages of existence, as well as of much which is invisible.... Possessing this gift, he is, in himself, the sum of earlier creations—he is able to get into touch with those kingdoms; and by this gift, he can frequently, through his scientific knowledge, reach out with prophetic vision. "Intellect is, in truth, the most precious gift bestowed upon man by the Divine Bounty. Man alone, among created beings, has this wonderful power."[25:41]

> This light of the intellect is the highest light that exists, for it is born of the Light Divine. [25:69]

> The power of the intellect is one of God's greatest gifts to men, it is the power that makes him a higher creature than the animal. [25:72]

INTERCALARY DAYS See **AYYÁM-I-HÁ**.

INTERCESSION 'Abdu'l-Bahá makes it clear that this is an important part of Bahá'í belief:

> The wealth of the other world is nearness to God. Consequently it is certain that those who are near the Divine Court are allowed to intercede, and this intercession is approved by God. But intercession in the other world is not like intercession in this world: it is another thing, another reality, which cannot be expressed in words. [106:329]

> The progress of man's spirit in the divine world, after the severance of its connection with the body of dust, is through the bounty and grace of the Lord alone, or through the intercession and the sincere prayers of other human souls, or through the charities and important good works which are performed in its name. [56:240]

INTERNATIONAL BAHÁ'Í BUREAU An office set up in Geneva by Mrs. Stannard at the request of Shoghi Effendi in March 1925 and that functioned as an intermediary between Haifa and other Bahá'í centers for many years. It was recognized by the League of Nations and published a bulletin, *Messenger Bahá'í*, in English, French and German. In 1925 and 1926 it hosted the international Esperanto Congresses, and it was at these that Lydia Zamenhof (q.v.) met the Faith, became a Bahá'í and for several years helped occasionally in the work of the Bureau. Its work was eventually taken over by the Bahá'í International Community (q.v.).

INTERNATIONAL BAHÁ'Í COUNCIL On 9 January 1951 Shoghi Effendi cabled, through the National Spiritual Assembly of United States:

> Proclaim National Assemblies East West weighty epoch-making decision formation first international Bahá'í Council, forerunner supreme administrative institution destined emerge fullness time within precincts beneath shadow World Spiritual Center Faith already established twin cities Akká Haifa.... most significant milestone evolution Administrative Order Faith Bahá'u'lláh course last thirty years ... invested threefold function—first, forge link authorities newly emerged State; second assist me discharge responsibilities involved erection mighty superstructure Báb's Holy Shrine, third, conduct negotiations related matters personal status civil authorities. [6:7]

To these were added others as the Council developed. Initially it had six members, two more were added and then another in 1955 raising the total to nine. In April 1961 it became an elected body of nine members to function in cooperation with the Hands of the Cause. All adult Bahá'ís in good standing were eligible, and the members of all the Regional and National Spiritual Assemblies elected in 1960 were called upon to cast their votes by mail. It ceased to exist when the Universal House of Justice was elected in 1963.

INTERNATIONAL TEACHING CENTER Established by the Universal House of Justice in 1973 when they announced:

> The time is indeed propitious for the establishment of the International Teaching Center, a development which, at

one and the same time, brings to fruition the work of the Hands of the Cause residing in the Holy Land and provides for its extension into the future, links the institution of the Boards of Counsellors even more intimately with that of the Hands of the Cause of God, and powerfully reinforces the discharge of the rapidly growing responsibilities of the Universal House of Justice. The duties now assigned to this nascent institution are:

To co-ordinate, stimulate and direct the activities of the Continental Boards of Counsellors and to act as liaison between them and the Universal House of Justice.

To be fully informed of the situation of the Cause in all parts of the world and to be able, from the background of this knowledge, to make reports and recommendations to the Universal House of Justice and give advice to the Continental Boards of Counsellors.

To be alert to possibilities, both within and without the Bahá'í community, for the extension of the teaching work into receptive or needy areas, and to draw the attention of the Universal House of Justice and the Continental Boards of Counsellors to such possibilities, making recommendations for action.

To determine and anticipate needs for literature, pioneers and traveling teachers and to work out teaching plans, both regional and global, for the approval of the Universal House of Justice. All the Hands of the Cause of God will be members of the International Teaching Center. Each Hand will be kept regularly informed of the activities of the Center through reports or copies of its minutes, and will be able, wherever he may be residing or traveling, to convey suggestions, recommendations and information to the Center and, whenever he is in the Holy Land, to take part in the consultations and other activities of the Center." [86:323]

It has its permanent seat in the Arc on Mount Carmel, Haifa.

INTERNATIONAL TEACHING CONFERENCES There have been several kinds of Bahá'í International Teaching Conferences—Inter-continental, such as the first four in 1953; in Kampala, Uganda; Chicago, United States; Stockholm, Sweden and New Delhi, India. A second series took place in 1958—in Kampala, Uganda; Sydney, Australia; Chicago, United States; Frankfurt, Germany; and in Djakarta/Singapore. Under the auspices of the

Universal House of Justice a new series of Intercontinental Conferences began—six in 1967—Chicago; Sydney; Kampala; Frankfurt; New Delhi; Panama City. In August 1968 the first Bahá'í Oceanic Conference took place in Palermo, Sicily to commemorate the centenary of the voyage of Bahá'u'lláh from Galipoli to 'Akká. In 1970-71 there was a Continental Conference in La Paz, Bolivia, and an Oceanic Conference in Rose Hall, Mauritius; a Continental Conference in Monrovia, Liberia; and the Oceanic Conferences of the South China Seas in Singapore; of the Caribbean in Kingston, Jamaica; of the South Pacific in Suva, Fiji Islands; of the North Pacific in Sapporo, Japan, of the North Atlantic in Reykjavik, Iceland. The first designated International Teaching Conference was held in Helsinki, Finland in July 1976 followed by Anchorage, Alaska; Paris, France; Nairobi, Kenya; and Hong Kong; in 1977 in Auckland, New Zealand; then in Bahia, Brazil and Merida, Mexico. In 1982 there were commemorative international conferences in Dublin, Ireland; in Quito, Ecuador; in Lagos, Nigeria; in Canberra, Australia and in Montréal Canada.

INTERNATIONAL TRIBUNAL Described sometimes as "a Supreme Tribunal," or a "World Tribunal." In 1931 Shoghi Effendi wrote about the world Super-State that the nations would need to adopt to achieve the Lesser Peace listed it as one of the institutions that would need to come into being:

> Such a state will have to include within its orbit an international executive adequate to enforce supreme and unchangeable authority on every recalcitrant member of the commonwealth; a world parliament whose members shall be elected by the people in their respective countries and whose election shall be confirmed by their respective governments; and a supreme tribunal whose judgment will have a binding effect even in such cases where the parties concerned did not voluntarily agree to submit their case to its consideration. [4:40f]

In describing some of the features of a future world Commonwealth, Shoghi Effendi wrote: "A world tribunal will adjudicate and deliver its compulsory and final verdict in all and any disputes that may arise between the various elements constituting this universal system." [4:203] 'Abdu'l-Bahá, while in America in 1912 said:

> The world is in greatest need of international peace. Until it is established, mankind will not attain composure and tranquillity. It is necessary that the nations and governments organize an international tribunal to which all their disputes and differences shall be referred. The deci-

> sion of that tribunal shall be final. Individual controversy will be adjudged by a local tribunal. International questions will come before the universal tribunal, and so the cause of warfare will be taken away. [26:300]

In answering a letter from an inquirer, Shoghi Effendi through his secretary wrote: "The Supreme Tribunal is an aspect of a world Super-State; the exact nature of its relationship to that state we cannot at present foresee. Supreme Tribunal is the correct translation; it will be a contributing factor in establishing the Lesser Peace." [104:69]

INTERPRETATION Bahá'u'lláh gave the right of interpretation of His Words only to His Eldest Son and Successor, 'Abdu'l-Bahá. On the passing of 'Abdu'l-Bahá His Will and Testament bestowed that same authority to His eldest grandson, Shoghi Effendi (q.v.) through his appointment, as the Guardian of the Bahá'í Faith. As no further Guardians could be appointed this function of authoritative interpretation came to an end with the death of Shoghi Effendi in 1957. The Writings of the Guardian and the Universal House of Justice are clear on this issue:

> There are those prerogatives and duties which lie exclusively within the sphere of the Guardian himself and, therefore, in the absence of a Guardian, are inoperative except insofar as the monumental work already performed by Shoghi Effendi continues to be of enduring benefit to the Faith. Such a function is that of authoritative interpretation of the Teachings. [86:310]

> A clear distinction is made in our Faith between authoritative interpretation and the interpretation or understanding that each individual arrives at for himself from his study of its teachings. While the former is confined to the Guardian, the latter, according to the guidance given to us by the Guardian himself, should by no means be suppressed. In fact such individual interpretation is considered the fruit of man's rational power and conducive to a better understanding of the teachings, provided that no disputes or arguments arise among the friends and the individual himself understands and makes it clear that his views are merely his own. Individual interpretations continually change as one grows in comprehension of the teachings. [86: p311]

INTERREGNUM After the death of Shoghi Effendi (q.v.) in 1957, with no will and testament or scope for the appointment of a successor, the affairs of the Faith were in the control of the Hands of the Cause (q.v.), referred to in the Guardian's last general message as "the Chief Stewards." This control was characterized by a complete devotion to what the Guardian had already made known, to the following out of his wishes to the letter and to the preparation for the election of the Universal House of Justice when the time was right. This interregnum period ceased with the election of the Universal House of Justice in 1963, which then, in accordance to the statements of Bahá'u'lláh and 'Abdu'l-Bahá, took over the control of the Faith.

IOAS, SYLVIA KUHLMAN (1895-1983) An early (1919) American believer of Czech parentage, she married Leroy Ioas (later a secretary to Shoghi Effendi and a Hand of the Cause of God). In May 1955 she was appointed the ninth member of the International Bahá'í Council by Shoghi Effendi. She was elected back onto the body in 1961 and served on it until 1963 when it was replaced by the Universal House of Justice. [11:611] See **IOAS, LEROY**.

IOAS, LEROY C. (1896-1965) (Hand of the Cause of God) Born in Wilmington, Ill. on 15 February 1896 of German parents; his father came from a Lutheran background, and his mother was a Roman Catholic. They accepted the Bahá'í Faith in 1898 and remained dedicated servants until their passing. They met 'Abdu'l-Bahá in Chicago in 1912, and it was Leroy who led his parents to greet Him in a crowded hotel lobby. It was in that same year he commenced working in the railway industry, which he continued for 40 years, rising from an insignificant position to a senior executive. He married Sylvia Kuhlman in 1919 and settled in San Francisco. Almost immediately he wrote to 'Abdu'l-Bahá begging for confirmation for all his family and children unborn and for his own severance, knowledge and steadfastness. Sylvia and Leroy opened their home for study classes, and he found himself almost unaided conducting classes of 100. This, along with his responsible job, the Chairmanship of the San Francisco local Spiritual Assembly and membership of the Western States Teaching Committee, began to affect his health. He determined to change the situation of being short of trained teachers and evolved three different plans of teaching—to develop very large unity conferences; to establish a teaching plan (which later found its consummation in the first Seven Year Plan) and to find a place where people could gather for a period of one or two weeks for the dual purpose of deepening their understanding of the Faith and preparing them for public teaching.

These ideas developed into projects that greatly influenced not only the growth of the Faith in America but throughout the Bahá'í world. Leroy had a creative vision, a practical sense and determination, and his hopes for the expansion of the Faith were boundless. With the support of Dr. David Starr Jordan, Rabbi Rudolf I. Coffee and other civic leaders he organized the first Conference for World Unity in the Palace Hotel, San Francisco on 20-22 March 1925. The Bahá'ís then sponsored a series of such conferences in 16 cities in the U.S. and Canada during the next two years. With John Bosch and George Latimer, Leroy planned and established the Geyserville Summer School, which opened in 1927. In 1932 he was elected to the National Spiritual Assembly (as its youngest member) and was at once appointed to the National Teaching Committee and served as its Chairman for 14 years.

In September 1935 he placed before Shoghi Effendi the Committee's plans for the teaching work and was a key worker throughout the subsequent Seven Year Plan (1937-1944), which achieved all its goals of establishing Spiritual Assemblies in the 34 states and provinces of the United States and Canada, trebled the number of localities where Bahá'ís lived and all its goals in Latin America. Leroy began to participate in international circles in 1948, and his reputation in groups outside the Bahá'í Faith was increasing. He was in the first contingent of Hands of the Cause appointed in December 1951 and was called to Haifa as Secretary General of the International Bahá'í Council, a position he held from 1952 to 1961. He represented the Guardian at the Kampala conference, 1953; the dedication of the Ḥaẓíratu'l-Quds, London, 1955; visited centers throughout Germany in 1956, participated in the Intercontinental Conferences, Chicago in April-May 1958 and Djakarta-Singapore, September 1958. He also toured Bahá'í communities in the British Isles in September-October 1961 and Scandinavia, Germany Luxembourg, July-September 1962.

On his arrival in Haifa in March 1952 he found himself not only one of the four Hands of the Cause to reside there and the Secretary General of the International Bahá'í Council, but also the Guardian's assistant secretary. All this entailed the consolidation of the Council's relationship with the civil authorities in Israel, negotiations for the purchase of a number of properties in Israel; the establishment of Israeli Branches of four National Spiritual Assemblies; and the supervision of the construction of the drum and dome of the Shrine of the Báb and the International Archives Building on Mount Carmel—working all the time under the close direction of the Guardian. His contact with non-Bahá'í organizations developed, and he lectured widely and gave press interviews, which resulted in much favorable publicity in the United States, South Africa and Europe. His crowning service in the Holy Land was, "the final and definite purification, after the lapse of no less than six decades, of the Outer Sanctuary of the Most Holy Shrine of the Bahá'í world" the securing, on 2 December 1957, of the title to the Shrine of Bahá'u'lláh, the Mansion at Bahjí and all other buildings and lands from those defectors and Covenant Breakers.

All of this heavy workload under enormous pressure took its toll on his health, and even by 1953 his heart was severely weakened. He became permanently troubled in health, in need of long periods of rest and cure that he had to seek almost annually in Europe or America. To him, however, teaching was, "the creative phase of the Faith," and following the passing of the Guardian he was called upon more and more to share with the friends his intimate knowledge of the Guardian and his works and what he had himself experienced though his life-long service to the Faith. He was able to "evoke the life, the spirit and the very presence of the Guardian" and as one writer said, "your spiritual power is ... entirely irresistible." [50:298] In February-April 1964 he traveled to meet the Bahá'ís of eight regions of the States: including Florida, Georgia, Arizona and California. A photograph taken at the time gave evidence of his increased frailty, with chronic bronchitis adding to his heart condition. This was such that he was unable to return to Haifa until October. However, his teaching contribution was unique, as he met nearly 1,600 Bahá'ís, many of them new believers. He returned to Haifa broken in health but rejoiced in spirit that he had been able to carry out a hope of the Guardian expressed long before, "You will, I am sure, persevere till the very end."

After some weeks in hospital he died on 22 July 1965 and was buried in the Mount Carmel Bahá'í Cemetery near to his life-long colleagues, Milly Collins (q.v.) and Horace Holley (q.v.). The Universal House of Justice cabled:

> Grieved announce passing outstanding Hand Cause Leroy Ioas. His long service Bahá'í Community United States crowned elevation rank Hand Faith paving way historic distinguished services Holy Land. Appointment first Secretary General International Bahá'í Council, personal representative Guardian Faith two intercontinental conferences, association his name by beloved Guardian octagon door Báb's Sepulcher, notable part erection International Archives building, all ensure his name immortal annals Faith. [8:157][50:291]

IOAS, MARIA B. (1865-1953) An early American believer and mother of Hand of the Cause of God Leroy Ioas. Shoghi Effendi wrote as follows on her passing: "Share your grief at passing of esteemed veteran of Faith, Maria Ioas. Soul rejoicing in the Abhá Kingdom at the services rendered by her dear son at the World Center of the Faith in the triple function of Hand of the Cause,

Secretary-General of the Council and supervisor of construction of the dome of the Báb's Sepulcher." [48:688][60:389]

ÍQÁN Certitude. [11:737]

ÍRÁN Also known as Persia, was the homeland of the Báb and Bahá'u'lláh.

IRÁQ The country in southwest Asia that has borders with Írán, Turkey, Saudi Arabia, Kuwait, Syria and Jordan. Its capital is Baghdád, to which Bahá'u'lláh was exiled from Írán and in which He declared His Mission in 1863 prior to His further exile to Turkey.

IRIZARRY, DOÑA MARÍA TETÉ (1903-1977) Born María Teressa Martín Quiñones in Puerto Rico, she was the first (c.1938) person to embrace the Cause in the Dominican Republic and the first Puerto Rican Bahá'í. She returned to Puerto Rico in 1949 and was for a time the only Bahá'í. [53:437]

'ISHQÁBÁD (Ashkhabad) The city in Russian Turkistán (Turkmenistan) where the first Bahá'í House of Worship was built (Mashriqu'l-Adhkár). At the time there was a large Bahá'í Community with schools, dispensary, travelers' hostel and other services in the area. In 1928 the Temple was seized by the government, converted to a museum 10 years later, then damaged in an earthquake and finally demolished in 1963. Since "perestroika" the Bahá'í Community has been reestablished.

ISHRÁQÁT Splendors: title of one of the Tablets of Bahá'u'lláh revealed after the Kitáb-i-Aqdas. [11:737]

'ISHRÁQÍ, 'INÁYATU'LLÁH (1922-1983) (Martyr), **'ISHRÁQÍ, "IZZAT JÁNAMI** (1926-1983) (Martyr) and **'ISHRÁQÍ, RU'YÁ** (1960-1983) (Martyr) A family of Íránian believers who, along with other coreligionists, were executed along with other coreligionists in Shíráz, Írán, by the government in June 1983, for refusing to recant their belief in Bahá'u'lláh. [11:596]

ISM Name. [11:738]

ISM-I-A'ẒAM The greatest name. [11:738]

ISMU'LLÁH Literally The Name of God. [11:738]

ISOLATED BELIEVERS The term given to Bahá'ís who are the only ones resident in a particular locality. When two or more are resident they may form a Bahá'í Group.

ISRÁFÍL Angel who sounds the trumpet on the Day of Judgment. [11:738]

IVES, HOWARD COLBY (1867-1941) An early American believer and author of *Portals to Freedom.* [114][45:608][83:155][59:340f][60:399]

J

JABAL Mountain. [11:738]

JABAL-I-BÁSIṬ, JABAL-I-SHADÍD The Open Mountain and The Grievous Mountain: the Báb's allusions to the fortress of Máh-Kú and the castle of Chihríq respectively. [11:738]

JACK, MARION (1866-1954) An early Canadian believer. She was much loved by both 'Abdu'l-Bahá and Shoghi Effendi. Miss Jack pioneered to Bulgaria in 1930 where she remained, despite considerable hardship, for 24 years until her passing. Shoghi Effendi wrote:

> Mourn loss of immortal heroine, Marion Jack, greatly loved and deeply admired by 'Abdu'l-Bahá, a shining example to pioneers of present and future generations of East and West, surpassed in constancy, dedication, self-abnegation and fearlessness by none except the incomparable Martha Root. Her unremitting, highly meritorious activities in the course of almost half a century, both in North America and Southeast Europe, attaining their climax in the darkest, most dangerous phase of the second World War, shed imperishable luster on contemporary Bahá'í history. This triumphant soul is now gathered to the distinguished band of her co-workers in the Abhá Kingdom; Martha Root, Lua Getsinger, May Maxwell, Hyde Dunn, Susan Moody, Keith Ransom-Kehler, Ella Bailey and Dorothy Baker, whose remains, lying in such widely scattered areas of the globe as Honolulu, Cairo, Buenos Aires, Sydney, Ṭihrán, Iṣfáhán, Tripoli and the depths of the Mediterranean Sea attest the magnificence of the pioneer services rendered by the North American Bahá'í Community in the Apostolic and Formative Ages of the Bahá'í Dispensation. Advise arrange in association with the Canadian National Assembly and the European Teaching Committee a befitting memorial gathering in the Mashriqu'l-Adhkár. Moved to share with the United States and Canadian National Assemblies the expenses of the erection, as soon as circumstances permit, of a worthy monument at her grave, destined to confer eternal benediction on a country already honored by its close proximity to the sacred city associated with the proclamation of the Faith of Bahá'u'lláh. Share message with all national assemblies. [48:674][60:405]

JÁHILÍYYIH The Age of Ignorance: denotes the state of paganism prevailing in Arabia before the advent of Muḥammad. [11:738📖]

JAMÁL-I-MUBÁRAK Literally The Blessed Beauty. [11:738📖]

JANKKO, GRETA (1902-1973) (Knight of Bahá'u'lláh) A Canadian believer (1951) of Finnish birth. She pioneered to the Marquesas Islands in 1953 (for which service she was designated a Knight of Bahá'u'lláh). In 1955 she pioneered to Finland, living successively in Helsinki, Hyvinkää, Lahti and Tampere. In 1957 she pioneered to Oslo, Norway for one year. During the period 1961-1963 she pioneered to both the Swedish and Finnish areas of Lapland. Within a 10 year period she served on all of the Spiritual Assemblies that existed in Finland. She translated a great many Bahá'í Writings into Finnish. [51:543]

JANSSEN, ALYCE BARBARA MAY (1900-1964) (Knight of Bahá'u'lláh) An American believer who pioneered to Switzerland, Italy, the Canary Islands and Ceuta, Spanish Morocco (1953) for which later service she was designated a Knight of Bahá'u'lláh. [50:315]

JESSUP, HENRY Prepared a paper while he was the Director of the Presbyterian Missionary Operations in Syria in which he uses the words of Bahá'u'lláh when He granted an interview with Edward Granville Browne (q.v.) in 1890. At the World Parliament of Religions (1893), the Chairman of the closing session read these words. This was the first major public mention of the Bahá'í Faith in America. [5:256]

JIHÁD Literally striving, endeavor; crusade; holy war, enjoined in the Qur'án, abrogated by Bahá'u'lláh. [11:738📖]

JINÁB Literally threshold; placed before a name is a courtesy title signifying "His Excellency," "His Honor." [11:738📖]

JÖRGENSEN, ELSE (1907-1977) A Norwegian Bahá'í who embraced the Cause in 1945 in Guayaquil, Ecuador and in so doing helped form the first local Spiritual Assembly of that town. In 1948 she returned to Norway and in April that year became a member of the first local Spiritual Assembly of Oslo. In 1949 she pioneered to Madrid, Spain. In 1953 she returned to Norway and married Roberto Cazcarra, only to pioneer again, this time to Portugal, in 1954. In 1956 she joined her husband in Montevideo, Uruguay, where she was immediately elected to the local Spiritual Assembly of Montevideo. In 1957, along with her husband, she was elected to the National Spiritual Assembly of Argentina, Chile, Uruguay, Paraguay and Bolivia. She was immediately asked by the Assembly to visit every local Spiritual Assembly under the purview of the National Spiritual Assembly (a task that took her five months and saw her give numerous public addresses and talks). On her return she found a letter appointing her an

Auxiliary Board member for Latin America—an appointment that saw her embark yet again on a lengthy and exhausting series of travels. [53:428]

JOSHI, ASANAND CHAGLA (1910-1982) An early (1945) Indian believer who served for many years as a member of the local Spiritual Assembly of Karachi. In 1948 he was elected to the National Spiritual Assembly of India, Pákistán and Burma. With the formation of the National Spiritual Assembly of Pákistán in 1958 he was elected its Chairman until his appointment as an Auxiliary Board member in 1974. Having learned 11 languages (mastering nine) he was a powerful advocate of the Cause. In 1972 he was instrumental in acquiring government recognition of the Faith as a separate minority religion—the first to be achieved in an Islamic country. He also secured tax exemption for Bahá'í properties. A lawyer by training, he served as honorary legal advisor to the Bahá'í administration for 30 years. [2:796]

JUBBIH An outer coat to cloak. [11:738📖]

JUBILEE, GREAT AND MOST GREAT The centenary of the Declaration of the Báb was in retrospect referred to by Shoghi Effendi as the first Jubilee. The second, described by him as the "Great" Jubilee was the centenary of the assumption by Bahá'u'lláh of His prophetic Mission in the Siyáh-Chál (q.v.) in Ṭihrán in summer 1852, was observed as a "Holy Year" and included four Continental Conferences as well as the launching of the Ten Year Plan/Global Crusade (q.v.). The Jubilee culminated in the "Most Great Jubilee" and saw the election of the Universal House of Justice.

Shoghi Effendi wrote, in outlining some of the aspects of the decade-long period between the two Jubilees, of the preeminent rôle to be played by the Bahá'ís of the North American continent:

> May this community—the spiritual descendants of the dawn-breakers of the Heroic Age of the Bahá'í Faith, the chief repository of the immortal Tablets of 'Abdu'l-Bahá's Divine Plan, the foremost executors of the Mandate issued by the Center of Bahá'u'lláh's Covenant, the champion-builders of a divinely conceived Administrative Order, the standard-bearers of the all-conquering army of the Lord of Hosts, the torchbearers of a future divinely inspired world civilization—arise, in the course of the momentous decade separating the Great from the Most Great Jubilee to secure, as befits its rank, the lion's share in the prosecution of a global crusade designed to diffuse the light of God's revelation over the surface of the entire planet. [3:109]

Referring to the rapid progress being made from the Centenary of the Declaration of the Báb to the closing weeks of the first year of the Crusade, Shoghi Effendi wrote:

> The total number of virgin areas, inscribed on the scroll with the names of conquerors since the launching of the World Crusade last Riḍván, has mounted to fifty. The number of territories included in the orbit of the Faith has been raised within an unbelievably short time to one hundred and seventy-eight, marking an increase of one hundred countries since the celebration of the first Jubilee nine years ago. [6:173]

Further clarification of the Holy Year was given by the Guardian through his secretary:

> The "Year Nine" is an abbreviation of 1269 A.H. The beginning of the Year Nine occurred about two months after His (Bahá'u'lláh) imprisonment in that dungeon. We do not know the exact time He received this first intimation.... We therefore regard the entire Year Nine as a Holy Year, and the emphasis should be placed ... on the entire year, which started in October, 1852. This means our Centenary Year of Celebration will be from October, 1952 to October, 1953. [104:84]

In a cable announcing the Crusade, 8 October 1952 Shoghi Effendi included in its objectives: "Convocation of a World Bahá'í Congress in the vicinity of the Garden of Riḍván, Bag͟hdád, third holiest city of Bahá'í world, on the occasion of the worldwide celebrations of the Most Great Jubilee, commemorating the Centenary of the Ascension of Bahá'u'lláh to the Throne of His Sovereignty." [6:43]

JUSTICE The following brief selections from Bahá'í Scripture demonstrate the preeminent place this occupies in Bahá'í understanding:

> The best beloved of all things in My sight is Justice; turn not away therefrom if thou desirest Me, and neglect it not that I may confide in thee. By its aid thou shalt see with thine own eyes and not through the eyes of others, and shalt know of thine own knowledge and not through the knowledge of thy neighbor. Ponder this in thy heart; how it behooveth thee to be. Verily justice is My gift to thee and the sign of My loving-kindness. Set it then before thine eyes. [92:A2]

A prayer of Bahá'u'lláh reads: "O God, my God! Attire mine head with the crown of justice, and my temple with the ornament of equity. Thou, verily, art the Possessor of all gifts and bounties." [70:12]

Shoghi Effendi on this theme wrote:

> "The light of men is Justice," He (Bahá'u'lláh) moreover states, "Quench it not with the contrary winds of oppression and tyranny. The purpose of justice is the appearance of unity among men." "No radiance," He declares, "can compare with that of justice. The organization of the world and the tranquillity of mankind depend upon it." "O people of God!" He exclaims, "That which traineth the world is Justice, for it is upheld by two pillars, reward and punishment. These two pillars are the sources of life to the world." "Justice and equity," is yet another assertion, "are two guardians for the protection of man. They have appeared arrayed in their mighty and sacred names to maintain the world in uprightness and protect the nations." "Bestir yourselves, O people," is His emphatic warning, "in anticipation of the days of Divine justice, for the promised hour is now come. Beware lest ye fail to apprehend its import, and be accounted among the erring." "The day is approaching," He similarly has written, "when the faithful will behold the daystar of justice shining in its full splendor from the dayspring of glory."[39:27]

The stress placed on this virtue is reflected in the future designation of "Houses of Justice," to be given to the local and national Spiritual Assemblies, to the name, "Universal House of Justice" given to the supreme administrative body of the Faith, and to the command of Bahá'u'lláh to the individual: "And if thine eyes be turned towards justice, choose thou for thy neighbor that which thou choosest for thyself." [77:64] "Whoso cleaveth to justice, can, under no circumstances, transgress the limits of moderation. He discerneth the truth in all things, through the guidance of Him Who is the All-Seeing." [85:342] "Be fair to yourselves and to others, that the evidences of justice may be revealed, through your deeds, among Our faithful servants." [85:278]

K

KA'BIH The Kaaba: ancient shrine at Mecca, chosen by Muḥammad to be the center of pilgrimage for Muslims. The most holy shrine in Islám and the Qiblih of the Muslim world. [11:738📖]

KABÍR Literally great, big, old. [11:738📖]

KABÍR-I-AFNÁN See ḤÁJÍ MÍRZÁ MUḤAMMAD-TAQÍ.

KABU, TOMMY (1922-1969) The first (c.1964) Papuan believer. [51:459]

KACHWALLA, GHULÁM-'ALÍ IBRÁHÍMJÍ (Kurlawala) (Knight of Bahá'u'lláh) (1896-1978) A Hindu Indian believer who embraced the Cause in 1926 and served as Vice-Chairman of the local Spiritual Assembly of Andheri from 1937 until 1942. In 1942 he pioneered to Bhopal before moving on to Ujjain. In 1949 he pioneered to Jaipur where he stayed for two years and assisted in the formation of the first local Spiritual Assembly of Jaipur. In 1953 he pioneered to Daman, Portuguese Goa, for which service he was designated a Knight of Bahá'u'lláh. He ended his Bahá'í service in Bombay in 1978. [53:461]

KAD-KHUDÁ Chief of a ward or parish in a town; headman of a village. [11:738]

KAHALOA, SOLOMON (1932-1980) His family was the first to accept the faith in Hawaii and were instrumental in the formation of the first local Spiritual Assembly of Puna. In the early 1970s he and his family moved to South Hilo on the Big Island for the purpose of promoting the Cause. In 1975 he and his family pioneered to Guam. He was killed in a car accident while visiting the Mariana Island of Rota in 1980. [2:740]

KALÁNTAR Mayor. [11:738]

KALÍM Speaker, interlocutor. Title given by Bahá'u'lláh to His faithful brother, Mírzá Músá (q.v.). [11:738]

KALÍMU'LLÁH He Who Conversed With God: title of Moses, given Him in the Islámic Dispensation. [11:738]

KÁMIL 'ABBAS See **'ABBAS-RIḌA, KÁMIL.**

KAMÁLÍ-SARVISTÁNÍ, MÍRZÁ ÁQÁ KHÁN (1924-1983) (Knight of Bahá'u'lláh) An Íránian believer who pioneered to the island of Socotra during the Ten Year Crusade for which service he was designated a Knight of Bahá'u'lláh. [2:817]

KAPPES, LILLIAN F. (-1920) (Disciple of 'Abdu'l-Bahá.) She was among that first group of American Bahá'ís who were teaching the Faith at the turn of the century. She pioneered to Persia where she became a distinguished teacher in the first Bahá'í school in Ṭihrán—the Tarbíyat School. She was much loved, and her services highly valued, by 'Abdu'l-Bahá. She passed away at an early age, in Ṭihrán, on 1 December 1920.

KAVELIN, HOWARD BORRAH (1906-1988) (Charter Member, Universal House of Justice) He was born in Russia to a distinguished Jewish family on 16 March 1906, the sixth of seven children. The family immigrated to the United States when he was three years old and remained in Denver, Colorado. His father was a greatly beloved rabbi in Denver, a pillar of the Jewish commu nity and well known as a healer. He lost his life caring for others during an influenza epidemic. His mother was founder of the Beth Israel Hospital and Old Folks' Home in Denver. As a young boy, Borrah had obtained a job as an usher at an opera house. His love for music drew him to New York City, and his debut as an operatic tenor occurred on the stage of Carnegie Hall. Through music, he met Martha Hamilton, a pianist studying at the Juilliard School of Music in New York. They were married in 1936. Those were difficult financial times for everyone during the Great Depression, and a singer's life could not support a family. So he turned from his musical career to become a secretary to the director of a real estate firm. His diligence and ability were soon recognized, and he became a partner in that original firm. He had an untarnished reputation for trustworthiness and honesty, considered by some to be rather unusual qualities in the realty world. He met the Bahá'í Faith in the late 1930s, and he and his wife accepted after some years of study in 1940. From 1941 to 1950 he served on the Local Spiritual Assembly of New York City. In 1950, he was elected to the National Spiritual Assembly of the United States, where he served for 13 years, with a number of years as treasurer, and from 1958 to 1963 as chairman. In 1957, on their behalf he chaired the first national convention for the formation of the National Spiritual Assembly of the Benelux Countries (Belgium, the Netherlands and Luxembourg), and represented them at the international conference held the following year in Kampala, Uganda. Shoghi Effendi, to whom Borrah Kavelin was deeply and personally devoted, invited him to come on pilgrimage directly after the conference. He had never had the bounty of meeting Shoghi Effendi personally, and he was deeply touched by the opportunity to pay homage to him. However, this meeting was never to occur. The greatest blow of his life came when he learned of Shoghi Effendi's untimely death in London, shortly before they were to meet. He grieved openly, as did so many others. After this, he dedicated increasing time to service to the Cause for which Shoghi Effendi had given his life. He was elected to the first International Bahá'í Council, and he served the Council as member-at-large rather than in residence in Haifa and was given permission to continue serving on the National Spiritual Assembly. He was elected to the Universal House of Justice in 1963 and served on that Body for a full quarter of a century, until 1988. He represented the Universal House of Justice on four significant missions to Írán to consult with the Bahá'ís in that country about the financial needs of the Faith. After the revolution in Írán in 1979, he again represented the Universal House of Justice at a time when the Bahá'í world was reeling from loss of income from the Íránian Bahá'í community. During a 10 week mission, he traveled throughout Europe,

Canada and the United States meeting with thousands of Bahá'ís who thronged to hear him. His mission was to explain the state of the Persian friends, and the financial impact on the Bahá'í world community of the persecutions. In 1987, after nearly 25 years of service, at 81 years of age, he asked to be excused from service as a member of the Universal House of Justice. Within two weeks from the time his retirement was announced he was hospitalized for cancer surgery, after which he recovered and felt ready to begin a life of retirement in the United States. The National Spiritual Assembly of the United States asked him to serve as a keynote speaker at six regional "Vision to Victory" conferences throughout the United States. This became the driving force of his day-to-day life. When the cancer recurred, and his health began to fail rapidly, he was even more driven to fulfill his commitment to these conferences. He was able to address the first conference in Boston, Massachusetts: his frail voice did not diminish the ardor with which he spoke to the friends of the imperative necessity to raise the Arc on Mount Carmel. However, by the time his plane arrived at the second conference site, in Chattanooga, Tennessee, he was so ill that he had to be rushed to the hospital in acute distress. His undeviating concern about making a presentation as he had promised was creatively solved by a doctor who asked if the Bahá'ís could videotape his talk there, in the hospital room. Mr. Kavelin agreed, and arrangements were swiftly made to tape his talk. Shortly after the talk, Mr. Kavelin lapsed into a coma. However, he recovered to the extent that two minor "miracles" were to occur. One was to give a Thanksgiving dinner to thank the doctor and all the many Bahá'í friends in Chattanooga who had been so kind to him. The other was to return home to Albuquerque. He lived another three weeks in his home in Albuquerque, then on 18 December 1988, he passed away. "You wander all your life in search of meaning and then you find at the end, at the core, there is only the Covenant." These were among the last words of Borrah Kavelin, a man who lived to his last breath the commitment he had made to Bahá'u'lláh. One of his favorite passages read at his funeral, attended by hundreds of friends, was "As ye have faith, so shall your powers and blessings be." He was laid to rest in the Fairview Memorial Park in Albuquerque, New Mexico. His epitaph reads simply: "Howard Borrah Kavelin, 1906-1988, Charter Member of the Universal House of Justice" (From an unpublished Memorial by Linda Kavelin Popov). The Universal House of Justice cabled on his passing:

> Hearts Laden With Sorrow Over Loss To Bahá'í World Our Dearly-Loved Former Colleague H. Borrah Kavelin Outstanding Servant Cause Bahá'u'lláh. Indomitable

Faith, Rigorous Conscientiousness, Irrepressible Optimism, Unfailing Reliability, Unblemished Trustworthiness Among Brilliant Qualities Which Shone Through His Nearly Half Century Monumental Services To Cause He Constantly Promoted And Defended To Last Days His Distinguished Life. His Extensive Involvement Bahá'í Administrative Affairs Began In 1941 With His Nine Years On Local Spiritual Assembly New York And Included 13 Years On National Spiritual Assembly United States, Two Years On International Bahá'í Council Followed By Quarter Century Membership On Universal House Of Justice. His Manifold Services Especially Marked By His Diligent Endeavors To Assist Development External Affairs Agencies Bahá'í International Community, His Deftness For Dignified Promotion Financial Interests Faith, His Lustrous Record In Connection Acquisition Important Properties Including Mansion Mazra'ih And House 'Abdu'lláh Páshá. Offering Ardent Supplications Holy Threshold That His Noble Soul May Be Richly Rewarded Abhá Kingdom And That Blessed Beauty May Surround His Beloved Wife Flore And Dear Children With Divine Mercy And Assistance. Advise Hold Memorial Gatherings In His Honor All Houses Worship And Throughout Bahá'í Community.

KAWTHAR Literally plentiful, abundant, sweet (potion); a river of Paradise, whence all other rivers derive their source. [11:738📖]

KELSEY, CURTIS DeMUDE (1894-1970) An early (1917) American believer who installed electric lighting at the Shrines of Bahá'u'lláh and the Báb (three lighting plants having been acquired by Roy Wilhelm). On first seeing the Shrine of the Báb illumined with light, 'Abdu'l-Bahá, in tears, said "In all the years of imprisonment (in Máh-Kú), the Báb spent all the nights in utter darkness. Yea, not even a candle was allowed (Him) ... Therefore, God willing, I shall illumine His Sublime Shrine with one hundred electric lamps." On his return to the United States he served tirelessly in many administrative and teaching capacities.[51:468][115]

KELSEY, OLIVIA (1889-1981) (Knight of Bahá'u'lláh) An early (1932) American believer who married Francis Arthur Kelsey (a Bahá'í) in 1929. In 1947 she compiled a book entitled *Bahá'í Answers*.[116] Following the death of her husband in 1937 she pioneered during the second Seven Year Plan to Louisville, Kentucky. In 1944 she moved to Kansas and in 1954, in response to the Ten Year Crusade goals she pioneered to Monaco, for which service she was designated a Knight of Bahá'u'lláh. Following the formation of the first local Spiritual Assembly of Monaco she moved to France where she lived for a time in Toulouse and then Montpelier. In 1964 she returned to the United States. In 1974 she undertook extensive teaching visits to South Carolina and West Virginia (she was then 85 years old).[2:775]

KEMPTON, HONOR (1892-1981) An early (1930s) American believer of English birth, she responded immediately to Shoghi Effendi's cable of 26 January 1939 calling for "Nine Holy Souls" to open the remaining virgin territories of North America (Alaska, Delaware, Nevada, South Carolina, Utah, Vermont, West Virginia, Manitoba and Nova Scotia) by moving to Alaska. She settled in Anchorage where she opened the town's first book shop ("The Book Cache"). She served on the first (1943) local Spiritual Assembly of Anchorage (also the first in Alaska). In 1947 she pioneered to Luxembourg the smallest of the still unopened second Seven Year Plan goal countries. In 1949 she moved to Geneva, Switzerland, to serve as the European Teaching Committee representative at the Bahá'í International Bureau. She also served as a member of the Italo-Swiss National Spiritual Assembly. When the Bahá'í International Bureau closed in 1957, she opened the French towns of Lille and Nancy to the Cause. She returned to Luxembourg in 1959 and was elected to the regional National Spiritual Assembly of the Benelux countries. [2:749]

KENNY, SARA M. (1900-1968) (Knight of Bahá'u'lláh) An early (1930) American believer who in 1953 pioneered, in the company of her mother Mrs. Ella Duffield, to the Madeira Islands for which service she was designated a Knight of Bahá'u'lláh. In 1954, with permission of Shoghi Effendi, she moved to France where in 1958 she was elected to the first National Spiritual Assembly and served as its Vice-Chairman until 1963. [51:441]

KEVORKIAN, HAIK (1916-1970) (Knight of Bahá'u'lláh) Born in Aleppo, Syria he moved in 1937 with his family to Argentina. During his years in Argentina he traveled widely to neighboring countries, and in 1953 he responded to the pioneer call of the Ten Year Crusade and moved to the Galápagos Islands (for which service he was designated a Knight of Bahá'u'lláh).[51:483]

KHÁDEM, DHIKRU'LLÁH (1904-1986) (Hand of the Cause of God) He was born into a distinguished Bahá'í family in Ṭihrán, Írán in 1904. He received as formal an education as was possible to the Bahá'ís of that time, becoming proficient in Persian, Arabic, English and French. For many years he was chief interpreter and director of the Education Department of the Anglo-Íránian Oil Company and developed an accelerated method of teaching Persian to English speakers. He later became Secretary of the Iráqi Embassy in Ṭihrán. He became known as an Old Testament scholar and was well versed in the history of the Bahá'í Faith and other world religions. He was author of several books about the Bahá'í Faith in Persian and English. In 1933 he married the secretary, friend and companion of Keith Ransom-Kehler, Javidukht Javid.

At the relatively young age of 34 he was elected to the National Spiritual Assembly of the Bahá'ís of Írán and served on that body for the next 21 years. He made trips to the Holy Land in 1939 and 1940. He was elevated to the rank of Hand of the Cause in the second contingent in February 1952, but before that time he had been acting for Shoghi Effendi in receiving and distributing communications from the Guardian for the Íránian believers—a service he joyfully carried out for 17 years. He was also instrumental in securing many precious archives for their safe preservation in the Holy Land. These included a famous sword wielded in defense of the Bábís by Mullá Ḥusayn at Bárfurúsh in 1848 (when with one stroke he had cut through a tree, the barrel of a gun and his adversary).

For the remainder of his life Khádem went on a vast number of assignments, encouraging the friends, promoting and protecting the Faith, and helping them to carry out their global teaching plans, first on behalf of Shoghi Effendi, then for the Hands of the Cause, and later for the Universal House of Justice. He was a most inspirational speaker, always conveying to his audience his deep love and knowledge of the Faith and his devotion to Shoghi Effendi and later, to the Universal House of Justice. These services to the Head of the Faith were always characterized by his instant, exact and complete obedience.

His worldwide travels included: 1953—attendance at all the four Intercontinental Conferences and visits to centers in Central and South America; in 1954-55—centers in India, Pákistán, Arabian Peninsula, Iráq and later in 1955—Pákistán, Japan, Taiwan, Hong Kong, Macau, Thailand, Burma and India; in 1957 he represented the Guardian at the Convention of Central America in Panama, and visited centers in Italy, Switzerland, Denmark, the United States, Panama, Costa Rica, Nicaragua, Honduras, El Salvador, Guatemala, British Honduras, Mexico, Canada, Sweden, Finland, Norway, Holland, Belgium, Luxembourg and France; in 1958 he participated in the Intercontinental Conference in Sydney, Australia and centers in Indonesia, Thailand, Burma and India; the Conference in Frankfurt followed by centers throughout Europe and the Conference in Djakarta-Singapore and then as a substitute member of the Nine Hands in the Holy Land in October to December; in 1959 he attended the inaugural Convention of the National Spiritual Assembly of Turkey followed by visits throughout Europe. In November he was asked to settle in the United States as a Hand of the Western Hemisphere, visiting centers in

Europe en route to his new home; in 1960 he again visited centers in Europe; in 1961 he was representative of the World Center at the Conventions of Costa Rica and of Panama followed by visits to England, Holland and Switzerland. During the next few years he attended conferences and conventions throughout the U.S., Canada and Alaska, with Jamaica, Trinidad and Tobago in 1971; and in 1973 and 1974, Írán. These trips, from November 1959, were from his new home in the United States (as he was asked to settle there as a Hand for the Western Hemisphere).

By August 1976 he had completed a most exacting task given to him by the Universal House of Justice—that of compiling an "International Registry of Bahá'í Holy Places and Historic Sites in the Holy Land," followed by a documented study of all the places visited by 'Abdu'l-Bahá in England, Scotland, the United States and Canada. He subsequently carried on his visits to National Spiritual Assemblies in the west and other visits to Írán and two significant events in 1979 in the United States—the 70th National Convention in April and a "Spiritual Enrichment" Conference in August-September.

In January 1981 he was attending a highly significant conference in Frankfurt, Germany, and later in the year attended a convention in Chicago. He continued attending conferences, conventions, summer schools and gatherings, where his inspired talks galvanized the Bahá'ís into making greater efforts in the promulgation of their Faith. These took him to every continent and back to Persia on several occasions to carry out special missions there.

Throughout his life Khádem had enjoyed good health, but in July 1986 it was discovered that he had a fatal illness that confined him to bed for much of his time, but he continued actively dictating his letters and talks. In October he wrote to the U.S. National Spiritual Assembly thanking the members "from the bottom of my heart for all the kindnesses you have shown to me over the past 26 years..." He passed away in the early hours of 13 November 1986 and the Universal House of Justice cabled:

> With sorrowful hearts announce passing indefatigable fearless defender Faith, deeply-loved Hand Cause Dhikru'lláh Khádem. His sterling services to the Cause, his total consecration to tasks assigned to him by beloved Guardian, his outstanding efforts as member National Spiritual Assembly Cradle Faith, his valuable soul-uplifting stimulation imparted body believers North America particularly United States Bahá'í Community, his untiring endeavors through his talks and writings in safeguarding Covenant and in instilling appreciation love for Shoghi Effendi shed undying lustre over period his

admirable stewardship Cause God. Offering prayers Holy Shrines progress his radiant soul Abhá Kingdom. Urge hold befitting memorial gatherings his name all Houses of Worship as well as in all local Bahá'í communities.

KHADÍJIH KHÁNUM The mother of Bahá'u'lláh. She was a widow with three children when she married Mírzá Buzurg, the father of Bahá'u'lláh, and had another five children by him, of whom Bahá'u'lláh was the eldest son. See appended **GENEALOGIES**.

KHADÍJIH-BAGUM The wife of the Báb. They were childhood playmates in Shíráz, were married in August 1842 and had one child, a son, who died in infancy. She was a devout and fervent Bábí and remained faithful after her Husband was martyred. She immediately accepted Bahá'u'lláh when she learned of His Declaration. She died in 1882. See appended **GENEALOGIES**.

KHÁDIMU'LLÁH Servant of God. [11:738]

KHALÍL Friend. [11:738]

KHALÍL'LLÁH Friend of God: title given to Abraham in the Qur'án. [11:738]

KHÁN Prince, lord, nobleman, chieftain. Originally used as a courtesy title for officers and high-ranking officials, Khán came to denote—placed after a given name—simple "gentleman." Also an exchange, market; inn, caravanserai: an inn constructed around a central court where caravans (trains of pack animals) may rest for the night. [11:738]

KHÁN, FLORENCE BREED (1875-1950) An early American believer. She met 'Abdu'l-Bahá on her way to Persia. She married Mírzá 'Alí-Kuli Khán (q.v.) in 1904. [48:703][59:146ff]

KHÁN, MÍRZÁ 'ALÍ-KULI (1879-1966) Íránian by birth he led a distinguished life with service given in many fields. He visited 'Abdu'l-Bahá in the Holy Land in 1899 and served as His amanuensis for over a year. In 1901 'Abdu'l-Bahá sent him to America to serve as interpreter for Mírzá Abu'l-Faḍl-i-Gulpáygání. In 1902 he became secretary to the Persian Minister at Washington, D.C. In 1906 he journeyed with his wife, Florence Breed Khán (q.v.), to Persia and returned to Washington as consul general. In 1910-1911 he was appointed chief diplomatic representative and chargé d'affaires in Washington. In 1912 he extended a befitting welcome to 'Abdu'l-Bahá during His visit to America. From 1921 to 1923 he was chief minister of the Crown Prince Regent's Court in Ṭihrán, and was then appointed minister plenipotentiary of the Five Republics of the Caucasus. He was a member of the National Spiritual Assembly of the United States and Canada in 1925 and 1926. [50:351][59:48ff]

KHÁNUM Lady; wife. Placed after a woman's name, Khánum is a courtesy title meaning "gentlewoman" comparable to Khán. [11:738]

KHÁZEH, COLONEL JALÁL (1897-1990) (Hand of the Cause of God) He was born in Ṭihrán, Persia in 1897. His father Ghulam-Ridá had suffered so many persecutions that he was always in poor health and died at age 35, when he was only seven and his sister, Farkhundíh, was only five. At the age of 17 he began his study of veterinary medicine at the military academy and in this profession he served in many parts of Írán reaching the rank of lieutenant at 19 and retired from the army with the rank of colonel in 1943.

He began serving the Faith when he was only 15 and in spite of his army service was able to serve on committees and spiritual assemblies. He married when he was 19 and had five children.

In 1944 he was elected to the National Spiritual Assembly of the Bahá'ís of Persia and served for five years, after which he was elected to the local Spiritual Assembly of the Bahá'ís of Ṭihrán, serving as its secretary for three years. He traveled extensively in Írán, reporting on the situation to Shoghi Effendi who praised and encouraged his works. He was strong, well built and very courageous and was outspoken to government officials if they failed in their duties. He resigned from the local Spiritual Assembly at the end of 1951 to give all his time to travel teaching, but on receiving permission to go on pilgrimage, he was able to go to Haifa in March, 1952. Shoghi Effendi advised him to concentrate on traveling throughout Persia to acquaint the Bahá'ís with the news of the teaching goals and arouse them to greater service, and this he did assiduously for two-and-a-half years.

On 23 October 1952, Shoghi Effendi called on him to attend the Kampala Conference in February 1953 to be followed by a tour of Africa and then to continue his touring of Persia. This he carried out to the letter, visiting Abyssinia, Eritrea, Kenya, Aden and the Gulf States before returning to his travels in Persia. His reports to the Guardian were greatly appreciated, who wrote that his "services are the cause of glory and honor," and they "set an example for the friends in Írán."

At the end of December 1953 Colonel Kházeh had returned to a certain town after a two-month teaching trip when he was awakened at about four A.M. by three Bahá'ís who wanted to congratulate him. On inquiring for the reason for the congratulations he was amazed and astonished to learn that a telegram had been following him around from Shoghi Effendi, dated 7 December, raising him to the rank of Hand of the Cause. Although he was again elected onto the National Spiritual Assembly, Shoghi Effendi encouraged him to continue to travel and stimulate the friends.

'Abdu'l-Bahá-The Center of the Covenant-The Mystery of God

Shoghi Effendi-The Guardian of the Faith-The Sign of God

Bahíyyih <u>Kh</u>ánum-The Greatest Holy Leaf

Mírzá Mihdí-The Purest Branch

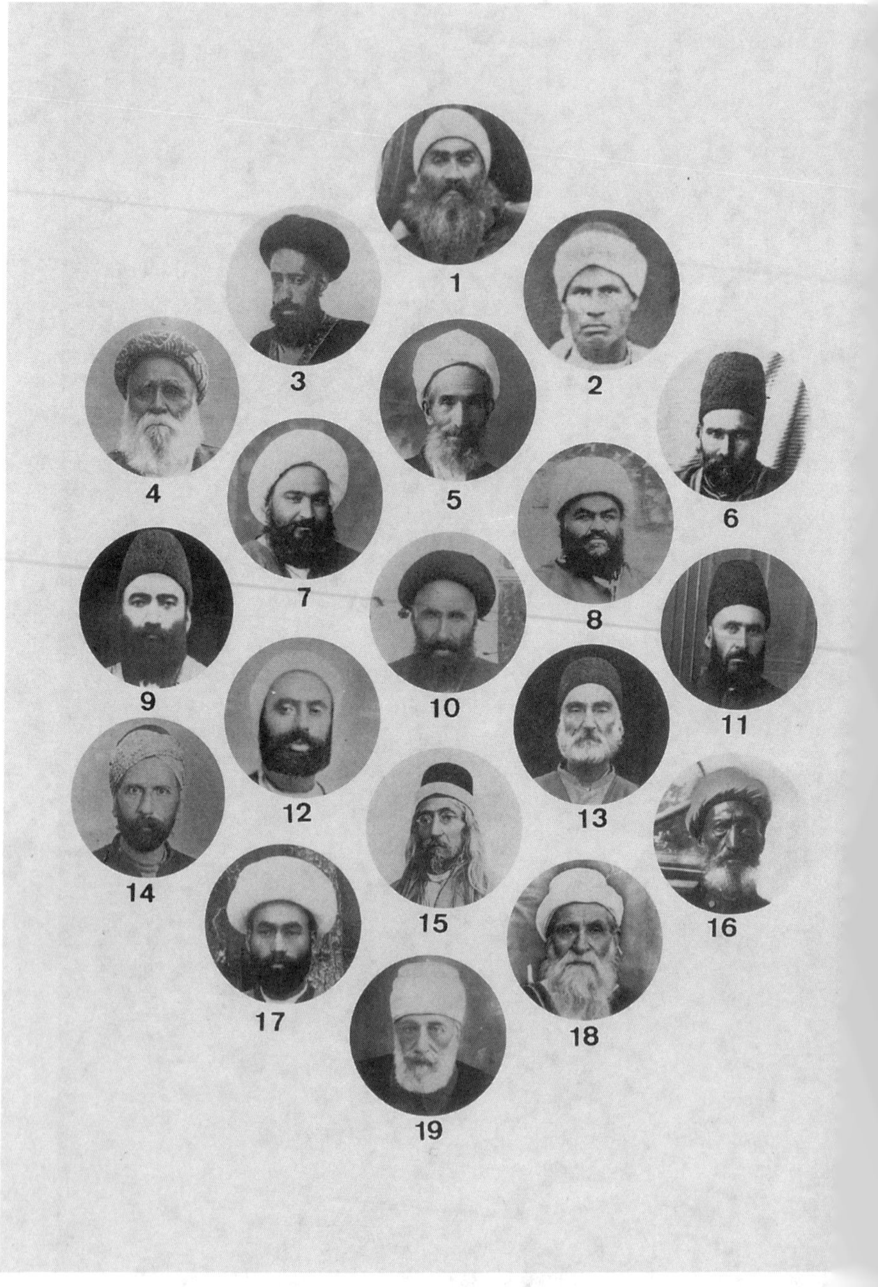

Apostles of Bahá'u'lláh: For names see numbered list on page 488.

Disciples of 'Abdu'l-Bahá: For names see numbered list on page 489.

Hands of the Cause of God: for names see numbered list on page 489f.

Hands of the Cause of God-for names see numbered list on page 489f.

38

39

40

41

42

43

44

45

46

47

48

49

Hands of the Cause of God: for names see numbered list on page 489f.

50

Mirzá Buzurg   Father of Bahá'u'lláh

He represented Shoghi Effendi at the Convention of Northeast Asia in 1957 and then visited centers in Japan, Korea, Taiwan, Hong Kong, Burma and Pákistán.

After the passing of Shoghi Effendi he was one of the Nine Hands of the Cause of God to be chosen to be resident in the Holy Land until the election of the Universal House of Justice. Notwithstanding this, he also traveled widely in visits to Europe, India and Ceylon. After the election of the Universal House of Justice he made his headquarters in South America for some years and traveled extensively throughout the Americas, as well as visiting centers in Europe and Persia. He initiated a newsletter in Spanish for use in Latin America. Under the guidance of the Universal House of Justice he and his wife returned to live in Írán in 1969, but he continued to represent the Universal House of Justice in many conventions and conferences, including those in West Africa (1970) and Malaysia (1972.) When back in Írán he concentrated on teaching and protection duties. During 1973-74 he made some globe-encircling tours.

By the time of the International Convention in Haifa in 1978 he had become quite weak and then, after his wife had passed away in Bábulshár, Írán, the Revolutionary Guards attacked his home, and his writings, documents and books were confiscated. He was moved to Ṭihrán and from place to place for his protection as the authorities wanted to arrest him. In 1984, at the age of 87, he moved to Canada and during the next six years was mostly confined to his house due to ill-health and failed eyesight. He passed away on February 21, 1990, and the Universal House of Justice cabled:

> Deeply grieved announce passing staunch tireless promoter Faith Hand Cause God Jalál Kházeh. His strenuous endeavors Cradle Faith, Holy Land, Latin America and world-wide travels after passing beloved Guardian set shining example of unshakable dedication and courage, of undeviating loyalty and perseverance. Imperishable record his sterling services as gifted teacher, defender Cause never to be forgotten. His noble spirit now Abhá Kingdom will undoubtedly intercede behalf Persian Bahá'í community whose vital interest he served with such high distinction over several decades. Fervently praying Holy Shrines for progress his illumined soul in realms on high. Advise friends everywhere hold befitting memorial gatherings his honor particularly all Houses of Worship. [105:April 1990]

KHAZRAI, FEREYDOUN (1914-1994) (Knight of Bahá'u'lláh) An Íránian believer who pioneered to Romania during the Ten Year Crusade, for which service he was designated a Knight of Bahá'u'lláh. [11:321]

KING, MALCOLM (1885?-1966) (Knight of Bahá'u'lláh) An American believer who traveled and pioneered extensively (Nicaragua, Haiti, Dominican Republic, Antigua, British Guiana and Jamaica.) He was designated a Knight of Bahá'u'lláh for his move to British Guiana in 1953. [50:316]

KING, MELBA M. CALL (1910-1979) The first (1943) full-blooded Yupik Eskimo believer; she traveled widely among both Eskimo and Indian peoples in the promotion of the Cause. [2:688]

KINGSHIP, STATION OF Bahá'u'lláh wrote:

> Although a republican form of government profiteth all the peoples of the world, yet the majesty of kingship is one of the signs of God. We do not wish that the countries of the world should remain deprived thereof. If the sagacious combine the two forms into one, great will be their reward in the presence of God. [77:28]

> One of the signs of the maturity of the world is that no one will accept to bear the weight of kingship. Kingship will remain with none willing to bear alone its weight. That day will be the day whereon wisdom will be manifested among mankind. Only in order to proclaim the Cause of God and spread abroad His Faith will anyone be willing to bear this grievous weight. Well is it with him who, for love of God and His Cause, and for the sake of God and for the purpose of proclaiming His Faith, will expose himself unto this great danger, and will accept this toil and trouble. [44:71]

Shoghi Effendi wrote:

> Let none, however, mistake or unwittingly misrepresent the purpose of Bahá'u'lláh. Severe as has been His condemnation pronounced against those sovereigns who persecuted Him, and however strict the censure expressed collectively against those who failed signally in their clear duty to investigate the truth of His Faith and to restrain the hand of the wrongdoer, His teachings embody no principle that can, in any way, be construed as a repudiation, or even a disparagement, however veiled, of the institution of kingship. The catastrophic fall, and the extinction of the dynasties and empires of those monarchs whose disastrous end He particularly prophesied, and the de

clining fortunes of the sovereigns of His Own generation, whom He generally reproved—both constituting a passing phase of the evolution of the Faith—should, in no wise, be confounded with the future position of that institution. Indeed if we delve into the writings of the Author of the Bahá'í Faith, we cannot fail to discover unnumbered passages in which, in terms that none can misrepresent, the principle of kingship is eulogized, the rank and conduct of just and fair-minded kings is extolled, the rise of monarchs, ruling with justice and even professing His Faith, is envisaged, and the solemn duty to arise and ensure the triumph of Bahá'í sovereigns is inculcated. [44:71]

KINNEY, CARRIE (Vaffa) (1878-1959) (A Pillar of the Cause of God) An early American believer. 'Abdu'l-Bahá bestowed the name "Vaffa" on her. Designated, along with her husband ("Saffa") a "Pillar of the Cause of God." [47:864][83:43]

KINNEY, EDWARD BEADLE (Saffa) (1863-1950) (A Pillar of the Cause of God) An early American believer. Shoghi Effendi wrote on his passing: "Grieve at passing of dearly loved, highly admired, greatly trusted, staunch, indefatigable, self-sacrificing teacher, pillar of Faith, Saffa Kinney. His leonine spirit, exemplary steadfastness, notable record of services enriched annals of closing period of Heroic Age and opening phase of Formative Age of Bahá'í Dispensation. Beautiful reward assured in Abhá Kingdom beneath the shadow of the Master he loved so dearly, served so nobly, defended so heroically until last breath." [48:677][83:43]

KINNEY, HOWARD M. (1905-1938) An early American believer. 'Abdu'l-Bahá conferred His own name on him ('Abdu'l-Bahá) during a visit his family made to 'Akká in 1909. [42:670]

KITÁB Book. [11:738🕮]

KITÁB-I AQDAS Bahá'u'lláh's book of laws. It is described in part by Shoghi Effendi:

> In this Charter of the future world civilization its Author ... announces to the kings of the earth the promulgation of the "Most Great Law," pronounces them to be His vassals; proclaims Himself the "King of Kings;" disclaims any intention of laying hands on their kingdoms; reserves for Himself the right to "seize and possess the hearts of men;" warns the world's ecclesiastical leaders not to weigh the "Book of God" with such standards as are current amongst them; and affirms that the Book itself is the "Unerring Balance" established amongst men. In it He formally ordains the institution of the "House of Justice," defines its functions, fixes its revenues, and designates its

members as the "Men of Justice," the "Deputies of God," the "Trustees of the All-Merciful," alludes to the future Center of His Covenant, and invests Him with the right of interpreting His holy Writ; anticipates by implication the institution of Guardianship; bears witness to the revolutionizing effect of His World Order; enunciates the doctrine of the "Most Great infallibility" of the Manifestation of God; asserts this infallibility to be the inherent and exclusive right of the Prophet; and rules out the possibility of the appearance of another Manifestation ere the lapse of at least one thousand years. In this Book He, moreover, prescribes the obligatory prayers; designates the time and period of fasting; prohibits congregational prayer except for the dead; fixes the Qiblih; institutes the Ḥuqúqu'lláh (Right of God); formulates the law of inheritance; ordains the institution of the Ma<u>sh</u>riqu'l-A<u>dh</u>kár; establishes the Nineteen Day Feasts, the Bahá'í festivals and the Intercalary Days; abolishes the institution of priesthood; prohibits slavery, asceticism, mendicancy, monasticism, penance, the use of pulpits and the kissing of Hands of the Cause; prescribes monogamy; condemns cruelty to animals, idleness and sloth, backbiting and calumny; censures divorce; interdicts gambling, the use of opium, wine and other intoxicating drinks; specifies the punishments for murder, arson, adultery and theft; stresses the importance of marriage and lays down its essential conditions; imposes the obligation of engaging in some trade or profession, exalting such occupation to the rank of worship; emphasizes the necessity of providing the means for the education of children; and lays upon every person the duty of writing a testament and of strict obedience to one's government. Apart from these provisions Bahá'u'lláh exhorts His followers to consort, with amity and concord and without discrimination, with the adherents of all religions; warns them to guard against fanaticism, sedition, pride, dispute and contention; inculcates upon them immaculate cleanliness, strict truthfulness, spotless chastity, trustworthiness; hospitality, fidelity, courtesy, forbearance, justice and fairness; counsels them to be "even as the fingers of one hand and the limbs of one body;" calls upon them to arise and serve His Cause; and assures them of His undoubted aid. He, furthermore, dwells upon the instability of human affairs; declares that true liberty consists in man's submission to His commandments; cautions them not to be indulgent in carrying out His statutes; prescribes the twin inseparable duties of recognizing the "Dayspring of God's Revelation" and of observing all the ordinances revealed by Him, neither of which, He affirms, is acceptable without the other. [5:214f]

And again,

the Laws revealed by Bahá'u'lláh in the Aqdas are, whenever practical and not in direct conflict with the Civil laws of the land, absolutely on every believer or Bahá'í institution whether in the East of in the West. Certain laws, such as fasting, obligatory prayers, the consent of the parents before marriage, avoidance of alcoholic drinks, monogamy, should be regarded by all believers as universally and vitally applicable at the present time. Others have been formulated in anticipation of a state of society destined to emerge from the chaotic conditions that prevail today. [104:8]

KITÁB-I'AHDÍ Bahá'u'lláh's Will and Testament in which He appointed 'Abdu'l-Bahá as His Successor.

KITÁB-I-ÍQÁN The *Book of Certitude* was written by Bahá'u'lláh, in answer to some questions, two years before His Declaration in Baghdád. It was described by Shoghi Effendi as the "Foremost among the priceless treasures cast forth from the billowing ocean of Bahá'u'lláh's Revelation. A model of Persian prose, of a style at once original, chaste and vigorous, and remarkably lucid, both cogent in argument and matchless in its irresistible eloquence." [5:138]

KNIGHT OF BAHÁ'U'LLÁH When a Bahá'í arose to move to a different place to help promote the Faith he or she became known as a "pioneer," and the success of the Bahá'í teaching Plans has been mainly due to the large number of pioneers who had arisen since the Plans first started in 1937. When the first truly "global" plan (as opposed to country-specific) was announced in 1953, and the Guardian gave all the National Spiritual Assemblies specific goals to achieve, he announced the need, on 28 May 1953, for 130 pioneers, "the number required to fill the gaps in the still unconquered territories of the globe" and then, "Planning to inscribe, in chronological order, the names of the spiritual conquerors on an illuminated Roll of Honor, to be deposited at the entrance door of the inner Sanctuary of the Tomb of Bahá'u'lláh, as a permanent memorial of the contribution by the champions of His Faith at the victorious conclusion of the opening campaign of the Global Crusade..." [6:49] Within four months he was able to announce that over 300 offers of pioneers had been made with 40 assigned to virgin areas and with almost a quarter of those required for the opening phase already inscribed on the Roll of Honor. By 8 February 1954 he cabled the Bahá'í world: "The nine months which have elapsed since the launching of the spiritual world-encompassing Crusade have witnessed the entry of the Knights of Bahá'u'lláh in well-nigh four score and ten territories throughout the planet" [6:49:55] and by 21 March "Ninety-one virgin areas have been opened to the Faith since the launching of the Crusade" [6:49:57] By 4 May 1954 he cabled that the Roll of Honor, one year after, the launching of the Crusade was closed except for those "first arriving in the few remaining virgin territories inside and outside Soviet Republics and satellites." [6:49:69] As these remaining territories were opened the new Knights of Bahá'u'lláh were enrolled, with the Knight for Mongolia arriving in December 1988 and the two for Sakhalin reaching their goal from Japan in March 1990. The Roll of Honor was placed in its allotted site, in the presence of the members of the Universal House of Justice, the Hands of the Cause, most of the surviving Knights and a vast group of Bahá'ís selected to represent every territory of the world, at an impressive ceremony at the Shrine of Bahá'u'lláh held during the Holy Year commemorations (1992) that marked the Centenary of the Passing of Bahá'u'lláh.

KNOBLOCH, ALMA (-1943) An early American believer who pioneered at the request of 'Abdu'l-Bahá to Germany. [45:641]

KNOBLOCH, FANNIE A. (1859-1949) An early American believer of German birth. She was among the group of pilgrims who visited 'Abdu'l-Bahá in 'Akká in 1908. [84:473]

KNOWLEDGE Three aspects of knowledge receive a great deal of attention in Bahá'í Scripture—the knowledge of God; the acquisition of knowledge and self-knowledge, as the following typical quotations illustrate:

> The beginning of all things is the knowledge of God, and the end of all things is strict observance of whatsoever hath been sent down from the empyrean of the Divine Will that pervadeth all that is in the heavens and all that is on the earth. [85:5]

> The spirit that animateth the human heart is the knowledge of God, and its truest adorning is the recognition of the truth that "He doeth whatsoever He willeth, and ordaineth that which He pleaseth. [85:291]

> The glory of man is in the knowledge of God, spiritual susceptibilities, attainment to transcendent powers and the bounties of the Holy Spirit. The glory of man is in being informed of the teachings of God. This is the glory of humanity. [26:312]

The knowledge of the Reality of the Divinity is impossible and unattainable, but the knowledge of the Manifestations of God is the knowledge of God, for the bounties, splendors, and divine attributes are apparent in them. Therefore if man attains to the knowledge of the Manifestations of God, he will attain to the knowledge of God; and if he be neglectful of the knowledge of the Holy Manifestation, he will be bereft of the knowledge of God. [106:323]

True knowledge, therefore, is the knowledge of God, and this is none other than the recognition of His Manifestation in each Dispensation. [65:89]

The source of all learning is the knowledge of God, exalted be His Glory, and this cannot be attained save through the knowledge of His Divine Manifestation. [77:156]

For man's knowledge of God cannot develop fully and adequately save by observing whatsoever hath been ordained by Him and is set forth in His heavenly Book. [77:268]

Whatever duty Thou hast prescribed unto Thy servants of extolling to the utmost Thy majesty and glory is but a token of Thy grace unto them, that they may be enabled to ascend unto the station conferred upon their own inmost being, the station of the knowledge of their own selves. [85:4-5]

Arts, crafts and sciences uplift the world of being, and are conducive to its exaltation. Knowledge is as wings to man's life, and a ladder for his ascent. Its acquisition is incumbent upon everyone. The knowledge of such sciences, however, should be acquired as can profit the peoples of the earth, and not those which begin with words and end with words. [70:26]

KOESTLIN, ANNA (1884-1972) An early (1907) German believer. She met 'Abdu'l-Bahá in Paris in 1911 and again in 1913 in Esslingen. She served as a member of the National Spiritual Assembly of Austria and Germany for a great many years. [51:511]

KRISHNAN, G. S. SANTHANAM (1945-1975) Although only a believer for four years before his untimely passing, Mr. Krishnan promoted the Cause widely throughout his native India. He traveled extensively without thought for his own well-being and, in the words of the Universal House of Justice was a "...devoted, brave and steadfast pioneer..." whose "...passing in the field of service to the Cause of God…" would undoubtedly "…confer upon him a special bounty which will be the cause of the progress of his soul in the eternal Kingdom of God." [52:563]

KRUKA, AMINDA JOSEPHINE (1892-1971) An early (1935) American believer designated by Shoghi Effendi as the "Mother of Finland." She pioneered to Cuba during the first Seven Year Plan and following several visits to Finland she moved there in 1950—spending the summer months in that country and returning to Cuba each winter. In 1957 she moved for six years to Finland and served as a member of the first National Spiritual Assembly of Finland (1962).[51:493]

KULÁH The Persian lambskin hat worn by government employees and civilians. [11:738□]

KULL-I SHAY' Literally all things: the term, whose numerical value is 361, signifies 19 cycles of 19 years in the Badí' calendar. [11:738□]

KUNZ, ANNA (1889-1973) An early (c.1914) American believer of Swiss birth. She met 'Abdu'l-Bahá in 1921 while on pilgrimage in Haifa and 'Akká. At the age of 58 she pioneered to Switzerland. In 1953 she was elected a member of the Italo-Swiss Regional Spiritual Assembly and served as its Secretary for nine years. In 1962 she was elected to the first National Spiritual Assembly of Switzerland and following service for one year as Secretary, she continued a member until her 80th when she asked to be allowed to stand down. [52:520][60:409]

L

LAITE, GORDON (1925-1978) An American believer (1955), he lived and traveled among the Navajo, Zuni, Hopi, Taos and other southwest Indian tribes over a long period of his Bahá'í life. He also pioneered to Honduras and Puerto Rico, where he and his wife (Jeanne Sánchez de Laite) served as members of the National Spiritual Assembly. [53:457]

LAMPRILL, GRETTA STEVENS (1890-1972) (Knight of Bahá'u'lláh) The first (1924) Tasmanian believer, she was designated by Shoghi Effendi as the "Mother of Tasmania." She served as the first Secretary of the first Spiritual Assembly of Hobart. While serving as Secretary of the National Spiritual Assembly of Australia she pioneered at the beginning of the Ten Year Crusade (1953) to Tahiti for which service she was designated a Knight of Bahá'u'lláh. She later pioneered during the Ten Year Plan in Australia to Devonport, Tasmania and in so doing allowed the first Spiritual Assembly of Devonport to be formed. [51:534]

LAWḤ Literally slate, sheet, table; Tablet. [11:738]

LAWRENCE, LOYCE DRUGAN (1905-1968) (Knight of Bahá'u'lláh) An early (1930s) American believer who pioneered in 1953 to Svolvaer in the Lofoten Islands, for which she was designated a Knight of Bahá'u'lláh. She served on the first local Spiritual Assembly of Svolvaer as well as on the National Spiritual Assembly of Norway. [51:446]

LAWS The Bahá'í Writings are explicit with regard to obedience to law and the prohibition of all forms of subversion. Religious law is seen to be composed of two kinds or degrees—laws that have eternal application and that are restated in each Dispensation—such as the need to acknowledge and worship God, to love one's fellow man—often referred to as the "Golden Rule"; and "secondary" or social laws that particularly address the needs of the age. These include dietary laws and those affecting marriage, fasting and prayer. These are equally binding on the followers of the Faith, but it is recognized that they may be changed or modified by another Manifestation of God.

Simplistically, humanity has throughout history ordered its affairs according to two prime methods: the rule of force and/or the rule of law. One general definition of "law" might read that it constitutes those rules for the conduct of human affairs in society as derived from an absolute basis and by a definite prescribed method (jurisprudence). The basis of law is that it is the point beyond which one cannot pass. In other words, there cannot be a law where one can imagine a more basic starting point—if a more basic starting point can be imagined, then the law has been undercut and rendered ineffective. The law offers a way of ordering life on an ultimate basis. Of course, people's perspective on what constitutes the ultimate basis of the law may differ, but it must be accepted as the ultimate basis. Law by definition carries authority and is self-authenticating. When human society was composed mainly of isolated groups and/or physically dominant groupings, the law was relatively straightforward and largely unquestioned. However, by and large, the peoples of our modern age no longer live in isolation or without knowledge of what is happening elsewhere. As such they are able to compare their own circumstances to those of other peoples and in so doing lay open to question the "ultimate" basis of their own law. This inevitably leads to contention as to which "ultimate basis" is truly ultimate. Usually any difference of opinion is settled by force, or the threat of force. In short, humanity suffers unmercifully from the instruments of its own making. In the words of the Universal House of Justice in the Peace Statement issued to the peoples of the world:

> Those who care for the future of the human race may well ponder this advice. If long-cherished ideals and time-honored institutions, if certain social assumptions and religious formulae have ceased to promote the welfare of the generality of mankind, if they no longer minister to the needs of a continually evolving humanity, let them be swept away and relegated to the limbo of obsolescent and forgotten doctrines. Why should these, in a world subject to the immutable law of change and decay, be exempt from the deterioration that must needs overtake every human institution? For legal standards, political and economic theories are solely designed to safeguard the interests of humanity as a whole, and not humanity to be crucified for the preservation of the integrity of any particular law or doctrine. [117]

Yet humanity, despite its suffering, continues stubbornly to hold to outworn belief systems. Bahá'u'lláh elucidates the reasons for mankind's confusion and resultant suffering as well as offering insight into how such suffering can be alleviated in the following Words:

> Behold the disturbances which, for many a long year, have afflicted the earth, and the perturbation that hath seized its peoples. It hath either been ravaged by war, or tormented by sudden and unforeseen calamities. Though the world is encompassed with misery and distress, yet no man hath paused to reflect what the cause or source of that may be. Whenever the True Counsellor uttered a word in admonishment, lo, they all denounced Him as a mover of mischief and rejected His claim. How bewildering, how confusing is such behaviour! No two men can be found who may be said to be outwardly and inwardly united. The evidences of discord and malice are apparent everywhere, though all were made for harmony and union. [118:163f]

He goes on to say:

> If the rulers and kings of the earth, the symbols of the power of God, exalted be His glory, arise and resolve to dedicate themselves to whatever will promote the highest interests of the whole of humanity, the reign of justice will assuredly be established amongst the children of men, and the effulgence of its light will envelop the whole earth. [118:163]

Concomitantly, large blocks of society no longer seem to feel that because something is legal (i.e., governed by law), it is necessarily right, moral or good. Where are they to turn for an absolute unimpeachable source of legal authenticity and authority? The Bahá'í Writings would say that the ultimate basis of law in any given age or era can be found only in the Word of God as revealed through His historically chosen Divine Manifestation. Given that Bahá'ís believe Bahá'u'lláh to be God's Spokesperson for the age in which we now live He is therefore seen as the Point toward which humanity must turn in its search for ultimate Truth and the foundation of Law.

Devoid of Divine input, the law is an empty letter; when it draws its source from Revelation, it is the spirit that moves men's hearts and drives their actions in ways that are both pleasing to their Creator and conducive to the well-being, prosperity and development of the entire planet. In this regard, Bahá'u'lláh posits religion as the source of law:

> The purpose of religion as revealed from the heaven of God's holy Will is to establish unity and concord amongst the peoples of the world; make it not the cause of dissension and strife. The religion of God and His divine law are the most potent instruments and the surest of all means for the dawning of the light of unity amongst men. The progress of the world, the development of nations, the tranquillity of peoples, and the peace of all who dwell on earth are among the principles and ordinances of God. Religion bestoweth upon man the most precious of all gifts, offereth the cup of prosperity, imparteth eternal life, and showereth imperishable benefits upon mankind. It behoveth the chiefs and rulers of the world, and in particular the Trustees of God's House of Justice, to endeavour to the utmost of their power to safeguard its position, promote its interests and exalt its station in the eyes of the world. It is incumbent upon everyone to firmly adhere to and observe that which hath streamed forth from Our Most Exalted Pen. God, the True One, beareth Me witness, and every atom in existence is moved to testify that such means as lead to the elevation, the advancement, the education, the protection and the regeneration of the peoples of the earth have been clearly set forth by Us and are revealed in the Holy Books and Tablets by the Pen of Glory. [118:129f]

Clearly, for Bahá'ís, the ultimate basis for law must be the Word of God. It is the only point that cannot be transcended or transgressed—the source of law.

LAWS, ELIZABETH S. (1888-1977) (Knight of Bahá'u'lláh) An American believer (c1938) who pioneered with her husband (Frederick Laws) to Basutoland (now Lesotho) for which service they were designated Knights of Bahá'u'lláh. They also lived for a time in The Gambia and Liberia before returning in 1957 to the United States. In 1976 they returned to Africa as pioneers in Tanzania, but due to visa problems they returned to the Unites States after only eight months. They settled in the Yakima Indian Reservation in Wapato, Washington. [53:459]

LEACH, BERNARD (1887-1979) A potter, artist and painter of international renown, he first heard of the Bahá'í Faith 1914 but it was not until he met Mark Tobey (q.v.) in the early 1930s that his faith took root. From 1909 to 1920 he lived in Japan and for his cultural services to that country he received the highest honor to be conferred upon a British commoner by the Japanese government: The Order of the Sacred Treasure, second class. In 1962 he was made a Commander of the British Empire (CBE), by Her Majesty Queen Elizabeth II; in 1973 he was the first craftsman to be made a Companion of Honour (CH) in a private audience with Her Majesty. Through his art he taught the Bahá'í Faith and sought to bring greater unity between East and West. [2:670][119]

LEARNED, THE In Bahá'í Administration there is the "elected" and the "appointed" arms. The former include the Universal House of Justice and the national and local Spiritual Assemblies while the "appointed" arm includes the Hands of the Cause, the Continental Boards of Counsellors and the Auxiliary Board Members. These appointed members are referred to as the "learned" while the elected members are the "rulers." The elected institutions function as bodies while the appointed members act as individuals and have no administrative powers but have an advisory and inspirational rôle.

LESSER PEACE See **PEACE, LESSER.**

LETTERS OF THE LIVING The first 18 followers of the Báb. Mullá Ḥusayn was the first and was known as "the Bábu'l-Báb" (Gate of the Gate) and the last one was Quddús. Half of them had suffered martyrdom before the Báb Himself was shot in 1850. See appended listing of the **LETTERS OF THE LIVING.**

LIBERTY In the Kitáb-i-Aqdas Bahá'u'lláh wrote:

> True liberty consisteth in man's submission unto My commandments, little as ye know it. Were men to observe that which We have sent down unto them from the Heaven of Revelation, they would, of a certainty, attain unto perfect liberty. Happy is the man that hath apprehended the Purpose of God in whatever He hath revealed from the Heaven of His Will, that pervadeth all created things. Say: The liberty that profiteth you is to be found nowhere except in complete servitude unto God, the Eter

nal Truth. Whoso hath tasted of its sweetness will refuse to barter it for all the dominion of earth and heaven.[85:335]

The Ancient Beauty hath consented to be bound with chains that mankind may be released from its bondage, and hath accepted to be made a prisoner within this most mighty Stronghold that the whole world may attain unto true liberty. [85:99]

Liberty must, in the end, lead to sedition, whose flames none can quench. Thus warneth you He Who is the Reckoner, the All-Knowing. Know ye that the embodiment of liberty and its symbol is the animal. That which beseemeth man is submission unto such restraints as will protect him from his own ignorance, and guard him against the harm of the mischief-maker. Liberty causeth man to overstep the bounds of propriety, and to infringe on the dignity of his station. It debaseth him to the level of extreme depravity and wickedness.... Regard men as a flock of sheep that need a shepherd for their protection. This, verily, is the truth, the certain truth. We approve of liberty in certain circumstances, and refuse to sanction it in others.... True liberty consisteth in man's submission unto My commandments, little as ye know it. Were men to observe that which We have sent down unto them from the Heaven of Revelation, they would, of a certainty, attain unto perfect liberty. Happy is the man that hath apprehended the Purpose of God in whatever He hath revealed from the Heaven of His Will, that pervadeth all created things. Say: The liberty that profiteth you is to be found nowhere except in complete servitude unto God, the Eternal Truth. Whoso hath tasted of its sweetness will refuse to barter it for all the dominion of earth and heaven. [85:336]

Shoghi Effendi wrote:

He, furthermore, dwells upon the instability of human affairs; declares that true liberty consists in man's submission to His commandments; cautions them not to be indulgent in carrying out His statutes; prescribes the twin inseparable duties of recognizing the "Dayspring of God's Revelation" and of observing all the ordinances revealed by Him, neither of which, He affirms, is acceptable without the other. [5:215]

LIFEBLOOD OF THE CAUSE Bahá'í Funds. See **FUNDS OF THE FAITH.**

LINFOOT, CHARLOTTE MAY (1895-1976) A leading figure in the growth and development of the Cause in America for nearly 50 years. In 1953 until her death in 1976 she served as a member and assistant Secretary of the National Spiritual Assembly of the United States. Simultaneously she served on the editorial committees of *Bahá'í News* and the *Bahá'í World.* [53:424]

LITH, JACOB EDUARD VAN (1922-1983) An early (1952) Dutch believer who served on the National Spiritual Assembly of the Benelux countries (1957-1962) until the formation of the National Spiritual Assembly of Belgium came into existence (1962) at which time he was elected to that body. In 1975 he pioneered with his wife (Marijke) and three children to Suriname where he was elected to the first National Spiritual Assembly of that country. [2:818]

LITTLE, MARION (1891-1973) An early (c.1915) American believer, she was actively involved for many years as secretary of the Bahá'í publishing committee; she produced Volume III of the *Bahá'í World* for which service she won "the unqualified gratitude" of Shoghi Effendi "in producing such a noteworthy publication." She also contributed greatly toward the publication of *The Dawn-Breakers*, which again earned her an accolade in a cable dated 12 April 1932 from Shoghi Effendi: "Excellent Production Eminently Satisfactory Every Respect Abiding Gratitude" followed by a handwritten note on 5 May 1932: "It is a striking and abiding evidence of the efficiency, competence and exemplary devotion which characterizes your work for the cause ..." In 1933, as part of the second Seven Year Plan (1946-1953), she pioneered to Western Europe where she traveled extensively. She was a member of the first Italo-Swiss Regional Spiritual Assembly. [51:547]

LJUNGBERG, ESKIL JOACHIM (1886-1984) (Knight of Bahá'u'lláh) A Swedish believer who embraced the Cause in Stockholm in 1947. He served on the newly formed local Spiritual Assemblies of Stockholm and later Gothenburg. In 1953, after several attempts to pioneer to "somewhere warm" he eventually settled in the Faroe Islands, for which service he was designated a Knight of Bahá'u'lláh. In 1973 he served on the first local Spiritual Assembly of Tórshavn. [11:658]

LOCAL SPIRITUAL ASSEMBLY The elected body of nine adult Bahá'ís responsible for the administration of the Faith in a locality. Each year in any locality where the number of adult Bahá'ís in good standing exceed nine in number a local Spiritual Assembly is elected on the 21st day of April. All adult Bahá'ís are eligible. Once elected, by secret ballot, without any electioneering or names be ing mentioned and by plurality vote, the Assembly elects its officers by majority vote. It functions by consultation, and its officers have only the powers given to them in session. Its duties are to promote and oversee the teaching work; conduct marriages and funerals; provide for the Bahá'í education of the whole community; ensure that the Bahá'í Calendar is observed with Feast and Holy Days properly conducted; give guidance and assistance to those in difficulty; accept new believers; consult closely with its community every 19 days and be responsible for the Bahá'í Funds. The authority for its existence lies in Bahá'u'lláh's own words:

> The Lord hath ordained that in every city a House of Justice be established wherein shall gather counsellors to the number of Bahá, and should it exceed this number it does not matter. It behooveth them to be the trusted ones of the Merciful among men and to regard themselves as the guardians appointed of God for all that dwell on earth. It is incumbent upon them to take counsel together and to have regard for the interests of the servants of God, for His sake, even as they regard their own interests, and to choose that which is meet and seemly. [120:21]

See **ADMINISTRATIVE ORDER**.

LOCKE, ALAIN LeROY (1886-1954) An early American believer who was a noted black author and educator. Two of his works appear in Bahá'í World volumes: vol. III *Impression of Haifa*[36:280] and volume V, *The Orientation of Hope*. [37:527]

LOFT, ALFRED JAMES (1908-1973) A Mohawk Indian who was born in Hiawatha, Ontario, Canada. When he was a young boy he was sitting on a fence watching a train pass by. As it passed him he saw a man clothed in flowing white robes wave to him. The memory stayed with him, and in 1948 when he embraced the Cause (through the efforts of his wife, Sarah Melba Whetung) he recognized the "man" to have been 'Abdu'l-Bahá. Following guidance from Shoghi Effendi he returned to share his new-found faith with his fellow Indians. Over the course of the remaining years of his life he promoted the Cause with vigor among the Mohawk peoples. [52:514][60:417]

LOFT, SARAH MELBA WHETUNG (Kinaaj-Kwe) An Ojibwa Indian, born on the Curve Lake Indian Reserve, near Peterborough, Ontario, Canada she was the first (1938) native Indian believer to embrace the Cause in Canada. She served on the first (1979) local Spiritual Assembly of Tyendinaga. She was active in the promotion of the Cause among the Indian peoples throughout her entire Bahá'í life and also traveled as far as Europe in 1978 (visiting

Denmark, United Kingdom, Ireland, Austria and Switzerland).[11:697]

LORD OF HOSTS Refers to Bahá'u'lláh. In His own words: "The Promised Day is come and the Lord of Hosts hath appeared. Rejoice ye with great joy by reason of this supreme felicity. Aid Him then through the power of wisdom and utterance." [77:239] 'Abdu'l-Bahá explained: "The blessed Person of the Promised One is interpreted in the Holy Book as the Lord of Hosts, i.e., the heavenly armies. By heavenly armies those souls are intended who are entirely freed from the human world, transformed into celestial spirits and have become divine angels. Such souls are the rays of the Sun of Reality who will illumine all the continents." [106:423]

LOVE Bahá'u'lláh described how the source of all creation is love and that mankind needs to reciprocate that love, while 'Abdu'l-Bahá enlarged upon the four kinds of love. Bahá'u'lláh wrote:

> Veiled in My immemorial being and in the ancient eternity of My essence, I knew My love for thee; therefore I created thee, have engraved on thee Mine image and revealed to thee My beauty.... I loved thy creation, hence I created thee. Wherefore, do thou love Me, that I may name thy name and fill thy soul with the spirit of life.... Love Me, that I may love thee. If thou lovest Me not, My love can in no wise reach thee. Know this, O servant.... Thy Paradise is My love; thy heavenly home, reunion with Me. Enter therein and tarry not. This is that which hath been destined for thee in Our kingdom above and Our exalted Dominion. If thou lovest Me, turn away from thyself; and if thou seekest My pleasure, regard not thine own; that thou mayest die in Me and I may eternally live in thee. [92:3-7]

'Abdu'l-Bahá wrote:

> Were it not for the love of God, the hearts would not be illumined. Were it not for the love of God, the pathway of the Kingdom would not be opened. Were it not for the love of God, the Holy Books would not have been revealed. Were it not for the love of God, the divine Prophets would not have been sent to the world. The foundation of all these bestowals is the love of God. Therefore, in the human world there is no greater power than the love of God. It is the love of God which has brought us together here tonight. It is the love of God which is affiliating the East and the West. It is the love of God which has resuscitated the world. [65:257]

In the Gospel it is said God is love. There are four kinds of love. The first is the love that flows from God to man; it consists of the inexhaustible graces, the Divine effulgence and heavenly illumination. Through this love the world of being receives life. Through this love man is endowed with physical existence, until, through the breath of the Holy Spirit—this same love—he receives eternal life and becomes the image of the Living God. This love is the origin of all the love in the world of creation. The second is the love that flows from man to God. This is faith, attraction to the Divine, enkindlement, progress, entrance into the Kingdom of God, receiving the Bounties of God ... This love is the origin of all philanthropy; this love causes the hearts of men to reflect the rays of the Sun of Reality. The third is the love of God towards the Self or Identity of God.... This is the reality of love, the Ancient Love, the Eternal Love. Through one ray of this Love all other love exists. The fourth is the love of man for man. The love which exists between the hearts of believers is prompted by the ideal of the unity of spirits. This love is attained through the knowledge of God, so that men see the Divine Love reflected in the heart.... This love will make all men the waves of one sea, this love will make them all the stars of one heaven and the fruits of one tree. This love will bring the realization of true accord, the foundation of real unity. [25:180]

LUNT, ALFRED EASTMAN (-1937) An early American believer. Shoghi Effendi cabled on his death: "Shocked distressed premature passing esteemed beloved Lunt. Future generations will appraise his manifold outstanding contributions to rise and establishment Faith Bahá'u'lláh American Continent." [37:531][83:121]

LUQMÁNÍ, MUḤAMMAD IBRÁHÍMJÍ (1896-1981) One of the best-known and well-respected early (1920) Bahá'ís of India. He served as a member of the local Spiritual Assembly of Bombay and was elected to the National Spiritual Assembly of India in the 1930s. In the 1940s he pioneered to Hyderabad after which he moved to Surat and Sholapur. In 1949 he pioneered to Sri Lanka (Ceylon) for which service Shoghi Effendi later referred to him as the spiritual "Conqueror" of Ceylon. In 1956 he returned to India and settled in Aurangabad. [2:772]

M

MADRISHI Seminary, school, religious college. [11:738]

MacARTHUR, EDYTHE (1906-1994) (Knight of Bahá'u'lláh) An early (1944) Canadian believer who introduced the Faith to the Queen Charlotte Islands for which service she was designated a Knight of Bahá'u'lláh. In 1954 she pioneered to South Africa where she served on the first local Spiritual Assembly of Cape Town. She then returned to Canada where her pioneering helped raise up five new local Spiritual Assemblies. [11:321]

MacNUTT, HOWARD (1898-1926) (Disciple of 'Abdu'l-Bahá) It was in January 1898 that Howard and his wife Mary, heard of the Bahá'í Faith, and they soon became believers. After some four years in New York City they moved to a larger house in Eastern Parkway, Brooklyn, to enable them better to serve their Faith. Howard became a powerful and convincing teacher, particularly after they went on pilgrimage to the Holy Land in 1905. The MacNutts hosted meetings for 'Abdu'l-Bahá on several occasions during His visit to America, and on every occasion he heard 'Abdu'l-Bahá speak Howard took copious notes as well as collecting all he could in the way of photographs and reports of all the Master's meetings. Desiring to make a permanent record of all this priceless material, he sought 'Abdu'l-Bahá's approval and in giving it He wrote on 20 July 1919, "Name the book which Mr. MacNutt is compiling, 'The Promulgation of Universal Peace.' As to its Introduction, it should be written by Mr. MacNutt himself when in heart he is turning toward the Abhá Kingdom, so that he may leave a permanent trace behind him." [83:11:41] The MacNutts died as a result of accidents in Miami, Florida, he on the 16 December 1926 and she a month later.

MAHDÍ See **MIHDÍ**. [11:739]

MAHD-I-'ULYÁ See **FÁṬIMIH KHÁNUM.**

MÁH-KÚ One of the fortresses in which the Báb was imprisoned during the last three years of His brief ministry. Shoghi Effendi refers to this period of His life:

> The period of the Báb's banishment to the mountains of Ádhirbáyján, lasting no less than three years, constitutes the saddest, the most dramatic, and in a sense the most pregnant phase of His six year ministry. It comprises His nine months' unbroken confinement in the fortress of Máh-Kú, and His subsequent incarceration in the fortress of Chihríq, which was interrupted only by a brief yet memorable visit to Tabríz. [5:17]

The fortress of Máh-Kú, not far from the village of that same name, whose inhabitants had long enjoyed the patronage of the Grand Vizír, situated in the remotest north-western corner of Ádhirbáyján, was the place of incarceration assigned by Muḥammad Sháh, for the Báb. No more than one companion and one attendant from among His followers were allowed to keep Him company in those bleak and inhospitable surroundings. [5:16]

On His way to that fortress the Báb passed a number of days in Tabríz, days that were marked by such an intense excitement on the part of the populace that, except for a few persons, neither the public nor His followers were allowed to meet Him.... So great, indeed, became the clamor that the town crier was ordered to warn the inhabitants that any one who ventured to seek the Báb's presence would forfeit all his possessions and be imprisoned. Upon His arrival in Máh-Kú, surnamed by Him Jabal-i-Básiṭ (the Open Mountain) no one was allowed to see Him for the first two weeks except His amanuensis, Siyyid Ḥusayn, and his brother. So grievous was His plight while in that fortress that, in the Persian Bayán, He Himself has stated that at night-time He did not even have a lighted lamp, and that His solitary chamber, constructed of sun-baked bricks, lacked even a door, while, in His Tablet to Muḥammad Sháh, He has complained that the inmates of the fortress were confined to two guards and four dogs. Secluded on the heights of a remote and dangerously situated mountain on the frontiers of the Ottoman and Russian empires; imprisoned within the solid walls of a four-towered fortress; cut off from His family, His kindred and His disciples; living in the vicinity of a bigoted and turbulent community who, by race, tradition, language and creed, differed from the vast majority of the inhabitants of Persia ... the Prisoner of Máh-Kú seemed in the eyes of His adversary to be doomed to languish away the flower of His youth, and witness, at no distant date, the complete annihilation of His hopes. That adversary was soon to realize, however, how gravely he had misjudged both his Prisoner and those on whom he had lavished his favors. An unruly, a proud and unreasoning people were gradually subdued by the gentleness of the Báb, were chastened by His modesty, were edified by His counsels, and instructed by His wisdom. They were so carried away by their love for Him that their first act every morning, notwithstanding the remonstrations of the domineering 'Alí Khán, and the repeated threats of disciplinary measures received from Ṭihrán, was to seek a place where they could catch a glimpse of His face, and beseech from afar His benediction upon their daily work. In cases of dispute it was their wont to hasten to the foot of the fortress, and, with their eyes fixed upon His abode, invoke His name, and adjure one another to speak the truth. [5:18]

The great bulk of the writings emanating from the Báb's prolific mind was, however, reserved for the period of His confinement in Máh-Kú and Chihríq. To this period must probably belong the unnumbered Epistles which, as attested by no less an authority than Bahá'u'lláh, the Báb specifically addressed to the divines of every city in Persia, as well as to those residing in Najaf and Karbilá, wherein He set forth in detail the errors committed by each one of them. It was during His incarceration in the fortress of Máh-Kú that He ... revealed no less than nine commentaries on the whole of the Qur'án—commentaries whose fate, alas, is unknown, and one of which, at least the Author Himself affirmed, surpassed in some respects a book as deservedly famous as the Qayyúmu'l-Asmá. Within the walls of that same fortress the Bayán (Exposition)—that monumental repository of the laws and precepts of the new Dispensation and the treasury enshrining most of the Báb's references and tributes to, as well as His warning regarding, "Him Whom God will make manifest"—was revealed.[5:24] See **BADASHT** and **CHIHRÍQ**.

MAḤMÚDNIZHÁD, MÚNÁ (1965-1983) (Martyr) A young Bahá'í who was executed along with other coreligionists in Shíráz, Írán, by the government in June 1983, for refusing to recant her belief in Bahá'u'lláh. [11:600]

MANTON, ERIC (1911-1984) An early (1946) British believer who served on the first local Spiritual Assembly of Edinburgh, Scotland. In 1952 he pioneered to Africa and had the distinction of being the first Bahá'í to set foot in Northern Rhodesia (now Zambia). He served on the first (1956) local Spiritual Assembly of Luanshya, Northern Rhodesia. In 1964 he was elected to the first National Spiritual Assembly of South Central Africa and served as Chairman until 1967 when the Universal House of Justice called for the election of the first National Spiritual Assembly of Zambia. He served as Chairman for nine consecutive years and then on other occasions until his retirement in 1982).[11:647]

MANY BEARS, EDMOND (1905-1968) and **JEAN** (1910-1968) The first Canadian Indians from the Blackfoot tribe to embrace the Cause. They traveled extensively among the Indian peoples sharing their faith. [50:357]

MAN-YUẒHIRUHU'LLÁH He Whom God Will Make Manifest: title given by the Báb to the Promised One (Bahá'u'lláh).[11:739]

MARANGELLA, PHILIP ANTONIO (1895-1974) An early (1921) American believer of Italian birth who traveled extensively throughout the United States promoting the Cause. In 1947 he pioneered for one year to Italy before returning to the United States. In 1953 he again left America as a pioneer, this time to Japan, where he spent the next 20 years. In 1971, at the request of the Universal House of Justice, he visited 20 established and four newly formed National Spiritual Assemblies. In 1972 he pioneered to Hong Kong. Throughout the period of his stay in the Far East he traveled extensively in the promotion of the Cause. [52:525]

MARḤABÁ Welcome! Bravo! Well Done! [11:739]

MARIE OF ROMANIA, QUEEN (1875-1938) Granddaughter of Queen Victoria; The first crowned head to be a supporter of the Bahá'í Faith. [42:269][60:427]

MARRIAGE Is not obligatory but is highly recommended. Both parties to a marriage must be at least 15 years old; must first make their own decision and then obtain consent of all living natural parents. Plurality of wives is forbidden. Bahá'ís must have a Bahá'í marriage ceremony, which may be as simple or as elaborate as the parties wish providing the basic requirements are met. These are that the bride and bridegroom both say, in the presence of witnesses, "We will all, verily, abide by the Will of God."[81:105] A spiritual assembly must be assured that this has been done; that neither party is already married; that consent of the parents has been obtained and that, in places where Bahá'í marriage is not legally recognized, a civil marriage has taken place within the previous 24 hours. Describing Bahá'í marriage 'Abdu'l-Bahá said:

> As for the question regarding marriage under the Law of God: first thou must choose one who is pleasing to thee, and then the matter is subject to the consent of father and mother. Before thou makest thy choice, they have no right to interfere.... Bahá'í marriage is the commitment of the two parties one to the other, and their mutual attachment of mind and heart. Each must, however, exercise the utmost care to become thoroughly acquainted with the character of the other, that the binding covenant between them may be a tie that will endure forever. Their purpose must be this: to become loving companions and comrades and at one with each other for time and eter-

> nity.... The true marriage of Bahá'ís is this, that husband and wife should be united both physically and spiritually, that they may ever improve the spiritual life of each other, and may enjoy everlasting unity throughout all the worlds of God. This is Bahá'í marriage. [65:118]

When one of the partners is not a Bahá'í, the Bahá'í may participate in the religious service of the other providing it does not involve a declaration of faith in the other religion nor commit the Bahá'í to allow any children to be brought up as non-Bahá'ís. In the Kitáb-i-Aqdas Bahá'u'lláh gives instructions about the length of engagement and the payment of a dowry. See **DIVORCE; DOWRY.**

MARTYR One who submits to death rather than renounce his/her faith. Also one whose sacrifices for the Faith merits this special designation. The first martyr in the Bahá'í era was Mullá 'Alí-i-Bastámí. Shoghi Effendi said that he was followed by no fewer than 20,000 martyrs who gave their lives in the early days, and these martyrdoms continue up to the present time. Bahá'u'lláh explained that it was possible to live and still be counted as a martyr.

MASEHLA, WILLIAM MMUTLE An early (1954) South African believer who served on the first (1956) local Spiritual Assembly of Alexandra. He went on to serve on the local Spiritual Assemblies of Dube, Soweto (1957), Dube/Mofolo (1958). In 1956 he was elected to the first National Spiritual Assembly of South and West Africa. He chaired the final session of the first Bahá'í World Congress in London in 1963. In 1968 he was appointed an Auxiliary Board member, and in 1976 he was raised to the rank of Continental Counsellor in which positions he traveled widely throughout the southern half of Africa in the promotion of the Cause. [11:607]

MASHRIQU'L-ADHKÁR (The Dawning Place of the Praise of God) The Bahá'í House of Worship (Bahá'í Temple). This Arabic term implies much more than a simple building—it covers several institutions built around a central house for worship that together cater for the various needs of the community. There are presently some seven of the central Houses of Worship in the world, some of which have one or more of the satellite buildings. These are in Wilmette, Ill.; Kampala, Uganda; Frankfurt, Germany; Sydney, Australia; Western Samoa; Panama and New Delhi, India. While the styles or architecture are widely varied, each central building must be nine-sided and have a dome; it must be open to all peoples of all races and religions; only the human voice will be used reading, singing or chanting from the world's religious scriptures. 'Abdu'l-Bahá said:

The Ma<u>sh</u>riqu'l-A<u>dh</u>kár is one of the most vital institutions in the world, and it hath many subsidiary branches. Although it is a House of Worship, it is also connected with a hospital, a drug dispensary, a traveler's hospice, a school for orphans, and a university for advanced studies. Every Ma<u>sh</u>riqu'l-A<u>dh</u>kár is connected with these five things. [65:99]

Shoghi Effendi wrote:

From the Ma<u>sh</u>riqu'l-A<u>dh</u>kár, ordained as a house of worship by Bahá'u'lláh in the Kitáb-i-Aqdas, the representatives of Bahá'í communities, both local and national, together with the members of their respective committees, will, as they gather daily within its walls at the hour of dawn, derive the necessary inspiration that will enable them to discharge, in the course of their day-to-day exertions in ... their administrative activities—their duties and responsibilities as befits the chosen stewards of His Faith. [5:340]

MASJID Mosque: a Muslim place of worship. [11:739🕮]

MATERIALISM The present time is obsessed by the pursuit of material possessions to the exclusion of spiritual objectives, and this is strongly condemned in Bahá'í Writings, though the desire for wealth and beautiful things is not in itself blameworthy:

The crass materialism, which lays excessive and everincreasing emphasis on material well-being, forgetful of those things of the spirit on which alone a sure and stable foundation can be laid for human society. It is this same cancerous materialism, born originally in Europe, carried to excess in the North American continent, contaminating the Asiatic peoples and nations, spreading its ominous tentacles to the borders of Africa, and now invading its very heart, which Bahá'u'lláh in unequivocal and emphatic language denounced in His Writings, comparing it to a devouring flame and regarding it as the chief factor in precipitating the dire ordeals and world-shaking crises that must necessarily involve the burning of cities and the spread of terror and consternation in the hearts of men.... It is this same all-pervasive, pernicious materialism against which the voice of the Center of Bahá'u'lláh's Covenant was raised, with pathetic persistence, from platform and pulpit, in His addresses to the heedless multitudes, which, on the morrow of His fateful visit to both Europe and America, found themselves suddenly swept into the vortex of a tempest which in its range and severity was unsurpassed in the world's history.... Collateral with this ominous laxity in morals, and this progressive stress laid on man's material pursuits and well-being, is the darkening of the political horizon, as witnessed by the widening of the gulf separating the protagonists of two antagonistic schools of thought which, however divergent in their ideologies, are to be commonly condemned by the upholders of the standard of the Faith of Bahá'u'lláh for their materialistic philosophies and their neglect of those spiritual values and eternal verities on which alone a stable and flourishing civilization can be ultimately established. [3:125] See **DETACHMENT**.

MATTHISEN, ANDREW F. (1885-1961) (Knight of Bahá'u'lláh) An early American believer who pioneered with his wife (Nina) to the Bahama Islands in 1953 for which they were designated Knights of Bahá'u'lláh.[51:529]

MATTHISEN, NINA Z. BENEDICT (1895-1972) (Knight of Bahá'u'lláh) The wife of Andrew Matthisen she embraced the Cause some six years after her marriage (1922; 1928.) She was designed a Knight of Bahá'u'lláh for her pioneer move to the Bahama Islands in 1953. [51:529]

MATTOON, EDWIN WHITAKER (-1956) An early American believer who visited 'Abdu'l-Bahá in Haifa during the summer of 1921. He served as Chairman of the National (U.S.) Bahá'í Archives Committee from 1934 to 1947; he also served on the Inter-American Teaching Committee for many years and made teaching trips to most countries in Central and South America. [47:926][60:435]

MATURITY The age of spiritual maturity in the Bahá'í Faith is set at 15 years. This is the age when a Bahá'í may get married and when the believer must begin to observe the obligations of prayer and fasting.

MAXWELL, MARION LORD (1889-1977) The first (1942) Jamaican believer to embrace the Cause in Jamaica. She was elected a member of the first (1943) local Spiritual Assembly of Kingston and became its first treasurer. [53:430]

MAXWELL, MARY See **'AMATU'L-BAHÁ RÚḤÍYYIH KHÁNUM**.

MAXWELL, MAY ELLIS BOLLES (1870-1940) (Martyr) Born in Englewood, New Jersey, 14 January 1870. From her earliest days she had a capacity for affectionate and enduring ties, an eagerness for truth and an independent nature. When she was 14 she declined further formal education. She said later: "I felt very distinctly there was another way of acquiring knowledge."

She spent many years in Paris, 11 of which were in residence for the benefit of her brother's architectural studies at the Ecôle des Beaux Arts. In spite of the beauty and comfort of her surroundings and the warmth of the relationship between herself, her mother and her brother, Randolph, she had a great deal of difficulty due to her health which was later referred to by her husband (Sutherland Maxwell [q.v.]): "May had courage and her sublime faith inspired her to carry on, very frequently under a handicap of health that would have daunted others." This weakness confined her to bed for two years before a close family friend, Mrs. Phoebe Hearst, brought a party of American tourists to her apartment on the Quai d'Orsay. Though their destination was to go up the Nile, May instinctively felt there was another purpose, and she learned from Lua Getsinger that they were to visit 'Abdu'l-Bahá in 'Akká, Palestine, being the first pilgrims from the West to visit Him. She joined the party and in the company of Mrs. Thornburgh, Lua Getsinger (q.v.), Robert Turner (q.v.) and a few others, she was in the party that reached 'Abdu'l-Bahá on 17 February 1899. She wrote of her experiences in Palestine and of the dedication to Him that characterized her whole life from that time (*An Early Pilgrimage*). [121]

On her return to Paris she began teaching the Faith and was responsible for introducing to it some of its early outstanding workers, including Charles Mason Remey (q.v.); Laura and Hippolyte Dreyfus-Barney (q.v.); Agnes Alexander (q.v.); Thomas Breakwell (q.v.); and, among many others, Juliet Thompson (q.v.).

After her marriage to William Sutherland Maxwell (q.v.) in 1902 they settled in Montréal, Canada. Their home became a center for teaching and for visitors from all over the world, many of them with the most distinguished Bahá'í names of that generation. From there she traveled widely, and always she carried with her the spirit of 'Abdu'l-Bahá. The writer of her superb *"In Memoriam"* wrote, "So potent was the force of His attraction on her heart that she in turn became a magnet of love drawing everyone to God. This alone was her method of teaching, the hidden source of an inimitable effect."[42:631] In addition to her wide teaching activities she was very active in the civic life of Montréal. She supported a Childrens' Court; maintained the Colbourne Milk Station; brought from New York a Montessori teacher and started the first school of this type in the top floor studio of her own home.

She became renowned in the East through the frequent mentions of her name by 'Abdu'l-Bahá, and it was on her second visit that the Holy Mother (Munírih Khánum, wife of 'Abdu'l-Bahá) said to her, "First as a young girl, now with your husband; on your next visit, you will come with your child." [42:631] A daughter, Mary (later to become the wife of Shoghi Effendi and designated by him as 'Amatu'l-Bahá Rúḥíyyih Khánum) was born to them in 1910.

In August 1912, after five months in the United States, 'Abdu'l-Bahá went to Montréal, Canada and stayed with the Maxwells for four days. Later He was to say, "May Maxwell is really a Bahá'í.... She breathed no breath and uttered no word save in service to the Cause of God.... Whosoever meets her feels from her association the susceptibilities of the Kingdom. Her company uplifts and develops the soul." [42:631] Her ceaseless services to the Faith took her to many parts of Canada and the United States, first carrying out the wishes of 'Abdu'l-Bahá and then for the Guardian. Of the tributes none can match those of 'Abdu'l-Bahá, "...Thy Lord shall strengthen thee in a manner, whereby the Queens of the world will envy thy happy state, throughout all time and ages. Because, verily, the Love of God is as a glorious Crown upon thy head, the brilliant jewels of which are glistening forth unto all horizons. Its brilliancy, transparency and effulgence shall appear in future centuries when the signs of God will encompass the heart of all the people of the earth!" [42:631]

It was in response to Shoghi Effendi's appeal to the Bahá'ís of America to turn towards Europe that she, with her husband, daughter and two relatives, left for a "brief visit." In reality it was two years before her return. They traveled in Germany, Belgium and France. She then went to Haifa during which time she prayed in the Holy Shrines for martyrdom. It was while she was there that she had the bounty of witnessing her daughter's marriage to Shoghi Effendi. After she left in May 1937 she never saw her daughter again nor experienced the Guardian's immediate, revitalizing force, "yet in a deeper sense she lived there, hour by hour to her last day." For many years she had been deeply attracted to South America but when the Guardian called upon the American Bahá'ís to settle in that part of the continent she was "immediately captivated," and she at one stage mentioned this to her daughter and was astonished when the Guardian responded by cable, "heartily approved winter visit to Buenos Aires." [42:631]

Securing the consent of her husband and physician she sailed on 24 January 1940 with her niece, Jeanne Bolles. In the cities of Rio de Janeiro, Montevideo and Buenos Aires she had fine teaching experiences, and her niece wrote, "As we drove through the streets, precious Aunt May was like a girl of sixteen in her joyous enthusiasm.... She leaned out of the taxi and exclaimed words of delight." [42:631] On the morning of 1 March, she had a terrible pain and passed away that afternoon. To her husband, Shoghi Effendi said in his cable of condolence, "Her tomb designed by yourself, erected by me, on spot she fought, fell gloriously, will become his toric center pioneer Bahá'í activity." Shoghi Effendi's announcement to Bahá'í world summarizes this outstanding life:

> 'Abdu'l-Bahá's beloved handmaid, distinguished disciple May Maxwell gathered glory Abhá Kingdom. Her earthly life, so rich, eventful, incomparably blessed, worthily ended. To sacred tie her signal services had forged, priceless honor martyr's death now added. Double crown deservedly won. Seven Year Plan, particularly South American campaign, derive fresh impetus example her glorious sacrifice. Southern outpost Faith greatly enriched through association her historic resting-place destined remain poignant reminder resistless march triumphant army Bahá'u'lláh Advise believers both Americas hold befitting memorial gathering. [42:631]

In his message to the American Convention in April that year appeared the following paragraph:

> And now as this year, so memorable in the annals of the Faith, was drawing to its close, there befell the American Bahá'í community, through the dramatic and sudden death of May Maxwell, yet another loss, which viewed in retrospect will come to be regarded as a potent blessing conferred upon the campaign now being so diligently conducted by its members. Laden with the fruits garnered through well-nigh half a century of toilsome service to the Cause she so greatly loved, heedless of the warnings of age and ill-health, and afire with the longing to worthily demonstrate her gratitude in her overwhelming awareness of the bounties of her Lord and Master, she set her face towards the southern outpost of the Faith in the New World, and laid down her life in such a spirit of consecration and self-sacrifice as has truly merited the crown of martyrdom. [38:69][42:631][59:151ff]

MAXWELL, WILLIAM SUTHERLAND (1874-1952) (Hand of the Cause of God) Born of Scottish descent, in Montréal, Canada in 1874. He demonstrated an ability for drawing and design at an early age and in 1899 went to Paris where he studied architecture. It was here that he met the sister of a fellow student, May Bolles, who later became his wife. May was a Bahá'í who had just returned from a pilgrimage to 'Akká where she had met 'Abdu'l-Bahá. Mr. Maxwell had to return to Canada, but Miss Bolles refused to leave Paris where she was needed as one of the earliest Bahá'ís. 'Abdu'l-Bahá approved the move of May to Canada and blessed the proposed marriage. They were married in 1902 so that

May Maxwell "opened" Canada to the Faith, and the Maxwell home became a center for Bahá'í activities.

Entering into partnership with his brother, Edward, their firm—Edward and W. S. Maxwell, became by the start of WW I the largest and most famous firm of architects in Canada: with many public landmarks, offices and private homes to their credit. In 1909, Sutherland and May went on pilgrimage to 'Akká, where Sutherland became a believer and was later host to 'Abdu'l-Bahá when He visited Montréal in 1912. Their only child, Mary Sutherland Maxwell (q.v.) was born in 1910.

It was written of him that "He was upright, truthful and never approached a human being except in courtesy, friendliness and that graciousness that is the essence of the democratic spirit." [40:641] His achievements and talents brought many honors in the fields of art and architecture. The greatest change in his life came in 1937 when he was called to Haifa to be present at the marriage of his daughter Mary to Shoghi Effendi.

The health of his wife, May, which for all their 35 years of marriage had bordered on invalidism, was deteriorating, and in 1940, on a teaching trip to South America, May suffered a heart attack and died in Buenos Aires. He was invited to Haifa where he spent the next 12 years in service to his beloved Guardian and son-in-law. Quiet, unassuming, like a rock Sutherland stood by Shoghi Effendi during some of the most difficult times of his Guardianship.

His crowning glory was when Shoghi Effendi asked him to design the outside structure for the Shrine of the Báb as the original building erected by 'Abdu'l-Bahá needed to be completed with a dome and an arcade. Studies were submitted to the Guardian in 1942 and a model of the completed and accepted design were exhibited to those who had gathered at the Shrine on the Centenary of His Declaration.

By 1946 Sutherland was in full charge of all the Guardian's outside work, dealing with visitors, mail, government contracts and other aspects of the Guardian's work. The pressure of the work eventually proved too much for him, and he suffered a broken blood vessel in his ear, which left him deaf, shaken and dizzy for weeks on end. Nevertheless, in 1948 he flew to Italy to place the contract for the stonework for the Shrine's superstructure. In spite of failing health he continued to work on the detailed working drawings until he broke down completely in 1949. During a series of collapses and partial recoveries, with no hope offered at all by the best doctors, he was kept alive by the reciprocating love between him and the Guardian until he was able to visit the completed Arcade of the Shrine. Sutherland's cherished wish was again to visit Montréal, and arrangements were made for him to spend the summer there of 1951 and to return to Haifa in the autumn. The food he needed to keep him from relapsing could not be obtained in Israel so he remained in Canada through the winter, and it was during this time that he was elevated to rank of Hand of the Cause. He passed away on 25 March 1952 with his nurse and favorite nephew at his bedside. As was the case with her mother, his daughter Mary was unable to be present when he passed away. Shoghi Effendi cabled the Bahá'í world:

> With sorrowful heart announce through National Spiritual Assemblies Hand of the Cause of Bahá'u'lláh highly esteemed dearly beloved Sutherland Maxwell gathered into the glory of the Abhá Kingdom. His saintly life extending well-nigh four-score years, enriched during the course of 'Abdu'l-Bahá 's ministry by services in the Dominion of Canada, ennobled during Formative Age of the Faith by decade of service in Holy Land, during darkest days of my life, doubly honored through the association with the crown of martyrdom won by May Maxwell and incomparable honor bestowed upon his daughter, attained consummation through his appointment as architect of the Arcade and Superstructure of the Báb's Sepulcher as well as his elevation to the front ranks of the Hands of the Causc of God.... The mantle of Hand of the Cause now falls upon the shoulders of his distinguished daughter, 'Amatu'l-Bahá Rúḥíyyih, who has already rendered and is still rendering no less meritorious self-sacrificing services at World Center of Faith of Bahá'u'lláh. [40:640][48:657][60:437]

MAIDEN A square or open place. [11:739📖]

MAZRA'IH The summer mansion some four miles north of 'Akká that 'Abdu'l-Bahá rented for Bahá'u'lláh and to which He moved in June 1877. He lived there for two years before moving into Bahjí. It was eventually purchased by the Universal House of Justice and renovated as one of the places of pilgrimage.

McDANIEL, ALLEN B. (1879-1965) An early (1915) American believer. He was elected a member of the National Spiritual Assembly of the United States and Canada in 1925 and continued to serve (mostly as Chairman) until 1946. It was his company that received the contract to construct the superstructure of the Wilmette Temple in 1930. [50:364]

McKINLEY, VIOLET JESSIE (1882-1959) (Knight of Bahá'u'lláh) An early (c.1925) British believer. She was a member of the first (1946) local Spiritual Assembly of Torquay. A year later she moved to Cardiff and helped form the first (1947) local Spiritual Assembly in that town. She pioneered along with her son (Hugh) to Cyprus in the first year of the Ten Year Crusade (for which they both were designated Knights of Bahá'u'lláh).[52:512]

McNEILL, LILIAN VAUGHAN (1879-1949) She was born into a military family on 1 December 1879. While her father was Acting Governor of Malta and the then-Duke of Edinburgh, second son of Queen Victoria, was Commander of the British Fleet in the Mediterranean, she met and played with the four daughters of the Duke. One of them was Marie (q.v. **MARIE, QUEEN**) the first member of Royalty to accept the Bahá'í Faith. Later the five girls continued their friendship at Buckingham Palace and Clarence House, London. All were married while they were quite young, Marie to King Ferdinand I of Romania and Lilian to a young officer who was killed in action in the Sudan while Lilian was carrying his son in 1898. Queen Victoria was the godmother to the new baby, and Lilian lived very quietly as a young widow. Eventually she married again—to her husband's fellow officer, Angus McNeill. In 1922 the McNeills went to Palestine where Angus was called upon to open and develop a stock-breeding project near 'Akká. Lilian became acquainted with the Bahá'í Faith in Palestine at about the same time that Queen Marie was meeting with Martha Root (q.v.). In 1929 the McNeills discovered a run-down old house with a Bedouin family living in tents in the garden. It had a great attraction for Lilian, and in May 1931 the McNeills took a lease on the house and were able to restore it. The House turned out to be the one that Bahá'u'lláh first visited and lived on leaving 'Akká. On learning of the association with Bahá'u'lláh they kept the floor that Bahá'u'lláh had used untouched. Lilian had hoped to renew her friendship with Queen Marie when she visited Palestine but it was not to be, and afterwards they exchanged correspondence during which the Queen wrote to Lilian saying, "to think that you are of all things living near Haifa and are, as I am, a follower of the Bahá'í Faith. It interests me that you are living in that special house." From the correspondence it would seem that Shoghi Effendi visited the McNeills on many occasions. Lilian died in August 1949, and Angus wrote to Shoghi Effendi saying that she had hoped that she and her old school friend, Queen Marie, could have visited the Shrines together. He died in Cyprus some six months after Lilian. Shoghi Effendi was able to obtain the Mansion on lease from the Israeli Government and the Universal House of Justice purchased it in March 1973. Lilian's first son was killed in Tanzania in 1946 and the son from Angus, Major-General John McNeill, collaborated closely with the writer of the article from which the above notes were taken and warmly gave his approval for the Universal House of Justice to erect an appropriate memorial stone over the grave of Lillian, discovered in 1981. [11:779ff]

MEDITATION While no set form of meditation is prescribed in Bahá'í Writings and the Bahá'ís are warned against allowing superstitious ideas creeping into it, its rôle in Bahá'í practice is emphasized:

> Meditate profoundly, that the secret of things unseen may be revealed unto you, that you may inhale the sweetness of a spiritual and imperishable fragrance, and that you may acknowledge the truth that from time immemorial even unto eternity the Almighty hath tried, and will continue to try, His servants, so that light may be distinguished from darkness, truth from falsehood, right from wrong, guidance from error, happiness from misery, and roses from thorns. [64:8]

> Do thou meditate on that which We have revealed unto thee, that thou mayest discover the purpose of God, thy Lord, and the Lord of all worlds. In these words the mysteries of Divine Wisdom have been treasured. [85:153]

> Meditation is the key for opening the doors of mysteries. In that state man abstracts himself: in that state man withdraws himself from all outside objects; in that subjective mood he is immersed in the ocean of spiritual life and can unfold the secrets of things-in-themselves.... This faculty of meditation frees man from the animal nature, discerns the reality of things, puts man in touch with God.... This faculty brings forth from the invisible plane the sciences and arts. Through the meditative faculty inventions are made possible, colossal undertakings are carried out; through it governments can run smoothly. Through this faculty man enters into the very Kingdom of God. [25:175]

> The inspiration received through meditation is of a nature that one cannot measure or determine. God can inspire into our minds things that we had no previous knowledge of, if He desires to do so. [104:77]

MEJIA, BLANCA VICTORIA (1911-1975) The first (1941) Nicaraguan to become a Bahá'í she shared her faith with many people from all walks of life. She was a member of the first local Spiritual Assembly of León. [52:550]

MIESSLER, EDMUND (1902-1977) An American believer who learned of the Faith from Hand of the Cause of God Dorothy Baker in Lima, Ohio. Following the death of his wife (Muriel Auble, 1945) he pioneered to São Paulo, Brazil where he helped form the first (1947) local Spiritual Assembly of São Paulo. He was later elected to the first and succeeding regional National Spiritual Assembly of South America. In 1961 he was elected to the first National Spiritual Assembly of Brazil. He was later appointed an Auxiliary Board member. [53:431][60:441]

MIGETTE, LUCIENE (1903-1983) An early (1936) French believer who came into the Cause through the efforts of May Maxwell (q.v.). She worked closely with the Bahá'í International Bureau in Geneva. In 1940 she served on the first local Spiritual Assembly of Lyon. She served after WW II on the local Spiritual Assembly of Paris and in 1958 was elected to the first National Spiritual Assembly of France. She remained a member of the National Assembly until her appointment as an Auxiliary Board member in 1965. [11:610]

MIHDÍ Literally directed, guided; one who is rightly guided; The Mahdi: a designation of the Twelfth Imám; a title of the Manifestation expected by Islám. [11:739📖]

MILLS, MARY OLGA KATHERINE (1882-1974) (Knight of Bahá'u'lláh) An early (mid-1920s) American believer of German birth. She met Shoghi Effendi while on pilgrimage sometime before 1930. She spent the war years in Leipzig and at the request of Shoghi Effendi, moved to the British Isles in early 1948. She was adamant in her desire to serve her Faith, and placed herself entirely at the disposal of the National Teaching Committee. She was always ready to move in the best interests of the Faith and she carried out no fewer that six important pioneer projects in the last two years of the Six Year Plan. In 1953 she pioneered to Malta, for which service she was designated a Knight of Bahá'u'lláh. At the age of 91 she was elected to the first local Spiritual Assembly of Malta. [52:531]

MILLS, MOUNTFORD (-1949) An early American believer who made two pilgrimages to 'Akká to meet 'Abdu'l-Bahá. He also met 'Abdu'l-Bahá during His historic visit to America. He was the first Chairman of the National Spiritual Assembly of the United States and Canada when it formed in 1922. The first draft of the Declaration of Trust and By-Laws adopted by the National Spiritual Assembly in 1927 was prepared by Mr. Mills. He was instrumental in drawing up the appeal to the League of Nations concerning the House of Bahá'u'lláh. [84:509][59:311ff]

MIND 'Abdu'l-Bahá deals at great length with the powers of the mind:

> The human spirit, unless assisted by the spirit of faith, does not become acquainted with the divine secrets and the heavenly realities. It is like a mirror which, although

clear, polished, and brilliant, is still in need of light. Until a ray of the sun reflects upon it, it cannot discover the heavenly secrets. But the mind is the power of the human spirit. Spirit is the lamp; mind is the light which shines from the lamp. Spirit is the tree, and the mind is the fruit. Mind is the perfection of the spirit, and is its essential quality, as the sun's rays are the essential necessity of the sun. [106:317]

Now concerning mental faculties, they are in truth of the inherent properties of the soul, even as the radiation of light is the essential property of the sun. The rays of the sun are renewed but the sun itself is ever the same and unchanged. Consider how the human intellect develops and weakens, and may at times come to naught, whereas the soul changeth not. For the mind to manifest itself, the human body must be whole; and a sound mind cannot be but in a sound body, whereas the soul dependeth not upon the body. It is through the power of the soul that the mind comprehendeth, imagineth and exerteth its influence, whilst the soul is a power that is free. The mind comprehendeth the abstract by the aid of the concrete, but the soul hath limitless manifestations of its own. The mind is circumscribed, the soul limitless. It is by the aid of such senses as those of sight, hearing, taste, smell and touch, that the mind comprehendeth, whereas, the soul is free from all agencies. [106:337] Though in infancy the signs of the mind and spirit appear in man, they do not reach the degree of perfection; they are imperfect. Only when man attains maturity do the mind and the spirit appear and become evident in utmost perfection. So also the formation of man in the matrix of the world was in the beginning like the embryo; then gradually he made progress in perfectness, and grew and developed until he reached the state of maturity, when the mind and spirit became visible in the greatest power. In the beginning of his formation the mind and spirit also existed, but they were hidden; later they were manifested. In the womb of the world mind and spirit also existed in the embryo, but they were concealed; afterward they appeared. [56:198]

The spirit is the power of life, the mind is the power which apprehendeth the reality of things, and the soul is an intermediary between the Supreme Concourse (or Spiritual World) and the lower concourse (or material world).[100:612]

MÍR A contraction of amír, used, when prefixed to a name, to denote descent from the House of the Prophet. See **SIYYID.** [11:739📖]

MIRACLES These are not regarded by Bahá'ís as being any proof of the divinity of Bahá'u'lláh, for as 'Abdu'l-Bahá wrote:

> Though if I wish to mention the supernatural acts of Bahá'u'lláh, they are numerous; they are acknowledged in the Orient, and even by some non-Bahá'ís. But these narratives are not decisive proofs and evidences to all; the hearer might perhaps say that this account may not be in accordance with what occurred ... From what evidence may we know that those are false and that these are true? ...Consequently, these accounts are not satisfactory proofs. Yes, miracles are proofs for the eyewitness only, and even he may regard them not as a miracle but as an enchantment. [100:37]

The greatest miracles of Bahá'u'lláh are the ways in which He changes the hearts of people, turns hatred into love; brings unity and peace where there was discord and war and has laid the foundations for a new civilization and a new human race: literally the effects of His Words on the hearers.

MIRANDA, ROQUE CENTURION (-1957) The first person to accept the Cause in Paraguay. [47:917]

MI'RÁJ The Ascent: Muḥammad's mystic vision of the "night journey" in which He ascended into heaven. [11:739📖]

MÍRZÁ A contraction of amír-zádih, meaning "son of an amír." When affixed to a name it signifies "Prince"; when prefixed, it either denotes a clerk, secretary, scribe or scholar, or conveys a merely honorific sense: Mister. [11:739📖]

MÍRZÁ ḌÍYÁ'U'LLÁH The second son of Fáṭimih Khánum was a weak, vacillating individual entirely under the influence of his elder brother, lived and died prematurely in the property adjacent to the Mansion of Bahjí, which was in the hands of the covenant-breaking family of Muḥammad-'Alí.

MÍRZÁ ḤUSAYN See **MISHKÍN-QALAM.**

MÍRZÁ ḤUSAYN 'ALÍ-I-NÚRÍ The name of Bahá'u'lláh (q.v.) before the Conference of Badasht, and by which He was generally known outside the Bábí community.

MÍRZÁ 'ALÍ MUḤAMMAD (Ibn-i-Aṣdaq) (—) (Hand of the Cause of God and Apostle of Bahá'u'lláh) As a young boy in the company of his father, he met Bahá'u'lláh in Baghdád. Soon after their return to Persia they were arrested for being Bábís (q.v.), put into chains, tortured and thrown into the Siyáh-Chál (q.v.), where Bahá'u'lláh Himself had been chained before He was exiled to Baghdád.

Father and son remained chained together in that foul dungeon for over two years, and young 'Alí Muḥammad became seriously ill. The chief jailer agreed to send for a physician, but none could be found who would treat a Bábí. He finally found a Jewish doctor, Ḥakim Masih, who treated the boy for two months and after his recovery spent hours in the prison learning about the Faith, which he then accepted, thereby becoming one of the earliest of Jewish background to become a believer. Ibn-i-Aṣdaq traveled widely throughout Persia with his father, teaching the Faith. As he matured he grew in spirit. When he was about 30 years of age he wrote to Bahá'u'lláh begging Him to confer upon him the state of "utter self-sacrifice" and pleaded for the crown of martyrdom. In January 1880 Bahá'u'lláh responded saying that He would pray that he may attain the station of the most great martyrdom; that service to the Cause is the greatest of all deeds; that martyrdom is not confined to the shedding of blood and that it is possible to live a life of service and sacrifice and still be counted as a martyr in the sight of God. Two years later he again wrote along similar lines to Bahá'u'lláh, Who replied with words of appreciation and praise for his devoted services and called upon him always to live a saintly life. He bestowed upon this young man the title Shahíd-ibn-i-Shahíd. (martyr, son of the martyr), and He subsequently appointed him a Hand of the Cause. He was also designated an Apostle of Bahá'u'lláh.

MÍRZÁ 'ALÍ MUḤAMMAD See **VARQÁ, MÍRZÁ 'ALÍ-MUḤAMMAD.**

MÍRZÁ 'ALÍ-MUḤAMMAD (a Hand of the Cause of God and an Apostle of Bahá'u'lláh) Known as "Varqá," he was a Bahá'í teacher and poet. He was killed in front of his 12-year-old son, who was then in turn strangled with a rope for refusing to recant. He was named a Hand of the Cause by 'Abdu'l-Bahá.

MÍRZÁ ABU'L-FAḌL-I-GULPÁYGÁNÍ (1844-1914) (Apostle of Bahá'u'lláh) Outstanding scholar and of rare erudition, unequaled amongst the followers of Bahá'u'lláh, in the East or in the West, in the first century of the Bahá'í Faith. Born in 1844, he embraced the Faith in 1876 and devoted the rest of his 70 years to traveling, teaching and writing about the Bahá'í Faith. He compiled a *Genealogies of Bahá'u'lláh*. He spent almost four years in America at the turn of the century. [59:80ff] Among the books he wrote that have been translated into English are *The Bahá'í Proofs*, *The Brilliant Proof* [122] and *Miracles and Metaphors* [123]

MÍRZÁ BADÍ'U'LLÁH (1890-1950) The youngest son of Fáṭimih Khánum, he supported fully all the early machinations of his brother Muḥammad-'Alí (q.v.), being his chief accomplice. He later betrayed him and published a signed denunciation of his actions against Bahá'u'lláh. Sometime later he again joined forces with Muḥammad-'Alí only to become alienated from him a second time. He died in 1950 after almost 60 years of acts of treachery and deceit, which sorely stained the history of the Faith established by his own illustrious Father.

MÍRZÁ BUZURG See **BADÍ'**.

MÍRZÁ HÁDÍ 15th Letter of the Living.

MÍRZÁ MAḤMÚD (an Apostle of Bahá'u'lláh) A staunch fearless defender of the Faith.

MÍRZÁ MAḤMÚD FURÚGHÍ (Apostle of Bahá'u'lláh) A staunch fearless defender of the Faith; he was designated an Apostle of Bahá'u'lláh.

MÍRZÁ MIHDÍ (the Purest Branch) (1848-1870) The second son of Bahá'u'lláh, he was born in Ṭihrán in 1848. He was exiled along with his family and died while incarcerated in the prison in 'Akká in June of 1870. His tragic and untimely death is described by Shoghi Effendi in these words:

> To the galling weight of these tribulations was now added the bitter grief of a sudden tragedy—the premature loss of the noble, the pious Mírzá Mihdí, the Purest Branch, 'Abdu'l-Bahá's twenty-two year old brother, an amanuensis of Bahá'u'lláh and a companion of His exile from the days when, as a child, he was brought from Ṭihrán to Baghdád to join his Father after His return from Sulaymáníyyih. He was pacing the roof of the barracks in the twilight, one evening, wrapped in his customary devotions, when he fell through the unguarded skylight onto a wooden crate, standing on the floor beneath, which pierced his ribs, and caused, twenty-two hours later, his death, on the 23rd of Rabí'u'l-Avval 1287 A.H. (June 23, 1870.) His dying supplication to a grieving Father was that his life might be accepted as a ransom for those who were prevented from attaining the presence of their Beloved. In a highly significant prayer, revealed by Bahá'u'lláh in memory of His son—a prayer that exalts his death to the rank of those great acts of atonement associated with Abraham's intended sacrifice of His son, with the crucifixion of Jesus Christ and the martyrdom of the Imám Ḥusayn—we read the following: "I have, O my Lord, offered up that which Thou hast given Me, that Thy servants may be quickened, and all that dwell on earth be united." And, likewise, these prophetic words, addressed to His martyred son: "Thou art the Trust of God and His Treasure in this Land. Erelong will God reveal through

thee that which He hath desired." After he had been washed in the presence of Bahá'u'lláh, he "that was created of the light of Bahá," to whose "meekness" the Supreme Pen had testified, and of the "mysteries" of whose ascension that same Pen had made mention, was borne forth, escorted by the fortress guards, and laid to rest, beyond the city walls, in a spot adjacent to the shrine of Nabí Ṣáliḥ, from whence, seventy years later, his remains, simultaneously with those of his illustrious mother, were to be translated to the slopes of Mt. Carmel, in the precincts of the grave of his sister, and under the shadow of the Báb's holy sepulcher. [5:188f]

MÍRZÁ MUḤAMMAD RAWḌIH-KHÁN-I-YAZDÍ Eighth Letter of the Living.

MÍRZÁ MUḤAMMAD-ḤASAN (Siyyid Ḥasan) (an Apostle of Bahá'u'lláh) One of two brothers of Iṣfáhán, given the title Sulṭánu'sh-Shuhadá,' the King of the Martyrs, was given a special mission to prepare for the journey to 'Akká of Fáṭimih, the wife-to-be of 'Abdu'l-Bahá. He and his brother, Mírzá Muḥammad-Ḥusayn, the Beloved of Martyrs, both well-loved and respected in Iṣfáhán for their generosity, trustworthiness, kindliness and piety, were, while Bahá'u'lláh was still imprisoned in 'Akká, denounced as Bábís. All their possessions were confiscated and they were placed in chains, decapitated and dragged through the streets of the town. For several years Bahá'u'lláh in His Tablets continued to extol their virtues and voice His grief at their passing.

MÍRZÁ MUḤAMMAD-'ALÍY-I-QAZVÍNÍ 16th Letter of the Living.

MÍRZÁ MUḤAMMAD-QULÍ A half-brother of Bahá'u'lláh who accompanied Him into exile in January 1853, then to Turkey and finally to 'Akká. When Bahá'u'lláh passed away, Mírzá Muḥammad-Qulí remained firm in the Covenant, devoting himself entirely to God, supplicating and praying. He was known for calling to mind the days of Bahá'u'lláh and expressing his grief because he himself lived on. One poignant testimony stated, "After the departure of Bahá'u'lláh, he did not draw an easeful breath; he kept company with no one, but stayed by himself most of the time, alone in his small refuge, burning with the fires of separation." [124:71]

MÍRZÁ MÚSÁ (Áqáy-i-Kalím) (-1887) (Apostle of Bahá'u'lláh) The younger blood brother of Bahá'u'lláh who became a firm follower of Bahá'u'lláh and was later designated as one of the Apostles of Bahá'u'lláh. He remained a most devoted follower of Bahá'u'lláh throughout his life, undertaking many missions at His request, until he passed away in 1887. Most notably, at the request of Bahá'u'lláh, he concealed the casket containing the remains of the

Báb and the faithful disciple who had shared His Martyrdom. He accompanied Bahá'u'lláh into exile and for many years acted as Bahá'u'lláh's deputy in meeting with officials and religious leaders. He remained to the end of his life a staunch and valued supporter, the ablest and most distinguished among His brothers and sisters, and one of the "only two persons who," according to Bahá'u'lláh's testimony, "were adequately informed of the origins" of His Faith (the other was Mírzá Muḥammad-Qulí, a half-brother, who, in spite of the defection of some of his relatives, remained loyal to the end to the Cause he had espoused).

MÍRZÁ YAḤYÁ (Ṣubḥ-i-Azal—Morning of Eternity) (-1912) A younger half-brother of Bahá'u'lláh who was the son of the fourth wife of Mírzá Buzurg, the father of Bahá'u'lláh. The Báb had, while in prison in Máh-Kú, written a letter to Bahá'u'lláh requesting Him to be responsible for the upbringing of Mírzá Yaḥyá. Subsequently the Báb appointed Yaḥyá as the nominal head of the Bábí community but after the exile of Bahá'u'lláh, notwithstanding his high calling, Yaḥyá fled the country in disguise and later joined the exiles in Ba<u>gh</u>dád. He turned away from Bahá'u'lláh and though he followed Him into exile in Turkey he constantly plotted again Him and even attempted to kill Him with poison, the aftereffects of which remained with Bahá'u'lláh until the end of His life. Led in his delusions by Siyyid Muḥammad-i-Iṣfáhání (q.v.), who was later to become notorious as the "Antichrist of the Bahá'í Revelation," Yaḥyá first claimed to be the successor of the Báb and, after Bahá'u'lláh had openly announced that He was indeed the "Promised One," advance that same claim for himself. He had a few followers who became known as Azalís. They instigated so much unrest in Adrianople that the government took drastic action against all the exiles and their families. Bahá'u'lláh was sent with some of His faithful followers and some Azalís to the penal city of 'Akká. Yaḥyá, with the remainder of his followers and some Bahá'ís, was sent in exile to Cyprus. Yaḥyá, regarded by Bahá'í historians as the Arch-Breaker of the Covenant of the Báb, lived long enough to witness, while eking out a miserable existence in Cyprus, termed by the Turks "the Island of Satan," every hope he had so maliciously conceived reduced to naught. A pensioner first of the Turkish and later of the British government, he was subjected to the further humiliation of having his application for British citizenship refused. Eleven of the 18 "witnesses" he had appointed forsook him and turned in repentance to Bahá'u'lláh. He himself became involved in a scandal that besmirched his reputation and that of his eldest son, deprived that son and his descendants of the successorship with which he had previously invested him, and appointed, in his stead, the perfidious Mírzá

Hádíy-i-Dawlat-Abádí, [90:73]—a notorious Azalí, who on one occasion was seized with such fear that during four consecutive days he proclaimed from the pulpit-top, and in a most vituperative language, his complete repudiation of the Bábí Faith, as well as of Mírzá Yaḥyá, his benefactor, who had reposed in him such implicit confidence. Yaḥyá died in Cyprus in 1912.

MISHKÍN-QALAM (musk-scented pen) (-1921) (Apostle of Bahá'u'lláh) Also known as Mírzá Ḥusayn and Áqá Ḥusayn-i-Iṣfahání. He was a notable calligrapher, holding, before he became a Bahá'í in Iṣfáhán, a high position in the court of the Sháh in Ṭihrán. He did not return to the Court but went to Adrianople to join the Bahá'í exiles where he met with Bahá'u'lláh. He was sent on an important mission by Him to Constantinople, where he was imprisoned; from there he was then sent on to Galipoli. When Bahá'u'lláh arrived in that port on His way to the prison in 'Akká, Mishkín-Qalam, to his great distress, was sent with three other of Bahá'u'lláh's disciples into exile with the Azalís to Cyprus. So deep was his devotion to Bahá'u'lláh that although he was for about nine years in close association with Azal, he remained true to the Faith and on his release rejoined the Bahá'ís in 'Akká. He passed away in the Holy Land in about 1912. Mishkín-Qalam has been described as "...unsurpassed as a calligrapher, and a genius in the creation of exquisite designs from letters and words..."[71:27] He was also designated an Apostle of Bahá'u'lláh.

MITCHELL, JOHN GEORGE (1907-1957) (Knight of Bahá'u'lláh) A member of the British National Spiritual Assembly from 1952 to 1954, during which time he served as treasurer. He pioneered to Malta in 1954 for which service he was designated a Knight of Bahá'u'lláh. [47:901]

MITCHELL, WILLIAM ARTHUR WELLESLEY (1907-1985) The second Jamaican to embrace the Cause (two days after Marian Lord Maxwell). He served on the first (1943) local Spiritual Assembly of Jamaica (formed in Kingston). In 1961 he was elected to the first National Spiritual Assembly of Jamaica. He was the first (1965-69) native believer to be appointed an Auxiliary Board member. [11:684]

MKHIZE, NHLUMBA BERTHA (1889-1981) An early (1959) South African believer who at the age of 70 arose to teach the cause in Natal and Zululand (where she lived as a pioneer in Gezinsila, Eshowe). During the nine years she lived in KwaZulu, she helped to raise up some 28 Bahá'í communities. In 1968 she was elected to the National Spiritual Assembly of South and West Africa. She also translated Bahá'í literature into Zulu. [2:773]

MOFFETT, RUTH J. (1880-1978) An early (1912) American believer and noted Bahá'í lecturer and writer. She first saw 'Abdu'l-

Bahá from a train platform in Chicago in 1912. She attended one of His lectures and took up active service in 1919. Her early teaching efforts were instrumental in establishing the Bahá'í community in America. Her teaching took her throughout the Americas, Europe, the Near East, Asia, Egypt and Canada. She often used the name "Rúḥáníyyih" (connoting spirituality, joy and beauty), which had been given to her by the greatest Holy Leaf (Bahíyyih Khánum).[53:463][60:443]

MOHAPI, CHADWICK (1888-1978) Led by his wife Mary, he was the first (1954) of the Bakoena clan (the royal clan of Lesotho, descendants of Mohoeshoe I, the father of the Basuto nation) to accept the Faith in Lesotho (formerly Basutoland).[53:449][60:445]

MOHAPI, MARY (-1968) Along with her husband she was the first (1954) of the Bataung clan, a direct descendant of the famous chieftain, Molestane, to become a Bahá'í in Lesotho.[53:451] See **MOHAPI, CHADWICK.**

MONUMENT GARDENS The area on Mount Carmel in the vicinity of the Shrine of the Báb where, in beautiful gardens, monuments have been raised over the tombs of the mother, sister, brother and wife of 'Abdu'l-Bahá. See **GREATEST HOLY LEAF; MOUNT CARMEL; MUNÍRIH KHÁNUM; NAVVÁB; PUREST BRANCH.**

MOODY, SUSAN I. (1851-1934) ('Amatu'l-A'lá—Handmaid of the Most High) She was born in Amsterdam, New York, of Scots-Covenanter parents on 20 November 1851. She received a good education, became a teacher and then entered the Women's Medical College, New York City. She later studied music, painting and sculpture in Chicago, New York and Paris and finally concluded her study of medicine in Chicago. She accepted the Bahá'í Faith in 1903 and conducted the first Bahá'í Sunday School in Chicago. Following the visit to Írán in 1908 of a party of Americans, when some doctors asked if it would be possible for a woman doctor to go to Ṭihrán to care for women who were at that time deprived of skilled medical care, she received a message from 'Abdu'l-Bahá saying that she had been chosen for this great medical work in Írán, and she proceeded immediately to comply. En route to Írán she visited 'Abdu'l-Bahá in the Holy Land and arrived in Ṭihrán on 26 November 1908. She served there for 15 years, suffering many difficulties and hardships but remembering throughout that 'Abdu'l-Bahá had said she would need patience. She became fluent in the Persian language and kept up a frequent correspondence with her friends in America describing the situation of the women in Írán. Not only was she much appreciated for her medical work, she was also acclaimed for founding the Tarbíyat School for Girls. Dr. Moody was the first and longest serving of four American Bahá'í women to work for the Faith in Persia.

She visited Haifa on her journey back to America in late 1924 and reached New York to a tremendous reception in January 1925 and remained in the States, where, among her lecturing visits, she took up the study of Esperanto at the age of 75.

At age 77 she returned to Írán in November 1928, accompanied by Miss Adelaide Sharp of San Francisco. They traveled via Haifa, where they received an outstanding welcome. She continued her devoted services, but her health gradually deteriorated and on her passing on 23 October 1934 Shoghi Effendi cabled on 28 October:

> Passing dearly beloved Susan Moody deprives Bahá'í world far-famed pioneer who, through her indomitable spirit, ceaseless services, earned unique distinction forge first link in chain uniting spiritual destinies Cradle of our Faith and community stalwart defenders in great American Republic. Instructing Persia rear monument perpetuate memory her noble mission. Am gladly defraying whatever expense incurred as token my admiration for community to which she originally belonged and on which her sacred life shed imperishable lustre. Advise hold Memorial gathering Temple Foundation Hall. [23:483][59:174ff]

MORTENSEN, FRED (1887-1946) An early American believer. He traveled across America to meet 'Abdu'l-Bahá "riding the rods" of railway carriages. Shoghi Effendi included the story of this journey in *God Passes By*. [5:290][84:483][83:111]

MOST GREAT BRANCH One of the titles given by Bahá'u'lláh to 'Abdu'l-Bahá.

MOST GREAT PEACE See **PEACE, MOST GREAT**.

MOST GREAT PRISON The designation given by Bahá'u'lláh to the Citadel in 'Akká where He was imprisoned on His arrival in 1868.

MOST HOLY SHRINE The Shrine of Bahá'u'lláh, Bahjí, Israel.

MOTHER TEMPLE The term used by Shoghi Effendi for the first House of Worship (Mashriqu'l-Adhkár [q.v.]) to be built in any specific geographical area. e.g., The Mother Temple of the West is in Wilmette, Ill. and the Mother Temple of Africa is in Kampala, Uganda.

MOUNT CARMEL The mountain in Israel that is referred to by Isaiah as the "mountain of the Lord" on and around which stands the modern city of Haifa. On its northern slopes, leading down to the Bay of Haifa, the World Center of the Bahá'í Faith is established. Bahá'u'lláh Himself pitched His tent there on several occasions, and in 1891 He revealed the Tablet of Carmel (q.v.) and pointed out to 'Abdu'l-Bahá the spot where the Shrine of the Báb should be built. Plots of land around that site have been purchased first by 'Abdu'l-Bahá, then by Shoghi Effendi and after his death by the Universal House of Justice to permit the development of a befitting world center. See **ARC; ARCHIVES; HAIFA.**

MUFTÍ Expounder of Muslim law; gives a fatvá or sentence on a point of religious jurisprudence. [11:739]

MUḤAMMAD ḤASAN-I-BUSHRÚ'Í (brother of Mullá Ḥusayn) second Letter of the Living.

MUḤAMMAD BÁQIR-I-BUSHRÚ'Í (nephew of Mullá Ḥusayn) third Letter of the Living.

MUḤAMMAD MUṢṬAFÁ (an Apostle of Bahá'u'lláh) He was reported to be a brave and vigilant custodian and bearer of the remains of the Báb that, along with those of His disciple, Mírzá Muḥammad-'Alí,(surnamed Anís), were retrieved after His martyrdom, wrapped in silk, placed in a casket and then hidden until they were secretly transported from Írán to 'Akká via Baghdád, Damascus and Beirut, reaching there on 31 January 1899—50 lunar years after the Martyrdom. He was also designated an Apostle of Bahá'u'lláh.

MUḤAMMAD TAQÍY-I-IṢFÁHÁNÍ (-1946) (Hand of the Cause of God) A Persian Bahá'í who accepted the Faith in its early days and who visited Egypt via 'Akká in 1878. From there he made many more trips to the Holy Land and on the second, Bahá'u'lláh advised him to settle permanently in Egypt. During 'Abdu'l-Bahá's visit to Egypt in 1910-1912 he was His host, and many other distinguished believers were received at his home. Mírzá Abu'l-Faḍl-i-Gulpáygání (Apostle of Bahá'u'lláh) 1914, and Mrs. Lua Getsinger ("the mother teacher of the West"), 1916, both spent the last few days of their respective lives in his house. He was a very fine teacher and introduced many Egyptians to the Faith; he was also a stalwart in the Covenant protecting the Faith from serious opposition. He was a dedicated translator and author. On his passing on 13 December 1946 when he was in his mid-90s the Guardian cabled the Bahá'í world: "Hearts grief stricken passing beloved outstanding steadfast promoter Faith, Muḥammad Taqíy-i-Iṣfáhání. Long record his magnificent exemplary services imperishable deserves rank (him among the) Hands Cause of God." [40:632]

MUḤAMMAD-'ALÍ (The Greater Branch) (-1937) The eldest son of Fáṭimih Khánum was born in Baghdád, nine years after the birth of 'Abdu'l-Bahá—the Most Great Branch. From his earliest days he showed himself to be jealous of 'Abdu'l-Bahá, Who was surnamed by Bahá'u'lláh "the Master," and sought to occupy the same eminence as his distinguished brother.

After the passing of Bahá'u'lláh his opposition to 'Abdu'l-Bahá increased immensely, and while accepting the authenticity of Bahá'u'lláh's Will, he tried by interpolation and corruption of other Writings and by forged documents, to discredit 'Abdu'l-Bahá. Initially undertaken covertly, this opposition grew into a most vicious campaign of open hostility that created a most serious crisis in Bahá'í development. Describing a distressing period of this opposition, it was said that

> All that 'Abdu'l-Bahá could do, during a period of four distressful years, His incessant exhortations, His earnest pleadings, the favors and kindnesses He showered upon him, the admonitions and warnings He uttered, even His voluntary withdrawal in the hope of averting the threatening storm, proved to be of no avail. Gradually and with unyielding persistence, through lies, half-truths, calumnies and gross exaggerations, this "Prime Mover of sedition" succeeded in ranging on his side almost the entire family of Bahá'u'lláh, as well as a considerable number of those who had formed his immediate entourage. Bahá'u'lláh's two surviving wives, His two sons, the vacillating Mírzá Ḍíyá'u'lláh and the treacherous Mírzá Badí'u'lláh, with their sister and half-sister and their husbands, one of them the infamous Siyyid 'Alí, a kinsman of the Báb, the other the crafty Mírzá Majdi'd-Dín, together with his sister and half-brothers—the children of the noble, the faithful and now deceased Áqáy-i-Kalím—all united in a determined effort to subvert the foundations of the Covenant which the newly proclaimed Will had laid. [5:247]

Had he remained firm in the Faith he would have, according to the Will and Testament of Bahá'u'lláh, become Head of the Faith after the passing of 'Abdu'l-Bahá in 1921. Instead, he continued to work against it and died, alone and unsupported and buried in an unmarked grave, in 1937.

MUHÁJIR, RAḤMATU'LLÁH (1923-1979) (Hand of the Cause of God) He was born in Írán in 1923 into a distinguished and dedicated Bahá'í family. From his earliest childhood he was involved in the continual succession of meetings held in his parents' home. As such, he was infused with the concept of pioneering and deferred his university training for two years to live and teach the Faith in Á<u>dh</u>irbáyján. Studying medicine he surprised all his friends by leaving off a few months before graduation to spend three months in a needy teaching area and then returning to complete his studies, graduating with honors.

He married in 1951 a few months before graduation and, with his wife, went on pilgrimage to the Holy Land in 1952 where Shoghi Effendi spoke with him at length about the potential for Bahá'í teaching in the Malaysian Peninsular and the Pacific Islands. When it was announced at the Intercontinental Conference in New Delhi in 1953 that a physician was needed to fill a goal in Mentawai Islands, Raḥmat volunteered immediately, resigned from his job and within two months set off with his wife to Indonesia without a permit to stay or a job to go to, arriving in the Island of Muara Siberut in February 1954. He was immediately employed by the Ministry of Health, given a permanent residence visa and assigned to the Mentawai Islands! In spite of the most inhospitable living conditions, among a people ridden with tropical diseases of all kinds, with no other medical help available, he won their respect and real affection, improved their living and their environmental circumstances, instituted schools and securely established the Bahá'í Faith there.

During the next few years he received many letters and cables of praise and encouragement from Shoghi Effendi, though the letters were delivered only every six to eight months by government mail-boat. He was appointed a Hand in the last contingent in October 1957, and although he had intended to remain in his pioneer post for the rest of his life, the untimely passing of the Guardian changed all his plans. It was not possible for him in the critical years that lay ahead to remain in a place without telephone or telegram service and cut off from the rest of the world except by means of a boat, which for most of the year was out of service. It was only after months of persuasion by the other Hands of the Cause, and many hours of prayer, that he agreed to leave the people he loved so much and had served so well. He left in 1958 after four years of work and witnessing the acceptance of some 4,000 native believers. A United Nations WHO Committee that visited Mentawai in 1960 paid tribute not only to his medical work but to his contribution to the development of the islands, the schools he established, his work in the eradication of disease, and to the cleanliness and order he brought to the villages.

The next 20 years of his life were dedicated to traveling, inspiring individuals and administrative bodies to teach, to establish concrete plans for massive enrollments, and putting into practice his extraordinary qualities of recognizing the needs of an area and suggesting valuable and practical methods for first establishing goals and then achieving them. In the years between 1958 and 1979 he visited all the Bahá'í national centers and in three years between 1974 and 1977 visited no fewer than 50 countries, traveling by sea and air, in buses and bullock carts, on foot and hitchhiking, always choosing the most economical way in the time al lowed, with moderately priced hotels and always living most austerely. He had utter reliance on and submission to the Will of God and was never discouraged. Wherever he went his emphasis was on mass teaching, with his greatest successes in India and the Philippines. In India in 1961 there were on record a mere 850 Bahá'ís, as a direct result of Dr. Muhájir's work and encouragement there were within two years no fewer than 65,000.

Publishing Bahá'í writings in the local languages was another favorite theme, and he initiated the production of a simple information folder as an important tool for proclamation; he proposed and helped prepare a Bahá'í correspondence course and wrote a book on methods of Bahá'í education of children. He used the media extensively, appearing frequently on television, giving radio talks, having interviews with dignitaries at every level, from royalty and prime ministers down to local mayors and frequently lectured in universities in many countries.

His death came in the way he had always wanted—while in service to the Faith. Remote from home but among Bahá'í friends he had traveled to Quito, Ecuador, arriving extremely fatigued, for a special teaching conference. He suffered a heart attack on the second day and passed away at the end of October 1979, in one of his most loved cities and among people for whom he had a deep and selfless affection to which they responded unreservedly. The Universal House of Justice cabled on 29 October 1979:

> Profoundly lament untimely passing in Quito Ecuador beloved Hand Cause Raḥmatu'lláh Muhájir following heart attack course his latest South American tour. Unstinted unrestrained outpouring of physical spiritual energies by one who offered his all path service has now ceased. Posterity will record his devoted services youthful years Cradle Faith, his subsequent unique exploits pioneering field Southeast Asia where he won accolade Knighthood Bahá'u'lláh, his ceaseless efforts over two decades since his appointment Hand Cause stimulating in many lands East West process entry by troops. Friends all continents who mourn this tragic loss now suddenly deprived collaboration one who endeared himself to them through his gentleness, his luminous personality, his exemplary unflagging zeal, his creative enthusiastic approach to fulfillment assigned goals. Urge friends everywhere hold memorial gatherings befitting his high station unique achievements. May his radiant soul Abhá Kingdom reap rich harvest his dedicated self-sacrificing services Cause God. [2:652]

MÜHLSHLEGEL, ADELBERT (1897-1977) (Hand of the Cause of God) He was born on 16 June 1897 in Berlin, where his father was a military doctor and his mother the daughter of a pastor. The combination of the two influenced him in his choice of profession and imbued him with a deep sense of spiritual values. He served in the German Medical Corps during the First World War and studied medicine in Freiburg, Greifswald and Tübingen. In 1920 he received a letter from his mother telling him of the new Faith she had accepted, it aroused his interest, and he himself soon became a Bahá'í He opened his first medical practice in Stuttgart in 1922 and married in 1926.

He and his wife went on pilgrimage to the Holy Land in 1936. Throughout WW II he practiced as a doctor in Stuttgart, where their apartment was bombed. In 1945 when the Occupation authorities rescinded the prohibition on the Faith imposed in 1937, their new home became a true center for Bahá'í activities with a warm atmosphere full of humor and hospitality.

He had a working knowledge of several European languages and was fluent in Esperanto. He translated much Bahá'í literature into German and had many articles on the Faith accepted for publication. He served for many years as a member of the National Spiritual Assembly of the Bahá'ís of Germany and Austria.

He was appointed a Hand in February 1952 and served with distinction in Europe. He had a profound spiritual experience that moved him to an even greater degree of service when, on the sudden passing of the Guardian, he was called by 'Amatu'l-Bahá Rúḥíyyih Khánum to fly at once to London to wash Shoghi Effendi's body and prepare it for interment. The following sentences are taken from his description of that experience:

> My first impression was the contrast between the body left behind and the majestic, transfigured face, a soul-stirring picture of the joyous victory of the eternal over the transient. My second impression ... was that in this degree of consecration to the work of God I should work all my life, and mankind should work a thousand years, in order to construct "the Kingdom" on earth; and my third thought was, as I washed each member of his body and anointed it, that I thanked those beloved hands which had worked and written to establish the Covenant, those feet that had walked for us, that mouth that had spoken to us, that head that had thought for us, and I prayed and meditated and supplicated that in the short time left to me, the members of my body might hasten to follow in his path of service ... a great deal of mercy, love and wisdom were hidden in that hour. [2:612]

His devoted wife, Herma, was his constant supporter and companion, and he cared for her with loving attention throughout a long and severe illness that preceded her death in 1964. He subsequently moved to Vienna to help the struggling national community, and after a year he married the Secretary of the National Spiritual Assembly, Ursula. In 1970 he registered in the University of Freiburg, Switzerland, and he and Ursula established a strong community there and traveled extensively throughout Europe. In 1969 he had made his first trip to other continents when at the request of the Universal House of Justice he had visited Persia, India, West Pákistán (Bangladesh) and Nepal; he and Ursula later traveled to Africa in 1971 and 1972 and to South America in 1975. In 1974 they settled in Hoffheim, Germany, where their home became a center of hospitality and study.

Although his heart began to fail, he developed a yearning again to serve in a challenging pioneer post, and, in 1977, at the age of 80 he settled in Athens where yet again the Mühlschlegel's home became a center of harmony and learning. On 29 July 1980 he passed away and was buried on the shores of the Mediterranean. The Universal House of Justice cabled:

> With sorrowful hearts announce passing beloved Hand Cause Adelbert Mühlschlegel. Grievous loss sustained entire Bahá'í world particularly felt Europe, main area his distinguished service Cause God. Serving for many years National Spiritual Assembly Germany he became, after elevation rank Hand Cause one of champion builders emerging European Bahá'í community constantly traveling encouraging raising spirits friends, residing wherever services most needed, finally pioneering Greece and surrendering his soul pioneer post. His constant willingness serve, his ability endear himself believers and others alike by his loving gentleness, serene humility, radiant cheerfulness, his never ceasing pursuit knowledge and total dedication Blessed Beauty provide wonderful example Bahá'í life. Advise friends commemorate his passing and request befitting memorial services all Mother Temples. [2:613]

MUJTAHID Muslim doctor-of-law. [11:739]

MULLÁ Muslim trained in theology and Islámic jurisprudence; theologian, priest. [11:739]

MULLÁ 'ALÍ-AKBAR (Apostle of Bahá'u'lláh) Described as "a flame of zeal and devotion" and designated an Apostle of Bahá'u'lláh.

MULLÁ 'ALÍY-I-BASṬÁMÍ Fourth Letter of the Living.

MULLÁ AḤMAD-I-IBDÁL-I-MARÁGHI'Í 12th Letter of the Living.

MULLÁ ABU'L-ḤASAN-I-ARDAKÁNÍ (-1928) (a Hand of the Cause of God and an Apostle of Bahá'u'lláh) Known also as Ḥájí Amín and Amín-Iláhí, he was a faithful steward of both Bahá'u'lláh and 'Abdu'l-Bahá and was the first pilgrim to meet Bahá'u'lláh while He was in a public bath in 'Akká, though unable to approach Him or give any sign of recognition. He collected the Ḥuqúqu'lláh (Right of God) for the first Trustee, Ḥájí Sháh-Muḥammad Manshadí and was himself appointed Trustee on Manshadí's death in 1880. He died in 1928 and was posthumously named a Hand of the Cause; he was also designated an Apostle of Bahá'u'lláh.

MULLÁ ÁQÁ MUḤAMMAD-I-QÁ'INÍ (-c.1892) (Hand of the Cause of God and Apostle of Bahá'u'lláh) He was also known as Fadil-i-Qá'iní—the Learned One of Qá'in. He was considered a prodigy amongst scholars and acknowledged as one of the most outstanding men of learning in Persia. He became a Bábí in about 1853 and some six years later visited Bahá'u'lláh in Baghdád and quickly recognized His supreme knowledge. Bahá'u'lláh instructed him to return to Persia and teach the Faith, which he did with great devotion and in the face of much persecution, being arrested three times. Bahá'u'lláh gave him the title Nabíl-i-Akbár. He died in Bukhara soon after the passing of Bahá'u'lláh in 1892. 'Abdu'l-Bahá designated him a Hand of the Cause; he was also designated an Apostle of Bahá'u'lláh.

MULLÁ BÁQIR-I-TABRÍZÍ 13th Letter of the Living.

MULLÁ JALÍL-I-URÚMÍ 11th Letter of the Living.

MULLÁ ḤUSAN-I-BAJISTÁNÍ Sixth Letter of the Living.

MULLÁ ḤUSAYN-I-BUSHRÚ'Í (Bábu'l-Báb—gate of the Gate) The first one to believe in the Báb when He made His Declaration to him during the night of 22 May 1844. He thereby became the first of the Letters of the Living (q.v.). He was killed during the siege of the Fort of Shaykh Ṭabarsí on 2 February 1849, but his heroism has been recorded for posterity. Shoghi Effendi wrote:

> The audacity of Mullá Ḥusayn who, at the command of the Báb, had attired his head with the green turban worn and sent to him by his Master, who had hoisted the Black Standard, the unfurling of which would, according to the Prophet Muḥammad, herald the advent of the vicegerent of God on earth, and who, mounted on his steed, was marching at the head of two hundred and two of his fellow-disciples to meet and lend his assistance to Quddús in the Jazíriy-i-Khaḍrá (Verdant Isle)—his audacity was the signal for a clash the reverberations of which were to resound throughout the entire country. The contest lasted

no less than eleven months. Its theater was for the most part the forest of Mázindarán. Its heroes were the flower of the Báb's disciples. Its martyrs comprised no less than half of the Letters of the Living, not excluding Quddús and Mullá Ḥusayn, respectively the last and the first of these Letters. [5:38]

We are struck with wonder as we contemplate the superhuman prowess of Mullá Ḥusayn which enabled him, notwithstanding his fragile frame and trembling hand, to slay a treacherous foe who had taken shelter behind a tree, by cleaving with a single stroke of his sword the tree, the man and his musket in twain. [5:40]

Nabíl, in his immortal narrative—*The Dawnbreakers*—writes of him: "The traits of mind and of character which, from his very youth, he displayed, the profundity of his learning, the tenacity of his faith, his intrepid courage, his singleness of purpose, his high sense of justice and unswerving devotion, marked him as an outstanding figure among those who, by their lives, have borne witness to the glory and power of this new Revelation." [10:383] See **BÁB**.

MULLÁ KAẒIM-I-SAMANDAR See **SHAYKH KÁẒIM-I-RASHTÍ**.

MULLÁ KHUDÁ-BAKJSH-I-QÚCHÁNÍ (subsequently known as Mullá 'Alí.) Fifth Letter of the Living.

MULLÁ MAḤMÚD-I-KHU'I 10th Letter of the Living.

MULLÁ MUḤAMMAD-I-ZARANDI See **NABÍL-I-A'ẒAM**.

MULLÁ ṢÁDIQ-I-MUQADDAS (Ismu'lláhu'l-Aṣdaq) (Hand of the Cause of God) The father of the Apostle of Bahá'u'lláh, Ibn-i-Aṣdaq (q.v. Mírzá 'Alí Muḥammad) was one of the early followers of the Báb. As a Shaykhí he had met the Báb in Karbilá prior to His declaration and had wondered at the reverence shown by the leader of the Shaykhí community, Siyyid Káẓim, to this young man. He was introduced to the Writings of the Báb by Mullá Ḥusayn (q.v.) shortly after His declaration in 1844 and became an ardent Bábí. Although a most distinguished Muslim divine, he suffered persecution and was one of the first three Bábís to be severely tortured. He was then old and frail and withstood the lashes, which exceeded 900, with serenity, calm and even with laughter. This was just the first of many tortures suffered as he traveled throughout Persia teaching the Faith.

He met Bahá'u'lláh in Baghdád and immediately recognized Him as the One promised by the Báb. He then returned to Persia to teach with increased fervor and was again imprisoned, at one time in the Siyáh-Chál where he was responsible for introducing the Faith to the first member of the Jewish faith. He was summoned by Bahá'u'lláh to visit Him, probably in the early part of 1874, when he was well advanced in years and after almost 30 years of sufferings and hardships. Many special letters were revealed by Bahá'u'lláh in his honor and in naming him, posthumously, as a Hand, 'Abdu'l-Bahá wrote:

> He was like a surging sea, a falcon that soared high. His visage shone, his tongue was eloquent, his strength and steadfastness astounding. When he opened his lips to teach, the proofs would stream out; when he chanted or prayed, his eyes shed tears like a spring cloud. His face was luminous, his life spiritual, his knowledge both acquired and innate; and celestial was his ardor, his detachment from the world, his righteousness, his piety and fear of God. [124:8]

MULLÁ YÚSUF-I-ARDIBÍLÍ 14th Letter of the Living.

MULLÁ ZAYNU'L-'ÁBIDÍN (Jináb-i-Zaynu'l-Muqarrabín) (Apostle of Bahá'u'lláh) One of the most assiduous and trusted scribes of Bahá'u'lláh. Before his acceptance of the Bábí Faith he was an outstanding mujtahid (doctor of Islamic law) in his native town of Najaf-Abad. Following his conversion he was persecuted by the very people who had previously respected him. He moved to Baghdád where he met Bahá'u'lláh and became a most ardent follower. He took such great care in his transcription of the voluminous Writings of Bahá'u'lláh that anything in his handwriting is considered to be accurate. He was the one who received permission from Bahá'u'lláh to ask the questions on the laws of the Kitáb-i-Aqdas that form part of that essential part of Bahá'í Scripture. He joined Mishkín-Qalam (q.v.) in being noted for his great sense of humor. He was also designated an Apostle of Bahá'u'lláh.

MUNÍRIH KHÁNUM (Fáṭimih) (The Holy Mother) (1848-1938) Came from an illustrious Bábí family and was born while her father and uncle were at the Conference of Badasht (June/July, 1848.) During her wedding feast, her new husband, apparently in perfect health, suddenly collapsed, became gravely ill and died soon afterwards. Fáṭimih then spent her days in prayer and meditation until an emissary from Bahá'u'lláh, then still in prison in 'Akká, called her, with her relatives, to join the exiles. In somewhat miraculous circumstances she reached the prison city and after almost five months received the gift of a new name from Bahá'u'lláh Himself—Munírih (Illumined) and the call to marry His Eldest Son, 'Abdu'l-Bahá. When she entered the presence of Bahá'u'lláh He said, "O thou My blessed leaf and maid-servant. We have chosen thee and accepted thee to be the companion of the

Greatest Branch and to serve Him ... thou must be very thankful, for thou has attained to this most great favor and bestowal." [42:261-2] The marriage took place in 1873. Of her marriage with 'Abdu'l-Bahá she wrote, "If I were to write the details of the fifty years of my association with the Beloved of the world, of His love, His mercy and bounty, I would need fifty more years of time and opportunity in order to write it...." [42:262] She died in Haifa at age 90 in 1938 and was buried by Shoghi Effendi in the Monument Gardens on Mount Carmel; her shrine is on a level below that of the Greatest Holy Leaf and those of Navváb and the Purest Branch.

MUQÍMÍ-ABYÁNIH, ZARRIN (1954-1983) (Martyr) A young Bahá'í who was executed along with other coreligionists in Shíráz, Írán, by the government in June 1983, for refusing to recant her belief in Bahá'u'lláh. [11: 600]

MURRAY, ETHEL (1884-1972) An early (1920s) American believer who was among the first to respond to the call to teach the Indian peoples—from 1954 until 1970 she lived (in conditions of hardship) on the Cherokee Reserve in North Carolina. This move was especially meaningful since Shoghi Effendi had chosen the Cherokee language as the first of the North American languages into which Bahá'í Writings should be translated.[51:520]

MURRAY, FRED (1884-1963) The first Australian Aborigine to embrace the Cause (1961).[50:368][60:459]

MUṢṬAFÁ, MUḤAMMAD (1898-1981) (Knight of Bahá'u'lláh) An Egyptian believer who in 1914 embraced the Cause. He received three Tablets from 'Abdu'l-Bahá. He was a member of the first National Spiritual Assembly of Egypt (for many years its Secretary, and later its Chairman.) He was the first to marry in an exclusively Bahá'í ceremony without Muslim rites; he was the first Egyptian Bahá'í to register his children as Bahá'ís from birth; he was the first Egyptian appointed an Auxiliary Board member as well as the first to be elevated to the rank of a Continental Counsellor. In 1953 he pioneered to the Spanish Sahara for which service he was designated a Knight of Bahá'u'lláh. Denied permanent residence in that region he pioneered on to Benghazi, Libya. Between 1954 and 1960 he traveled extensively throughout north, east and west Africa. In 1958 he returned to Egypt ands suffered a number of imprisonments for his faith. He continued to travel extensively throughout Africa for the remaining years of his life. [2:769]

MUSTAGHÁTH He Who Is Invoked (for Help), God: term used by the Báb in Reference to the advent of Bahá'u'lláh on the Day of the Latter Resurrection. [11:739📖]

MUTAṢARRIF Governor: lower in rank than a valí. [11:739📖]

MYSTERY OF GOD (Sirru'lláh) One of the titles given by Bahá'u'lláh to 'Abdu'l-Bahá. Shoghi Effendi wrote as follows on the subject:

> Upon Him that loving and unerring Father had chosen to confer the unique title of 'Sirru'lláh' (the Mystery of God), a designation so appropriate to One Who, though essentially human and holding a station radically and fundamentally different from that occupied by Bahá'u'lláh and His Forerunner, could still claim to be the perfect Exemplar of His Faith, to be endowed with super-human knowledge, and to be regarded as the stainless mirror reflecting His light. [5:242]

> He is, above and beyond these appellations, the "Mystery of God"—an expression by which Bahá'u'lláh Himself has chosen to designate Him, and which, while it does not by any means justify us to assign to Him the station of Prophethood, indicates how in the person of 'Abdu'l-Bahá the incompatible characteristics of a human nature and superhuman knowledge and perfection have been blended and are completely harmonized. [4:134]

N

NABÍL Learned, noble. [11:739]

NABÍL-I-A'ẒAM(-1892) (Apostle of Bahá'u'lláh) One of the followers of the Báb who would call on Bahá'u'lláh at His home in Ṭihrán. He became not only a renowned teacher of the Faith, but an outstanding poet and historian, recording in detail the lives of the early believers. His epic, *The Dawnbreakers*, was one of the earliest works translated by Shoghi Effendi into English. He described it, among other things, as "a source of inspiration in all literary and artistic pursuits, an indispensable preliminary to future pilgrimage to Bahá'u'lláh's native land, and as an unfailing instrument to allay distress and resist attacks of a critical, disillusioned humanity." [38:5] On the passing of Bahá'u'lláh he was so grief-stricken that he ended his life by throwing himself into the sea at 'Akká. He was also designated an Apostle of Bahá'u'lláh.

NABÍL-I-AKBAR See **MÍRZÁ MUḤAMMAD**.

NAKHJAVÁNÍ, JALÁL (1917-1982) Born in Baku, Southern Russia, but raised in the Holy Land under the watchful eye and guidance of Shoghi Effendi, he went on to become a pioneer and staunch servant of the Cause. In 1937, at the request of Shoghi Effendi, he left the Holy Land for Írán. In 1943 he married Darajhshandih Na'ímí, and in 1950 he pioneered to Africa (being the first pioneer to set foot on the soil of East Africa.) He settled in Dar-es-Salaam, Tanganyika (now Tanzania) and was joined in June 1951 by his wife and family. He served on the first (1952) local Spiritual Assembly of Dar-es-Salaam and was elected to the first (1954) Regional Spiritual Assembly of Central and East Africa. In 1954 he was appointed one of nine Auxiliary Board members and traveled extensively for the Cause in the following years. In 1967 he and his family moved to West Germany where he was a valued member of the local Spiritual Assembly Hamburg/Eimsbuttel. He later pioneered to Neumuenster, West Germany to enable the formation of the first local Spiritual Assembly of that town. In 1978 he and his wife moved to Canada where he took up service on the local Spiritual Assembly of Selkirk, Manitoba. During the last years of his life he traveled extensively throughout Canada in the promotion of the Cause. [2:797]

NATIONAL SPIRITUAL ASSEMBLIES While Bahá'u'lláh Himself created the institutions of the Universal House of Justice and the local Spiritual Assemblies, it was 'Abdu'l-Bahá Who in His Will and Testament announced the need to establish "secondary houses of justice" and indicated that these Bodies would provide the members who would elect the Universal House of Justice.

Their functions were developed by Shoghi Effendi, who explained the qualifications for membership; outlined the method of their election at an annual Convention; called on them to become legally incorporated and to hold endowments and dealt directly with them and encouraged them from their formation. In 1944, when there were seven such bodies functioning, he wrote:

> In countries where the local Bahá'í communities had sufficiently advanced in number and in influence measures were taken for the initiation of National Assemblies, the pivots round which all national undertakings must revolve. Designated by 'Abdu'l-Bahá in His Will as the "Secondary Houses of Justice," they constitute the electoral bodies in the formation of the International House of Justice, and are empowered to direct, unify, co-ordinate and stimulate the activities of individuals as well as local Assemblies within their jurisdiction. Resting on the broad base of organized local communities, themselves pillars sustaining the institution which must be regarded as the apex of the Bahá'í Administrative Order, these Assemblies are elected, according to the principle of proportional representation, by delegates representative of Bahá'í local

> communities assembled at Convention during the period of the Riḍván Festival; are possessed of the necessary authority to enable them to insure the harmonious and efficient development of Bahá'í activity within their respective spheres; are freed from all direct responsibility for their policies and decisions to their electorates; are charged with the sacred duty of consulting on the views, of inviting the recommendations and of securing the confidence and co-operation of the delegates and of acquainting them with their plans, problems and actions; and are supported by the resources of national funds to which all ranks of the faithful are urged to contribute. [5:332]

By 1996 there were some 174 National Spiritual Assemblies in the Bahá'í global community.

See **ADMINISTRATIVE ORDER.**

NATIONALISM Bahá'u'lláh stated: "The world is but one country, and mankind its citizens"; "Let not a man glory in that he loves his country; let him rather glory in this, that he loves his kind"; "Ye are the fruits of one tree, and the leaves of one branch"; "Bend your minds and wills to the education of the peoples and kindreds of the earth, that haply all mankind may become the upholders of one order, and the inhabitants of one city." [44:114]

In many of his writings, Shoghi Effendi condemned a "capricious and militant nationalism" but not "a sane and intelligent patriotism." He goes on to say:

> Let there be no misgivings as to the animating purpose of the world-wide Law of Bahá'u'lláh. Far from aiming at the subversion of the existing foundations of society, it seeks to broaden its basis, to remold its institutions in a manner consonant with the needs of an ever-changing world. It can conflict with no legitimate allegiances, nor can it undermine essential loyalties. Its purpose is neither to stifle the flame of a sane and intelligent patriotism in men's hearts, nor to abolish the system of national autonomy so essential if the evils of excessive centralization are to be avoided. It does not ignore, nor does it attempt to suppress, the diversity of ethnical origins, of climate, of history, of language and tradition, of thought and habit, that differentiate the peoples and nations of the world. It calls for a wider loyalty, for a larger aspiration than any that has animated the human race. It insists upon the subordination of national impulses and interests to the imperative claims of a unified world. It re

> pudiates excessive centralization on one hand, and disclaims all attempts at uniformity on the other. Its watchword is unity in diversity. [4:41]

He further describes the kind of world in which this healthy patriotism may flourish:

> A world community in which all economic barriers will have been permanently demolished and the interdependence of Capital and Labor definitely recognized; in which the clamor of religious fanaticism and strife will have been forever stilled; in which the flame of racial animosity will have been finally extinguished; in which a single code of international law—the product of the considered judgment of the world's federated representatives—shall have as its sanction the instant and coercive intervention of the combined forces of the federated units; and finally a world community in which the fury of a capricious and militant nationalism will have been transmuted into an abiding consciousness of world citizenship—such indeed, appears, in its broadest outline, the Order anticipated by Bahá'u'lláh, an Order that shall come to be regarded as the fairest fruit of a slowly maturing age. [4:41]

NAVVÁB (Grace, Highness) (Ásíyih Khánum, Exalted Leaf) (-1886) The first wife of Bahá'u'lláh; she was married to Him in Ṭihrán in 1835 (when He was 18 years old). There were seven children of this marriage, of whom only three survived—'Abdu'l-Bahá; Bahíyyih Khánum and Mihdí. She was outstanding in her devotion to Bahá'u'lláh and suffered a great deal at the hands of those within her family who subsequently opposed her beloved Husband, but her faith remained resolute and unshakable. As one writer testified: "Among those who shared His exile was His wife, the saintly Navváb, entitled by Him the 'Most Exalted Leaf,' who, during almost forty years, continued to evince a fortitude, a piety, a devotion and a nobility of soul which earned her from the pen of her Lord the posthumous and unrivaled tribute of having been made His 'perpetual consort in all the worlds of God.' " [5:108] 'Abdu'l-Bahá stated that the 54th chapter of Isaiah referred to Navváb. She passed away in 'Akká in 1886. [5:348] See **GENEALOGIES**.

NAW-RÚZ (New Day—New Year) This is one of the nine Bahá'í Holy days and coincides with Bahá, the first month of the Bahá'í Year. It occurs on the Spring Equinox, which is normally on 21 March. Should the equinox fall after sunset on 21 March, Naw-Rúz is celebrated on the 22nd. It marks the end of the month of fasting and is a Holy Day of joyous celebration.

NICHOLS, VALERIA LAMB (1903-1985) An American believer (1937) who served on the first (1940) local Spiritual Assembly of Beverley Hills, California. During the second Seven Year Plan she pioneered in 1947 to Europe. After a brief stay in Holland she pioneered to Portugal where she remained until 1951 and where she assisted in the formation of the first local Spiritual Assembly of Lisbon. In 1953 she pioneered to Latin America where she remained for the balance of her life. Initially she stayed in Costa Rica but then moved to Mexico, settling first in Mexico City and then, in 1964, in Merida, Yucatan. She served on the National Spiritual Assembly of Mexico for a number of years. [11:690]

NICKLIN, EVE BLANCHE (1895-1985) An early American believer who in 1941 pioneered to Lima, Peru (the first believer to do so), an action that earned her the accolade "spiritual mother of Peru." She served on the first (1944) local Spiritual Assembly of Lima (the first also in Peru). In 1948, with the approval of Shoghi Effendi, she pioneered to Punta Arenas, Chile to assist with the strengthening of the work in that country. On her return to Peru she settled in Callao and served on the first (1949) local Spiritual Assembly of that town. In 1951 she was elected to the National Assembly of South America. She moved for a year to Uruguay (1952-53) and two and a half years in Paraguay (1953-55). In 1955 she returned to Peru but in 1958 went back to Paraguay where she remained until 1962, when she again moved to Peru. In 1965 she was appointed an Auxiliary Board member. By the time of her death in 1985 there were almost 600 local Spiritual Assemblies in Peru. [11:670]

NINETEEN DAY FEAST See **FEAST, NINETEEN DAY.**

NÍRÚMAND, MAHSHÍD (1955-1983) (Martyr) A young Bahá'í who was executed along with other coreligionists in Shíráz, Írán, by the government in June 1983, for refusing to recant her belief in Bahá'u'lláh. [11:600]

NJANG, ELIZABETH IDANG (1928-1983) An early (1956) Nigerian believer who served as a member (1967) of the National Spiritual Assembly of West Central Africa. She was a notable teacher of the Cause and was referred to as "Ṭáhirih of Nigeria" by the Hands of the Cause of God attending the 1960 Annual Convention. [2:819][60:463]

NJIKI, SAMUEL NJENJI (1935-1983) (Knight of Bahá'u'lláh) The first (1954) Bamilike tribesman in Batala-Bangante, Nde Division, Western Province, Republic of Cameroon, to embrace the Cause. In April 1954 he arose and pioneered to Doula in French Cameroon for which service he was designated a Knight of Bahá'u'lláh. [11:615]

NOLEN, RICHARD H. (1914-1964) (Knight of Bahá'u'lláh) An American believer who pioneered with his family to the Azores

Islands for which service he was designated a Knight of Bahá'u'lláh. [50:317]

NORDSTROM, ADDIE (1885-1968) An American believer (c.1940) who at the advanced age of 78 pioneered to the Aleutian Islands. [51:444]

NOURSE, CATHERINE ELIZABETH (1904-1985) An early American believer; her mother Elizabeth Nourse, was 'Abdu'l-Bahá's hostess on a number of occasions during His 1912 visit to America. In 1937 she pioneered to Hawaii where she served on the local Spiritual Assembly of Honolulu. In 1957 she served on the first local Spiritual Assembly of Hilo, the Big Island. [11:680]

NUQṬIY Point. [11:739📖]

NUQṬIY-I-ÚLÁ The Primal Point: a title of the Báb. [11:739📖]

NÚRÁNÍ, 'SHÍRÍN (1918-1984) (Knight of Bahá'u'lláh) An Indian believer born into a Bahá'í family of Zoroastrian background. She pioneered to Karikal during the Ten Year Crusade for which service she was designated a Knight of Bahá'u'lláh. [11:636]

NÚSHÚGATÍ, MALAKAT (-1937) An early Egyptian Bahá'í. Her burial was the first in Egypt to be performed solely according to Bahá'í burial law. [37:550]

O

OBER, ELIZABETH MERIEL KIDDER (1902-1979) The identical twin sister of **ALICE GERTRUDE KIDDER**. Both ladies heard of the Bahá'í Faith in 1934 at the same time but in different cities and from different people. On hearing of the Faith they shared the news with each other only to discover it was already known and embraced. Elizabeth married Harlan Ober (q.v.) in 1941. In 1954 Alice pioneered to South Africa and set up a medical practice. In 1956 she was joined by Elizabeth and Harlan. In April 1956 they formed the first local Spiritual Assembly of Pretoria, to be followed in 1958 by the first local Spiritual Assembly of Atteridgeville. In 1958 Alice moved to Haifa to serve as personal physician to 'Amatu'l-Bahá Rúḥíyyih Khánum. In 1969 the sisters returned to the United States but in 1975 they pioneered to Guadalajara, Mexico. In 1978 they were elected to the local Spiritual Assembly of Zapopan. [2:678]

OBER, HARLAN FOSTER (1881-1962) An early American believer. He met 'Abdu'l-Bahá during His visit to America and received several Tablets. 'Abdu'l-Bahá, Himself married Harlan and his wife Grace Robarts (of Canada) on 17 July 1912. [42:656][91:118] He made three pilgrimages to the Holy Land. After the third pilgrimage he pioneered (with his second wife, Dr. Elizabeth Kidder Ober) to South Africa (1956) where he helped form the first all-African local Spiritual Assembly in Pretoria. He was appointed a member of the Auxiliary Board for protection in October 1957.[47:866][91:118][59:176ff]

OBLIGATORY PRAYER Bahá'u'lláh revealed three special prayers, one of which must be used each day by all believers who are over the age of maturity (15 years). The prayer should be said privately, after the performance of ablutions and facing the Qiblih and with any other requirements made in the Kitáb-i-Aqdas. The believer is free to use whichever one he/she wishes. The short one is recited between noon and sunset; the medium one is recited three times per day and the long one is used once in 24 hours.

OLINGA, ENOCH (1926-1979) (Hand of the Cause of God and Knight of Bahá'u'lláh) He was born in the province of Teso, North East Uganda on 24 June 1926. A year later his father moved the family back to his native village of Tilling—a village whose name will for ever be associated with the first substantial expansion of the Faith in the Bahá'í world, with Africa's only native Hand of the Cause and with the first Bahá'í school to be established on the African continent. In August 1951, Enoch, who was at that time working in the Department of Education in Kampala, learned of the Faith through Crispin Kajubi (the first Muganda to become a Bahá'í). In February 1952, Enoch became the first of the Teso tribe and the fourth Ugandan to enroll, enabling him to be the ninth member of the first local Spiritual Assembly of the Bahá'ís of Kampala on 21 April 1952. Shortly afterwards he returned to Tilling on vacation and began to teach the Faith and, with the help of some of the pioneers, began the process that led to the large-scale enrollment, which was hailed with great joy by Shoghi Effendi in his subsequent messages to the Bahá'í world.

In August 1953, responding to the call for pioneers for west and central Africa, Enoch and two other new African Bahá'ís, with Violette Nakhjavání in a car purchased by her father, Mr. Banání, and driven by 'Alí Nakhjavání, set off on an epic journey across Africa. They left one African to pioneer in the Belgian Congo (Zaire), the second one to pioneer in French Equatorial Africa (Congo Republic) and then for the longest part of the journey they drove through deep tropical jungles and disease-decimated areas of Gabon, with the car breaking down frequently or sticking in the mud and making little progress—one day they only made 100 kilometers in 16 hours. When, on one occasion the car broke down completely, Enoch volunteered to walk 50 miles to the nearest garage but 'Alí eventually got the car to limp along and caught up with Enoch after he had walked 35 miles. By this time all three travelers were ill, and Enoch had to spend two days in the hospital and could not travel for a week. On 10 October they reached French Cameroons but pushed on, as Enoch's goal was to reach British Cameroons, which he did only within hours of the deadline date to "open" that country and become its "Knight of Bahá'u'lláh." On 16 October 1953 the party reached Victoria where Enoch was to live for the next 10 years.

Accommodation was eventually found for Enoch in the home of David Tanyi, who subsequently became the first native of the Cameroons to accept the Faith and the Knight of Bahá'u'lláh for French Cameroons. Dedicated to teaching new believers, Enoch began to enroll each one imbued with the same spirit of teaching. Among these were many who became, like Enoch, stalwarts in the Faith. In February 1957 Enoch had the privilege of a pilgrimage, after which he taught with renewed zeal, and Shoghi Effendi gave him the title Abu'l-Futúh (the "Father of Victories"). In the last contingent of Hands of the Cause, Enoch was elevated to that rank which made him the only African Hand, the second of his race to be granted that honor and the first Native African Bahá'í to obtain a pilgrimage.

Although the formalities required to get to London prevented Enoch from attending the funeral of Shoghi Effendi, he was able to get to the Holy Land for the first Conclave of the Hands of the Cause immediately following Shoghi Effendi's passing. In 1958 he was able to attend the Intercontinental Conference in Kampala and participate in the laying of the foundation stone for the Kampala House of Worship. He finally returned to Tilling and built a house there for his family, but he traveled in every continent and visited many countries and attended conferences on behalf of the Universal House of Justice. He was selected by the other Hands to be the chairman of the opening session of the 1963 World Congress in the Albert Hall, London.

Although he was the youngest ever to be appointed a Hand, he traveled as widely as the other Hands (with the exception of 'Amatu'l-Bahá Rúḥíyyih Kh̲ánum). After attending the Singapore Conference in 1958 he toured Australia, New Zealand, Fiji, Samoa, and Pakistan; in 1960 he went to many places in West and North Africa, Sicily and Italy; in 1961 to Jamaica, Dominican Republic and Cuba. Subsequent travels included the Greater Antilles and Central America; in 1962 East Africa, the Sudan, Ethiopia and the Congo, and on behalf of the Universal House of Justice, to many Conventions in Africa and the outlying Islands and to the large Mediterranean Conference in Palermo, Sicily in 1968 and was later received by the Dalai Lama in his Indian headquarters; in 1970 to many parts of Africa, an extensive tour of South and Central America, the Antilles and the United States and from there on to many parts of the Pacific islands and Japan; in 1971 to Iceland, Scandinavia, British Isles and then to Írán. For the next few years he spent a great deal of time in different African countries, with other visits to Brazil and Mexico, finally returning to Uganda to help in his home country, where the Faith had been officially banned and was in great turmoil with civil war, terrorism and chaos. Not only was Enoch known as a Bahá'í of international repute, but he was also a well-known, capable and prosperous businessman with relatives and friends in high places and as such, was a target of subversive elements. He was aware he was on a list for "elimination" but refused to leave his home. He had, at one stage, purchased the house in Kampala where he had studied the Faith, where he had learned of his appointment as a Hand and that was so interwoven with the early history of the Faith in Uganda. It was a family custom of the Olingas to gather together on special days. Such a day was called for 16 September 1979 to have a picnic in the grounds of the House of Worship and then all to meet in the Kampala house. It was a very joyous occasion, with Enoch and his wife joining in the singing and dancing that followed the Bahá'í service in the Temple. Due to various unforeseen circumstances several members of the family were unable to reach Kampala that night and only Enoch, his wife Elizabeth and three children (Ṭáhirih, Lennie and Badí') were present. The family had their evening meal and then, at about 8.30 P.M., five or six armed men entered the compound, and all five were brutally murdered. Every night afterwards during curfew hours heavy gunfire was heard, and during that week many other entire families were wiped out. These were acts of terrorism, and it is not known who the murderers were nor their motive in killing the Olinga family. The Universal House of Justice announced to the Bahá'í world:

> With grief-stricken hearts announce tragic news brutal murder dearly loved greatly admired Hand Cause God Enoch Olinga by unknown gunmen courtyard his Kampala home. His wife Elizabeth and three of his children Badí', Lennie and Ṭáhirih have also fallen innocent victims this cruel act. Motive attack not yet ascertained. His radiant spirit his unwavering faith his all-embracing love his leonine audacity in the teaching field his titles Knight Bahá'u'lláh, Father Victories conferred beloved Guardian all combine distinguish him as pre-eminent member his race in annals Faith African continent. Urge friends everywhere hold memorial gatherings befitting tribute his imperishable memory. Fervently praying Holy Shrines

progress his noble soul and souls four members his precious family. [2:634][60:471]

OLSEN, HENDRIK (-1967) The first (1965) indigenous Greenland believer. [50:369]

ONENESS OF MANKIND Shoghi Effendi has written at some length on this central principle of the Bahá'í Faith. Commenting as long ago as 1931 on the implications of what both Bahá'u'lláh and 'Abdu'l-Bahá had said, he wrote:

> Are not these intermittent crises that convulse present-day society due primarily to the lamentable inability of the world's recognized leaders to read aright the signs of the times, to rid themselves once for all of their preconceived ideas and fettering creeds, and to reshape the machinery of their respective governments according to those standards that are implicit in Bahá'u'lláh's supreme declaration of the Oneness of Mankind—the chief and distinguishing feature of the Faith He proclaimed? For the principle of the Oneness of Mankind, the cornerstone of Bahá'u'lláh's world-embracing dominion, implies nothing more nor less than the enforcement of His scheme for the unification of the world—the scheme to which we have already referred. "In every Dispensation," writes 'Abdu'l-Bahá, "the light of Divine Guidance has been focused upon one central theme.... In this wondrous Revelation, this glorious century, the foundation of the Faith of God and the distinguishing feature of His Law is the consciousness of the Oneness of Mankind." The principle of the Oneness of Mankind—the pivot round which all the teachings of Bahá'u'lláh revolve—is no mere outburst of ignorant emotionalism or an expression of vague and pious hope. Its appeal is not to be merely identified with a reawakening of the spirit of brotherhood and good-will among men, nor does it aim solely at the fostering of harmonious co-operation among individual peoples and nations. Its implications are deeper, its claims greater than any which the Prophets of old were allowed to advance. Its message is applicable not only to the individual, but concerns itself primarily with the nature of those essential relationships that must bind all the states and nations as members of one human family.... It implies an organic change in the structure of present-day society, a change such as the world has not yet experienced. It constitutes a challenge, at once bold and universal, to outworn shibboleths of national creeds—creeds that have had their day and which must give way to a new gospel,

> fundamentally different from, and infinitely superior to, what the world has already conceived. It calls for no less than the reconstruction and the demilitarization of the whole civilized world—a world organically unified in all the essential aspects of its life, its political machinery, its spiritual aspiration, its trade and finance, its script and language, and yet infinite in the diversity of the national characteristics of its federated units. [4:36,42]

ORBISON, VIRGINIA (1902-1985) (Knight of Bahá'u'lláh) An American believer (1933) who pioneered to Santiago, Chile in 1942 and in so doing helped form the first (1943) local Spiritual Assembly of Santiago (the first in Chile). In the following four-year period she traveled relentlessly in the promotion of the Cause: In 1943 she visited Argentina, Paraguay and Bolivia; in 1944 she visited Peru, Bolivia and Ecuador; in 1945 she returned for six months to Wilmette for "hospitalization and rest" only to travel from there back to Brazil where she stayed until December 1946. In 1947 she responded to a call for pioneers to go to Europe by moving to Spain where she was the first believer to arrive. By 1948 there were sufficient believers to form the first local Spiritual Assembly of Madrid (on which Virginia served as Corresponding Secretary). A second local Spiritual Assembly in Barcelona followed in 1949. By 1954 there were Spiritual Assemblies in Murcia and Tarrasa. In 1953 she pioneered to the Balearic Islands for which service she was designated a Knight of Bahá'u'lláh. In 1954 she was imprisoned and questioned by police in Barcelona during the Iberian Teaching Conference. In 1956 she moved to Lisbon. In 1957 she was elected to the first Iberian Regional Spiritual Assembly. In May 1959 she was expelled from Portugal on Police order for "Bahá'í activities." She then moved to Dudelange, Luxembourg, to help maintain the local Spiritual Assembly. In 1962 she served on the first National Spiritual Assembly of Luxembourg. In 1968, on doctor's orders to move to a warmer climate, she returned to Malaga, Spain. In 1972 she was elected to the first local Spiritual Assembly of Malaga. For her services in the Iberian Peninsula she earned the accolade "the Mother of Spain." [11:691]

OUTHEY, JEANNETTE (-1980) The first (1961) Caledonian believer, she served on the first (1961) local Spiritual Assembly of Noumea (for a period of 19 years). In 1971 she was elected to the National Spiritual Assembly of the South West Pacific Ocean. In 1977 she replaced her mother as Custodian of the National Ḥaẓíratu'l-Quds in Noumea. [2:722]

P

PALU, JOHANNES (1913-1994) Along with his wife Raia, the first (1968) Estonian Bahá'ís. He served on the first (1990) local Spiritual Assembly of Tallinn. [11:321]

PARKE, GLADYS IRENE (-1969) (Knight of Bahá'u'lláh) An Australian believer who embraced the Cause in Tasmania (the first to do so in Northern Tasmania). In 1953 she pioneered to Tahiti in the Society Islands for which service she was designated a Knight of Bahá'u'lláh. She later returned to Tasmania where she remained active in the teaching field. [51:457]

PARSONS, AGNES (1861-1934) In about 1861, Agnes, daughter of General and Mrs. Royal, was born into a beautiful and sheltered world with every advantage that social position and material wealth could bring. Until she heard of the Bahá'í Faith, circa 1908, it is believed she had not known nor associated with anyone outside her immediate social circle, which makes her outstanding future services even more remarkable. She was then living happily with her husband Arthur Jeffrey Parsons and their two children, Jeffrey and Royal, in Washington, D.C. Two years later she made a pilgrimage to Haifa to meet 'Abdu'l-Bahá, and it was in that environment that she accepted and became confirmed in her Faith. During 'Abdu'l-Bahá's visit to Washington in the spring of 1912 she entertained Him and worked indefatigably to make His visit the success that has been recorded in the history of that time. Many talks that He gave are recorded in *Promulgation of Universal Peace*, but there were numerous visits to Him by groups and individuals in her home, some of which were noted in her own records. In August 'Abdu'l-Bahá visited her again but in her home in Dublin, N.H.; the pattern was repeated, and He Himself referred to her spirituality and significant services to her Faith. She visited 'Abdu'l-Bahá again in late 1919 or early 1920, and it was during this second pilgrimage that she received His instructions, which not only caused her considerable surprise but gave her a specific mission. She had long been closely associated with societies working for the improvement of the relationships between America and Persia,[87:vol.II,No.1] but when she received the command from 'Abdu'l-Bahá, "I want you to arrange a Convention for unity of the colored and white races. You must have people to help you." [37:413] She carried out His wishes implicitly and with a group of eminent Bahá'ís organized the First Racial Amity Convention, which opened on 19 May 1921 in the First Congregational Church, Washington, D.C. with the pastor opening it with a prayer and with William H. Randall (q.v.) as Chairman of the first session.

One of Agent's coworkers on the convening committee had been a Mr. Mountford Mills, who was in Haifa when the Convention opened but returned in time to be the Chairman of one of its sessions. He brought with him a message from 'Abdu'l-Bahá: "Say to this Convention that never since the beginning of time has a Convention of more importance been held. It will become the cause of the removal of hostility between the races. It will become the cause of the enlightenment of America. It will, if rightly managed and continued, check the deadly struggle between these races which otherwise will inevitably break out." [87:volXII,No.6,115] Immediately on receipt of a cable from Mrs. Parsons: "Convention successful. Meetings crowded. Hearts comforted." 'Abdu'l-Bahá replied: "The white/colored Convention produced happiness. Hoping will establish same in all America." Subsequently an eminent Bahá'í said, "'Abdu'l-Bahá gave to this first convention for amity the station of 'mother' and said that its spirit would spread to other cities." [20:282] At the Annual Convention of the Bahá'ís of North America, Chicago 22-25 April 1922, the first National Spiritual Assembly of that continent was elected, and Agnes was a member for three consecutive years. She remained active in the field of racial amity and was for years the Chairman of the National Race Unity Committee (National Interracial Committee). On 19 January 1934 she was knocked down by a passing automobile and died on 23 January. Writing on *Progress in Racial Amity*, Nellie French wrote: "Whenever the thought of racial amity passes before the mind's eye there appears simultaneously the vision of that gentle and loving spirit, Mrs. Agnes S. Parsons.... Her memory will ever be kept alive by those who seek to follow in her footsteps and take up the mission laid down by her untimely demise." [37:111] Shoghi Effendi cabled: "Greatly deplore loss distinguished handmaid of Bahá'u'lláh Through her manifold pioneer services she has proved herself worthy of the implicit confidence reposed in her by 'Abdu'l-Bahá. Advise American believers hold befitting memorial gatherings. Assure relatives heartfelt sympathy, prayers." [37:410][91:76]

PÁSHÁ Honorary title formerly given to a Turkish officer of high rank such as a military commander or provincial governor. [11:739📖]

PATTERSON, ROBERT HENRY (1925-1975) An Australian believer (1956) of Scottish birth, he first pioneered within Australia and then in 1968 he went to Apia, Western Samoa. He was elected to the first National Spiritual Assembly of Samoa when it formed in 1970. His death in 1975 earned him the designation of being the first pioneer to Samoa to give up his life at his post. [52:549]

PAVÓN, RAÚL MEJÍA De (1933-1983) An early (1958) Ecuadorian believer who served on the local Spiritual Assemblies of Otavalo and Quito as well as on the National Spiritual Assembly of Ecua dor. In 1973 he was appointed a member of the Continental Board of Counsellors in South America and then (when the Boards were merged) as a member of the Americas Board. He played a lead rôle in the establishment of Radio Bahá'í, Ecuador—the first Bahá'í-owned and operated radio station in the world. Through his efforts, his parents also embraced the Faith. [11:616]

PEACE Bahá'í Scriptures abound in references to peace—world peace; Lesser Peace; Most Great Peace; inner peace—and the Bahá'í teaching emphasize that peace must be firmly established at every level of human society—from the individual to the family, society, the nation and to the whole world. Bahá'u'lláh wrote:

> The purpose underlying the revelation of every heavenly Book, nay, of every divinely-revealed verse, is to endue all men with righteousness and understanding, so that peace and tranquillity may be firmly established amongst them. Whatsoever instilleth assurance into the hearts of men, whatsoever exalteth their station or promoteth their contentment, is acceptable in the sight of God. [85:206]

'Abdu'l-Bahá wrote:

> Universal Peace is assured by Bahá'u'lláh as a fundamental accomplishment of the religion of God; that peace shall prevail among nations, governments and peoples, among religions, races and all conditions of mankind. This is one of the special characteristics of the Word of God revealed in this Manifestation. [106:247]

> When the banner of truth is raised, peace becomes the cause of the welfare and advancement of the human world. In all cycles and ages war has been a factor of derangement and discomfort whereas peace and brotherhood have brought security and consideration of human interests. This distinction is especially pronounced in the present world conditions, for warfare in former centuries had not attained the degree of savagery and destructiveness which now characterizes it. [107:20]

> The primary purpose, the basic objective, in laying down powerful laws and setting up great principles and institutions dealing with every aspect of civilization, is human happiness; and human happiness consists only in drawing closer to the Threshold of Almighty God, and in securing the peace and well-being of every individual member, high and low alike, of the human race; and the supreme agencies for accom-

plishing these two objectives are the excellent qualities with which humanity has been endowed.[125:60]

The time has come when all mankind shall be united, when all races shall be loyal to one fatherland, all religions become one religion and racial and religious bias pass away. It is a day in which the oneness of humankind shall uplift its standard and international peace like the true morning flood the world with its light. [107:17] See **PEACE, LESSER; PEACE, MOST GREAT**.

PEACE, LESSER According to Bahá'í Writings, world peace will be established in two stages the first being a political peace established by the governments of the world which, in turn, in the fullness of time, will evolve into "the Most Great Peace." Shoghi Effendi wrote:

In His Tablet to Queen Victoria He, (Bahá'u'lláh) moreover, invites these kings to hold fast to "the Lesser Peace," since they had refused "the Most Great Peace;" exhorts them to be reconciled among themselves, to unite and to reduce their armaments; bids them refrain from laying excessive burdens on their subjects, who, He informs them, are their "wards" and "treasures;" enunciates the principle that should any one among them take up arms against another, all should rise against him... [5:206]

Now that ye have refused the Most Great Peace," He, admonishing the kings and rulers of the earth, has written, "hold ye fast unto this the Lesser Peace, that haply ye may in some degree better your own condition and that of your dependants." Expatiating on this Lesser Peace, He thus addresses in that same Tablet the rulers of the earth: "Be reconciled among yourselves, that ye may need no more armaments save in a measure to safeguard your territories and dominions.... Be united, O kings of the earth, for thereby will the tempest of discord be stilled amongst you, and your peoples find rest, if ye be of them that comprehend. Should any one among you take up arms against another, rise ye all against him, for this is naught but manifest justice. [126:162]

Suffice it to say that this consummation will, by its very nature, be a gradual process, and must, as Bahá'u'lláh has Himself anticipated, lead at first to the establishment of that Lesser Peace which the nations of the earth, as yet unconscious of His Revelation and yet unwittingly enforcing the general principles which He has enunciated, will themselves establish. [44:123] See **PEACE; PEACE, MOST GREAT.**

PEACE, MOST GREAT Bahá'ís believe that after the Lesser Peace (q.v.) has been established by the governments of the world, and war has been forever forsworn, there will come a time when the problems facing the global community that have resulted from its warring past will have to be confronted. Gradually, through the slow spiritualization of the masses, the human race will become aware of its oneness, and a peace founded on universal love will evolve. This is repeatedly referred to in Bahá'í Writings, 'Abdu'l-Bahá wrote: "Today there is no greater glory for man than that of service in the cause of the 'Most Great Peace.' Peace is light whereas war is darkness. Peace is life; war is death. Peace is guidance; war is error. Peace is the foundation of God; war is satanic institution. Peace is the illumination of the world of humanity; war is the destroyer of human foundations." [106:231] This is the goal to which Bahá'ís dedicate their efforts: the building of the foundations of the Most Great Peace by carrying out their teaching plans, by endeavoring to live their lives in accordance with the teachings of Bahá'u'lláh and by establishing those institutions by which this Peace may function.

Shoghi Effendi described the process in some detail:

> Suffice it to say that this consummation will, by its very nature, be a gradual process, and must, as Bahá'u'lláh has Himself anticipated, lead at first to the establishment of that Lesser Peace which the nations of the earth, as yet unconscious of His Revelation and yet unwittingly enforcing the general principles which He has enunciated, will themselves establish. This momentous and historic step, involving the reconstruction of mankind, as the result of the universal recognition of its oneness and wholeness, will bring in its wake the spiritualization of the masses, consequent to the recognition of the character, and the acknowledgment of the claims, of the Faith of Bahá'u'lláh—the essential condition to that ultimate fusion of all races, creeds, classes, and nations which must signalize the emergence of His New World Order. Then will the coming of age of the entire human race be proclaimed and celebrated by all the peoples and nations of the earth. Then will the banner of the Most Great Peace be hoisted. Then will the world-wide sovereignty of Bahá'u'lláh—the Establisher of the Kingdom of the Father foretold by the Son, and anticipated by the Prophets

of God before Him and after Him—be recognized, acclaimed, and firmly established. Then will a world civilization be born, flourish, and perpetuate itself, a civilization with a fullness of life such as the world has never seen nor can as yet conceive. Then will the Everlasting Covenant be fulfilled in its completeness. Then will the promise enshrined in all the Books of God be redeemed, and all the prophecies uttered by the Prophets of old come to pass, and the vision of seers and poets be realized. Then will the planet, galvanized through the universal belief of its dwellers in one God, and their allegiance to one common Revelation, mirror, within the limitations imposed upon it, the effulgent glories of the sovereignty of Bahá'u'lláh... be made the footstool of His Throne on high, and acclaimed as the earthly heaven, capable of fulfilling that ineffable destiny fixed for it, from time immemorial, by the love and wisdom of its Creator. [44:123] See **PEACE; PEACE, LESSER.**

PEACE, THE PROMISE OF WORLD A statement by the Universal House of Justice addressed *To the Peoples of the World* in October 1985 for particular use during the United Nations International Year of Peace, 1986. [117] Copies were presented to heads of state and governments, either directly or through their ambassadors at the United Nations and to civic leaders, scholars and leaders of thought in most countries. In all, over one million copies in more than 90 languages were distributed during 1985 alone. The statement has been the basis for many books and media articles and the presentation of copies to influential people has been a continuing process. Among the issues it addresses are: the inevitability of world peace; the rôle of religion as a source of order, the results of the turning away from it and the rise of materialistic ideologies; the hopeful signs in the declarations and conventions of the United Nations; such root causes of war as racism, disparity between rich and poor, unbridled nationalism, religious strife, denial of full partnership between men and women, lack of education in many parts of the world and of full communication between peoples. It suggests the ways forward for establishing world order and directs attention to Bahá'u'lláh's call for a convocation of the "rulers and kings of the earth." It offers the Bahá'í experience as a model for study and ends on a high note of optimism. See **PEACE; PEACE, LESSER; PEACE, MOST GREAT.**

PERSECUTION From the birth of the Bahá'í Faith its followers have, in several countries, suffered persecution. This has been the most prolonged and intensive in Írán, by both state and the Islámic clergy. The most recent wave began with the Islámic

Revolution of 1979 and has included sentences of death, as well as lesser persecutions of being deprived of employment, pensions, food permits, schooling and attendance at university. Many cases of imprisonment, torture and execution have been brought to the attention of the United Nations Human Rights Commission. Persecution has also been suffered by Bahá'ís in North Africa, the Middle East and some Asian countries. Most cases are of religious origin with pressure on Bahá'ís to recant their faith. For detailed discussions of the persecutions suffered by the Bahá'ís in Írán see: *A Cry from the Heart: The Bahá'ís in Iran*;[127] *Iran's Secret Pogrom: The Conspiracy to Wipe Out the Bahá'ís*;[128] *The Bábí and Bahá'í Religions, 1844-1944: Some Contemporary Western Accounts*;[129] *The Baha'is of Iran.*[130]

PILGRIM A Bahá'í pilgrim is one who goes on a special pilgrimage organized by the Universal House of Justice or who visits the House of Bahá'u'lláh in Baghdád—which is not presently available to Bahá'ís. At one time it included a visit to the House of the Báb in Shíráz, Írán (before it was destroyed during anti-Bahá'í activities in 1978). Pilgrims in the early days of the Faith visited Bahá'u'lláh in 'Akká and later 'Abdu'l-Bahá in Haifa. From time to time, groups of pilgrims are allowed to go on a "nine-day" pilgrimage, which combines visits on a planned schedule to "special" places in Haifa and 'Akká with private prayer in the Shrines of Bahá'u'lláh, the Báb and 'Abdu'l-Bahá, the Most Great Prison, the Mansion at Bahjí, Mazra'ih, the tombs in the Monument Gardens and other holy places as desired. See **HOLY PLACES**.

PINCHON, FLORENCE E. (—) An early (1916) British believer, she came into the Cause through the efforts of Dr. Esslemont. She received a Tablet from 'Abdu'l-Bahá in 1920. She wrote extensively (for *Star of the West* and *World Order* magazines) and published the volume *The Coming of the Glory.*[131][50:370]

PIONEER A Bahá'í pioneer is a believer who moves from his/her home to another place in the interests of the Faith. Bahá'ís consider it a great bounty to be able to pioneer, and in some instances it is a service that takes precedence over all others.

The Universal House of Justice wrote in 1965:

> The duties of teaching and pioneering are enjoined upon all believers. There are no special categories of believers for these functions. Any Bahá'í who spreads the Message of Bahá'u'lláh is a teacher, any Bahá'í who moves to another area to spread the Faith is a pioneer.[86:572]

The Guardian wrote through his secretary in 1954:

> While it carries great responsibilities; and difficulties; yet its spiritual blessings are so great, they overshadow eve-

rything else; and the opportunities for special victories of the Faith so abundant; the soul who once tastes the elixir of pioneering service, seldom will do anything else.

To a National Spiritual Assembly he wrote:

The principle is that pioneers entering the pioneer field should realize that they are going there to represent the Cause, in fact, to be the Cause. Their minds and their hearts should be centered in their new tasks and in their new environment. They should not be thinking of when they can return home, or when they can go somewhere else. Only when the Faith is firmly established should they give any thought to moving.[86:578]

In 1966 the Universal House of Justice wrote: "The perseverance of the pioneers in their posts, however great the sacrifices involved, is an act of devoted service, which as attested by our teachings, will have an assured reward in both worlds." [86:579]

The pioneer is not an employee nor a minister, as there is no professional clergy in the Bahá'í Faith. The call of the Guardian in May 1953, however, proved irresistible for an army of volunteers:

The hour is ripe to disencumber themselves of worldly vanities, to mount the steed of steadfastness, unfurl the banner of renunciation, don the armor of utter consecration to God's Cause, gird themselves with the girdle of a chaste and holy life, unsheathe the sword of Bahá'u'lláh's utterance, buckle on the shield of His love, carry as sole provision implicit trust in His promise, flee their homelands, and scatter far and wide to capture the unsurrendered territories of the entire planet. [86:570] See **KNIGHTS OF BAHÁ'U'LLÁH.**

PLANS, TEACHING The 14 *Tablets of the Divine Plan* from 'Abdu'l-Bahá written to the American Bahá'í Community towards the end of His life set in place the overall world vision of the rôle of the North American Bahá'ís. Beginning in October 1935, Shoghi Effendi began to prepare the American believers to take on "nation-wide, systematic sustained efforts in the teaching field [112:5] followed three months later by such stirring words as "an effort unexampled in its scope and sustained vitality is urgently required." [112:6] Four months later he followed with this statement: "Humanity entering outer fringes most perilous stage its existence. Opportunities of present hour unimaginably precious. Would to God every State within American Republic and every Republic in American continent ... might embrace the light of the

Faith of Bahá'u'lláh." [112:6] Finally to the National Convention of 1937 he cabled:

> Dual gift providentially conferred American Bahá'í community invests recipients with dual responsibility fulfill historic mission. First prosecute uninterruptedly teaching campaign inaugurated last convention in accordance divine plan. Second resume with inflexible determination exterior ornamentation entire structure temple. Advise ponder message conveyed delegates esteemed coworker Fred Schopflocher. No triumph can more befittingly signalize termination first century Bahá'í era than accomplishment this twofold task. Advise prolongation convention sessions enable delegates consult national assembly to formulate feasible seven year plan to ensure success temple enterprise. No sacrifice too great for community so abundantly blessed repeatedly honored.[38:7, 9, 39, 40:385ff, 41:25]

It was this cable that prompted the creation and launch of the first Bahá'í Plan—The Six Year Plan. [112:9]

While the goals were set by the Guardian, the National Spiritual Assembly of India, Pákistán and Burma followed the North American example and launched its own Six Year Plan.

On learning of the success of the American plan, the British National Convention of 1944 adopted a Six Year Plan. They cabled the Guardian asking for Goals and were quickly assigned a goal of raising the number of local Spiritual Assemblies from five to 19. Following a tremendous effort the British Bahá'ís achieved a sixfold increase by 1950, and Shoghi Effendi gave them another plan for opening some new territories in British Africa by 1953.

Following a two-year respite, a second American plan, the Seven Year Plan, was launched in April 1946. It contained the following goals:

> A twofold responsibility urgently calls vanguard dawnbreakers west champion builders Bahá'u'lláh's order torchbearers world civilization executors 'Abdu'l-Bahá's mandate arise simultaneously bring fruition tasks already undertaken launch fresh enterprises beyond borders western hemisphere. First objective new plan consolidation victories won throughout Americas involving multiplication Bahá'í centers bolder proclamation faith masses. Second objective completion interior ornamentation holiest house worship Bahá'í world designed coincide fiftieth anniversary inception historic enterprise. Third objective formation three national assemblies pillars Universal House Justice Dominion Canada Central South

America. Fourth objective initiation systematic teaching activity war torn spiritually famished European continent cradle world famed civilizations twice blest 'Abdu'l-Bahá's visits whose rulers Bahá'u'lláh specifically collectively addressed aiming establishment assemblies in Iberian Peninsula Low Countries Scandinavian States and Italy. [38:87ff][40:395][41:33]

On 14 April 1944, Shoghi Effendi wrote to the first National Spiritual Assembly of Canada (about to be formed during Convention later that month) congratulating them and urging them to adopt a Five Year Plan:

Hearts uplifted in thanksgiving to Bahá'u'lláh for the epoch-making event of the coming of age of the dearly beloved Canadian Bahá'í community, the formation of the first National Convention in the City of Montreal and the forthcoming election of Canada's National Assembly constituting the ninth pillar of the institution of the Universal House of Justice.... I am moved to appeal to assembled delegates to arise in conjunction with the first Canadian National Assembly, as a token of gratitude for the manifold blessings of Divine Providence, to initiate in the hour of the birth of their national activities a Five Year Plan designed to associate them, formally and systematically and independently, with their sister community of the United States, in the common task of the prosecution of their world- encompassing mission. The fulfillment of this collective task confronting the rapidly maturing community necessitates the incorporation of the Canadian National Assembly, the establishment of National Bahá'í Endowments, doubling the number of Local Assemblies throughout the Dominion and raising to one hundred the total number of localities where Bahá'í reside throughout the Provinces, the constitution of a group in Newfoundland and the formation of a nucleus of the Faith in the Territory of Greenland, singled out for special mention by the Author of the Divine Plan, and the participation of Eskimos and Red Indians in membership to share administrative privileges in local institutions of the Faith in Canada.[40:409][46:7]

On 14 March 1947, Shoghi Effendi wrote to the National Spiritual Assembly of Australia and New Zealand encouraging them to adopt a Plan (Six Year Plan (1947—1953)):

I wish to appeal, through you, to the members of the entire community in both Australia and New Zealand, to arise, in these opening years of the Second Bahá'í century, and lend, through their concerted, their sustained, and determined efforts, an unprecedented impetus to the growth of the Faith, the multiplication of its administrative centers, and the consolidation of its nascent institutions. The initiation of a Plan, carefully devised, universally supported, and designed to promote effectively the vital interests of the Faith, and attain a definite objective within a specified number of years, would seem, at the present hour, highly desirable and opportune, and will, as a magnet, attract, to an unprecedented degree, the blessings of Bahá'u'lláh on the members of both communities, both individually and collectively. [9:69f][40:407]

Three months later he wrote praising them in these words:

The Plan, on which the National elected representatives of the Bahá'í communities of Australia and New Zealand have spontaneously embarked marks a turning-point, of great spiritual significance, in the evolution of the Faith in those far-off lands, and is an evidence of the truly remarkable spirit that animates them as well as the communities they represent. I welcome this mighty step they have taken with joy, pride and gratitude, and have hastened to transmit to them my contribution as a token of my keen appreciation of their high endeavors, of my confidence in their ability, and of my admiration for their zeal and noble determination in the service of the Faith. The attention of the members of both communities must henceforth be focused on the Plan, its progress, its requirements, its significance and immediate objectives. All must participate without exception without reserve, without delay. The Administrative Order which they have labored to establish must henceforth, through its organs and agencies be utilized for the promotion of this vital purpose, this supreme end. For no other purpose was it created. That it may serve this end, that the Plan may speedily develop and yield its destined fruit and demonstrate through its consummation the worthiness, the capacity and high-mindedness of the organized body of the followers of Bahá'u'lláh in those distant lands are the objects of my fervent and constant prayers at the Holy Shrines.[9:69f][40:407]

In April 1950 Shoghi Effendi announced to the British National Convention that they were to launch what was subsequently called the *Africa Plan* (1951-1953):

Heart Flooded Joy Striking Evidence Bountiful Grace Bahá'u'lláh Enabling Valorous Dearly Loved Bahá'í Community British Isles Triumphantly Conclude First Historic Plan Half Century British Bahá'í History. Herald Author Faith Centre Covenant Concourse On High Acclaim Superb Collective Achievement Immortalising Opening Decade Second Bahá'í Century Unprecedented History Faith British Isles Unrivalled Annals Any Bahá'í Community European Continent Unparalleled Percentage Members Community Responding Pioneer Call Throughout Bahá'í World Since Termination Apostolic Age Bahá'í Dispensation. Historic Pledge British Bahá'í Community Nobly Redeemed. Tribute Memory Martyr Prophet Faith Worthily Paid. Spiritual Potentialities Prosecute Subsequent Stage Unfolding Mission Fully Acquired. Triumphant Community Now Standing Threshold Catching First Glimpse Still Dimly Outlined Future Enterprises Overseas. Hour Propitious Galvanised Firmly Knit Body Believers Brace Itself Embark After One Year Respite Yet Another Historic Undertaking Marking Formal Inauguration Two Year Plan Constituting Prelude Initiation Systematic Campaign Designed Carry Torch Faith Territories Dark Continent Whose Northern Southern Fringes Were Successively Illuminated Course Ministries Bahá'u'lláh 'Abdu'l-Bahá. Hour Struck Undertake Preliminary Steps Implant Banner Faith Amidst African Tribes Mentioned Tablet Centre Covenant Signalising Association Victorious British Bahá'í Community With Sister Communities United States Egypt Designed Lay Structural Basis Bahá'í Administrative Order Scale Comparable Foundation Already Established North South American European Australian Continents. Projected Plan Itself Prelude Double Task To Be Undertaken Course Future Plans Destined Simultaneously Broaden Base Operations Home Front And Prosecute Systematic Campaign Dependencies British Isles. First Objective Two Year Plan Consolidation Nineteen Assemblies Painstakingly Established England Scotland Wales North Ireland Eire. Second Objective Formation Nuclei Three Dependencies British Crown Either East West Africa. Third Objective Translation Publication Dissemination Bahá'í Literature Through Publishing Trust Three African Languages Addition Three Already Undertaken Course First Plan. Successful Prosecution Contemplated Plan Will Pave Way Large Scale Operations Calculated Lay Foundation Promised Kingdom Earth Through Establishment Administrative Order Infi nitely More Glorious Empire Built Rulers British Isles Throughout That Continent And Will Enable British Bahá'í Community Share Honour Sister Community Across Atlantic Prosecuting Successfully Two Successive Plans Registering Double Victory Laying Twice Repeated Sacrifice Altar Faith Anticipation Approaching Celebrations Commemorating Centenary Birth Bahá'u'lláh's Prophetic Mission. Contributing One Thousand Pounds First Contribution Furtherance Noble Purpose. [9:245f][40:413]

The American second Seven Year Plan, a Five Year Plan of the newly resurgent National Spiritual Assembly of Germany and Austrian; a Four-and-one-half Year Plan of India, Pákistán and Burma; an Íránian Four Year Plan; an Australia and New Zealand Six Year Plan, an Iráqi Three Year Plan; an Egyptian Five Year Plan; a 19-Month Plan adopted by the Persian National Spiritual Assembly in 1951 and a Five Year Plan adopted by the Canadian National Spiritual Assembly in 1948, all terminated successfully by 1953, thereby enabling Shoghi Effendi to launch, in April of that year, a global Ten Year Plan or Global Crusade aimed at opening wherever possible all the territories in the world mentioned by 'Abdu'l-Bahá in His Divine Plan.

Hail, with feelings of humble thankfulness and unbounded joy, opening of the Holy Year commemorating the centenary of the rise of the Orb of Bahá'u'lláh's most sublime Revelation marking the consummation of the six thousand year cycle ushered in by Adam, glorified by all past prophets and sealed with the blood of the Author of the Bábí Dispensation.... Feel hour propitious to proclaim to the entire Bahá'í world the projected launching on the occasion of the convocation of the approaching Intercontinental Conferences on the four continents of the globe the fate-laden, soul-stirring, decade-long, world-embracing Spiritual Crusade involving the simultaneous initiation of twelve national Ten Year Plans and the concerted participation of all National Spiritual Assemblies of the Bahá'í world aiming at the immediate extension of Bahá'u'lláh's spiritual dominion as well as the eventual establishment of the structure of His administrative order in all remaining Sovereign States, Principal Dependencies ... The four-fold objectives of the forthcoming Crusade, marking the third and last phase of the initial epoch of the evolution of 'Abdu'l-Bahá's Divine Plan are destined to culminate in the world-wide festivities commemorating the fast-approaching Most Great Jubilee. First, development

> of the institutions at the World Center of the Faith in the Holy Land. Second, consolidation, through carefully devised measures on the home front of the twelve territories destined to serve as administrative bases for the operations of the twelve National Plans. Third, consolidation of all territories already opened to the Faith. Fourth, the opening of the remaining chief virgin territories on the planet through specific allotments to each National Assembly functioning in the Bahá'í world.[3][40:417ff][47]

The successful completion of all these plans, under the continued encouragement of Shoghi Effendi during his lifetime and faithfully pursued by the Hands of the Cause, in their capacity as the Chief Stewards during the interregnum period (1957-1963), enabled the election of the Universal House of Justice to take place during the Most Great Jubilee period (Riḍván 1963). Immediately following their election, the Universal House of Justice launched its first global plan—a Nine Year Plan to maintain the momentum of a triumphant global community. Since that time there have been a succession of Global plans, with each newly emerging National Spiritual Assembly being given its share of the systematic teaching campaign as foreseen by 'Abdu'l-Bahá. Following the Nine Year Plan, there have been four other Global Plans—of Five, Seven, Six, Three and Four years duration. See **GOALS, TABLETS OF THE DIVINE PLAN; TIMELINES—SHOGHI EFFENDI; THE UNIVERSAL HOUSE OF JUSTICE.**

POLITICS While in the strict meaning of the word—the science or art of government—the Bahá'í approach to government is very political, and indeed the Bahá'í Faith has a great deal to say about government, the conduct of the Faith eschews any involvement in "party" or competitive types of government. Bahá'ís are forbidden to participate in partisan politics, as Shoghi Effendi emphasized:

> To enter the arena of party politics is surely detrimental to the best interests of the Faith and will harm the Cause. [86:441]

> No loyal believer should under any circumstances commit himself in any way to a political program or policy formulated and upheld by a political party for affiliation with such a party necessarily entails repudiation of some principles and teachings of the Cause, or partial recognition of some of its fundamental verities. The friends should, therefore, keep aloof from party politics. What they should mainly keep away from under all circumstances and in all its forms is partisanship. [86:443]

We see, therefore, that we must do two things—shun politics like the plague, and be obedient to the government in power in the place where we reside. We cannot start judging how a particular government came into power, and therefore whether we should obey it or not. This would immediately plunge us into politics. We must obey in all cases except where a spiritual principle is involved such as denying our Faith. For these spiritual principles we must be willing to die. [86:445]

Though loyal to their respective governments, though profoundly interested in anything that affects their security and welfare, though anxious to share in whatever promotes their best interests, the Faith with which the followers of Bahá'u'lláh stand identified is one which they firmly believe God has raised high above the storms, the divisions, and controversies of the political arena. Their Faith they conceive to be essentially non-political, supranational in character, rigidly non-partisan, and entirely dissociated from nationalistic ambitions, pursuits, and purposes. Such a Faith knows no division of class or of party. It subordinates, without hesitation or equivocation, every particularistic interest, be it personal, regional, or national, to the paramount interests of humanity, firmly convinced that in a world of inter-dependent peoples and nations the advantage of the part is best to be reached by the advantage of the whole, and that no abiding benefit can be conferred upon the component parts if the general interests of the entity itself are ignored or neglected. [4:198]

Let them refrain from associating themselves, whether by word or by deed, with the political pursuits of their respective nations, with the policies of their governments and the schemes and programs of parties and factions. In such controversies they should assign no blame, take no side, further no design, and identify themselves with no system prejudicial to the best interests of that world-wide Fellowship which it is their aim to guard and foster. [4:64]

It must characterize the attitude of every loyal believer towards non-acceptance of political posts, non-identification with political parties, non-participation in political controversies, and non-membership in political organizations and ecclesiastical institutions. [39:26]

PÖLLINGER, FRANZ (1895-1979) An early (1914) Austrian believer, he received two Tablets from 'Abdu'l-Bahá and was mentioned by name in another to Alma Knobloch. He was a member of the first (1926) local Spiritual Assembly of Vienna and the first (1959) National Spiritual Assembly of Austria. [2:701][60:481]

POOR The Universal House of Justice wrote in 1985:

> The inordinate disparity between rich and poor, a source of acute suffering, keeps the world in a state of instability, virtually on the brink of war. Few societies have dealt effectively with this situation. The solution calls for the combined application of spiritual, moral and practical approaches.... It is an issue that is bound up not only with the necessity for eliminating extremes of wealth and poverty but also with those spiritual verities the understanding of which can produce a new universal attitude. [117:10]

In a statement to the Copenhagen Summit, 1995, entitled *The Prosperity of Humankind*, the Bahá'í International Community dealt in some depth with the problem of poverty. [94:22f] While recognizing that the trend towards the latter part of the 20th century is for the rich to become richer and the poor poorer, and the nations of the world must address this challenging issue, Bahá'ís speak to the rich and to the poor as well as seeking at the same time to bring about a more just and caring society, as the following quotations indicate.

Bahá'u'lláh wrote:

> Bestow My wealth upon My poor, that in heaven thou mayest draw from stores of unfading splendor and treasures of imperishable glory. [92:57]

> To the poor be a treasure of wealth, and to the sick a remedy and healing. Be a helper of every oppressed one, the protector of every destitute one, be ye ever mindful to serve any soul of mankind. [106:216]

> Be generous in prosperity, and thankful in adversity. Be worthy of the trust of thy neighbor, and look upon him with a bright and friendly face. Be a treasure to the poor, an admonisher to the rich, an answerer to the cry of the needy, a preserver of the sanctity of thy pledge. Be fair in thy judgment, and guarded in thy speech. Be unjust to no man, and show all meekness to all men. [70:93]

> Know ye that the poor are the trust of God in your midst. Watch that ye betray not His trust, that ye deal not unjustly with them and that ye walk not in the ways of the treacherous. Ye will most certainly be called upon to an

> swer for His trust on the day when the Balance of Justice shall be set, the day when unto every one shall be rendered his due, when the doings of all men, be they rich or poor, shall be weighed. [78:9]
>
> Be not troubled in poverty nor confident in riches, for poverty is followed by riches, and riches are followed by poverty. Yet to be poor in all save God is a wondrous gift, belittle not the value thereof, for in the end it will make thee rich in God, and thus thou shalt know the meaning of the utterance, "In truth ye are the poor," and the holy words, "God is the all-possessing," shall even as the true morn break forth gloriously resplendent upon the horizon of the lover's heart, and abide secure on the throne of wealth. [92:51]

'Abdu'l-Bahá wrote: "That is why, in the religion of God, it is prescribed and established that wealthy men each year give over a certain part of their fortune for the maintenance of the poor and unfortunate." [106:284]

PRAYER Bahá'u'lláh and 'Abdu'l-Bahá left a wealth of prayers not only to cover almost every exigency but for praise, thanksgiving and for meditation. Bahá'u'lláh wrote:

> Intone, O My servant, the verses of God that have been received by thee, as intoned by them who have drawn nigh unto Him, that the sweetness of thy melody may kindle thine own soul, and attract the hearts of all men. [85:295]
>
> We have commanded you to pray and fast from the beginning of maturity; this is ordained by God, your Lord and the Lord of your forefathers. [104:27]

In the long Obligatory Prayer, Bahá'u'lláh writes:

> I beseech Thee by them Who are the Day-Springs of Thine invisible Essence, the Most Exalted, the All-Glorious, to make of my prayer a fire that will burn away the veils which have shut me out from Thy beauty, and a light that will lead me unto the ocean of Thy Presence.... [132:317]

'Abdu'l-Bahá wrote:

> Thou spiritual friend! Thou hast asked the wisdom of prayer. Know thou that prayer is indispensable and obligatory, and man under no pretext whatsoever is excused from performing the prayer unless he be mentally unsound, or an insurmountable obstacle prevent him. The

> wisdom of prayer is this: That it causeth a connection between the servant and the True One, because in that state man with all heart and soul turneth his face towards His Highness the Almighty, seeking His association and desiring His love and compassion. The greatest happiness for a lover is to converse with his beloved, and the greatest gift for a seeker is to become familiar with the object of his longing; that is why with every soul who is attracted to the Kingdom of God, his greatest hope is to find an opportunity to entreat and supplicate before his Beloved, appeal for His mercy and grace and be immersed in the ocean of His utterance, goodness and generosity. Besides all this, prayer and fasting is the cause of awakening and mindfulness and conducive to protection and preservation from tests. [106:368]

> Shoghi Effendi wrote through his secretary:

> The daily prayers are to be said each one for himself, aloud or silent makes no difference. There is no congregational prayer except that for the dead. We read healing and other prayers in our meetings, but the daily prayer is a personal obligation, so someone else reading it is not quite the same thing as saying it for yourself. [104:59]

> The important thing that should always be borne in mind is that with the exception of certain specific obligatory prayers, Bahá'u'lláh has given us no strict or special rulings in matters of worship, whether in the Temple or elsewhere. Prayer is essentially a communion between man and God, and as such transcends all ritualistic forms and formulae. [104:78]

> For prayer is absolutely indispensable to their inner spiritual development, and this ... is the very foundation and purpose of the religion of God. [104:87]

Prayers are usually said in private though they are used during the 19-Day Feast and publicly at meetings, unity Feasts, Holy Days, special devotional meetings and at the Ma<u>sh</u>riqu'l-A<u>dh</u>kár. See **OBLIGATORY PRAYERS; INTERCESSION**.

PREJUDICE, ELIMINATION OF All forms of prejudice are condemned in the Bahá'í Writings. 'Abdu'l-Bahá said:

> His Holiness Bahá'u'lláh addressing all humanity, said that ... Inasmuch as your origin was one, you must now be united and agreed; you must consort with each other in joy and fragrance. He pronounced prejudice, whether re

ligious, racial, patriotic, political, the destroyer of the body-politic. He said that man must recognize the oneness of humanity, for all in origin belong to the same household and all are servants of the same God. [106:233]

Among the teachings of Bahá'u'lláh is, that religious, racial, political, economic and patriotic prejudices destroy the edifice of humanity. As long as these prejudices prevail, the world of humanity will not have rest. [106:286]

But there is need of a superior power to overcome human prejudices, a power which nothing in the world of mankind can withstand and which will overshadow the effect of all other forces at work in human conditions. That irresistible power is the love of God. [26:68]

Religion is a mighty stronghold, but that it must engender love, not malevolence and hate. Should it lead to malice, spite, and hate, it is of no value at all. For religion is a remedy, and if the remedy bring on disease, then put it aside. Again, as to religious, racial, national and political bias: all these prejudices strike at the very root of human life; one and all they beget bloodshed, and the ruination of the world. So long as these prejudices survive, there will be continuous and fearsome wars. [65:248]

Shoghi Effendi wrote:

The call of Bahá'u'lláh is primarily directed against all forms of provincialism, all insularities and prejudices. If long-cherished ideals and time-honored institutions, if certain social assumptions and religious formulae have ceased to promote the welfare of the generality of mankind, if they no longer minister to the needs of a continually evolving humanity, let them be swept away and relegated to the limbo of obsolescent and forgotten doctrines. [4:42]

PRIMAL POINT A title by which the Báb was known.

PRINCIPLES, BAHÁ'Í The basic principles enunciated by Bahá'u'lláh and enlarged upon by 'Abdu'l-Bahá during His visits to Europe and America were listed by Shoghi Effendi:

The independent search after truth, unfettered by superstition or tradition; the oneness of the entire human race, the pivotal principle and fundamental doctrine of the Faith; the basic unity of all religions; the condemnation of all forms of prejudice, whether religious, racial, class or

> national; the harmony which must exist between religion and science; the equality of men and women, the two wings on which the bird of human kind is able to soar; the introduction of compulsory education; the adoption of a universal auxiliary language; the abolition of the extremes of wealth and poverty; the institution of a world tribunal for the adjudication of disputes between nations; the exaltation of work, performed in the spirit of service, to the rank of worship; the glorification of justice as the ruling principle in human society, and of religion as a bulwark for the protection of all peoples and nations; the establishment of a permanent and universal peace as the supreme goal of all mankind... [5:281]

'Abdu'l-Bahá said in one of His talks in America in November 1912:

> Everyone who truly seeks and justly reflects will admit that the teachings of the present day emanating from mere human sources and authority are the cause of difficulty and disagreement amongst mankind, the very destroyers of humanity, whereas the teachings of Bahá'u'lláh are the very healing of the sick world, the remedy for every need and condition. In them may be found the realization of every desire and aspiration, the cause of the happiness of the world of humanity, the stimulus and illumination of mentality, the impulse for advancement and uplift, the basis of unity for all nations, the fountain source of love amongst mankind, the center of agreement, the means of peace and harmony, the one bond which will unite the East and the West. [26:440]

PRINTEZIS, NIKOLAS (1921-1984) An early (1960) Greek believer who served on the first (1977) National Spiritual Assembly of Greece. He was the first Bahá'í born in Greece to have his religion stated on his Greek registration card. [11:649]

PROGRESSIVE REVELATION A fundamental Bahá'í belief that Revelation from God is never final and that the Founders of the world's religions, the Manifestations of God (q.v.), have each revealed the laws and teachings of the one Creator according to the needs and conditions of the world of Their Day. Shoghi Effendi wrote:

> That Bahá'u'lláh should ... be regarded as essentially one of these Manifestations of God, never to be identified with that invisible Reality, the Essence of Divinity itself, is one of the major beliefs of our Faith—a belief which should never be obscured and the integrity of which no one of its

followers should allow to be compromised.... Nor does the Bahá'í Revelation ... attempt, under any circumstances, to invalidate those first and everlasting principles that animate and underlie the religions that have preceded it. The God-given authority, vested in each one of them, it admits and establishes as its firmest and ultimate basis. It regards them in no other light except as different stages in the eternal history and constant evolution of one religion, Divine and indivisible, of which it itself forms but an integral part. It neither seeks to obscure their Divine origin, nor to dwarf the admitted magnitude of their colossal achievements. It can countenance no attempt that seeks to distort their features or to stultify the truths which they instill. Its teachings do not deviate a hairbreadth from the verities they enshrine, nor does the weight of its message detract one jot or one tittle from the influence they exert or the loyalty they inspire.... It should also be borne in mind that, great as is the power manifested by this Revelation and however vast the range of the Dispensation its Author has inaugurated, it emphatically repudiates the claim to be regarded as the final revelation of God's will and purpose for mankind. To hold such a conception of its character and functions would be tantamount to a betrayal of its cause and a denial of its truth. It must necessarily conflict with the fundamental principle which constitutes the bedrock of Bahá'í belief, the principle that religious truth is not absolute but relative, that Divine Revelation is orderly, continuous and progressive and not spasmodic or final.... "To believe that all revelation is ended, that the portals of Divine mercy are closed, that from the daysprings of eternal holiness no sun shall rise again, that the ocean of everlasting bounty is forever stilled, and that out of the tabernacle of ancient glory the Messengers of God have ceased to be made manifest" must constitute in the eyes of every follower of the Faith a grave, an inexcusable departure from one of its most cherished and fundamental principles. [4:114] See **GOD, MANIFESTATION OF; REVELATION; PROMISED ONE OF ALL AGES.**

PROMISED ONE OF ALL AGES, THE This title has a double significance in Bahá'í Scripture. The Báb (q.v.) was the promised Qá'im of Shí'ih Islám; Bahá'u'lláh, was the Promised One of all religions as well as being more specifically the One promised by the Báb as "Him Who God shall make Manifest."

Under the first heading we have the statement made by Mullá Ḥusayn when recalling the first hours he had with the Báb when He made His Declaration:

> I felt possessed of such courage and power that were the world, all its peoples and its potentates, to rise against me, I would, alone and undaunted, withstand their onslaught. The universe seemed but a handful of dust in my grasp. I seemed to be the voice of Gabriel personified, calling unto all mankind: "Awake, for, lo! the morning Light has broken. Arise, for His Cause is made manifest. The portal of His grace is open wide; enter therein, O peoples of the world! For He Who is your promised One is come!" [5:6]

Off the wider significance Bahá'u'lláh Himself writes:

> Mighty, inconceivably mighty is this Day!... Every Prophet hath announced the coming of this Day, and every Messenger hath groaned in His yearning for this Revelation—a Revelation which, no sooner had it been revealed than all created things cried out saying, "The earth is God's, the Most Exalted, the Most Great!"
>
> The Day of the Promise is come, and He Who is the Promised One loudly proclaimeth before all who are in heaven and all who are on earth, "Verily there is none other God but He, the Help in Peril, the Self-Subsisting!" I swear by God! That which had been enshrined from eternity in the knowledge of God, the Knower of the seen and unseen, is revealed. Happy is the eye that seeth, and the face that turneth towards, the Countenance of God, the Lord of all being. Great indeed is this Day! The allusions made to it in all the sacred Scriptures as the Day of God attest its greatness. The soul of every Prophet of God, of every Divine Messenger, hath thirsted for this wondrous Day. All the divers kindreds of the earth have, likewise, yearned to attain it. [39:77f]
>
> Verily I say, this is the Day in which mankind can behold the Face, and hear the Voice, of the Promised One. The Call of God hath been raised, and the light of His countenance hath been lifted up upon men. It behoveth every man to blot out the trace of every idle word from the tablet of his heart, and to gaze, with an open and unbiased mind, on the signs of His Revelation, the proofs of His Mission, and the tokens of His glory. [85:10]

Shoghi Effendi, when writing on this theme, wrote of Bahá'u'lláh's letter to Pope Pius IX:

> It was to him who regarded himself as the Vicar of Christ that Bahá'u'lláh wrote that "the Word which the Son (Jesus) concealed is made manifest," that "it hath been sent down in the form of the human temple," that the Word was Himself, and He Himself the Father. It was to him who styling himself "the servant of the servants of God" that the Promised One of all ages, unveiling His station in its plenitude, announced that "He Who is the Lord of Lords is come overshadowed with clouds." It was he, who, claiming to be the successor of St. Peter, was reminded by Bahá'u'lláh that "this is the day whereon the Rock (Peter) crieth out and shouteth ... saying: 'Lo, the Father is come, and that which ye were promised in the Kingdom is fulfilled.'" It was he, the wearer of the triple crown, who later became the first prisoner of the Vatican, who was commanded by the Divine Prisoner of 'Akká to "leave his palaces unto such as desire them," to "sell all the embellished ornaments" he possessed, and to "expend them in the path of God," and to "abandon his kingdom unto the kings," and emerge from his habitation with his face "set towards the Kingdom." [44:52f] See **PROGRESSIVE REVELATION.**

PROSELYTIZING Bahá'ís are forbidden to proselytize: to attempt to convert someone on the basis of a threat (e.g., that they will suffer eternal damnation if they do not accept) or a promised reward (e.g., they will go to heaven and or be among the "saved"). Bahá'ís are enjoined to share their faith as if offering a gift to a king. Bahá'u'lláh wrote:

> Consort with all men, O people of Bahá, in a spirit of friendliness and fellowship. If ye be aware of a certain truth, if ye possess a jewel, of which others are deprived, share it with them in a language of utmost kindliness and good-will. If it be accepted, if it fulfill its purpose, your object is attained. If anyone should refuse it, leave him unto himself, and beseech God to guide him. Beware lest ye deal unkindly with him. A kindly tongue is the lodestone of the hearts of men. [70:15]

'Abdu'l-Bahá wrote:

> This activity (teaching) should be tempered with wisdom—not that wisdom which requireth one to be silent and forgetful of such an obligation, but rather that which

requireth one to display divine tolerance, love, kindness, patience, a goodly character, and holy deeds. [65:268]

Shoghi Effendi wrote:

Care, however, should, at all times, be exercised, lest in their eagerness to further the international interests of the Faith they frustrate their purpose, and turn away, through any act that might be misconstrued as an attempt to proselytize and bring undue pressure upon them, those whom they wish to win over to their Cause. [39:66]

See **TEACHING**.

PROSPERITY The Bahá'í International Community Statement for the 1995 World Summit for Social Development, Copenhagen, *The Prosperity of Humankind*,[94] deals in some depth with the Bahá'í approach to the issues that are far wider than merely increasing the material wealth of people. It may be summarized in the following excerpt:

[The] rising impulses for change must be seized upon and channeled into overcoming the remaining barriers that block realization of the age-old dream of global peace. The effort of will required for such a task cannot be summoned up merely by appeals for action against the countless ills afflicting society. It must be galvanized by a vision of human prosperity in the fullest sense of the term—an awakening to the possibilities of the spiritual and material well-being now brought within grasp. Its beneficiaries must be all of the planet's inhabitants, without distinction, without the imposition of conditions unrelated to the fundamental goals of such a reorganization of human affairs. [94:1]

PUBLISHING TRUSTS, BAHÁ'Í A substantial number of National Spiritual Assemblies have publishing houses whose main work is the publishing and distribution of Bahá'í Scripture, books about the Faith, biographies, history and even audio-visual materials.

PUREST BRANCH, THE See **MÍRZÁ MIHDÍ**.

Q

QÁḌÍ Muslim judge—civil, criminal, or ecclesiastic. [11:739]

QÁ'IM He Who Shall Arise: title designating the promised One of Islám. [11:739]

QALAM Pen. [11:739]

QALAM-I-ALÁ' The Pen of the Most High: a designation of Bahá'u'lláh. [11:740📖]

QAYYÚMU'L-ASMÁ The commentary on the Qur'ánic 'Súrih of Joseph, made by the Báb, the first chapter of which was made to Mullá Ḥusayn during the night of 22 May 1844 when He made His Declaration. Written in Arabic, comprising more than 9,300 verses, it was later translated in full into Persian by Ṭáhirih. See **BÁB; SÚRIH OF JOSEPH**.

QIBLIH The "Point of Adoration"—the place to which believers turn when in prayer. With the Christians it was Jerusalem; with Muslims it is Mecca and for Bahá'ís it is the Most Holy Shrine (of Bahá'u'lláh) at Bahjí, near 'Akká. [11:740📖]

QUDDÚS (Pure, Holy, Blessed [11:740📖]) (-1849) (Ḥájí Mullá Muḥammad-'Alí-i-Bárfurú<u>sh</u>í) The 18th Letter of the Living. He ranks next in lineage and in spiritual capacity to The Báb Himself. He was given the name Quddús by Bahá'u'lláh during the Conference of Bada<u>sh</u>t (q.v.). His father died while he was still in his teens, and he devoted himself then to the pursuit of learning becoming the outstanding pupil of Siyyid Káẓim in Karbilá. The Báb had intimated to Mullá Ḥusayn (q.v.) that on the day following His Declaration 18 holy souls (Letters of the Living [q.v.]) would arise unbidden and declare their belief in Him. A few days after Mullá Ḥusayn's meeting with the Báb on 23 May 1844 Quddús approached him saying to him (Mullá Ḥusayn), "Why do you seek to hide Him from me? I can recognise Him by His gait." [12:23f] In so doing he became the last of the Letters of the Living. He accompanied the Báb on pilgrimage to Mecca, he was later tortured and finally done to death in appalling circumstances. Shoghi Effendi spoke of him as follows:

> Quddús, immortalized by Him (Bahá'u'lláh) as Ismu'lláhi'l-Á<u>kh</u>ir (the Last Name of God); on whom Bahá'u'lláh's Tablet of Kullu'ṭ-Ṭa'ám later conferred the sublime appellation of Nuqṭiy-i-U<u>kh</u>rá (the Last Point); whom He elevated, in another Tablet, to a rank second to none except that of the Herald of His Revelation; whom He identifies, in still another Tablet, with one of the "Messengers charged with imposture" mentioned in the Qur'án; whom the Persian Bayán extolled as that fellow-pilgrim round whom mirrors to the number of eight Vaḥíds revolve; on whose "detachment and the sincerity of whose devotion to God's will God prideth Himself amidst the Concourse on high;" whom 'Abdu'l-Bahá designated as the "Moon of Guidance;" and whose appearance the Revelation of St. John the Divine anticipated as one of the

two "Witnesses" into whom, ere the "second woe is past," the "spirit of life from God" must enter—such a man had, in the full bloom of his youth, suffered, in the Sabzih-Maydán of Bárfurúsh, a death which even Jesus Christ, as attested by Bahá'u'lláh, had not faced in the hour of His greatest agony.[5:49f]

QUEEN MARIE OF ROMANIA, HRH See **MARIE, QUEEN.**

QURBÁN Sacrifice. [11:740]

QURRATU'L-AYN Literally Solace of the Eyes. (1) A title conferred upon Ṭáhirih (q.v.) by Siyyid Káẓim. (2) Term used by the Báb in the Qayyúmu'l-Asmá' to refer to both Bahá'u'lláh and Himself. [11:740]

R

RABBÁNÍ The Persian family name given to Shoghi Effendi by 'Abdu'l-Bahá so that he would not be confused with his cousins, as they were all of the family of the Báb—the Afnán. It was also used as a family name by Shoghi Effendi's brothers and sisters. See **SHOGHI EFFENDI.**

RABBÁNÍ, MADAME See **'AMATU'L-BAHÁ RÚḤÍYYIH KHÁNUM.**

RABB-I-A'LÁ Exalted Lord: one of the designations of the Báb. [11:740]

RACISM All forms of racism are condemned by Bahá'ís, as it is the antithesis of the most basic of Bahá'í teachings—the oneness of mankind. It was particularly addressed by 'Abdu'l-Bahá when He was in America. At one meeting He said:

> Today I am most happy, for I see here a gathering of the servants of God. I see the white and colored people together. In the estimation of God there is no distinction of color; all are one in the color and beauty of servitude to Him. Color is not important; the heart is all-important. It matters not what the exterior may be if the heart be pure and white within. God does not behold differences of hue and complexion; He looks at the hearts. He whose morals and virtues are praiseworthy is preferred in the presence of God; he who is devoted to the Kingdom is most beloved. In the realm of genesis and creation the question of color is of least importance. [107:34]

Shoghi Effendi wrote:

> To discriminate against any race, on the ground of its being socially backward, politically immature, and numeri

cally in a minority, is a flagrant violation of the spirit that animates the Faith of Bahá'u'lláh ... "God," 'Abdu'l-Bahá Himself declares, "maketh no distinction between the white and the black. If the hearts are pure both are acceptable unto Him. God is no respecter of persons on account of either color or race. All colors are acceptable unto Him, be they white, black, or yellow. Inasmuch as all were created in the image of God, we must bring ourselves to realize that all embody divine possibilities." [39:35,37]

The theories and policies, so unsound, so pernicious, which deify the state and exalt the nation above mankind, which seek to subordinate the sister races of the world to one single race, which discriminate between the black and the white, and which tolerate the dominance of one privileged class over all others—these are the dark, the false, and crooked doctrines for which any man or people who believes in them, or acts upon them, must, sooner or later, incur the wrath and chastisement of God. [44:113]

RAFÍ'Í, SHÁYISTIH (1907-1992) (Knight of Bahá'u'lláh) An Íránian believer who pioneered with her family to Morocco for which service they were designated Knights of Bahá'u'lláh. [57:275]

RAFSANJÁNÍ, 'ALÍ AKBAR RAFÍ'Í (1882-1965) (Knight of Bahá'u'lláh) An Íránian believer who pioneered with his family to Tangiers, Morocco, for which service he was designated a Knight of Bahá'u'lláh. [50:318]

RA'ÍS President, head, leader. [11:740📖]

RANDALL, WILLIAM (Harry) (-1929) (Disciple of 'Abdu'l-Bahá) One of the early Bahá'ís of America, known as a most eloquent upholder of the Faith. He and his wife and daughter visited 'Abdu'l-Bahá in Haifa among the groups of pilgrims that began to arrive in the Holy Land immediately following WW I. On his passing in February 1929 the Guardian wrote, "I wish to refer ... to the sad and untimely death of our dearly beloved and highly distinguished brother and fellow-worker, Mr. Harry Randall. The unsparing efforts which he exerted for the promotion of the Faith, the passionate eloquence with which he diffused its teachings, the mature judgment and ripe experience he contributed to its councils ... and above all his upright and generous character, are traits that will long live after him, and which bodily separation can never remove..." [4]

RANDRIANARIVO, DANIEL (1924-1985) The first Malagasy (Madagascar) to embrace the Cause (1954), he served on the first (1955) local Spiritual Assembly of Tananarive. [11:669]

RANSOM-KEHLER, KEITH (1878-1933) (Martyr) (Hand of the Cause of God) She was born in America in 1878 and died suddenly of smallpox in Iṣfáhán, Persia on 23 October 1933, thereby becoming America's first Bahá'í martyr and first Hand of the Cause of God. After traveling for the Faith for two years in China, Japan, Australia and India she visited Haifa in mid-1932 where Shoghi Effendi chose her to take on a most important mission—he asked her to go to Persia to make personal representations to His Majesty Reza Sháh Pahlaví on behalf of the persecuted Bahá'ís of that land. She carried impeccable credentials from the National Spiritual Assembly of the Bahá'ís of the United States and Canada, and her purpose was to ask for permission for Bahá'í books and magazines published in the West to be released to their fellow Bahá'ís in Persia. On 20 August 1932 she cabled: "Mission successful." The Court Minister in Ṭihrán was cabled a message of gratitude, and a press release was issued in America. Keith received a tremendous welcome from Bahá'í communities throughout Persia, but it soon became obvious that changes had been made in the office of the Court Minister, and Keith had to start again. In spite of most moving appeals written to His Majesty and powerful letters to every cabinet minister and the president of parliament, it soon became apparent that the Sháh himself never received any communication. In the meantime the American National Spiritual Assembly was making similar representations through diplomatic channels, but without success. From her correspondence with her friends in the West, it was becoming obvious that Keith, with her intensive work-load of letter writing, interviewing of officials, and traveling to meet with Bahá'í communities, was suffering from frustration with the authorities. Exhausted from her journeys and her constant battle against ill-health, she fell victim to smallpox and died within a few hours during a visit to the Bahá'ís of Iṣfáhán.

The American press reported in detail the news of her death, and the following extract from the *New York American* of 28 October 1933 illustrates the depth of the coverage:

> In August, 1932 Mrs. Ransom-Kehler ... went to Persia on a special mission to represent the American Bahá'ís in appealing to the Shah's government for removal of the ban on entry of Bahá'í literature into the country of the origin of the world religion established by Bahá'u'lláh nearly seventy years ago. From the Court Minister, Mrs. Keith Ransom-Kehler received assurance that the prohibition, passed under the former regime while the Muhammedan clergy were at the height of their power, would be rescinded. This promise, was, however, unful

filled and Mrs. Ransom-Kehler devoted the remaining months of her life to the task of penetrating the imperial entourage and presenting to the Shah in person a formal petition prepared by the American Bahá'í Assembly on behalf of the sixty Bahá'í communities of the United States and Canada."

The following message from Shoghi Effendi to the Bahá'í world, dated October 30, remains the most poignant testimonial to Keith's supreme service to her Faith:

> Keith's precious life offered up in sacrifice to beloved Cause in Bahá'u'lláh's native land. On Persian soil, for Persia's sake, she encountered, challenged and fought the forces of darkness with high distinction, indomitable will, unswerving, exemplary loyalty. The mass of her helpless Persian brethren mourns the sudden loss of their valiant emancipator. American believers grateful and proud of the memory of their first and distinguished martyr. Sorrow stricken, I lament my earthly separation from an invaluable collaborator, an unfailing counsellor, an esteemed and faithful friend. I urge Local Assemblies befittingly to organize memorial gatherings in memory of one whose international services entitled her to an eminent rank among the Hands of the Cause of Bahá'u'lláh. [40:473-4][17:389]

RAWḤÁNÍ, SHÁPÚR ISFANDÍYÁR (1931-1985) (Knight of Bahá'u'lláh) An Indian believer (of Íránian parentage) he pioneered in 1954 to Bhutan for which service he was designated a Knight of Bahá'u'lláh. [11:689]

RAYNOR, ALLAN (1910-1979) A Canadian believer (1945), he was twice a member of the National Spiritual Assembly of Canada (1954-1960; 1963-1964) and a member of the first local Spiritual Assembly of North York. He was renowned for his knowledge of the "Covenant" and traveled widely throughout Canada "deepening" the believers in this crucial aspect of Bahá'í life. In 1971 he served as the first member of the Legal Affairs Department of the National Spiritual Assembly of Canada. [2:693][60:485]

RECTITUDE OF CONDUCT Shoghi Effendi wrote:

> A rectitude of conduct, an abiding sense of undeviating justice, unobscured by the demoralizing influences which a corruption-ridden political life so strikingly manifests; a chaste, pure, and holy life, unsullied and unclouded by the indecencies, the vices, the false standards, which an inherently deficient moral code tolerates, perpetuates,

> and fosters; a fraternity freed from that cancerous growth of racial prejudice, which is eating into the vitals of an already debilitated society—these are the ideals which the ... believers must, from now on, individually and through concerted action, strive to promote, in both their private and public lives, ideals which are the chief propelling forces that can most effectively accelerate the march of their institutions, plans, and enterprises, that can guard the honor and integrity of their Faith.... This rectitude of conduct, with its implications of justice, equity, truthfulness, honesty, fair-mindedness, reliability, and trustworthiness, must distinguish every phase of the life of the Bahá'í community.... Such a rectitude of conduct must manifest itself, with ever-increasing potency, in every verdict which the elected representatives of the Bahá'í community, in whatever capacity they may find themselves, may be called upon to pronounce. It must be constantly reflected in the business dealings of all its members, in their domestic lives, in all manner of employment, and in any service they may, in the future, render their government or people. [39:23,26]

RELIGION There are many facets of "religion" that are treated in depth in Bahá'í Writings. They embrace the origin of religion and its purpose, for the individual and for society and emphasize its rôle in personal spiritual development and in peace and order among people. Some of these facets may be gleaned from the following quotations. From Bahá'u'lláh:

> The purpose of religion as revealed from the heaven of God's holy Will is to establish unity and concord amongst the peoples of the world; make it not the cause of dissension and strife. The religion of God and His divine law are the most potent instruments and the surest of all means for the dawning of the light of unity amongst men. The progress of the world, the development of nations, the tranquillity of peoples, and the peace of all who dwell on earth are among the principles and ordinances of God. Religion bestoweth upon man the most precious of all gifts, offereth the cup of prosperity, imparteth eternal life, and showereth imperishable benefits upon mankind. It behoveth the chiefs and rulers of the world, and in particular the Trustees of God's House of Justice, to endeavor to the utmost of their power to safeguard its position, promote its interests and exalt its station in the eyes of the world. [77:129]

In truth, religion is a radiant light and an impregnable stronghold for the protection and welfare of the peoples of the world, for the fear of God impelleth man to hold fast to that which is good, and shun all evil. Should the lamp of religion be obscured, chaos and confusion will ensue, and the lights of fairness and justice, of tranquillity and peace cease to shine. [77:125]

Religion is, verily, the chief instrument for the establishment of order in the world, and of tranquillity amongst its peoples. The weakening of the pillars of religion hath strengthened the foolish, and emboldened them, and made them more arrogant. Verily I say: The greater the decline of religion, the more grievous the waywardness of the ungodly. This cannot but lead in the end to chaos and confusion. [70:28]

From 'Abdu'l-Bahá:

We should earnestly seek and thoroughly investigate realities, recognizing that the purpose of the religion of God is the education of humanity and the unity and fellowship of mankind. Furthermore, we will establish the point that the foundations of the religions of God are one foundation. This foundation is not multiple, for it is reality itself. Reality does not admit of multiplicity, although each of the divine religions is separable into two divisions. One concerns the world of morality and the ethical training of human nature. It is directed to the advancement of the world of humanity in general; it reveals and inculcates the knowledge of God and makes possible the discovery of the verities of life. This is ideal and spiritual teaching, the essential quality of divine religion, and not subject to change or transformation. It is the one foundation of all the religions of God. Therefore, the religions are essentially one and the same. The second classification or division comprises social laws and regulations applicable to human conduct. This is not the essential spiritual quality of religion. It is subject to change and transformation according to the exigencies and requirements of time and place. [26:364]

The essential purpose of the religion of God is to establish unity among mankind. The divine Manifestations were Founders of the means of fellowship and love. [26:202]

Religion must be conducive to love and unity among mankind; for if it be the cause of enmity and strife, the absence of religion is preferable. [26:128]

Religion must be the source of unity and fellowship in the world. If it is productive of enmity, hatred and bigotry, the absence of religion would be preferable. [26:434]

If it is the cause of discord and hostility, if it leads to separation and creates conflict, the absence of religion would be preferable in the world. [26:454]

Religion, moreover, is not a series of beliefs, a set of customs; religion is the teachings of the Lord God, teachings which constitute the very life of humankind, which urge high thoughts upon the mind, refine the character, and lay the groundwork for man's everlasting honor. [65:52]

REMEY, CHARLES MASON (1874-1974) (Covenant Breaker) One of the earliest American believers, he was born on 15 May 1874 in Burlington, Vermont. A well-known architect by profession, he accepted the Faith in Paris on 31 December 1899.

He received much love and praise from both 'Abdu'l-Bahá and Shoghi Effendi and gave sterling service to the Faith in the United States, and in Hawaii, and made teaching visits to several countries including Japan. In November 1950, the Guardian appointed him to the newly formed Bahá'í International Council and called him to live in Haifa. He was elevated to the rank of Hand of the Cause of God (q.v.) in the first contingent in December 1951 and then as President of the Bahá'í International Council. He was among the Hands of the Cause present at all the 1953 Intercontinental Conferences, being the Guardian's representative at the one in New Delhi. He was also appointed to represent the Guardian at the Conference in Sydney, Australia in March 1958 and was present at the Conference in Wilmette in May of that year. Under the close guidance of the Guardian Mason Remey designed the Bahá'í Houses of Worship for Kampala, Uganda, and Sydney, Australia. In spite of all these distinguished services he lost the respect of the whole Bahá'í world and will be remembered in Bahá'í history as one who fell from the highest rank to a pitiful soul, shunned by all but a handful of his one-time fellow believers when he claimed to be the second Guardian, and thereby relinquished his right to be regarded as a Hand of the Cause of God. He was declared a Covenant Breaker (q.v.) on 26 July 1960. About 15 Bahá'ís initially followed Remey and were themselves declared Covenant Breakers, but Remey himself died alone and isolated in his old age and was buried by his young secretary who was not a

Bahá'í. Like any branch cut off from its root, the Remey incident withered away. He was 100 years old at his death. A day after his passing on 4 February 1974, the Universal House of Justice noted the occasion with the following cablegram: "Charles Mason Remey Whose Arrogant Attempt Usurp Guardianship After Passing Shoghi Effendi Led To His Expulsion From Ranks Faithful Has Died In Florence Italy In Hundredth Year Of His Life Without Religious Rite Abandoned By Erstwhile Followers." See **BAHÁ'U'LLÁH, COVENANT OF; COVENANT BREAKERS.**

RESURRECTION Bahá'ís believe in the spiritual rather than the physical significance of resurrection. It may refer to the return of qualities or characteristics as when a perfect rose again blossoms on the bush that produced one on the previous season. It may also refer to the appearance of a Manifestation of God. These two instances may apply to the resurrection of the dead on the Day of Judgment.

Bahá'u'lláh wrote: "This is the Day that hath been illumined by the effulgent light of the Countenance of God—the Day when the Tongue of Grandeur is calling aloud: The Kingdom is God's, the Lord of the Day of Resurrection." [77:253]

Referring to the resurrection of Christ 'Abdu'l-Bahá explained:

> The meaning of Christ's resurrection is as follows: the disciples were troubled and agitated after the martyrdom of Christ. The Reality of Christ, which signifies His teachings, His bounties, His perfections and His spiritual power, was hidden and concealed for two or three days after His martyrdom, and was not resplendent and manifest. No, rather it was lost, for the believers were few in number and were troubled and agitated. The Cause of Christ was like a lifeless body; and when after three days the disciples became assured and steadfast, and began to serve the Cause of Christ, and resolved to spread the divine teachings, putting His counsels into practice, and arising to serve Him, the Reality of Christ became resplendent and His bounty appeared; His religion found life; His teachings and His admonitions became evident and visible. In other words, the Cause of Christ was like a lifeless body until the life and the bounty of the Holy Spirit surrounded it. [56:104]

Emphasizing the spiritual meanings of miracles in general 'Abdu'l-Bahá said:

> The outward miracles have no importance for the people of Reality. If a blind man receives sight, for example, he will finally again become sightless, for he will die and be

deprived of all his senses and powers. Therefore, causing the blind man to see is comparatively of little importance, for this faculty of sight will at last disappear. If the body of a dead person be resuscitated, of what use is it since the body will die again? But it is important to give perception and eternal life—that is, the spiritual and divine life. For this physical life is not immortal, and its existence is equivalent to non-existence. So it is that Christ said to one of His disciples: "Let the dead bury their dead;" for "That which is born of the flesh is flesh; and that which is born of the Spirit is spirit." Observe: those who in appearance were physically alive, Christ considered dead; for life is the eternal life, and existence is the real existence. Wherever in the Holy Books they speak of raising the dead, the meaning is that the dead were blessed by eternal life; where it is said that the blind received sight, the signification is that he obtained the true perception; where it is said a deaf man received hearing, the meaning is that he acquired spiritual and heavenly hearing. [56:101]

REVELATION Bahá'ís believe that the way by which the Founders of the World Religions have conveyed the Word of God to mankind has been by means of revelation. Shoghi Effendi writes at length of Bahá'u'lláh's experience:

"One night in a dream," He Himself, calling to mind, in the evening of His life, the first stirrings of God's Revelation within His soul, has written, "these exalted words were heard on every side: 'Verily, We shall render Thee victorious by Thyself and by Thy pen. Grieve Thou not for that which hath befallen Thee, neither be Thou afraid, for Thou art in safety. Ere long will God raise up the treasures of the earth—men who will aid Thee through Thyself and through Thy Name, wherewith God hath revived the hearts of such as have recognized Him.'"In another passage He describes, briefly and graphically, the impact of the onrushing force of the Divine Summons upon His entire being. "During the days I lay in the prison of Ṭihrán," are His own memorable words, "though the galling weight of the chains and the stench-filled air allowed Me but little sleep, still in those infrequent moments of slumber I felt as if something flowed from the crown of My head over My breast, even as a mighty torrent that precipitateth itself upon the earth from the summit of a lofty mountain. Every limb of My body would, as a result, be set afire. At such moments My tongue recited what no man could bear to hear." In His Epistle to Náṣiri'd-Dín

Sháh ... occur these passages which shed further light on the Divine origin of His mission: "O King! I was but a man like others, asleep upon My couch, when lo, the breezes of the All-Glorious were wafted over Me, and taught Me the knowledge of all that hath been. This thing is not from Me, but from One Who is Almighty and All-Knowing. And he bade Me lift up My voice between earth and heaven, and for this there befell Me what hath caused the tears of every man of understanding to flow ... This is but a leaf which the winds of the will of Thy Lord, the Almighty, the All-Praised, have stirred ... His all-compelling summons hath reached Me, and caused Me to speak His praise amidst all people. I was indeed as one dead when His behest was uttered. The hand of the will of Thy Lord, the Compassionate, the Merciful, transformed Me." "By My Life!" He asserts in another Tablet, "Not of Mine own volition have I revealed Myself, but God, of His own choosing, hath manifested Me." And again: "Whenever I chose to hold My peace and be still, lo, the Voice of the Holy Spirit, standing on My right hand, aroused Me, and the Most Great Spirit appeared before My face, and Gabriel overshadowed Me, and the Spirit of Glory stirred within My bosom, bidding Me arise and break My silence."[5:101]

See **BAHÁ'U'LLÁH; GOD, MANIFESTATION OF; PROGRESSIVE REVELATION.**

REVELATION, BIRTH OF BAHÁ'Í See **SIYÁH-CHÁL.**

REVELL, ETHEL COWAN (1897-1984) She was only 10 years old when she embraced the Cause after hearing of it from Annie McKinley (her mother's sister) at the same time as her mother (Mary Revell [q.v.]) and older sister Jessie Revell (q.v.). She met 'Abdu'l-Bahá when He visited America and received a number of Tablets from Him. In 1936 she, along with her sister, bought a car to allow them better "teaching" access to neighboring towns and villages. On 14 November 1950 Shoghi Effendi cabled the American National Spiritual Assembly as follows: "Appreciate extend financial assistance Revell sisters come Haifa require their services." On 22 November he sent a second cable to Ethel and her sister: "Welcome your presence Haifa." On 2 March 1951 he cabled the Bahá'í world to advise them of the formation of the International Bahá'í Council and the membership thereof: both Ethel and Jessie were among those named. Ethel served in the household of Shoghi Effendi and 'Amatu'l-Bahá Rúḥíyyih Khánum as well as acting as "guide" to the many pilgrim groups that visited in the years after her arrival. She continued to serve almost to the very end of her long life. [11:627]

REVELL, JESSIE (1891-1966) An early (1906) American believer she met 'Abdu'l-Bahá in Philadelphia and New York in 1912. In 1921 she received permission to visit 'Abdu'l-Bahá in 'Akká. Sadly, 'Abdu'l-Bahá passed away before she could make the trip. In 1951 she and her sister, Ethel Revell (q.v.), were asked by Shoghi Effendi to move to Haifa to assist him in his work. She was appointed by Shoghi Effendi to membership of the first International Bahá'í Council (on which body she served as Treasurer and continued to serve when it became an elected position). On the passing of Shoghi Effendi she served as a companion to 'Amatu'l-Bahá Rúḥíyyih Kh̲ánum both at home and during her travels. [50:300]

REVELL, MARY J. (1859-1943) An early American believer, she hosted 'Abdu'l-Bahá on several occasions during His visit to the United States and was later addressed by Him as "Thou Ensign of Peace and Salvation." She was the mother of Ethel and Jessie Revell. (qq.v).[45:602]

RHEIN, OTTILIE (1903-1979) (Knight of Bahá'u'lláh) An American believer (1941) of German birth, she pioneered to Mauritius in 1953 for which service she was designated a Knight of Bahá'u'lláh. She enrolled the first believer (Mr. Him Lin) within a few months, and in 1956, when her visa expired, there were 40 Bahá'ís on the island: enough to form three local Spiritual Assemblies. [2:704]

RIḌVÁN The 12-day Festival that commemorates the days spent by Bahá'u'lláh in the Najíbíyyih garden preparing for His exile from Bag̲h̲dád to Constantinople in 1863 and during which time He announced that He was the "Promised One of all ages."(q.v.). Shoghi Effendi described the event as follows:

> The arrival of Bahá'u'lláh in the Najíbíyyih Garden, subsequently designated by His followers the Garden of Riḍván, signalizes the commencement of what has come to be recognized as the holiest and most significant of all Bahá'í festivals, the festival commemorating the Declaration of His Mission to His companions.... As to the significance of that Declaration let Bahá'u'lláh Himself reveal to us its import. Acclaiming that historic occasion as the "Most Great Festival," the "King of Festivals," the "Festival of God," He has, in His Kitáb-i-Aqdas, characterized it as the Day whereon "all created things were immersed in the sea of purification," whilst in one of His specific Tablets, He has referred to it as the Day whereon "the breezes of forgiveness were wafted over the entire creation." "Rejoice, with exceeding gladness, O people of Bahá!," He, in another Tablet, has written, "as ye call to

remembrance the Day of supreme felicity, the Day whereon the Tongue of the Ancient of Days hath spoken, as He departed from His House proceeding to the Spot from which He shed upon the whole of creation the splendors of His Name, the All-Merciful." And again: "The Divine Springtime is come, O Most Exalted Pen, for the Festival of the All-Merciful is fast approaching.... The Day-Star of Blissfulness shineth above the horizon of Our Name, the Blissful, inasmuch as the Kingdom of the Name of God hath been adorned with the ornament of the Name of Thy Lord, the Creator of the heavens.... This is the Day whereon the unseen world crieth out: 'Great is thy blessedness, O earth, for thou hast been made the footstool of thy God, and been chosen as the seat of His mighty throne' ... Say ... He it is Who hath laid bare before you the hidden and treasured Gem, were ye to seek it. He it is who is the One Beloved of all things, whether of the past or of the future." [5:151,153]

The First, Ninth and 12th Days are three of the nine Holy Days when work is suspended. On the First Day of Riḍván all elections for local Spiritual Assemblies take place, while during the remaining 11 days all the National Spiritual Assemblies are elected, and once in five years the election for the Universal House of Justice takes place.

RIḌVÁN, GARDEN OF (NA'MAYN) A garden near the walls of 'Akká, Israel, first rented in 1875 and then purchased in 'Abdu'l-Bahá's name for Bahá'u'lláh. It became a favorite retreat for Him. He, Himself described it: "One day of days We repaired unto Our Green Island. Upon Our arrival, We beheld its streams flowing, and its trees luxuriant, and the sunlight playing in their midst. Turning Our face to the right, We beheld what the pen is powerless to describe; nor can it set forth that which the eye of the Lord of Mankind witnessed in that most sanctified, that most sublime, that blest, and most exalted Spot." [70:136]

RICE, EMMA MANDELL (1898-1985) (Knight of Bahá'u'lláh) An American believer (1942) who pioneered in 1953 to Sicily for which service she was designated a Knight of Bahá'u'lláh. [11:677]

RICHARDSON, DORIS (1901-1976) (Knight of Bahá'u'lláh) An early (1939) Canadian believer who pioneered to Grand Manan Island in 1953 for which service she was designated a Knight of Bahá'u'lláh. She was a member of the first local Spiritual Assembly of Scarborough, Ontario, and in 1948 she was elected to the first National Spiritual Assembly of Canada. [53:411]

RITUAL In general, ritual is minimized in the Bahá'í Faith. The teachings are summarized by the Universal House of Justice:

> Concerning rituals, the beloved Guardian's secretary wrote on his behalf to an individual believer on 24 June 1949: "Bahá'u'lláh has reduced all ritual and form to an absolute minimum in His Faith. The few forms that there are—like those associated with the two longer obligatory daily prayers, are only symbols of the inner attitude. There is a wisdom in them, and a great blessing but we cannot force ourselves to understand or feel these things, that is why He gave us also the very short and simple prayer, for those who did not feel the desire to perform the acts associated with the other two." Thus it can be seen that the Faith has certain simple rites prescribed by Bahá'u'lláh, such as the obligatory prayers, the marriage ceremony and the laws for the burial of the dead, but its teachings warn against developing them into a system of uniform and rigid rituals incorporating man-made forms of practices, such as exists in other religions where rituals usually consist of elaborate ceremonial practices performed by a member of the clergy. In another letter written on behalf of the Guardian his secretary stated: "In these days the friends should, as much as possible, demonstrate through their deeds the independence of the Holy Faith of God, and its freedom from the customs, rituals and practices of a discredited and abrogated past." [86:476]

ROBARTS, JOHN ALDHAM (1901-1991) (Hand of the Cause of God) He was born on 2 November 1901 in Waterloo, Ontario, Canada. He was for many years member of the National Spiritual Assembly of the Bahá'ís of Canada, often as its Chairman. In 1950 he accepted an invitation from the British National Teaching Committee to undertake an intensive teaching trip to the British Isles where he witnessed the acceptance of many new Bahá'ís—thereby playing a significant rôle in the victories achieved in the British first Six Year Plan.

He was elevated to the rank of Hand of the Cause in the last contingent, October 1957.

He pioneered from Canada to South Africa in 1953 and, along with his wife Audrey, became a Knight of Bahá'u'lláh for Bechuanaland when he moved there in February 1954. He was among the first to be appointed as an Auxiliary Board Member for Hand of the Cause Músá Banání (q.v.). He participated in the Intercontinental Conferences in Kampala, Chicago and Frankfurt in 1958 and in January and July 1960 visited almost all the Bahá'í centers then extant in the Dominion of Canada. Throughout the years 1959 to 1966 he traveled extensively in Africa, Europe, the United States, Canada and Alaska before returning to Canada where he settled in Rawdon, Québec.

In 1971 he represented the Universal House of Justice at the North Atlantic Oceanic Conference in Reykjavik, Iceland. During the ensuing years he carried on his travels to many parts of the world and attended conferences and conventions, including the International Conventions in Haifa every five years. Following the 1973 Haifa Convention he flew to Kenya and London and attended the annual conventions of the United Kingdom and Canada. He attended many summer schools and conferences in Canada and the United States. In 1976 he attended the International Teaching Conferences in Anchorage, Paris and Nairobi; after which he undertook assignments in Southern and East Africa. In 1978 he visited the American South followed a year later by a visit to Mexico.

At an exceptionally large convention in the United States in April 1979 he joined forces with Hands of the Cause William Sears and Dhikru'lláh Khádem (q.v.) in inspiring more than 1,800 Bahá'ís. From there he traveled on in September to Italy. In 1980 he attended the first International Conference of the Canadian Association for Bahá'í Studies. Glowing reports of his teaching activities in various parts of Canada during 1980 were followed by visits to the United Kingdom and South Africa in 1981. In 1982 he represented the Universal House of Justice at an International Teaching Conference in Lagos, Nigeria and at International Conferences in Dublin, Ireland and Montréal, Canada. In the following year he attended the dedication of land for a Bahá'í House in Yukon and visited North American Indian areas. Two years later he attended the actual dedication of the Yukon House. He was adopted as an elder into the Johns clan of the Tlingit people with the name of "Gooch Ooxu" (Wolf Teeth.)

Suffering from rapidly deteriorating health, he nevertheless made a final international trip to 11 cities in Ireland, in 1986; attended a conference in Montréal in 1987 and the Canadian National Convention in 1989—his last public appearance. He passed away quietly in June 1991. On 19 June the Universal House of Justice cabled:

> With saddened hearts announce passing much-loved staunch promoter Faith, Knight Bahá'u'lláh, Hand Cause God, John Robarts. His distinguished administrative teaching pioneering activities in his native Canada, in Africa and Europe, during ministry beloved Guardian and subsequently on world scale through his international travels were source abundant inspiration countless

friends many lands. His reliance and emphasis on prayer in all efforts promotion Cause and his sustained service path love for Blessed Beauty were characterised by spirit certitude, self-effacement and vigour which set a standard of stewardship that has enriched annals Faith. He has assuredly earned bountiful reward Abhá Kingdom. Praying Holy Shrines progress his radiant soul. Advise hold befitting memorial gatherings in his honour throughout world including all Houses Worship. (Unpublished letter.)

ROBERTS, CHARLEY (-1969) The first Athabascan Indian north of the Arctic Circle to embrace the Cause, he taught widely among Indian peoples throughout the north. [51:454][60:487]

ROBOMAN, ANDREW (-1992) A Chief of the Council of Chiefs, Yap Island, Micronesia, he embraced the Cause in 1970. [57:275]

RODRIGUES, JOSÉ C. XAVIER (1931-1985) (Knight of Bahá'u'lláh) In September 1953 he pioneered, along with his wife (Hilda), to Bissau, Portuguese Guinea for which service they were designated Knights of Bahá'u'lláh. In 1955 they were forced to leave and returned to Portugal. In 1956 they pioneered to Luanda, Angola, where they helped form the first local Spiritual Assembly of that town. They returned to Amadora, Portugal, in 1960 and Xavier served on the first National Spiritual Assembly of Portugal when it formed in 1961. [11:686]

ROOT, MARTHA L. (1872-1939) (Hand of the Cause of God) She was born in Richwood, Ohio on 10 August 1872. During her youth she studied traditional classical subjects: Latin, Greek, French and German, English literature, psychology, mathematics and the Bible. After starting her professional career as a teacher, school administrator and lecturer, she began writing, and in 1900 her future as a newspaper reporter really commenced with an editorship followed by the first of her travels—to France as an automobile magazine editor in 1902. She was introduced to the Bahá'í Faith by Roy C. Wilhelm (q.v.) in 1908 and embraced it in early 1909. Another of Martha's mentors was the first American Bahá'í, Thornton Chase (q.v.).

Her first newspaper article on the Faith appeared in the *Pittsburgh Post* on 26 September 1909. She obtained several hundred copies and mailed them to people all around the world, including many to her new Bahá'í friends to be used for local publicity.

Her dedication to her Faith was confirmed during the visit of 'Abdu'l-Bahá to the United States in 1912 when Martha attended as many meetings as possible including two private interviews. A high point in her life was a picnic for 'Abdu'l-Bahá at the home of the Wilhelms, West Englewood, New Jersey on 29 June.

At the age of 40 she embarked on a new career. She had long wanted to travel to other lands to spread the Faith, and the first of her round-the-world trips began on 30 January 1915—a feat that she accomplished four times, with extensive stays in China and Japan—four visits; and India—three visits. These tours included every major city in South America; 26 States in America; Canada; Europe; Asia; Middle East; Africa; Australia and Central America.

By 1912, Martha was eagerly studying Esperanto and later used it extensively during her travels. She addressed many audiences in and helped in the translation of Bahá'í literature into that language. She attended some 12 international Esperanto Congresses and even taught for a while in an Esperanto school in China. In his history of the first Bahá'í century, *God Passes By*, Shoghi Effendi wrote of Martha,

> Not only through her preponderating share in initiating measures for the translation and dissemination of Bahá'í literature, but above all through her prodigious and indeed unique exertions in the international teaching field, has covered herself with a glory that has not only eclipsed the achievements of the teachers of the Faith among her contemporaries the globe around but has outshone the feats accomplished by any of its propagators in the course of the entire century. To Martha Root, that archetype of Bahá'í itinerant teachers and the foremost Hand Raised by Bahá'u'lláh since 'Abdu'l-Bahá's passing, must be awarded, if her manifold services and the supreme act of her life are to be correctly appraised, the title of Leading Ambassadress of His Faith and Pride of Bahá'í teachers, whether men or women, in both the East and the West. [5:386f]

> [She] transmitted the message of the New Day to kings, queens, princes and princesses, presidents of republics, ministers and statesmen, publicists, professors, clergymen and poets, as well as a vast number of people in various walks of life, and contacted, both officially and informally, religious congresses, peace societies, Esperanto associations, socialist congresses, Theosophical societies, women's clubs and other kindred organizations. [5:387f]

Her eight successive audiences with Queen Marie of Romania resulted in the Queen embracing the Cause.

After an accident to her back in her youth she suffered its effects throughout her life. As she traveled around the world, the pain it caused her increased and, as was subsequently diagnosed not long before her death, she gradually succumbed to a cancer that had first manifested itself in 1912 and that had, over many years caused her excruciating pain in her back, legs and neck.

After an intensive 15-month teaching tour in India she set sail on 29 December 1938 for Australia and New Zealand where, during the course of 40 lectures and several broadcasts in Sydney in four weeks, she had a minor heart attack. She continued with her intensive teaching schedule and sailed from New Zealand for San Francisco at the end of May 1939 and reached Honolulu on 7 June, in such pain that she could not address the many friends who had gathered to greet her. She had to go to the hospital and on 28 September 1939 gently, peacefully and finally out of pain, passed away. The Guardian of the Faith cabled:

> Martha's unnumbered admirers throughout Bahá'í world lament with me earthly extinction her heroic life. Concourse on high acclaim her elevation rightful position galaxy Bahá'í immortals.... Advise hold befitting memorial gathering Temple honor one whose acts shed imperishable lustre American Bahá'í community.[112:29][42:643][60:491][32][33]

ROSENBERG, ETHEL JENNER (1858-1930) One of the pioneers of the Cause in the Western world. She was born in Bath, England, on 6 August 1858 and became a Bahá'í in mid-1899. She was well known in the London art world as a prolific and accomplished miniature portrait painter and was much in demand in social circles. One of these ladies, Mrs. Thornburgh-Cropper (q.v.), the first Bahá'í in England, introduced her to the Bahá'í Faith. Over the coming years she devoted ever increasing time to its promotion. She went on pilgrimage in 1901, staying in the Holy Land for four months and then traveling to America with Mírzá Abu'l-Faḍl-i-Gulpáygání. In all, she made three visits to the United States and visited Paris frequently (during one such visit she taught the Faith to Lady Blomfield [q.v.]), meeting with the small but growing French community, and working with Mrs. Thornburgh-Cropper. She accompanied Laura Clifford Barney to 'Akká for eight months in 1904 and during that time assisted in the compilation of *Some Answered Questions* (q.v.). She was a gifted lecturer and wrote several pieces of introductory literature. She met 'Abdu'l-Bahá when He arrived in England and later assisted Lady Blomfield in the production and distribution of *Paris Talks*. She was on the first Bahá'í administrative body in England and went to the Holy Land again in early December 1921 to find 'Abdu'l-Bahá had passed away. She remained for a time in Haifa and was able to be of great assistance to Shoghi Effendi and the ladies of the Holy Family. She was treated with the greatest respect by Shoghi Effendi and in his letters to her after her return would refer to her as "dear and precious Rosa." On her return to England, despite declining health, she worked ceaselessly for the Faith, being Secretary of the London local Assembly, a member of the National Spiritual Assembly. She returned to Haifa where she worked as a secretary and collaborator to Shoghi Effendi, leaving finally in 1927. In October of that year he wrote to her: "I grieve to learn of your failing health and mental restlessness. How much I miss you this year. I will most assuredly pray for you from the bottom of my heart. Your past services are engraved upon my heart and mind." She passed away on 17 November 1931, and the Guardian cabled: "Deeply grieved passing Rosenberg England's outstanding Bahá'í pioneer worker. Memory her glorious service will never die. 'Abdu'l-Bahá's family join me in expressing heartfelt condolences her brother relatives. Urge friends hold befitting memorial service. [9:90][17:262][83:55][133]

ROWLING, MARGARET (1897-1981) An early (1938) Australian believer, she pioneered to Noumea in 1954. Throughout the period 1956 to 1975 she traveled extensively throughout the islands of the Pacific in the promotion of the Cause. In 1957 she was appointed an Auxiliary Board member, and in 1963 she was elected to the National Spiritual Assembly of the South Pacific. [2:758]

RULERS In His public proclamation to the *Rulers and Kings of the World,* Bahá'u'lláh called upon them to hold a convocation to establish world peace, to reduce their armaments, to recognize His Mission and made specific appeals to several of them. Within the Bahá'í Administration "rulers" refers to the elected bodies—the Universal House of Justice, the National Spiritual Assemblies and the local Spiritual Assemblies ("Spiritual Assemblies" is a designation which will eventually be replaced by local and national "Houses of Justice" Their rôle is to legislate and make decisions on the application of the Bahá'í Teachings in the Bahá'í Communities under their jurisdiction.) See **LEARNED ARM**; **TABLETS TO THE KINGS.**

RÚMÍ, SIYYID MUṢṬAFÁY (1846-1945) (Hand of the Cause of God) was of an Iráqi family resident in Madras, India, when, in his early 20s, he came into contact with Sulaymán Khán Ilyas (Jamál Effendi) the teacher sent by Bahá'u'lláh in 1875 to develop the Faith in India. He soon became a Bahá'í and began to travel with his new teacher, reaching Burma in 1878 where he settled in Rangoon and married into a rich family. Being an erudite scholar and well versed in Muslim theology he was able to develop the small Bahá'í groups in Rangoon and Mandalay into strong communities. In 1899 he carried the marble sarcophagus in which the bodies of the Báb and His companion were to be entombed to the Holy Land. In 1910 the business with which he was associated failed, and a little later his wife died, and he was able to devote his whole time in service to the Faith. Invited to the village of Daidanaw by the headman, who had been assisted in a court case by some Bahá'ís, Muṣṭafáy Rúmi so impressed the elders of the village that the whole village embraced the Faith, and he devoted much time to its development as a Bahá'í village. After the passing of Bahá'u'lláh and 'Abdu'l-Bahá, he was a tower of strength in observing the Covenant and protecting purity of the Faith. When he passed away in 1945 as he approached his 99th birthday the Guardian cabled: "Hearts grief-stricken passing Supreme Concourse distinguished pioneer Faith Bahá'u'lláh, dearly loved staunch high minded noble soul Siyyid Mustafa. Long record his superb services both teaching administrative fields shed lustre on both heroic and formative ages Bahá'í Dispensation. His magnificent achievements fully entitle him join ranks Hands Cause Bahá'u'lláh." [40:589][19:517]

RUTFJÄLL, NILS (1895-1970) He and his wife Sigrid were the first *Samer* (Lapps) to embrace the Cause (1961).[51:483]

S

SA'AD, 'ABDU'L-JALÍL BEY (-1933) (Hand of the Cause of God) Taught in Egypt by Mírzá Abu'l-Faḍl-i-Gulpáygání, Sa'ad was an early Egyptian believer. He was a distinguished judge of the civil courts and as such was able to render significant services to the Faith. He wrote extensively advocating the principle that all religions should be treated equally. In spite of much opposition he was able to ensure that the Bahá'í Declaration of Trust for legal recognition of the Faith was accepted. After writing a series of articles in defense of the Faith he was transferred, as a disciplinary measure, to a remote locality in upper Egypt, where he used the opportunity to translate, *The Dawn Breakers* and *Bahá'u'lláh and the New Era* into Arabic. For many years chairman of the National Spiritual Assembly of the Bahá'ís of Egypt and the Sudan, he served not only as a wise and learned teacher but as a capable administrator. He obtained the permission to build a Bahá'í headquarters in Cairo and was often found to be on site supervising the work. He died suddenly on 25 May 1942 and was appointed posthumously by Shoghi Effendi, in 1943, as Egypt's first and only Hand of the Cause of God. [45:597]

ṢÁBIRÍ, SÍMÍN (1958-1983) (Martyr) A young Bahá'í who was executed along with other coreligionists in Shíráz, Írán, by the government in June 1983, for refusing to recant her belief in Bahá'u'lláh. [11:600]

SABRI, ISOBEL (Locke) (1924-1992) An American believer (1945), she pioneered to the United Kingdom in 1946 as a Bahá'í pioneer and teacher. She moved with her husband (Ḥasan Sabri) to East Africa following a call from Shoghi Effendi for pioneers. They served the Cause in Tanganyika, Uganda and Kenya. She served on the regional Spiritual Assembly of Central and East Africa before being appointed in 1968 a member of the Continental Board of Counsellors in Africa. In 1983 she was appointed a member of the International Teaching Center (of which she remained a member until her death in England).[57:275][60:151]

SACRIFICE According to Bahá'í teachings there are many aspects of sacrifice. In addition to the giving up of one's life there is also the voluntary relinquishing of home, position, wealth and even family and health in certain pioneer circumstances and, without being a pioneer, one can sacrifice time, wealth, position to serve the Faith. 'Abdu'l-Bahá said, referring to Christ:

> Notwithstanding His knowledge of what would befall Him, He arose to proclaim His message, suffered all tribulation and hardships from the people and finally offered His life as a sacrifice in order to illumine humanity—gave His blood in order to guide the world of mankind. He accepted every calamity and suffering in order to guide men to the truth. Had He desired to save His own life, and were He without wish to offer Himself in sacrifice, He would not have been able to guide a single soul. There was no doubt that His blessed blood would be shed and His body broken. Nevertheless, that Holy Soul accepted calamity and death in His love for mankind. This is one of the meanings of sacrifice. As to the second meaning: There could be no question that the physical body was born from the womb of Mary. But the reality of Christ, the Spirit of Christ, the perfections of Christ all came from heaven. Consequently, by saying He was the bread which came from heaven He meant that the perfections which He showed forth were divine perfections, that the blessings within Him were heavenly gifts and bestowals, that His light was the light of Reality. He said, "If any man eat of this bread, he shall live for ever." That is to say, whosoever assimilates these divine perfections which are within me will never die; whosoever has a share and partakes of these heavenly bounties I embody

will find eternal life; he who takes unto himself these divine lights shall find everlasting life. How manifest the meaning is! How evident! For the soul which acquires divine perfections and seeks heavenly illumination from the teachings of Christ will undoubtedly live eternally. This is also one of the mysteries of sacrifice.... Christ outwardly disappeared. His personal identity became hidden from the eyes, even as the identity of the seed disappeared; but the bounties, divine qualities and perfections of Christ became manifest in the Christian community which Christ founded through sacrificing Himself. When you look at the tree, you will realize that the perfections, blessings, properties and beauty of the seed have become manifest in the branches, twigs, blossoms and fruit; consequently, the seed has sacrificed itself to the tree. Had it not done so, the tree would not have come into existence. Christ, like unto the seed, sacrificed Himself for the tree of Christianity. Therefore, His perfections, bounties, favors, lights and graces became manifest in the Christian community, for the coming of which He sacrificed Himself. [26:450]

'Abdu'l-Bahá continued:

For instance, consider the substance we call iron. Observe its qualities; it is solid, black, cold. These are the characteristics of iron. When the same iron absorbs heat from the fire, it sacrifices its attribute of solidity for the attribute of fluidity. It sacrifices its attribute of darkness for the attribute of light, which is a quality of the fire. It sacrifices its attribute of coldness to the quality of heat which the fire possesses so that in the iron there remains no solidity, darkness or cold. It becomes illumined and transformed, having sacrificed its qualities to the qualities and attributes of the fire.... Likewise, man, when separated and severed from the attributes of the world of nature, sacrifices the qualities and exigencies of that mortal realm and manifests the perfections of the Kingdom, just as the qualities of the iron disappeared and the qualities of the fire appeared in their place. [26:452]

See **MARTYR**.

SADRATU'L-MUNTAHÁ The Divine Lote Tree, The Tree beyond which there is no passing: symbolic of the Manifestation of God. [11:740]

ṢADR-I-A'ẒAM Grand Vizier, prime minister. [11:740]

ṢÁḤIBU'Z-ZAMÁN Lord of the Age: one of the titles of the promised Qá'im. [11:740]

SA'ÍD-I-HINDÍ Ninth Letter of the Living.

SALA, ROSEMARY (Mary Scott Gillies) (1902-1980) An early Canadian believer (1927) of Scottish birth. Shortly after learning of the Faith in Montréal she attended the Bahá'í School in Greenacre where she was one of three 'Marys' and was given the name Rosemary by George Spendlove—the name by which she was known for the rest of her life. She served as a member of the first (1948) National Spiritual Assembly of Canada for a period of six years. She went on pilgrimage in 1952 during which time she met Shoghi Effendi. Following the announcement of the Ten Year Crusade she and her husband (Emeric) pioneered in 1954 to Zululand. When their visas were not renewed they moved the following year to Port Elizabeth, South Africa where they remained for some 13 years (serving during that time as a member of the National Spiritual Assembly of South and West Africa) before returning to Canada. In 1971 they moved to Guadalajara, Mexico. [2:713]

SALÁM Peace, salutation. Salámun 'Alaykum, Peace Be With You! a greeting among Muslims. Va's Salám And Peace (be with you). [11:740]

SALSABÍL Pure, limpid water. A fountain in Paradise. [11:740]

SAMADAR Literally salamander; phoenix. A mythical creature indestructible by fire. [11:740]

SAMANDARÍ, ṬARÁẒU'LLÁH (1874-1968) (Hand of the Cause of God) He was born in 1874 in Qazvín, Persia, of illustrious Bábí parents, his father being the Apostle of Bahá'u'lláh, Mullá Káẓim-i-Samandar (q.v.). Samandarí is unique not only among the Hands of the Cause but in the whole Bahá'í community in that he had the privilege of actively serving the Faith under Bahá'u'lláh Himself at a very young age, under 'Abdu'l-Bahá throughout the whole of His ministry, the whole of Shoghi Effendi's Guardianship, the whole of the Ministry of the Custodians and five years under the Universal House of Justice. He was 17 years old when he first met Bahá'u'lláh and was in His entourage for six months before His passing in 1892, during which time he was given the name Ṭarázu'lláh. 'Abdu'l-Bahá referred to him as "Mírzá Taráz," while Shoghi Effendi addressed him as "Jináb-i-Samandarí."

Taught at home, he became a noted calligrapher, and throughout his life he copied the Bahá'í Scriptures. Regarded as a well-educated man he was in fact without formal education but deeply immersed in the Scriptures he had copied and memorized. He spent most of his life in traveling for the Faith and undertaking commissions of great importance for 'Abdu'l-Bahá and the Guardian. Tributes to his steadfastness and dedication appear in a large number of their letters.

Mr. Samandarí was among the first contingent of living Hands of the Cause appointed 24 December 1951, and he continued to serve with distinction right up to his passing on 2 September 1968. He attended the Intercontinental Conferences in Kampala, Wilmette, Stockholm and New Delhi in 1953; visiting many centers in the U.S. in that year; the Arabian Peninsular Convention in 1957 and the Intercontinental Conferences of Kampala, and Singapore, 1958, Convention of Burma, 1959 and carried out extensive travels throughout Iráq, Írán, Pákistán, India, Ceylon, Burma and Turkey, 1959-1963. In 1967 he represented the Universal House of Justice at an Intercontinental Conference in Wilmette where as the only surviving Hand who had met Bahá'u'lláh and with his neat small upright figure, his clear and resonant voice, his courtesy, dignity and kindliness, he thrilled and inspired the more than 3,000 Bahá'ís attending the Conference. During this visit to the West he also met Bahá'ís and addressed meetings, at the age of 92, in Alaska, Canada, United States, England and Germany.

In late August 1968 he visited the Holy Land to attend the commemorations of the centenary of Bahá'u'lláh's arrival on those shores, but his health deteriorated and he went into the hospital. Many of the friends visited him and found his mind lucid and his radiance undimmed, and he passed away content. In a report of the funeral it is written, "nearly 1,000 souls attended, most of them joining the funeral cortège proceeding from the Master's House, where the service was held, to the Bahá'í Cemetery at the foot of Mt. Carmel ... The funeral was one of the largest and most impressive since the time of the Master." The Universal House of Justice cabled:

> With sorrowful hearts announce passing Hand Cause God, Shield His Faith, dearly-loved Ṭaráẓu'lláh Samandarí ninety- third year his life on morrow commemoration centenary Bahá'u'lláh 's arrival Holy Land. Faithful to last breath instructions his Lord, his Master, his Guardian, he continued selfless devoted service unabated until falling ill recent teaching mission. Unmindful illness he proceeded Holy Land participate centenary. Ever remembered hearts believers East West to whose lands he traveled bearing message his Lord whose communities he faithfully served. this precious remnant Heroic Age who attained presence Blessed Beauty year His Ascension, now laid rest foot mountain God throng believers assembled vicinity very spot Bahá'u'lláh first trod these sacred

shores. Request all National Assemblies hold memorial services including four Mother Temples Bahá'í World befitting long life dedicated exemplary service Lord Hosts by one assured Center Covenant loving welcome presence Bahá'u'lláh Abhá Kingdom. Extend loving sympathy assurance prayers members distinguished family. [51:416]

SÁM KHÁN The officer in charge of the Armenian regiment that made the first unsuccessful attempt to execute the Báb. See **BÁB, MARTYRDOM OF.**

SARKÁR-ÁQÁ Literally The Honorable Master. A designation of 'Abdu'l-Bahá. [11:740]

SCHOLARSHIP Towards the middle of this century Shoghi Effendi gave guidance to many individuals who had written to him on the subject of scholarship:

> Young men and women in the Faith must be deep and thoughtful scholars of its teachings, so that they can teach in a way that will convince people that all the problems facing them have a remedy. They must grasp the Administration, so that they can wisely and efficiently administer the ever-growing affairs of the Cause; and they must exemplify the Bahá'í way of living. [104:84]

> As to correlating philosophy with the Bahá'í teachings; this is a tremendous work which scholars in the future can undertake. [9:445]

The Universal House of Justice wrote to an individual in 1983 listing several objectives of the Bahá'í community: "a fourth is the promotion of Bahá'í scholarship, so that an increasing number of believers will be able to analyze the problems of mankind in every field and to show how the Teachings solve them." [86:435] In 1974 the Universal House of Justice called upon the Canadian Bahá'í community to cultivate opportunities for formal presentations, courses and lectureships on the Bahá'í Faith in universities and other institutions of higher learning and a "Canadian Association for Studies on the Bahá'í Faith" was established. Several other countries followed the Canadian example, and Associations for Bahá'í Studies were set up, some using languages other than English. These associations publish papers from their annual and theme conferences, and other Bahá'í "Agencies" and "Fora" have become affiliated. A periodical, *Bahá'í Studies* and a quarterly publication *The Journal of Bahá'í Studies* were initiated.

SCHEFFLER, CARL (1883-1962) An early American believer. He became a Bahá'í at the age of 16; he was the 665th to have declared his faith in Chicago. In 1907 he visited 'Abdu'l-Bahá in 'Akká. He was a member of the first "House of Justice" of Chicago. In 1925 he was elected to the National Spiritual Assembly of the United States and Canada, on which he served until 1938.[47:939][59:65ff]

SCHERER, CARL A. (1900-1982) and **SCHERER, LORETTA L.** (1907-1980) (Knights of Bahá'u'lláh) American believers (1949) who pioneered during the Ten Year Crusade to Macao for which service they were designated Knights of Bahá'u'lláh. In 1959 they pioneered to Portugal where Mr. Scherer was elected to the National Spiritual Assembly. [2:739]

SCHMIDT, EUGEN (1901-1982) An early (1924) German believer, he was a member of the National Spiritual Assembly of Germany from 1932 onwards. He was also a member of the local Spiritual Assemblies of Stuttgart and then Leinfelden-Echterdingen. He served as editor of *Bahá'í Nachrichten* (a monthly Bahá'í newsletter) and of *Sonne der Wahrheit* (a Bahá'í periodical). He contributed greatly to the raising up of the German national Ḥaẓíratu'l-Quds (1952) and the building of the Mother Temple of Europe (Mas͟hriqu'l-Ad͟hkár) (1964), both of which are in Langenhain. In later years he served as an Auxiliary Board member. [2:800]

SCHOPFLOCHER, FLORENCE (Kitty or Lorol) (1886-1970) An early (early 1920s) Canadian believer who is reputed to have traveled around the world nine times sharing the Bahá'í Message. [87:vol.XVIII,Nos.3,5&6,pp.90,150,186)] She was the wife of Hand of the Cause of God Siegfried Schopflocher. [51:488]

SCHOPFLOCHER, SIEGFRIED (Fred) (1877-1953) (Hand of the Cause of God) Although he was born in Germany of Jewish parents, he drifted away from orthodoxy and later, when he moved to Canada, embraced the Cause.

The first of his many visits to the Holy Land as a Bahá'í was in 1922. He became devoted to Shoghi Effendi and carried out many future assignments for him. He visited many parts of the globe, frequently on business, meeting the Bahá'ís. His main concerns in North America were the building of the first House of Worship in the West (Wilmette, Chicago), for which the Guardian named him "The Chief Temple Builder"; and the repair, development and expansion of the permanent Bahá'í Summer School at Green Acre and later the one at Geyserville. Beginning in 1924 he was elected for 15 of the next 23 years to the National Spiritual Assembly of the United States and Canada, and when Canada formed a separate national body in 1948, he was elected to that Body and remained a member until his death.

He was appointed a Hand of the Cause by Shoghi Effendi in the second contingent, on 29 February 1952 and went on his last pilgrimage to Haifa in January 1953. He attended the Canadian National Convention the following April and planned to attend the Indian International Conference later that year in New Delhi but passed away in Montréal on 27 July. Shoghi Effendi cabled:

> Profoundly grieved passing dearly-loved, outstandingly staunch Hand Cause Fred Schopflocher. His numerous, magnificent services extending over 30 years administrative teaching spheres United States, Canada, Institutions Bahá'í World Center greatly enrich annals Formative Age Faith. Abundant reward assured Abhá Kingdom. Advising American National Assembly hold befitting memorial gathering Temple he generously helped raise. Advise hold memorial gathering Maxwell home to commemorate his eminent part rise Administrative Order Faith Canada. Urge ensure burial close neighborhood resting place distinguished Hand of Cause Sutherland Maxwell. [40:647][48:664]

SCHUBARTH, JOHANNA (1877-1952) The founding member of the Norwegian Bahá'í community—entitled the "mother of the Norwegian community" by Shoghi Effendi. [48:694][60:499]

SCHWARTZ, ALBERT (1871-1931) (Disciple of 'Abdu'l-Bahá) Born 14 December 1871, Consul Schwartz became a most active promoter of the Bahá'í Faith in Germany and was the Chairman of its National Spiritual Assembly from its formation up to the time he passed away on 13 January 1931. During the visit of 'Abdu'l-Bahá to Germany in 1913, he and his wife Alice (See **SCHWARZ-SOLIVO, ALICE)** entertained Him on several occasions. They took Him to the hotel and mineral bath he owned at Bad Mergentheim, some 60 miles from Stuttgart. Later he followed 'Abdu'l-Bahá to Paris and enjoyed several days in His presence. He had planned to visit 'Abdu'l-Bahá in Haifa but He passed away unexpectedly before the Consul and his wife were able to make the journey, and they later went on pilgrimage at the invitation of the Guardian. On his passing the Guardian cabled Albert's family: "Inexpressibly sad profoundly deplore passing Germany's outstanding Bahá'í pioneer worker. Memory his distinguished service imperishable. Greatest Holy Leaf joins me assurance affectionate prayer, heartfelt condolences." [36:264]

SCHWARZ-SOLIVO, ALICE (1875-1965) An early German believer, she learned of the Cause in 1912 from Edwin Fisher, an American dentist and the first Bahá'í to go to Germany. She met 'Abdu'l-Bahá in 1913 in Stuttgart and received Him in her home as a guest (she was the wife of Consul Schwarz). She later received a Tablet from Him. [50:377]

SCHWEIZER, ANNEMARIE (1884-1957) One of the earliest German believers. She met 'Abdu'l-Bahá several times, and he stayed in her home when visiting Stuttgart. She visited Shoghi Effendi in 1934. During the prohibition of the Bahá'í faith by Hitler she was arrested by the Gestapo, tried before a court and sentenced to imprisonment for her belief. [47:890]

SCIENCE Bahá'u'lláh wrote:

> Arts, crafts and sciences uplift the world of being, and are conducive to its exaltation. Knowledge is as wings to man's life, and a ladder for his ascent. Its acquisition is incumbent upon everyone. The knowledge of such sciences, however, should be acquired as can profit the peoples of the earth, and not those which begin with words and end with words. Great indeed is the claim of scientists and craftsmen on the peoples of the world. [77:52]

> It is permissible to study sciences and arts, but such sciences as are useful and would redound to the progress and advancement of the people. [77:26]

> The source of crafts, sciences and arts is the power of reflection. Make ye every effort that out of this ideal mine there may gleam forth such pearls of wisdom and utterance as will promote the well-being and harmony of all the kindreds of the earth. [77:72]

'Abdu'l-Bahá said:

> Encourage the children from their earliest years to master every kind of learning, and make them eager to become skilled in every art—the aim being that through the favoring grace of God, the heart of each one may become even as a mirror disclosing the secrets of the universe, penetrating the innermost reality of all things; and that each may earn world-wide fame in all branches of knowledge, science and the arts. [86:144]

> No individual should be denied or deprived of intellectual training although each should receive according to capacity. None must be left in the grades of ignorance, for ignorance is a defect in the human world. All mankind must be given a knowledge of science and philosophy; that is, as much as may be deemed necessary. All cannot be scientists or philosophers but each should be educated according to his needs and deserts. [86:211]

> Thus for the first time religion will become harmonized with science and science will be the handmaid of religion, both showering their material and spiritual gifts on all

humanity. In this way the people will be lifted out of the quagmires of slothfulness and bigotry. [86:606]

SCIENCE AND RELIGION 'Abdu'l-Bahá said:

There is no contradiction between true religion and science. When a religion is opposed to science it becomes mere superstition: that which is contrary to knowledge is ignorance.... How can a man believe to be a fact that which science has proved to be impossible? If he believes in spite of his reason, it is rather ignorant superstition than faith. The true principles of all religions are in conformity with the teachings of science. [25:141]

Religion and science are in complete agreement. Every religion which is not in accordance with established science is superstition. Religion must be reasonable. If it does not square with reason, it is superstition and without foundation. It is like a mirage, which deceives man by leading him to think it is a body of water. God has endowed man with reason that he may perceive what is true. If we insist that such and such a subject is not to be reasoned out and tested according to the established logical modes of the intellect, what is the use of the reason which God has given man?[26:63]

Religion must stand the analysis of reason. It must agree with scientific fact and proof so that science will sanction religion and religion fortify science. Both are indissolubly welded and joined in reality. If statements and teachings of religion are found to be unreasonable and contrary to science, they are outcomes of superstition and imagination. [26:175]

In describing the future world civilization, Shoghi Effendi wrote: "In such a world society, science and religion, the two most potent forces in human life, will be reconciled, will cooperate, and will harmoniously develop."[4:203] See **WORLD COMMONWEALTH; PRINCIPLES, BAHÁ'Í.**

SEARS, WILLIAM BERNARD PATRICK MICHAEL TERRANCE (Bill) (1911-1992) (Hand of the Cause of God) He was born on 28 March 28 1911 in Duluth, Minnesota, of an Irish father and a mother of mixed European background. He was brought up in a Roman Catholic environment and from a very early age was interested in deeply religious questions. His mother had become a Catholic on her marriage, but his grandfather was an inquiring Protestant who introduced Bill to the Bible.

He was not very old when he began writing poetry and later some one-act plays.

He married and had two children, but his wife died very young, and his younger son, Michael, had to be placed in a sanitarium. Bill eventually found work as a radio announcer, first as a newsreader and later as a sports commentator. After a few years he was introduced to the Bahá'í Faith by a young lady, Marguerite Reimer, who became his wife in 1940. He soon became a Bahá'í, and they served the Faith together for the next 50 years. It was when he was researching his first full-sized book *Thief in the Night*,[134] that he became a Bahá'í. Bill progressed in the world of media, becoming a well-known sportscaster and then in television, in a regular feature, *In The Park*. In 1951 *The Bill Sears Show* won an Emmy award as the best sports series of the year. In 1953 Marguerite attended the first Intercontinental Conference in Kampala and fell in love with Africa. Later, at the Chicago Conference they responded to the call for overseas pioneers and settled in South Africa. The move came at a time when he had achieved financial success, awards and fame both locally and nationally, and new contract offers and opportunities which, such was the development of the television industry, would have assured him of superstar status. The decision to move to Africa for his faith called for him to walk away from his hard earned fame and fortune.

Soon after his arrival in Africa he had a heart attack but recovered and took a job in radio. In 1954 he made his first pilgrimage to the Holy Land. He was one of the first Auxiliary Board members appointed by Hand Músá Banání and was himself elevated to the rank of Hand of the Cause by the Guardian in his last contingent in October 1957. Although he had periods of serious ill health he continued to travel widely, attending the Kampala Conference in 1958, followed by visits to the Convention in France, centers throughout France, Italy and Greece, six months as one of the Nine resident in Haifa; and Egypt, Sudan, Uganda, Kenya, Zanzibar, Tanzania, Northern and Southern Rhodesia, Mozambique, South Africa, Swaziland, Basutoland, and Mauritius, all in that same year. In 1959 he was assigned to the Western Hemisphere and returned to the Americas, where he toured, during the next few years, North, Central and South America, Costa Rica, Jamaica, Haiti, Dominican Republic, Alaska, El Salvador and Guatemala, frequently as representative of the World Center.

He was a member of the Nine Hands of the Cause resident in the Holy Land from 1961 to 1963. In 1963 he attended the Jubilee World Conference in the Albert Hall, London, where he shared the platform with Philip Hainsworth (a British pioneer to Uganda) at the public meeting which had an audience of more than 7,000. After this he visited Hawaii, Australia and Africa, returning to the United States in February 1964. In 1966 he returned yet again to Africa when Hand John Robarts returned to Canada. He traveled widely during the next few years in Europe, the Americas, Persia, Africa, and from his temporary new base in Canada in 1974, continued his writing, the production of audio cassettes, radio and television programs and visits to Korea, Japan, Hawaii, Samoa, Iceland, the Scottish Islands, centers throughout Canada and the United States. He attended conferences, summer schools, conventions and meetings with National Spiritual Assemblies and the Continental Board of Counsellors, often as the representative of the Universal House of Justice. He launched and inspired many teaching campaigns, galvanizing the friends to tremendous activity with his vivid presentations and powerful oratory. Examples of these were seen at an International Convention in Haifa and the Conference that followed the Dedication of the Indian House of Worship, New Delhi. His book on the persecutions of the Bahá'ís of Írán, *A Cry from the Heart,* [127] released in early 1982, became a potent force in raising the consciousness of its readers to the sufferings and the steadfastness of the Íránian believers, and it was widely used in most parts of the English-speaking Bahá'í communities. A dramatic appeal for support for a Bahá'í radio station in South Carolina was taped by Bill and broadcast in more than 1,000 Bahá'í communities on 12 December 1983. This resulted in an unprecedented outpouring of funds.

He was a most powerful speaker, and when it was known he was to speak, there would be standing room only at his meeting. Bill tackled the problems of ill-health and aging with characteristic courage and ingenuity.

During the later years of his life when he was unable to travel widely, he continued to inspire conferences and gatherings of all kinds with his taped messages, which always conveyed his dedication to the Faith, his deep love for the Guardian, his comprehensive knowledge of the Bahá'í Scripture, his vision of the future development of the Cause and his supreme optimism for its triumph. In October 1991 he began an intensive tour, stopping in Massachusetts; Arizona; California; and Oregon and in February of the following year he visited New York City; Cleveland, Ohio; Washington, D.C.; and Chicago, Ill. In March he was in Atlanta, Georgia; and Minneapolis, Minnesota. This exhausting itinerary does not convey the additional pressures of hours of waiting in airports in the middle of the night, the missed connections, the terrible weather conditions or the traveling in a wheel-chair. March 28

1992 would have been his 81st birthday, but he passed away in the morning of the 25th, and the Universal House of Justice cabled:

> Our hearts deeply saddened, Bahá'í world greatly deprived, by passing Hand Cause God William Sears, vibrant, consecrated, stout-hearted Standard-Bearer Faith Bahá'u'lláh. His more than half century unbroken service marked by unflinching devotion to beloved Guardian, infectious enthusiasm for teaching, galvanizing sense drama, disarming humor, special love for children, unflagging determination in face difficulties. He will ever be remembered for dedicating full range his creative and energetic capacities as writer, editor, lecturer, radio and television program director, to his various services as traveling teacher to numerous countries, particularly in the Americas, and as pioneer to Africa where he was member of Auxiliary Board and of National Spiritual Assembly South and West Africa when in 1957 he was elevated rank Hand Cause. He later served a member body Hands Holy Land. His loss acutely felt in North America where he expended last measure his ebbing strength promotion teaching activities. Dynamic effects his work will endure through his many books and recordings. Generations to come will rejoice in rich legacy left them through his historic accomplishments. Fervently praying Holy Shrines progress his illustrious soul Abhá Kingdom. Advise friends throughout world commemorate his passing. Request befitting memorial services in his honor all Houses of Worship. [105:May 1992]

SEEPE, LOT MAX (1908-1982) The first (1955) "colored" believer to embrace the Cause in South Africa, he served as chairman of the local Spiritual Assembly for Western, Newclare and Sophiatown Townships. In 1956 he was elected to the first Regional Spiritual Assembly of South and West Africa and served in that capacity for 25 years until his passing in 1982. He traveled widely throughout the region in the promotion of the Cause. [2:807]

SEEPE, MAY MARTHA Along with her husband (Lot Max Seepe [q.v.]) she was the first "colored" believer to accept the Faith in South Africa. She was a polyglot (English, Afrikaans, Sesotho, Zulu and Xhosa) a skill that enhanced her teaching activities, which stretched over seven countries in Southern Africa. She served on the first local Spiritual Assembly of Johannesburg for some 30 years. [11:322]

SENNE, DOROTHY KEDIBONE (1931-1977) The first (1955) African woman in South Africa to embrace the Cause. [53:435][60:503]

SERVICE Much attention is paid in the Bahá'í Faith to service to others, to society and to the work of the Faith. Bahá'u'lláh wrote:

> That one indeed is a man who, today, dedicateth himself to the service of the entire human race. The Great Being saith: Blessed and happy is he that ariseth to promote the best interests of the peoples and kindreds of the earth.... Wert thou to consider this world, and realize how fleeting are the things that pertain unto it, thou wouldst choose to tread no path except the path of service to the Cause of thy Lord. [85:250, 314]

> Man's merit lieth in service and virtue and not in the pageantry of wealth and riches. [77:138]

'Abdu'l-Bahá said: "Consecrate and devote yourselves to the betterment and service of all the human race." [26:448] "Forget thou entirely the ease, tranquillity, composure and living of this transitory world and occupy thyself with the well-being and the service of the human world and conduct thyself in accord with the advices and exhortations of God." [100:659]

Shoghi Effendi through his secretary wrote: "Every individual, no matter how handicapped and limited he may be, is under the obligation of engaging in some work or profession, for work, especially when performed in the spirit of service, is according to Bahá'u'lláh, a form of worship." [104:83] And again: "Vie ye with each other in the service of God and of His Cause. This is indeed what profiteth you in this world, and in that which is to come. Your Lord, the God of Mercy, is the All-Informed, the All-Knowing." [39:83]

SETO, MAMIE LORETTA O'CONNOR (1885-1970) An early American believer who pioneered with her husband (Anthony Yuen Seto (1890-1957) [47:886]) to Honolulu, Hawaii in 1916. 'Abdu'l-Bahá revealed at least one Tablet for them. She was a devoted teacher and traveled widely for the Cause. In 1932 they left Hawaii and settled in San Francisco, followed in 1944 by a move to Prince Edward Island, Canada. She later traveled widely and lived as a pioneer with her husband in Hong Kong. Following the death of her husband she returned to the United States. [51:479]

SHÁH King. [11:740]

SHÁH-BAHRÁM World Savior and Promised One of the Zoroastrians, identified by Bahá'ís with Bahá'u'lláh. [11:740]

SHAHÍD Martyr. [11:740]

SHAHÍD-IBN-I-SHAHÍD See **MÍRZÁ 'ALÍ-MUḤAMMAD.**

SHARI'AT, SHARI'AH Literally path, way, custom. Law. Muslim canonical law. [11:740] and returned to the Americas, where he toured, during the next few years, North, Central and South America, Costa Rica, Jamaica, Haiti, Dominican Republic, Alaska, El Salvador and Guatemala, frequently as representative of the World Center.

He was a member of the Nine Hands of the Cause resident in the Holy Land from 1961 to 1963. In 1963 he attended the Jubilee World Conference in the Albert Hall, London, where he shared the platform with Philip Hainsworth (a British pioneer to Uganda) at the public meeting which had an audience of more than 7,000. After this he visited Hawaii, Australia and Africa, returning to the United States in February 1964. In 1966 he returned yet again to Africa when Hand John Robarts returned to Canada. He traveled widely during the next few years in Europe, the Americas, Persia, Africa, and from his temporary new base in Canada in 1974, continued his writing, the production of audio cassettes, radio and television programs and visits to Korea, Japan, Hawaii, Samoa, Iceland, the Scottish Islands, centers throughout Canada and the United States. He attended conferences, summer schools, conventions and meetings with National Spiritual Assemblies and the Continental Board of Counsellors, often as the representative of the Universal House of Justice. He launched and inspired many teaching campaigns, galvanizing the friends to tremendous activity with his vivid presentations and powerful oratory. Examples of these were seen at an International Convention in Haifa and the Conference that followed the Dedication of the Indian House of Worship, New Delhi. His book on the persecutions of the Bahá'ís of Írán, *A Cry from the Heart,*[127] released in early 1982, became a potent force in raising the consciousness of its readers to the sufferings and the steadfastness of the Íránian believers, and it was widely used in most parts of the English-speaking Bahá'í communities. A dramatic appeal for support for a Bahá'í radio station in South Carolina was taped by Bill and broadcast in more than 1,000 Bahá'í communities on 12 December 1983. This resulted in an unprecedented outpouring of funds.

He was a most powerful speaker, and when it was known he was to speak, there would be standing room only at his meeting. Bill tackled the problems of ill-health and aging with characteristic courage and ingenuity.

During the later years of his life when he was unable to travel widely, he continued to inspire conferences and gatherings of all kinds with his taped messages, which always conveyed his dedication to the Faith, his deep love for the Guardian, his comprehensive knowledge of the Bahá'í Scripture, his vision of the future development of the Cause and his supreme optimism for its triumph. In

Shí'ahs reject the first three Caliphs, believing that the successorship in Islám belonged by divine right to 'Alí (first Imám and fourth Caliph) and to his descendants. Originally, the successorship was the vital point of difference, and Islám was divided because Muḥammad's (albeit verbal) appointment of 'Alí was disregarded. See **SUNNAH; IMÁM.** [11:741]

SHÍ'Í, SHIITE Member of the Shí'ah (or Party) of 'Alí; Muslim of the Shí'ah branch of Islám.

SHÍRÁZ The city in Írán where the Bahá'í Era began with the Báb making His Declaration to Mullá Ḥusayn during the night of 22-23 May 1844.

SHOGHI EFFENDI (RABBÁNÍ) (1897-1957) (Guardian of the Bahá'í Faith) (The Sign of God on Earth) The great grandson of Bahá'u'lláh and the grandson of 'Abdu'l-Bahá (his mother being Díyá'íyyih Khánum, 'Abdu'l-Bahá's eldest daughter). His father was Mírzá Hádí Shírází, a relative of the Báb. He was born on 1 March 1897 in 'Akká, Palestine. He went to school first in Haifa and then in Beirut where in 1918 he received a B.A. at the American University. 'Abdu'l-Bahá sent him to Oxford University, England, where he entered Balliol College in the spring of 1920. The whole of his education, he believed, was to equip himself better to serve his beloved grandfather, but he, in common with all his family, had no idea that he was being prepared for the rôle that 'Abdu'l-Bahá had decreed for him in His Will and Testament. This Will and Testament was handed to Shoghi Effendi on his arrival in Haifa by train just one month after 'Abdu'l-Bahá had passed away in the early hours of the 28th November 1921. The Will was in three parts and even in the first section, which had been written when Shoghi Effendi was but a small child, as well as in the other two, he was named as the "Guardian of the Cause of God," "the sign of God," "the chosen branch," and the "Center of the Cause." Bahá'u'lláh had appointed 'Abdu'l-Bahá as His Successor as Head of the Bahá'í Faith with authority to provide for further succession. On the death of 'Abdu'l-Bahá His Will and Testament, as stated above, designated Shoghi Effendi as the Guardian of the Bahá'í Faith. 'Abdu'l-Bahá wrote:

> O my loving friends! After the passing away of this wronged one, it is incumbent upon the Aghṣán (Branches), the Afnán (Twigs) of the Sacred Lote-Tree, the Hands (pillars) of the Cause of God and the loved ones of the Abhá Beauty to turn unto Shoghi Effendi—the youthful branch branched from the two hallowed and sacred Lote-Trees and the fruit grown from the union of the two offshoots of the Tree of Holiness,—as he is the sign of God, the chosen branch, the guardian of the Cause of God,

> he unto whom all the Aghṣán, the Afnán, the Hands of the Cause of God and His loved ones must turn. He is the expounder of the words of God and after him will succeed the first-born of his lineal descendants.... The sacred and youthful branch, the Guardian of the Cause of God, as well as the Universal House of Justice, to be universally elected and established, are both under the care and protection of the Abhá Beauty, under the shelter and unerring guidance of His Holiness, the Exalted One (may my life be offered up for them both.) Whatsoever they decide is of God. Whoso obeyeth him not, neither obeyeth them, hath not obeyed God; whoso rebelleth against him and against them hath rebelled against God; whoso opposeth him hath opposed God; whoso contendeth with them hath contended with God; whoso disputeth with him hath disputed with God; whoso denieth him hath denied God; whoso disbelieveth in him hath disbelieved in God; whoso deviateth, separateth himself and turneth aside from him hath in truth deviated, separated himself and turned aside from God.... The mighty stronghold shall remain impregnable and safe through obedience to him who is the Guardian of the Cause of God. It is incumbent upon the members of the House of Justice, upon all the Aghṣán, the Afnán, the Hands of the Cause of God to show their obedience, submissiveness and subordination unto the Guardian of the Cause of God, to turn unto him and be lowly before him. [96:6f]

Bahá'u'lláh Himself had written about the ultimate establishment of the Universal House of Justice and anticipated the Guardianship. In describing their relative functions Shoghi Effendi, as Guardian, wrote:

> From these statements it is made indubitably clear and evident that the Guardian of the Faith has been made the Interpreter of the Word and that the Universal House of Justice has been invested with the function of legislating on matters not expressly revealed in the teachings. The interpretation of the Guardian, functioning within his own sphere, is as authoritative and binding as the enactments of the International House of Justice, whose exclusive right and prerogative is to pronounce upon and deliver the final judgment on such laws and ordinances as Bahá'u'lláh has not expressly revealed. Neither can, nor will ever, infringe upon the sacred and prescribed domain of the other. Neither will seek to curtail the specific and undoubted authority with which both have been divinely

invested.... Though the Guardian of the Faith has been made the permanent head of so august a body he can never, even temporarily, assume the right of exclusive legislation. He cannot override the decision of the majority of his fellow-members, but is bound to insist upon a reconsideration by them of any enactment he conscientiously believes to conflict with the meaning and to depart from the spirit of Bahá'u'lláh's revealed utterances. He interprets what has been specifically revealed, and cannot legislate except in his capacity as member of the Universal House of Justice. He is debarred from laying down independently the constitution that must govern the organized activities of his fellow-members, and from exercising his influence in a manner that would encroach upon the liberty of those whose sacred right is to elect the body of his collaborators. [4:149f]

It was a grievous blow to him to learn of the passing of his grandfather, as he had not been aware that He was ill. But when this was added to the news of his appointment when he reached Haifa and was handed 'Abdu'l-Bahá's Will, it was almost more than he could bear. Added to these twin blows were the attacks made upon him by ill-wishers, Covenant Breakers and later, by those who unsuccessfully challenged the authenticity of the Will. From the beginning it became clear to those around him how wise had been 'Abdu'l-Bahá's choice of a Successor, as we read from *Twenty-five Years of Guardianship*:

We beheld a young man of only 24 standing at the helm of the Cause and some of the friends felt impelled to advise him about what it would be wise for him to do next. It was then that we began to know not only the nature of our first Guardian but the nature of the entire Institution of Guardianship, for we quickly discovered that Shoghi Effendi was "unreachable." Neither relatives, old Bahá'ís or new Bahá'ís, well wishers or ill wishers could sway his judgment or influence his decisions. We quickly came to realize that that he was not only divinely guided but had been endowed by God with just those characteristics needed to build up the Administrative Order, unite the believers in common endeavor and co-ordinate their world-wide activities.[61]

In her tribute written after the passing of the Guardian, Millie Collins wrote that she first met him in 1923 and found him:

A young man ... full of determination to carry forward the great work entrusted to his care. He was so spontaneous,

> so trusting and loving and outgoing in the buoyancy of his beautiful heart. Through the years we all watched with wonder.... the unfoldment of Bahá'u'lláh's Divine Order which he built up so patiently and wisely all over the world. But ... at what great cost to himself! In 1951 I began to learn what he had passed through. His face was sad, one could see his very spirit had been heavily oppressed by the agony he went through for years during the period when the family pursued their own desires and finally abandoned the work of the Faith and went their own way ... for a number of years we ... seldom saw him smile ... I do not know in any great detail the day to day afflictions of Bahá'u'lláh and 'Abdu'l-Bahá, but I sometimes wonder if they could have been any more heartbreaking than those of our beloved Shoghi Effendi.... after his final separation from them, there came a new joy and hope to our beloved Guardian. The rapid progress made in the attainment of so many of the goals of the World Crusade lifted him up.... His conscientiousness was like a fire burning in him; from his earliest childhood he showed the sensitive, noble, painstaking qualities that characterized him, and grew stronger as he matured and throughout his Guardianship. [135:1]

Shoghi Effendi married Mary Maxwell in 1937 (later named by him as 'Amatu'l-Bahá Rúḥíyyih Khánum [q.v.]).

Because all living members of Bahá'u'lláh's family broke the Covenant, Shoghi Effendi could not, in conformity with the provisions of 'Abdu'l-Bahá's Will and Testament, appoint a Successor. When he passed away in November 1957, the Faith was then left without a Guardian. As an institution, however, the Guardianship lived on through the voluminous writings and guidance of Shoghi Effendi and in those areas that were jointly the responsibility of the Guardian and the Universal House of Justice, by the Universal House of Justice since its inauguration in April 1963.

Outstanding among Shoghi Effendi's achievements are: the spread of the Faith to all parts of the world through his plans; the development of the Administrative Order; the vast number of letters of guidance, encouragement, explanation, interpretation,; the translations of numerous passages from Bahá'í Scripture; the massive amount of research that went into the writing of the history of the first Bahá'í century, *God Passes By*; the translation of such works as *Nabíl's Narrative*; the defense of the Faith from the attacks and actions of the Covenant Breakers; the acquisition of the lands and properties in 'Akká and Haifa, their development for future pilgrimages and the landscaping of the sites on Mount

Carmel and the construction of the superstructure of the Shrine of the Báb and of the International Archives building; the establishment of the close relationships with the local and national government officials in the State of Israel.

Shoghi Effendi died of Asiatic flu in London on 4 November, 1957. His funeral took place on 9 November with the cortege of well over 60 cars leaving the British Ḥaẓíratu'l-Quds (27 Rutland Gate, Knightsbridge) at 10.30 A.M. The burial was in the Great Northern London Cemetery, New Southgate, London (now the New Southgate Cemetery) and was preceded by a service in the chapel in the presence of a host of grieving Bahá'ís from every corner of the world.

For a true appreciation of the life and works of Shoghi Effendi, particular reference should be given to the biographical works of his wife, 'Amatu'l-Bahá Rúḥíyyih Khánum. These include *The Priceless Pearl* [31] and *The Guardian of the Bahá'í Faith.* [30] (The book written by Hand of the Cause of God Ugo Giachery, *Shoghi Effendi* is also of great value in understanding his genius). [136]

In the *Priceless Pearl* Amatu'l-Bahá Rúhíyyih Khánum's wrote a magnificent summary of his achievements, from which the following few sentences are taken:

> The Guardian had fused in the alembic of his creative mind all the elements of the Faith of Bahá'u'lláh into one great indivisible whole; he had created an organized community of His followers which was the receptacle of His teachings, His laws and His Administrative Order; the teachings of the twin Manifestations of God and the Perfect Exemplar had been woven into a shining cloak that would clothe and protect man for a thousand years, a cloak on which the fingers of Shoghi Effendi had picked out the pattern, knitted the seams, fashioned the brilliant clasps of his interpretations of the Sacred Texts, never to be sundered, never to be torn away until that day when a new Law-giver comes to the world and once again wraps His creature man in yet another divine garment.... It would be hard indeed to find a comparable figure in history who, in a little over a third of a century, set so many different operations in motion, who found the time to devote his attention to minute details on one hand and on the other to cover the range of an entire planet with his plans, his instructions, his guidance and his leadership. [31:436]

SHOGHI EFFENDI, RESTING PLACE OF The only Holy Place in the Western world. It is situated in the New Southgate Cemetery (originally the Great Northern London Cemetery), New Southgate, London. It is in a central position of an area owned by the Bahá'í Faith with many graves of Bahá'ís in the vicinity. The tomb itself is beneath a white marble column, crowned by a Corinthian capital on which rests a globe, with a map of Africa facing the Qiblih. Bahá'ís from all over the world visit the grave for prayer and meditation.

SIMPLE, PETER (1899-1971) The second Athabascan Indian north of the Arctic Circle to embrace the Cause. [51:498][60:510]

SIMS, ELLEN CATHERINE An American believer (1938) who pioneered with her husband (Stuart) extensively throughout South America: Paraguay, Colombia and Bolivia. She was a member of the Regional National Spiritual Assembly of Argentina, Bolivia, Chile, Paraguay and Uruguay, as well as the National Spiritual Assembly of Colombia and then, separately, the National Spiritual Assembly of Bolivia. [11:322]

SIN In the Bahá'í teachings there is no such thing as "original sin." Evil is the absence of good; confession of sins before another is forbidden (though consultation with a spiritual assembly about dealing with personal problems is not in this category); no sin is unforgivable, and the concealing of the sins of others is a personal responsibility. Baptism is not practiced. From the vast number of passages in Bahá'í Scripture the following give some insight on this subject.

Bahá'u'lláh wrote:

> If ye become aware of a sin committed by another, conceal it, that God may conceal your own sin." [70:55]
>
> Breathe not the sins of others so long as thou art thyself a sinner. Shouldst thou transgress this command, accursed wouldst thou be.... Know thou of a truth: He that biddeth men be just and himself committeth iniquity is not of Me, even though he bear My name. [92:27]
>
> Wherefore, hearken ye unto My speech, and return ye to God and repent, that He, through His grace, may have mercy upon you, may wash away your sins, and forgive your trespasses. The greatness of His mercy surpasseth the fury of His wrath, and His grace encompasseth all who have been called into being and been clothed with the robe of life, be they of the past or of the future. [85:130]

With all his heart he should avoid fellowship with evil-doers, and pray for the remission of their sins. He should forgive the sinful, and never despise his low estate, for none knoweth what his own end shall be. How often hath a sinner attained, at the hour of death, to the essence of faith, and, quaffing the immortal draught, hath taken his flight unto the Concourse on high! [85:266]

Forgive me, O my Lord, my sins which have hindered me from walking in the ways of Thy good-pleasure, and from attaining the shores of the ocean of Thy oneness. [132:29]

When the sinner findeth himself wholly detached and freed from all save God, he should beg forgiveness and pardon from Him. Confession of sins and transgressions before human beings is not permissible, as it hath never been nor will ever be conducive to divine forgiveness. Moreover such confession before people results in one's humiliation and abasement, and God—exalted be His glory—wisheth not the humiliation of His servants. Verily He is the Compassionate, the Merciful. The sinner should, between himself and God, implore mercy from the Ocean of mercy, beg forgiveness from the Heaven of generosity. [77:24]

'Abdu'l-Bahá wrote:

If there was no wrong how would you recognize the right? If it were not for sin how would you appreciate virtue? If evil deeds were unknown how could you commend good actions? If sickness did not exist how would you understand health? Evil is non-existent; it is the absence of good; sickness is the loss of health; poverty the lack of riches. [107:78]

Evil is imperfection. Sin is the state of man in the world of the baser nature, for in nature exist defects such as injustice, tyranny, hatred, hostility, strife: these are characteristics of the lower plane of nature. These are the sins of the world, the fruits of the tree from which Adam did eat. Through education we must free ourselves from these imperfections. The Prophets of God have been sent, the Holy Books have been written, so that man may be made free. Just as he is born into this world of imperfection from the womb of his earthly mother, so is he born into the world of spirit through divine education. When a man is born into the world of phenomena he finds the universe; when he is born from this world to the world of the spirit, he finds the Kingdom. [25:177]

The principle of baptism is purification by repentance. John admonished and exhorted the people, and caused them to repent; then he baptized them. Therefore, it is apparent that this baptism is a symbol of repentance from all sin: its meaning is expressed in these words: "O God! as my body has become purified and cleansed from physical impurities, in the same way purify and sanctify my spirit from the impurities of the world of nature, which are not worthy of the Threshold of Thy Unity!" [56:91]

All sin comes from the demands of nature, and these demands, which arise from the physical qualities, are not sins with respect to the animals, while for man they are sin. The animal is the source of imperfections, such as anger, sensuality, jealousy, avarice, cruelty, pride: all these defects are found in animals but do not constitute sins. But in man they are sins. [56:119]

SINGH, PRITAM (1881-1959) Professor Singh was the first (c.1908) member of the Sikh Faith in the Indian subcontinent to become a Bahá'í. [47:874]

ṢIRÁT Lote Tree. See **SADRATU'L-MUNTAHÁ**. [11:741📖]

SIRR Secret, mystery. Arḍ-i-Sirr. Literally The Land of Mystery: Adrianople. [11:741📖]

SIRRU'LLÁH The Mystery of God: a designation of 'Abdu'l-Bahá, conferred on Him by Bahá'u'lláh. [11:741📖]

SIYÁH-CHÁL The "Black Pit," the underground dungeon in Ṭihrán, Írán where Bahá'u'lláh was imprisoned for four months in the autumn of 1852 along with a number of other Bábís and where, chained and in the most appalling circumstances, He received the Call from God to be the "Promised One." (q.v.). We have Bahá'u'lláh's own description of this event:

Nevertheless, they apprehended Us, and ... conducted Us, on foot and in chains, with bared head and bare feet, to the dungeon of Ṭihrán....We were consigned for four months to a place foul beyond comparison. As to the dungeon in which this Wronged One and others similarly wronged were confined, a dark and narrow pit were preferable. Upon Our arrival We were first conducted along a pitch-black corridor, from whence We descended three steep flights of stairs to the place of confinement assigned to Us. The dungeon was wrapped in thick darkness, and Our fellow-prisoners numbered nearly a hundred and fifty souls: thieves, assassins and highwaymen. Though crowded, it had no other outlet than the passage by which We entered. No pen can depict that place, nor any tongue describe its loathsome smell. Most of these men had neither clothes nor bedding to lie on. God alone knoweth what befell Us in that most foul-smelling and gloomy place! [5:72]

Shoghi Effendi described it as follows:

A Revelation, hailed as the promise and crowning glory of past ages and centuries, as the consummation of all the Dispensations within the Adamic Cycle ... signalizing the end of the Prophetic Era and the beginning of the Era of Fulfillment, unsurpassed alike in the duration of its Author's ministry and the fecundity and splendor of His mission—such a Revelation was, as already noted, born amidst the darkness of a subterranean dungeon in Ṭihrán—an abominable pit that had once served as a reservoir of water for one of the public baths of the city. Wrapped in its stygian gloom, breathing its fetid air, numbed by its humid and icy atmosphere, His feet in stocks, His neck weighed down by a mighty chain, surrounded by criminals and miscreants of the worst order ... painfully aware of the dire distress that had overtaken its champions, and of the grave dangers that faced the remnant of its followers—at so critical an hour and under such appalling circumstances the "Most Great Spirit," as designated by Himself ... descended upon, and revealed itself, in the form of a "Maiden," to the agonized soul of Bahá'u'lláh. [5:100f]

Was not the Bearer of such a Revelation, at the instigation of Shí'ah ecclesiastics and by order of the Sháh himself forced, for no less than four months, to breathe, in utter darkness, whilst in the company of the vilest criminals and freighted down with galling chains, the pestilential air of the vermin-infested subterranean dungeon of Ṭihrán—a place which, as He Himself subsequently declared, was mysteriously converted into the very scene of the annunciation made to Him by God of His Prophethood? [44:10] See **BAHÁ'U'LLÁH**.

SIYÁVUSHÍ, JAMSHÍD (1944-1983) (Martyr) **SIYÁVUSHÍ, ṬÁHIRIH ARJUMANDI** (1951-1983) (Martyr) A husband and wife who were executed along with other coreligionists in Shíráz,

Írán, by the government in June 1983, for refusing to recant their belief in Bahá'u'lláh. [11:598]

SIYYID Literally chief, lord, prince: descendant of the Prophet Muḥammad. [11:741📖]

SIYYID ḤUSAYN-I-YAZDÍ An amanuensis to the Báb and surnamed by Him, 'Azíz; he shared the Báb's imprisonments in both Máh-Kú and Chihríq; seventh Letter of the Living.

SIYYID YAḤYÁY-I-DÁRÁBÍ See **VAḤÍD**.

SMOKING 'Abdu'l-Bahá wrote:

> [There are] the things forbidden by an absolute prohibition and of which the perpetration is a grave sin; they are so vile that even to mention them is shameful. There are other forbidden things which do not cause an immediate evil and of which the pernicious effect is only gradually produced. They are also abhorred, blamed and rejected by God, but their prohibition is not recorded in an absolute way, although cleanliness and sanctity, spotlessness and purity, the preservation of health and independence are required by these interdictions.... One of these last prohibitions is the smoking of tobacco, which is unclean, malodorous, disagreeable and vulgar and of which the gradual harmfulness is universally recognized. All clever physicians have judged, and have also shown by experiment, that one of the constituents of tobacco is a mortal poison and that smokers are exposed to different indispositions and maladies. That is why cleanly people have a marked aversion for its use. [106:334]
>
> I wish to say that, in the sight of God, the smoking of tobacco is a thing which is blamed and condemned, very unclean, and of which the result is by degrees injurious. Besides it is a cause of expense and of loss of time and it is a harmful habit. So, for those who are firm in the Covenant, it is a thing reprobated by the reason and by tradition, the renouncement of which giveth gradual repose and tranquillity, permitteth one to have stainless hands and a clean mouth, and hair which is not pervaded by a bad odor.... Without any doubt, the friends of God on receiving this epistle will renounce this injurious habit by all means, even if it be necessary to do so by degrees. This is my hope. [106:335]

SNIDER, HOWARD J. (1884-1970) (Knight of Bahá'u'lláh) An early (1915) American believer. In 1953, he pioneered to Key West, Florida for which service he was designated a Knight of

Bahá'u'lláh. At the age of 70 (1954) he pioneered to Switzerland followed in 1965 by a move to Barbados. [51:481][60:514]

SOMBEEK, GEORGETTE STRAUB-VAN BLEYSWIJK VAN (1906-1979) One of the first (1946) Bahá'ís in the Netherlands. Along with her sister (**SOMBEEK, RITA VAN BLEYSWIJK** [q.v.]), who introduced Georgette to the Faith, she translated Bahá'í literature into the Dutch language, including *The Hidden Words of Bahá'u'lláh, Bahá'u'lláh and the New Era*, and the various "prayers." [53:475]

SOMBEEK, LUDMILA (OTT) VAN (1893-1979) An early (1922) American believer of Austrian birth who worked tirelessly throughout the southern United States for the promotion of racial unity. She was a member of the first (1962) local Spiritual Assembly of Durham, North Carolina. She traveled extensively behind the (then) Iron Curtain countries of Czechoslovakia, Hungary and Bulgaria (1958, 1963, 1965 and 1967.) In 1958 she toured Russia and in 1967 visited Írán, both in the promotion of the Cause. [2:689]

SOMBEEK, RITA VAN BLEYSWIJK (1903-1981) One of the first (1945) Dutch believers, she embraced the Cause in America after attending a lecture by Stanwood Cobb. In 1946 she pioneered to Europe, where she lived for varying times in Holland, Italy and Luxembourg. She helped raise up the first (1947) local Spiritual Assembly of Amsterdam and later (1970) served on the first local Spiritual Assembly of Doesburg, Luxembourg, in 1973 on the first local Spiritual Assembly of Zeist. [2:763]

SOME ANSWERED QUESTIONS This was one of the three books that Shoghi Effendi said "...should be mastered by every Bahá'í. They should read these books over and over again." [137:27] The other two are the *Kitáb-i-Íqán* and *The Dawnbreakers* (Nabíl's Narrative). See **DREYFUS-BARNEY, LAURA CLIFFORD**.

SOUL The Bahá'í Scriptures contain a great many references to the soul, its development, its relation to the body and its progress after death. Each human soul comes into existence at conception and is unique and eternal. The purpose of human life on this earth is to develop spiritual qualities that will equip the soul for its eternal life after physical death. After "death" it continues to progress according to the mercy of God, the prayers and intercession of its friends and relatives and even through charity performed in its name. A few passages have been selected to illustrate the Bahá'í concept of the soul.

Bahá'u'lláh wrote:

> Know thou that the soul of man is exalted above, and is independent of all infirmities of body or mind.... Every malady afflicting the body of man is an impediment that

preventeth the soul from manifesting its inherent might and power. When it leaveth the body, however, it will evince such ascendancy, and reveal such influence as no force on earth can equal. Every pure, every refined and sanctified soul will be endowed with tremendous power, and shall rejoice with exceeding gladness. [85:153]

Know thou, of a truth, that if the soul of man hath walked in the ways of God, it will, assuredly, return and be gathered to the glory of the Beloved. By the righteousness of God! It shall attain a station such as no pen can depict, or tongue describe. The soul that hath remained faithful to the Cause of God, and stood unwaveringly firm in His Path shall, after his ascension, be possessed of such power that all the worlds which the Almighty hath created can benefit through him. *[85:154,161]*

He hath endowed every soul with the capacity to recognize the signs of God. How could He, otherwise, have fulfilled His testimony unto men, if ye be of them that ponder His Cause in their hearts. He will never deal unjustly with any one, neither will He task a soul beyond its power. He, verily, is the Compassionate, the All-Merciful. *[85:105]*

Know thou of a truth that the soul, after its separation from the body, will continue to progress until it attaineth the presence of God, in a state and condition which neither the revolution of ages and centuries, nor the changes and chances of this world, can alter. It will endure as long as the Kingdom of God, His sovereignty, His dominion and power will endure. It will manifest the signs of God and His attributes, and will reveal His loving kindness and bounty.... The honor with which the Hand of Mercy will invest the soul is such as no tongue can adequately reveal, nor any other earthly agency describe. Blessed is the soul which, at the hour of its separation from the body, is sanctified from the vain imaginings of the peoples of the world. Such a soul liveth and moveth in accordance with the Will of its Creator ... the Prophets of God and His chosen ones will seek its companionship. With them that soul will freely converse, and will recount unto them that which it hath been made to endure in the path of God, the Lord of all worlds. If any man be told that which hath been ordained for such a soul in the worlds of God, ... his whole being will instantly blaze out in his great longing to attain that most exalted, that sanctified and resplendent station.... The nature of the soul after death can never be described, nor is it meet and permissible to reveal its whole character to the eyes of men. [85:155f]

I loved thy creation, hence I created thee. Wherefore, do thou love Me, that I may name thy name and fill thy soul with the spirit of life. [92:4]

'Abdu'l-Bahá explained:

The human spirit which distinguishes man from the animal is the rational soul; and these two names—the human spirit and the rational soul—designate one thing. This spirit, which in the terminology of the philosophers is the rational soul, embraces all beings, and as far as human ability permits discovers the realities of things and becomes cognizant of their peculiarities and effects, and of the qualities and properties of beings. But the human spirit, unless assisted by the spirit of faith, does not become acquainted with the divine secrets and the heavenly realities. It is like a mirror which, although clear, polished, and brilliant, is still in need of light. Until a ray of the sun reflects upon it, it cannot discover the heavenly secrets. *[106:317]* But the mind is the power of the human spirit. Spirit is the lamp; mind is the light which shines from the lamp. Spirit is the tree, and the mind is the fruit. Mind is the perfection of the spirit and is its essential quality, as the sun's rays are the essential necessity of the sun. [56:208f]

Shoghi Effendi wrote through his secretary:

What the Bahá'ís do believe though is that we have three aspects of our humanness, so to speak, a body, a mind and an immortal identity—soul or spirit. We believe the mind forms a link between the soul and the body, and the two interact on each other. [113:89] See **DEATH, LIFE AFTER.**

SPENDLOVE, F. ST. GEORGE (1897-1962) An early Canadian believer. He traveled widely in the promotion of the Cause and was a founder member of the first (1927) organized Bahá'í youth group in North America. He spent some time in London and served on the National Spiritual Assembly of the British Isles. [47:895][60:515]

ST. BARBE, RICHARD BAKER See **BAKER, RICHARD St. BARBE.**

STAMP, ELIZABETH (1887-1970) (Knight of Bahá'u'lláh) An early (1939) American believer of Irish birth. She pioneered in 1954 to the island of St. Helena for which service she was designated a Knight of Bahá'u'lláh. [51:490]

STAR OF THE WEST This was the first Bahá'í magazine published in the West. It was printed in the United States from 1910 until 1924.

STEFFES, MARIAN (1900-1978) Among the first Oneida Indians to embrace the Cause. She was an outstanding teacher of the Cause among the Indian peoples. [53:458]

STEINMETZ, ELSA (-1970) An early American believer who pioneered to Switzerland in 1947 and assisted in the formation of the first Bahá'í community in Berne (later the first local Spiritual Assembly (1949).) She served on the first Italo-Swiss National Spiritual Assembly and then on the National Spiritual Assembly of Switzerland. [51:475]

STEVENSON, MARGARET BEVERIDGE (-1941) The first believer in New Zealand. [45:600][60:520]

STOUT, JANET WHITENACK (1907-1985) Although born in Pelham, New York she was the first (1939) person to embrace the Cause in Alaska. In 1943 she moved from her pioneer post in the Eskimo village of Tulaksak to Anchorage in order to form the first local Spiritual Assembly in Alaska. In 1957 she was elected to the first National Spiritual Assembly of Alaska. Shortly thereafter she pioneered with her husband (Verne) as the first Bahá'ís in Palmer; they then moved five miles outside the town to "open" the Matanauska Valley. She also served as the first editor of the monthly newsletter *Alaska Bahá'í News*. [11:661]

STRUVEN, EDWARD (1875-1965) An early (1904) American believer, he was among those who welcomed 'Abdu'l-Bahá on His arrival in New York. He worked professionally on the construction of the Wilmette temple. [50:380][59:214ff]

ṢUFÍ An exponent of Ṣufism, a Muslim mystic or darví<u>sh</u>. [11:741📖]

SULṬÁN Sovereignty; King, sovereign, monarch, sultan.

SULṬÁNU'SH-<u>SH</u>UHADÁ' King of Martyrs. See **MÍRZÁ MUḤAMMAD-ḤASAN**.

SUMMER SCHOOLS, BAHÁ'Í These are sessions of instruction, frequently in residential accommodation, which may last for a few days or for one or more weeks. Different aspects of the Faith are studied in depth, and those attending enjoy the experience of Bahá'í fellowship. Some are dedicated to a particular theme, others focus on the arts, all are participatory, and experts, Bahá'í and non-Bahá'í, are invited to give lectures or run the training sessions. Some countries have permanent establishments where courses can run all through the year. Most of them are open to the public for those who wish to investigate the Faith.

SUNNAH Literally way, custom, practice; The Way of the Prophet as reported in the Ḥadíth. Designates by far the largest sect of Islám, which includes the four so-called orthodox sects: Hanbalites, Hanafites, Malakites and Shafiites. Sunnis accept the Caliphs as legitimate, believing that the position of Caliph is elective. See **SHÍ'AH; CALIPH.** [11:741]

SUNNÍ, SUNNITE Muslim of the Sunnah branch of Islám. [11:741]

SUPREME CONCOURSE See **CONCOURSE ON HIGH.**

SÚRIH Name of a chapter of the Qur'án; used by the Báb and Bahá'u'lláh in the titles of some of Their Own Writings. [11:741]

SÚRIH OF JOSEPH This was a chapter from the Qur'án that Mullá Ḥusayn had selected as a test he would submit to the "Promised One" for whom he was searching. On the evening he met the Báb (22 May 1844), unasked, the Báb revealed His commentary on this chapter with great power. From a description of that event by Shoghi Effendi we read:

> A more significant light, however, is shed on this episode, marking the Declaration of the Mission of the Báb, by the perusal of that "first, greatest and mightiest" of all books in the Bábí Dispensation, the celebrated commentary on the Súrih of Joseph, the first chapter of which, we are assured, proceeded, in its entirety, in the course of that night of nights from the pen of its divine Revealer. The description of this episode by Mullá Ḥusayn, as well as the opening pages of that Book attest the magnitude and force of that weighty Declaration. [5:6] See **BÁB; QAYYÚMU'L-ASMÁ.**

SZÁNTÓ-FELBERMANN, RENÉE (1900-1984) She was the first (1936) Hungarian to embrace the Cause some three years after listening to a lecture by Martha Root in Budapest. In 1956 she managed to flee (two months after the uprising) to London. In 1980 she published her memoirs in a book entitled *Rebirth—The Memoirs of Renée Szanto-Felbermann.* [138] In 1981 she moved to Germany where she passed away on 28 February 1984. [11:633]

T

ṬÁ The 19th letter of the Persian alphabet, with a numerical value of nine. Arḍ-i-Ṭá. Literally Land of Ṭá: Ṭihrán. [11:741]

TABARSÍ, FORT OF SHAYKH Noted in Bahá'í history for the superhuman power of Mullá Ḥusayn, the heroism of its defenders and their cruel betrayal. Excerpts from Shoghi Effendi's history describe some of these events:

> We remember with thrilling hearts that memorable encounter when, at the cry "Mount your steeds, O heroes of God!" Mullá Ḥusayn, accompanied by two hundred and two of the beleaguered and sorely-distressed companions, and preceded by Quddús, emerged before daybreak from the Fort, and, raising the shout of "Yá Ṣáḥibu'z-Zamán!", rushed at full charge towards the stronghold of the Prince, and penetrated to his private apartments, only to find that, in his consternation, he had thrown himself from a back window into the moat, and escaped barefooted, leaving his host confounded and routed. We see relived in poignant memory that last day of Mullá Ḥusayn's earthly life, when, soon after midnight, having performed his ablutions, clothed himself in new garments, and attired his head with the Báb's turban, he mounted his charger, ordered the gate of the Fort to be opened, rode out at the head of three hundred and thirteen of his companions, shouting aloud "Yá Ṣáḥibu'z-Zamán!", charged successively the seven barricades erected by the enemy, captured every one of them, notwithstanding the bullets that were raining upon him, swiftly dispatched their defenders, and had scattered their forces when, in the ensuing tumult, his steed became suddenly entangled in the rope of a tent, and before he could extricate himself he was struck in the breast by a bullet ... We acclaim the magnificent courage that, in a subsequent encounter, inspired nineteen of those stout-hearted companions to plunge headlong into the camp of an enemy that consisted of no less than two regiments of infantry and cavalry ... Nor can we fail to note the superb fortitude with which these heroic souls bore the load of their severe trials; when their food was at first reduced to the flesh of horses brought away from the deserted camp of the enemy; when later they had to content themselves with such grass as they could snatch from the fields whenever they obtained a respite from their besiegers; when they were forced, at a later stage, to consume the bark of the trees and the leather of their saddles, of their belts, of their scabbards and of their shoes; when during eighteen days they had nothing but water of which they drank a mouthful every morning; when the cannon fire of

> the enemy compelled them to dig subterranean passages within the Fort, where, dwelling amid mud and water, with garments rotting away with damp, they had to subsist on ground up bones; and when, at last, oppressed by gnawing hunger, they, as attested by a contemporary chronicler, were driven to disinter the steed of their venerated leader, Mullá Ḥusayn, cut it into pieces, grind into dust its bones, mix it with the putrefied meat, and, making it into a stew, avidly devour it.... Nor can reference be omitted to the abject treachery to which the impotent and discredited Prince eventually resorted, and his violation of his so-called irrevocable oath ... whereby he ... undertook to set free all the defenders of the Fort, pledged his honor that no man in his army or in the neighborhood would molest them, and that he would himself, at his own expense, arrange for their safe departure to their homes. And lastly, we call to remembrance, the final scene ... when, as a result of the Prince's violation of his sacred engagement, a number of the betrayed companions of Quddús were assembled in the camp of the enemy, were stripped of their possessions, and sold as slaves, the rest being either killed by the spears and swords of the officers, or torn asunder, or bound to trees and riddled with bullets, or blown from the mouths of cannon and consigned to the flames, or else being disembowelled and having their heads impaled on spears and lances. [5:40]

TABLET Remembering the Tablets of Moses, the word has been used in Bahá'í terminology to refer to the written words of Bahá'u'lláh, the Báb and 'Abdu'l-Bahá to imply the permanency of Their Works.

TABLET OF THE BRANCH Revealed by Bahá'u'lláh describing the station of 'Abdu'l-Bahá. [5:242]

TABLET OF CARMEL Probably revealed by Bahá'u'lláh during His fourth and last visit to Haifa in 1891 when He pointed out to 'Abdu'l-Bahá the spot where the Tomb of the Báb should be built. Written in Arabic, it is described by Shoghi Effendi as one of the three "Charters" for the worldwide development of the Faith. See **THREE CHARTERS**.

TABLETS OF THE DIVINE PLAN During WW I 'Abdu'l-Bahá wrote 14 messages to the Bahá'ís of North America, who received them in 1919. These constituted one of the three Charters mentioned above and about them Shoghi Effendi wrote:

> And yet during these somber days, the darkness of which was reminiscent of the tribulations endured during the

> most dangerous period of His incarceration in the prison-fortress of 'Akká, 'Abdu'l-Bahá, whilst in the precincts of His Father's Shrine, or when dwelling in the House He occupied in 'Akká, or under the shadow of the Báb's sepulcher on Mt. Carmel, was moved to confer once again, and for the last time in His life, on the community of His American followers a signal mark of His special favor by investing them, on the eve of the termination of His earthly ministry, through the revelation of the Tablets of the Divine Plan, with a world mission, whose full implications even now, after the lapse of a quarter of a century, still remain undisclosed, and whose unfoldment thus far, though as yet in its initial stages, has so greatly enriched the spiritual as well as the administrative annals of the first Bahá'í century. [5:305]

Outstanding among those who reacted immediately to 'Abdu'l-Bahá's call were Martha Root (q.v.), and Clare and Hyde Dunn (q.v.) but it was only in 1937, with the launching of the American Seven Year Plan that a beginning was made for a planned stage-by-stage response. See **THREE CHARTERS**.

TABLETS OF VISITATION Special Prayers and Readings to be used in certain Holy Places or on Holy Days. The one frequently used in the Shrines of Bahá'u'lláh and the Báb [132:310] and on the Holy Days associated with Their lives is actually a compilation of passages from the Writings of Bahá'u'lláh made by Nabíl on the instruction of 'Abdu'l-Bahá. [65:319] One used frequently in private prayer, at meetings, on the commemorations associated with 'Abdu'l-Bahá and in His Shrine was revealed by Him and commences with the words: "Whoso reciteth this prayer with lowliness and fervor will bring gladness and joy to the heart of this servant; it will be even as meeting Him face to face." [65:319]

TABLETS TO THE KINGS [78] Bahá'u'lláh addressed a series of letters to the kings and rulers of the time. The first was His Tablet to the Sultan of Turkey written while He was in Constantinople; some were addressed to individuals others to them collectively. These dated from His exile in Turkey after His Declaration in Bag͟hdád in 1863 and continued though into his exile in Palestine. Those addressed included Náṣiri'd-Dín S͟háh; Napoleon III; Queen Victoria; Kaiser Wilhelm I; Franz Joseph of Austria and Hungary; Czar Alexander II; Pope Pius IX and the "Rulers of America and the Presidents of the Republics therein." In all of these He publicly proclaimed His Message, and as Shoghi Effendi wrote:

> In His Tablet to Queen Victoria He, moreover, invites these kings to hold fast to "the Lesser Peace," since they

had refused "the Most Great Peace;" exhorts them to be reconciled among themselves, to unite and to reduce their armaments; bids them refrain from laying excessive burdens on their subjects, who, He informs them, are their "wards" and "treasures;" enunciates the principle that should any one among them take up arms against another, all should rise against him; and warns them not to deal with Him as the "King of Islám" and his ministers had dealt. [5:206f]

TABRÍZ City in northwest Írán where the Báb was held for 40 days before His imprisonment in the fortress of Máh-Kú and where He was again taken to be questioned, tortured and finally, on 9 July 1850, suffered martyrdom See **CHIHRÍQ**; **MÁH-KÚ**; **MARTYRDOM OF THE BÁB**.

TAFFA, TERESA PIA (1915-1984) An Italian believer who served as the only woman member on the first (1962) National Spiritual Assembly of Italy. She served as its Secretary for five of her 13 years on that body. In 1966 she pioneered to the Aeolian Islands. [11:644]

ṬÁHIRIH (the Pure One) (1817-1853) She was born Fáṭimih Umm-Salamih. The title Ṭáhirih was given to her by Bahá'u'lláh during the Conference of Badasht (q.v.). She was also known as Qurratu'l-'Ayn (Solace of the Eyes) and Zarrín-Táj (Crown of Gold). She was the 17th Letter of the Living (q.v.) and the only woman to be so designated. She became the first woman "suffragette" to be martyred. Shoghi Effendi gives some of her extraordinary story:

> A poetess, less than thirty years of age, of distinguished birth, of bewitching charm, of captivating eloquence, indomitable in spirit, unorthodox in her views, audacious in her acts, immortalized as Ṭáhirih (the Pure One) by (Bahá'u'lláh) and surnamed Qurratu'l-'Ayn (Solace of the Eyes) by Siyyid Káẓim, her teacher, she had, in consequence of the appearance of the Báb to her in a dream, received the first intimation of a Cause which was destined to exalt her to the fairest heights of fame, and on which she, through her bold heroism, was to shed such imperishable lustre.... [In the conference of Badasht] ... One day ... Ṭáhirih, regarded as the fair and spotless emblem of chastity and the incarnation of the holy Fáṭimih, appeared suddenly, adorned yet unveiled, before the assembled companions, seated herself on the right-hand of the affrighted and infuriated Quddús, and, tearing through her fiery words the veils guarding the sanctity of the ordinances of Islam, sounded the clarion-call, and pro-

claimed the inauguration, of a new Dispensation. The effect was electric and instantaneous. She, of such stainless purity, so reverenced that even to gaze at her shadow was deemed an improper act, appeared for a moment, in the eyes of her scandalized beholders, to have defamed herself, shamed the Faith she had espoused, and sullied the immortal Countenance she symbolized. Fear, anger, bewilderment, swept their inmost souls, and stunned their faculties.... Undeterred, unruffled, exultant with joy, Ṭáhirih arose, and, without the least premeditation and in a language strikingly resembling that of the Qur'án, delivered a fervid and eloquent appeal to the remnant of the assembly, ending it with this bold assertion: "I am the Word which the Qá'im is to utter, the Word which shall put to flight the chiefs and nobles of the earth!" [5:32f]

Her meteoric career, inaugurated in Karbilá, culminating in Badasht, was now about to attain its final consummation in a martyrdom that may well rank as one of the most affecting episodes in the most turbulent period of Bahá'í history.... A scion of the highly reputed family of Ḥájí Mullá Ṣáliḥ-i-Baraqání ... designated as Zarrín-Táj (Crown of Gold) and Zakíyyih (Virtuous) by her family and kindred; born in the same year as Bahá'u'lláh; regarded from childhood, by her fellow-townsmen, as a prodigy, alike in her intelligence and beauty; highly esteemed even by some of the most haughty and learned 'ulamás of her country, prior to her conversion, for the brilliancy and novelty of the views she propounded ... established her first contact with a Faith which she continued to propagate to her last breath, and in its hour of greatest peril, with all the ardor of her unsubduable spirit. Undeterred by the vehement protests of her father; contemptuous of the anathemas of her uncle; unmoved by the earnest solicitations of her husband and her brothers... [5:82]

'Abdu'l-Bahá tells of her martyrdom:

She was sentenced to death. Saying she was summoned to the Prime Minister's, they arrived to lead her away from the Kalántar's house. She bathed her face and hands, arrayed herself in a costly dress, and scented with attar of roses she came out of the house.... They brought her into a garden, where the headsmen waited; but these wavered and then refused to end her life. A slave was found, far gone in drunkenness; besotted, vicious, black of heart.

> And he strangled Ṭáhirih. He forced a scarf between her lips and rammed it down her throat. Then they lifted up her unsullied body and flung it in a well, there in the garden, and over it threw down earth and stones. But Ṭáhirih rejoiced; she had heard with a light heart the tidings of her martyrdom; she set her eyes on the supernal Kingdom and offered up her life. [124:202f]

Shoghi Effendi completes her story: "Thus ended the life of this great Bábí heroine, the first woman suffrage martyr, who, at her death, turning to the one in whose custody she had been placed, had boldly declared: 'You can kill me as soon as you like, but you cannot stop the emancipation of women.'" [5:75][13]

TÁJ Literally crown. Tall felt head-dress adopted by Bahá'u'lláh in 1863 on the day of His departure from His Most Holy House in Baghdád. [11:741]

TAJALLÍYÁT Effulgences: title of one of the Tablets of Bahá'u'lláh revealed after the Kitáb-i-Aqdas. [11:741]

TAKYIH Religious house, monastery; hostel for pilgrims; religious theater for presenting Muslim passion-plays; specifically, the place at which the martyrdom of Ḥusayn is commemorated. See **ḤUSAYNÍYYIH.** [11:741]

TAMASESE, SAIALALA LEALOFI II (1912-1965) The first indigenous Samoan to embrace the Cause. [50:382]

ṬÁRÁZÁT Ornaments: title of one of the Tablets of Bahá'u'lláh revealed after the Kitáb-i-Aqdas. [11:741]

TEACHING Bahá'ís look at two aspects of teaching. There is teaching as a profession, and there is the teaching of the Bahá'í Faith. Bahá'u'lláh's words are quite clear on the latter—it is an obligation for every Bahá'í. Shoghi Effendi writes most emphatically on this subject:

> To teach the Cause of God, to proclaim its truths, to defend its interests, to demonstrate, by words as well as by deeds, its indispensability, its potency, and universality, should at no time be regarded as the exclusive concern or sole privilege of Bahá'í administrative institutions, be they Assemblies, or committees. All must participate, however humble their origin, however limited their experience, however restricted their means, however deficient their education, however pressing their cares and preoccupations, however unfavorable the environment in which they live. "God," Bahá'u'lláh, Himself, has unmistakably revealed, "hath prescribed unto everyone the duty of teaching His Cause." "Say," He further has written, "Teach ye the Cause of God, O people of Bahá, for God hath pre-

scribed unto everyone the duty of proclaiming His Message, and regardeth it as the most meritorious of all deeds." [39:45]

Bahá'u'lláh describes the prerequisites for teaching:

Whoso ariseth among you to teach the Cause of his Lord, let him, before all else, teach his own self, that his speech may attract the hearts of them that hear him. Unless he teacheth his own self, the words of his mouth will not influence the heart of the seeker. Take heed, O people, lest ye be of them that give good counsel to others but forget to follow it themselves. [85:277]

Should any one among you be incapable of grasping a certain truth, or be striving to comprehend it, show forth, when conversing with him, a spirit of extreme kindliness and good-will. Help him to see and recognize the truth, without esteeming yourself to be, in the least, superior to him, or to be possessed of greater endowments. [85:8]

Due to the emphasis given to teaching and especially to the teaching of children, teaching as a profession is highly regarded in the Bahá'í Faith. See **PROSELYTIZING**.

TEACHING INSTITUTES In order to deepen (q.v.) believers in their Faith and increase their knowledge of its history, teachings, laws and the constituent elements of Bahá'í life, teaching institutes are established. These may be conducted in Bahá'í Centers, homes, rented accommodation or, where a community has adequate resources, in permanent establishments with regular courses and published curricula. When a national Bahá'í Community is strong enough to maintain permanent training centers, such institutes can make a substantial contribution to the education and deepening of the Bahá'ís and in poorer countries where the community needs education in basic skills, literacy, hygiene, etc., outside financial assistance can provide such institutes and so provide help for the Bahá'ís and for the wider society as well.

TEO, GEOK LENG (1907-1986) The first (1952) Chinese believer in Singapore, he served on the first (1952) local Spiritual Assembly of Singapore as well as serving on the first (1972) National Spiritual Assembly of Singapore (for eight years as Treasurer). From 1973 to 1984 he was appointed by the government of Singapore to solemnize marriages and in that capacity solemnized a great many Bahá'í marriages. [11:701]

TEN YEAR CRUSADE Originally Shoghi Effendi had anticipated three Seven Year Plans for the North American Bahá'ís—the First (1937-1944), the Second (1946-1953) and the Third, (1956-1963.)

However, the outstanding success of the Two Year Plan of the British Bahá'ís in their coordination of the efforts of their sister National Spiritual Assemblies in the African Campaign, and the victories being won by the American Bahá'ís in the prosecution of their second Seven Year Plan influenced him to change the American Third Plan, cut out the three-year respite and launch a Ten Year Plan for all existing National Spiritual Assemblies to coincide with the Centenary of the birth of Bahá'u'lláh's Mission (1953). It was also known as "The Global Crusade."

See **GOALS; KNIGHTS OF BAHÁ'U'LLÁH; PLANS.**

THÁBIT, AKHTAR (1958-1983) (Martyr) A young Bahá'í who was executed along with other coreligionists in Shíráz, Írán, by the government in June 1983, for refusing to recant her belief in Bahá'u'lláh. [11:600]

THACHER, CHESTER I. (Disciple of 'Abdu'l-Bahá) One of the earliest American believers and a most zealous worker for the Faith.

THOMAS, WILMA (1913-1977) An early American believer. She served as a pioneer in Ecuador, Peru, Colombia and Venezuela throughout the period 1955 until her passing in 1977. She was elected to the first National Spiritual Assembly of Colombia in 1961. In 1973 she was appointed an Auxiliary Board member for Venezuela. [53:436]

THOMPSON, JULIET (1873-1956) (Disciple of 'Abdu'l-Bahá) She was born in Washington, D.C., in 1873 and at a very early age displayed a talent for painting. Her father died when she was 12, leaving very little money, but she was able to sell her pastel portraits and by the age of 16 had already gained a fine reputation for her work. When a small child, she was on the verge of death with diphtheria when she overheard the doctor telling her mother of his prognosis. As she lay there she "dreamed" that a wonderful looking man assured her she would get well, and when she awoke the fever had broken, and she recovered. Many years later, while studying art in Paris, she saw a picture of 'Abdu'l-Bahá and immediately recognized Him as the man who had come to her in her dream. In 1901 she was associating with May Bolles (Maxwell) (q.v.), Lua Getsinger (q.v.), and others of that circle of early Bahá'ís and embraced the Cause during that period. Returning to the States after completing her studies at the Sorbonne, she began to teach the Faith in New York. In 1909 she was able to visit the Holy Land and kept a diary of her encounters with 'Abdu'l-Bahá. This included her "awesome" experience of being invited by Him to be present when He was dictating to His secretary.

When 'Abdu'l-Bahá visited New York City she was there to meet Him at the boat and followed Him to many places. While in

New York He invited her to paint His portrait and promised three sittings. She describes these occasions vividly in her diary. She was known to be an excellent teacher, with a radiant love of 'Abdu'l-Bahá and held meetings in her home to the end of her life. Many photographs were made of her painting of the Master, but it was in pastels, and the original was eventually lost. She passed away on 9 December 1956 and the Guardian cabled:

> Deplore loss much-loved greatly admired Juliet Thompson, outstanding, exemplary hand-maid 'Abdu'l-Bahá. Over half-century record manifold meritorious services, embracing concluding years Heroic opening decades Formative Age Bahá'í Dispensation won her enviable position glorious company triumphant disciples beloved Master Abhá Kingdom. Advise hold memorial gathering Mas͟hriqu'l-Ad͟hkár pay befitting tribute imperishable memory one so wholly consecrated Faith Bahá'u'lláh fired such consuming devotion Centre His Covenant. [47:862][83:73]

THORNBURGH, Mrs. (Disciple of 'Abdu'l-Bahá); **THORNBURGH-CROPPER, MARY VIRGINIA (Maryam K͟hánum)** (-1938) Mrs. Thornburgh was staying with her daughter, Mrs. Mary Virginia Thornburgh-Cropper, in London when they heard of the Bahá'í Faith by mail from a friend in San Francisco (Mrs. Phoebe Hearst) who promised to tell them more when she came to London en route to 'Akká, Palestine. The outcome was that they accompanied Mrs. Hearst on the first pilgrimage from the West to 'Abdu'l-Bahá in December 1898. Mrs. Thornburgh-Cropper visited the Holy Land again in 1906 and by that time had an active group meeting in London, she being the first resident Bahá'í in the British Isles. During the visits of 'Abdu'l-Bahá to London in 1911 and 1912-13 she placed her car at His disposal and with her close friend, Lady Blomfield (q.v.), arranged the very intensive schedule of visitors for Him.

Mrs. Thornburgh-Cropper was associated with the administration of the Faith in the British Isles from its beginning. On 6 June 1922 the first meeting of a Bahá'í Spiritual Council for England met in her house, and she was one of the seven members from London (with one each from Bournemouth and Manchester) on that body. The National Spiritual Assembly of the Bahá'ís of the British Isles, which replaced the Council, met for the first time in her house on the 13 October 1923. Notwithstanding her failing health, in January 1932 it was reported that she, Lady Blomfield and Mrs. George had commenced work on a history of the Faith in England. Sadly, however, by that time she was an invalid and unable to participate in any active sense. She passed away on 15 March 1938 in London. [42:649][91:17][60:521]

THREE CHARTERS Shoghi Effendi identified three separate documents as Charters for the creation of the Bahá'í Faith:

> the triple impulse generated through the revelation of the Tablet of Carmel by Bahá'u'lláh and the Will and Testament as well as the Tablets of the Divine Plan bequeathed by the Center of His Covenant—the three Charters which have set in motion three distinct processes, the first operating in the Holy Land for the development of the institutions of the Faith at its World Center and the other two, throughout the rest of the Bahá'í world, for its propagation and the establishment of its Administrative Order.... [6:84] See **'ABDU'L-BAHÁ, WILL & TESTAMENT OF; TABLET OF CARMEL; TABLETS OF THE DIVINE PLAN.**

ṬIHRÁN Capital city of Írán. Home of Bahá'u'lláh for many years and the city in which He received the message from the Báb (q.v.) via Mullá Ḥusayn (q.v.). The scene of many of the martyrdoms of the Bábís and the site of the infamous Siyáh-Ch͟ál where He experienced His Revelation in 1852.

TOBEY, MARK (1890-1976) An early (1918) American believer who was renowned for his genius as a painter. Although his main services to the faith have been through his art and public association with the Bahá'í Faith, he also served as a member of several local Spiritual Assemblies (Seattle, Washington; Victoria, B.C.; Basel, Switzerland) and for three years served as a member of the National Spiritual Assembly of the British Isles. He gave countless lectures and talks wherever he went. [139][53:401]

TOBIN, ESTHER (Nettie) (-1944) An early American believer. Mrs. Tobin found and delivered the stone used by 'Abdu'l-Bahá as the cornerstone of the Mas͟hriqu'l-Ad͟hkár in Wilmette. [19:543][60:525]

TORMO, SALVADOR (-1960) (Knight of Bahá'u'lláh) He and his wife (Adela) established the first Spiritual Assembly on the Island of Juan Fernandez (Robinson Crusoe Island) in 1953 for which service they were designated Knights of Bahá'u'lláh. [47:908]

TOWNSHEND, GEORGE (1876-1957) (Hand of the Cause of God) Born in Dublin, of distinguished Irish parents on 14 June 1876 he was destined to become the only Irish Hand of the Cause of God and one of the three to be appointed from Europe in the first contingent on 24 December 1951. He was the eldest of seven children of his father's second wife, the first wife having died at the early age of 43 after also giving birth to seven children. In his youth he was a notable athlete, studied classics and English, first at Uppingham Public School and later at Hertford College, Oxford, from which he graduated with a modest B.A. and a good collection of trophies for his athletic prowess. Living in the family home in Dublin, George took a degree in law and was called to the bar. At the same time his literary talents were developing, and he became a leader-writer for the *Irish Times* while officially practicing as a barrister between 1903 and 1920. In fact, he never argued a case, disliking the narrow life of Dublin and the grave social problems of Ireland. With his father's support, he spent from early 1904 until the end of 1905 riding around the Rocky Mountains, ending up in Salt Lake City where he studied and was ordained as a priest in the Episcopal Church of America. Eventually he abandoned the ministry for a new ethical movement and made a living by teaching at the Salt Lake City High School (while living with his sister Kathleen, who was nursing at the hospital). He returned to Ireland in 1916, and an eye trouble reoccurred that led to complete blindness for a while. This prevented him from returning to America and so he took up employment with the Church of Ireland.

In the winter of 1916, with his sight returning, he learned of the Bahá'í Faith from some pamphlets sent by a librarian in Sewanee, Tennessee with whom he had boarded. He sent off for more literature, which eventually arrived in July 1917 on the very day he met Nancy Maxwell, whom he married in 1918. Shortly after he was appointed to the incumbency of Ahascragh, Ballinasloe, Co. Galway which became their home for the next 28 years.

On 10 June 1919 he wrote his first letter to 'Abdu'l-Bahá and received a reply six weeks later. A few months later George accepted the Faith by writing a poem to 'Abdu'l-Bahá from which the following verse is culled:

> Thy words are to me as fragrances borne from the garden of heaven,
>
> Beams of a lamp that is hid in the height of a holier world, Arrows of fire that pierce and destroy with the might of the levin,
>
> Into our midnight hurled...[140:49]

In His response 'Abdu'l-Bahá included a phrase that was to become the guiding light for the remainder of George's life, "It is my hope that thy church will come under the Heavenly Jerusalem" [140:50]

He resigned formally from the church in 1947 and moved with his family into a bungalow in Dundrum, Dublin. His letter, primarily addressed to the clergy, *The Old Churches and the New World Faith* was printed as a pamphlet and was widely distributed in February 1949, with some 10,000 copies being sent to

Christian clergymen throughout the British Isles; 5,000 went to Australia, 2,000 to the United States and 4,000 to Canada. He subsequently traveled to several British Bahá'í communities to teach the Faith but due to failing health was able to attend only one of the Intercontinental Conferences in Stockholm.

During the last years of his life he spent varying periods in different nursing homes, including his old home in Dublin which had been turned into a clinic. He passed away, with one of the first copies of his last book, *Christ and Bahá'u'lláh* in his hands, in the Baggot Street Hospital on 25 March 1957. The Guardian cabled:

> Deeply mourn passing dearly loved much admired greatly gifted outstanding Hand Cause George Townshend. His death morrow publication his crowning achievement robs British followers Bahá'u'lláh their most distinguished collaborator and Faith itself one its stoutest defenders. His sterling qualities his scholarship his challenging writings his high ecclesiastical position unrivaled any Bahá'í western world entitle him with Thomas Breakwell, Dr. Esslemont one of three luminaries shedding brilliant lustre annals Irish, English, Scottish Bahá'í communities. His fearless championship Cause he loved so dearly, served so valiantly constitutes significant landmark British Bahá'í history ... confident his reward inestimable Abhá Kingdom. [140:365][47:841][60:529]

TRIGG, MARTHA 'NAKIYA' NOYAKUK (1944-1978) An Eskimo born in Mary's Igloo, Alaska, she embraced the Cause in 1961. When her husband (Jerome) became a Bahá'í (1967) they were the first Bahá'í Eskimo couple in the world. She and her husband promoted the Cause extensively among the Eskimo peoples. [53:448][60:536]

TRUE, CORINNE KNIGHT (1861-1961) (Hand of the Cause of God) Born in Oldham County, Kentucky on 1 November 1861, she married Moses Adams True in 1882 and had eight children. Although brought up in a strictly orthodox Presbyterian family, she soon embraced the Bahá'í Faith after hearing of it in 1899 and turned to 'Abdu'l-Bahá for a set of guiding principles and in response received the first of more than 50 letters from Him. Early in 1907 she made the first of her nine pilgrimages to the Holy Land. Her last was in 1952 after her appointment as a Hand of the Cause.

During all her Bahá'í life she dedicated herself to carrying out explicitly the guidance given to her by 'Abdu'l-Bahá with respect to the construction of the Mashriqu'l-Adhkár (q.v.) in Wilmette, Ill. He had said to her during her first pilgrimage: "Devote yourself to this project—make a beginning and all will come right...." and He gave her a description of what it should incorporate. She returned from her pilgrimage to the Holy Land in 1922 to attend the first Convention for the election of the National Spiritual Assembly of United States and Canada, to which she was duly elected.

During her last pilgrimage Shoghi Effendi remarked that "Mrs. True is to be regarded as the most venerable figure among the pioneers of the Faith of Bahá'u'lláh in the West." [47:848] Although her name will always be linked with the development of the House of Worship, she was an outstanding teacher of the Faith, and though she had no training and was shy before the public, she remembered 'Abdu'l-Bahá, Who had told her to turn her heart and mind to Him, and He would never fail her.

Encouraged by the Guardian, she spent many years in the training of teachers and during the years 1948-1952 visited many new centers in Western Europe and, as Shoghi Effendi's representative, attended, at the age of 95, the Convention of the Greater Antilles in April 1957.

While it was in 1907 that 'Abdu'l-Bahá had given Corinne the Temple mandate, she had the privilege of being hostess to Him when He came to Chicago to dedicate the ground selected for its construction. It was her crowning joy to see its completion in 1953 and be present at its dedication on 2 May of that year. On the passing of Shoghi Effendi, Corinne True was, at the age of 96, unable to travel to the Holy Land for the Conclave of the Hands of the Cause, but was able to sign an affidavit approving the Proclamation, thus making it a unanimous document of all 27 living Hands of the Cause.

She died in her 100th year on 2 April 1961. On 4 April 1961 the following cable was received from the Hands resident in the Holy Land:—"Grieved loss distinguished disciple 'Abdu'l-Bahá Hand Cause Corinne True. Her long association early history Faith America, raising Mother Temple West, staunch unfailing championship Covenant, steadfast support beloved Guardian every stage unfoldment World Order unforgettable enrich annals Faith western world. Urge hold befitting memorial gathering Mashriqu'l-Adhkár." [32:257][47:846][59:5ff][60:537]

TRUE, GEORGE RUSSELL (1911-1984) (Knight of Bahá'u'lláh) An American believer (1936) who, along with his wife Marguerite (known as Peggy) pioneered to the Canary Islands for which service they were designated Knights of Bahá'u'lláh. He served on the first (1955) local Spiritual Assembly of Santa Cruz de Tenerife until he and his wife again pioneered to Valle Gran Rey on the island of La Gomera in April 1979, thereby opening it to the Faith. [11:635]

TRUE, KATHERINE KNIGHT (1893-1963) An early American believer who at the age of nine wrote to 'Abdu'l-Bahá. She wrote several times to the Master and received several responses. She was elected to the National Spiritual Assembly of the United States for the period 1956 to 1960. [50:383]

TRUE SEEKER In the Kitáb-i-Íqán Bahá'u'lláh states clearly the requirements of the true seeker. These include:

> O my brother, when a true seeker determineth to take the step of search ... he must, before all else, cleanse and purify his heart, which is the seat of the revelation of the inner mysteries of God, from the obscuring dust of all acquired knowledge, and the allusions of the embodiments of satanic fancy.... That seeker should also regard backbiting as grievous error, and keep himself aloof from its dominion, inasmuch as backbiting quencheth the light of the heart, and extinguisheth the life of the soul.... With all his heart should the seeker avoid fellowship with evil doers, and pray for the remission of their sins. He should forgive the sinful, and never despise his low estate, for none knoweth what his own end shall be.... He must purge his breast, which is the sanctuary of the abiding love of the Beloved, of every defilement, and sanctify his soul from all that pertaineth to water and clay, from all shadowy and ephemeral attachments. He must so cleanse his heart that no remnant of either love or hate may linger therein, lest that love blindly incline him to error, or that hate repel him away from the truth.... When the detached wayfarer and sincere seeker hath fulfilled these essential conditions, then and only then can he be called a true seeker.... Then will the manifold favors and outpouring grace of the holy and everlasting Spirit confer such new life upon the seeker that he will find himself endowed with a new eye, a new ear, a new heart, and a new mind. He will contemplate the manifest signs of the universe, and will penetrate the hidden mysteries of the soul. [64:192ff]

TRUSTWORTHINESS Bahá'u'lláh places great emphasis on this virtue:

> Adorn your temples with the adornment of trustworthiness and piety. Help, then, your Lord with the hosts of goodly deeds and a praiseworthy character. [70:135]

> The purpose of the one true God in manifesting Himself is to summon all mankind to truthfulness and sincerity, to

piety and trustworthiness, to resignation and submissiveness to the Will of God, to forbearance and kindliness, to uprightness and wisdom. [85:299]

Adorn your heads with the garlands of trustworthiness and fidelity, your hearts with the attire of the Fear of God, your tongues with absolute truthfulness, your bodies with the vesture of courtesy. These are in truth seemly adornings unto the temple of man, if ye be of them that reflect. [141:21]

Trustworthiness is the greatest portal leading unto the tranquillity and security of the people. In truth the stability of every affair hath depended and doth depend upon it. All the domains of power, of grandeur and of wealth are illumined by its light. [77:37]

TSAO, Y. S. (-1937) An early Chinese believer (who heard of the Faith through Martha Root when he was President of Tsing Hua College, the Boxer Indemnity College).[37:548]

TÚMÁN Discontinued unit of Íránian currency. [11:741📖]

TURNER, ROBERT (—) (Disciple of 'Abdu'l-Bahá) Mr. Turner was a butler holding a highly responsible position in the household of Mrs. Phoebe Hearst who had become, in 1891, a very wealthy widow at age 48, her late husband having being a senator of California and a very successful businessman. Shortly before 1898 she received at her home in San Francisco a visiting Bahá'í teacher, Mrs. Lua Getsinger, who introduced the Faith to her while Robert was serving tea. He and Mrs. Hearst were deeply moved, and she decided to go for her own investigations to visit 'Abdu'l-Bahá in the Holy Land and in 1898 arranged for the first group of pilgrims to visit Haifa. The party of 15 for security reasons traveled from Port Said in three separate groups, Lua and Mrs. Thornburgh-Cropper (an American living in London) in the first group on 10 December, May Bolles—the Canadian who took the Faith to France and Robert Turner being among the second, arriving on 16 February 1899 and the rest of the party reaching there a few days later. Robert was most warmly received by 'Abdu'l-Bahá Who raised him to his feet and embraced him when, on first seeing the Master, he had dropped to his knees calling out, "My Lord! My Lord! I am not worthy to be here." On a later occasion 'Abdu'l-Bahá said, "Robert, your Lord loves you."[121:20] Robert later encountered many difficulties, but he remained staunch in his faith, and he died not many years after his return from the Holy Land. [83:13]

TURVEY, REGINALD (1882-1968) An early South African believer designated by Shoghi Effendi as "the spiritual father of South Africa."[50:385][60:542]

TWIGS See **AFNÁN**.

U

'ULAMÁ Literally learned men, scholars; clerical authorities, theologians, divines; the Muslim religious hierarchy. [11:741📖]

ULLRICH, CLARENCE (1894-1969) An early (1922) American believer who worked for many years developing the gardens surrounding the Wilmette Temple. He pioneered with his wife (Marguerite (q.v.) to Cuba during the Ten Year Crusade. In 1960 they assisted with the teaching work in Curaçao, Netherland Antilles before moving to Jamaica (where they served on the first National Spiritual Assembly). For reasons of health they returned to the United States in 1963. [51:465]

ULLRICH, MARGARITE HOPE IAOS (1898-1984) The daughter of Hand of the Cause of God Leroy Ioas (q.v.), she met 'Abdu'l-Bahá in Chicago when she was a young girl of 13 and later (1920) received a Tablet from Him. She married Clarence Ullrich (q.v.) in 1922. In 1940, in order to make up the ninth member of the first local Spiritual Assembly of Oak Park, Michigan, he embraced the Cause. In 1941 the family moved to Mansfield, Ohio then moved back to Oak Park in 1945. In 1959 they pioneered to Camaguey, Cuba and in 1960 formed the first local Spiritual Assembly of that town that, in turn, led to the formation in 1961 of the first National Spiritual Assembly of Cuba. While away from Cuba, visiting family, they learned that the U.S. government would not permit their return to Cuba, so they pioneered to Jamaica. In 1961 both Marge (as she was known) and her husband were elected to the first National Spiritual Assembly of Jamaica. Sometime after the Bahá'í World Congress (1963) they moved for health reasons to Florida, where Marge was elected to the local Spiritual Assembly of Manatee County in 1966 and remained in that position until forced to retire in 1975. [11:622]

UMM Mother. [11:741📖]

UNITED NATIONS, BAHÁ'ÍS AND THE See **BAHÁ'Í INTERNATIONAL COMMUNITY**.

UNITY The Bahá'í Faith emphasizes the unity of God, of religion and of mankind. It is a fundamental concept around which all the other Teachings revolve. Bahá'u'lláh wrote:

The light of men is Justice. Quench it not with the contrary winds of oppression and tyranny. The purpose of justice is the appearance of unity among men. [39:27]

The Divine Messengers have been sent down, and their Books were revealed, for the purpose of promoting the knowledge of God, and of furthering unity and fellowship amongst men. [70:12, 14]

With the utmost unity, and in a spirit of perfect fellowship, exert yourselves, that ye may be enabled to achieve that which beseemeth this Day of God.... It beseemeth all men, in this Day, to take firm hold on the Most Great Name, and to establish the unity of all mankind.... Set your faces towards unity, and let the radiance of its light shine upon you. Gather ye together, and for the sake of God resolve to root out whatever is the source of contention amongst you. [85:196,203,217,288]

Please God, that we avoid the land of denial, and advance into the ocean of acceptance, so that we may perceive, with an eye purged from all conflicting elements, the worlds of unity and diversity, of variation and oneness, of limitation and detachment, and wing our flight unto the highest and innermost sanctuary of the inner meaning of the Word of God. [64:160]

From the beginning of time the light of unity hath shed its divine radiance upon the world, and the greatest means for the promotion of that unity is for the peoples of the world to understand one another's writing and speech.... The tabernacle of unity hath been raised; regard ye not one another as strangers. Ye are the fruits of one tree, and the leaves of one branch. [77:164]

'Abdu'l-Bahá wrote:

The prophets of God have been divine shepherds of humanity. They have established a bond of love and unity among mankind, made scattered peoples one nation and wandering tribes a mighty kingdom. They have laid the foundation of the oneness of God and summoned all to universal peace. All these holy, divine Manifestations are one. They have served one God, promulgated the same truth, founded the same institutions and reflected the same light. [107:14]

The first candle is unity in the political realm, the early glimmerings of which can now be discerned. The second candle is unity of thought in world undertakings, the consummation of which will erelong be witnessed. The third candle is unity in freedom which will surely come to pass. The fourth candle is unity in religion which is the cornerstone of the foundation itself, and which, by the power of God, will be revealed in all its splendor. The fifth candle is the unity of nations—a unity which, in this century, will be securely established, causing all the peoples of the world to regard themselves as citizens of one common fatherland. The sixth candle is unity of races, making of all that dwell on earth peoples and kindreds of one race. The seventh candle is unity of language, i.e., the choice of a universal tongue in which all peoples will be instructed and converse. Each and every one of these will inevitably come to pass, inasmuch as the power of the Kingdom of God will aid and assist in their realization. [44:121]

Shoghi Effendi wrote:

Of the principles enshrined in these Tablets the most vital of them all is the principle of the oneness and wholeness of the human race, which may well be regarded as the hall-mark of Bahá'u'lláh's Revelation and the pivot of His teachings. Of such cardinal importance is this principle of unity that it is expressly referred to in the Book of His Covenant, and He unreservedly proclaims it as the central purpose of His Faith. "We, verily," He declares, "have come to unite and weld together all that dwell on earth." "So potent is the light of unity," He further states, "that it can illuminate the whole earth." [5:216f]

World Unity the Goal Unification of the whole of mankind is the hall-mark of the stage which human society is now approaching. Unity of family, of tribe, of city-state, and nation have been successively attempted and fully established. World unity is the goal towards which a harassed humanity is striving. Nation-building has come to an end. The anarchy inherent in state sovereignty is moving towards a climax. A world, growing to maturity, must abandon this fetish, recognize the oneness and wholeness of human relationships, and establish once for all the machinery that can best incarnate this fundamental principle of its life. [4:202]

UNITY FEAST Unlike a 19-Day Feast (q.v.), a Unity Feast is open to the public. Bahá'í Scriptures are read or chanted, and the emphasis is on fellowship in a devotional atmosphere. It is inspirational and is usually accompanied by refreshments. It is not a part of the Bahá'í administrative structure; there is nothing in Bahá'í writings as to how it might be conducted, as it is just one way adopted by some communities to bring Bahá'ís and non-Bahá'ís together in a happy environment. 'Abdu'l-Bahá Himself hosted some such "Feasts" while He was in America. Occasionally, if a non-Bahá'í is present at a 19-Day Feast making it improper to have the consultative part of the Feast, rather than cause unhappiness to the visitor with a request to leave, the meeting continues as a Unity Feast. See **NINETEEN-DAY FEAST**.

UNITY IN DIVERSITY The Bahá'í understanding of unity does not imply uniformity. On the contrary, there is an emphasis on diversity, the keynote being absolute unity in essentials but the widest diversity possible in nonessentials. Shoghi Effendi outlines these concepts and quotes 'Abdu'l-Bahá:

> Its watchword is unity in diversity such as 'Abdu'l-Bahá Himself has explained: "Consider the flowers of a garden. Though differing in kind, color, form and shape, yet, inasmuch as they are refreshed by the waters of one spring, revived by the breath of one wind, invigorated by the rays of one sun, this diversity increaseth their charm and addeth unto their beauty. How unpleasing to the eye if all the flowers and plants, the leaves and blossoms, the fruit, the branches and the trees of that garden were all of the same shape and color! Diversity of hues, form and shape enricheth and adorneth the garden, and heighteneth the effect thereof. In like manner, when divers shades of thought, temperament and character, are brought together under the power and influence of one central agency, the beauty and glory of human perfection will be revealed and made manifest. Naught but the celestial potency of the Word of God, which ruleth and transcendeth the realities of all things, is capable of harmonizing the divergent thoughts, sentiments, ideas and convictions of the children of men." [4:42]

> It is not uniformity which we should seek in the formation of any national or local assembly. For the bedrock of the Bahá'í administrative order is the principle of unity in diversity, which has been so strongly and so repeatedly emphasized in the writings of the Cause. Differences which are not fundamental and contrary to the basic teachings of the Cause should be maintained, while the underlying unity of the administrative order should be at

any cost preserved and insured. Unity, both of purpose and of means is, indeed, indispensable to the safe and speedy working of every Assembly, whether local or national. [43:47]

The diversity in the human family should be the cause of love and harmony, as it is in music where many different notes blend together in the making of a perfect chord.... Bahá'ís should obviously be encouraged to preserve their inherited cultural identities, as long as the activities involved do not contravene the principles of the Faith. The perpetuation of such cultural characteristics is an expression of unity in diversity. [86:527, 553]

See **UNITY** and **NATIONALISM.**

UNITY OF GOD See **GOD, UNITY OF.**
UNITY OF MANKIND See **ONENESS OF MANKIND.**
UNITY OF RELIGION See **PROGRESSIVE REVELATION.**
UNIVERSAL AUXILIARY LANGUAGE 'Abdu'l-Bahá stated:

One of the great steps towards universal peace would be the establishment of a universal language. Bahá'u'lláh commands that the servants of humanity should meet together, and either choose a language which now exists, or form a new one. [25:155]

Bahá'u'lláh advocated one language as the greatest means of unity and the basis of international conference. He wrote to the kings and rulers of the various nations, recommending that one language should be sanctioned and adopted by all governments. According to this each nation should acquire the universal language in addition to its native tongue. The world would then be in close communication, consultation would become general, and dissensions due to diversity of speech would be removed. [26:232]

UNIVERSAL HOUSE OF JUSTICE Ordained by Bahá'u'lláh in His Kitáb-i-Aqdas, the Universal House of Justice is unique in religious history; its duties and functions are clearly outlined in many passages in Bahá'í Writings. Shoghi Effendi, quoting 'Abdu'l-Bahá and Bahá'u'lláh had this to say:

And now, concerning the House of Justice which God hath ordained as the source of all good and freed from all error, it must be elected by universal suffrage, that is, by the believers. Its members must be manifestations of the fear of God and daysprings of knowledge and understanding, must be steadfast in God's faith and the well-wishers of all mankind. By this House is meant the Universal House of Justice, that is, in all countries, a secondary House of Justice must be instituted, and these secondary Houses of Justice must elect the members of the Universal one. Unto this body all things must be referred. It enacteth all ordinances and regulations that are not to be found in the explicit Holy Text. By this body all the difficult problems are to be resolved and the guardian of the Cause of God is its sacred head and the distinguished member for life of that body. [120:10]

What has not been formulated in the Aqdas, in addition to matters of detail and of secondary importance arising out of the application of the laws already formulated by Bahá'u'lláh, will have to be enacted by the Universal House of Justice. This body can supplement but never invalidate or modify in the least degree what has already been formulated by Bahá'u'lláh. Nor has the Guardian any right whatsoever to lessen the binding effect much less to abrogate the provisions of so fundamental and sacred a Book.... [104:3]

He has ordained and established the House of Justice, which is endowed with a political as well as a religious function, the consummate union and blending of church and state. This institution is under the protecting power of Bahá'u'lláh Himself. A universal, or international, House of Justice shall also be organized. Its rulings shall be in accordance with the commands and teachings of Bahá'u'lláh, and that which the Universal House of Justice ordains shall be obeyed by all mankind. This international House of Justice shall be appointed and organized from the Houses of Justice of the whole world, and all the world shall come under its administration. [26:455]

It is incumbent upon the members of the House of Justice, "Bahá'u'lláh ... declares ... to take counsel together regarding those things which have not outwardly been revealed in the Book, and to enforce that which is agreeable to them. God will verily inspire them with whatsoever He willeth, and He verily is the Provider, the Omniscient." "Unto the Most Holy Book" (the Kitáb-i-Aqdas), 'Abdu'l-Bahá states in His Will, "every one must turn, and all that is not expressly recorded therein must be referred to the Universal House of Justice. That which this body,

> whether unanimously or by a majority doth carry, that is verily the truth and the purpose of God Himself. Whoso doth deviate therefrom is verily of them that love discord, hath shown forth malice, and turned away from the Lord of the Covenant." [4:149]
>
> The men of God's House of Justice have been charged with the affairs of the people. They, in truth, are the Trustees of God among His servants and the daysprings of authority in His countries.... O people of God! That which traineth the world is Justice, for it is upheld by two pillars, reward and punishment. These two pillars are the sources of life to the world. Inasmuch as for each day there is a new problem and for every problem an expedient solution, such affairs should be referred to the Ministers of the House of Justice that they may act according to the needs and requirements of the time. They that, for the sake of God, arise to serve His Cause, are the recipients of divine inspiration from the unseen Kingdom. It is incumbent upon all to be obedient unto them. All matters of State should be referred to the House of Justice, but acts of worship must be observed according to that which God hath revealed in His Book.... It is incumbent upon the Trustees of the House of Justice to take counsel together regarding those things which have not outwardly been revealed in the Book, and to enforce that which is agreeable to them.... First: It is incumbent upon the ministers of the House of Justice to promote the Lesser Peace so that the people of the earth may be relieved from the burden of exorbitant expenditures. This matter is imperative and absolutely essential, inasmuch as hostilities and conflict lie at the root of affliction and calamity. [77:26, 68, 89]

The successful conclusion of the Ten Year Crusade provided a sufficiently strong foundation for the election of this body, and the members of the 56 National Spiritual Assemblies in existence in 1962 served as its electors. The election was announced to the Bahá'í world on 5 November 1961 by the Hands of the Cause, to take place on the 1st through the 3rd Days of Riḍván 1963. The duly elected Universal House of Justice presented their first Message at the Most Great Jubilee at the Albert Hall, London (28 April-2 May). Its first major concern was to effect the complete transfer of the administrative responsibilities that the Hands of the Cause had had to assume as Chief Stewards during the interregnum period, including the legal transfer of all rights and properties, and to terminate the legal entity of the "Custodians" (Completed by 7 June 1963). In its earliest meetings it decided to have no officers and it planned to announce its first detailed plan of expansion for the whole Bahá'í community to be launched at Riḍván, 1964. By June it announced details of the offices it had taken over in Haifa and the continuation of pilgrimages. It also had to confirm that "...there is no way to appoint or to legislate to make it possible to appoint a second Guardian to succeed Shoghi Effendi." [8:11] By October it had announced that the "Plan" for the following April would be for the duration of nine years. Also during its first five years of office it made announcements for the development of the institution of the Hands of the Cause; the Auxiliary Board Members; clarified the relationship between the Guardianship and the Universal House of Justice; launched a campaign to commemorate the Proclamation of Bahá'u'lláh to the kings and rulers; the First Oceanic conference in Sicily to commemorate the Centenary of Bahá'u'lláh's transfer to the Most Great Prison and the appointment of the Continental Board of Counsellors. On 26 November 1972 it signed the declaration of Trust and By-Laws for its Constitution [142] in which it confirmed the existing administrative principles for the formation and functioning of local and national Spiritual Assemblies and established that its own elections would take place every five years at an International Bahá'í Convention (q.v.). In the ensuing years it has continued to guide the Bahá'í community through the launching of global plans; ensuring the preservation of the Sacred Texts and safeguarding their inviolability; enacting laws and ordinances not expressly recorded in the Sacred Texts; issuing compilations on vital issues; answering questions from individuals and institutions; ruling on disputes; protecting the Faith; and dealing with a wide range of matters at international level. [53:285ff] See **ADMINISTRATIVE ORDER; HOUSES OF JUSTICE; INTERNATIONAL BAHÁ'Í COUNCIL; JUSTICE; KITÁB-I AQDAS; NATIONAL SPIRITUAL ASSEMBLIES; SEAT OF THE UNIVERSAL HOUSE OF JUSTICE.**

UNIVERSAL HOUSE OF JUSTICE, SEAT OF The building that is the administrative seat of the Universal House of Justice as anticipated by Shoghi Effendi in his message to the Bahá'í world on 27 November 1954 and that, in addition to its council chamber, houses its offices and ancillary services, banqueting facilities, storage vaults and a concourse for the reception of pilgrims and dignitaries. In its own words, it is "a building that will not only serve the practical needs of a steadily consolidating administrative center but will, for centuries to come, stand as a visible expression of the majesty of the divinely ordained institutions of the Administrative Order of Bahá'u'lláh." [52:398]

In 1973 at the third International Convention, the delegates were shown the site of the proposed Seat; in 1978 at the fourth International Convention the delegates gathered on a special platform erected to enable them to witness the placing of a casket containing dust from the Shrines of the Báb and Bahá'u'lláh in a niche in the new building at a dedication ceremony; the inauguration took place on 17 July 1982, and during January 1983 the members of the Universal House of Justice transferred their offices to the Seat. At the fifth International Convention in April 1983, the actual election of the Universal House of Justice took place in the Reception Concourse. In October, 1983 the first guest to be honored with a banquet was the president of Israel, Chaim Herzog. The Seat comprises six stories, is clad in marble and provides 11,000 square meters of floor space. In 1978 the Italian firm of marble carvers, the Industria dei Marmi Vicentini of Chiampo, (which also produced the carved marble for the Bahá'í International Archives building) issued an impressive brochure that pointed out that their quarries will provide 85,000 cubic feet of "Caesar's White" marble of Pentelikon quality, the same marble that was used in the Parthenon in Athens, that the Parthenon has 46 columns each 31.5 feet high while the new Seat has "a peristyle of 58 columns, each 33 feet high ... decorated with magnificent entablatures and surmounted by a great dome." Its architect was Ḥusayn Amanat (a Persian Bahá'í now resident in the United States). See **ARC**.

'URVATU'L-VUTHQÁ The Sure Handle, Firm Cord: a Qur'ánic term, used in the Bahá'í Writings to symbolize the Covenant and Testament. [11:741📖]

USTÁD Teacher, professor; mechanic, artisan, craftsman. [11:741📖]

V

VAḤDAT, YADU'LLÁH (1910-1981) (Martyr) An Íránian believer who (along with his wife Qudsíyyih) was arrested in Shíráz in February 1981 for his belief in Bahá'u'lláh. He was executed in May 1981. [2:759]

VÁḤID Literally unity, one, single; The One, Invisible God. [11:741📖] It is used in the Badí' calendar for a period or cycle of 19 years. In its Arabic original its numerical value is 19, and it symbolizes the unity of God. See **CALENDAR, BAHÁ'Í**.

VAḤÍD Single, unique, peerless. [11:742📖] The title given to an outstanding scholar, Siyyid Yaḥyáy-i-Dárábí, about whom Shoghi Effendi wrote:

The commotion had assumed such proportions that the Sháh, unable any longer to ignore the situation, delegated the trusted Siyyid Yaḥyáy-i-Dárábí, surnamed Vaḥíd, one of the most erudite, eloquent and influential of his subjects—a man who had committed to memory no less than thirty thousand traditions—to investigate and report to him the true situation. Broad-minded, highly imaginative, zealous by nature, intimately associated with the court, he, in the course of three interviews, was completely won over by the arguments and personality of the Báb.... Vaḥíd, pronounced in the Kitáb-i-Íqan to be the "unique and peerless figure of his age," a man of immense erudition and the most preeminent figure to enlist under the banner of the new Faith, to whose "talents and saintliness," to whose "high attainments in the realm of science and philosophy" the Báb had testified in His Dalá'il-i-Sab'ih (Seven Proofs), had already, under similar circumstances, been swept into the maelstrom of another upheaval, and was soon to quaff in his turn the cup drained by the heroic martyrs of Mázindarán. [5:11,50]

VAKÍL, 'ABBÁS (1911-1984) (Knight of Bahá'u'lláh) A Turkish born believer whose family was closely associated with the development of the Cause in both Iráq and Írán. In 1953 he and his wife (Samírá) pioneered to Nicosia, Cyprus for which service they were designated Knights of Bahá'u'lláh. In c.1963 they returned to Turkey where 'Abbás served for a time on the National Spiritual Assembly of Turkey. [11:646]

VAKÍL, MUNÍR (1900-1976) (Knight of Bahá'u'lláh) A third-generation Iráqi believer (his grandfather and father accepted the Faith during Bahá'u'lláh's time in Baghdád), he met 'Abdu'l-Bahá when he was a young boy, and his mother and sister served in His house for a period. On the death of his father he inherited responsibility for the care of the House of Bahá'u'lláh in Baghdád. He was a member of the first National Spiritual Assembly of Iráq. In 1953 he pioneered to the Kuria Muria Islands for which service he was designated a Knight of Bahá'u'lláh. Following service in those islands he pioneered to the Seychelles Islands in 1955 and stayed until the formation of the first local Spiritual Assembly in Victoria, Mahe. Before his departure he purchased and maintained the Ḥaẓíratu'l-Quds in Victoria. In 1962 he returned to Iráq. [52:565]

VAKIL, NARAYENRAO RANGNATH (1866-1943) The first Hindu believer in India. [45:637]

VALÍ Guardian. [11:742]

VÁLÍ Governor of a province. [11:742]

VALÍ-'AHD Crown prince, heir to the throne. [11:742]

VARAQIH Leaf; often used metaphorically in the Bahá'í Writings to refer to a woman. [11:742]

VARAQIY-I-'ULYÁ Literally The Most Exalted Leaf; The Greatest Holy Leaf: title of Bahá'íyyih (or more commonly Bahíyyih) Khánum, saintly daughter of Bahá'u'lláh and the "outstanding heroine of the Bahá'í Dispensation."[11:742] See **BAHÍYYIH KHÁNUM.**

VARQÁ Bird, nightingale; The Heavenly Dove. [11:742]

VARQÁ, 'ALÍ MUḤAMMAD (1912-) (Hand of the Cause of God; Trustee Ḥuqúqu'lláh) He was born in Ṭihrán, Írán, in 1912. His father was Valíyu'lláh Varqá, the third son of Mírzá 'Alí Muḥammad, the martyr (qq.v.). Valíyu'lláh Varqá had attended the American University in Beirut, deepening his knowledge of the Bahá'í teachings under the guidance of 'Abdu'l-Bahá during his summer vacations. Later, he accompanied the Master on His historic journey to Europe and America, serving as an interpreter. 'Alí-Muḥammad was born while his father was in the United States.

'Alí-Muḥammad attended primary and secondary school in Ṭihrán, and always participated in Bahá'í activities. As a youth, he served on many committees and was a teacher of Bahá'í children's classes. The government of Írán sent him to France to study geomorphology, a branch of science that deals with the land and submarine relief features of the earth's surface. On his return to Írán, he became of professor of geology at the University of Ṭihrán.

He continued his academic career at the university, becoming the head of the Department of Geography. His services to the Faith were never-ending, encouraged by his father, who was a Trustee of Ḥuqúqu'lláh and who was in the first contingent of Hands of the Cause of God appointed by Shoghi Effendi on 24 December 1951. His father, Valíyu'lláh Varqá (q.v.) died on 12 November 1955, following a long illness. In the cable announcing his passing, sent on 15 November, Shoghi Effendi included the statement: "His mantle as Trustee Huquq now falls on 'Alí-Muḥammad, his son.... Newly appointed Trustee Huquq now elevated rank Hand Cause." [6:173]

He represented the Guardian at the convention of the Region of Argentina, Chile, Uruguay, Paraguay and Bolivia in Buenos Aires, April 1957 and then visited centers in Argentina and Chile. His international travels then included the Intercontinental Conference, Djakarta-Singapore 1958; centers in France, 1961 Convention of Belgium and Luxembourg in 1962 and centers in the British Isles in 1962 and 1963. He continued his professorial duties at the University of Ṭihrán with outside travels during his vacations. In the summers of 1973, 1974 and 1975 he was on teaching tours in Western Europe and in 1974 visited West Africa. During the period 1976 to 1979 he carried on his developing work of Trustee of the Ḥuqúqu'lláh; spent a great deal of his time in assembling historical data at the request of the Universal House of Justice; traveled extensively in the Caribbean and parts of central Africa and in 1978 in Western Europe and Canada. [47][11]

Dr. Varqá had retired from his post as head of the department at the university, and was on a teaching trip to Francophile countries in Europe when the Islámic Revolution broke out in Írán in 1978. While he was in Luxembourg he received a cable suggesting that he not return to Írán "for a while." He and his wife went to live in Montréal, Canada, where they still maintain a residence. Since 1992, Dr. Varqá has also spent part of each year in Haifa.

The persecution of the Bahá'í community of Írán has caused immense problems to be dealt with in relation to the safeguarding and sale of properties donated for the Ḥuqúqu'lláh as well as a multitude of other historic tasks. Dealing with these problems has fallen to the lot of Dr. Varqá in his capacity as a Hand of the Cause of God. The universal application of the Law of Ḥuqúqu'lláh, beginning at Riḍván 1992, required the establishment of an Office of Ḥuqúqu'lláh in the Holy Land and the appointment of Deputies and representatives in many countries of the world. This task fell on Dr. Varqá as the Trustee of Ḥuqúqu'lláh.

While living in North America, Dr. Varqá has often attended gatherings of the friends at conventions, summer schools, or other meetings. He has also traveled to represent the Universal House of Justice at the elections of the first National Spiritual Assembly of Czechoslovakia in April 1991; of Greenland in May 1992; also of the Ukraine, Belarus and Moldova in May 1992; and of Slovenia and Croatia in May 1994.

VARQÁ, MÍRZÁ 'ALÍ-MUḤAMMAD (Hand of the Cause of God) A Bahá'í teacher and poet who, along with several other Bahá'ís, was falsely charged with involvement in the assassination of the Sháh. Although the charges were completely spurious, he and his coreligionists were executed by the Íránian authorities in Ṭihrán on 1 May 1896. The execution took place in front of his 12-year-old son, Rúḥu'lláh, who was subsequently strangled with a rope because he refused to recant. Varqá was named a Hand of the Cause by 'Abdu'l-Bahá; he was also designated an Apostle of Bahá'u'lláh.

VARQÁ, VALÍYU'LLÁH (1884-1955) (Hand of the Cause of God; Trustee Ḥuqúqu'lláh) Although born in 1884 in Tabríz, Írán into a distinguished Bahá'í family (his father and brother were both martyrs) his grandmother was a committed Moslem who endeavored to turn him against his father. Eventually, his welfare was taken over by his uncle, who was a devout Bahá'í, thereby securing his education in the Faith.

He studied Arabic and English and spent some time in the Holy Land, where he met with 'Abdu'l-Bahá, and continued his studies in Beirut until he was asked by 'Abdu'l-Bahá to return on a special mission to Ṭihrán. Completing the mission, he married and had 10 children, seven of whom survived and became active believers.

He was employed in the Russian Embassy as a secretary and was able to obtain permission from 'Abdu'l-Bahá and his employers to travel with 'Abdu'l-Bahá on His visit to America. On his return he was employed as First Secretary Translator at the Turkish Embassy. During all these years, beginning at the age of 20 until his death at age 71, he continued with unabated zeal and enthusiasm to serve the Cause, particularly after the death of Amín Amín in 1938, when Shoghi Effendi appointed him as Trustee of the Ḥuqúqu'lláh (q.v.). He was appointed a Hand of the Cause in the first contingent on 24 December 1951. He attended the Intercontinental Conference in Kampala, 1953 as well as the one in Chicago, and then on Shoghi Effendi's directions did some travel teaching in Brazil and Chile. After attending the Conference in Stockholm, Sweden, he visited a large number of Bahá'í centers in Germany. While in Stuttgart he became ill, spent a week in the hospital and then a month in Ulm, where he had surgery. He left to attend the New Delhi Conference, cutting down on his convalescence and then proceeded to Iráq, where his illness worsened. After a short recovery, he visited several centers in Egypt and from there went to Turkey, where his suffering increased, and Shoghi Effendi instructed him to return to Írán. Shoghi Effendi then permitted him to go on pilgrimage, during which he was inspired with new life. He then went on to Germany to complete his course of treatment and from there to Austria; in Vienna he addressed large audiences prior to his return to Írán. In March 1955 he again experienced severe pain and left for treatment in Germany, calling on the way to teach in Paris and Italy. He went into the hospital in Tübingen where, after 41 days, teaching from his bed whenever he could, he passed away on 12 November 1955. On 15 November Shoghi Effendi cabled:

> Profoundly grieved loss outstanding Hand Cause God, exemplary Trustee Ḥuqúq, distinguished representative most venerable community Bahá'í world, worthy son brother twin immortal martyrs Faith, dearly beloved disciple Center Covenant. Shining record services extending

over half century enriched annals heroic formative ages Bahá'í Dispensation. His reward Abhá Kingdom inestimable. Advise erect my behalf befitting monument his grave. His mantle as trustee funds Ḥuqúq now falls on 'Alí Muḥammad, his son. Instruct Rowhani Ṭihrán arrange befitting memorial gatherings capital provinces honor memory mighty pillar Faith Bahá'u'lláh. Newly-appointed trustee Ḥuqúq now elevated rank Hand Cause. [47:831]

From a letter addressed to those who had attended the funeral, the following extract written on behalf of the Guardian by his secretary is of particular interest: "...The Bahá'ís could not have a better example before them of nobility and faithfulness than this distinguished Hand of the Cause; and it is a blessing for the German friends that their country should have received his dust. The Guardian urges you all to follow in the footsteps of this beloved Hand." [47:834]

VAZÍR Vizír, minister (of state), vizier. Vazír-i-A'ẓam: Grand Vizier, Prime Minister. [11:742📖]

VENTO, ELSA MATILDA (Hellstrom) (1886-1955) An early Canadian believer of Finnish birth. She pioneered to her native Finland in 1950 and died there in 1955. She had a wide correspondence, both in Finland and internationally, and translated many of the Bahá'í Writings into Finnish. [47:900]

VENTURINI, VERENA (1878-1975) An early (1915) Italian believer she served on the first local Spiritual Assembly in Italy (Rome 1948).[52:560]

VERMEESCH, ARIANE DROLLET (1901-1964) The first (1920) Tahitian to embrace the Cause. [50:388]

VIERA, EDUARDO DUARTE (1921-1966) (The First African Martyr) Born in Portuguese Guinea, he embraced the Cause while on a visit to Lisbon in the mid-1950s. He was arrested for his beliefs and died under "mysterious circumstances" while in prison. [50:389][52:568]

VILÁYAT Guardianship. [11:742📖]

VOELZ, GENEVIEVE E. An early (1904) American believer. The funeral of her mother (Mrs. Laura Thime) in 1905 (who accepted the Cause at the same time as her daughter) is thought to be the first Bahá'í funeral in America. She met 'Abdu'l-Bahá in 1912 when he visited Kenosha. All of her five children became Bahá'ís (with one serving on the National Spiritual Assembly of the United States for 40 years).[11:637]

VUJDÁNÍ, BAHÁR (1922-1979) (Martyr) An Íránian believer who was executed by the Íránian authorities on 27 September 1979 for his belief in Bahá'u'lláh. [2:699]

W

WAQF Literally bequeathing (for charitable uses); pious bequest, religious endowment, estate held in mortmain. Denotes landed property endowed to the Muslim community; in Írán, the estate of the expected Imám. [11:742📖]

WARD, NAIRNE FORSYTH (1897-1969) An early (1921) American believer who for many years (1927-1941) directed summer school activities during the summer months at Geyserville. In 1959 he and his wife (Janet) set out as pioneers to Uganda. Enroute they made a pilgrimage to the Holy Land where they were asked, and accepted, to become Custodians of the Shrine of Bahá'u'lláh at Bahjí—a service he performed until he passed away while walking in the Gardens at Bahjí in 1969. [51:451]

WAYENECE, EMMA (1927-1976) The first (1961) Melanesian woman of New Caledonia and the Loyalty Islands to embrace the Cause. She was elected to the first (1962) local Spiritual Assembly of Nouméa; and in 1971 she pioneered with her husband (Georges) to Yahoué to assist in the formation of the first local Spiritual Assembly of that town. [53:415]

WEALTH AND POVERTY, ELIMINATION OF EXTREMES OF 'Abdu'l-Bahá addressed many of His talks on this subject:

> Wealth is most commendable, provided the entire population is wealthy. If, however, a few have inordinate riches while the rest are impoverished, and no fruit or benefit accrues from that wealth, then it is only a liability to its possessor. If, on the other hand, it is expended for the promotion of knowledge, the founding of elementary and other schools, the encouragement of art and industry, the training of orphans and the poor—in brief, if it is dedicated to the welfare of society—its possessor will stand out before God and man as the most excellent of all who live on earth and will be accounted as one of the people of paradise. [125:24]

> Organize in an effort to help them and prevent increase of poverty. The greatest means for prevention is that whereby the laws of the community will be so framed and enacted that it will not be possible for a few to be millionaires and many destitute. One of Bahá'u'lláh's teachings

is the adjustment of means of livelihood in human society. Under this adjustment there can be no extremes in human conditions as regards wealth and sustenance. For the community needs financiers, farmers, merchants and laborers just as an army must be composed of commanders, officers and privates. All cannot be commanders; all cannot be officers or privates. Each in his station in the social fabric must be competent; each in his function according to ability; but justness of opportunity for all. [107:36]

Shoghi Effendi wrote through his secretary:

Social inequality is the inevitable outcome of the natural inequality of man. Human beings are different in ability and should, therefore, be different in their social and economic standing. Extremes of wealth and poverty should, however, be abolished.... The Master has definitely stated that wages should be unequal, simply because men are unequal in their ability and hence should receive wages that would correspond to their varying capacities and resources. [104:19]

We must be like the fountain or spring that is continually emptying itself of all that it has and is continually being refilled from an invisible source. To be continually giving out for the good of our fellows undeterred by fear of poverty and reliant on the unfailing bounty of the Source of all wealth and all good—this is the secret of right living.[104:31]

WEEDEN, BENJAMIN DUNHAM (1892-1979) (Knight of Bahá'u'lláh) An American believer who embraced the Cause in 1948. He moved that same year to Haifa to assist in the construction of the superstructure of the Shrine of the Báb. While in Haifa he met and married Miss Gladys Anderson (q.v. Gladys Weedon) in what was the first Bahá'í marriage within the newly formed State of Israel.

In 1950 Shoghi Effendi advised Ben and his wife that they were to be members of the first International Bahá'í Council. Regrettably, ill health forced Ben to return to the United States in 1951, and, therefore, the appointment did not take effect. In 1952, at the request of Shoghi Effendi, he and his wife traveled to all the then 48 states and visited 75 major Bahá'í communities. In 1953 he pioneered with his wife to Antigua, for which service he was designated a Knight of Bahá'u'lláh. [51:478]

WEEDON, GLADYS ANDERSON (1906-1979) (Knight of Bahá'u'lláh) An American believer (1937) she was taught the Faith by 'Amatu'l-Bahá Rúḥíyyih Khánum (then Mary Maxwell). During the later part of the Seven Year Plan (1942) she pioneered to Brattleboro, Vermont (where she was the first Bahá'í) and served on the first local Spiritual Assembly of that town when it formed in 1943. In 1847 she received a cable from Shoghi Effendi asking her to come to Haifa to assist him in administrative matters and act as a companion to 'Amatu'l-Bahá Rúḥíyyih Khánum. It was during this period that she met her (second) husband (q.v. Benjamin Dunham Weedon). After her marriage she and her husband often represented Shoghi Effendi at social and official functions.

In 1951 Shoghi Effendi advised her that she and her husband were to be members of the first International Bahá'í Council; due to her husband's ill health and forced return to the United States the appointment did not take effect. After journeying to the United States to ensure proper medical attention for her husband, she returned to Haifa for several months to hand over her administrative duties to coworkers. In 1953 she pioneered with her husband to Antigua for which service she was designated a Knight of Bahá'u'lláh. In 1973 she returned to Haifa for five months to assist 'Amatu'l-Bahá Rúḥíyyih Khánum with the renovation of the House of 'Abdu'l-Bahá in Haifa. [2:693]

WELLS, ARNOLD (-1986) The second (early 1950s) Bahamian believer, he served on the first (1955) local Spiritual Assembly of Nassau. [11:702]

WESSON, VIVIAN (1895-1994) (Knight of Bahá'u'lláh) An early (1921) American believer, she pioneered in 1954 to French Togoland (now Togo) for which service she was designated a Knight of Bahá'u'lláh. [11:322]

WHITAKER, OSWALD ALFRED (-1941) The first Australian believer. [45:606]

WHITE, ROGER (1929-1993) A Canadian believer (1952), he pioneered in 1966 to Nairobi until 1969, when he moved to Palm Springs, California, as secretary and research assistant to Hand of the Cause of God William Sears. From 1971 to 1991 he served as the head of the publishing department at the Bahá'í World Center. He was known for his fine poetry and prose, some of which has been published. [57:276][60:543]

WILES, GEORGIE BROWN (1899-1939) An early American believer who worked in the field of race relations. [42:673][60:553]

WILHELM, ROY C. (1875-1951) (Hand of the Cause of God) He was born in Zanesville, Ohio, 17 September 1875. His parents moved from Ohio to West Englewood, New Jersey, they opened an import business in New York City, which Roy actively conducted until the last few years of his life. Already a Bahá'í, he and his mother visited 'Abdu'l-Bahá in 'Akká in 1907. From his earliest days as a

Bahá'í he was involved in making Bahá'í writings available. He printed hundreds of thousands of pamphlets during his lifetime, and quotations were used in his business advertisements in trade magazines. He personally received many messages from 'Abdu'l-Bahá and was also responsible for the receipt and distribution of letters from 'Abdu'l-Bahá addressed to Bahá'í groups and individuals throughout North America. The first Bahá'í national administrative body in America was elected in 1909, and with the exception of one year of ill health, he was elected annually for the next 37 years onto that body and to the National Spiritual Assembly that replaced it, serving as treasurer for many years. The author of his obituary writes, "No other American believer has achieved a comparable record..." After the passing of 'Abdu'l-Bahá in 1921 Roy Wilhelm and Mr. Mountford Mills were summoned by Shoghi Effendi to Haifa for discussion. Sadly, he died on 20 December 1951. On 24 December, the very day Shoghi Effendi announced the first of the Hands to be appointed by him in their own lifetime, Mr. Wilhelm was posthumously raised to this station. Shoghi Effendi issued the following cable to the Bahá'í world on Roy's passing:

> Heart filled sorrow loss greatly prized much loved highly admired herald Bahá'u'lláh's Covenant. Distinguished career enriched annals concluding years Heroic and opening years Formative age Faith. Sterling qualities endeared him to his beloved Master, 'Abdu'l-Bahá. His saintliness indomitable faith outstanding services local national international, his exemplary devotion, qualify him join ranks Hands of Cause, insure him everlasting reward Abhá Kingdom. Advise hold memorial gathering Temple befitting his unforgettable services and lofty rank.[40:645][48:662][83:87][59:317ff]

WILKS, HELEN HAZEL (1903-1980) An American believer (1934) who pioneered to Africa (Swaziland) in 1963. She was appointed an Auxiliary Board member, first in Swaziland and later in Rhodesia (now Zimbabwe). She traveled extensively throughout South Africa, Lesotho, Botswana, Zambia, Malawi, Seychelles and Mauritius in the promotion of the Cause. [2:708]

WILLS Bahá'ís are enjoined by Bahá'u'lláh in His Kitáb-i-Aqdas to execute a Will. They are free to leave their possessions and make bequests in any way they wish, but should a Bahá'í die intestate, Bahá'u'lláh has specified the allocation of any inheritance among relatives and teachers.

WINDUST, ALBERT ROBERT (1874-1956) (Disciple of 'Abdu'l-Bahá) An early American believer designated by 'Abdu'l-Bahá as a "Herald of the Covenant." He was a member of the first local

Spiritual Assembly of Chicago. He was the first publisher of the Writings of the Faith in America. [47:873][59:25ff]

WINE Shoghi Effendi wrote:

> "The drinking of wine," writes 'Abdu'l-Bahá, "is, according to the text of the Most Holy Book, forbidden; for it is the cause of chronic diseases, weakeneth the nerves, and consumeth the mind." [39:33]
>
> Deliver them from alcohol and tobacco, and save them from opium, the purveyor of madness! [106:336]
>
> It requires total abstinence from all alcoholic drinks, from opium, and from similar habit-forming drugs. [39:30]
>
> The believers should certainly, under no circumstances, drink any alcoholic beverages as this has been forbidden in the Aqdas. [82: Vol. ii, 68] See **ALCOHOL; DRUGS**.

WISDOM Bahá'u'lláh wrote:

> As the body of man needeth a garment to clothe it, so the body of mankind must needs be adorned with the mantle of justice and wisdom.... Take heed, O concourse of the rulers of the world! There is no force on earth that can equal in its conquering power the force of justice and wisdom.... Blessed is the king who marcheth with the ensign of wisdom unfurled before him, and the battalions of justice massed in his rear. He verily is the ornament that adorneth the brow of peace and the countenance of security. There can be no doubt whatever that if the day star of justice, which the clouds of tyranny have obscured, were to shed its light upon men, the face of the earth would be completely transformed. [85:81,219]
>
> Above all else, the greatest gift and the most wondrous blessing hath ever been and will continue to be Wisdom. It is man's unfailing Protector. It aideth him and strengtheneth him. Wisdom is God's Emissary and the Revealer of His Name the Omniscient. Through it the loftiness of man's station is made manifest and evident. It is all-knowing and the foremost Teacher in the school of existence. It is the Guide and is invested with high distinction. Thanks to its educating influence earthly beings have become imbued with a gem-like spirit which outshineth the heavens.... The beginning of Wisdom and the origin thereof is to acknowledge whatsoever God hath clearly set forth, for through its potency the foundation of

statesmanship, which is a shield for the preservation of the body of mankind, hath been firmly established. [77:151]

WOLCOTT, CHARLES (1906-1987) (Member Universal House of Justice) He was born in Flint, Michigan, on 29 September 1906. His father, Frederick Charles Wolcott, whose business interests were overshadowed by his love for music, formed a small-town orchestra in which his son participated, on the piano and accordion, from an early age. By the time Charles reached high school he had his own four-piece orchestra (piano, banjo, saxophone, drums) that played at school dances. When he attended the University of Michigan, his larger band, "Charley Wolcott and his Wolverines," played for faculty (ballroom) dances and his smaller bands for fraternity and sorority (tea) dances. In the 1920s he went to the larger city of Detroit to play piano in hotels and ballrooms with the Jean Goldkette Organization and also performed on radio shows.

He married Harriett Marshall on 30 August 1928, and they moved from Flint to New York, where he was always able to find work as a pianist, composer, arranger, or conductor with the Paul Whiteman Band, Benny Goodman, the Dorsey brothers, Columbia Records, and network radio programs such as Burns and Allen (George and Gracie), Kate Smith and Bob Hope.

Fascinated by the color and sound developments in motion pictures, he moved the family to Hollywood, California, in 1937 and soon began working at the Walt Disney Studios, writing music for cartoon shorts, then feature films, such as *Pinocchio* and *Bambi*.

In about 1935 both he and his wife were introduced to the Bahá'í Faith but did not embrace it until August 1938 in Los Angeles (where they remained until 1960). During this period he composed music as a setting for some of the prayers of Bahá'u'lláh including *From the Sweet Scented Streams*, *O Thou by Whose Name* and *Blessed Is the Spot*. By 1944 he had become general musical director at Disney Studios. In 1950 he transferred to Metro-Goldwyn-Mayer (MGM) Studios as associate general musical director and in 1958 became general musical director. In 1955, after he placed Bill Haley's song *Rock around the Clock* in the MGM movie *Blackboard Jungle*, the "rock and roll" music craze spread worldwide.

He was appointed to be a member of the Inter-America Bahá'í Teaching Committee (1942-1944); served as chairman of the National Audio-Visual Education Committee (1946-1948); and was elected to the Los Angeles Local Spiritual Assembly (1948-1960). In 1953, he was elected to the National Spiritual Assembly of the United States, where he served as vice-chairman until 1960. When

Hand of the Cause of God Horace Holley was called to the Bahá'í World Centre as one of the nine Hands to serve in the Holy Land, Charles was elected secretary of the National Assembly in 1960. In January 1960 he resigned his position as head of the music department at MGM Studios, and he and his wife moved to Wilmette, Illinois, so he could take up his duties in the National Bahá'í Center.

At Riḍván 1961, he was one of the nine elected to the International Bahá'í Council, which then elected him to be its Secretary-General. He moved to the Bahá'í World Centre in 1961 to take up his two-year post on the International Bahá'í Council, not knowing that his service to the Faith would keep him in that Holy Spot for another 26 years, until his death.

In 1963 he was elected a member of the Universal House of Justice and re-elected to subsequent terms in 1968, 1973, 1978 and 1983. He died suddenly, toward the end of his last term, on 26 January 1987 and was buried in the Bahá'í Cemetery at the foot of Mount Carmel.

WOMEN, STATUS OF Bahá'ís hold the raising of the status of women to be a central feature in the establishment of world peace. In 1985, in its contribution to the peace process, the Universal House of Justice wrote:

> The emancipation of women, the achievement of full equality between the sexes, is one of the most important, though less acknowledged pre-requisites of peace. The denial of such equality perpetrates an injustice against one half of the world's population and promotes in men harmful attitudes and habits that are carried from the family to the workplace, to political life, and ultimately to international relations. There are no grounds, moral, practical, or biological, upon which such denial can be justified. Only as women are welcomed into full partnership in all fields of human endeavor will the moral and psychological climate be created in which international peace can emerge. [86:618]

Should financial constraints exist in a family that allow for the education of only some of the children, then the education of girl children must first receive priority. During His visit to the West, 1911-1913, 'Abdu'l-Bahá addressed this issue on many occasions, and the Universal House of Justice seeks constantly to encourage the Bahá'ís to put it into practice:

> The world in the past has been ruled by force, and man has dominated over women by reason of his more forceful and aggressive qualities both of body and mind.... But the

balance is already shifting—force is losing its weight and mental alertness, intuition, and the spiritual qualities of love and service, in which woman is strong, are gaining ascendancy. Hence the new age will be an age, less masculine, and more permeated with the feminine ideals—or, to speak more exactly, will be an age in which the masculine and feminine elements of civilization will be more evenly balanced. [86:615]

Therefore, strive to show in the human world that women are most capable and efficient, that their hearts are more tender and susceptible than the hearts of men, that they are more philanthropic and responsive toward the needy and suffering, that they are inflexibly opposed to war and are lovers of peace. Strive that the ideal of international peace may become realized through the efforts of womankind, for man is more inclined to war than woman, and a real evidence of woman's superiority will be her service and efficiency in the establishment of universal peace. [86:618]

The decision-making agencies involved would do well to consider giving first priority to the education of women and girls, since it is through educated mothers that the benefits of knowledge can be most effectively and rapidly diffused throughout society. In keeping with the requirements of the times, consideration should also be given to teaching the concept of world citizenship as part of the standard education of every child. [86:616]

The duty of women in being the first educators of mankind is clearly set forth the Writings. It is for every woman, if and when she becomes a mother, to determine how best she can discharge on the one hand her chief responsibility as a mother and on the other, to the extent possible, to participate in other aspect of the activities of the society of which she forms a part. [86:619]

The equality of men and women is not, at the present time, universally applied. In those areas where traditional inequality still hampers its progress we must take the lead in practicing this Bahá'í principle. Bahá'í women and girls must be encouraged to take part in the social, spiritual and administrative activities of their communities. [86:619]

See **EQUALITY OF MEN AND WOMEN.**

WORK Bahá'ís are called upon by Bahá'u'lláh to engage in useful trades, crafts and professions that are of benefit to mankind and such work, done to the best of one's ability and in the spirit of service to humanity is ranked as worship. Begging and the giving of alms to beggars are both forbidden. The implications of these teachings to society, to work relations, to involvement in strikes and to idleness are far-reaching. Shoghi Effendi, writing through his secretary, explained:

> With reference to Bahá'u'lláh's command concerning the engagement of the believers in some sort of profession; the Teachings are most emphatic on this matter, particularly the statement in the "Aqdas" to this effect which makes it quite clear that idle people who lack the desire to work can have no place in the new World Order. As a corollary of this principle, Bahá'u'lláh further states that mendacity should not only be discouraged but entirely wiped out from the face of society. It is the duty of those who are in charge of the organization of society to give every individual the opportunity of acquiring the necessary talent in some kind of profession, and also the means of utilizing such a talent, both for its own sake and for the sake of earning the means of his livelihood. Every individual, no matter how handicapped and limited he may be, is under the obligation of engaging in some work or profession, for work, specially when performed in the spirit of service, is according to Bahá'u'lláh a form of worship. It has not only a utilitarian purpose, but has a value in itself, because it draws us nearer to God, and enables us to better grasp His purpose for us in this world. It is obvious, therefore, that the inheritance of wealth cannot make anyone immune from daily work. [86:623]

See **BEGGING** and **SERVICE**.

WORLD CENTRE, BAHÁ'Í Shoghi Effendi referred in numerous places to the great significance of the raising of the buildings of the Bahá'í world administrative system in the vicinity of the Shrines on Mount Carmel. In 1944 he announced:

> Moreover, as a further testimony to the majestic unfoldment and progressive consolidation of the stupendous undertaking launched by Bahá'u'lláh on that holy mountain, may be mentioned the selection of ... the precincts of the Shrine of the Báb as a permanent resting-place for the Greatest Holy Leaf ... (comparable in rank to those immortal heroines such as Sarah, Ásiyih, the Virgin Mary,

> Fáṭimih and Ṭáhirih, each of whom has outshone every member of her sex in previous Dispensations.) And lastly, ... the transfer, a few years later, to that same hallowed spot ... of the Purest Branch, the martyred son of Bahá'u'lláh ... To this same burial-ground, and on the same day the remains of the Purest Branch were interred, was transferred the body of his mother, the saintly Navváb, she ... whom Bahá'u'lláh in His Tablet, has destined to be "His consort in every one of His worlds." ... The conjunction of these three resting-places, under the shadow of the Báb's own Tomb, embosomed in the heart of Carmel, facing the snow-white city across the bay of 'Akká, the Qiblih of the Bahá'í world, set in a garden of exquisite beauty, reinforces, if we would correctly estimate its significance, the spiritual potencies of a spot, designated by Bahá'u'lláh Himself the seat of God's throne. It marks, too, a further milestone in the road leading eventually to the establishment of that permanent world Administrative Center of the future Bahá'í Commonwealth, destined never to be separated from, and to function in the proximity of, the Spiritual Center of that Faith, in a land already revered and held sacred alike by the adherents of three of the world's outstanding religious systems. [5:347f]

In November 1954, Shoghi Effendi painted a vision of future developments that subsequently became the goal for the Universal House of Justice:

> The raising of this Edifice (the International Archives building), will in turn herald the construction, in the course of successive epochs of the Formative Age of the Faith, of several other structures ... in the shape of a far-flung arc, and following a harmonizing style of architecture, surround the resting-places of the Greatest Holy Leaf, ranking as foremost among the members of her sex in the Bahá'í Dispensation, of her Brother ... and of their Mother ... The ultimate completion of this stupendous undertaking will mark the culmination of the development of a world-wide divinely-appointed Administrative Order whose beginnings may be traced as far back as the concluding years of the Heroic Age of the Faith. This vast and irresistible process, unexampled in the spiritual history of mankind, and which will synchronise with two no less significant developments—the establishment of the Lesser Peace and the evolution of Bahá'í national and local institutions—the one outside and the other within the

Bahá'í world—will attain its final consummation, in the Golden Age of the Faith, through the raising of the standard of the Most Great Peace, and the emergence, in the plenitude of its power and glory, of the focal Center of the agencies constituting the World Order of Bahá'u'lláh. The final establishment of this seat of the future Bahá'í World Commonwealth will signalize at once the proclamation of the sovereignty of the Founder of our Faith and the advent of the Kingdom of the Father repeatedly lauded and promised by Jesus Christ. [6:74f] See **ARC; ARCHIVES, BAHÁ'Í INTERNATIONAL; HAIFA; MOUNT CARMEL.**

WORLD COMMONWEALTH Described by Shoghi Effendi as a world community of nations governed by a world federation:

> The unity of the human race, as envisaged by Bahá'u'lláh, implies the establishment of a world commonwealth in which all nations, races, creeds and classes are closely and permanently united, and in which the autonomy of its state members and the personal freedom and initiative of the individuals that compose them are definitely and completely safeguarded. This commonwealth must, as far as we can visualize it, consist of a world legislature, whose members will, as the trustees of the whole of mankind, ultimately control the entire resources of all the component nations, and will enact such laws as shall be required to regulate the life, satisfy the needs and adjust the relationships of all races and peoples. A world executive, backed by an international Force, will carry out the decisions arrived at, and apply the laws enacted by, this world legislature, and will safeguard the organic unity of the whole commonwealth. A world tribunal will adjudicate and deliver its compulsory and final verdict in all and any disputes that may arise between the various elements constituting this universal system. A mechanism of world inter-communication will be devised, embracing the whole planet, freed from national hindrances and restrictions, and functioning with marvelous swiftness and perfect regularity. A world metropolis will act as the nerve center of a world civilization, the focus towards which the unifying forces of life will converge and from which its energizing influences will radiate. A world language will either be invented or chosen from among the existing languages and will be taught in the schools of all the federated nations as an auxiliary to their mother

> tongue. A world script, a world literature, a uniform and universal system of currency, of weights and measures, will simplify and facilitate intercourse and understanding among the nations and races of mankind. In such a world society, science and religion, the two most potent forces in human life, will be reconciled, will cooperate, and will harmoniously develop. [4:203f]

Among the many other references of the Guardian on this subject, the following excerpts are both informative and representative:

> During this Formative Age of the Faith, and in the course of present and succeeding epochs, the last and crowning stage in the erection of the framework of the Administrative Order of the Faith of Bahá'u'lláh ... will have been completed ... the Lesser Peace will have been established, the unity of mankind will have been achieved and its maturity attained, the Plan conceived by 'Abdu'l-Bahá will have been executed, the emancipation of the Faith from the fetters of religious orthodoxy will have been effected, and its independent religious status will have been universally recognized, whilst in the course of the Golden Age, destined to consummate the Dispensation itself, the banner of the Most Great Peace, promised by its Author, will have been unfurled, the World Bahá'í Commonwealth will have emerged in the plenitude of its power and splendor, and the birth and efflorescence of a world civilization, the child of that Peace, will have conferred its inestimable blessings upon all mankind. [3:6]

> It is the creative energies which His Revelation has released ... to all mankind, that have instilled into humanity the capacity to attain this final stage in its organic and collective evolution. It is with the Golden Age of His Dispensation that the consummation of this process will be forever associated. It is the structure of His New World Order, now stirring in the womb of the administrative institutions He Himself has created, that will serve both as a pattern and a nucleus of that world commonwealth which is the sure, the inevitable destiny of the peoples and nations of the earth. [44:118]

> To the general character, the implications and features of this world commonwealth, destined to emerge, sooner or later ... I have already referred in my previous communications. Suffice it to say that this consummation will, by

its very nature, be a gradual process, and must, as Bahá'u'lláh has Himself anticipated, lead at first to the establishment of that Lesser Peace which the nations of the earth, as yet unconscious of His Revelation and yet unwittingly enforcing the general principles which He has enunciated, will themselves establish. This momentous and historic step, involving the reconstruction of mankind, as the result of the universal recognition of its oneness and wholeness, will bring in its wake the spiritualization of the masses, consequent to the recognition of the character, and the acknowledgment of the claims, of the Faith of Bahá'u'lláh—the essential condition to that ultimate fusion of all races, creeds, classes, and nations which must signalize the emergence of His New World Order.... Then will the coming of age of the entire human race be proclaimed and celebrated by all the peoples and nations of the earth. Then will the banner of the Most Great Peace be hoisted. Then will the world-wide sovereignty of Bahá'u'lláh—the Establisher of the Kingdom of the Father foretold by the Son, and anticipated by the Prophets of God before Him and after Him—be recognized, acclaimed, and firmly established. Then will a world civilization be born, flourish, and perpetuate itself, a civilization with a fullness of life such as the world has never seen nor can as yet conceive. Then will the Everlasting Covenant be fulfilled in its completeness. Then will the promise enshrined in all the Books of God be redeemed, and all the prophecies uttered by the Prophets of old come to pass, and the vision of seers and poets be realized. [44:123] See **MOST GREAT PEACE.**

WORLD CONGRESS (First and Second) The First World Congress was called to commemorate the Centenary of the Declaration of Bahá'u'lláh (Riḍván 1963), the conclusion of the Ten Year Crusade; and the election of the Universal House of Justice. Shoghi Effendi had hoped that it would be possible to have it in Bag͟hdád but the situation in Iráq was such that the Hands of the Cause changed the venue to London and were able to hire the Albert Hall which was filled to capacity by more than 7,000 Bahá'ís.

The Second World Congress was called by the Universal House of Justice for November 1992 (Holy Year) commemorating the Centenary of the Passing of Bahá'u'lláh. It was held in the Jacob Javits Convention Center, New York City—the "City of the Covenant" and commemorated the Centenary of the Covenant of 'Abdu'l-Bahá. Nearly 30,000 Bahá'ís made it the largest ever Bahá'í gathering, and the total number of Bahá'í participation was increased enormously by satellite Conferences, held simultaneously in Apia, Western Samoa; Buenos Aires, Argentina; Sydney, Australia; New Delhi, India; Nairobi, Kenya; Panama City, Panama; Bucharest, Romania; Moscow, Russia; and Singapore.

WORLD ORDER OF BAHÁ'U'LLÁH See **BAHÁ'U'LLÁH, WORLD ORDER.**

WORLD PARLIAMENT OF RELIGIONS The Conference, held in Chicago on 23 September 1893, though ambitious and historically significant, did not achieve the objectives of its organizers. Each representative of the many Faiths presenting papers seemed more concerned in justifying their own beliefs, even somewhat aggressively, than in seeking to find common ground and a basis for working together. It was in an effort to bring some harmony into the proceedings that the Rev. George A. Ford introduced Henry Jessup's paper. It was featured in Shoghi Effendi's history of the first Bahá'í century:

> It was on September 23, 1893, a little over a year after Bahá'u'lláh's ascension, that, in a paper written by Rev. Henry H. Jessup, DD, Director of Presbyterian Missionary Operations in North Syria, and read by Rev. George A. Ford of Syria, at the World Parliament of Religions, held in Chicago, in connection with the Colombian Exposition, commemorating the four-hundredth anniversary of the discovery of America, it was announced that "a famous Persian Sage," "the Bábí Saint," had died recently in 'Akká, and that two years previous to His ascension "a Cambridge scholar" had visited Him, to whom He had expressed "sentiments so noble, so Christ-like" that the author of the paper, in his "closing words," wished to share them with his audience. [5:256]
>
> Extracts from the interview with Bahá'u'lláh follow:
>
> We desire but the good of the world and the happiness of the nations ... that all nations should become one in faith and all men as brothers; that the bonds of affection and unity between the sons of men should be strengthened; that diversity of religion should cease, and differences of race be annulled. [39:37]
>
> These fruitless strifes, these ruinous wars shall pass away, and the "Most Great Peace" shall come.... These strifes and this bloodshed and discord must cease, and all men be as one kindred and one family. [44:116]

This was the first public mention of the Bahá'í Faith in America, and it aroused the interest of several people who were moved to investigate further. Within a few years several hundred supporters were reported in Chicago and Kenosha. At the Centenary of that first Interfaith Conference, held in Chicago in 1993, there was a much larger gathering, much more sincere dialogue was witnessed and members of the Bahá'í community presented several papers. See **JESSUP, HENRY**.

WORSHIP Given that there is no fixed form of service, minimal rituals and no clergy, worship is largely a private and personal concern. Bahá'ís worship God in prayer; by action in daily life in accordance with Bahá'í Teachings; and by work carried out in the spirit of service. It is in the Mashriqu'l-Adhkárs that forms of service are observed but these are carried out as planned by a committee appointed for the purpose by a Spiritual Assembly with each service, therefore, taking on a specifically unique form. Common elements may well be the inclusion of passages from Bahá'í Scriptures: that may be read, chanted or sung *a cappella*. A Spiritual Assembly may occasionally arrange a meeting where Scriptural passages are used, but these do not conform to any regular pattern. In answering questions about the form of worship to be followed in the Mashriqu'l-Adhkár Shoghi Effendi wrote through his secretary:

> Shoghi Effendi wishes in this connection to urge the friends to avoid all forms of rigidity and uniformity in matters of worship. There is no objection to the recital or chanting of prayers in the Oriental language, but there is also no obligation whatsoever of adopting such a form of prayer at any devotional service in the auditorium of the Temple. It should neither be required nor prohibited. The important thing that should always be borne in mind is that with the exception of certain specific obligatory prayers, Bahá'u'lláh has given us no strict or special rulings in matters of worship, whether in the Temple or elsewhere. Prayer is essentially a communion between man and God, and as such transcends all ritualistic forms and formulae. [104:78]

In answer to a question about the study of agriculture, 'Abdu'l-Bahá wrote:

> Strive as much as possible to become proficient in the science of agriculture for in accordance with the Divine Teachings, the acquisition of sciences and the perfection of arts is considered as acts of worship. If a man engages with all his power in the acquisition of a science or in the perfection of an art, it is as if he has been worshipping God in the churches and temples. Thus as thou enterest a

school of agriculture and strivest in the acquisition of that science thou art day and night engaged in acts of worship—acts that are accepted at the threshold of the Almighty. What bounty greater than this that science should be considered as an act of worship and art as service to the Kingdom of God. [106:377f] See **PRAYER; WORK; MASHRIQU'L-ADHKÁR**.

WRIGHT, IONITA (1915-1968) The first inhabitant of San Andrés Island to become a believer. [51:434]

WRITINGS While this is generally understood to be a reference to Bahá'í Scripture, "Bahá'í Writings" include those which have come from the Guardian (which are themselves not a part of Bahá'í Scripture). Those "Writings" that Bahá'u'lláh calls upon the believers to read daily are solely from Bahá'í Scripture. In relation to copyright, however, the Universal House of Justice referred to both:

> The Universal House of Justice has ... (made) it clear that the Spiritual Assemblies and individual believers are free to quote in their publications from any of the Writings of the three Central Figures of the Faith or from the writings of the beloved Guardian, whether in the original language or in translation, without obtaining clearance from the copyright holder, unless the copyright holder in the case of a translation is an individual or is a non-Bahá'í institution.... The ruling is made to ensure that the Sacred Scriptures of our Faith and the writings of the beloved Guardian may be freely used by the believers; it does not change the existing requirements for individual believers to submit their works on the Faith for review before publication, neither does it relieve Spiritual Assemblies of their responsibility to protect the dignity of the Faith and uphold the proper standard of reverence in the use of its Sacred Scriptures. [86:105]

Y

YÁ Vocative particle meaning "O."[11:742📖]

YÁ BAHÁ'U'L-ABHÁ O Thou the Glory of the Most Glorious. [11:736📖]

YALDÁ'Í, BAHRÁM (1955-1983) (Martyr) A Bahá'í who was executed along with other coreligionists in Shíráz, Írán, by the government in June 1983, for refusing to recant his belief in

Bahá'u'lláh. His mother, Nuṣrat (see next entry), was also executed for refusing to recant her faith. [11:600]

YALDÁ'Í, NUṢRAT GHUFRÁNÍ (1929-1983) (Martyr) A Bahá'í who was executed (following severe torture that included at least 200 lashes) along with other coreligionists in Shíráz, Írán, in June 1983 for refusing to recant her belief in Bahá'u'lláh. Her son, Bahrám (see previous entry), was also executed for refusing to recant his faith. [11:600]

YAMAMOTO, KANICHI (1879-1961) The first (1902) Japanese Bahá'í to embrace the Cause in Hawaii. In 1903 he moved to America as a butler in the Goodall (q.v.) household. In 1912 he met 'Abdu'l-Bahá in Oakland. He received four tablets from 'Abdu'l-Bahá. [47:931][91:176][60:556]

YAZDÍ, ḤÁJÍ 'ALÍ (1845-1943) An early Persian who arrived in 'Akká a few days after Bahá'u'lláh was removed from the Barracks and who stayed until the end of his life. He is remembered for the gift he made of the tract of land in Bahjí on which Bahá'u'lláh's Tomb was built. [45:624]

YEAR OF WAITING—YEAR OF PATIENCE This "year" is essential before the granting of Bahá'í divorce. Applying the guidance given in the Bahá'í writings we find:

> When a Spiritual Assembly receives an application for divorce its first duty is to try to reconcile the couple. When it determines that this is not possible, it should then set the date of the beginning of the year of waiting. That could be the date on which the Assembly reaches the decision, unless the couple are still living together, in which case it must be postponed until they separate. If the couple had already separated some time before, the Assembly may back-date the beginning of the year; however, the earliest date on which it can be set is the date on which the couple last separated with the intention of obtaining a divorce.... Thus the date of the beginning of the year of patience normally commences when one of the parties notifies the Assembly that they have separated with the intention of divorce. However, the Assembly may establish the beginning of the year of patience on a prior date provided it is satisfied such prior date reflects the actual date of separation and there is good reason for so doing.... The parties to a divorce must live apart in separate residences during the year of waiting. Any cohabitation of the parties stops the running of the year of waiting. If thereafter a divorce is desired a new date for the beginning of a new year of waiting must be set by the Assembly.... It is the responsibility of the husband to provide support for

his wife and children during the year of waiting.... It is the responsibility of the Assembly to assist the divorced couple to arrive at an amicable settlement of their financial affairs and arrangement for the custody and support of the children rather than let these matters be a subject of litigation in the civil courts. If the Assembly is unable to bring the couple to an agreement on such matters then their only recourse is to civil court.... It is not possible to shorten the period of waiting as this is a provision of the Kitáb-i-Aqdas. However, a Spiritual Assembly may, if circumstances justify it, back-date the beginning of the year provided that this is not earlier than the date the parties last separated with the intention of obtaining a divorce.... the Assembly should determine, before setting the date of the beginning of the year of waiting, that irreconcilable antipathy exists.... it is the Assembly's responsibility to conduct its own investigation and come to a decision. Assemblies are, of course, discouraged from probing unnecessarily into details of personal lives and the examination of a divorce problem should not go beyond what is necessary to ascertain whether or not such antipathy does, indeed, exist. [86:395ff] See **DIVORCE**.

YEN, HILDA YANK SING (1905-1970) Born in a wealthy, prominent family that held an indisputably high profile in the new China that emerged after the revolution of Sun Yatsen, she became a Bahá'í in 1944. At the end of WW II she was part of the Chinese Delegation at the Dumbarton Oaks Conference, and in 1945 she joined the department of public information when the United Nations was formed. She was instrumental in assisting the recognition of the Bahá'í International Community as a non-governmental organization. [51:476]

YOUTH The present adult age for a Bahá'í to have administrative rights (q.v.) is 21. However, a Bahá'í youth is, according to Bahá'u'lláh, mature, for obedience to the obligatory laws, such as fasting, prayer and marriage, at age 15. Young Bahá'ís, however, continue to be involved in youth activities into their late twenties. Throughout its history the Bahá'í Faith has been noted for the outstanding contributions made by its youth. These range from the youthfulness of the Báb when He declared His Mission to the tender ages of many of its martyrs, of its pioneers and teachers in opening new places, even new countries, to the Faith, and even its administrators. The Universal House of Justice recognized this when they wrote in May 1975:

> The endurance of youth under arduous conditions, their vitality and vigor, and their ability to adapt

themselves to local situations, to meet new challenges, and to impart their warmth and enthusiasm to those they visit, combined with the standard of conduct upheld by Bahá'í youth, make them potent instruments for the execution of the contemplated projects. Indeed, through these distinctive qualities they can become the spearhead of any enterprise and the driving force of any undertaking in which they participate, whether local or national. Our expectant eyes are fixed on Bahá'í youth! ... From the very beginning of the Bahá'í Era, youth have played a vital part in the promulgation of God's Revelation. The Báb Himself was but twenty-five years old when He declared His Mission, while many of the Letters of the Living were even younger. The Master, as a very young man, was called upon to shoulder heavy responsibilities in the service of His Father in 'Iraq and Turkey, and His brother, the Purest Branch, yielded up his life to God in the Most Great Prison at the age of twenty-two that the servants of God might "be quickened, and all that dwell on earth be united." Shoghi Effendi was a student at Oxford when called to the throne of his guardianship, and many of the Knights of Bahá'u'lláh, who won imperishable fame during the Ten Year Crusade, were young people. Let it, therefore, never be imagined that youth must await their years of maturity before they can render invaluable services to the Cause of God. [85:632]

In 1944 Shoghi Effendi wrote:

The greatest need of youth today is character training. Prayer is only one factor in this; they must learn to live up to the ethical teachings of the Faith.... Once young people become convinced of the existence of the soul they should not need much convincing that material training and material progress are not sufficient. The soul needs training and help too. He [Shoghi Effendi] feels that teaching the Faith to the youth is of the utmost importance in these days, as they will not only become the workers of the future but will be able to widely spread the Message among their own generation. [85:630]

A few years later he wrote through his secretary:

He urges you to make up your minds to do great, great deeds for the Faith; the condition of the world is steadily growing worse, and your generation must provide the saints, heroes, martyrs and administrators of future years. With dedication and will power you can rise to great heights. [85:630]

In 1982 the Universal House of Justice wrote:

As to Bahá'í youth, legatees of the heroic early believers and now standing on their shoulders, we call upon them to redouble their efforts, in this day of widespread interest in the Cause of God, to enthuse their contemporaries with the divine Message and thus prepare themselves for the day when they will be veteran believers able to assume whatever tasks may be laid upon them. We offer them this passage from the Pen of Bahá'u'lláh: "Blessed is he who in the prime of his youth and the heyday of his life will arise to serve the Cause of the Lord of the beginning and of the end, and adorn his heart with His love. The manifestation of such a grace is greater than the creation of the heavens and of the earth. Blessed are the steadfast and well is it with those who are firm." [85:628]

Z

ZÁDIH Born; offspring, son. Used as a suffix after a proper name it means "Son of —."[11:742📖]

ZAMENHOF, LYDIA (1904-1944) An early European believer and the daughter of Dr. Ludwig L. Zamenhof, the inventor of Esperanto. Miss Zamenhof, along with members of her family, was executed by the Nazis during WW II (she perished in Treblinka concentration camp in August 1944).[19:533][143][60:561]

ZAMZAN Literally copious (water): sacred well within the precincts of the Great Mosque in Mecca. Though salty, its water is much esteemed for pious uses, such as ablutions, and drinking after a fast. [11:742📖]

ZARRÍN-TÁJ. See **ṬÁHIRIH**.

ZAWRÁ' A term signifying Ba<u>gh</u>dád. [11:742📖]

ZAYNU'L-ÁBIDÍN, FAWZÍ (1911-1975) (Knight of Bahá'u'lláh) An Egyptian believer who pioneered (1953) with his wife (Bahíyyih 'Alí Sa'd'id-Dín) to Spanish Morocco for which service they were designated Knights of Bahá'u'lláh. [52:544]

ZAYNU'L-MUQARRABÍN Literally Ornament of the Near (or Favored) Ones. [11:742📖]

ZONNEVELD, ARNOLD (1933-1983) A Dutch believer (1961) who pioneered first to Spitzbergen Island (1961-1963) and then to Bolivia with his wife (Gisela) and family (1966-1983).[2:825]

Bibliography

If this dictionary had been written only 20 years ago the compilation of a bibliography would have been a very much easier task. With the exception of the Writings (q.v.) the bulk of the titles that follow have been published in the last two decades. As it is, even a partial listing of English language Bahá'í literature would fill a volume some three to four times the length of this dictionary! The most complete bibliographic work currently available is William Collins's excellent work, *Bibliography of English-Language Works on the Bábí and Bahá'í Faiths 1844-1985*. No serious researcher will want to be without this meticulous book.

In all but a few cases we have listed the most recent date of publication. Sadly, a great many interesting works are now long out of print and generally unavailable although some may be located through good libraries. Where a book is out of print but thought to be of interest and/or value, it has been included in the listing.

We have structured the bibliography according to the following groupings:

1. **Scriptures—The Central Figures**
   a) The Báb (in English)
   b) The Báb (original language titles)
   c) Bahá'u'lláh (in English)
   d) Bahá'u'lláh (original language titles)
   e) 'Abdu'l-Bahá (in English)
   f) 'Abdu'l-Bahá (original language titles)
   This section contains all known English-language works by the Central Figures. To assist readers who may be unfamiliar with Arabic and/or Persian titles (which are frequently referred to in texts) we have listed the original language titles of the major works of the Báb, Bahá'u'lláh and 'Abdu'l-Bahá with source references as to where their English-language equivalent can be found.
2. **Shoghi Effendi**
   A complete English-language listing of the published works of Shoghi Effendi.
3. **Universal House of Justice.**
   A partial English-language listing of the published works of the Universal House of Justice. The bulk of written materials from the Universal House of Justice is contained in letters to the Institutions of the Bahá'í Faith and/or to individual believers and is not, therefore, available for study. Some letters have, however, been made generally available, and these are listed in this section.

4. **Bahíyyih Khánum**
5. **Compilations**: The Writings of the Báb; Bahá'u'lláh; 'Abdu'l-Bahá; Shoghi Effendi; Universal House of Justice
6. **Hands of the Cause of God**
7. **Works Related to the Central Figures and Other Key Figures**
   a) The Báb
   b) Bahá'u'lláh
   c) 'Abdu'l-Bahá
   d) Shoghi Effendi
   e) Bahíyyih Khánum
   f) Ásíyih Khánum
   g) Munríhih Khánum
8. **Bibliographies**
9. **Yearbooks, Journals, Magazines**
   These works form the core of publicly available historical reference materials, although a growing number of scholars are now engaged in original historical research (see next Section).
10. **Historical Reference Materials**
    a) Bábí
    b) Bahá'í
    c) Other
    The reader interested specifically in the development of the North American Bahá'í Community is referred to the excellent history series written by Dr. Robert Stockman. Also of significance for historical researchers is the series produced by Kalimát Press, which was first published as Studies in Bábí and Bahá'í History, but which now goes under the heading of Studies in the Bábí and Bahá'í Religions.
11. **Biographies**
    Given that history devolves from the actions of people, we have prepared a substantial list of biographical works in the knowledge that historians and researchers will be able to glean much that is of interest from the pages of these works—insofar as they are in many cases the only available record of Bahá'í activities in a given area (and will remain so until Bahá'í archives can be made available to researchers).
12. **Bahá'í International Community**
    Various statements and other documents relating to the work of the Bahá'í International Community (primarily with the agencies of the United Nations).
13. **Treatise on Bahá'í Subjects—Theological/apologetic works.**

14. **Electronic Media**
   a) Bahá'í Scriptures
15. **WWW Sites**
   a) Bahá'í Scriptures
   b) Bahá'í International Community Statements
   c) Bibliographies
   d) General Resources
   e) Introductory Material
   f) Images—Graphics

1. Scripture—The Central Figures

a) The Báb (in English)

The Báb's Address to the Letters of the Living. Trans. Unknown. New York: Bahá'í Publishing Committee, 1930s.

A Compilation of Passages from the Writings of the Báb. New Delhi: Bahá'í Publishing Trust, 1980.

Selections of the Writings of the Báb. Trans. Ḥabíb Taherzadeh. Haifa: Bahá'í World Center, 1978.

b) The Báb (original language titles)[1]

Bayán, The Arabic Bayán, [145] 1847, Máh-Kú.

Bayán, The Persian Bayán, 1847, Máh-Kú.

Dalá'il-i-Sab'ih, Seven Proofs, [146:115] Máh-Kú.

Khasa'il-i-Sab'ih, Supplementary to the Seven Proofs. [145]

Kitáb-i-Asmá', The Book of Names, [146:127] Chihríq.

Kitáb-i-Panj-Sha'n, The Book of Five Grades. [145]

Kitabu'r-Rúh, The Book of the Spirit. [145]

Lawḥ-i-Ḥurúfát, Tablet of the Letters, [145] revealed in honor of Dayyán (a prominent official of some literary standing), Chihríq.

Qayyúmu'l-Asmá,' Commentary on the Súrih of Joseph (the first chapter of which was revealed to Mullá Ḥusayn 23 May 1844), [72:179, 147:306] 1844, Shíráz.

Risáliy-i-'Adlíyyih, Treatise on Justice, [145] Third Year of Báb's Ministry.

Risáliy-i-Dhahabíyyih, The Golden Treatise, [145] Third Year of Báb's Ministry.

Risáliy-i-Fiqhíyyih, Treatise on Jurisprudence, [145] early Ministry, Búshihr.

Risáliy-i-Furú'i-'Adlíyyih, Treatise on Aspects of Jurisprudence, [145] mid-Ministry.

1. English language translation are cited where known.

Ṣahífatu'l-Ḥaramayn, Epistle Between the Two Shrines (Mecca and Medina) in answer to questions put by Mírzá Muḥíṭ-I-Kirmání (a leader in the Shaykhí movement),[145] January 1845.

Ṣahífiy-i-Ja'fariyyih, Epistle to Ja'far,[145] early Ministry.

Ṣahífiy-i-Makhdhúmíyyih, Treatise on Prayer,[145] early Ministry.

Ṣahífiy-i-Raḍavíyyih, Treatise on Paradise. [145]

Súriy-i-Tawḥíd, Verse of Divine Unity,[145] early to mid-Ministry.

Tafsír-i-Nubuvvat-i-Khaṣṣih, Treatise on the Prophethood of Muḥammad,[145] 1847.

Tafsír-i-Súrih of Kawthar, Commentary on the Súrih of Kawthar. [145] During three interviews with Him by Siyyid Yaḥyá Dárábí (Vaḥíd), Shíráz.

Tafsír-i-Súrih of Va'l-'Aṣr, Commentary on the Súrih of Va'l-'Aṣr, [145] At the request of Mírzá Siyyid Muḥammad, the Sulṭánu'l-'Ulamá Imám-Jum'ih, Iṣfáhán.

Zíyárat-i-Sháh-'Abdu'l-'Aẓím, Verse of Visitation—Resting Place of the Sister of the Báb (Okht).[145]

c) Bahá'u'lláh (in English)

Epistle to the Son of the Wolf. Trans. Shoghi Effendi. Wilmette, Ill.: Bahá'í Publishing Trust, 1979.

Gleanings from the Writings of Bahá'u'lláh. Wilmette, Ill.: Bahá'í Publishing Trust, 1988.

The Hidden Words of Bahá'u'lláh. rev. ed. Wilmette, Ill.: Bahá'í Publishing Trust, 1985.

Kitáb-i-Aqdas—The Most Holy Book. Trans. A Committee of the Universal House of Justice. Haifa: Bahá'í World Center, 1992.

Kitáb-i-Íqan, the Book of Certitude. Trans. Shoghi Effendi. 2nd ed. Wilmette, Ill.: Bahá'í Publishing Trust, 1981.

Meditations of the Blessed Beauty. London: Bahá'í Publishing Trust, 1992.

Prayers and Meditations by Bahá'u'lláh. Trans. Shoghi Effendi. Wilmette, Ill.: Bahá'í Publishing Trust, 1979.

The Proclamation of Bahá'u'lláh to the Kings and Leaders of the World. Haifa: Bahá'í World Center, 1978.

The Seven Valleys and the Four Valleys. Trans. Ali Kuli Khan, Marzieh Gail. 3rd. ed. rev. Wilmette, Ill.: Bahá'í Publishing Trust, 1984.

Synopsis and Codification of the Laws and Ordinances of the Kitáb-i-Aqdas. Haifa: Bahá'í World Center, 1973.

Tablets of Bahá'u'lláh Revealed After The Kitáb-i-Aqdas. Wilmette, Ill.: Bahá'í Publishing Trust, 1988.

d) Bahá'u'lláh (original language titles)[2]

Alváḥ-i-Laylatu'l-Quds, Tablet of Holy Night, [72:164] 'Akká.
Aṣl-i-Kullu'l-Khayr, Words of Wisdom, [77:154] 'Akká
Az-Bágh-i-Illáhí, From the Garden of God, [71:218] Baghdád.
Báz-Áv-u-Bidih-Jámí, A Poem, [148] Baghdád.
Bishárat, Glad Tidings, [74:161] Baghdád.
Chihár-Vádí, Four Valleys, [71:104] Baghdád.
Haft-Vádí, Seven Valleys, [71:96] Baghdád.
Halih-Halih-Yá-Bishárát, Glad Tidings, [71:219] Baghdád.
Ḥúr-i-'Ujáb, Wondrous Maiden, [71:218] Baghdád.
Ḥurúfát-i-Állíyát, Exalted Letter, [71:122] Baghdád, 1886-03-19.
Ishráqát, Splendors. [73:145]
Kalimát-i-Firdawsíyyih, Words of Paradise. [77:57-58]
Kalimát-i-Makúnih, Hidden Words. [92]
Kitáb-i-'Ahd, Book of Covenant. [77:219]
Kitáb i-Aqdas, Most Holy Book. [81]
Kitáb-i-Badí', Wondrous Book, [72:370] Adrianople, 1867.
Kitáb-i-Íqán, Book of Certitude. [64]
Lawḥ-i-'Abdu'l-'Azíz-Va-Vakulá, Tablet of 'Abdu'l-'Azíz. [148]
Lawḥ-i-'Abdu'l-Vahháb, Tablet of 'Abdu'l-Vahháb, [74:41] 'Akká.
Lawḥ-i-'Abdu'r-Razzáq, Tablet of 'Abdu'r-Razzáq. [148]
Lawḥ-i-Aḥbáb, Tablet of the Friends. [73:258]
Lawḥ-i-Aḥmad, Tablet of Aḥmad. [72:137]
Lawḥ-i-Amjad, Tablet of the Most Glorious, [[148] 'Akká.
Lawḥ-i-Amváj, Tablet of the Waves. [148]
Lawḥ-i-Anta'l-Káfí, Long Healing Prayer. [149:84]
Lawḥ-i-Aqdas, The Most Holy Tablet (Tablet to the Christians), [77:9ff] 'Akká.
Lawḥ-i-Ard-I-Bá, Tablet of the Land of Bá. [77:227]
Lawḥ-i-Ashraf, Tablet of Ashraf, [72:230] 'Akká.
Lawḥ-i-'Áshiq-va-Ma'shúq, Tablet of the Lover of the Beloved, [148] 'Akká.
Lawḥ-i-Áyiy-i-Núr, Tablet of Light, [71:125] 'Akká.
Lawḥ-i-Ayyúb, Tablet of Job, [71:263] Baghdád.
Lawḥ-i-Bahá, Tablet of Bahá, [72:171]Adrianople.
Lawḥ-i-Baqá, Tablet of Eternity, [148] 'Akká.
Lawḥ-i-Basíṭatu'l-Ḥaqiqih, Tablet of Uncompounded Reality, [148] 'Akká.
Lawḥ-i-Bismilih, Tablet in the Name of God, [148] 'Akká.
Lawḥ-i-Bulbulu'l-Firáq, Tablet of the Nightingale of Separation, [71:244] Baghdád.

2. English language translation are cited where known.

Lawḥ-i-Burhán, Tablet of Proofs, [77:205] 'Akká.
Lawḥ-i-Dahat, Tablet of Mehdi Dahat. [77:195]
Lawḥ-i-Dunyá, Tablet of the World, [77] 'Akká.
Lawḥ-i-Fitnih, Tablet of Test, [71:128] Baghdád.
Lawḥ-i-Ghulámu'l-Khuld, Tablet of the Youth of Paradise, [71:213] Baghdád.
Lawḥ-i-Ḥabíb, Tablet of the Beloved, [148] 'Akká.
Lawḥ-i-Haft-Purshish, Tablet of Seven Questions. [73:272]
Lawḥ-i-Ḥajj, Tablet of Pilgrimage, Adrianople. 1863.
Lawḥ-i-Hawdaj, Tablet of the Howdah,[72:6] en route Constantinople, 1863.
Lawḥ-i-Ḥikmat, Tablet of Wisdom. [77:137]
Lawḥ-i-Hirtík, Tablet to Hardegg. [73:28-9]
Lawḥ-i-Ḥúríyyih, Tablet of the Maiden, [71:125] 1858.
Lawḥ-i-Ḥusayn, Tablet of Ḥusayn, [148] 'Akká.
Lawḥ-i-Ibn-i-Dhi'b, Epistle to the Son of the Wolf, [70] Bahjí, 1891.
Lawḥ-i-Ittiḥád, Tablet of Unity, [73:191] 'Akká.
Lawḥ-i-Iḥtaraq, The Fire Tablet. See *Lawḥ-i-Qad-Iḥtaraqa'l-Mukhliṣún*. [149:214]
Lawḥ-i-Jamál, Tablet to Jamál Brujerdi (Bahá'í Studies), 'Akká.
Lawḥ-i-Khalil, Tablet of the Word of God. [72:260]
Lawḥ-i-Karím, Tablet to Karím, [148] 'Akká.
Lawḥ-i-Karmil, Tablet of Carmel, [77:2-5] Haifa.
Lawḥ-i-Kullu'ṭ-Ṭa'ám, Tablet of All Food, [71:55] Baghdád, 1854.
Lawḥ-i-Malikih, Tablet to Queen Victoria, [78:31] 'Akká.
Lawḥ-i-Malik-i-Rús, Tablet to the Czar of Russia, [78:25] 'Akká.
Lawḥ-i-Malláḥu'l-Quds, Tablet of the Holy Mariner, [71:228] 'Akká, 1863.
Lawḥ-i-Mánikjí-Ṣáḥib, Tablet of Seven Questions (Zora), [73:270] 'Akká.
Lawḥ-i-Maqṣúd, Tablet of Intention, [74:227] 'Akká.
Lawḥ-i-Maryam, Tablet to Maryam, [150] Baghdád.
Lawḥ-i-Mawlúd, Tablet of Birth, [148] 'Akká.
Lawḥ-i-Mabáhilih, Tablet of Confirmation, [148] Adrianople.
Lawḥ-i-Nápulyún, First Tablet to Napoleon III, [78:17] 'Akká.
Lawḥ-i-Nápulyún, Second Tablet to Napoleon III, [78:39] 'Akká.
Lawḥ-i-Náṣir, Tablet to Náṣir, [72:245] 'Akká.
Lawḥ-i-Náqús, Tablet of the Bell, [72:23] Baghdád.
Lawḥ-i-Nuqṭih, Tablet of the Point, [148] Adrianople.
Lawḥ-i-Páp, Tablet to Pope Pius, [78:81] 'Akká.
Lawḥ-i-Pisar-'Amm, Tablet to the Cousin. [73:216]
Lawḥ-i-Qad-Iḥtaraqa'l-Mukhliṣún, The Fire Tablet. See *Lawḥ-i-Iḥtaraq*. [149:214]

Lawḥ-i-Qiná', Tablet of the Veil, [71:334] 'Akká.
Lawḥ-i-Quds, Tablet of Holiness (I & II), [148] 'Akká.
Lawḥ-i-Rafí', Tablet of Elevation, [148] 'Akká.
Lawḥ-i-Ra'ís, Tablet to Ra'ís, [72:411] en route to 'Akká.
Lawḥ-i-Rashá, Tablet of the Fawn, [148] en route to 'Akká.
Lawḥ-i-Rasúl, Tablet of the Prophet, [148] en route to 'Akká.
Lawḥ-i-Rúḥ, Tablet of the Spirit, [72:181] Adrianople.
Lawḥ-i-Ru'yá, Tablet of Vision, [73:221] 1837.
Lawḥ-i-Saḥáb, Tablet of the Companion, [148] 'Akká.
Lawḥ-i-Salmán I, Tablet to Salmán I, [73:89-90] 'Akká.
Lawḥ-i-Salmán II, Tablet to Salmán II, [73:89-90] 'Akká.
Lawḥ-i-Sámsún, Tablet to Sámsún (Bahá'í Studies), Constinople
Lawḥ-i-Sayyáh, Tablet of the Traveler; [72:210] there are several Tablets with this name revealed at different times to different recipients.
Lawḥ-i-Shaykh-Fání, Tablet to Shaykh-Fání,[148] 'Akká.
Lawḥ-i-Sulṭán, Tablet to Náṣiri'd-Din Sháh. [72:337]
Lawḥ-i-Siráj, Tablet to Siráj. [72:262]
Lawḥ-i-Tawḥíd, Tablet of Divine Unity, [148] 'Akká.
Lawḥ-i-Ṭibb, Tablet of Medicine. [73:358]
Lawḥ-i-Tuqá, Tablet of the Fear of God, [148] Adrianople.
Lawḥ-i-Varqá, Tablet of Varqá, [74:64] 'Akká.
Lawḥ-i-Yúsuf, Tablet of Joseph, 'Akká.
Lawḥ-i-Zaynu'l-Muqarrabín, Tablet to Zayn, [148] 'Akká.
Lawḥ-i-Ziyárih, Tablet of Visitation. [149:230]
Madínatu'r-Riḍá, Tablet of the Radiant Acquiesence, [71:108] Baghdád.
Madínatu't-Tawḥíd, Tablet of the City of Divine Unity, [71:109] Baghdád.
Mathnaví, Poetical Forms, [72:30] Constinople.
Munájátháy-i-Ṣiyám, Prayer for the Fast, [149:238] 'Akká.
Qad-Iḥtaraqa'l-Mukhliṣún, Fire Tablet. [73:223]
Qaṣídy-i-Varqá'íyyih, Ode of the Dove. [73:206]
Rashḥ-i-'Amá, Sprinkling of the Divine Cloud (Bahá'í Studies), 1852.
Riḍvánu'l-'Adl, The Paradise of Justice, [148] 'Akká.
Riḍvánu'l-Iqrár, The Paradise of Acknowledgment, [148] 'Akká.
Ṣaḥiffiy-i-Shaṭṭíyyih, Treaty of the Torrent (Stream), [71:105] Baghdád.
Ṣalát-i-Mayyit, Prayer for the Dead. [149:40]
Sáqá-Az-Ghayb-i-Baqá, The Gift of Invisible Eternity, [148] Baghdád.
Shikkar-Shikan-Shavand, Allusions to Shaykh Abdu'l Ḥusayn. [71:147]
Subḥána-Rabbíya'l-A'lá, Praised Be To God—The Most Exalted, [71:211] Baghdád, 1863.
Subḥána-Yá-Hú, Praised Be Thou Oh God, [72:18] Baghdád, 1863.

Súratu'lláh, Verse of God, [71:245] Baghdád.
Súriy-i-Aḥzán, Verse of Affliction, [148] Baghdád.
Súriy-i-Amín, Verse of Trustworthiness, [148] Baghdád.
Súriy-i-Amr, Verse of Command, [72:162] Adrianople.
Súriy-i-A'ráb, Verse of the Arabs, [148] 'Akká.
Súriy-i-Aṣḥáb, Verse of the Companion, [72:65] Adrianople.
Súriy-i-Asmá,' Verse of the Names, [71:280] 'Akká.
Súriy-i-Bayán, Verse of Exposition, [148] Adrianople.
Súriy-i-Damm, Verse of Blood, [72:236] Adrianople.
Súriy-i-Dhabíḥ, Verse of Sacrifice, [148] Adrianople.
Súriy-i-Dhikr, Verse of Remembrance, [148] Adrianople.
Súriy-i-Faḍl, Verse of Knowledge, [148] Adrianople.
Súriy-i-Fatḥ, Verse of Opening, [148] Adrianople.
Súriy-i-Fu'ád, Verse of the Heart, [73:87] 'Akká, 1873.
Súriy-i-Ghuṣn, Verse of the Branch. [72:240]
Súriy-i-Ḥajj I, Verse of Pilgrimage I, Adrianople.
Súriy-i-Ḥajj II, Verse of Pilgrimage II, [148] Adrianople.
Súriy-i-Haykal, Verse of the Temple. [73:132]
Súriy-i-Ḥifẓ, Verse of Preservation, [148] Adrianople.
Súriy-i-Hijr, Verse of Separation, [148] Baghdád.
Súriy-i-'Ibád, Verse of the Servant, [72:272] 'Akká.
Súriy-i-Ism, Verse of the Name, [148] 'Akká.
Súriy-i-Ismuna'l-Mursil, Verse of the Greatest Name of God, [148] 'Akká.
Súriy-i-Javád, Verse of Javád, [148] 'Akká.
Súriy-i-Khiṭáb, Verse of Oration, [148] Adrianople.
Súriy-i-Ma'ání, Verse of Inner Meaning, [148] 'Akká.
Súriy-i-Man,' Verse of Bounty, [148] 'Akká.
Súriy-i-Mulúk, Verse of the Kings, [73:109] Constantinople.
Súriy-i-Nidá, Verse of the Announcement, [148] 'Akká.
Súriy-i-Nuṣḥ, Verse of the Announcement, [71:137] Baghdád.
Súriy-i-Qadír, Verse of Omnipotence, [71:119] 'Akká.
Súriy-i-Qahir, Verse of Wrath, [148] 'Akká.
Súriy-i-Qalam, Verse of the Pen, [148] Adrianople.
Súriy-i-Qamíṣ, Verse of the Robe, [148] Adrianople.
Súriy-i-Ṣabr, Verse of Patience, [71:265-68] Baghdád, 1863.
Súriy-i-Sulṭán, Verse of the Kings, [148] 'Akká.
Súriy-i-Vafá, Verse of Fidelity, [74:205] 'Akká.
Súriy-i-Zíyárih, Verse of Visitation for Zíyárih, [148] 'Akká.
Súriy-i-Zabur, Verse of Psalms, [148] 'Akká.
Súriy-i-Ẓuhúr, Verse of the Manifestation, [151] Adrianople.
Tafsír-i-Hú, Commentary of He Who Is, [148] Baghdád, 1860.

Tafsír-i-Ḥurúfát-i-Muqaṭṭa'ih, Commentary on the Disconnected Letters, [148] Baghdád, 1860.

Tafsír-i-Súriy-i-Va'sh-Shams, Commentary on the Verse of the Sun, (Bahá'í Studies), 'Akká.

Tajallíyát, Effulgences. [77:47ff]

Ṭarázát, Ornaments. [77:33f]

Zíyárat-Námih, The Tablet of Visitation. [148]

Zíyárat-Námiy-i-Awlíyá, The Tablet of the Comprehensive Visitation, [148] 'Akká.

Zíyárat-Námiy-i-Bábu'l-Báb va Quddús, The Tablet of Visitation for the Shrines of Mullá Ḥusayn and Quddús, [148] 'Akká.

Zíyárat-Námiy-i-Bayt, The Tablet of Visitation for the House, [148] 'Akká.

Zíyárat-Námiy-i-Maryam, The Tablet of Visitation of Mary, [148] 'Akká.

Zíyárat-Námiy-i-Siyyidu'sh-Shuhadá,' The Tablet of Visitation for the Prince of Martyrs, Imám Ḥusayn, [18] 'Akká.

e) 'Abdu'l-Bahá (in English)

'Abdu'l-Bahá on Divine Philosophy. Boston: The Tudor Press, 1916.

America's Spiritual Mission. Trans. Ahmad Sohrab. New York: Bahá'í Publishing Committee, 1936.

Contentment: Jewels from the Words of Abdu'l-Bahá. Ed Gordon Kerr. London: Bahá'í Publishing Trust, 1995.

The Divine Art of Living. New York: Brentano's, 1926.

Foundations of World Unity. Wilmette, Ill.: Bahá'í Publishing Trust, 1979.

Friendship and Love: Jewels from the Words of Abdu'l-Bahá. Ed Gordon Kerr. London: Bahá'í Publishing Trust, 1994.

Happiness: Jewels from the Words of Abdu'l-Bahá. Ed Gordon Kerr. London: Bahá'í Publishing Trust, 1995.

Memorials of the Faithful. Trans. Marzieh Gail. Wilmette, Ill.: Bahá'í Publishing Trust, 1975.

The Mystery of God. New Delhi: Bahá'í Publishing Trust, 1971.

Notes Taken at Acca: Table Talks by Abdul Baha Taken Down in Persian by Mirza Hadi at Acca, Feb. 1907. Notes Taken by Corinne True. Trans. A. U. Fareed. Chicago: Bahá'í Publishing Society, 1907.

Paris Talks: Addresses Given by Abdu'l-Bahá in Paris in 1911-1912. 9th ed. London: Bahá'í Publishing Trust, 1951.

The Promulgation of Universal Peace. 2nd ed. Vol. 1 & 2. Wilmette, Ill.: Bahá'í Publishing Trust, 1982. 2 vols.

The Reality of Man. New York: Publishing Committee of the Bahá'ís of the United States and Canada, 1931.

The Secret of Divine Civilization. Trans. Marzieh Gail. Wilmette, Ill.: Bahá'í Publishing Trust, 1957.

Selections from the Writings of Abdu'l-Bahá. Trans. A Committee at the Bahá'í World Center and Marzieh Gail. Haifa: Bahá'í World Center, 1978.

Some Answered Questions. Trans. and comp. by Laura Clifford Barney. 1981 ed. Wilmette, Ill.: Bahá'í Publishing Trust, 1982.

Table Talks at Acca by Abdul Baha Abbas (as expressed by Mirza Moneer and Mirza Nur-ed-Din interpreters). Trans. Mirza Moneer Mirza Nur-ed-Din. Chicago: Bahá'í Publishing Society, 1907.

Tablets of Abdul-Baha Abbas. Vol. 1, 2, 3. Chicago: Bahá'í Publishing Society, 1919.

Tablets of the Divine Plan. Wilmette, Ill.: Bahá'í Publishing Trust, 1980.

Tablets to Japan. New York: Bahá'í Publishing Committee, 1928.

Talks by 'Abdu'l-Bahá Given in Paris: Supplementary Historical Note and Introduction. London, 1936. (Compiled by Helen Pilkington Bishop.)

A Traveler's Narrative to Illustrate the Episode of the Báb. Trans. Edward Granville Browne. New and corrected ed. Wilmette, Ill.: Bahá'í Publishing Trust, 1980.

A Traveler's Narrative Written to Illustrate the Episode of the Bab. Trans. Edward Granville Browne. 2 vols. Cambridge: Cambridge University Press, 1891.

The Will and Testament of Abdu'l-Bahá. Wilmette, Ill.: Bahá'í Publishing Trust, 1971.

f) 'Abdu'l-Bahá (original language titles)

Ad'íyyih va Munáját, Prayers & Supplications.

Alváḥ-I-Tablíghí-i-Ámríká, Tablets of the Divine Plan. [106:400]

Alváḥ-I-Vaṣáyá, Will and Testament. [111]

Khiṭábát dar Urúpá va Ámríká, Address to Europe America. [87:vol.II,No.6]

Lawḥ-i-Aflákíyyih, Tablet of the Sphere.

Lawḥ-i-'Ahd va Mitháq (Ámríká), Will & Testament. [152]

Lawḥ-I-'Ammih, Tablet to the Aunt. [152]

Lawḥ-i-Áyát, Tablet of the Verses . [152]

Lawḥ-i-Du-Nidáy-i-Faláḥ-va-Najáḥ, Tablet of Supplication. [152]

Lawḥ-i-Dr. Forel, Tablet to Dr. Forel. [153]

Lawḥ-i-Haft Sham, Tablet of the Seven Candles. [65:32]

Lawḥ-i-Hizár-Baytí, Tablet of the One Thousand Verses. [152]

Lawḥ-i-Khurásán, Tablet of Khurásán. [152]

Lawḥ-i-Láhih, Tablet to the Central Organization for a Durable Peace, The Hague. [154]

Lawḥ-i-Maḥfil-Shawr, Tablet to the Assembly of the East. [152]

Lawḥ-i-Maḥabbat, Tablet of Love (Four Kinds of Love). [25:180]

Lawḥ-i-Tanzíh va Taqdís, Tablet of Purity. [106:333]
Lawḥ-i-Tarbíyat, Tablet of Education. [152]
Madaníyyih, The Secret of Divine Civilization. [125]
Makátíb-i-'Abdu'l-Bahá, Tablets of 'Abdu'l-Bahá. [152]
Maqáliy-i-Sayyáh, A Traveler's Narrative. [63]
Mufávidát, Some Answered Questions. [56]
Sharḥ-i-Faṣṣ-i-Nigín-i-Ism-A'ẓam, Commentary on the Ring Symbol—Greatest Name.
Sharḥ-i-Shuhadáy-i-Yazd va Iṣfáhán, The Martyrs of Yazd. [71:321-326]
Síyásíyyih, Treatise on Politics. [152]
Tadhkirat'l-Vafá, Memorials of the Faithful. [124]
Tafsír-i-Bushmi'lláh-'r-Raḥmáni'r-Raḥím, Commentary in the name of God—The Merciful, The Compassionate. [152]
Tafsír-i-Kuntu Kanzan Makhfíyyan, Commentary on "I Was A Hidden Treasure" (Bahá'í Studies).
Ziyárat Námih, Tablet of Visitation for Námih. [152]

2. Shoghi Effendi

The Advent of Divine Justice. Wilmette, Ill.: Bahá'í Publishing Trust, 1984.
America and the Most Great Peace. New York: Bahá'í Publishing Trust, 1933.
Arohanui: Letters from Shoghi Effendi to New Zealand. Suva, Fuji: Bahá'í Publishing Trust, 1982.
The Ascension of 'Abdu'l-Bahá. London: Bahá'í Publishing Trust, 1985.
Bahá'í Administration. Wilmette, Ill.: Bahá'í Publishing Trust, 1974.
The Bahá'í Faith, 1844-1952: Information Statistical and Comparative. Wilmette, Ill.: Bahá'í Publishing Committee, 1953.
The Bahá'í Life. Wilmette, Ill.: Bahá'í Publishing Trust, 1981.
Bahá'í Youth: A Compilation. Wilmette, Ill.: Bahá'í Publishing Trust, 1973.
Bahá'u'lláh's Ground Plan of World Fellowship. London: World Congress of Faiths, 1936.
Call to the Nations. Haifa: Bahá'í World Center, 1977.
Centers of Bahá'í Learning. Wilmette, Ill.: Bahá'í Publishing Trust, 1980.
The Challenging Requirements of the Present Hour. Wilmette, Ill.: National Spiritual Assembly of the Bahá'ís of the United States and Canada, 1947.
Charter of a Divine Civilization: A Compilation. Wilmette, Ill.: National Spiritual Assembly of the Bahá'ís of the United States, 1956.

Citadel of Faith: Messages to America, 1947-1957. Wilmette, Ill.: Bahá'í Publishing Trust, 1980.

Dawn of a New Day. New Delhi: Bahá'í Publishing Trust, 1970.

Directives from the Guardian. New Delhi: Bahá'í Publishing Trust, 1973.

The Dispensation of Bahá'u'lláh. New York: Bahá'í Publishing Committee, 1981.

The Functions of the Institutions of the Continental Boards of Counsellors and Their Auxiliary Boards. London: Bahá'í Publishing Trust, 1981.

The Future World Commonwealth. Wilmette, Ill.: National Spiritual Assembly of the Bahá'ís of the United States and Canada, 1936.

The Generation of the Half-Light: A Compilation for Bahá'í Youth. New Delhi: Bahá'í Publishing Trust, 1974.

The Goal of a New World Order. Wilmette, Ill.: Bahá'í Publishing Trust, 1976.

God Passes By. Wilmette, Ill.: Bahá'í Publishing Trust, 1979.

The Golden Age of the Cause of Bahá'u'lláh. New York: Bahá'í Publishing Committee, 1932.

The Greatest Holy Leaf: A Tribute to Bahíyyih Khánum. London: National Spiritual Assembly of the Bahá'ís of the United Kingdom, 1980.

The Guardian's Message for the Centenary of the Martyrdom of the Báb. Wilmette, Ill.: National Spiritual Assembly of the United States, 1950.

Guidance for Today and Tomorrow. London: Bahá'í Publishing Trust, 1953, 1973.

High Endeavors: Messages to Alaska. Anchorage: National Spiritual Assembly of the Bahá'ís of Alaska, 1976.

Importance and Methods of Close Collaboration Amongst the Institutions of the Faith. Ed. Continental Board of Counsellors in Africa: No publisher, 1982.

The Importance of Teaching Indigenous Peoples. Toronto: National Spiritual Assembly of the Bahá'ís of Canada, 1968.

Letters from Shoghi Effendi to the Believers of Central America and the Antilles from March 28, 1949 to October 6, 1957. Mimeographed ed. San José, Costa Rica: National Spiritual Assembly of the Bahá'ís of Central America and the Antilles, 196?

Letters from Shoghi Effendi, January 21, 1922—November 27, 1924. New York: Bahá'í Publishing Trust, 1925.

Letters from the Guardian to Australia and New Zealand, 1923-1957. Sydney, NSW, Australia: National Spiritual Assembly of the Bahá'ís of Australia and New Zealand, 1971.

Lifeblood of the Cause. London: Bahá'í Publishing Trust, 1975.

The Light of Divine Guidance: The Messages from the Guardian of the Bahá'í Faith to Individual Believers, Groups and Bahá'í Communities of Germany and Austria. Hofheim-Langenhain: Bahá'í-Verlag, 1982.

Living the Life. London: Bahá'í Publishing Trust, 1974, 1984.

Messages from the Guardian: Letters and Cablegrams Received by the National Spiritual Assembly from June 21, 1932 to July 21, 1940. New York: Bahá'í Publishing Committee, 1940.

Messages of Shoghi Effendi to the Indian Subcontinent. New Delhi: Bahá'í Publishing Trust, 1995.

Messages to America: Selected Letters and Cablegrams Addressed to the Bahá'ís of North America, 1932-1946. Wilmette, Ill.: Bahá'í Publishing Committee, 1947.

Messages to Canada (1923-1957). Toronto, Ont.: National Spiritual Assembly of the Bahá'ís of Canada, 1965.

Messages to the Bahá'í World 1950-1957. Wilmette, Ill.: Bahá'í Publishing Trust, 1971.

A Mysterious Dispensation of Providence: A Message from the Guardian on the Persecution of the Bahá'ís in Írán. Wilmette, Ill: National Spiritual Assembly of the Bahá'ís of the United States, 1955.

Political Non-Involvement and Obedience to Government: A Compilation of Some of the Messages of the Guardian and the Universal House of Justice. Mona Vale, NSW, Australia: Bahá'í Publications Australia, 1984.

Principles of Bahá'í Administration. London: Bahá'í Publishing Trust, 1976.

The Passing of the Greatest Holy Leaf: A Tribute. Haifa: No publisher, 1932.

The Promised Day is Come. Wilmette, Ill.: Bahá'í Publishing Trust, 1980.

The Rising World Commonwealth. London: Bahá'í Publishing Trust, 1945.

Selected Writings of Shoghi Effendi. Wilmette, Ill.: Bahá'í Publishing Trust, 1975.

The Unfolding Destiny of the British Bahá'í Community: The Messages from the Guardian of the Bahá'í Faith to the Bahá'ís of the British Isles. London: Bahá'í Publishing Trust, 1981.

The Unfoldment of World Civilization. New York: Bahá'í Publishing Committee, 1936.

The World Order of Bahá'u'lláh. Wilmette, Ill.: Bahá'í Publishing Trust, 1982.

World Government & Collective Security: A Collection of Some Bahá'í Quotations. New Delhi: National Spiritual Assembly of the Bahá'ís of India, Pakistan and Burma, 1953.

3. Universal House of Justice

Analysis of the Five Year International Teaching Plan 1974-1979. Haifa: Universal House of Justice, 1975.

Analysis of the Nine Year International Plan 1964-1973. Wilmette, Ill.: Bahá'í Publishing Trust, 1964.

Analysis of the Seven Year Plan 1979-1986: Second Phase Goals, 1981. Haifa: Universal House of Justice, Statistics Department, 1981.

The Bahá'í Faith (Statistical Information) 1844-1968: Showing Current Status and Outstanding Goals of the Nine Year International Teaching Plan, 1964-1973. Haifa: Universal House of Justice, 1968.

The Bahá'í Holy Places at the World Center. Haifa: Universal House of Justice, 1968.

Canada and the Five Year Plan (Le Canada et le Plan de Cinq Ans). Thornhill, Ont.: National Spiritual Assembly of the Bahá'ís of Canada, 1974.

The Constitution of the Universal House of Justice. Haifa: Bahá'í World Center, 1972.

The Continental Boards of Counsellors: Letters, Extracts from Letters, and Cables from the Universal House of Justice. An Address by Edna M. True. Ed Compiled and edited by the National Spiritual Assembly of the Bahá'ís of the United States. Wilmette, Ill.: Bahá'í Publishing Trust, 1981.

Five Year Plan Given to the Bahá'ís of East & West Malaysia. Kuala Lumpur: National Spiritual Assembly of the Bahá'ís of Malaysia, 1974.

The Five Year Plan, 1974-1979: Statistical Report, Riḍván 1978. Haifa: Bahá'í World Center, 1978.

The Five Year Plan, 1974-1979: Statistical Report, Riḍván 1979. Haifa: Bahá'í World Center, 1979.

The Five Year Plan: Messages from the Universal House of Justice to the Bahá'ís of the World and of the United States. Naw-Rúz 1974 Announcing the Objectives of the Third Global Teaching Campaign. Wilmette, Ill.: Bahá'í Publishing Trust, 1974.

Individual Rights and Freedoms in the World Order of Bahá'u'lláh. Haifa, Israel: Universal House of Justice, 1988. 22.

Messages from the Universal House of Justice 1968-1973. Wilmette, Ill.: Bahá'í Publishing Trust, 1976.

Messages from the Universal House of Justice: 1963-1986 The Third Epoch of the Formative Age. Wilmette, Ill.: Bahá'í Publishing Trust, 1996.

The Mission of this Generation: Messages from the Universal House of Justice to Bahá'í Youth. London: Bahá'í Publishing Trust, 1996.

The Nine Year Plan, 1964-1973: Statistical Report, Riḍván 1973. Haifa: Universal House of Justice, 1973.

The Promise of World Peace. Wilmette, Ill.: Bahá'í Publishing Trust, 1985.

The Seven Year Plan, 1979-1986: Statistical Report, Riḍván 1983. Haifa: Bahá'í World Center, 1983.

The Seven Year Plan. Wilmette, Ill.: Bahá'í Publishing Trust, 1980, 1981.

Wellspring of Guidance: Messages 1963-1968. Wilmette, Ill.: Bahá'í Publishing Trust, 1976.

A Wider Horizon: Selected Messages of the Universal House of Justice (1983-1992.) Riviera Beach, Fla: Palabra Publications, 1992.

4. Bahíyyih Khánum

Bahíyyih Khánum. *The Greatest Holy Leaf: Bahíyyih Khánum*. Compilation. Haifa: The Research Department, Bahá'í World Center, 1982.

5. Compilations: Writings of the Báb, Bahá'u'lláh, 'Abdu'l-Bahá, Shoghi Effendi and the Universal House of Justice

Arise to Serve. New Delhi: Bahá'í Publishing Trust, 1971.

Bahá'í Answers—A Compilation from the Words of the Báb, Bahá'u'lláh, 'Abdu'l-Baha and Shoghi Effendi. Compiled by Olivia Kelsey. Chicago: NSA Bahá'ís of the US and Canada, 1947.

Bahá'í Answers: A Compilation. Independence, Mo.: Lambert Moon Printers and Publishers, 1947.

Bahá'í Code of Conduct: Selections from the Sacred Writings: Guidance Two, Proclamation. Kuala Lumpur: National Bahá'í Information Service, 1967.

Bahá'í Consultation. Auckland: National Spiritual Assembly of the Bahá'ís of New Zealand, 1978.

Bahá'í Daybook: Passages for Deepening and Meditation. Wilmette, Ill.: Bahá'í Publishing Trust, 1985.

Bahá'í Education: A Compilation. Wilmette, Ill.: Bahá'í Publishing Trust, 1978.

Bahá'í Institutions: A Compilation. New Delhi: Bahá'í Publishing Trust, 1973.

Bahá'í Marriage and Family Life: Selections from the Writings of the Bahá'í Faith. Thornhill, Ont.: Bahá'í Canada Publications, 1983.

Bahá'í Prayers. Wilmette, Ill.: Bahá'í Publishing Trust, 1954.

Bahá'í Prayers. New, expanded and revised ed. Wilmette, Ill.: Bahá'í Publishing Trust, 1982.

Bahá'í Quotations on Education. Honolulu: National Spiritual Assembly of the Bahá'ís of the Hawaiian Islands, 1971.

Bahá'í Readings: Selections from the Writings of the Báb, Bahá'u'lláh and Abdu'l-Bahá for Daily Meditation. Thornhill, Ont.: Bahá'í Canada Publications, 1984.

Bahá'í References on Education. Ed. Advisory Committee on Education. Vol. 1. Bahá'í Teacher's handbook. Wilmette, Ill.: Bahá'í Publishing Trust, 1970. 1 vols.

The Bahá'í Revelation. London: Bahá'í Publishing Trust, 1955.

Bahá'í Scriptures. New York: Brentano's, 1923.

Bahá'í Teachings on Economics: A Compilation. Bahá'í Teaching Committee (Committee on Economics. New York: Bahá'í Publishing Committee, 1934.

Bahá'í World Faith. (Bahá'u'lláh & 'Abdu'l-Bahá) Wilmette, Ill.: Bahá'í Publishing Trust, 1976.

Bahíyyih Khánum, the Greatest Holy Leaf: A Compilation from the Bahá'í Sacred Texts and Writings of the Guardian of the Faith and Bahíyyih Khánum's Own Letters. Haifa: Bahá'í World Center, 1982.

Be As I Am: A Compilation (Anecdotes about 'Abdu'l-Bahá.) Trans. Compiled by Elias Zohoori. Kingston: National Spiritual Assembly of the Bahá'ís of Jamaica, 1983.

The Chalice of Immortality. New Delhi: Bahá'í Publishing Trust, 1978.

A Compilation of Bahá'í Writings on Music. London: Bahá'í Publishing Trust, 1983.

A Compilation on Bahá'í Education. London: Bahá'í Publishing Trust, 1976.

Compilation of Compilations. Vol. 1, 2. Maryborough, Victoria, Australia: Bahá'í Publications Australia, 1991.

Compilation of the Holy Utterances of Baha'o'llah and Abdul Baha Concerning the Most Great Peace, War and Duty of the Bahais Toward Their Government. 2nd ed. Boston: The Tudor Press, 1918.

A Compilation on the Importance of Deepening Our Understanding and Knowledge of the Faith. London: Bahá'í Publishing Trust, 1983.

A Compilation on the Importance of Prayer, Meditation and the Devotional Attitude. London: Bahá'í Publishing Trust, 1981.

Consultation: A Compilation. Wilmette, Ill.: Bahá'í Publishing Trust, 1980.

The Covenant of Bahá'u'lláh: A Compilation. Manchester: Bahá'í Publishing Trust, 1950.

The Declaration of the Báb: A Compilation. Los Angeles: Kalimát Press, 1992.

Death, the Messenger of Joy. London: Bahá'í Publishing Trust, 1980.

The Desire of the World: Materials for the Contemplation of God and His Manifestation for this Day. Compiled by Rúḥíyyih Rabbání. Oxford: George Ronald, 1984.

Distinctive Characteristics of a Bahá'í Life: A Compilation. Continental Board of Counsellors in Africa, 1974.

The Divine Art of Living. Wilmette, Ill.: Bahá'í Publishing Trust, 1979.

Divorce: A Compilation Dealing with the Bahá'í Attitude Towards the Subject of Divorce. Mona Vale, NSW, Australia: Bahá'í Publications Australia, 1985.

Enkindle the Souls: Raising the Quality of Teaching. Nairobi: Continental Board of Counsellors in Africa, 1982.

The Establishment of the Universal House of Justice. London: Bahá'í Publishing Trust, 1984.

Excellence in All Things. London: Bahá'í Publishing Trust, 1981.

Family Life. Mona Vale, NSW, Australia: Bahá'í Publications Australia, 1982.

Fasting. Auckland: National Spiritual Assembly of the Bahá'ís of New Zealand, 1983.

The Gift of Teaching. London: Bahá'í Publishing Trust, 1977.

The Glad Tidings of Bahá'u'lláh. London: John Murray, 1949, 1956.

The Glorious Journey to God: Selections From Sacred Scriptures on the Afterlife. Mt. Pleasant, Michigan: Global Perspective, 1996.

The Heaven of Divine Wisdom. London: Bahá'í Publishing Trust, 1978.

Huqúqu'lláh. Auckland, NZ: National Spiritual Assembly of the Bahá'ís of New Zealand, 1985.

Inspiring the Hearts: Selections from the Writings of the Báb, Bahá'u'lláh and 'Abdu'l-Bahá. London: Bahá'í Publishing Trust, 1981.

The Institution of the Hands of the Cause of God: Its Origin and Unfoldment, Auxiliary Boards, Relation to National Spiritual Assemblies. United States of America: No publisher, 1957.

Japan Will Turn Ablaze! Tablets of Abdu'l-Bahá, Letters of Shoghi Effendi and the Universal House of Justice, and Historical Notes About Japan. Compiled by Barbara Sims. Tokyo, Japan: Bahá'í Publishing Trust, Japan, 1992.

Justice & Peace: A Compendium of Quotations from the Bahá'í Writings. Paddington, NSW, Australia: National Spiritual Assembly of the Bahá'ís of Australia, 1968.

Life After Death. Honolulu: Hawaii Bahá'í Press, 1976.

Life Eternal: Extracts from the Writings of Bahá'u'lláh and 'Abdu'l-Bahá. East Aurora, N.Y.: Roycroft Shops, 1936, 1937.

Lights of Guidance: A Bahá'í Reference File. 2nd ed. New Delhi, India: Bahá'í Publishing Trust, 1988.

Local Spiritual Assemblies. London: Bahá'í Publishing Trust, 197?
The Most Great Peace. Boston: Tudor Press, 1916.
Naw-Rúz, New Day: A Compilation. Los Angeles: Kalimát Press, 1992.
The Oneness of Mankind. New York: Bahá'í Publishing Trust, 1927.
The Onward March of the Faith. London: Bahá'í Publishing Trust, 1975.
The Pattern of Bahá'í Life. 3rd ed. London: Bahá'í Publishing Trust, 1983.
Peace. London: Bahá'í Publishing Trust, 1985.
The Power of Divine Assistance. London: Bahá'í Publishing Trust, 1981.
Prayers and Meditations. Bahá'u'lláh and 'Abdu'l-Bahá. New York: Bahá'í Publishing Committee, 1929.
Prayers Revealed by Bahá'u'lláh, the Báb, and 'Abdu'l-Bahá. Trans. Shoghi Effendi. New York: Bahá'í Publishing Committee, 1939.
Proclaiming the Faith: A Compilation of Quotations from the Bahá'í Writings. Wilmette, Ill.: Office of Public Affairs, Bahá'í National Center, 1982.
Prohibition of Intoxicating Drinks. Lagos: Publishing Committee of the National Spiritual Assembly of the Bahá'ís of Nigeria, 1982.
The Pupil of the Eye: African Americans in the World Order of Bahá'u'lláh: Selections from the Writings of Bahá'u'lláh, the Báb, 'Abdu'l-Bahá, Shoghi Effendi and the Universal House of Justice Compiled by Bonnie J. Taylor. Riviera Beach, Fla: Palabra Publications, 1995.
Quotations from the Bahá'í Writings on Prayer. Anchorage: National Spiritual Assembly of the Bahá'ís of Alaska, 1973.
Racial Amity. United States: No publisher, 1924.
The Reality of Man. 1962 ed. Wilmette, Ill.: Bahá'í Publishing Trust, 1979.
A River of Life: A Selection from the Teachings of Baha Ullah and Abdul Baha. Trans. Yuhanna Dawud. London: Cope & Fenwick, 1914.
Seeking the Light of the Kingdom: Compilations Issued by the Universal House of Justice on the Nineteen Day Feast and Bahá'í Meetings. London: Bahá'í Publishing Trust, 1977.
Selections from Bahá'í Scripture. Manchester, England: Bahá'í Publishing Trust, 1941.
Some Aspects of Health and Healing: Selections from the Bahá'í Writings. Auckland, NZ: National Spiritual Assembly of the Bahá'ís of New Zealand, 1981.
Some Quotations from the Bahá'í Writings Relating to Socio-Economic Development and Human Progress. Banjul: National Spiritual Assembly of the Bahá'ís of the Gambia, 1984.

Spiritual Assemblies and Consultation. New Delhi: Bahá'í Publishing Trust, 1978.

The Splendor of God: Being Extracts from the Sacred Writings of the Bahais. London: John Murray, 1909, 1910, 1911.

The Straight Path: Dedicated to Shoghi Effendi, First Guardian of the Bahá'í Faith on the Occasion of the Twenty-Fifth Anniversary of the Inception of the Guardianship. United States of America: No publisher, 1947.

The Supreme Gift of God to Man: Selections from the Bahá'í Writings on the Value, Development and Use of the Intellect. Wilmette, Ill.: Bahá'í Publishing Trust, 1980.

Teaching the Cause: Cornerstone of the Foundation of All Bahá'í Activity. New Delhi: Bahá'í Publishing Trust, 1977.

The Throne of the Inner Temple. Kingston, Jamaica: University Printery and School Printing, University of West Indies, 1985.

Unto Him Shall We Return: Selections from the Bahá'í Writings on the Reality and Immortality of the Human Soul. Wilmette, Ill.: Bahá'í Publishing Trust, 1985.

Victory Promises. Honolulu: National Spiritual Assembly of the Bahá'ís of the Hawaiian Islands, 1978.

Waging Peace: Selections from the Bahá'í Writings on Universal Peace. Los Angeles: Kalimát Press, 1984.

Why Our Cities Burn: Views on the Racial Crisis in the United States from the Writings of the Bahá'í Faith. Wilmette, Ill.: Bahá'í Publishing Trust, 1968.

6. Hands of the Cause of God

The Bahá'í Faith, 1844-1963: Information and Statistical Comparison. Compiled by Hands of the Cause of God Residing in the Holy Land. Ramat Gan: Peli, P.E.C. Printing Works (Hands of the Cause of God), 1963. Vol. 128.

Addenda to Statistical Information Published by the Hands of the Cause in the Holy Land in Riḍván 1963: Countries Opened to the Faith of Bahá'u'lláh and Supplementary Accomplishments. Compiled by Hands of the Cause of God Residing in the Holy Land. Haifa: Bahá'í World Center, 1964.

The Ministry of the Custodians 1957-1963—An Account of the Stewardship of the Hands of the Cause—With an Introduction by the Hand of the Cause Amatu'l-Bahá Rúhíyyih Khánum. Hands of the Cause of God, Haifa: Bahá'í World Center, 1992.

7. Works Related to Central Figures & Other Key Figures

a) The Báb

Balyuzi, H. M. *Khadíjih Bagum, the Wife of the Báb*. Oxford: George Ronald, 1981, 1982.

———— *The Báb, the Herald of the Day of Days*. Oxford: George Ronald, 1973, 1974, 1975, 1994.

Nabíl-i-A'zam. *The Dawn Breakers: Nabil's Narrative of the Early Days of the Bahá'í Revelation*. Ed. and trans. Shoghi Effendi. Wilmette. Ill.: Bahá'í Publishing Trust, 1970.

Sears, William. *Release the Sun*. Wilmette, Ill.: Bahá'í Publishing Trust, 1975.

———— *The Martyr-Prophet of a World Faith*. Wilmette, Ill.: Bahá'í Publishing Trust, 1950.

b) Bahá'u'lláh

Balyuzi, H. M. *Bahá'u'lláh, the King of Glory*. Oxford: George Ronald, 1980.

———— *Bahá'u'lláh*. London: Bahá'í Publishing Trust, 1938.

———— *Bahá'u'lláh: A Brief Life: Followed by an Essay on the Manifestation of God Entitled The Word Made Flesh*. London, Oxford: George Ronald, 1963, 1968, 1970, 1972, 1973, 1974, 1976 1984.

Buck, Christopher. *Symbol and Secret: Qur'án Commentary in Bahá'u'lláh's Kitáb-i-Iqán*, ed. Anthony A. Lee, Studies in the Bábí and Bahá'í Religions, vol. 7 (Los Angeles: Kalimát Press, 1995.)

Furútan, 'Ali-Akbar. *Stories of Bahá'u'lláh*. Trans. Katayoon and Robert Crerar. Oxford: George Ronald, 1986.

Hofman, David. *Bahá'u'lláh: The Prince of Peace*. Oxford: George Ronald, 1992.

Johnson, Lowell. *Remember My Days: The Life Story of Bahá'u'lláh*. 2nd rev. ed. Johannesburg: National Spiritual Assembly of the Bahá'ís of South and West Africa, 1985.

Kheiralla, Ibrahim George, and Howard MacNutt. *Beha'u'llah—The Glory of God*. Chicago: I.G. Kheiralla Publisher, 1900.

Muhammad-Aliy-i-Salmani, Ustad. *My Memories of Bahá'u'lláh*. Trans. Marzieh Gail. Los Angeles: Kalimát Press, 1982.

Perkins, Mary. *Day of Glory: The Life of Bahá'u'lláh*. Oxford: George Ronald, 1992.

Ruhe, David S. *Robe of Light: The Persian Years of the Supreme Prophet Bahá'u'lláh 1817-1853*. Oxford: George Ronald, 1994.

Salmání, Ustád Muhammad. *Memories of Bahá'u'lláh*. Trans. Marzieh Gail. Los Angeles: Kalimát Press, 1982.

Samandarí, Ṭaráẓu'lláh. *Moments With Bahá'u'lláh: Memoirs of the Hand of the Cause of God Ṭaráẓu'lláh Samandarí*. Trans. Mehdi Samandarí Marzieh Gail. Los Angeles: Kalimát Press, 1995.

Taherzadeh, Adib. *The Covenant of Bahá'u'lláh*. Oxford: George Ronald, 1992.

———. *The Revelation of Bahá'u'lláh 'Akká, The Early Years 1868-77*. Vol. 3. Oxford: George Ronald, 1988. 4 vols.

———. *The Revelation of Bahá'u'lláh Adrianople 1863-68*. Paperback ed. Vol. 2. Oxford: George Ronald, 1988. 4 vols.

———. *The Revelation of Bahá'u'lláh Mazra'ih and Bahjí 1877-92*. Vol. 4. Oxford: George Ronald, 1988. 4 vols.

———. *The Revelation of Bahá'u'lláh Baghdád 1853-63*. Paperback ed. Vol. 1. Oxford: George Ronald, 1988. 4 vols.

Ward, Allan L. *'Abdu'l-Bahá's Journey in America*. Wilmette, Ill.: Bahá'í Publishing Trust, 1979.

Yazdí, 'Alí M. "Memories of 'Abdu'l-Bahá." *Bahá'í Year Book 1979-1983*. Haifa: Bahá'í World Center, 1986. Vol. 18.

c) 'Abdu'l-Bahá

'Abdu'l-Bahá in Edinburgh. London: National Spiritual Assembly of the Bahá'ís of the British Isles, 1963.

'Abdu'l-Bahá in London. London: Longmans Green & Co., 1912.

'Abdu'l-Bahá in New York, the City of the Covenant, April-December 1912. New York: Bahá'í Assembly, 1912.

Ahdieh, Hussein, and Elaine A. Hopson, eds. *'Abdu'l-Baha in New York—The City of the Covenant—Commemorating the 75th Anniversary of the Visit of 'Abdu'l-Baha to America*. New York: Spiritual Assembly of the Bahá'ís of New York, 1987.

Balyuzi, H. M. *'Abdu'l-Bahá, the Center of the Covenant of Bahá'u'lláh*. London: George Ronald, 1973.

Brown, Ramona Allen. *Memories of 'Abdu'l-Bahá: Recollections of the Early Days of the Bahá'í Faith in California*. Wilmette, Ill.: Bahá'í Publishing Trust, 1980.

Cobb, Stanwood. *Memories of 'Abdu'l-Bahá*. Washington, D.C.: The Avalon Press, 1962.

Goodall, Helen S., and Ella Goodall Cooper. *Daily Lessons Received at Acca, January 1908*. Rev. ed. Chicago: Bahá'í Publishing Trust, 1979.

Grundy, Julia M. *Ten Days in the Light of Acca*. Rev. ed. Wilmette, Ill.: Bahá'í Publishing Trust, 1907, 1979.

Hannen, Joseph H. *Akka Lights*. n.p., 1909.

Haydar-'Alí, Hájí Mírzá. *Stories from the Delight of Hearts: the Memoirs of Hájí Mírzá Haydar-'Alí*. Trans. A. Q. Faizi. Los Angeles: Kalimát Press, 1980.

Hofman, David. *Commentary on the Will and Testament of 'Abdu'l-Bahá*. 4th rev. ed. Oxford: George Ronald, 1982.

Khursheed, Anjam. *The Seven Candles of Unity: The Story of 'Abdu'l-Bahá in Edinburgh*. London: Bahá'í Publishing Trust, 1991.

Lee, Anthony A. ed., *The Black Rose: A Story About 'Abdu'l-Bahá in America*. Los Angeles: Kalimát Press, 1979.

——— *The Cornerstone: A Story About 'Abdu'l-Bahá in America*. Los Angeles: Kalimát Press, 1979.

——— *The Proud Helper: A Story About 'Abdu'l-Bahá in the Holy Land*. Los Angeles: Kalimát Press, 1979.

——— *The Scottish Visitors: A Story About 'Abdu'l-Bahá in Britain*. Los Angeles: Kalimát Press, 1980.

——— *The Unfriendly Governor: A Story About 'Abdu'l-Bahá in the Holy Land*. Los Angeles: Kalimát Press, 1979.

——— *In His Presence: Visits to 'Abdu'l-Baha. Memoirs of Roy Wilhelm, Stanwood Cobb and Genevieve Coy*. Los Angeles: Kalimát Press, 1989.

Mahmúd (Zarqání, Mírzá Mahmúd-i.) *Mahmúd's Diary (Kitáb-i-Badáyi'u'l-áthár.)* Vol. 1 1914; Vol. 2 1921. Bombay, 1921. 2 vols.

Phelps, Myron H. *The Life and Teachings of Abbas Effendi (Cover Title: Abbas Effendi, His Life and Teachings.)* New York: G.P. Putnam's Sons: Knickerbocker Press, 1903.

——— *The Master in 'Akká, Including Recollections of the Greatest Holy Leaf*. Los Angeles: Kalimát Press, 1985.

Sohrab, Mirza Ahmad. *Abdul-Baha in Egypt*. New York: J.H. Sears & Co., for The New History Foundation, 1929.

——— *I Heard Him Say—Words of 'Abdu'l-Baha*. New York: The New History Foundation, 1937.

Thompson, Juliet. *The Diary of Juliet Thompson*. Los Angeles: Kalimát Press, 1983.

d) Shoghi Effendi

Association for Bahá'í Studies. *The Vision of Shoghi Effendi*. Ottawa: Association for Bahá'í Studies, 1984.

Collins, Amelia. *A Tribute to Shoghi Effendi*. Wilmette, Ill.: Bahá'í Publishing Trust, 1960.

Giachery, Ugo. *Shoghi Effendi, Recollections*. Oxford: George Ronald, 1973, 1974.

Rabbání, Rúḥíyyih. *Poems of the Passing*. Oxford: George Ronald, 1996.

———*The Guardian of the Bahá'í Faith*. London: Bahá'í Publishing Trust, 1988.

———*The Priceless Pearl*. London: Bahá'í Publishing Trust, 1969.

———*Twenty-Five Years of the Guardianship*. Wilmette, Ill.: Bahá'í Publishing Trust, 1948.

Rabbání, Rúḥíyyih, and John Ferraby. *The Passing of Shoghi Effendi*. London: Bahá'í Publishing Trust, 1958.

e) Bahíyyih Khánum

Gail, Marzieh. *Khánum, the Greatest Holy Leaf.* Oxford: George Ronald, 1981, 1982.

f) Ásíyih Khánum

Ma'ani, Baharieh. *Ásíyih Khánum, The Most Exalted Leaf entitled Navváb.* Oxford: George Ronald, 1993.

g) Munríhih Khánum

Khánum, Munríhih. *Episodes in the Life of the Moneereh Khanum.* Trans. Ahmad Sohrab. Los Angeles: Persian-American Publishing Co., 1924.

8. Bibliographies

Afsharian, Payam. *Dictionary of Bahá'í Book Collectors, Bibliophiles, & Researchers.* Los Angelos: Afsharian, 1984.

Bjorling, Joel. *The Bahá'í Faith: A Historical Bibliography.* (Sects and Cults in America: Bibliographical Guides). Garland Reference Library of the Humanities, New York; London: Garland, 1985.

Collins, William P. *Bibliography of English-Language Works on the Bábí and Bahá'í Faiths 1844-1985.* Oxford: George Ronald, 1990.

Momen, Moojan. *The Works of Shaykh Ahmad al-Ahsa'i: A Bibliography.* Newcastle Upon Tyne: Bahá'í Studies Bulletin Monograph, 1992.

9. Yearbooks, Journals, Magazines

Bahá'í News Index—No. 1 to No. 172. Ed. and Comp. by May Prentiss Stebbins. Vol. 1 Wilmette, Ill.: Bahá'í Publishing Trust, 1956; *Bahá'í News Index—No. 173 to No. 322.* Ed. and Comp. by May Prentiss Stebbins. Vol. 2 Wilmette, Ill.: Bahá'í Publishing Trust, 1959; *Bahá'í News Index—No. 323 to No. 393.* Ed. and Comp. by Amine DeMille. Vol. 3 Wilmette, Ill.: Bahá'í Publishing Trust, 1966; *Bahá'í News Index—No. 394 to No. 453.* Ed. and Comp. by Amine DeMille. Vol. 4 Wilmette, Ill.: Bahá'í Publishing Trust, 1970; *Bahá'í News Index—No. 454 to No. 513.* Vol. 5 Wilmette, Ill.: Bahá'í Publishing Trust, 1978.

Bahá'í News/Star of the West. *Star of the West (Bahá'í News; The Bahá'í Magazine)* 1-25 (1910-1935); Reprinted: *Star of the West (Reprinted Compendium Edition.)* Oxford: George Ronald, 1978, 1984.

Bahá'í Year Book. *Bahá'í Year Book (1925-1926) Vol. 1 An International Record.* New York: Bahá'í Publishing Committee, 1926; *Bahá'í World (1926-1928) Vol. 2 An International Record.* New York: Bahá'í Publishing Committee, 1928; *Bahá'í World (1928-1930) Vol. 3 An International Record.* New York: Bahá'í Publishing

Committee, 1930; *Bahá'í World (1930-1932) Vol. 4 An International Record*. New York: Bahá'í Publishing Committee, 1933; *Bahá'í World (1932-1934) Vol. 5 An International Record*. New York: Bahá'í Publishing Committee, 1936; *Bahá'í World (1934-1936) Vol. 6 An International Record*. New York: Bahá'í Publishing Committee, 1937; *Bahá'í World (1936-1938) Vol. 7 An International Record*. New York: Bahá'í Publishing Committee, 1939; *Bahá'í World (1938-1940) Vol. 8 An International Record*. Wilmette, Ill.: Bahá'í Publishing Committee, 1942; *Bahá'í World (1940-1944) Vol. 9 An International Record*. Wilmette, Ill.: Bahá'í Publishing Committee, 1945; *Bahá'í World (1944-1946) Vol. 10 An International Record*. Wilmette, Ill.: Bahá'í Publishing Committee, 1949; *Bahá'í World (1946-1950) Vol. 11 An International Record*. Wilmette, Ill.: Bahá'í Publishing Committee, 1952; *The Bahá'í World (1950-1954) An International Record*. Wilmette, Ill.: Bahá'í Publishing Trust, 1956; *Bahá'í World (1950-1954) Vol. 12 An International Record*. Wilmette, Ill.: Bahá'í Publishing Trust, 1956; *Bahá'í World (1954-1963) Vol. 13 An International Record*. Haifa: The Universal House of Justice, 1970; *Bahá'í World (1963-1968) Vol. 14 An International Record*. Haifa: The Universal House of Justice, 1974; *Bahá'í World (1968-1973) Vol. 15 An International Record*. Haifa: Bahá'í World Center, 1976; *Bahá'í World (1973-1976) Vol. 16 An International Record*. Haifa: Bahá'í World Center, 1979; *Bahá'í World (1976-1979) Vol. 17 An International Record*. Haifa: Bahá'í World Center, 1982; *Bahá'í World (1979-1983) Vol. 18 An International Record*. Haifa: Bahá'í World Center, 1986; *Bahá'í World (1983-1986) Vol. 19 An International Record*. Haifa: Bahá'í World Center, 1994.

Bahá'í Year Book. *Bahá'í World Reprint of Vols. 1-12*. Wilmette, Ill.: Bahá'í Publishing Trust, 1980-1981.

Bahá'í Year Book. *A Compendium of Volumes of the Bahá'í World, An International Record, Vols. 1-12, 82-110 of the Bahá'í Era*. Ed. and Comp. by Roger White. Oxford: George Ronald, 1981.

Bahá'í Year Book, New Series. *Bahá'í World (1992-1993) An International Record*. Haifa: Bahá'í World Center, 1993; *Bahá'í World (1993-1994) An International Record*. Haifa: Bahá'í World Center, 1994; *Bahá'í World (1994-1995) An International Record*. Haifa: Bahá'í World Center, 1996; Bahá'í Year Book, *Bahá'í World (1995-1996) An International Record*. Haifa: Bahá'í World Center, 1997.

10. Historical Reference Materials

a) Bábí

Ali, Maulana Muhammad. *History and Doctrines of the Babi Movement*. Lahore: Ahmadiyya Anjuman Isha'at-i-Islam, 1933.

Ali, U. *Babism and Bahaism Explained*. New Kotwali, Agra: S.R. & Bros., 1956.

Amanat, Abbas. *Resurrection and Renewal: The Making of the Babi Movement in Iran, 1844-1850*. Ithaca and London: Cornell University Press, 1989.

Browne, Edward Granville. *Materials for the Study of the Bábí Religion*. Cambridge: Cambridge University Press, 1918, 1961.

b) Bahá'í

Armstrong-Ingram, R. Jackson, ed. *Music, Devotions, and Mashriqu'l-Adhkár: Studies in Bábí and Bahá'í History*. 4 vols. Los Angeles: Kalimát Press, 1987.

Bahá'í Centenary (1944: Chicago.) *Bahá'í Centenary 1844-1944 All America Program*. National Spiritual Assembly of the Bahá'ís of the United States and Canada, 1944.

Bahá'í Centenary (1944: London.) *The Centenary of the Bahá'í Faith. May 23rd 1944*. London: National Spiritual Assembly of the Bahá'ís of the British Isles, 1944.

Bahá'í Centenary (1953: Chicago.) *Centenary Birth of the Bahá'í Revelation, 1853-1953*. Wilmette, Ill.: National Spiritual Assembly of the Bahá'ís of the United States, 1953.

Bahá'í Committee of Investigation, Washington, D.C. *General Letters, Kircher Affair. 1917-1918*. 1918.

———*Report of the Bahai Committee of Investigation, 1917-18*. 1918.

Bahá'í European Teaching Committee of the American NSA. *Record of First Bahá'í European Teaching Conference, May 22-27, 1948*. Geneva, Switzerland, 1948. 33.

Bahá'í Intercontinental Conference. *Bahá'í Centenary 1853-1953*. New Delhi, 8th & 12th October 1953: National Spiritual Assembly of the Bahá'ís of India, 1953. 4.

——— *Bahá'í Centenary, 1867-1967: Commemorating the 100th Anniversary of Bahá'u'lláh's Tablets to the Kings*. Chicago and Wilmette, Ill.: National Spiritual Assembly of the Bahá'ís of the United States, 1967. 12.

Bahá'í Temple Unity Convention. *Bahai Congress and Fifteenth Annual Convention of the Bahai Temple Unity*. Chicago: Bahai Temple Unity, 1923. 4.

——— *Eleventh Annual Mashrekol-Azkar Convention and Bahai Congress*. Chicago: Bahá'í Temple Unity, 1918.

——— *Program, Bahai Temple Unity Convention, Chicago, April 27th to May 2nd 1912*. Chicago: Bahá'í Temple Unity, 1912.

——— *Mashriq'ul-Adhkar Report, 1909-1925*. 1925.

Bausani, A. "The Bahá'í Perspective on the History of Religion," in *The Bahá'í Faith and Islám*, ed. H. Moayyad. Ottawa: Bahá'í Studies Publications, 1990.

Bourgeois, Louise. *The Bahai Temple: Press Comments, Symbolism.* Chicago, 1921.

Braun, Eunice, and Hugh E. Chance. *A Crown of Beauty: The Bahá'í Faith and the Holy Land*. Oxford: George Ronald, 1982, 1987, 1992.

———— *From Strength to Strength: The First Half Century of the Formative Age of the Bahá'í Era*. Wilmette, Ill.: Bahá'í Publishing Trust, 1978.

———— *From Vision to Victory: Thirty Years of the Universal House of Justice*. Oxford: George Ronald, 1993.

———— *The March of the Institutions: A Commentary on the Interdependence of the Rulers and the Learned*. Oxford: George Ronald, 1984.

Cole, Juan R., and Moojan Momen, eds. *From Írán East and West: Studies in Bábí and Bahá'í History*. Los Angeles: Kalimát Press, 1984.

Hall, E. T. *Continuation of "The Bahá'í Dawn: Manchester,"* 1933.

———— *The Beginning of the Bahá'í Cause in Manchester (Cover title: The Bahá'í Dawn, Manchester)*. Manchester, U.K.: Manchester Bahá'í Assembly, 1925.

Himes-Cox, Florence. *The Dawn-Breakers: Chronological Study Outline.* Wilmette, Ill.: Study Outline Committee, 195?

History Calendar. *Bahá'í History Calendar*. National Spiritual Assembly of the Bahá'ís of the Hawaiian Islands, 1978, 1979, 1980, 1981, 1992, 1993, 1994, 1995.

Hollinger, Richard, ed. *Community Histories: Studies in the Bábí and Bahá'í Religions*. Los Angeles: Kalimát Press, 1992.

Hornby, Helen. *Heroes of God: History of the Bahá'í Faith in Ecuador, 1940-1979*. Quito, Ecuador: Arqtelier, 1984.

Ioas, Monroe C. *Bahá'í Publicity in the Berwyn-Cicero Life Newspaper, 1979-1980*. Berwyn, Ill.: Monroe C. Ioas, 1980.

Jání Káshání, Hájí Mírzá. *Kitáb-i-Nuqtatu'l-Káf: Being the Earliest History of the Bábís*. Ed. Edward G. Browne: Leydon: E. J. Brill; London: Luzac & Co., 1910.

Lee, Anthony A. "The Rise of the Bahá'í Community of 'Ishqábád." *Bahá'í Studies*. Ottawa: Canadian Association for Bahá'í Studies on the Bahá'í Faith, 1979. Vol. 5: The Bahá'í Faith in Russia: Two Early Instances..

Martin, Douglas. "The Missionary as Historian." *Bahá'í Studies 4*. (December 1978): 1-29.

———— "The Persecution of the Bahá'ís of Iran, 1844-1984." *Bahá'í Studies* 12-13 (1984): 86.

McCormick, Jim. *The History and Doctrines of the Bahá'í Faith*. Belfast, Northern Ireland: Great Joy Publications, 1985.

Momen, Moojan, ed. *Selections from the Writings of E. G. Browne on the Bábí and Bahá'í Religions*. Oxford: George Ronald, 1987.

———— *Studies in Bábí and Bahá'í History*. Los Angeles: Kalimát Press, 1982.

———— *Studies in Honor of the Late Hasan M. Balyuzi: Studies in the Bábí and Bahá'í Religions*. Los Angeles: Kalimát Press.

———— *The Bábí and Bahá'í Religions, 1844-1944: Some Contemporary Western Accounts*. Oxford: George Ronald, 1981.

Piff, David. Ed. Conference. *Proceedings of the UCLA Bahá'í History Conference, August 5-7, 1983*. Los Angeles, UCLA, 1983. 88.

Sims, Barbara R. *Traces That Remain: A Pictorial History of the Early Days of the Bahá'í Faith Among the Japanese*. Tokyo, Japan: Bahá'í Publishing Trust, Japan, 1989.

Sims, Barbara R. *Raising the Banner in Korea: An Early Bahá'í History*. Tokyo, Japan, 1996.

Smith, Melanie, and Paul Lample. *The Spiritual Conquest of the Planet: Our Response to Plans*. Riviera Beach, Fla: Palabra Publications, 1993.

Smith, Peter, ed. *Bahá'ís in the West: Studies in Bábí and Bahá'í History*. Los Angeles: Kalimát Press.

———— ed. *The Development and Influence of the Bahá'í Administrative Order in Great Britain, 1914-1950*. Los Angeles: Kalimát Press, 1992.

———— *In Írán: Studies in Bábí and Bahá'í History*. Los Angeles: Kalimát Press.

———— *The Bahá'í Religion: A Short Introduction to its History and Teachings*. Oxford: George Ronald, 1988.

———— ed. *A Short History of the Bahá'í Faith*. Oneworld: Oxford, 1996.

———— *What Was a Bahá'í? Concerns of British Bahá'ís, 1900-1920*. Los Angeles: Kalimát Press, 1988.

Stockman, Robert H. *The Bahá'í Faith in America: Early Expansion 1900-1912*. Vol. 2. Oxford: George Ronald, 1995. 3 vols.

———— *The Bahá'í Faith in America: Origins 1892-1900*. Vol. 1. Wilmette, Ill.: Bahá'í Publishing Trust, 1985. 3 vols.

The Centenary of a World Faith: The History of the Bahá'í Faith and Its Development in the British Isles. Ed. National Spiritual Assembly of the Bahá'ís of the UK. London, 1944.

The Guardian's Seven Year Plan for the American Bahá'ís, 1946-1953. Wilmette, Ill.: National Spiritual Assembly of the Bahá'ís of the United States and Canada, 1946.

The Seven Year Plan and Canada's Goals for Phase I and II. National Spiritual Assembly of Canada, 1981.

The Ten Year Crusade: A Program of Action for the Second Year. National Spiritual Assembly of the British Isles, 1954.

Whitmore, Bruce W. *The Dawning Place: The Building of a Temple, the Forging of the North American Bahá'í Community*. Wilmette, Ill.: Bahá'í Publishing Trust, 1984.

c) Other

Balyuzi, H. M. *Edward Granville Browne and the Bahá'í Faith*. Oxford: George Ronald, 1970, 1975, 1980.

11. Biographies

Alexander, Agnes Baldwin. *History of the Faith in Japan 1914-1938*. Osaka: Bahá'í Publishing Trust, 1977.

———— *Personal Recollections of a Bahá'í Life in the Hawaiian Islands: Forty Years of the Bahá'í Cause in Hawaii, 1902-1942*. Honolulu: National Spiritual Assembly of the Bahá'ís of the Hawaiian Islands, 1971.

Anderson, Angela. *Valley of Search*. Cornwall: Wordens of Cornwall Ltd., 1968.

Austin, Elsie. *Above All Barriers: The Story of Louis G. Gregory*. Wilmette, Ill.: Bahá'í Publishing Trust, 1976.

Balyuzi, H. M. *Eminent Bahá'ís in the Time of Bahá'u'lláh: with Some Historical Background*. Oxford: George Ronald, 1985.

Baram, A., ed. *Martha Root, Herald of the Kingdom: A Compilation*. New Delhi: Bahá'í Publishing Trust, 1983.

Barney, Laura Clifford. *God's Heroes*. London: Kegan Paul Trench Truber & Co.; Philadelphia: Lippincott, 1910.

Blomfield, Lady Sarah Louisa. *The Chosen Highway*. London: Bahá'í Publishing Trust, 1940.

Caldwell, Jenabe. *From Night to Knight*. Oxford: Oneworld Publishing, 1992.

Chase, Thornton, and Arthur S. Agnew. *In Galilee and In Spirit and In Truth*. Chicago: Bahai Publishing Society, 1908.

Freeman, Dorothy. *From Copper to Gold: The Life of Dorothy Baker*. Oxford: George Ronald, 1984.

Gail, Marzieh. *Summon Up Remembrance*. Oxford: George Ronald, 1987.

Garis, M. R. *Martha Root, Lioness at the Threshold*. Wilmette, Ill.: Bahá'í Publishing Trust, 1983.

Heller, Wendy. *Lidia: The Life of Lidia Zamenhof, Daughter of Esperanto*. Oxford: George Ronald, 1985.

Hendry, Derald E. *In the Hollow of His Hand: the Story of Ethel Murray*. Morganstown, N.C.: Derald E. Hendry, 1984.

Hofman, David. *George Townshend, Hand of the Cause of God (Sometime Canon of St. Patrick's Cathedral, Dublin, Archdeacon of Clonfert.)* Oxford: George Ronald, 1983.

Honnold, Annamarie, ed. *Why They Became Bahá'ís: First Generation Bahá'ís by 1963*. New Delhi: Bahá'í Publishing Trust, 1994.

Hunt, Ethel M. M., and A. J. Weinber. *A Journey from Judaism to the Bahá'í Faith (with a statement on the spread of the Bahá'í teachings among the Jews in Persia by A. J. Weinberg)*, n.p., n.d. 1941.

Ives, Howard Colby. *Portals to Freedom*. Wilmette, Ill.: Bahá'í Publishing Trust, 1967.

Labíb, Muhammad. *The Seven Martyrs of Hurmuzak*. Oxford: George Ronald, 1981.

Leach, Bernard. *My Religious Faith*. London: National Spiritual Assembly of the Bahá'ís of the United Kingdom, 1979.

Matthews, Loulie A. *Not Every Sea Hath Pearls*. Milford, N.H.: The Cabinet Press, 1951.

Maxwell, May (Bolles). *An Early Pilgrimage*. Chicago: Bahá'í Publishing Society, 1917.

Mayberry, Florence. *The Great Adventure*. Manotick, Ontario: Nine Pines Publishing, 1994.

McKay, Doris, and Paul Vreeland. *Fires in Many Hearts*. Manotick, Ontario: Nine Pines Publishing, 1993.

Mehrabkhani, R. *Mullá Husayn, Disciple at Dawn*. Los Angeles: Kalimát Press, 1987.

Momen, Moojan. *Dr. John Ebenezer Esslemont, M.B., Ch.B., SBEA, Hand of the Cause of God*. London: Bahá'í Publishing Trust, 1975.

Morrison, Gayle. *To Move the World: Louis G. Gregory and the Advancement of Racial Unity in America*. Wilmette, Ill.: Bahá'í Publishing Trust, 1982.

Nakhjavání, Violette. *Amatu'l-Bahá Visits India*. New Delhi: Bahá'í Publishing Trust, 1966, 1984.

Nelson-McDermott, Catherine. "Tahirih." *Bahá'í Studies Notebook* 1:1 (1980.)

Parsons, Agnes. *Agnes Parsons' Diary: Supplemented with Episodes from Maḥmúd's Diary April 11, 1912-November 11, 1912*. Ed. by Richard Hollinger. Los Angeles: Kalimát Press, 1996.

Roohizadegan, Olya. *Olya's Story: A Survivor's Dramatic Account of the Persecution of the Bahá'ís of Iran*. Oxford: Oneworld Publications, 1993.

Root, Martha L. *Táhirih the Pure, Irán's Greatest Woman*. Rev. ed. Los Angeles: Kalimát Press, 1981.

Rowdon, Larry. *Hidden Bounties: Memories of Pioneering on the Magdalen Archipelago*. Manotick, Ontario: Nine Pines Publishing, 1994.

Ruhe, David S. *Door of Hope: A Century of the Bahá'í Faith in the Holy Land*. Rev. ed. Oxford: George Ronald, 1986.

Rutstein, Nathan. *Corinne True: Faithful Handmaiden of 'Abdu'l-Bahá*. Oxford: George Ronald, 1987.

——— *He Loved and Served: The Story of Curtis Kelsey.* Oxford: George Ronald, 1982.

Schopflocher, Lorol. *Sunburst.* London: Ryder & Co., 1937.

Sears, William, and Robert Quigley. *The Flame (Cover Title: The Flame: The Story of Lua).* Oxford: George Ronald, 1973.

——— *All Flags Flying!* Johannesburg: National Spiritual Assembly of the Bahá'ís of South and West Africa, 1985.

——— *God Loves Laughter.* Oxford: George Ronald, 1984.

Szanto-Felbermann, Renee. *Rebirth: The Memoirs of Renee Szanto-Felbermann.* London: Bahá'í Publishing Trust, 1980.

Vreeland, Claire. *And the Trees Clapped their Hands: Stories of Bahá'í Pioneers.* Oxford: George Ronald, 1994.

Weinberg, Robert. *Ethel Jenner Rosenberg: The Life and Times cf England's Outstanding Bahá'í Pioneer Worker.* Oxford: George Ronald, 1995.

West, Marion. *Letters from Bonaire.* Oxford: George Ronald, 1990.

Whitehead, O. Z. *Some Baha'is to Remember.* Oxford: George Ronald, 1983.

——— *Some Early Bahá'ís of the West.* Oxford: George Ronald, 1976.

——— *Portraits of Some Bahá'í Women.* Oxford: George Ronald, 1996.

Winckler, Bahíyyih Randall. *My Pilgrimage to Haifa November 1919* Wilmette, Ill., Bahá'í Publishing Trust, 1996

Winckler, Bahíyyih Randall and Garis, M. R. *William Henry Randall: Disciple of 'Abdu'l-Bahá.* Oxford: Oneworld, 1996.

Yazdi, A. M. *Blessings Beyond Measure: Recollections of 'Abdu'l-Bahá and Shoghi Effendi.* Wilmette, Ill.: Bahá'í Publishing Trust, 1988.

Zohoori, Elias. *A Wondrous World: A Collection of Bahá'í Sacred Writings and Accounts of Dreams and Visions from Bahá'í History.* Kingston, Jamaica: Zoohoori, 1992.

12. Bahá'í International Community

A Bahá'í Declaration of Human Rights and Obligations: Presented to the United Nations Human Rights Commission. New York: Bahá'í International Community, 1947.

Bahá'í International Community Quadrennial Report to the UN Economic & Social Council (ECOSOC) 1977-1981. New York: Bahá'í International Community, 1981.

Bahá'í International Community Quadrennial Report to the UN Economic & Social Council (ECOSOC) October 1981 to September 1985. New York: Bahá'í International Community, 1985.

Bahá'í International Community Quadrennial Report to the UN Economic & Social Council (ECOSOC) October 1985 to September 1989. New York: Bahá'í International Community, 1989.

Bahá'í International Community Quadrennial Report to the UN Economic & Social Council (ECOSOC) October 1989 to June 1994. New York: Bahá'í International Community, 1994.

The Bahá'í Question: Iran's Secret Blueprint for the Destruction of a Religious Community; An Examination of the Persecution of the Bahá'ís of Írán 1979-1993. New York: Bahá'í International Community, 1993. Vol. 55.

The Bahá'ís in Iran: A Report on the Persecution of a Religious Minority. New York: Bahá'í International Community, 1982.

Chronological Summary of Individual Acts of Persecution Against Bahá'ís in Iran (from August 1978). New York: Bahá'í International Community, 1981.

The Environment and Human Values: A Bahá'í View. Wilmette, Ill.: Bahá'í Publishing Trust, 1983.

Equality of Men and Women: A New Reality. Wilmette, Ill.: Bahá'í Publishing Trust, 1983.

A Pattern of Justice. New York: Bahá'í International Community, 1974.

The Promise of Disarmament and Peace. New York: Bahá'í International Community, 1982.

Proposals for Charter Revision Submitted to the United Nations by the Bahá'í International Community. New York: Bahá'í International Community, 1961.

Proposals for Charter Revision Submitted to the United Nations by the Bahá'í International Community. New York: Bahá'í International Community, 1954.

The Prosperity of Humankind. New York: Bahá'í International Community, Office of Public Information, 1995.

Science and Technology for Human Advancement. New York: Bahá'í International Community, 1979.

The Spiritual Basis of Equality. New York: Bahá'í International Community, 1985.

Systematic Torture of Bahá'ís in Iranian Prisons. New York: Bahá'í International Community, 1984.

Towards Universal Tolerance in Matters Relating to Religion or Belief: Submission by the Bahá'í International Community to the Seminar on the Encouragement of Understanding, Tolerance and Respect in Matters Relating to Freedom of Religion or Belief. Geneva: Bahá'í International Community, 1984.

Turning Point For All Nations: A Statement of the Bahá'í International Community on the Occasion of the 50th Anniversary of the

United Nations. New York: Bahá'í International Community, United Nations Office, 1995.

Universal Values for the Advancement of Women. New York: Bahá'í International Community, 1983.

The Work of Bahá'ís in Promotion of Human Rights: A Statement Prepared for the United Nations Conference on Human Rights. Wilmette, Ill.: Bahá'í International Community, 1948.

World Citizenship: A Global Ethic for Sustainable Development. New York: Bahá'í International Community, 1993.

World Conference to Combat Racism and Racial Discrimination: New York: Bahá'í International Community, 1978.

13. Treatise on Bahá'í Subjects

Áfáqí, S., *Proofs from the Holy Qur'án (Regarding the Advent of Bahá'u'lláh)*. New Delhi: Mir'át Publications, 1993.

Abu'l-Fadl Gulpáygani, Mirzá. *Letters and Essays, 1886-1913*. Trans. Juan R.I. Cole. Los Angeles: Kalimát Press, 1985.

——— *Miracles and Metaphors*. Trans. Juan Ricardo Cole. Los Angeles: Kalimát Press, 1981.

——— *The Bahá'í Proofs (Hujaja'l-Bahíyyih); and A Short Sketch of the History of the Lives of the Leaders of This Religion*. Trans. Ali-Kuli Khan (Ishti'al Ibn-i-Kalántar). Facsimile of the 1929 ed. Wilmette, Ill.: Bahá'í Publishing Trust, 1983.

——— *The Brilliant Proof, Burhäne Lämé*. Chicago: Baha News Service, 1912.

Afnan, Ruhi. *Mysticism and the Bahá'í Revelation*. New York: Bahá'í Publishing Committee, 1934.

Backwell, Richard. *The Christianity of Jesus*. Portlaw, Ireland: Volturna Press, 1972.

Badiee, Julie. *An Earthly Paradise: Bahá'í Houses of Worship Around the World*. Oxford: George Ronald, 1992.

Balyuzi, H. M. *Muhammad and the Course of Islam*. Oxford: George Ronald, 1976.

Bowes, Eric. *Great Themes of Life*. Wilmette, Ill.: Bahá'í Publishing Trust, 1958.

Bryson, Alan. *Light After Death: A Comparison of the Near Death Experience and the Teachings of the Bahá'í Faith on Life After Death*. India: Sterling Publishers Private, Limited, 1993.

Buck, Christopher, ed. *Symbol and Secret: Qur'án Commentary in Bahá'u'lláh's Kitáb-i-Íqan: Studies in the Bábí and Bahá'í Religions*. Los Angeles: Kalimát Press, 1995.

Bushrui, *The Style of the Kitáb-i-Aqdas: Aspects of the Sublime*. Bethesda, Maryland: University Press of Maryland, 1995.

Cameron, G. and W. Momen, *A Basic Bahá'í Chronology*. Oxford: George Ronald, 1996.

Chase, Thornton. *The Bahá'í Revelation*. New York: Bahá'í Publishing Trust, 1920.

Chew, Phyllis Ghim Lian. *The Chinese Religion and the Bahá'í Faith*. Oxford: George Ronald, 1993.

Cole, Juan Ricardo. "The Concept of Manifestation in the Bahá'í Writings." *Association for Bahá'í Studies: Bahá'í Studies* 9 (1982): 38.

Cole, Owen W., ed. *World Religions: A Handbook for Teachers*. 2nd Reprint ed. London: Commission for Racial Equality, in conjunction with The SHAP Working Party on Religions in Education, 1980.

Cooper, Roger. "The Baha'is of Iran." London: Minority Rights Group, 1982.

The Covenant: Its Meaning and Origin and Our Attitude Towards It. Ed. National Teaching Committee. Riviera Beach, Fla: Palabra Publications, 1988.

Dahl, Arthur L. *Mark Tobey, Art and Belief*. Oxford: George Ronald, 1984.

Danesh, Hossain B. *The Psychology of Spirituality*. Manitock, Ontario: Nine Pines Publishing, 1994.

———— *The Violence Free Society: A Gift for Our Children*. Vol. 6. Ottawa: Canadian Association for Studies on the Bahá'í Faith, 1979.

Dreyfus, Hippolyte. *The Universal Religion: Bahaism*. Trans. (Essai sur le Béhaïsme.) Chicago: Bahá'í Publishing Company, 1909.

Education, Advisory Committee on. "Bahá'í School Lesson Plans Grade 1: History, Teachings for the Individual, Social Teachings (*Bahá'í Teacher's Handbook*)." Wilmette, Ill.: Bahá'í Publishing Trust, 1968, 1976. 105; "Bahá'í School Lesson Plans Grade 2: History, Teachings for the Individual, Social Teachings (*Bahá'í Teacher's Handbook*)." Wilmette, Ill.: Bahá'í Publishing Trust, 1968. 89; "Bahá'í School Lesson Plans Grade 3: History, Teachings for the Individual, Social Teachings (*Bahá'í Teacher's Handbook*)." Wilmette, Ill.: Bahá'í Publishing Trust, 1970. 109; "Bahá'í School Lesson Plans Grade 4: History, Teachings for the Individual, Social Teachings (*Bahá'í Teacher's Handbook*)." Wilmette, Ill.: Bahá'í Publishing Trust, 1970. 92; "Bahá'í School Lesson Plans Grade 5: History, Teachings for the Individual, Social Teachings (*Bahá'í Teacher's Handbook*)." Wilmette, Ill.: Bahá'í Publishing Trust, 1970. 90; "Bahá'í School Lesson Plans Grade 6: History, Teachings for the Individual, Social Teachings (*Bahá'í Teacher's Handbook*)." Wilmette, Ill.: Bahá'í Publishing Trust, 1968. 93; "Bahá'í School Lesson Plans Grade 7: History, Teachings for the Individual, Social Teachings (*Bahá'í Teacher's Handbook*)." Wilmette, Ill.: Bahá'í Publishing Trust, 1968. 131; "Bahá'í School Lesson Plans Grade 8: History, Teachings for the Individual, Social Teachings (*Bahá'í Teacher's Handbook*)." Wilmette, Ill.: Bahá'í Publishing Trust, 1968. 104; "Bahá'í School Lesson Plans Grade 9: History, Teachings for the Individual, Social Teachings (*Bahá'í Teacher's Handbook*)." Wilmette, Ill.: Bahá'í Publishing Trust, 1970. 92; "Bahá'í School Lesson Plans Grade K: History, Teachings for the Individual, Social Teachings (*Bahá'í Teacher's Handbook*)." Wilmette, Ill.: Bahá'í Publishing Trust, 1976.

Esslemont, John Ebenezer. *Bahá'u'lláh and the New Era*. 4th rev. ed. Wilmette, Ill.: Bahá'í Publishing Trust, 1980.

Gail, Marzieh. *Bahá'í Glossary*. Wilmette, Ill.: Bahá'í Publishing Trust, 1976.

———— *Other People, Other Places*. Oxford: George Ronald, 1982.

———— *The Sheltering Branch*. Wilmette, Ill.: Bahá'í Publishing Trust, 1970.

Hainsworth, Philip, and Mary Perkins. *The Bahá'í Faith*. London: Ward Lock Educational, 1985.

Hainsworth, Philip. *Bahá'í Focus on Human Rights*. London: Bahá'í Publishing Trust, 1985.

———— *The Bahá'í Faith and the United Nations*. Paper written for the National Spiritual Assembly of the Bahá'ís of the United Kingdom Bahá'í community, 1995.

Hatcher, John S. "The Metaphysical Nature of Physical Reality." *Bahá'í Studies (Canadian Association of Bahá'í Studies)* 3 (1977): 27.

———— *The Arc of Ascent: The Purpose of Physical Reality II*. Oxford: George Ronald, 1994.

———— *The Purpose of Physical Reality: The Kingdom of Names*. Wilmette, Ill.: Bahá'í Publishing Trust, 1987.

———— "The Concept of Spirituality." *Bahá'í Studies (Association for Bahá'í Studies)* 11 (1982): 35.

———— "The Science of Religion." *Bahá'í Studies (Canadian Association for Bahá'í Studies)* 2 (1977): 45.

Hatcher, William S., and J. Douglas Martin. *The Bahá'í Faith: The Emerging Global Religion*. San Francisco, Calif.: Harper & Row, 1984, 1985.

Huddleston, John. *The Earth Is But One Country*. 2nd ed. London: Bahá'í Publishing Trust, 1976, 1980.

Kheiralla, Ibrahim George. *The Door of True Religion (Bab-Ed-din): 1, Za-ti-et Al-lah, 2, El Fi-da: Revelation from the East: Rational Argument.* Chicago: Chas. H. Kerr and Company, 1897.

———— *The Identity and the Personality of God: Za-Ti-Et Allah*. Chicago: Grant's Printery, 1896.

Kolstoe, J. *Developing Genius: Getting the Most Out of Group Decision-Making*. Oxford: George Ronald, 1995.

Lee, Anthony A., ed. *Circle of Unity: A Proclamation to the Native Americans from the Bahá'í Faith*. Wilmette, Ill.: Bahá'í Publishing Trust, 1980.

———— *Circle of Unity: Bahá'í Approaches to Current Social Issues*. Los Angeles: Kalimát Press, 1984.

Loehle, Craig. *On the Shoulders of Giants*. Oxford: George Ronald, 1994.

Marks, Geoffrey W. *Call to Remembrance: Connecting the Heart to Bahá'u'lláh*. Wilmette, Ill.: Bahá'í Publishing Trust.

Matthews, Gary L. *The Challenge of Bahá'u'lláh*. Oxford: George Ronald, 1993.

McDaniel, Allen Boyer. *The Spell of the Temple*. New York: Vantage Press, 1953.

McLean, J. A. *Dimensions in Spirituality*. Oxford: George Ronald, 1994.

McLean, J. *Revisioning the Sacred: New Perspectives on a Bahá'í Terminology*. Studies in the Bábí and Bahá'í Religions, ed. A.A. Lee. Vol. 8 Kalimat Press: Los Angeles, 1997.

Metalmann, V.P. *Lua Getsinger: Herald of the Covenant*. Oxford: George Ronald, 1997.

Momen, Wendi, ed. *A Basic Bahá'í Dictionary*. Oxford: George Ronald, 1989.

Mustafa, M. *Bahá'u'lláh: The Great Announcement of the Qur'an*. Dhaka, Bangladesh: Bahá'í Publishing Trust, 1995.

Nakhjavání, Bahíyyih. *Asking Questions: A Challenge to Fundamentalism*. Oxford: George Ronald, 1990.

———— *Responses*. Oxford: George Ronald, 1983.

Nash, Geoffrey. *Iran's Secret Pogrom: The Conspiracy to Wipe Out the Bahá'ís*. Suffolk, U.K.: Neville Spearman, 1982.

Pinchon, Florence E. *The Coming of "the Glory": (As Described in the Bahai Writings.)* London: Simpkin Marshall Ltd., 1928.

Sabet, Huschmand. *The Heavens Are Cleft Asunder*. Oxford: George Ronald, 1975.

Schaefer, Udo. *The Imperishable Dominion: The Bahá'í Faith and the Future of Mankind*. Trans. Janet Rawling-Keitel, David Hopper and Patricia Crampton. Oxford: George Ronald, 1983.

———— *The Light Shineth in Darkness: Five Studies in Revelation After Christ*. Trans. Helene Momtaz Neri, Oliver Coburn. Oxford: George Ronald, 1980.

Sears, William. *A Cry from the Heart: The Bahá'ís in Írán*. Oxford: George Ronald, 1982.

———— *The Prisoner and the Kings*. Toronto: General Publishing Company, 1971.

———— *The Wine of Astonishment*. Oxford: George Ronald, 1983.

———— *Thief in the Night, or the Strange Case of the Missing Millennium*. Oxford: George Ronald, 1985.

Shook, Glenn A. *Mysticism, Science and Revelation*. Wilmette, Ill.: Bahá'í Publishing Trust, 1970.

Sours, Michael W. *Understanding Biblical Evidence*. Preparing for a Bahá'í/Christian Dialogue. Vol. 1. Oxford: Oneworld, 1997.

———— *Understanding Christian Beliefs*. Preparing for a Bahá'í/Christian Dialogue. Vol. 2. Oxford: Oneworld, 1997.

———— *Understanding Biblical Prophecy*. Preparing for a Bahá'í/Christian Dialogue. Vol. 3. Oxford: Oneworld, 1997.

———— *The Prophecies of Jesus*. Oxford: Oneworld, 1990.

———— Jesus Christ in Sacred Bahá'í Literature: A Compilation. Oxford: Oneworld, 1990.

———— *Bahá'u'lláh's Tablet to the Christians*. Oxford: Oneworld, 1990.

Wallbridge, J. *Sacred Acts, Sacred Space, Sacred Time*. Oxford: George Ronald, 1996.

The Word of God. Ed. National Teaching Committee. Riviera Beach, Fla: Palabra Publications, 1987.

14. Electronic Media

a) Bahá'í Scriptures

Nelson, Lee. *Refer—Multiple Author Refer System: Indexing and Retrieval Software*. (CD ROM version 1.2) San Juan Capistrano, CA: Crimson Publications, 1995.

Schooley, Bernal. *Immerse: The Electronic Bahá'í Library*. (Beta version 0.92) St. Charles, Ill.: Bernal Schooley III, 1997.

15. WWW Sites

a) Bahá'í Scriptures

ftp://ftp.bwc.org/bahai
mirrored at: ftp://oneworld.wa.com/pub/bwc;
HTML format at: http://www.bcca.org/~kalantar/writings/)

b) Bahá'í International Community Statements

http://www.bahai.org (The official Bahá'í International Community web site).

c) Bibliographies

ftp://rtfm.mit.edu/pub/usenet/soc.religion.bahai/Baha_i_Faith_Annotated_Bibliography

d) General resources

http://www.bcca.org/srb/resources.html (maintained by Gordon Lane laneg@cadvision.com)

http://www.bcca.org/glittle/

e) Introductory Material

ftp://rtfm.mit.edu/pub/usenet/soc.religion.bahai/Baha_i_Faith_Introduction

http://www.primenet.com/~rmcdonld/intro.html

http://oneworld.wa.com/bahai/magazine/cover.html

http://www.miracles.win-uk/Bahai/BasicFacts/basic1.html

f) Images—Graphics

ftp://ftp.icis.on.ca/pub/pc/windows/text/bahai/bahaipics (100+ Images)

http://www.nwark.com

http://www.bcca.org/akka

http://aloha.net/hol/home/lizhm/bahaiyou.htm (GIF format)

http://www.nwark.com/~bstover

http://ian-vink.icis.on.ca/bahai/ianvink

Appendices

Genealogy—Bahá'u'lláh-Descended from Yazdgird III

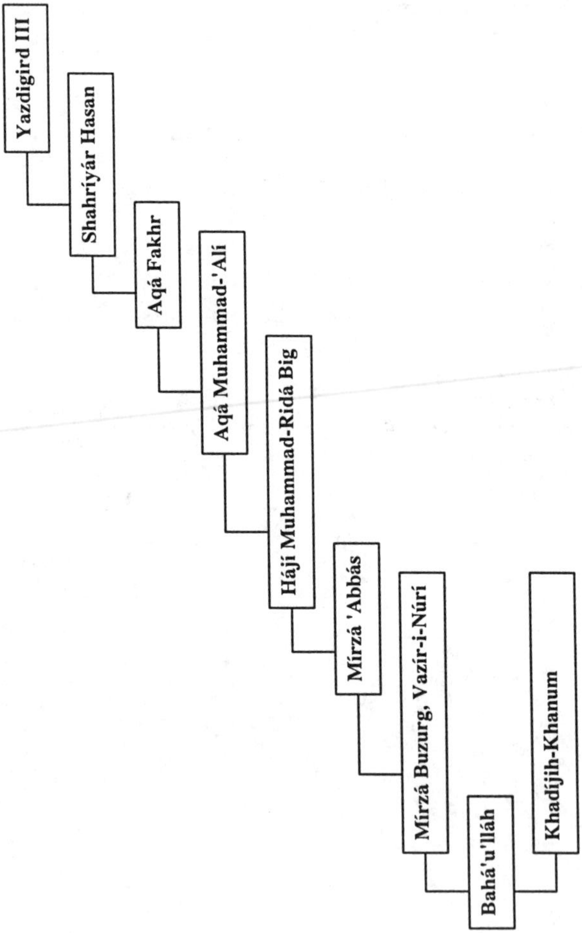

Genealogy—Bahá'u'lláh-First Generation Descendants

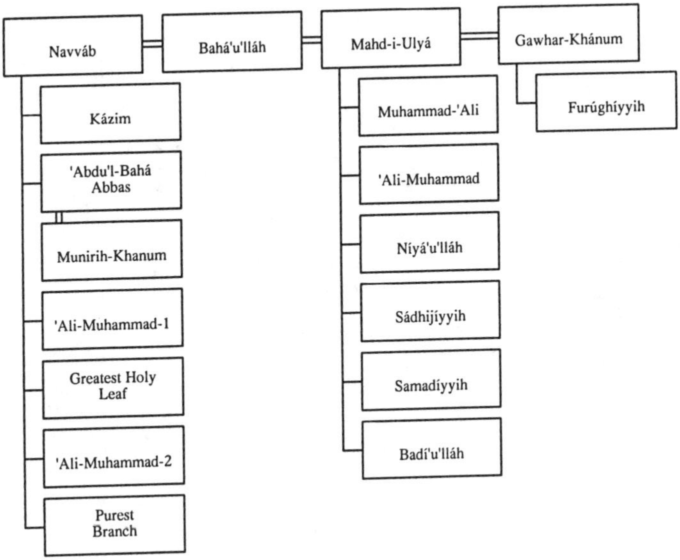

Genealogy—'Abdu'l-Bahá-First Generation Descendants

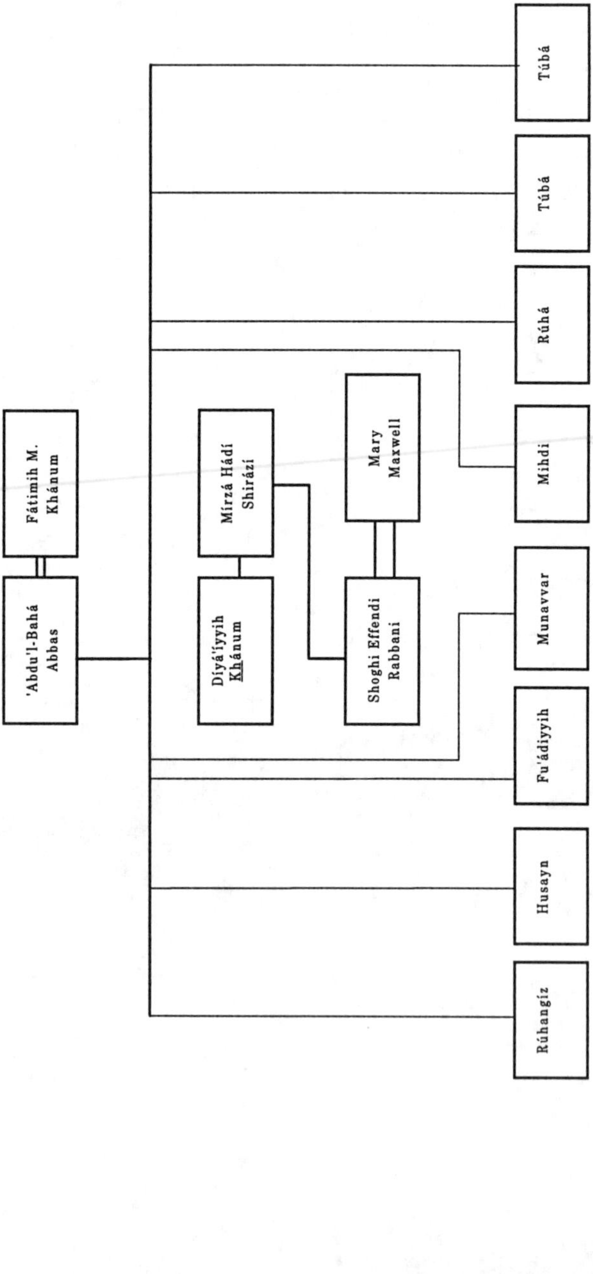

Genealogy of the Báb-Relationship to Shoghi Effendi

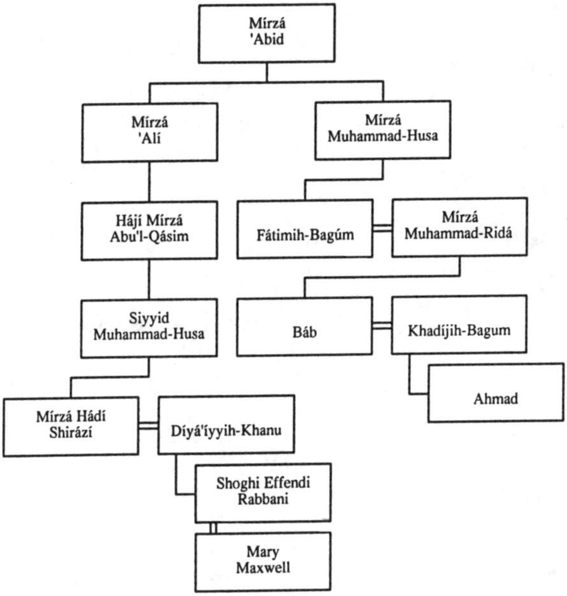

Genealogy-Bahá'u'lláh-Kinship Listing

Name	Relationship with Bahá'u'lláh
Ḥusayn-'Alí - Bahá'u'lláh	Self
'Abdu'l-Bahá 'Abbás	Son
Mírzá 'Abbás	Grandfather
'Alí-Muḥammad	Son
'Alí-Muḥammad (1)	Son
'Alí-Muḥammad (2)	Son
Mírzá Áqá	Half-brother
Áqáy-i-Kalím	Brother
Ásiyih-Khánum	Wife
Badí'u'lláh	Son
Bahíyyih-Khánum	Daughter
Hájí Muḥammad-Ridá Big	Great-grandfather
Vazír-i-Núrí Mírzá Buzurg	Father
Díyá'íyyih-Khánum	Granddaughter
Áqá Fakhr	3rd great-grandaughter
Fátimih-Khánum	Daughter-in-law
Fátimih-Khánum	Wife
Fátimih-Sultán-Khánum	Half-sister
Fu'ádiyyih	Granddaughter
Furúghíyyih	Daughter
Gawhar-Khánum	Wife
Sháhríyár Hasan	4th great-grandfather
Ḥusayn	Grandson
Husníyyih-Khánum	Half-sister
Mírzá Ibráhím	Half-brother
'Izzíyih-Khánum	Half-sister
Kázim	Son
Khadíjih-Khánum	Mother
Khan-Nanih	Wife of the father
Kúchik-Khánum	Wife of the father
Kulthúm-Khánum-i-Núrí	Wife of the father
Mahd-i-Ulyá	Wife
Mary Maxwell	Wife of the great-grandson
Mihdí	Grandson
Mírzá Mihdí	Son
Mírzá Mihdí	Brother
Muḥammad-'Alí	Son
Áqá Muḥammad-'Alí	2nd great-grandfather
Mírzá Muḥammad-'Alí	Half-brother
Mírzá Muḥammad-Hasan	Half-brother
Mírzá Muḥammad-Qulí	Half-brother
Munavvar	Granddaughter

Munírih-Khánum	Daughter-in-law
Mírzá Músá	Brother
Nabát-Khánum	Wife of the father
Navváb	Wife
Nisá-Khánum	Sister
Níyá'u'lláh	Daughter
Paríshán	Half-brother
Shoghi Effendi Rabbání	Great-grandson
Hájí Mírzá Ridá-Qulí	Half-brother
Rúhá	Granddaughter
Rúhangíz	Granddaughter
Sádhijíyyih	Daughter
Sakínih-Khánum	Half-sister
Samadíyyih	Daughter
Sárih-Khánum	Sister
Fath 'Alí Sháh	Wife of the father
Sháh-Sultan	Half sister
Mírzá Hádí Shírází	Husband of the granddaughter
Sughrá-Khánum	Half-sister
Mírzá Taqí	Half-brother
Túbá	Granddaughter
Túbá	Granddaughter
Turkamáníyyih	Wife of the father
Mírzá Yaḥyá	Half-brother
Yazdigird III	5th great-grandfather

Letters of the Living

1. Mullá Ḥusayn-i-Bushrú'í (q.v.) (Bábu'l-Báb).
2. Muḥammad Ḥasan-i-Bushrú'í (brother of Mullá Ḥusayn).
3. Muḥammad Báqir-i-Bushrú'í (nephew of Mullá Ḥusayn).
4. Mullá 'Alíy-i-Basṭámí.
5. Mullá Khudá-Bakjsh-i-Qúchání (subsequently known as Mullá 'Alí).
6. Mullá Ḥusan-i-Bajistání.
7. Siyyid Ḥusayn-i-Yazdí (an amanuensis to the Báb and surnamed by Him, 'Azíz; he shared the Báb's imprisonments in both Máh-Kú and Chihríq).
8. Mírzá Muḥammad Rawḍih-Khán-i-Yazdí.
9. Sa'íd-i-Hindí.
10. Mullá Maḥmúd-i-Khu'i.
11. Mullá Jalíl-i-Urúmí.
12. Mullá Aḥmad-i-Ibdál-i-Marághi'í.
13. Mullá Báqir-i-Tabrízí.
14. Mullá Yúsuf-i-Ardibílí.
15. Mírzá Hádí.
16. Mírzá Muḥammad-'Alíy-i-Qazvíní.
17. Fáṭimih Umm-Salamih (titled Ṭáhirih [q.v.] [the Pure One] during the Conference of Badasht; also known as Qurratu'l-Ayn [Solace of the Eyes] and Zarrín-Táj [Crown of Gold]).
18. Ḥájí Muḥammad-'Alíy-Bárfurúshí (titled Quddús [q.v.] [the Most Holy] during the Conference of Badasht).

Apostles of Bahá'u'lláh

1. Mírzá Músá, surnamed Kalím; the only full brother of Bahá'u'lláh.
2. Mírzá Buzurg, surnamed Badí; executed following delivery of a letter from Bahá'u'lláh to the Náṣiri'd-Dín Sháh.
3. Siyyid Ḥasan, surnamed Sulṭánu'sh-Shuhadá' one of two brothers from Iṣfáhán, who was executed for his faith.
4. Mullá Abu'l-Ḥasan, surnamed Amín; steward to Bahá'u'lláh.
5. Mírzá Abu'l-Faḍl; designated by Bahá'ís as the "foremost and authoritative expounder of the Bahá'í Revelation."
6. Mírzá 'Alí-Muḥammad, surnamed Varqá; a poet and teacher of the Bahá'í Faith; the first Trustee of the Ḥuqúqu'lláh.
7. Adíb. See Mírzá Ḥasan.
8. Mírzá Maḥmúd.
9. Mírzá Muḥammad, surnamed Nabíl-i-Akbar.

10. Ḥájí Mírzá Muḥammad Taqí, surnamed Kabír-i-Afnán. An Apostle of Bahá'u'lláh. A cousin of the Báb and the principle builder of the Mashriqu'l-Adhkár of 'Ishqábád.
11. Ḥájí Mírzá Muḥammad Taqí. An Apostle of Bahá'u'lláh.
12. Mullá Muḥammad, surnamed Nabíl-i-A'ẓam.
13. Shaykh Káẓim, surnamed Samadar.
14. Muḥammad Muṣṭafá. The custodian and bearer of the remains of the Báb.
15. Mírzá Ḥusayn, surnamed Mishkín-Qalam. An Apostle of Bahá'u'lláh and a distinguished calligraphist.
16. Mírzá Ḥasan, surnamed Adíb. An Apostle of Bahá'u'lláh.
17. Shaykh Muḥammad 'Alí.
18. Zaynu'l-'Ábidín, noted scribe.
19. Mírzá 'Alí Muḥammad, surnamed Shahíd-ibn-i-Shahíd.

Disciples of 'Abdu'l-Bahá-Heralds of the Covenant

1. Dr. John E. Esslemont.
2. Mr. Thornton Chase.
3. Mr. Howard McNutt.
4. Miss Sarah Farmer.
5. Monsieur Hippolyte Dreyfus-Barney.
6. Miss Lilian Kappes.
7. Mr. Robert Turner.
8. Consul A. Schwartz
9. Mr. William H. Randall.
10. Mrs. Lua M. Getsinger.
11. Mr. Joseph Hannan.
12. Mr. C. I. Thacher.
13. Mr. Charles Greenleaf.
14. Mrs. J. D. Brittingham.
15. Mrs. E. Rosenberg
16. Mrs. Helen S. Goodall.
17. Mr. Arthur P. Dodge.
18. Mr. William H. Hoar.
19. Dr. A. J. Augur.
20. Mrs. Thornburgh-Cropper.

Hands of the Cause of God (by Contingent)

Bahá'u'lláh

1. Ḥájí Mullá 'Alí-Akbar-i-Shahmirzádí, surnamed Ḥájí Ákhúnd.
2. Ḥájí Mírzá Muḥammad-Taqiy-i-Abhari, surnamed Ibn-i-Abhar.
3. Ḥájí Abu'l-Ḥasan, surnamed Adíb.
4. Mírzá 'Alí Muḥammad, surnamed Ibn-i-Aṣdaq.

'Abdu'l-Bahá (Posthumously by 'Abdu'l-Bahá)

5. Áqá Muḥammad-i-Qá'iní, surnamed Nabíl-i-Akbar.
6. Mírzá 'Alí-Muḥammad, surnamed Varqá.
7. Shaykh Muḥammad Riḍáy-i-Yazdí.
8. Mullá Ṣádiq-i-Muqaddas, known as Ismu'lláhu'l-Aṣdaq.

Posthumously by Shoghi Effendi

9. Ḥájí Abu'l-Ḥasan, surnamed Amín and known alternatively as Mullá Abu'l-Ḥasan, July 1928.
10. John E. Esslemont, 30 November 1925
11. Lewis G. Gregory, 5 August 1951.
12. Keith Ransom-Kehler,
13. Martha L Root,
14. Siyyid Muṣṭafá Rúmí, 14 July 1945
15. 'Abdu'l-Jalíl Bey Sa'd, 25 June1942.
16. Roy C. Wilhelm, 23 December 1951.
17. John Henry Hyde-Dunn, 26 April 1954.
18. Muḥammad Taqíy-i-Iṣfahání, 12 December 1946.

1st Contingent—Shoghi Effendi (24 December 1951)

19. Dorothy B. Baker.
20. Amelia E. Collins.
21. 'Alí-Akbar Furútan.
22. Ugo Giachery.
23. Hermann Grossman.
24. Horace Holley.
25. Leroy Ioas.
26. William Sutherland Maxwell.
27. Charles Mason Remey (q.v.) (later expelled as a Covenant Breaker.)
28. Ṭarázu'lláh Samandarí.
29. George Townshend.
30. Valíyu'lláh Varqá.

2nd Contingent—Shoghi Effendi (29 February 1952)

31. Shu'á'u'lláh 'Alá'í.
32. Músá Banání.
33. Clara Dunn.
34. Dhikru'lláh Khadem.
35. Adelbert Mühlschlegel.
36. Siegfried Schopflocher.
37. Corrine Knight True.

Individual single appointments—Shoghi Effendi

38. 'Amatu'l-Bahá Rúḥíyyih Khánum, 26 March 1952.
39. Jalál Khazeh, 7 December 1953
40. Paul E. Haney, 19 March 1954
41. 'Alí-Muḥammad Varqá, 15 November 1955
42. Agnes B. Alexander, 27 March 1957

3rd (Final) Contingent—Shoghi Effendi (2 October 1957)

43. Enoch Olinga.
44. William Sears.
45. Ḥasan Muvaqqar Bályúzí.
46. John Robarts.
47. John Ferraby.
48. Collis H. Featherstone.
49. Raḥmatu'lláh Muhájir.
50. Abu'l-Qásim Faiẓí.

Badí' Calendar

Event	Arabic	English	First day
1st month	Bahá	Splendor	March 21
2nd month	Jalál	Glory	April 9
3rd month	Jamál	Beauty	April 28
4th month	'Aẓamat	Grandeur	May 17
5th month	Núr	Light	June 5
6th month	Raḥmat	Mercy	June 24
7th month	Kalimát	Words	July 13
8th month	Kamál	Perfection	August 1
9th month	Asmá'	Names	August 20
10th month	'Izzat	Might	September 8
11th month	Mashíyyat	Will	September 27
12th month	'Ilm	Knowledge	October 16
13th month	Qudrat	Power	November 4
14th month	Qawl	Speech	November 23
15th month	Masá'il	Questions	December 12
16th month	Sharaf	Honor	December 31
17th month	Sulṭán	Sovereignty	January 19
18th month	Mulk	Dominion	February 7
Intercalary Days	Ayyám-i-Há	Intercalary Days	Feb 26—March 1
19th month	'Alá'	Loftiness	March 2
Fast		19 Day Fast	March 2—20
1st weekday	Jalál	Glory	Saturday
2nd weekday	Jamál	Beauty	Sunday
3rd weekday	Kamál	Perfection	Monday
4th weekday	Fiḍál	Grace	Tuesday
5th weekday	'Idál	Justice	Wednesday
6th weekday	Istijlál	Majesty	Thursday
7th weekday	Istiqlál	Independence	Friday
Holy Day	Naw-Rúz	New Year	March 21
Holy Day		1st Day of Riḍván	April 21
Holy Day		9th Day of Riḍván	April 29
Holy Day		12th Day of Riḍván	May 2
Holy Day		Declaration of the Báb	May 23
Holy Day		Ascension of Bahá'u'lláh	May 29
Holy Day		Martyrdom of the Báb	July 9
Holy Day		Birth of the Báb	October 20
Holy Day		Birth of Bahá'u'lláh	November 12
Holy Day		Day of the Covenant	November 26
Holy Day		Ascension of 'Abdu'l-Bahá	November 28
Holy Days	Riḍván	Feast of Riḍván (Paradise)	April 21—May 2

Statistics[144:317]

Worldwide Bahá'í population	+5 million
Countries where Bahá'í Faith is established	190
Dependent territories where Bahá'í Faith is established	45
Continental Counsellors	81
Auxiliary Board members	990
National Spiritual Assemblies	174
Local Spiritual Assemblies	17,148
• Africa	4,828
• Americas	4,515
• Asia	5,954
• Australasia	901
• Europe	950
Localities where Bahá'ís reside	121,058
Tribes, races & ethnic groups represented in Bahá'í Faith	2,112
Languages into which Bahá'í literature has been translated	802
Bahá'í Publishing Trusts	30

279

to prosecute the siege.—

The Founder of this sect has been executed at Tabreez. He was killed by a volley of musketry, and his death was on the point of giving his religion a lustre which would have largely increased its proselytes. When the smoke and dust cleared away after the volley, Báb was not to be seen, and the populace proclaimed that he had ascended to

the

Facsimile of a letter written by Martin Sheil (from a camp near Tehran) to The British Foreign Office, London, 22 July 1850, concerning the execution of the Báb.

Partial text of Martin Sheil's letter to Lord Palmerston, The British Foreign Office, London, 22 July 1850 concerning the execution of the Báb.

Camp near Tehran,
July 22nd. 1850

The Right Honorable The Viscount Palmerston G.C.B.

My Lord,

There has been an intermission in the contest at Gengan between the Shah's troops and the Bâbees of that city—The Chief of the sect in Gengan, a mollah of high station, wrote to me a short time ago, declaring that he had been falsely accused of Bâbeeism and begging me to intercede and save himself and his companions from military violence. He enclosed a letter of the same purport to the Ameer i Nizam—The Persian Minister replied to their person that he was willing to accept his declaration but that in proof of his sincerity he must present himself at the Shah's Court. No notice having been taken of this condition a further body of troops has been summoned to prosecute the siege.

The founder of this sect has been executed at Tabreez. He was killed by a volley of musketry, and his death was on the point of giving his religion a lustre which would have largely increased its proselytes. When the smoke and dust had cleared away after the volley, Bâb was not to be seen, and the populace proclaimed that he had ascended to the skies. The balls had broken the ropes by which he was bound, but he was dragged from the recess where after some search he was discovered and shot.

His death according to the belief of his disciples will make no difference, as Bâb must always exist.

....

I have the honor to be with the greatest respect—My Lord, Your Lordship's Most obedient humble servant

Martin Sheil

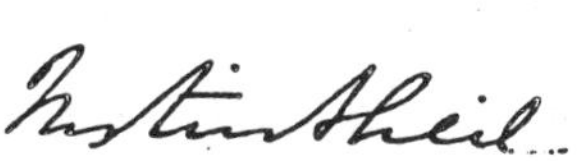

Citations

1. Collins, W. P., *Bibliography of English-Language Works on the Bábí and Bahá'í Faiths 1844-1985*. 1990, Oxford: George Ronald.
2. Bahá'í Year Book, *Bahá'í World (1979-1983). Vol. XVIII: An International Record*. Vol. XVIII. 1986, Haifa: Bahá'í World Centre Publications.
3. Effendi, S., *Citadel of Faith: Messages to America, 1947-1957*. 1980, Wilmette, Ill.: Bahá'í Publishing Trust.
4. Effendi, S., *The World Order of Bahá'u'lláh*. 2nd rev. ed. 1982, Wilmette, Ill.: Bahá'í Publishing Trust.
5. Effendi, S., *God Passes By*. 1979 rev. ed. 1979, Wilmette, Ill.: Bahá'í Publishing Trust.
6. Effendi, S., *Messages to the Bahá'í World 1950-1957*. 1971, Wilmette, Ill.: Bahá'í Publishing Trust.
7. *Bahá'í News Index—No. 173 to No. 322*, Comp. M. P. Stebbins. Vol. II. 1959, Wilmette, Ill.: Bahá'í Publishing Trust.
8. Universal House of Justice, *Wellspring of Guidance: Messages 1963-1968*. 1st rev. ed. 1976, Wilmette, Ill.: Bahá'í Publishing Trust.
9. Effendi, S., *The Unfolding Destiny of the British Bahá'í Community: The Messages from the Guardian of the Bahá'í Faith to the Bahá'ís of the British Isles*. 1981, London: Bahá'í Publishing Trust.
10. Nabíl-i-A'zam, *The Dawn Breakers: Nabil's Narrative of the Early Days of the Baha'i Revelation*, ed. S. Effendi. 1970, Wilmette. Ill.: Bahá'í Publishing Trust.
11. Bahá'í Year Book, *Bahá'í World (1983-1986) Vol. XIX: An International Record*. Vol. XIX. 1994, Haifa: Bahá'í World Centre Publications.
12. Balyuzi, H. M., *The Báb, the Herald of the Day of Days*. 1994, Oxford: George Ronald.
13. Root, M. L., *Táhirih the Pure, Irán's Greatest Woman*. Rev. ed. 1981, Los Angeles: Kalimát Press.
14. Balyuzi, H. M., *Bahá'u'lláh, the King of Glory*. 1980, Oxford: George Ronald.
15. Effendi, S., *The Bahá'í Faith, 1844-1952: Information Statistical and Comparative*. 1953, Wilmette, Ill.: Bahá'í Publishing Committee.
16. Balyuzi, H. M., *'Abdu'l-Bahá, the Centre of the Covenant of Bahá'u'lláh*. 1973, London: George Ronald.
17. Bahá'í Year Book, *Bahá'í World (1930-1932) Vol. IV: An International Record*. Vol. IV. 1933, .: Bahá'í Publishing Committee.

18. Stockman, R. H., *The Bahá'í Faith in America: Origins 1892-1900*. Vol. 1. 1985, Wilmette, Ill.: Bahá'í Publishing Trust.
19. Bahá'í Year Book, *Bahá'í World (1944-1946) Vol. X: An International Record*. Vol. X. 1949, Wilmette, Ill.: Bahá'í Publishing Committee.
20. Bahá'í Year Book, *Bahá'í World (1926-1928) Vol. II: An International Record*. Vol. II. 1928, .: Bahá'í Publishing Committee.
21. Phelps, M. H., *The Life and Teachings of Abbas Effendi (Cover Title: Abbas Effendi, His Life and Teachings.)* 1903, New York: G. P. Putnam's Sons: Knickerbocker Press.
22. Bahá'í Year Book, *Bahá'í Year Book (1925-1926) Vol. I: An International Record*. Vol. I. 1926, Wilmette, Ill.: Bahá'í Publishing Committee.
23. Bahá'í Year Book, *Bahá'í World (1934-1936) Vol. VI: An International Record*. Vol. VI. 1937, Wilmette, Ill.: Bahá'í Publishing Committee.
24. 'Abdu'l-Bahá, *Abdu'l-Bahá in London*. 1912, London: Longmans Green & Co.
25. 'Abdu'l-Bahá, *Paris Talks: Addresses Given by Abdu'l-Bahá in Paris in 1911-1912*. 9th ed. 1951, London: Bahá'í Publishing Trust.
26. 'Abdu'l-Bahá, *The Promulgation of Universal Peace*. 2nd ed. Vol. 1 & 2. 1982, Wilmette, Ill.: Bahá'í Publishing Trust.
27. Thompson, J., *The Diary of Juliet Thompson*. 1983, Los Angeles: Kalimát Press.
28. 'Abdu'l-Bahá, *'Abdu'l-Bahá in Canada*. 1962, Toronto: National Spiritual Assembly of the Bahá'ís of Canada.
29. Khursheed, A., *The Seven Candles of Unity: The Story of 'Abdu'l-Bahá in Edinburgh*. 1991, London: Bahá'í Publishing Trust.
30. Rabbani, R., *The Guardian of the Bahá'í Faith*. 1988, London: Bahá'í Publishing Trust.
31. Rabbani, R., *The Priceless Pearl*. 1969, London: Bahá'í Publishing Trust.
32. Hands of the Cause of God, *The Ministry of the Custodians 1957-1963—An Account of the Stewardship of the Hands of the Cause—With an Introduction by the Hand of the Cause Amatu'l-Bahá Rúhíyyih Khánum*. 1992, Haifa: Bahá'í World Centre Publications.
33. Baram, A., ed. *Martha Root, Herald of the Kingdom: A Compilation*. Comp. K. Zinky. 1983, New Delhi: Bahá'í Publishing Trust.
34. Conference, *Where Eagles Soar: Martha Root, Agnes Alexander, Dr Augur*. in *Bahá'í International Youth Conference*. 1974. Hilo, Hawaii: National Spiritual Assembly of the Bahá'ís of the Hawaiian Islands.

35. Garis, M. R., *Martha Root, Lioness at the Threshold*. 1983, Wilmette, Ill.: Bahá'í Publishing Trust.
36. Bahá'í Year Book, *Bahá'í World (1928-1930) Vol. III: An International Record*. Vol. III. 1930, Wilmette. Ill.: Bahá'í Publishing Committee.
37. Bahá'í Year Book, *Bahá'í World (1932-1934) Vol. V: An International Record*. Vol. V. 1936, Wilmette. Ill.: Bahá'í Publishing Committee.
38. Effendi, S., *Messages from the Guardian: Letters and Cablegrams Received by the National Spiritual Assembly from June 21, 1932 to July 21, 1940*. 1940, Wilmette, Ill.: Bahá'í Publishing Committee.
39. Effendi, S., *The Advent of Divine Justice*. 1984 ed., ed. 1984, Wilmette, Ill.: Bahá'í Publishing Trust.
40. Bahá'í Year Book, *A Compendium of Volumes of the Bahá'í World, an International Record, I-XII, 82-110 of the Bahá'í Era*. Comp. R. White. 1981, Oxford: George Ronald.
41. Braun, E., *From Strength to Strength: The First Half Century of the Formative Age of the Bahá'í Era*. 1978, Wilmette, Ill.: Bahá'í Publishing Trust.
42. Bahá'í Year Book, *Bahá'í World (1938-1940) Vol. VIII: An International Record*. Vol. VIII. 1942, Wilmette, Ill.: Bahá'í Publishing Committee.
43. Effendi, S., *Dawn of a New Day*. Cover title: *Dawn of a New Day: Messages to India. 1923-1957*. 1970, New Delhi: Bahá'í Publishing Trust.
44. Effendi, S., *The Promised Day is Come*. 1980, Wilmette, Ill.: Bahá'í Publishing Trust.
45. Bahá'í Year Book, *Bahá'í World (1940-1944) Vol. IX: An International Record*. Vol. IX. 1945, Wilmette, Ill.: Bahá'í Publishing Committee.
46. Effendi, S., *Messages to Canada (1923-1957)*. 1965, Toronto: National Spiritual Assembly of the Bahá'ís of Canada.
47. Bahá'í Year Book, *Bahá'í World (1954-1963) Vol. XIII: An International Record*. Vol. XIII. 1970, Haifa: The Universal House of Justice.
48. Bahá'í Year Book, *Bahá'í World (1950-1954) Vol. XII: An International Record*. Vol. XII. 1956, Wilmette, Ill.: Bahá'í Publishing Trust.
49. Universal House of Justice, *Messages from the Universal House of Justice 1968-1973*. 1976, Wilmette, Ill.: Bahá'í Publishing Trust.
50. Bahá'í Year Book, *Bahá'í World (1963-1968) Vol. XIV: An International Record*. Vol. XIV. 1974, Haifa: The Universal House of Justice.

51. Bahá'í Year Book, *Bahá'í World (1968-1973) Vol. XV: An International Record*. Vol. XV. 1976, Haifa: Bahá'í World Centre Publications.
52. Bahá'í Year Book, *Bahá'í World (1973-1976) Vol. XVI: An International Record*. Vol. XVI. 1979, Haifa: Bahá'í World Centre Publications.
53. Bahá'í Year Book, *Bahá'í World (1976-1979) Vol. XVII: An International Record*. Vol. XVII. 1982, Haifa: Bahá'í World Centre Publications.
54. Universal House of Justice, *A Wider Horizon: Selected Messages of the Universal House of Justice (1983-1992)*. 1992, Riviera Beach, Fla: Palabra Publications.
55. Blomfield, S. L., *The Chosen Highway*. 1940, London: Bahá'í Publishing Trust.
56. 'Abdu'l-Bahá, *Some Answered Questions*. 1981 ed. 1982, Wilmette, Ill.: Bahá'í Publishing Trust.
57. Bahá'í Year Book, *Bahá'í World (1992-1993) An International Record*. 1993, Haifa: Bahá'í World Centre Publications.
58. Compilation, *Japan Will Turn Ablaze: Tablets of 'Abdu'l-Bahá, Letters of Shoghi Effendi and Historical Notes About Japan*. 1974, Osaka: Bahá'í Publishing Trust.
59. Stockman, R. H., *The Bahá'í Faith in America: Early Expansion 1900-1912*. Vol. 2. 1995, Oxford: George Ronald.
60. Honnold, A., ed. *Why They Became Bahá'ís: First Generation Bahá'ís by 1963*. 1994, New Delhi :Bahá'í Publishing Trust.
61. Rabbani, R., *Twenty-Five Years of the Guardianship*. 1948, Wilmette, Ill.: Bahá'í Publishing Trust.
62. 'Abdu'l-Bahá, *Tablets of the Divine Plan*. 3rd. rev. ed. 1980, Wilmette, Ill.: Bahá'í Publishing Trust.
63. 'Abdu'l-Bahá, *A Traveller's Narrative to Illustrate the Episode of the Báb*. New and corrected ed. 1980, Wilmette, Ill.: Bahá'í Publishing Trust.
64. Bahá'u'lláh, *Kitáb-i-Íqan, the Book of Certitude*. 2nd ed. 1981, Wilmette, Ill.: Bahá'í Publishing Trust.
65. 'Abdu'l-Bahá, *Selections from the Writings of Abdu'l-Bahá*. Lightweight ed. 1982, Haifa: Bahá'í World Centre Publications.
66. Effendi, S., *Principles of Bahá'í Administration*. 4th ed. 1976, London: Bahá'í Publishing Trust.
67. Compilation, *The Covenant of Bahá'u'lláh: A Compilation*. 1950, Manchester: Bahá'í Publishing Trust.
68. Compilation, *The Pattern of Bahá'í Life*. 3rd ed. 1983, London: Bahá'í Publishing Trust.
69. Backwell, R., *The Christianity of Jesus*. 1972, Portlaw, Ireland: Volturna Press.

70. Bahá'u'lláh, *Epistle to the Son of the Wolf*. 1979, Wilmette, Ill.: Bahá'í Publishing Trust.
71. Taherzadeh, A., *The Revelation of Bahá'ulláh Baghdád 1853-63*. Paperback ed. Vol. 1. 1988, Oxford: George Ronald.
72. Taherzadeh, A., *The Revelation of Bahá'u'lláh Adrinople 1863-68*. Paperback ed. Vol. 2. 1988, Oxford: Geroge Ronald.
73. Taherzadeh, A., *The Revelation of Bahá'lláh 'Akká, The Early Years 1868-77*. Vol. 3. 1988, Oxford: George Ronald.
74. Taherzadeh, A., *The Revelation of Bahá'u'lláh Mazra'ih and Bahjí 1877-92*. Vol. 4. 1988, Oxford: George Ronald.
75. Hofman, D., *Bahá'u'lláh: The Prince of Peace*. 1992, Oxford: George Ronald.
76. Ruhe, D. S., *Robe of Light: The Persian Years of the Supreme Prophet Bahá'u'lláh 1817-1853*. 1994, Oxford: George Ronald, Publisher.
77. Bahá'u'lláh, *Tablets of Bahá'u'lláh Revealed After the Kitáb-i-Aqdas*. Lightweight ed. 1982, Haifa: Bahá'í World Centre Publications.
78. Bahá'u'lláh, *The Proclamation of Bahá'u'lláh to the Kings and Leaders of the World*. 1978, Haifa: Bahá'í World Centre Publications.
79. Effendi, S., *The Greatest Holy Leaf: A Tribute to Bahíyyih Khánum*. 1980, London: National Spiritual Assembly of the Bahá'ís of the United Kingdom.
80. Freeman, D., *From Copper to Gold: The Life of Dorothy Baker*. 1984, Oxford: George Ronald.
81. Bahá'u'lláh, *Kitáb-i-Aqdas—The Most Holy Book*. 1992, Haifa: Bahá'í World Centre Publications.
82. Effendi, S., *The Light of Divine Guidance: The Messages from the Guardian of the Bahá'í Faith to Individual Believers, Groups and Bahá'í Communities of Germany and Austria*. 1982, Hofheim-Langenhain: Bahá'í-Verlag.
83. Whitehead, O. Z., *Some Early Bahá'ís of the West*. 1976, Oxford: George Ronald.
84. Bahá'í Year Book, *Bahá'í World (1946-1950) Vol. XI: An International Record*. Vol. XI. 1952, Wilmette, Ill.: Bahá'í Publishing Committee.
85. Bahá'u'lláh, *Gleanings from the Writings of Bahá'u'lláh*. 1988, Wilmette, Ill.: Bahá'í Publishing Trust.
86. Compilation, *Lights of Guidance: A Bahá'í Reference File*. 2nd ed. 1988, New Delhi: Bahá'í Publishing Trust.
87. *Bahá'í News / Star of the West, Star of the West.* (Bahá'í News; The Bahá'í Magazine), 1910-1935. 1-25.
88. Effendi, S., *Principles of Bahá'í Administration*. 1st ed. 1950, London: Bahá'í Publishing Trust.

89. Goodall, H. S., and E. G. Cooper, *Daily Lessons Received at Acca, January 1908*. Rev. ed. 1979, Chicago: Bahá'í Publishing Trust.
90. Taherzadeh, A., *The Covenant of Bahá'u'lláh*. 1992, Oxford: George Ronald.
91. Whitehead, O. Z., *Some Baha'is to Remember*. 1983, Oxford: George Ronald.
92. Bahá'u'lláh, *The Hidden Words of Bahá'u'lláh*. rev. ed. 1985, Wilmette, Ill.: Bahá'í Publishing Trust.
93. Bahá'u'lláh, *Gleanings from the Writings of Bahá'u'lláh*. 1982, Wilmette, Ill: Bahá'í Publishing Trust.
94. Bahá'í International Community, *The Prosperity of Humankind*, 1995, New York: Bahá'í International Community, Office of Public Information.
95. Bahá'í International Community, *World Citizenship: A Global Ethic for Sustainable Development*, 1993, New York: Bahá'í International Community.
96. Effendi, S., *Bahá'í Administration*. 1974 ed., Wilmette, Ill.: Bahá'í Publishing Committee.
97. Association for Bahá'í Studies. *The Vision of Shoghi Effendi*. In *Association for Bahá'í Studies Ninth Annual Conference*. 1984. Ottawa: Association for Bahá'í Studies.
98. Compilation, *Compilation of Compilations*. Vol. 1, 2. 1991, Maryborough, Victoria, Australia: Bahá'í Publications Australia.
99. Esslemont, J. E., *Bahá'u'lláh and the New Era*. 4th rev. ed. 1980, Wilmette, Ill.: Bahá'í Publishing Trust.
100. 'Abdu'l-Bahá, *Tablets of Abdul Baha Abbas*. Vol. 3. 1919, Chicago: Bahá'í Publishing Society.
101. Compilation, *Seeking the Light of the Kingdom: Compilations Issued by the Universal House of Justice on the Nineteen Day Feast and Bahá'í Meetings*. Compilation Series No. 8. 1977, London: Bahá'í Publishing Trust.
102. British Bahá'í Journal, *John Ferraby—In Memoriam*. Bahá'í Journal, 1973 (October).
103. Compilation, *The Gift of Teaching*. Compilation Series No. 9. 1977, London: Bahá'í Publishing Trust.
104. Effendi, S., *Directives from the Guardian*. 1973, New Delhi: Bahá'í Publishing Trust.
105. National Spiritual Assembly of the Bahá'ís of the British Isles. *Bahá'í Journal*.
106. Bahá'u'lláh and 'Abdu'l-Bahá, *Bahá'í World Faith*. 2nd ed. 1976, Wilmette, Ill.: Bahá'í Publishing Trust.
107. 'Abdu'l-Bahá, *Foundations of World Unity*. 1979, Wilmette, Ill.: Bahá'í Publishing Trust.
108. Hannen, J. H., *Akka Lights*. 1909: n.p.

109. Effendi, S., *High Endeavors: Messages to Alaska*. 1976, Anchorage: National Spiritual Assembly of the Bahá'ís of Alaska.
110. Bahá'í International Community, *A Bahá'í Declaration of Human Rights and Obligations Presented to the United Nations Human Rights Commission*, 1947, New York: Bahá'í International Community.
111. 'Abdu'l-Bahá, *The Will and Testament of Abdu'l-Bahá*. 1971, Wilmette, Ill.: Bahá'í Publishing Trust.
112. Effendi, S., *Messages to America: Selected Letters and Cablegrams Addressed to the Bahá'ís of North America, 1932-1946*. 1947, Wilmette, Ill.: Bahá'í Publishing Committee.
113. Effendi, S., *Letters from the Guardian to Australia and New Zealand, 1923-1957*. 1971, Sydney, NSW, Australia: National Spiritual Assembly of the Bahá'ís of Australia and New Zealand.
114. Ives, H. C., *Portals to Freedom*. 1967, Wilmette, Ill.: Bahá'í Publishing Trust.
115. Rutstein, N., *He Loved and Served: The Story of Curtis Kelsey*. 1982, Oxford: George Ronald.
116. Compilation, *Bahá'í Answers: A Compilation*. 1947, Independence, Mo.: Lambert Moon Printers and Publishers.
117. Universal House of Justice, *The Promise of World Peace*. 1985, Wilmette, Ill.: Bahá'í Publishing Trust.
118. Bahá'u'lláh, *Tablets of Bahá'u'lláh Revealed after the Kitáb-i-Aqdas*. 1988, Wilmette, Ill.: Bahá'í Publishing Trust.
119. Leach, B., *My Religious Faith*. 1979, London: National Spiritual Assembly of the Bahá'ís of the United Kingdom.
120. Effendi, S., *Bahá'í Administration*. 1974 ed. Wilmette, Ill.: Bahá'í Publishing Trust.
121. Maxwell, M. B., *An Early Pilgrimage*. 1917, Chicago: Bahá'í Publishing Society.
122. Abu'l-Fadl Gulpáyganí, M., *The Brilliant Proof, Burhäne Lämé*. 1912, Chicago: Bahá'í News Service.
123. Abu'l-Fadl Gulpáyganí, M., *Miracles and Metaphors*. 1981, Los Angeles: Kalimát Press.
124. 'Abdu'l-Bahá, *Memorials of the Faithful*. 1975, Wilmette, Ill.: Bahá'í Publishing Trust.
125. Abdu'l-Bahá, *The Secret of Divine Civilization*. 1957, Wilmette, Ill.: Bahá'í Publishing Trust.
126. Effendi, S., *The World Order of Bahá'u'lláh*. Paperback ed. 1955, Wilmette, Ill.: Bahá'í Publishing Trust.
127. Sears, W., *A Cry from the Heart: The Bahá'ís in Írán*. 1982, Oxford: George Ronald.
128. Nash, G., *Iran's Secret Pogrom: The Conspiracy to Wipe Out the Bahá'ís*. 1982, Suffolk, U.K.: Neville Spearman.

129. Momen, M., ed. *The Bábí and Bahá'í Religions, 1844-1944: Some Contemporary Western Accounts*. 1981, Oxford: George Ronald.
130. Cooper, R., *The Baha'is of Iran*. 1982, London: Minority Rights Group.
131. Pinchon, F. E., *The Coming of "the Glory": (As Described in the Bahai Writings.)* 1928, London: Simpkin Marshall Ltd.
132. Bahá'u'lláh, *Prayers and Meditations by Bahá'u'lláh*. 1979, Wilmette, Ill.: Bahá'í Publishing Trust.
133. Weinberg, R., *Ethel Jenner Rosenberg: The Life and Times of England's Outstanding Bahá'í Pioneer Worker*. 1995, Oxford: George Ronald.
134. Sears, W., *Thief in the Night, or the Strange Case of the Missing Millenium*. 1985, Oxford: George Ronald.
135. Collins, A., *A Tribute to Shoghi Effendi*. 1960, Wilmette, Ill.: Bahá'í Publishing Trust.
136. Giachery, U., *Shoghi Effendi, Recollections*. 1974, Oxford: George Ronald.
137. Compilation, *A Compilation on the Importance of Deepening Our Understanding and Knowledge of the Faith*. Cover title: Deepening; Compilation Series No. 15. 1983, London: Bahá'í Publishing Trust.
138. Szanto-Felbermann, R., *Rebirth: The Memoirs of Renee Szanto-Felbermann*. 1980, London: Bahá'í Publishing Trust. 185.
139. Dahl, A. L., *Mark Tobey, Art and Belief*. 1984, Oxford: George Ronald.
140. Hofman, D., *George Townshend, Hand of the Cause of God (Sometime Canon of St Patrick's Cathedral, Dublin, Archdeacon of Clonfert.)* 1983, Oxford: George Ronald.
141. Bahá'u'lláh, *Synopsis and Codification of the Laws and Ordinances of the Kitáb-i-Aqdas*. Cover title: *A Synopsis and codification of the Kitáb-i-Aqdas, the Most Holy Book of Bahá'u'lláh*. 1973, Haifa: Bahá'í World Centre Publications.
142. Universal House of Justice, *The Constitution of the Universal House of Justice*. 1972, Haifa: Bahá'í World Centre Publications.
143. Heller, W., *Lidia: The Life of Lidia Zamenhof, Daughter of Esperanto*. 1985, Oxford: George Ronald.
144. Bahá'í Year Book, *Bahá'í World (1994-1995): An International Record*. 1996, Haifa: Bahá'í World Centre Publications.
145. Báb, *Untranslated work*.
146. Báb, *Selections from the Writings of the Báb*. Lightweight ed. 1982, Haifa: Bahá'í World Centre Publications.
147. Browne, E.G., *Materials for the Study of the Bábí Religion*. 1961, Cambridge: Cambridge University Press.
148. Bahá'u'lláh, *Untranslated work*.

149. Compilation, *Bahá'í Prayers*. New expanded and revised ed. 1982, Wilmette, Ill.: Bahá'í Publishing Trust.
150. Momen, M., ed. *Selections from the Writings of E. G. Browne on the Bábí and Bahá'í Religions*. 1987, Oxford: George Ronald.
151. Compilation, *Bahá'í Scriptures*. 1923, New York: Brentano's.
152. 'Abdu'l-Bahá, *Untranslated work*.
153. 'Abdu'l-Bahá, *Tablet to Dr. August Forel*.
154. 'Abdu'l-Bahá, *Tablet to the Hague*. 195?, London: Bahá'í Publishing Trust.
155. Balyuzi, H. M., *Edward Granville Browne and the Bahá'í Faith*. 1980, Oxford: George Ronald.
156. Balyuzi, H. M., *Muhammad and the Course of Islam*. 1976, Oxford: George Ronald.

About the Authors

HUGH CARSWELL ADAMSON (B.A. Sir George Williams University, Montréal; M.A. and M.B.A. Concordia University, Montréal; F.Inst.D., F.I.Mgt., F.R.S.A.) was elected Secretary General of the National Spiritual Assembly of the Bahá'ís of the United Kingdom in 1987 and is currently serving in that position. He was born in the U.K. but moved to Canada as a young man. He was educated in Canada where he obtained Master's degrees in business administration and the history and philosophy of comparative religion. He has wide business experience, including senior executive posts in Canada, the United States and the U.K. He is currently pursuing his Ph.D. at Coventry University, Transformation Studies Group, where he is a Research Fellow. He is Chairman of the World Congress of Faiths—The Interfaith Fellowship; Patron, World Conference of Religions for Peace (UK); a council member, The Wyndham Place Trust; an Executive Committee member, The InterFaith Network and an Hon. Vice-President, United Nations Association (UK). He is a Trustee of the International Interfaith Centre and a Trustee and Hon. Secretary of the Bahá'í Agency for Social and Economic Development (U.K.). He is a Fellow of the Institute of Directors, a Fellow of the British Institute of Management and a Fellow of the Royal Society for the Encouragement of Arts, Manufactures & Commerce. He is also a member of the Royal Institute for International Affairs, the European Atlantic Group, the Refugee Council, the United Nations Environmental & Development Committee (UK) and the Association of Chief Executives of National Voluntary Organizations. He is also Chairman of the Institute for the Healing of Racism.

PHILIP HAINSWORTH accepted the Bahá'í Faith in 1938 and has served on Bahá'í national administrative bodies for 43 years. He has lectured in over 40 countries from the United States to India, from Scandinavia to the Falkland Islands and from St. Petersburg to the Black Sea. He was in the Overseas Civil Service in Uganda for 15 years, followed by 20 years as a fellow of the Life Insurance Association, and is presently a consultant with the National Spiritual Assembly of the Bahá'ís of the U.K. He has served on a wide variety of voluntary organizations involved in interfaith activities, religious education, the United Nations and others working towards global governance. He compiled and edited an extensive work, *The Unfolding Destiny* (Bahá'í Publishing Trust, United Kingdom 1981); co-authored the Ward Lock publication *The Bahá'í Faith* with Mary Perkins (1980), which has been translated into several European languages and is a basic textbook in Germany, Russia and other Eastern European countries. Other works include *The Bahá'í Focus on Human Rights*, *The Bahá'í Focus on Peace*, *Beyond Disarmament*, all published by the Bahá'í Publishing Trust (U.K.); *A New World Order—Some Further Considerations* (National Spiritual Assembly of the Bahá'ís of the United Kingdom, 1991). He has also written the Bahá'í sections for several other major works between 1978 and 1986 including, *Initiation Rites in World Faiths*, *Death in World Faiths*, *Festivals in World Religions*, *Marriage and the Family*, and has made numerous contributions to magazines and periodicals. He has represented the Bahá'í community at international conferences in India, Germany, France, Kenya, Sicily, Republic of Ireland, Luxembourg and Russia, and at the European Parliament, Strasbourg (in relation to the persecution of the Bahá'ís of Írán in 1980). He is a Trustee and Chairman of the Bahá'í Agency for Social and Economic Development (UK).